# The New Social Theory Reader

The last decade has seen a dramatic shift in the nature of social theory. The disciplinary divisions which used to divide the social sciences from the humanities are breaking down, as are the divisions between theory and ethical and political issues of social justice and the good society.

This ambitious reader will give students and scholars access to the writers and perspectives that are shaping some of the most exciting social thinking today. The text is made lively by placing key figures in debate with each other. The first section sets out some of the main schools of thought, including Habermas and Honneth on New Critical Theory, Jameson and Hall on Cultural Studies, and Foucault and Laclau and Mouffe on Poststructuralism. The sections that follow trace debates as they become more issues-based and engaged, looking at:

- concepts such as justice and truth
- the social meaning of nationalism, multiculturalism, globalization
- identity debates around gender, sexuality, race, post-coloniality

*The New Social Theory Reader* is an essential, reliable guide to current theoretical debates.

**Steven Seidman** is Professor of Sociology at State University of New York, Albany. **Jeffrey C. Alexander** is Professor of Sociology at Yale University.

**Contributors:** Norma Alarcón, Jeffrey C. Alexander, Benedict Anderson, Arjun Appadurai, Anthony Appiah, Zygmunt Bauman, Ulrich Beck, Robert N. Bellah *et al.*, Seyla Benhabib, Homi Bhabha, Rogers Brubaker, Judith Butler, James Clifford, Jean L. Cohen and Andrew Arato, Michel Foucault, Nancy Fraser, Diana Fuss, Anthony Giddens, Jürgen Habermas, Stuart Hall, David Halperin, Donna Haraway, David Harvey, Axel Honneth, Fredric Jameson, Will Kymlicka, Ernesto Laclau and Chantal Mouffe, Jean-François Lyotard, Alasdair MacIntyre, Michael Omi and Howard Winant, John Rawls, Richard Rorty, Marshall Sahlins, Edward Said, Steven Seidman, Charles Taylor, Michael Walzer, Iris Marion Young.

# The New Social Theory Reader

## Contemporary Debates

Edited and introduced by

## Steven Seidman and Jeffrey C. Alexander

London and New York

First published 2001
by Routledge
11 New Fetter Lane, London EC4P 4EE

Simultaneously published in the USA and Canada
by Routledge
29 West 35th Street, New York, NY 10001

*Routledge is an imprint of the Taylor & Francis Group*

Typeset in Perpetua and Bell Gothic by
Florence Production Ltd, Stoodleigh, Devon
Printed and bound in Great Britain by
TJ International Ltd, Padstow, Cornwall

*British Library Cataloguing in Publication Data*
A catalogue record for this book is available from the British Library

*Library of Congress Cataloging in Publication Data*
The new social theory reader: contemporary debates/edited and
   introduced by Steven Seidman and Jeffrey C. Alexander.
      p. cm.
   Includes bibliographical references and index.
   1. Sociology.   I. Seidman, Steven.   II. Alexander, Jeffrey C.
   HM585.N46 2001
   301–dc21                                          00–051779

ISBN 0–415–18807–5 (hbk)
ISBN 0–415–18808–3 (pbk)

# Contents

# PART THREE
## Postdisciplinary debates: societies

# Acknowledgements

The publishers would like to thank the following for their permission to reprint their material:

The American Philosophical Association for permission to reprint Richard Rorty, 'Pragmatism, Relativism and Irrationalism', originally published in the *Proceedings and Addresses of the American Philosophical Association* 53(6), 1980: 719–38.

Arjun Appadurai, for permission to reprint 'Disjuncture and Difference in the Global Cultural Economy,' in *Modernity at Large*. Minneapolis: University of Minnesota Press, 1996, pp. 27–42. Total: 13 pages. This is an extract of the essay that originally appeared in *Public Culture* 2 (2), 1990.

K. Anthony Appiah for his permission to reprint 'African Identities', in Appiah, *In My Father's House: Africa in the Philosophy of Culture*, Oxford: Oxford University Press, 1992, pp. 173–80.

Ulrich Beck for permission to reprint Ulrich Beck, 'World Risk Society as Cosmopolitan Society? Ecological Questions in a Framework of Manufactured Uncertainties', *Theory, Culture and Society* 13, 1996: 3–10.

Blackwell Publishers for permission to reprint Jurgen Habermas, *Between Facts and Norms: Contributions to a Discourse Theory of Law and Democracy*, Cambridge, MA: MIT Press [1996] 1992, pp. xl–xliii, 3–8, 17–18, 25–7, 31–2, 35–7, 38–41; Axel Honneth, 'Personal Identity and Disrespect', in Honneth, *The Struggle for Recognition: The Moral Grammar of Social Conflicts,* London: Polity Press [1992] 1995, pp. 131–9; Zygmunt Bauman, *Postmodern Ethics*, Oxford: Basil Blackwell, 1993, pp. 32–5, 39–51, 53–4, 60; Anthony Giddens, *The Consequences of Modernity*, Palo Alto, CA: Stanford University Press, 1990, pp. 63–78; David Harvey, *The Condition of Postmodernity*, Oxford: Basil Blackwell, 1990, pp. vii, 113–18, 338–42, 344–5; Michael Walzer, *Spheres of Justice: A Defense of Pluralism and Equality*, New York: Basic Books, 1983, pp. 3–12, 17–20, 318–19.

Rogers Brubaker for his permission to reprint Brubaker, *Nationalism Reframed: Nationhood and the National Question in the New Europe*, Cambridge: Cambridge University Press, 1996, pp. 13–21, 69–75.

Cambridge University Press for permission to reprint Rogers Brubaker, *Nationalism Reframed: Nationhood and the National Question in the New Europe*, Cambridge: Cambridge University Press, 1996, pp. 13–21, 69–75.

Columbia University Press for permission to reprint John Rawls, *Political Liberalism*, New York: Columbia University Press, 1993, pp. 3–4, 8–12, 14, 23–6, 30–2.

Cornell University Press for permission to reprint Frederic Jameson, *The Political Unconscious: Narrative as Socially Symbolic Act*, © 1981 by Cornell University Press, 1981, pp. 10–11, 20–1, 23, 34–5, 68–70, 103–7, 112, 130–1, 134–5, 148, 150.

Gerald Duckworth and Co. for permission to reprint Alasdair MacIntyre, *Whose Justice? Which Rationality?* © 1988 by Alasdair MacIntyre, Notre Dame, IN: Notre Dame University Press, pp. 1–7, 351–2, 354–6, 361–2, 364–6.

Stuart Hall for his permission to reprint Hall, 'Cultural Studies and the Centre: Some Problematics and Problems', in Stuart Hall *et al.* (eds), *Culture, Media, Language*, London: Hutchinson & Co., 1980, pp. 27–39.

Harvard University Press for permission to reprint Charles Taylor, *Sources of the Self: The Making of Modern Identity*, Cambridge, MA: Harvard University Press, 1989, pp. 11–12, 22, 105, 368, 372, 374–6, 384–5, 389–90, 509, 511.

MIT Press for permission to reprint Jurgen Habermas, *Between Facts and Norms: Contributions to a Discourse Theory of Law and Democracy*, Cambridge, MA: MIT Press [1996] 1992, pp. xl–xliii, 3–8, 17–18, 25–7, 31–2, 35–7, 38–41; Jean L. Cohen and Andrew Arato, 'The Utopia of Civil Society', in Cohen and Arato, *Civil Society and Political Theory*, Cambridge, MA: MIT Press, 1992, pp. 1–2, 29–30, 451–62.

Oxford University Press for permission to reprint Will Kymlicka, *Multicultural Citizenship: A Liberal Theory of Minority Rights*, Oxford: Oxford University Press, 1995, pp. 10–15, 17–20, 26, 35–7, 40–1, 43–7; K. Anthony Appiah, 'African Identities', in Appiah *In My Father's House: Africa in the Philosophy of Culture*, Oxford: Oxford University Press, 1992, pp. 173–80. © 1992 by K. Anthony Appiah; David Halperin, 'The Queer Politics of Michel Foucault', in Halperin, *Saint Foucault: Towards a Gay Haglography*, New York: Oxford University Press, 1995, pp. 56–62, 66, 79–81, 86–8, 95–7, © 1997 by David M. Halperin.

Perseus Books Group for permission to reprint Michael Walzer, *Spheres of Justice: A Defence of Pluralism and Equality*, © 1983 by Basic Books, a member of Perseus Books, PLC, pp. 3–12, 17–20, 318–19.

Princeton University Press for permission to reprint Iris Marion Young, *Justice and the Politics of Difference*, © 1990, by Princeton University Press, pp. 159–68.

Random House Inc. for permission to reprint Edward Said, *Orientalism*, New York: Vintage, 1979, pp. 5–7, 12, 14, © 1978 by Edward Said, reprinted by permission of Pantheon Books, a division of Random House, Inc.; Michel Foucault, *Power/Knowledge*, New York: Pantheon, 1972, pp. 80–5, 104–8, © 1972, 1975, 1976, 1977 by Michel Foucault, reprinted by permission of Pantheon Books, a division of Random House, Inc.

Routledge Inc. for permission to reprint Nancy Fraser, 'From Redistribution to Recognition: Dilemmas of Justice in a "Postsocialist" Age', pp. 11–39 in Fraser, *Justice Interruptus: Critical Reflections on the 'Postsocialist' Condition*, New York and London: Routledge, 1997, pp. 11–16, 19–26. © 1996, reproduced by permission of Taylor & Francis, Inc; Donna Haraway, 'The Biopolitics of Postmodern Bodies: Constitutions of Self in Immune System Discourse', in Haraway, *Simians, Cyborgs, and Women*, New York: Routledge, 1991, pp. 203–12, © 1990, reproduced by permission of Taylor and Francis, Inc.; Michael Omi and Howard Winant, *Racial Formations in the US*, 2nd edn, New York: Routledge, 1994, pp. 54–61, 65–8, 71–2, 74–6, © 1994, reproduced by permission of Taylor & Francis, Inc.; Norma Alarcón, 'The Theoretical Subjects of *This Bridge Called My Back* and Anglo-American Feminism', in L. Nicholson (ed.), *The Second Wave*, New York: Routledge, 1997, pp. 289–99, © 1997, reproduced by permission of Taylor & Francis, Inc.; Diana Fuss, 'Introduction', in D. Fuss (ed.), *Inside/Out*, New York: Routledge, 1991, pp. 1–8, © 1991, reproduced by permission of Taylor & Francis, Inc.; Seyla Benhabib, 'Feminism and the Question of Postmodernism', in *Situating the Self*, New York: Routledge, 1992, pp. 203, 223–30, © 1992, reproduced by permission of Taylor & Francis, Inc.; Judith Butler, 'Imitation and Gender Subordination', in Diana Fuss, *Inside/Out*, New York: Routledge, 1991, pp. 13–29, © 1991, reproduced by permission of Taylor & Francis, Inc.; Stuart Hall, 'Cultural Studies and the Centre: Some Problematics and Problems', in Stuart Hall *et al.* (eds), *Culture, Media, Language*, London: Hutchinson & Co., 1980, pp. 27–39; Homi Bhahba, *The Location of Culture*, New York: Routledge, 1994, pp. 66–84.

Routledge (Methuen) for permission to reprint Frederic Jameson, *The Political Unconscious: Narrative as Socially Symbolic Act*, Ithaca, NY: Cornell University Press, 1981, pp. 10–11, 20–1, 23, 34–5, 68–70, 103–7, 112, 130–1, 134–5, 148, 150.

Sage Publications Ltd for permission to reprint Ulrich Beck, 'World Risk Society as Cosmopolitan Society? Ecological Questions in a Framework of Manufactured Uncertainties', *Theory, Culture and Society* 13, 1996: 3–10.

Stanford University Press for permission to reprint Anthony Giddens, *The Consequences of Modernity*, Palo Alto, CA: Stanford University Press, 1990, © 1990 by the Board of Trustees of the Leland Stanford Junior University.

University of California Press for permission to reprint James Clifford, 'On Ethnographic Allegory', in Clifford and George E. Marcus (eds), *Writing Culture: The Poetics and Politics of Ethnography,* Berkeley and Los Angeles: University of California Press, 1986, pp. 98–106; Robert N. Bellah, Richard Madsen, William M. Sullivan, Ann Swidler and Steven M. Tipton, *Habits of the Heart: Individualism and Commitment in American Life*, Berkeley and Los Angeles: University of California Press, l985, pp. 22–6, 75–80.

University of Chicago Press for permission to reprint Jeffrey C. Alexander, 'The Binary Discourse of Civil Society', in Michele Lamont and Marcel Fournier (eds), *Cultivating Difference*, Chicago: University of Chicago Press, 1992, pp. 289–300.

University of Manchester Press for permission to reprint Jean-François Lyotard, *The Postmodern Condition*, Minneapolis: University of Minnesota Press, 1984, pp. xxiv–xxv, 37–41, 65–7.

University of Minnesota Press for permission to reprint Jean-François Lyotard, *The Postmodern Condition: A Report on knowledge*, translated by Geoff Bennington and Brian Massumi (English edition published by University of Minnesota Press), Minneapolis: University of Minnesota Press, 1984, pp. xxiv–xxv, 37–41, 65–7.

University of Notre Dame Press for permission to reprint Alasdair MacIntyre, *Whose Justice? Which Rationality?* © 1988 by Alasdair MacIntyre, Notre Dame, IN: University of Notre Dame, pp: 1–7, 351–2, 354–6, 361–2, 364–6.

Verso for permission to reprint Benedict Anderson, *Imagined Communities: Reflections on the Origin and Spread of Nationalism*, London: Verso, [1981], 1991, pp. 1–3, 5–12, 22, 24–6, 33–6, 141–5; Ernesto Laclau and Chantal Mouffe, *Hegemony and Socialist Strategy: Towards a Radical Democratic Politics*, London: Verso, 1985, pp. 105–18, 121.

The Publishers have made every effort to contact authors and copyright holders of works reprinted in *The New Social Theory Reader*. This has not been possible in every case, however, and we would welcome correspondence from individuals or companies we have been unable to trace.

# Introduction

■  Steven Seidman and Jeffrey C. Alexander

**A** DRAMATIC SHIFT IN THE IDENTITY of social theory materialized in the course of the 1990s, although the origins of this sea change can
be traced to the decades before. To think systematically about these new
developments is to risk violating the intellectual spirit that has brought them about.
Yet we believe this risk is worth taking. By thematizing the links between these
disparate developments, we will try to clarify what is new about social theory today.

Thirty years ago, theoretical efforts in the social sciences were elaborated
almost entirely within disciplinary frameworks. This was especially true in the
American social sciences, where theory made strenuous efforts to cut itself off
from broader trends in intellectual and political life. Theorists aimed to establish
unimpeachable 'foundations' for a universalizing science of society.

By foundationalism, we mean the belief that the aim of theory is to establish the
most basic general concepts and categories that will unify and direct social research.
Foundationalist theorizing is inspired by an ideal of social analysis relatively
untouched – or uncontaminated – by social values, interests and politics. For example,
Marx sought to establish a 'materialist' foundation as the only sound basis for
a non-ideological, objective sociology. He proposed the concepts of labor, mode of
production, and social class as the core guiding concepts for analyzing any aspect
of social life, past or present and across all societies. Much foundationalist thinking
in the social sciences has been scientistic. It has pursued a scientific explanatory
framework for understanding social life, one that would parallel in precision and
objectivity the frameworks of the hard sciences. In this scientist version, social
theory aims to provide logical chains of propositions and models that can be
empirically tested and elaborated into systems of knowledge. Many classical and
contemporary social theorists have abandoned scientism, without however abandoning foundationalism. Some of these theorists have pursued a philosophical grounding

of social theory. They intend to establish the most basic general ideas about society that would then guide social analysis. Debates over whether society is to be viewed as an organism, a system, or a field of action or whether the individual or the group is the basic unit of social analysis are indicative of a philosophical effort to establish the conceptual foundations of an objective social science.

Abandoning foundationalism does not mean abandoning general thinking or arguing about social truths. Post-foundationalism is a view about social knowledge that states that we always theorize or do research from a socially situated point of view, that social interests and values shape our ideas, that our social understandings are also part of the shaping of social life. Accordingly, post-foundationalism is not a rejection of theory or rigorous social analysis but a position that defends a more complex, multidimensional type of argumentation. Instead of speaking of hard and fast truths, post-foundationalists might speak of credible or persuasive arguments; instead of speaking of research testing theory, they would be apt to speak of how social analysis involves a multi-levelled type of argumentation that moves between analytical reasoning, empirical data, normative clarification and remains reflective about its own practical social implications.

With the reappearance, in the United States and elsewhere, of massive social and political upheaval in the 1960s, the consensual façade supporting this foundational project dissolved. Yet, while the hegemony of functionalism in the social sciences was defeated, social theory remained scientifically orientated, specialized in disciplinary terms, foundational, and relatively abstracted from normative and political claims. In the 1970s, theory textbooks were dominated by discussions of disciplinary crises. Conflict theory, symbolic interactionism, ethnomethodolgy, and exchange theory were presented as alternative paradigms for resolving the crisis and building a new and more adequate social science. In the 1980s, as the specter of Parsonian domination receded into distant memory, such polarizing and fragmented discourses no longer dominated theoretical consciousness, even if they remained in the reified structures of textbook life. They gave way to grand efforts at theoretical synthesis that, while much less empiricist, more explicitly philosophical, and much less narrowly tied to specific disciplines, remained closely connected to the project of providing an effective framework for a universalizing social science. Debates about structure and agency, expressive and strategic action, positivism and postpositivism were the order of the day. Debates about structure and agency, expressive and strategic action, positivism and post-positivism were the order of the day.

These debates seem decidedly less relevant to the contemporary scene. While it is certainly not the case that these analytical concerns have been resolved, the conversation about them has assumed an entirely different form. The language of contemporary social theory has dramatically changed. The scientific project has been abandoned, not only in theory but also in some of the most influential empirical research. Not only has the disciplinary focus disappeared, but there has also been a marked shift away from the ambitions of a specifically social science.

To engage in theoretical reflections today one must enter directly into discussions that have emerged in philosophy and literary theory and engage in post-foundational debates that transcend disciplinary boundaries and the once firm divisions between humanities and social science. Theoretical work also has taken a decidedly normative turn. As political and moral philosophy have assumed center stage, debate has focused on issues of justice, democracy, equality, and authenticity – topics once considered too 'value laden' to be useful to social science theorizing.

Theoretical discussions are filled with unapologetic links to social movements and political change. Generalized and abstract discourse remains important, perhaps even more influential than before. What has changed is that general theories are offered in a spirit of anti-foundationalism. What we mean by this is that these theories now explicitly find their justification in connections to broader intellectual traditions and to the moral urgencies of political life.

This changing discourse of justification has been accompanied by what we call a 'downward shift' in social theory. Social reasoning has assumed a distinctively more pragmatic form, as generalizing and normative arguments are increasingly elaborated in the idiom of empirical and practical social science. Yet, even as general theorists of the 1970s and 1980s have turned towards empirical domains, the new wave of problem-orientated studies can hardly be understood as 'scientific' in the early, foundational sense. Not only are these investigations directly informed by metatheoretical concerns, but also their arguments are evaluated in terms that go beyond narrowly evidentiary criteria of scientific truth to embrace normative resonance, hermeneutic texture, and critical reflexivity. There is now a much more explicitly acknowledged, and far from delegitimating, relationship between social theory and social life. Just as dramatic shifts in actual social life have stimulated this transformation in theoretical reasoning, it is today widely believed that the new modes of theorizing, whether abstract or pragmatic in intent, can engage and shape social life.

## Part One: General theory without foundations

In this section, we highlight the break from scientific theory. This means not only going beyond disciplinary boundaries and arguing in an explicitly normative way, but the new theory has abandoned the limiting constraints of the foundational frameworks of theoretical traditions themselves. The result is that the boundaries of traditions have been blurred. For each of the four traditions we include in this section, the key figures have made decisive breaks from the classical vision presented by the founding figures and, in doing so, have drawn considerably from traditions that were previously viewed as their antagonists.

### New critical theory

If there is a single theorist whose recent work expresses both the downward shift in contemporary theory and the continuing importance of philosophical abstraction and macrosociological generalization, it is Jurgen Habermas. 'Critical Theory' originated in Germany as an attempt to radically revise Marxism. In the l960s,

Habermas started a second phase by proposing a self-consciously democratic and culturally orientated critical 'theory of communicative action'. His ideas differed profoundly from the institutionally reductionist approach of the original Frankfurt School. Only in the last decade, however, has Habermas fully abandoned the final romantic vestiges of neo-Marxism, for example, his earlier claim that modern 'systems' colonize human 'lifeworlds'. What is now much more firmly in place is a critical-liberal theory that emphasizes the emancipatory possibilities of legally regulated political democracy, a position that defines progress in terms of democratization rather than socialism. Over the last decade, Habermas has devoted himself to elaborating a 'discourse ethics' that can only be articulated in a constitutional democratic civil society.

This selection illustrates post-foundationalism or the downward shift in theorizing in that Habermas aims to justify his theorizing by its moral-practical imperative. While criticizing the injustices and suffering of the century, Habermas remains committed to the possibilities for freedom and justice in modern times. He claims that in the daily practices of modern people are structures of rationality. His discourse ethics is at one level an effort to retrieve this rationality as a democratic ideal in terms of which modern societies can be criticized. In contrast to earlier traditions of critical and Marxist theory, with its historical certainty about the future, discourse theory emphasizes the contingency of reason, explaining how it emerges from everyday, ordinary interaction. 'Whoever makes use of a natural language in order to come to an understanding with an addressee about something in the world', Habermas suggests, 'is required to take a performative attitude and commit herself to certain presuppositions'. What are presupposed are notions about the trustworthiness, autonomy, clear-headedness, and sincerity of speakers. In this way, Habermas suggests, 'unavoidable idealizations' enter into the mundane practice of everyday life, creating a tension between 'idea and reality' that, challenging mere 'facticity', raises implicitly normative 'validity claims'. While these claims revolve around general principles and do not, as such, provide blueprints for particular social actions, they provide both a practical core for democracy and a source for the immanent criticism of every attempt to institutionalize it. These considerations lead Habermas to emphasize the centrality of legal reasoning and institutions in democratic societies. It rests on and inspires reason, but it also refers to 'tradition', in the form of earlier legal precedents, and draws upon the coercion of the state. This duality of law, however, is what allows it to make possible the 'highly artificial communities' upon which universalism and democracy in modern and complex societies depend.

If Habermas started the second Frankfurt School, then Axel Honneth may well be said to be initiating a third. Honneth has responded to criticisms of Habermas's 'abstractness' and 'idealism' by making the downward theoretical shift in a more decisive and emphatic way.

At once philosophical, sociological, psychological, and political, Axel Honeth's work can no more be classified in disciplinary terms than his teacher's. Yet when Honneth draws upon ordinary language theory to provide an anti-foundationalist anchor, he is less moral and Kantian than psychological and Hegelian. While

Habermas concentrates on communication, suggesting it inspires a cognitive interest in consensual agreement, Honneth concentrates on recognition, linking it to emotional life and suggesting that it produces a special sensitivity not only to others' approval but to their disrespect. In elaborating the nature of disrespect, moreover, Honneth tries to connect his model to the central political and social controversies of our time. Physical disrespect means the loss of control over one's body; it is manifest in torture and rape. Moral disrespect means denigration and the denial of rights; it is expressed in racism and other stereotyping efforts at ostracism and domination. Evaluative disrespect relates to the denigration of ways of life; it is expressed in attacks on religious and sexual styles of life.

Utilizing the tools of cultural interpretation, Honneth observes that these forms of disrespect become articulated via metaphors of physical disease such as social death, emotional scars, and psychic injuries. These biological metaphors point to how one might conceptualize the requisites of a good society. Just as physical precautions are necessary to protect against biological illness, social guarantees must be institutionalized to protect against the various forms of disrespect. But it is not some statist 'social physician' who will provide such guarantees. On the contrary, Honneth argues that emotional responses to shame can produce new moral insights that will trigger social and cultural struggles for recognition.

## Semiotic-structuralism

Critical theory began as an effort to revise Marxism in the face of the flourishing of subjectively orientated thinking at the beginning of the twentieth century. Saussure's semiotics or Lévi-Strauss's 'structuralism' marked one of the highest achievements of this voyage of cultural discovery. Yet, like other cultural innovative theories such as psychoanalysis or ordinary language philosophy, it has hardly had an easy time. Defined in opposition to contingency and history, interpretation and subjectivity, semiotic structuralism has been criticized. Marshall Sahlins has achieved his position as a quintessential contemporary theorist by arguing that theory can remain structuralist only by transcending these structuralist-generated oppositions. To do so, he combines structuralism with pragmatism, its most ancient enemy. Sahlins makes structuralism practical in three different ways:

1    *methodologically*: rather than theorizing abstractly, without reference to concrete issues, Sahlins develops his neo-structuralist alternative via the 'downward shift' to real historical time. He considers, in fact, the empirical reinterpretation of a concrete historical case – the initial encounter between the British explorer Captain Cook and the native peoples of the Hawaiian Islands;

2    *epistemologically*: Sahlins insists that the practical and messy exigencies encountered in real historical time have the power fundamentally to alter pre-existent, structured meanings: 'People use and experience signs as the names of things, hence they condition and potentially revise the general conceptual values of linguistic terms and relation by reference to a world'. Thus, the

utterly unpredictable but implacable presence of two British ships in Waimea Bay on 20 January 1778 produced a series of physical, social, and psychological exigencies. While initially interpreted from within the pre-existing structural categories of Hawaiian culture, these exigencies eventually caused fundamental changes within it;

3   *ideologically*: in his choice of which changes to thematize, Sahlins substantiates his theoretical innovation by implicitly connecting it with contemporary social movements of our day. He shows, for example, how the natives' encounter with Cook triggered class and gender conflict within Hawaiian society, conflicts that eventually produced a more egalitarian status system.

Sahlins confronted the objectivism of 'classical' semiotics by challenging its theory of cultural determinism. James Clifford confronts classical semiotics by challenging its methodological objectivity. Like Sahlins, Clifford moves away from structure by adding pragmatism, demonstrating that ethnography is practical, situated, and interested. Yet just as Sahlins uses pragmatics to reassert the importance of symbolic structures, so does Clifford, in examining ethnography as a performance, find that symbolic figures such as allegories already structure the situated ethnographer's act.

By shifting attention away from the ethnographic object to the ethnographer himself, Clifford means to knock the 'foundations' from under scientific anthropology. Seeing the ethnographer as a writer rather than an observer, Clifford blurs the sharp dividing line between fact and fiction, and between social science and literary studies. In a prototypically downward shift, he argues that anthropological writing has always had an ethical intent, stimulated by an ambition to instruct one's contemporaries about what is right or wrong about their own time by 'observing' what existed in earlier or simpler societies. Having exposed this practical interest, however, Clifford does not move to 'ideology critique', arguing, for example, that anthropology therefore distorts reality. On the contrary, he suggests that the ethical and imaginative content of ethnography should be accepted as legitimate. What should change is not the 'non-scientific' quality of ethnographies but the way ethnographies are presented. Instead of the impersonal 'view from nowhere', the personal and practical should be acknowledged, the differences between narrator and narrated should be made an explicit part of the anthropological story. Clifford gives up the universal as a source of deduction to the particular, but he does not accept relativism. He believes that, properly understood, the ethnographer writes about issues of humanity by engaging the particular.

## Post-structuralism

Post-structuralism has at times been presented as a major break from the general theoretical positions outlined above. For some interpreters, post-structuralism is said to abandon a general theoretical perspective and the possibility of a forceful critical standpoint. We disagree. As we've argued, all of the above perspectives are aware of the ways social context and interests shape ideas. Moreover, recent formulations of these perspectives have abandoned earlier scientistic positions. From Habermas to Clifford, there is an awareness of the conventional, socially agreed upon and historically provisional basis of theoretical foundations. Post-structuralism shares this suspicion towards objective or unimpeachable truths without abandoning generalizing types of theorizing.

Furthermore, post-structuralism shares with the above positions a reorienting to the importance of cultural analysis. With its strong roots in semiotics and structuralism, it is not surprising that post-structuralism found its initial focus on the power of language and texts. Instead, however, of analyzing only how textual meaning is given coherence by transhistorical codes or structures, post-structuralists aim to show how coherence is arbitrary or contingent, shifting, and unstable. Furthermore, they intend to show how claims to textual coherence or closure are linked to social power and inequality. Deconstructing a text or showing how texts have multiple shifting meanings is meant to show how the social world is a realm of ongoing social conflict. Post-structuralism aims to bring textual and linguistic analysis into the heart of social analysis and politics.

Whereas some post-structuralists such as Derrida and Lacan focus on language and texts, Michel Foucault analyzes discursive formations – bounded bodies of knowledge such as the social sciences. He explores how discourses contribute to shaping 'human subjects'. Thus, he argues that, rather than seeing humans as born with sexual natures, Foucault asks how humans came to be thought of as sexual agents. The force of his argument is that the rise of discourses such as sexology, psychiatry, and psychoanalysis didn't discover but created the idea of a unified notion of sexuality and humans as having sexual identities. Foucault connects the making of sexual subjects to forms of sexual control and resistance.

Foucault's emphasis on discourse is paralleled in the work of Chantal Mouffe and Ernesto Laclau. They are also interested in the question of how to think about a human subject. They offer a more fluid, multiple concept of the self or subject than Foucault. Instead of assuming that individuals have an identity as, say, a woman or a black, or assuming that selves are produced by discourses in any simple way, they see individuals as being inserted into webs of discourses that always position us in multiple, intersecting ways. We are never simply a man or woman, white or black, but always assume many, intersecting subject positions or identities. Agency is always implicated in the way discourses position us – both constraining and enabling us. The work of Mouffe and Laclau are major bridges to social analyses that criticize the particularism and separatism of identity politics without rejecting their critical intent. A multiple, intersecting subject provides a rationale for a coalitional-based politics that demands equality and respect for differences.

## Cultural studies

Cultural studies is now a term used to cover a wide range of scholarly work that is both deeply literary and social theoretic. Cultural studies was originally associated with a group of British scholars who were mostly historians and sociologists. Emerging in the 1960s, British cultural studies was an effort to rethink Marxism in a world where, on the one hand, the mass media were central and, on the other hand, where social movements advocating gender, racial, and sexual justice were prominent. With its focus on political economy and class conflict, Marxism needed to be rethought in order to address contemporary developments.

Although much of the work of British cultural studies was collaborative, Stuart Hall was without doubt the leading figure. Drawing on a wide range of thinking from Foucault and Gramsci to classical and contemporary sociology, Hall developed a critical theory that made culture central to social analysis. Against a literary tradition that defined culture as the world of literature, music, and theatre, and against a Marxist tradition that reduced culture to class ideology, Hall and his associates argued that culture is the ensemble of meanings, beliefs, values, norms, and rituals, that structure a society. Culture is both a source of meaning for individuals and communities and an ideological force related to power dynamics. The aim of cultural studies is to analyze culture in relation to lived experience and in relation to social structural inequalities where it functioned as a force of both domination and resistance.

As cultural studies was transported from Britain to the United States in the 1970s and 1980s, it was not sociologists but humanities professors who took up its critical aims. And while cultural studies in America has many different forms and homes, one of its most powerful American formulations is by the literary theorist, Fredric Jameson.

In a move that typifies the hybrid nature of contemporary theory, Jameson embraces 'genre analysis', initiated by one of the twentieth century's most formidable critics, Northrup Frye. Using simplified narrative forms, such as romance, comedy, and tragedy, Frye argued that literature provides archetypical myths that modern readers employ to create meaning in their secular lives.

Jameson historicizes this literary theory by arguing that genres are a response to the fragmentations of modern capitalist life. Rather than providing an authentic meaning, they express the suppressed hope of the political unconscious. Against the traditional Marxist emphasis on the scientific realism of capitalist literature, Jameson shows that realism is itself not only a genre, a fictional form, but an inadequate and ultimately impoverishing one. He argues, in fact, that the imagination of capitalist writers and readers is much more consistently drawn to romanticism, not realism. Jameson shows how 'romance' provides a sense of utopian possibility, not only in high culture but in popular culture as well. But for Jameson this utopia can only exist as an unfulfilled possibility that could be realized only if capitalist life were radically changed.

Jameson has come to believe that modern capitalist societies have been transformed into post-modern ones. He described post-modernity as a social condition whose fragmentation and incoherence make the romantic reference to utopia impossible. While Stuart Hall participated in the same literary reconstruction of Marxism as Jameson and is attuned to the same postmodern condition, he finds that meaning-making continues to be possible. In fact, symbolic resistance has become ever more important and cultural creativity more central than ever to contemporary life.

## Part Two: The normative turn in social theory

In this section, we argue that the abandonment of foundational scientific theory has involved a turn to moral reasoning. In presenting these normative debates, we highlight the tension between more particularizing, local, and community-focused approaches and more universalizing modes. Such debates over the nature of the good society, between historically based formulations of a new social ethics, and foundational arguments over the criteria for ascertaining truth have in the contemporary period gained a pre-eminent place.

### Justice

Arguably it has been the 'normative turn', more than any other development, that has transformed the nature of general theoretical discussion. The rebirth of political commitment and radical social reform in the 1960s was given a theoretical statement in John Rawls's masterful *Theory of Justice*. This book almost single-handedly rekindled the field of political and moral philosophy. It can almost be said that modern versions of communitarian, hermeneutical, and libertarian theorizing were created to challenge Rawlsian 'foundationalism'.

Perhaps the most relevant of such efforts to a social scientific perspective was Michael Walzer's communitarian *Spheres of Justice*. Walzer was critical of Rawls's formalistic aim to establish principles of justice that applied to any society, past and present. Against the search for general principles of moral life, Walzer adopts an 'internalist' position that approaches justice by interpreting and reconstructing the self-critical standards that, he believes, are implicit in the cultures of actual communities. Thus, there can only be 'spheres of justice', and theories of justice, not a single set standard for distributing valued goods that will hold everywhere. Equality might be desirable in, say, the civil community but it will be inappropriate in, for example, the family unit, which depends on age inequality between parents and children, or in the economy, which depends on asymmetrical distributions and hierarchical control over resources to achieve efficiency. Exactly what justice is must be related to each sphere's specific and idiosyncratic goods and activities. Love, money, power, truth, art: all have their different sense of justice. Thus, although Walzer does not endorse inequality, he does suggest that monopolization of rewards in a particular sphere is defensible and not necessarily unjust if it corresponds to abilities and competences to produce this particular set of valued goods. By contrast, what is all-important for establishing justice is to eliminate domination, which Walzer defines as the effort of one sphere to replace another sphere's differentiated, independent criteria of distribution with its own. Examples would be a theocracy asserting religious control over the spheres of politics, love, and economics, or political or economic dictatorships that insert inappropriate monetary and political criteria into the workings of other spheres. The key to justice, in Walzer's view, is the pluralistic separation of spheres and the respect for the independence of their distributive criteria.

In response to criticisms such as Walzer's, John Rawls revised his theory of justice by shifting it 'downward'. In *Political Liberalism*, he presents a post-foundational approach to justice that, while embracing internalism, continues to maintain the importance of generalizable criteria. His goal is 'just cooperation', not justice *per se*. In establishing the fair terms of social cooperation, moreover, he highlights the importance of tolerating competing versions of the good. Indeed, Rawls emphasizes that the most important goods in life are particular goods, those produced by competing associations, including ideological and religious ones, in a civil society. Yet in order to preserve the ability of groups to pursue their own versions of the good, in their own particular spheres, Rawls insists that societies must commit to a thoroughly separated, free-standing sphere of 'political justice', one based on more abstract rightness than a particular goodness. Rightness aspires to universality. It is defined by the use of public reason, as compared to the non-public reason of comprehensive doctrines that develop community-centered rationales. Only the power of an independent public reason, and its associated legal and political institutions, can facilitate the kind of overlapping consensus upon which democracy depends. But how can political justice and public reason be developed without deducing them from some quasi-transcendental position, abstracted from history, place, and time? Rawls makes a surprisingly contextualist answer: they can be developed, via interpretation and criticism, only from values that are implicit in liberal forms of democratic culture. Paradoxically, it is only particular cultures that can develop universal political justice.

## Ethics

Rejecting both the notions of a universal public reason and a plurality of clearly defined moral spheres, Alasdair MacIntyre creates a normative theory even more closely tied to practical life and even more critical of abstract appeals to universal reason. In fact, MacIntyre aims to develop an historically delimited 'ethics' rather than a broad morality of justice. Behind the illusion of consensus in modern societies, he believes, there is radical conflict between what seem to be incommensurable notions of justice and rationalities. Rather than systematic debates in institutionalized public forums, disputes over controversial issues have been degraded to mere assertions and counter-assertions, with the result that convictions become dogmatically asserted independent of reasoned argument. MacIntyre blames the Enlightenment for this condition. Its narrowly rationalist viewpoint misleadingly suggested that disputants in moral arguments can abstract themselves completely from their cultural and social commitments. Against such 'liberal individualism', MacIntyre argues that one should abandon the effort to find a neutral, impartial, and universal point of view. He does not believe, however, that the ideals of rationality and consensus should for that reason be cast aside. Rather than adopting a relativist position, we need to understand rationality as emerging from within historically established traditions. Rationality does not demand that we step outside tradition; invention, responsibility, and reflexivity can emerge from disputes within and between traditions. Ethical traditions continually face newly emerging empirical problems, for which they must account by creating new ideas. They also continually encounter new arguments from competing ethical traditions, in relation to which they try to revise their positions and sometimes even abandon them entirely. Because success in these endeavors requires a keen understanding of other points of view, it seems possible that multiple traditions of justice can lead, if not to agreement and homogeneity, then at least to mutual sensitivity and cooperation.

There has been a downward conflation in contemporary ethical discussions, from the early foundationalist Rawls, to Walzer's pluralistic but still liberal response, to Rawls's later historically specific public reason, and then to MacIntyre's anti-liberal yet still rationalizing traditionalism. This reaches its logical conclusion in Zygmunt Bauman's post-modern ethics. Baumann argues that we must start from the messy world of everyday life in post-modern society, where there simply aren't any foundations to be found. Yet individuals do live morally in such a world. The challenge is to articulate this lived ethic. Bauman believes that morality has become re-personalized. Individual passions and beliefs can provide a basis for more authentic convictions and a sincere respect for others. A personal ethics rejects not only abstract universalism but the authoritarian claims of traditions and communities. For any postulate of a collective morality is based on the fraudulent claim that a social 'we' can be formed from the many 'I's that compose it. This abstraction from the irrevocably personal nature of the self must be rejected, for it has facilitated domination in pre-modern and modern societies. We must be willing to respect others, and even to sacrifice for them, without thinking that we are the same as they are, much less that they will owe us something in return.

## Truth

Just as debates over questions of justice and ethics have shifted to post-foundationalist types of arguments or arguments which take seriously the tradition-or-social context-based character of thinking and practice, so too in the debates over truth. To be sure, there are theorists who continue to search for ahistorical or transcendent ways of thinking about knowledge. However, the close link of reason and social interests, the view that thinking is shaped by social purpose, has compelled many theorists to imagine a type of rationality that is contextual yet able to retain its capacity forcefully to adjudicate disagreements and guide social practice.

Richard Rorty has defended the idea of a pragmatic critical reason. By pragmatism, he refers to the idea that truth is always to be assessed in terms of the way in which ideas or ways of thinking are useful or contribute to realizing social goals. Rorty maintains that beliefs or ideas are true if they are useful or if they help us achieve our purposes. He intends to shift the way we talk of knowledge away from the language of abstract reason, objectivity, and certainty. Ideas are true or false only in relation to the context in which they appear, the purposes for which they are intended, and in relation to their social consequences. This does not mean that all ideas are equally true or valid. It means that there are no hard and fast rules to tell us what is true and what is false; communities must determine for themselves what is true by arguing in a pragmatic way.

While Rorty's pragmatism has been welcomed by some for underscoring the close tie between social context, history and reason, others have felt that he makes the link to social practice too tightly, thereby undermining the power of reason to establish truths. While some critics appeal to a renewed transcendent view of reason against Rorty, Seyla Benhabib does not. She agrees with Rorty that a situated reason is all that is possible. Moreover, as someone associated with critical theory and feminism, she is sympathetic to Rorty's activist approach to knowledge. However, she believes that binding truth to utility does not give reason enough independence and critical force. Feminists, for example, need to be able to convince people of gender inequality by claiming that their ideas are true, not merely useful. She worries that a feminist argument for gender equality might be too easily dismissed in a pragmatic mode by linking it to women's social interests. Benhabib wishes to defend a stronger concept of reason, one that is both contextual and general, as a condition of making reason a social force for justice.

## Part Three: Post-disciplinary debates: societies

In the next two sections, we turn to the manner in which theoretical concerns increasingly have become expressed in investigations of an empirical kind. We argue that the above shifts in general theoretical discourse are connected to deep social transformations in institutional structure and identity formation. These social changes have become the sites of intense moral and political conflict and, thus, the natural foci for empirical investigation by theorists with a practical intent. This explains the 'downward shift' in contemporary theoretical debate, whose post-foundational and normative sensibility, and blurred boundaries, lead naturally into practical social studies. Concretized metatheory moves fluidly between philosophical, normative, and empirical, problem-orientated discussion, with the paradoxical result that empirical investigations in contemporary social science have actually undergone a corresponding 'upwards shift'. Not only do theorists themselves often conduct empirical investigations, but also practical and even policy-orientated studies are much more often explicitly related to issues of a metatheoretical kind. On the one hand, there is the necessity to justify the practices of post-foundational general theory by demonstrating its relevance to practical life. On the other, empirical research, now bereft of scientific foundations, feels compelled to find its justification in normative, theoretical and philosophical argument.

### Post-modernity

Such long-term structural trends as the shift to post-industrialism and globalization in the political, economic, and cultural spheres have been complemented by such radically contingent developments as the post-1989 democratic transitions in East Europe and elsewhere. The latter have led to the unexpected foregrounding of the notion of civil society, which has been contested, socially and intellectually, by renewed attention to nationalism. The emergence of holistic, ecological thinking about nature and the spread of multicultural rather than assimilative modes of incorporation seem also to be defining characteristics of post-modern societies.

Central to current theoretical debates is the question of whether social developments, at least in Europe and the United States, indicate a shift from a modern to a post-modern type of society. According to many social thinkers, modernity is an historical era characterized by the industrial revolution, the rise of the nation state, the nuclear family, clearly marked gender roles, and a faith in reason to establish general standards of truth, beauty, and rightness. Does the rise of an information- and service-based economy, multinational organizations, globalizing processes, relativizing, post-foundational discourses, and a decline in the belief in social progress underscore the arrival of postmodernity?

François Lyotard's *The Postmodern Condition* is one of the key texts in making the case for the coming of post-modernity. Lyotard describes modernity by, among other features, the power of the 'grand narrative', by which he means two things. First, Lyotard points to the great stories of modern times such as the Marxist tale of class conflict or the liberal story of social progress driven by enlightenment as creating a sense of unity and purpose to history. Second, from the philosophy of empiricism to rationalism and idealism, moderns have been convinced that philosophy could determine truth from falsity and right from wrong. Lyotard's claim is that today the grand narrative has lost its power. Such stories and discourses are no longer believed or they have the status of being just one story or interpretation among others. Post-modern culture is characterized not by the loss of belief but by the acceptance of the plurality of beliefs without the need – or credible effort – to create a hierarchy of truth. This sense of the contingent, uncertain, pluralistic, and open-ended character of knowledge is extended to identity and social ethics. This shift in the realm of culture is related to the development of societies that are more information driven, and therefore decentralized and contract based.

David Harvey both agrees and disagrees with Lyotard. He concurs that indeed there have been remarkable changes in the post-war period, in particular, cultural changes in ways that we can describe as post-modern. He disagrees, though, that such changes amount to the rise of a new type of society. From a neo-Marxist perspective, Harvey relates changes in the cultural sphere to political economic changes. He speaks of a shift from a highly centralized, mass-production, factory-based economy to a 'post-Fordist' economy characterized by decentralization, flexible production, enhanced worker autonomy, and a knowledge-driven economy. It is precisely this reconfigured global capitalist economy that creates fluid identities, promotes tolerance for differences as capital needs to focus on local markets, promotes cultural innovation as new sites of profit-making, and so on. In other words, post-modernity is a product of, and tied to, the modernity of a capitalist social order.

## Civil society

If post-modernity is one of the broad structural transformations that underlies the kinds of theoretical shifts we are identifying in this collection, the new focus on civil society is the result of much more contingent factors. It was the unanticipated uprising by the Polish workers movement, 'Solidarity', against its communist rulers in 1980–1 that recovered the concept, which had virtually disappeared from social theory since the mid-nineteenth century. That movement, and the anti-communist upheavals that culminated in the revolutionary year 1989, employed the slogan 'society against the state' to campaign for a civil society and against traditional socialism. Since then, as the socialist version of utopia has faded, not only new critical theories about contemporary societies, but even new conservative thinking, has made reference to the idealized principles of civil society.

Jean Cohen and Andrew Arato articulate the downward shift that characterizes contemporary utopian thinking. The earlier, foundationalist approach to utopian thought, classically embodied in Marx, posited a sweeping social 'rationality' as the ideal and believed that it would be possible to completely transform existing societies to achieve that goal. Cohen and Arato reject this 'totalizing' approach to social change, pointing to the brutalizing failed utopias of state socialism and, indeed, pure capitalism. In opposition to this utopian vision, they insist on the necessity of maintaining social differentiation and deepening pluralism. Such goals suggest that social movements should demand that the principles of democracy be institutionalized in ever more profound and radical ways.

Reflecting the post-foundational turn, Cohen and Arato abandon the idea that theory and practice should be guided by a concrete substantive democratic ideal. They transform the traditional democratic ideal of society as a 'free voluntary association' in a linguistic way, suggesting an ideal of civil society as establishing a more fully realized open communication. Following Habermas's discourse theory of ethics, Cohen and Arato advocate, not a substantive institution (socialism), but rather an increasing engagement in open discussion as against authoritative fiat. They see this utopian aspiration in the growth of a wide variety of 'publics', from the internal discussions generated by feminist and ecological movements to the political discussions in parliamentary debates and mass media.

Developing this newly recovered concept of civil society in a more empirical manner, Jeffrey Alexander studies how the ideal has been applied in existing societies. He finds that there has, indeed, been increasing social differentiation, association, and plurality, but also that institutionalizing these structures and principles has, historically, been accompanied by new kinds of exclusions and forms of domination. Focusing on cultural dynamics, Alexander points to contradictions inside the discourse of civil society itself. Modern exclusions from civil society result from its enthusiastic institutionalization, not from its failed effect.

In a deeply cultural analysis, Alexander reveals that the normative structure of civil society has a binary form. The positive side of its symbolic code describes civil qualities that allow a group to be legitimately included. The negative side of the code lays out qualities that are widely agreed to be anti-civil. In so far as groups of actors have been alleged to exhibit such qualities, Alexander suggests, it has been considered legitimate, perhaps even necessary, for core groups to 'protect' society by polluting and excluding them.

Rejecting empiricism, Alexander's sociological model is clearly animated by a normative commitment to justice. In this sense, it reflects the 'upward' shift of contemporary empirical studies. At the same time, his theoretical model also reflects the downward shift from universaliziing 'foundationalism'. In contrast to Cohen and Arato's decidedly 'normative' theorizing, Alexander asserts that universalism and particularism have, at least until now, always been disturbingly intertwined.

## Multiculturalism

One reason why the idea of civil society has moved into the center of social and political debates is that social movements of the last few decades have made this notion central to their politics. In Eastern Europe, the focus of social movements has been to establish a stable civil society against state power. In the US and Western Europe, social movements have focused on democratizing civil society, one aspect of which has meant creating a more pluralistic order. Identity-based movements, from feminism to gay liberationism, have emphasized the importance of group differences in shaping social norms and institutions. As a result, the question of how differences of gender, race, sexuality, nationality and religion shape and should shape social and political life is at the center of debates around multiculturalism.

Iris Young develops a radical defense of multiculturalism that asserts the importance of difference over and against universalism. She criticizes assimilationist theories for ignoring power, asserting that it is cultural domination that compels outgroups to reject their long-standing cultural identities, not the attractiveness of mainstream values themselves. Yet, despite their assimiliationist ambitions, modern societies do not actually succeed in eliminating cultural differences and establishing homogeneity; they succeed only in subjecting the cultural differences of less-powerful groups to prejudice and discrimination. Such injustice could be avoided if the liberal philosophy of universal humanism, which celebrates individuality, were replaced by an ethic that gave priority to sustaining particular cultural solidarities. If separatism were championed over integration, it would not necessarily lead to conflict and antagonism. If people can learn to respect the right of others to be different, multiculturalism will produce not only more justice but more legitimate cooperation.

Will Kymlicka develops a theory that also seeks to respect the growing social emphasis on cultural difference, but he does so within the humanistic philosophy that Young rejects. On the one hand, Kymlicka argues against the critics of multiculturalism, asserting that there are indeed circumstances in which groups must be allowed to sustain control over their own cultures. On the other hand, he argues that maintaining group rights cannot be the only goal a democratic society pursues. On many occasions, efforts to sustain solidarity threaten the freedom of individuals inside the group to choose their own values. Against the radical multicultural position, Kymlicka believes that liberal philosophy is basic to democracy. On these grounds, he rejects the notion that individual autonomy can be compromised in order to maintain the differences among groups. Multicultural policies are justified as a defense against external domination, but they must be limited in ways that prevent them from placing limits upon individual choice.

## Nationalism

Certainly it is a sobering reminder of the complexity of contemporary social development that nationalism has re-emerged at the very same time as movements of democratization. Nationalism, like the focus on civil society and multiculturalism, has the same relation to the decline of state communism. As the cold war ended, and the Soviet empire dissolved, new openings to democracy emerged, but new assertions of national interest also asserted themselves in virulent ways.

While the tendencies toward civil society and nationalism collide in contemporary reality, their treatment in contemporary social theory displays common intellectual concerns. Thus, Benedict Anderson rejects abstract and universalizing theories of nationalism, approaches that typically viewed national identity as reflecting a progressive phase of modernization and, eventually, a particularistic response against it. He emphasizes the continuity, not the distance, between traditional and modern societies. He turns away from universal assertions towards practical exigencies, and he discovers that in modern societies the same needs for community remain.

Writing after the linguistic turn, Anderson rejects naturalistic approaches to communities and their values; instead, he looks closely at the role that language performs. He finds that a new national language gradually filled the psychological space vacated by religion. It did so by linking social identity, which often promised a kind of secular salvation, to a delimited territory. The mass publication of books and newspapers in the post-Latinate vernacular – the new 'national' languages – were critical. Such publications allowed people to experience an impersonal yet rhetorically compelling solidarity with those millions of others who shared the same territory but would never meet. Anderson acknowledges that this linguistically 'imagined community' connected national identity to the quasi-naturalistic order of race, gender, parentage, and birth. Nevertheless, he contends that the love of nation does not, in fact, necessarily imply such restrictive and exclusive membership criteria. After all, he reasons, nations are conceived above all in language, not in blood.

Writing fifteen years after the initial publication of Anderson's book, Rogers Brubaker carries forward its cultural, constructivist emphasis. Warning against the 'realism of the group', Brubaker criticizes the still current tendency to accept the claims that nationalizing groups make for the ontological status of their national identities. Yet, in response to the dystopian disappointments of recent history, as well as the contemporary theoretical suspicion of linear, abstract arguments, Brubaker sharply rejects what he sees as Anderson's implicitly optimistic, perhaps even complacent, 'developmentalism'. Drawing on Bourdieu, he argues that nationalism should be seen more in more practical and contingent terms. The aim of nationalist 'practices' is to tie symbolic representations of the reality of national identity to situationally specific political and institutional struggles. In the breakup of the former Yugoslavia Brubaker finds this more 'eventful' approach to nationalism particularly relevant.

## Globalization

A fundamental assumption of Enlightenment traditions of social thinking has been the idea that certain social structures that have emerged in western modernity would become worldwide. From the *philosophes* to Marx, Weber and Habermas, the claim has been made that all nations would gradually be pulled into a process of modernization that would bring about human progress. Marx, for example, imagined that capitalism would become world-historical, unifying the globe thereby creating the conditions for a worldwide communist revolution. Durkheim emphasized universalizing processes of social differentiation and Weber pointed to bureaucracy, formal-rational law and science as exhibiting the same global drive.

The debate over globalization occurs then squarely within this Enlightenment tradition but with two qualifications. First, modernizing structures and processes, from notions of citizenship to bureaucratic principles and market exchanges, have in fact become global. The debate today is over what are the chief driving forces of globalization and its human costs and benefits. Second, despite some ambivalence, classical and many contemporary social theorists have assumed that globalization involves a universalizing of western structures which, despite some human costs, is a necessary condition of social progress. Today, we are less confident about the equation of westernization and progress and, at a minimum, acknowledge multiple paths of progress.

Anthony Giddens has proposed a synthesis of classical and contemporary ideas about globalization. Central to his approach is the claim that it is a product or extension of the chief features of modernity. The latter refers to societies organized around a capitalist economy, the nation-state, and a military-industrial complex. The combination of market exchanges and nation-state and military alliances between states have produced a globalized world: a world where societies are interconnected and where the local and the general are enmeshed. What makes such global processes possible is a process of time and space distaniation. With the development of clocks and maps, time and space can be approached in similar terms (as matters of quantification and 'geography') across very different societies. Globalization suggests neither simply progress nor regress but the continuous force of societal interconnectedness, the enmeshing of the local and the global, as social forces shape selves, societies, and history.

Giddens is very much in the classical tradition in that globalization is seen as driven by social structural factors. By contrast, Arjun Appadurai brings cultural processes into the center of analysis. He speaks of a complex cultural flow of people, technology, images, tropes, ideas, including religious or humanistic faiths, across the globe creating a transnational or global cultural economy. Moreover, there are disjunctures among the various objects of transnational circulation. That is, there is no necessary consistency or coherency between the exchange or circulation of these objects or people. The same nation that exports unskilled workers may be a major importer of tourists or high-tech machinery and brainpower. Today, analyzing the global cultural economy requires attention to the multiple levels of global exchange, their tensions or strains, and the complex mixes of local and transnational structures.

## Domination/liberation

Nancy Fraser paints a broad portrait of the manner in which the cultural turn in contemporary social theory, and its attention to the new social movements of difference, has redefined traditional approaches to the problem of social inequality. While acknowledging the compelling significance of these new social and intellectual developments, Fraser criticizes them for being one-sided approaches, accusing them of ignoring the more material forms of domination. While discrimination against gays may be confronted with purely cultural demands for recognition, such an identity-based approach does not address the kinds of economic deprivations that deny underprivileged economic classes of the basic means of life. These problems demand a focus on redistribution, not recognition.

Most contemporary conflicts fall somewhere between these extreme cases. Gender discrimination derives not only from cultural stereotypes about women's incapacities but from profound limitations on economic participation. The racial underclass is a product of inner-city economic decline and the disappearance of production line jobs in a post-industrial economy; at the same time, the existence of this underclass feeds into, and reflects, the cultural distortions of black–white identities. Yet, while problems of misrecognition and maldistribution are empirically intertwined, efforts to redress them often work at cross-purposes. Economic redistribution implies the need to treat different groups in a more egalitarian and homogeneous manner. Cultural recognition implies, to the contrary, the need to allow groups to maintain their differences. The challenge for a progressive political agenda, Fraser argues, is to develop a theoretical framework that shows how this tension can be resolved. Only if programs for change are radicalized so that they become less 'affirmative' and more 'transformational' can cultural and economic structures be changed in complementary ways.

In her argument for an emancipatory politics that emphasizes both redistribution and recognition, Fraser assumes that domination operates by means of material deprivation and cultural disrespect. However, social analysts have argued that the so-called new social movements are not only focused on winning material equality, civic rights and cultural respect; they are also engaged in struggles to refashion selves and to create new forms of solidarity and cultural expression.

Developing a Foucauldian notion of queer politics, David Halperin argues that social and cultural structures 'dominate' not only through denial but through productively shaping forms of personal and social life that restrict forms of selfhood, pleasure, intimate solidarity, cultural innovation and so on.

For example, modern societies compel selves to project a sexual identity and subject them to social controls that define sexual desires as normal or abnormal. Thus, gays are oppressed not only because they lack equal rights and recognition but because they have to signify their desire as an exclusive, unitary sexual identity. Accordingly, liberation is not only about equal rights and symbolic inclusion but about resistance to a system that compels us to mark our desires as sexual, to define our sexuality in mutually exclusive identity terms, to reduce our pleasures to sexuality, and to subject our behavior to ideas of normal sexuality. Accordingly, Halperin defends a queer position not as a new type of identity but as a position from which to criticize a regime of sexualization and normalization in favor of a social field that allows for desires to be expressed not as sexual identity but as pleasures, as bases for self-expression or the formation of new types of intimacies and cultural forms. From this perspective, liberation is less about rights or materiality than about the refashioning of selves and social life.

## Nature

The idea of the natural and the social have often stood in a relation of opposition in the history of social thought. Thus, in early contract theory, political theorists such as Hobbes, Locke, and Rousseau contrasted a state of nature, a hypothetical condition of the pure state of human nature, with society, a state inaugurated and sustained through at least a tacit social agreement. The contrast between nature and society reappears, for example, in the opposition between sex, which is often thought of as natural (we're assumed to be born male or female), and gender, which is socially learned roles and identities. But with the advent of an evolutionary view of nature in the early nineteenth century, it was possible to view nature and society as interconnected, or to view nature as always subject to social influence. Thus Marx asserted, before Darwin's breakthrough ideas, that nature, including human nature, is always subject to social historical forces – thus shifting a binary into a complex mediated relationship. Since Marx, many other thinkers have begun to enquire into the social making of nature.

Ulrich Beck challenges the social/natural division in the course of developing a theory of the risk society. The basic idea is that societies are structured by the risks and insecurities they create and their responses to them. In particular, Beck focuses on so-called environmental risks associated with the introduction of new biomedical and nuclear technologies. The dominant view, in evidence in the Frankfurt school, approaches environmental problems as indicating the natural limits or foundations of social life. Nature can, so to speak, strike back at human intervention in troubling ways. Similarly, current critical ecological perspectives often rely on notions of the integrity or autonomy of nature to criticize social practices that produce environmental problems or degradation.

Bech challenges these perspectives by questioning the nature and society dualism. There is, he argues, no natural order outside the social. The risks associated with nature are socially produced not in the simple sense that nature reacts to social intervention but that society forms or shapes the natural. For Bech, there is no nature in itself; nature is always already socially interpreted, formed, thought about, made into a norm or object of science or a site of tourism or a resource:

> The nature invoked is no longer there. What is there, and what creates
> such a political stir, are different forms of socialization and different
> symbolic mediations of nature [and the destruction of nature]. It is
> these cultural concepts of nature, these opposing views of nature . . .
> which have a determining influence on ecological conflicts.

In this regard, Bech departs from ecological-critical perspectives by claiming that the basic problems today are not of the environment or nature, and not a matter of simple social irresponsibility or lack of respect for nature. A critical social perspective should focus on social institutions and cultural dynamics. In particular, Bech holds that today ecological problems are global social problems, as risks have been made global through new technologies. A critical ecological practice should focus on making institutions more reflexive and accountable about the possible risks and consequences of their practices. Moreover, if such a global response to environmental problems is developing today it is, in part, because of the appearance of a transnational discourse which has helped to create a world public sphere and a global agenda.

Donna Haraway is, as Bech acknowledges, a pioneer in thinking through the blurring of the boundaries between the natural and the social. A former biologist, she does not intend to withdraw all agency or reality from nature or to see reality as only social. Instead, she looks to the ways in which nature inevitably becomes a screen for social meanings and conflict. Her focus is less on social interventions, risks, and unintended consequences than on the ways nature becomes symbolic or serves as a space to signify a thick sociocultural order.

Specifically, Haraway analyzes the way the immune system in medical-scientific writings on Aids serves as more than just an account of a natural phenomenon. These discourses create a social symbolic order, a map as it were of the way Americans differentiate the self from the non-self and the normal from the pathological. In short, the scientific mapping of the body in Aids discourse is simultaneously viewed as a mapping of the social body. It follows that this discourse is not only important for its medical truths and utility but has social and political implications. Haraway sketches how the immune system in this discourse serves as a site to mark normative boundaries and establish social hierarchies. In the end, Haraway views the biomedical discourse of AIDS as participating in a specific production of the post-modern individual and social body.

## Part Four: Postdisciplinary debates: identities

These macro shifts have given rise to micro-level transformations in the daily lives of contemporary social actors. New social movements have created not only new historical agents but also new subjects of knowledge. In a historically unprecedented manner, various aspects of the self have been denaturalized. Gender, sexuality, race and post-coloniality have become not only the sources of new identities but triggers for fundamentally new lines of empirical research.

### Self

At the core of the emerging focus on 'identities' is the perception that the social changes of recent decades have made the autonomous self — a self increasingly independent of both material and cultural constraint — more powerful and legitimate than ever before. Beyond this shared insight, however, there is sharp disagreement about what the consequences of this development might be, for society and personality alike.

Robert Bellah and Charles Taylor have both been 'general theorists' whose earlier work illuminated the implications of the linguistic turn. In the context of the downward shift in contemporary thought, however, these theoretical commitments have increasingly expressed themselves in highly textured studies of empirical discourse. For Bellah and his sociological colleagues, in-depth interviews provide the texts for empirical investigations. For Taylor, a philosopher, the sources are treatises in the history of political and religious thought.

In their interviews with hundreds of middle-class white Americans, Robert Bellah and his collaborators found that the ultimate idea of the good life boiled down to increasing the range of personal choice. Being on one's own, being left alone to act and feel as one wishes, has become an end in itself, detached from any substantive ideal of a good society. Criticizing this emphasis on freedom as creating an 'empty self', Bellah blames the exaggerated influence of the economic ideal of financial independence and the psychological ideal of emotional self-control. When 'utility replaces duty' and 'self-expression unseats authority', the image of a shared life with others becomes an impossibility. In American society today, the cultural resources for creating solidarity and community simply do not exist.

Charles Taylor wishes to develop a perspective on contemporary individualism by placing it in the broad context of the distinctive moral outlook of western modernity. In this religious and secular culture, there has emerged an emphatic sense that rights are rooted in the self rather than in communities. Accordingly, the true social good can be achieved only by exercising the capacity for individual agency. While Taylor notes that there is certainly an instrumental and economic version of this ideal, he is more interested in illuminating the dimension of autonomy that he calls 'expressive' individuality. Decisively influenced by the Romantic movement nearly two centuries ago, the central idea of expressivism is that every personality is distinctive and therefore each person has the obligation to develop his/her unique vision, creativity, and emotional power. That individuals do so for themselves rather than for a virtuous social cause, in Taylor's view, threatens neither authenticity nor community. The 'obligation to live up to our originality' can, to the contrary, lead not only to a 'new and fuller individuation' but to the need for directly experiencing a sense of community, a need reflected in developments that range from ecological movements to demands for preserving distinctive regional and national cultures. Taking issue with Bellah and his colleagues, Taylor suggests that the 'genuine moral resources' invoked by such expressivist aspirations should not be reduced to the 'least impressive, trivializing offshoots' of this important but so often neglected strand of the individualist tradition.

## Gender

Despite the multiple theoretical currents of second-wave feminism, its chief target of criticism was a naturalistic view of gender that legitimated men's social dominance.

Feminists sought to situate gender squarely in the realm of the social. Typically, this meant that they insisted upon a distinction between sex and gender: the former was viewed as natural, the latter as social. Individuals may be born female or male, but they learn and are coerced into becoming women and men. Framing gender as a social fact made possible a social movement aimed at changing social arrangements of gender inequality. Much of second-wave feminism assumed that, despite many differences, all women shared common experiences and values; for example, all women were subject to sexism.

However, the early 1980s witnessed challenges to this assumption — not only by anti-feminists but also by feminists. Some feminists argued that developing a movement on the assumption that women share a common natural or social essence had the effect of suppressing differences and creating inequalities among women. In particular, ideas of womanhood in the dominant traditions of feminism often reflected the values and social experiences of white, middle-class, highly educated, heterosexual women. The end of second-wave feminism is perhaps signaled by the turn of many feminists away from assumptions of the unity of women to assertions of their differences. Gender unity is now understood to be based on strategic political goals, not on foundational claims about the nature of women: another example of the post-foundational, pragmatic turn in social theory.

One direction a difference-based feminism has taken has been to emphasize 'intersectionality'. Instead of viewing gender as a distinct, independent basis of identity and oppression, some feminists such as Norma Alarcon argue that gender always intersects with class, race, sexuality, and so on. Viewing gender as intersectional means abandoning a notion of a separate autonomous unitary self that has been dominant in a male-centered Enlightenment tradition and much western feminism. Articulating a position which she sees in the writings of women of color, Alarcon proposes a view of a self who occupies simultaneous social axes of gender, class, race, and sexuality. Such a multiple-voiced subject points to a coalition-based politics, instead of a narrow identity politics.

A second direction taken by a difference-based feminism was towards a poststructural or post-modern feminism. While not rejecting identity politics, the effort to ground women's identity and politics in nature or a common social experience was contested. Instead of approaching gender as an identity deeply rooted in the psychology of the individual, Judith Butler views gender identity as discursive and performative. The former means that it is only in the opposition of man and woman that each term gets its meaning. The latter suggests that it is only through practices that individuals project a unified gender identity. In other words, gender identity is less the basis of action than its social effect. Accordingly, gender identity is unstable, multiple, and only appears to be solid, uniform, and singular by gender practices. Moreover, like Alarcon, Butler links gender to other aspects of identity and social dynamics. In this way, and reflecting a post-foundationalism that does not abandon general theorizing, the aim of both an intersectional and post-modern approach to gender is to broaden gender studies into a general social analysis.

## *Sexuality*

Sexuality has been historically difficult to dislodge from the realm of nature – and therefore from the realm of the universal. Not only have many social scientists assumed that sex is natural, but many feminists, sexual liberationists, and gay activists asserted that sexuality is a transhistorical phenomenon. Many analysts sought a general universalizing theory of sexuality. The claim that sexuality is natural was intended to justify a freer, more tolerant social environment. Scholars who claimed that sexuality was a social fact challenged this naturalistic view of sexuality in the 1970s and 1980s. The body, including its desires and pleasures, took a social shape and meaning under specific sociohistorical conditions. In the debates over sexuality we can observe a determined concretization of theorizing, as well as an explicit normative turn.

Debates between essentialist and constructionist approaches to sexuality were especially rich around the question of sexual identity. Constructionists criticized an essentialist perspective, which assumed that the figures of the homosexual and the heterosexual have existed throughout history. By contrast, they argued that sexuality becomes the basis of identities and communities only in some societies.

By the early 1990s, the terms of this debate were being criticized as too narrowly framed. That is, those who articulated both essentialists and constructionists tended to analyze these identities as if they were separate, distinct and rooted in a deep psychological reality, even if this reality was given meaning socially and historically. Queer perspectives criticized these standpoint positions for isolating sexual identities from non-sexual identities and from efforts to theorize sexuality as part of a larger social order.

Diana Fuss articulates many of these queer concerns. In particular, while she recognizes the importance of affirming a gay identity in a normatively heterosexual society, she argues for making such assertions more complex and open-ended. Fuss argues that homosexuality is defined less by the nature of its desire than by its contrast to heterosexuality. Fuss locates homosexuality more squarely in the realm of culture, as a discursive figure, and as such its meaning remains permanently open and contestable. One consequence of this queer move is to bring the analysis of heterosexuality into the center of critical sexual studies. In effect, Fuss urges a shift from theorizing sexual identity from a minority standpoint to analyzing the way the hetero/homo binary operates in discourses and practices as a principle of social organization.

If Fuss proposed an application of a post-structural theory, her ideas remain metatheoretical. Steven Seidman aims to concretize queer theory and clarify its normative position. Drawing on interviews, Seidman points to the rise of a post-closeted gay life. To explain and interpret the meaning of normalizing trends, he proposes to analyze the changing social dynamics of normative heterosexuality, which is understood as an institution or principle of social organization.

Specifically, Seidman argues that between the 1950s and today there has been a shift from a pollution to a normalizing social logic of normative heterosexuality. A pollution logic establishes a division between heterosexuality and homosexuality. These two sexualities are understood as the basis of individual identities. Citizens are divided into a heterosexual majority and a homosexual minority. This is a moral division: the heterosexual signifies a pure and good human status in contrast to the impure and dangerous homosexual. A pollution logic assumes a dynamic of moral contagion. To exclude the homosexual from the public world of visible, open communication, strategies involving censorship, civic disenfranchisement, and sequestration are deployed. By contrast, normalization constructs the homosexual as the psychological and moral equal of the heterosexual. Normalization implies the homosexual's incorporation into the national community with equal civic status to the heterosexual. Accordingly, the homosexual can freely and openly intermingle with heterosexuals. However, the normalized homosexual is compelled to exhibit what is considered to be 'normal' behaviors, traits, or identities in every way other than sexual orientation. For example, the normalized gay self is expected to be gender conventional, link sex to intimacy and love, defend family values, personify economic individualism, and display national pride. While normalization makes possible a life beyond the closet, it does not challenge the normative status of heterosexuality. For example, it leaves in place the norm of gender binary and the ideal of heterosexual marriage and family. Normalization makes possible the legitimation of a minority gay status but sustains the institution of heterosexuality. Finally, Seidman suggests that a pollution logic created the conditions of the so-called closet and this, at least in the US gave rise to various types of identity politics focused on self-purification and citizenship rights. As heteronormativity shifts to normalizing strategies, a queer anti-normalizing politics is one response. Seidman examines the meaning of queer politics and sketches a post-foundationalist queer sexual ethics.

## Race

The debates over race resemble closely those in the field of gender and sexuality. The key development in race theory in the twentieth century has been the substitution of sociohistorical for biological concepts of race. Social groups become racial groups as a result of historical traditions and social conflicts. The sociologist and social critic W.E.B. Du Bois is a pivotal figure. In his *The Philadelphia Negro* and other writings, Du Bois makes the case that racial differences and inequalities are social in origin. Henceforth, contemporary race theory should be a form of social theory.

Although Du Bois and others have insisted upon a social view of race, a critical race theory has often been foundationalist or inattentive to the complex histories and differences within racial groupings. Thus, Afrocentrism, which builds on thinking critical of biologism, makes the questionable assumption that the mere fact of an African heritage gives a social and political unity of social purpose to American blacks.

Much racial theory in the last decade or so has aimed to complicate the way racial identity is theorized. Closely paralleling gender debates, some thinkers have emphasized intersectionality. However, critics have pointed out that assuming interrelated identities preserves the assumption that each identity has a unity and coherence. Anthony Appiah has questioned that assumption. For example, he argues that the notion of African does not refer to a unitary, common experience, set of values, social conditions or set of beliefs. There is not one African identity but many conceptions of such an identity. It is less a basis of experience and politics than itself a political creation. If we assume that there is an African way of thinking or acting, this idea serves to control people and creates divisions and social hierarchies among 'Africans'. Reflecting the downward, pragmatic shift in theorizing, Appiah proposes to treat the notion of African identity as a strategic idea, useful for forming coalitions among nations in Africa and useful for mobilizing around certain goals.

Much race theory, and this holds true for gender and sexual theory as well, has focused on initially offering a constructionist view of identity and then deconstructing these identities as a way to promote a coalition-based politics and avoid the undesirable effects of identity politics. Nevertheless, as important as this theorizing has been, its preoccupation with identity and identity politics has meant that its analysis of social institutions has suffered. The focus has been on the discursive making of identities. In the work of Michael Omi and Howard Winant, racial identities are squarely situated in broader social institutional contexts. They offer an original viewpoint that approaches race as produced by social structure but also interlaced with the organization of a whole society. Thus, the state, law, the media, the university, and so on are all implicated in the racialization of identities and institutions. Anti-racist politics involves changing identities and institutions. Whereas the pragmatic basis of Appiah's metatheorizing on race is his promotion of a pan-Africanism, Omi and Winant's race theory aims to find common ground between racial identity movements and other critical forces by developing a social structural critical race theory.

## Post-colonialism

To adopt a post-colonial standpoint is both to claim a distinct social identity rooted in a colonial experience and to claim a unique social perspective. Against the grain of much social research and theory, post-colonial theory insists upon analyzing nations in their interdependence, in particular in relation to their history of colonialism.

Classical and contemporary theory, from Marx to Habermas and Foucault, has taken the nation-state as its starting point. Thus, Marx analyzed the modes of production of particular nation-states; similarly, although much of his work was comparative, Weber studied societies more or less in isolation from one another. Of course, Marx and Weber, like Foucault and Habermas, understood that nations interact. They did not take this national interdependence as theoretically foundational.

The neo-Marxism of Wallerstein and Dependency theorists have, on the contrary, assumed that societies can only be grasped if they are relations of unequal interconnection. Yet, for these theorists it was economic interdependence that mattered and relations between nations were flattened into relations of dominance and subordination.

Post-colonial theory has challenged both the materialist reductionism of neo-Marxism and its understanding of power as one-dimensionally repressive. Edward Said has been pivotal in bringing culture into the center of colonial dynamics. In a brilliant concretization of post-structural theory, Said argues that representations and discourses of the colonized nation as 'Other' or as different and inferior are both a condition of, and integral aspect of, the dynamics of political economic colonialism. Said's case study is western colonialism of Asian societies. He argues that discourses in European and Anglo-American nations constructed, indeed invented, the notion that the very diverse nations of the Near and Far East are part of a unified civilization: 'the Orient'. Interpreted as the opposite of the 'Occident', Oriental civilization was viewed as backward, static, child-like, despotic, and so on. Such interpretations stimulated and justified colonial intervention as part of social progress.

Said's highly influential analysis suffered from assuming a flat relation of domination and subordination between the Occident and Orient. The work of Homi Bhabha, among others, has made the case that the relation between colonizer and colonized is characterized by ambivalence. As much as the colonizer is repulsed by and repressive towards the colonized, the colonizer is also attracted to, influenced by, and open to the claims of the colonized. Colonial discourse is ambivalent and hybrid. The voice of the colonizer is both dominating and yet reveals traces of the colonized – and thus contains resistance or a potential for reversal or critique. Similarly, the colonizer's discourse is not simply disavowed by the colonized but is in part absorbed, thereby creating ambivalence and hybridity on the part of the colonized. Bhahbi makes the analysis of the subjectivity of the colonizing experience, of its unconscious, central to post-colonial discourse.

# PART ONE

# General theory without foundations

# NEW CRITICAL THEORY

- Jürgen Habermas, Contributions to a discourse theory of law and democracy

- Axel Honneth, Personal identity and disrespect

**Jürgen Habermas** was born in Dusseldorf, Germany on 18 June 1929. He studied philosophy, history and German literature at the universities in Göttingen, Zurich and Bonn. He obtained a doctorate in 1961 at the University of Marbug. He has held positions at various universities, including Heidelberg and Frankfurt am Main, and was director of the Max Planck Institute in Starnberg. Habermas is the author of *Knowledge and Human Interest* (1971) and *A Theory of Communicative Action* (1984).

**Axel Honneth** was born in Germany in 1949. Honneth is currently Professor of Philosophy at Goethe University in Frankfurt. He is the author of *Critique of Power* (1991) and *The Struggle for Recognition* (1997).

# Chapter 1

# Jürgen Habermas

## CONTRIBUTIONS TO A DISCOURSE
## THEORY OF LAW AND DEMOCRACY

[. . .]

**A** MORAL-PRACTICAL SELF-UNDERSTANDING of modernity as a whole is articulated in the controversies we have carried on since the seventeenth century about the best constitution of the political community. This self-understanding is attested to both by a universalistic moral consciousness and by the liberal design of the constitutional state.

Discourse theory attempts to reconstruct this normative self-understanding in a way that resists both scientistic reductions and aesthetic assimilations. The three dimensions of cognitive, evaluative, and normative validity that have been differentiated within the self-understanding of modernity must not be collapsed. After a century that, more than any other, has taught us the horror of existing unreason, the last remains of an essentialist trust in reason have been destroyed. Yet modernity, now aware of its contingencies, depends all the more on a procedural reason, that is, on a reason that puts itself on trial. The critique of reason is its own work: this double meaning, first displayed by Immanuel Kant, is due to the radically anti-Platonic insight that there is neither a higher nor a deeper reality to which we could appeal – we who find ourselves already situated in our linguistically structured forms of life.

Three decades ago I criticized Marx's attempt to transpose the Hegelian philosophy of right into a materialist philosophy of history:

> With his critique of ideology applied to the bourgeois constitutional
> state and with his sociological dissolution of the theoretical basis for
> natural rights, Marx so enduringly discredited . . . both the idea of
> legality and the intention of natural law, that the link between natural
> law and revolution has been broken ever since. The parties of an inter-

nationalized civil war have divided this heritage between themselves with fateful clarity: the one side has taken up the heritage of revolution, the other the ideology of natural law.

After the collapse of state socialism and the end of the 'global civil war,' the theoretical error of the defeated party is there for all to see: it mistook the socialist project for the design – and violent implementation – of a concrete form of life. If, however, one conceives 'socialism' as the set of necessary conditions for emancipated forms of life about which the participants *themselves* must first reach an understanding, then one will recognize that the democratic self-organization of a legal community constitutes the normative core of this project as well. On the other hand, the party that now considers itself victorious does not rejoice at its triumph. Just when it could emerge as the *sole* heir of the moral-practical self-understanding of modernity, it lacks the energy to drive ahead with the task of imposing social and ecological restraints on capitalism at the breathtaking level of global society. It zealously respects the systemic logic of an economy steered through markets; and it is at least on guard against overloading the power medium of state bureaucracies. Nevertheless, we do not even begin to display a similar sensibility for the resource that is *actually* endangered – a social solidarity preserved in legal structures and in need of continual regeneration.

In contemporary Western societies governed by the rule of law, politics has lost its orientation and self-confidence [. . .] what makes communicative reason possible is the linguistic medium through which interactions are woven together and forms of life are structured. This rationality is inscribed in the linguistic telos of mutual understanding and forms an ensemble of conditions that both enable and limit. Whoever makes use of a natural language in order to come to an understanding with an addressee about something in the world is required to take a performative attitude and commit herself to certain presuppositions. In seeking to reach an understanding, natural-language users must assume, among other things, that the participants pursue their illocutionary goals without reservations, that they tie their agreement to the intersubjective recognition of criticizable validity claims, and that they are ready to take on the obligations resulting from consensus and relevant for further interaction. These aspects of validity that undergird speech are also imparted to the forms of life reproduced through communicative action. Communicative rationality is expressed in a decentered complex of pervasive, transcendentally enabling structural conditions, but it is not a subjective capacity that would tell actors what they *ought* to do.

Unlike the classical form of practical reason, communicative reason is not an immediate source of prescriptions. It has a normative content only insofar as the communicatively acting individuals must commit themselves to pragmatic presuppositions of counterfactual sort. That is, they must undertake certain idealizations – for example, ascribe identical meanings to expressions, connect utterances with context-transcending validity claims, and assume that addressees are accountable, that is, autonomous and sincere with both themselves and others.

Communicatively acting individuals are thus subject to the 'must' of a weak transcendental necessity, but this does not mean they already encounter the prescriptive 'must' of a rule of action – whether the latter 'must' can be traced back deontologically to the normative validity of a moral law, axiologically to a constellation of preferred values, or empirically to the effectiveness of a technical rule.

A set of unavoidable idealizations forms the counterfactual basis of an actual practice of reaching understanding, a practice that can critically turn against its own results and thus *transcend* itself. Thus the tension between idea and reality breaks into the very facticity of linguistically structured forms of life. Everyday communicative practice overtaxes itself with its idealizing presuppositions, but only in the light of this innerworldly transcendence can learning processes take place at all.

Communicative reason thus makes an orientation to validity claims possible, but it does not itself supply any substantive orientation for managing practical tasks – it is neither informative nor immediately practical. On the one hand, it stretches across the entire spectrum of validity claims: the claims to propositional truth, personal sincerity, and normative rightness; to this extent it reaches beyond the realm of moral-practical questions. On the other hand, it pertains only to insights – to criticizable utterances that are accessible in principle to argumentative clarification – and thus falls short of practical reason aimed at motivation, at guiding the will. Normativity in the sense of the obligatory orientation of action does not coincide with communicative rationality. Normativity and communicative rationality *intersect* with one another where the justification of moral insights is concerned. Such insights are reached in a hypothetical attitude and carry only the weak force of rational motivation. In any case, they cannot themselves guarantee that insight will issue in motivated action.

One must keep these differences in view when I continue to use the concept of communicative reason in connection with a reconstructive social theory. In this new context, the received concept of practical reason also acquires a different, more or less heuristic status. It no longer provides a direct blueprint for a normative theory of law and morality. Rather, it offers a guide for reconstructing the network of discourses that, aimed at forming opinions and preparing decisions, provides the matrix from which democratic authority emerges. From this perspective, the forms of communication that confer legitimacy on political will-formation, legislation, and the administration of justice appear as part of a more encompassing process in which the lifeworlds of modern societies are rationalized (under the pressure of systemic imperatives). At the same time, such a reconstruction would provide a critical standard, against which actual practices – the opaque and perplexing reality of the constitutional state – could be evaluated.

In spite of the distance from traditional concepts of practical reason, it is by no means trivial that a contemporary theory of law and democracy still seeks to link up with classical concept formations at all. This theory starts with the socially integrating force of rationally motivating, hence noncoercive processes of reaching understanding. These provide a space for distance and recognized differences within a sustained commonality of convictions. Moral philosophers and philosophers of law adopt this perspective in the normative discourses they still carry on, indeed with greater vigor than ever before. Because they specialize in dealing with questions of normative validity in the performative attitude of participants, they usually remain inside the limited horizon of lifeworlds whose spell has been broken by the objectivating observations of social scientists for some time now. Normative theories are open to the suspicion that they take insufficient notice of the hard facts that have long contradicted the contractarian self-understanding of the modern constitutional state. From the objectivating viewpoint of the social sciences, a philosophical approach that still operates with the alternatives of *forcibly* stabilized versus *rationally* legitimated orders belongs to the transitional semantics of early modernity. Such terminology seemingly became obsolete once the transition from stratified to functionally differentiated societies was complete. Even when we adopt a theoretical approach that accords a central role to a communicative concept of 'practical reason,' we must, so it seems, single out a special and particularly demanding form of communication that covers only a small part of the broad spectrum of observable forms of communication: 'using such narrow channels one can hardly succeed, in the new paradigm of reaching understanding, in once again filling out a sufficiently complex theory of society.'

Tossed to and fro between facticity and validity, political theory and legal theory today are disintegrating into camps that hardly have anything more to say to one another. The tension between normative approaches, which are constantly in danger of losing contact with social reality, and objectivistic approaches, which screen out all normative aspects, can be taken as a caveat against fixating on one disciplinary point of view. Rather, one must remain open to different methodological standpoints (participant vs. observer), different theoretical objectives (interpretive explication and conceptual analysis vs. description and empirical explanation), the perspectives of different roles (judge, politician, legislator, client, and citizen), and different pragmatic attitudes of research (hermeneutical, critical, analytical, etc). [. . .] in explicating the meaning of linguistic expressions and the validity of statements, we touch on idealizations that are connected with the medium of language. Specifically, the ideal character of conceptual and semantic generality is accessible to a semantic analysis of language, whereas the idealization connected with validity claims is accessible to a pragmatic analysis of the use of language oriented to reaching understanding. These idealizations inhabiting language itself acquire, in addition, an *action-theoretic* meaning if the illocutionary binding forces of speech acts are enlisted for the coordination of the action plans of different actors.

With the concept of communicative action, which brings in mutual understanding as a mechanism of action coordination, the counterfactual presuppositions of actors who orient their action to validity claims also acquire immediate relevance for the construction and preservation of social orders; for these orders *exist* through the recognition of normative validity claims. This means that the tension between facticity and validity built into language and its use turns up again in the dynamics of the integration of communicatively socialized individuals. What is more, this tension must be worked off by the participants' own efforts. In the social integration achieved through enacted law, this tension is [. . .] stabilized in a special way.

Every social interaction that comes about without the exercise of manifest violence can be understood as a solution to the problem of how the action plans of several actors can be coordinated with each other in such a way that one party's actions 'link up' with those of others. An ongoing connection of this sort reduces the possibilities of clashes among the doubly contingent decisions of participants to the point where intentions and actions can form more or less conflict-free networks, thus allowing behavior patterns and social order in general to emerge. As long as language is used only as a medium for transmitting information, action coordination proceeds through the mutual influence that actors exert on each other in a purposive-rational manner. On the other hand, as soon as the illocutionary forces of speech acts take on an action-coordinating role, language itself supplies the primary source of social integration. Only in this case should one speak of 'communicative action.' In such action, actors in the roles of speaker and hearer attempt to negotiate interpretations of the situation at hand and to harmonize their respective plans with one another through the unrestrained pursuit of illocutionary goals. Naturally, the binding energies of language can be mobilized to coordinate action plans only if the participants suspend the objectivating attitude of an observer, along with the immediate orientation to personal success, in favor of the performative attitude of a speaker who wants to *reach an understanding* with a second person about something in the world. Under this condition, speech-act offers can achieve an action-coordinating effect because obligations relevant to further interaction result from the addressee's affirmative response to a serious offer.

Communicative action, then, depends on the use of language oriented to mutual understanding. This use of language functions in such a way that the participants either agree on the validity claimed for their speech acts or identify points of disagreement, which they conjointly take into consideration in the course of further interaction. Every speech act involves the raising of criticizable validity claims aimed at intersubjective recognition. A speech-act offer has a coordinating effect because the speaker, by raising a validity claim, concomitantly takes on a sufficiently credible guarantee to vindicate the claim with the right kind of reasons, should this be necessary [. . .] The embeddedness of communicative action in lifeworld contexts and the regulation of behavior through strong archaic institutions explain how social integration in small and relatively undifferentiated groups is at all possible on the improbable basis of processes of reaching understanding. Naturally in the course of social evolution the risk of dissension increases with the scope for taking yes/no positions on criticizable validity claims. The more societal complexity increases and originally ethnocentric perspectives widen, the more there develops a pluralization of forms of life accompanied by an individualization of life histories, while the zones of overlapping lifeworlds and shared background assumptions shrink. In proportion to their disenchantment, sacralized belief complexes fall apart, under differentiated validity aspects, into the more or less freely thematizable contents of a tradition set communicatively aflow. Above all, however, processes of *social* differentiation necessitate a multiplication and variation of functionally specified tasks, social roles, and interest positions. On the one hand, this allows communicative action to escape its narrowly circumscribed institutional boundaries for a wider range of opportunities. On the other hand, in a growing number of spheres social differentiation not only unshackles but requires the self-interested pursuit of one's own success.

This brief outline should suffice to indicate the *problem* that emerges in modern societies: how the validity and acceptance of a social order can be stabilized once communicative actions become autonomous and clearly begin to differ, in the view of the actors themselves, from strategic interactions. Naturally, self-interested action has always been fused with, or limited by, a normative order. In societies organized around a state, legal norms are already superimposed on a mature normative infrastructure. In these traditional societies, however, even the law still feeds on the self-authorizing force of the religiously sublimated sacred realm. For example, the notion of a higher law familiar in the medieval tradition of law was still rooted in the sacred fusion of facticity and validity. According to this idea, the law made by the ruler remained *subordinate* to the Christian natural law administered by the Church.

In what follows, I start from the modern situation of a predominantly secular society in which normative orders must be maintained without metasocial guarantees. Even lifeworld certainties, which in any case are pluralized and ever more differentiated, do not provide sufficient compensation for this deficit. As a result, the burden of social integration shifts more and more onto the communicative achievements of actors for whom validity and facticity – that is, the binding force of rationally motivated beliefs and the imposed force of external sanctions – have parted company as incompatible. This is true, at least, outside the areas of habitualized actions and customary practices. If, as I assume along with Parsons and Durkheim, complexes of interaction cannot be stabilized simply on the basis of the reciprocal influence that success-oriented actors exert on one another, then *in the final analysis* society must be integrated through communicative action.

Such a situation intensifies the problem: how can disenchanted, internally differentiated and pluralized lifeworlds be socially integrated if, at the same time, the risk of dissension is growing, particularly in the spheres of communicative action that have been cut loose from the ties of sacred authorities and released from the bonds of archaic institutions? According to this scenario, the increasing need for integration must hopelessly overtax the integrating capacity of communicative action, especially if the functionally necessary spheres of strategic interaction are growing, as is the case in modern economic societies. In the case of conflict, persons engaged in communicative action face the alternatives of either breaking off communication or shifting to strategic action – of either postponing or carrying out the unresolved conflict. One way out of this predicament, now, is for the actors themselves *to come to some understanding* about the *normative regulation of strategic interactions*. The paradoxical nature of such regulation is revealed in light of the premise that facticity and validity have split apart, for the acting subjects themselves, into two mutually exclusive dimensions. For self-interested actors, all situational features are transformed into facts they evaluate in the light of their own preferences, whereas actors oriented toward reaching understanding rely on a jointly negotiated understanding of the situation and interpret the relevant facts in the light of intersubjectively recognized validity claims. However, if the orientations to personal success and to reaching understanding exhaust the alternatives for acting subjects, then norms suitable as socially integrating constraints on strategic interactions must meet two contradictory conditions that, from the viewpoint of the actors, cannot be simultaneously satisfied. On the one hand, such rules must present de facto restrictions that alter the relevant information in such a way that the strategic actor feels compelled to adapt her behavior in the objectively desired manner. On the other hand, they must at the same time develop a socially integrating force by imposing obligations on the addressees – which, according to my theory, is possible only on the basis of intersubjectively recognized normative validity claims.

According to the above analysis, the type of norms required would have to bring about willingness to comply *simultaneously* by means of de facto constraint and legitimate validity. Norms of this kind would have to appear with an authority that once again equips validity with the force of the factual, only this time under the condition of the polarization already existing between action oriented to success and that oriented to reaching understanding, which is to say, under the condition of a *perceived* incompatibility of facticity and validity. As we have already assumed, the metasocial guarantees of the sacred have broken down, and these guarantees are what made the ambivalent bonding force of archaic institutions possible, thereby allowing an amalgam of validity and facticity in the validity dimension itself. The solution to this puzzle is found in the system of rights that lends to individual liberties the coercive force of law. We can then also see, from a historical perspective, that the core of modern law consists of private rights that mark out the legitimate scope of individual liberties and are thus tailored to the strategic pursuit of private interests. [. . .]

A legal order must not only guarantee that the rights of each person are in fact recognized by all other persons; the reciprocal recognition of the rights of each by all must in addition be based on laws that are legitimate insofar as they grant equal liberties to each, so that each's freedom of choice can coexist with the freedom of all. Moral laws fulfill these conditions per se, but for legal statutes, they must be satisfied by the political legislator. The process of legislation thus represents the place in the legal system where social integration first occurs. For this reason, it must be reasonable to expect those who participate in the legislative process, whether directly or indirectly, to drop the role of private subject and assume, along with their role of citizen, the perspective of members of a freely associated legal community, in which an agreement on the normative principles for regulating social life either has already been secured through tradition or can be brought about deliberatively in accordance with normatively recognized procedures. We have already clarified the unique combination of facticity and legitimacy in individual rights that equip legal persons with enforceable entitlements to pursue their own interests strategically. This combination requires a process of lawmaking in which the participating citizens are *not* allowed to take part simply in the role of actors oriented to success. To the extent that rights of political participation and rights of communication are constitutive for the production of legitimate statutes, they must not be exercised by persons who act merely as private subjects of civil law. Rather, these rights must be exercised in the attitude of communicatively engaged citizens. Hence, the concept of modern law, which both intensifies and behaviorally operationalizes the tension between facticity and validity, already harbors the *democratic idea* developed by Rousseau and Kant: the claim to legitimacy on the part of a legal order built on rights can be redeemed only through the socially integrative force of the 'concurring and united will of all' free and equal citizens [. . .]

To the extent that action coordination, and with it the formation of networks of interaction, takes place through processes of reaching understanding, intersubjectively shared convictions form the medium of social integration. Actors are convinced of what they understand and consider valid. This is why beliefs that have become problematic can be supported or revised only through reasons. Reasons, however, are not adequately described as dispositions to have opinions; rather, they are the currency used in a discursive exchange that redeems criticizable validity claims. Reasons owe their rationally motivating force to an internal relationship between the meaning and the validity of linguistic utterances. This makes them double-edged from the word go, because they can both reinforce and upset beliefs. With reasons, the facticity-validity tension inhabiting language and its use penetrates society. Insofar as it is supported by shared beliefs, the integration of a society is susceptible to the destabilizing effect of invalidating reasons (and is all the more susceptible to the invalidation of an entire category of reasons). The ideal tension breaking into social reality stems from the fact that the acceptance of validity claims, which generates and perpetuates social facts, rests on the context-dependent acceptability of reasons that are constantly exposed to the risk of being invalidated by better reasons and context-altering learning processes.

These properties of communicative action explain why the symbolically structured lifeworld, mediated by interpretations and beliefs, is shot through with fallible suppositions of validity. They help us see why behavioral expectations that depend on such fallible suppositions acquire at best a precarious kind of stability. This stability depends on achievements of social integration that ward off the ever-present danger of destabilization resulting from rationally motivated dissent. To be sure, reasons count only against the background of context-dependent standards of rationality; but reasons that express the results of context-altering learning processes can also undermine established standards of rationality. [. . .]

Under the modern conditions of complex societies, which require self-interested and hence normatively neutralized action in broad spheres, the paradoxical situation arises in which *unfettered* communicative action can neither unload nor seriously bear the burden of social integration falling to it. Using its own resources, it can control the risk of dissension built into it only by increasing the risk, that is, by making rational discourse permanent. What kind of mechanism might allow an unfettered communication to unburden itself of socially integrative achievements without compromising itself? One plausible solution to the puzzle would be to 'positivize' the law hitherto based in the sacred and interwoven with conventional forms of ethical life (*Sittlichkeit*), that is, completely transform it into enacted law. [. . .]

If one thus views modern law as a mechanism that, without revoking the principle of unhindered communication, removes tasks of social integration from actors who are already overburdened in their efforts at reaching understanding, then the two sides of law become comprehensible: the positivity of law means that a consciously enacted framework of norms gives rise to an artificial layer of social reality that exists only so long as it is not repealed, since each of its individual components can be changed or rendered null and void. In light of this aspect of changeability, the validity of positive law appears as the sheer expression of a will that, in the face of the ever-present possibility of repeal, grants specific norms continuance until further notice. [. . .]

Modern societies are integrated not only socially through values, norms, and mutual understanding, but also systemically through markets and the administrative use of power. Money and administrative power are systemic mechanisms of societal integration that do not necessarily coordinate actions via the intentions of participants, but objectively, 'behind the backs' of participants. Since Adam Smith, the classic example for this type of regulation is the market's 'invisible hand.' Both media of systemic integration, money and power, are anchored via legal institutionalization in orders of the lifeworld, which is in turn socially integrated through communicative action. In this way, modern law is linked with all three resources of integration. Through a practice of self-determination that requires citizens to make public use of their communicative freedoms, the law draws its socially integrating force from the sources of social solidarity. On the other hand, institutions of private and public law make possible the establishment of markets and governmental bodies, because the economic and the administrative system, which have separated from the lifeworld, operate inside the forms of law.

Because law is just as intermeshed with money and administrative power as it is with solidarity, its own integrating achievements assimilate imperatives of diverse origin. This does not mean that legal norms come with labels telling us *how* these imperatives are to be balanced. In the different subject areas of law, we can certainly see that the needs for regulation, to which politics and lawmaking respond, have different sources. But in the functional imperatives of the state apparatus, the economic system, and other social subsystems, normatively unfiltered interest positions often carry the day only because they are stronger and use the legitimating force of legal forms to cloak their merely factual strength. Therefore, as a means for organizing state activities related to the functional imperatives of a differentiated economic society, modern law remains a profoundly ambiguous medium of societal integration. Often enough, law provides illegitimate power with the mere semblance of legitimacy. At first glance, one cannot tell whether legal regulations deserve the assent of associated citizens or whether they result from administrative self-programming and structural social power in such a way that they independently generate the necessary mass loyalty.

The less the legal system as a whole can rely on metasocial guarantees and immunize itself against criticism, the less scope there is for this type of self-legitimation of law. Indeed, a law responsible for the brunt of social integration in modern societies comes under the *secular* pressure of the functional imperatives of social reproduction; however, it is simultaneously subject to what we might call the *idealistic* pressure to legitimate any regulations. Even the systemic integration achieved through money and power *ought*, in accordance with the constitutional self-understanding of the legal community, to remain dependent on the socially integrative process of civic self-determination. [. . .]

# Chapter 2

# Axel Honneth

## PERSONAL IDENTITY AND DISRESPECT

[. . .]

INHERENT IN OUR EVERYDAY use of language is a sense that human integrity owes its existence, at a deep level, to the patterns of approval and recognition that we have been attempting to distinguish. For up to the present day, in the self-descriptions of those who see themselves as having been wrongly treated by others, the moral categories that play a dominant role are those – such as 'insult' or 'humiliation' – that refer to forms of disrespect, that is, to the denial of recognition. Negative concepts of this kind are used to designate behaviour that represents an injustice not simply because it harms subjects or restricts their freedom to act, but because it injures them with regard to the positive understanding of themselves that they have acquired intersubjectively. Without the implicit reference to the claims to recognition that one makes to one's fellow human beings, there is no way of using these concepts of 'disrespect' and 'insult' meaningfully. In this sense, our ordinary language contains empirical indications of an indissoluble connection between, on the one hand, the unassailability and integrity of human beings and, on the other hand, the approval of others. What the term 'disrespect' [Miβachtung] refers to is the specific vulnerability of humans resulting from the internal interdependence of individualization and recognition, which both Hegel and Mead helped to illuminate. Because the normative, self-image of each and every individual human being – his or her 'me', as Mead put it – is dependent on the possibility of being continually backed up by others, the experience of being disrespected carries with it the danger of an injury that can bring the identity of the person as a whole to the point of collapse.

Admittedly, all of what is referred to colloquially as 'disrespect' or 'insult' obviously can involve varying degrees of depth in the psychological injury to a subject. There is a categorial difference between, say, the blatant degradation involved in the denial of basic human rights, on the one hand, and the subtle humiliation that accompanies a public allusion to a person's failings, on the other. And the use of a single term threatens to efface this difference. But even just the fact that we have been able to identify systematic gradations for the complementary concept of 'recognition' points to the existence of internal differences between individual forms of disrespect. If it is the case that the experience of disrespect signals the withholding or withdrawing of recognition, then the same distinctions would have to be found within the field of negative phenomena as was met with in the field of positive phenomena. In this sense, the distinctions between three patterns of recognition gives us a theoretical key with which to separate out just as many kinds of disrespect. Their differences would have to be measured by the various degrees to which they are able to disrupt a person's practical relation-to-self by denying him or her recognition for particular claims to identity. Only by proceeding from this set of divisions can one take on the question that neither Hegel nor Mead were able to answer: how is it that the experience of disrespect is anchored in the affective life of human subjects in such a way that it can provide the motivational impetus for social resistance and conflict, indeed, for a struggle for recognition?

In light of the distinctions worked out thus far it would appear sensible to start from a type of disrespect that affects a person at the level of physical integrity. The forms of practical maltreatment in which a person is forcibly deprived of any opportunity freely to dispose over his or her own body represent the most fundamental sort of personal degradation. This is because every attempt to gain control of a person's body against his or her will – irrespective of the intention behind it – causes a degree of humiliation that impacts more destructively than other forms of respect on a person's practical injury, as exemplified by torture and rape. It is not the purely physical pain but rather the combination of this pain with the feeling of being defencelessly at the mercy of another subject, to the point of feeling that one has been deprived of reality. Physical abuse represents a type of disrespect that does lasting damage to one's basic confidence (learned through love) that one can autonomously coordinate one's own body. Hence the further consequence, coupled with a type of social shame, is the loss of trust in oneself and the world, and this affects all practical dealings with other subjects, even at a physical level. Thus, the kind of recognition that this type of disrespect deprives one of is the taken-for-granted respect for the autonomous control of one's own body, which itself could only be acquired at all through experiencing emotional support as part of the socialization process. The successful integration of physical and emotional qualities of behaviour is, as it were, subsequently broken up from the outside, thus lastingly destroying the most fundamental form of practical relation-to-self, namely, one's underlying trust in oneself.

Since such forms of basic psychological self-confidence carry emotional preconditions that follow a largely invariant logic associated with the intersubjective balance between fusion and demarcation, this experience of disrespect also cannot simply vary with the historical period or the cultural frame of reference. Whatever the construction of the system of legitimation that tries to justify it, the suffering of torture or rape, is always accompanied by a dramatic breakdown in one's trust in the reliability of the social world and hence by a collapse in one's own basic self-confidence. By contrast, the other two types of disrespect in our tripartite division are embedded in a process of historical change. Here, what it is that is perceived, in each case, to be a moral injury is subject to the same historical transformations as the corresponding patterns of mutual recognition.

Whereas the first form of disrespect is inherent in those experiences of physical abuse that destroy a person's basic self-confidence, we have to look for the second form in those experiences of denigration that can affect a person's moral self-respect. This refers to those forms of personal disrespect to which an individual is subjected by being structurally excluded from the possession of certain rights within a society. We have initially construed the term 'rights', only roughly, as referring to those individual claims that a person can legitimately expect to have socially met because he or she participates, with equal rights, in the institutional order as a full-fledged member of a community. Should that person now be systematically denied certain rights of this kind, this would imply that he or she is not being accorded the same degree of moral responsibility as other members of society. What is specific to such forms of disrespect, as exemplified by the denial of rights or by social ostracism, thus lies not just in the forcible restriction of personal autonomy but also in the combination with the feeling of not enjoying the status of a full-fledged partner to interaction, equally endowed with moral rights. For the individual, having socially valid rights-claims denied signifies a violation of the intersubjective expectation to be recognized as a subject capable of forming moral judgements. To this extent, the experience of this type of disrespect typically brings with it a loss of self-respect, of the ability to relate to oneself as a legally equal interaction partner with all fellow humans. Thus, the kind of recognition that this type of disrespect deprives one of is the cognitive regard for the status of moral responsibility that had to be so painstakingly acquired in the interactive processes of socialization. This form of disrespect represents a historically variable quantity because the semantic content of what counts as a morally responsible agent changes with the development of legal relations. Therefore, the experience of the denial of rights is always to be measured not only in terms of the degree of universalization but also in terms of the substantive scope of the institutionally established rights.

Finally, this second type of disrespect, which injures subjects with regard to their self-respect, is to be set off from a third type of degradation, one that entails negative consequences for the social value of individuals or groups. Not until we consider these, as it were, evaluative forms of disrespect – the denigration of individual or collective ways of life – do we arrive at the form of behaviour ordinarily labelled 'insulting' or 'degrading' today. As we saw, a person's 'honour', 'dignity', or, to use the modern term, 'status' refers to the degree of social esteem accorded to his or her manner of self-realization within a society's inherited cultural horizon. If this hierarchy of values is so constituted as to downgrade individual forms of life and manners of belief as inferior or deficient, then it robs the subjects in question of every opportunity to attribute social value to their own abilities. For those engaged in them, the result of the evaluative degradation of certain patterns of self-realization is that they cannot relate to their mode of life as something of positive significance within their community. For individuals, therefore, the experience of this social devaluation typically brings with it a loss of personal self-esteem, of the opportunity to regard themselves as beings whose traits and abilities are esteemed. Thus, the kind of recognition that this type of disrespect deprives a person of is the social approval of a form of self-realization that he or she had to discover, despite all hindrances, with the encouragement of group solidarity. Of course, one can only relate these kinds of cultural degradation to oneself as an individual person once the institutionally anchored patterns of social esteem have been historically individuated, that is, once these patterns refer evaluatively to individual abilities instead of collective traits. Hence, this experience of disrespect, like that of the denial of rights, is bound up with a process of historical change.

It is typical of the three groups of experiences of disrespect analytically distinguished in this way that their individual consequences are always described in terms of metaphors that refer to states of deterioration of the human body. Psychological studies of the personal after-effects of torture or rape frequently speak of 'psychological death'. In research concerned with how victims of slavery collectively cope with (the denial of rights and exclusion from society) the concept of 'social death' is now well established. And with regard to the type of disrespect associated with the cultural denigration of forms of life, one regularly speaks of 'scars' and 'injuries'. These metaphorical allusions to physical suffering and death articulate the idea that the various forms of disregard for the psychological integrity of humans play the same negative role that organic infections take on in the context of the reproduction of the body. The experience of being socially denigrated or humiliated endangers the identity of human beings, just as infection with a disease endangers their physical life. If this interpretation suggested by our linguistic practice turns out to be not entirely implausible, then it contains two implicit suggestions that are relevant for our purposes. First, the comparison with physical illness prompts the idea of identifying, for the case of suffering social disrespect as well, a stratum of symptoms that, to a certain extent, make the subjects aware of the state they are in. The hypothesis here is that what corresponds to physical indications here are the sort of negative emotional reactions expressed in feelings of social shame. Second, however, the comparison also provides the opportunity to draw conclusions, on the basis of an overview of the various forms of disrespect, as to what fosters the 'psychological health' or integrity of human beings. Seen this way, the parallel to the preventive treatment of illnesses would be the social guarantees associated with those relations of recognition that are able to protect subjects most extensively from suffering disrespect. Although this second comparison will only be of interest to us when we examine the normative implications of this connection between personal integrity and disrespect [. . .] the first comparison is already significant for the argument to be developed here. For the negative emotional reactions accompanying the experience of disrespect could represent precisely the affective motivational basis in which the struggled-for recognition is anchored.

Neither in Hegel nor in Mead did we find any indication as to how experiencing social disrespect can motivate a subject to enter a practical struggle or conflict. There was, as it were, a missing psychological link that would lead from mere suffering to action by cognitively informing the person in question of his or her social situation. I would like to defend the thesis that this function can be performed by negative emotional reactions, such as being ashamed or enraged, feeling hurt or indignant. These comprise the psychological symptoms on the basis of which one can come to realize that one is being illegitimately denied social recognition. The reason for this can again be seen in the constitutional dependence of humans on the experience of recognition. In order to acquire a successful relation-to-self, one is dependent on the intersubjective recognition of one's abilities and accomplishments. Were one never to experience this type of social approval at some stage of one's development, this would open up a psychological gap within one's personality, into which negative emotional reactions such as shame or rage could step. Hence, the experience of disrespect is always accompanied by affective sensations that are, in principle, capable of revealing to individuals the fact that certain forms of recognition are being withheld from them. In order to give this complex thesis some plausibility, at least in outline, it would be advisable to connect it to a conception of human emotions of the sort developed by John Dewey in his pragmatist psychology.

In several early essays, Dewey turned against the widespread view that human states of emotional excitation had to be conceived of as expressions of inner feelings. He wanted to show that such a conception, which could still be found in William James, necessarily overlooks the function of emotions for action by assuming the psychological event to be something 'inner' and prior to actions, which it views as something directed 'outwards'. Against this, Dewey's argument proceeds from the observation that, within the human horizon of experience of particularly successful 'communications' (with people or things), emotions emerge as bodily states of excitement, or they emerge as the experience of being repelled by a failed, interrupted attempt to execute an action. The analysis of such experiences of being repelled provides Dewey with the key to devising an action-theoretical conception of human emotions. According to this conception, negative feelings such as anger, indignation, and sorrow constitute the affective side of the shift of attention towards one's own expectations that inevitably occurs as soon as one has difficulty making the step one planned to make upon completing an action. Positive feelings such as joy or pride, by contrast, arise when one is suddenly freed from a burdensome state of excitement, because one has been able to find a suitable, successful solution to a pressing action problem. In general, then, Dewey views feelings as the affective reactions generated upon succeeding or failing to realize our intentions.

Starting from this general point, we can differentiate emotions still further once we distinguish more precisely the types of 'disruptions' on which habitual human action can founder. Since these disruptions or failures are to be assessed against the background of the orienting expectations that precede the act in each case, we can make an initial, rough division on the basis of two different types of expectations. Routine human actions can come up against obstacles either in the context of expectations of instrumental success or in the context of normative behavioural expectations. Should actions oriented towards success fail as a result of unanticipated obstructions, this leads to 'technical' disruptions in the broadest sense. By contract, should actions guided by norms be repelled by situations because the norms taken to be valid are violated, this leads to 'moral' conflicts in the social lifeworld. This second class of disrupted actions constitutes the experiential horizon in which moral emotional reactions are situated practically. They can be understood, in Dewey's sense, as the emotional excitations with which human beings react to having their actions unexpectedly repelled owing to a violation of normative expectations. The differences between the individual feelings can be measured quite elementarily in terms of whether the violation of the norm hindering the action is caused by the subject or by the interaction partner. In the first case, the subject experiences the hindrance to the actions in feelings of guilt and, in the second case, in emotions of moral indignation. What is true of both cases, however, is something that Dewey considered to be typical of situations of emotionally experiencing one's action thrown back upon itself, namely, that with the shift of attention to one's own expectations, one also becomes aware of the cognitive components in this case, moral knowledge – that had informed the planned and (now) hindered action.

The most open of our moral feelings is shame – to the extent that it does not refer simply to the evidently deep-seated shyness about having one's body exposed. In the case of shame, it is not fixed from the outset which party to the interaction is responsible for violating the norm, a norm that the subject now lacks, as it were, for the routine continuation of an action. As both psychoanalytical and phenomenological approaches have shown, the emotional content of shame consists, to begin with, in a kind of lowering of one's own feeling of self-worth. Ashamed of oneself as a result of having one's action rejected, one experiences oneself as being of lower social value than one had previously assumed. In psychoanalytic terms, this means that what is negatively affected by the action-inhibiting violation of a moral norm is not the super-ego but the subject's ego-ideals. This type of shame – which is only experienced in the presence of a real or imaginary interaction partner, playing as it were the role of witness to the injured ego-ideals – can be caused by oneself or by others. In the first case, one experiences oneself as inferior because one has violated a moral norm, adherence to which had constituted a principle of one's ego-ideals. In the second case, however, one is oppressed by a feeling of low self-esteem because one's interaction partners violate moral norms that, when they were adhered to, allowed one to count as the person that, in terms of one's ego-ideals, one wants to be. Hence, the moral crisis in communication is triggered here by the agent being disappointed with regard to the normative expectations that he or she believed could be placed on another's willingness to respect him or her. In this sense, the second type of moral shame represents the emotion that overwhelms subjects who, as a result of having their ego-claims disregarded, are incapable of simply going ahead with an action. In these emotional experiences, what one comes to realize about oneself is that one's own person is constitutively dependent on the recognition of others.

In the context of the emotional responses associated with shame, the experience of being disrespected can become the motivational impetus for a struggle for recognition. For it is only by regaining the possibility of active conduct that individuals can dispel the state of emotional tension into which they are forced as a result of humiliation. But what makes it possible for the praxis thus opened up to take the form of political resistance is the opportunity for moral insight inherent in these negative emotions as their cognitive content. It is only because human subjects are incapable of reacting in emotionally neutral ways to social injuries – as exemplified by physical abuse, the denial of rights, and denigration – that the normative patterns of mutual recognition found in the social lifeworld have any chance of being realized. For each of the negative emotional reactions that accompany the experience of having one's claims to recognition disregarded holds out the possibility that the injustice done to one will cognitively disclose itself and become a motive for political resistance.

Of course, the weakness of this foothold of morality within social reality is shown by the fact that, in these affective reactions, the injustice of disrespect does not inevitably *have to* reveal itself but merely *can*. Empirically, whether the cognitive potential inherent in feeling hurt or ashamed becomes a moral-political conviction depends above all on how the affected subject's cultural-political environment is constructed; only if the means of articulation of a social movement are available can the experience of disrespect become a source of motivation for acts of political resistance. The developmental logic of such collective movements can, however, only be discovered via an analysis that attempts to explain social struggles on the basis of the dynamics of moral experiences.

# SEMIOTIC STRUCTURALISM

- Marshall Sahlins, Historical metaphors and mythical realities

- James Clifford, On ethnographic allegory

**Marshall Sahlins** was born in Chicago, Illinois on 27 December 1930. He taught at various universities in the United States, including Columbia University, University of Michigan and the University of Chicago. Sahlins is the author of various anthropological books, among them *Culture and Practical Reason* (1976) and *Islands of History* (1985).

**James Clifford** is currently a Professor of the History of Consciousness Program at the University of California, Santa Cruz. Among his publications are *Essays in Travel and Interculture* (1997) and *The Predicament of Culture* (1988).

# Chapter 3

# Marshall Sahlins

## HISTORICAL METAPHORS AND
## MYTHICAL REALITIES

[. . .]

STRUCTURAL ANTHROPOLOGY was founded in a binary opposition, of the kind that would later become its trademark: a radical opposition to history. Working from Saussure's model of language as a scientific object, structuralism similarly privileged system over event and synchrony over diachrony. In a way parallel to the Saussurean distinction between language (*la langue*) and speech (*la parole*), structural analysis seemed also to exclude individual action and worldly practice, except as they represented the projection or 'execution' of the system in place. I will argue here, mainly by concrete demonstration, that all these scruples are not really necessary, that one can determine structures in history – and vice versa.

For Saussure the disengagement of structure from history had seemed requisite, inasmuch as language could be systematically analyzed only as it was autonomous, referentially arbitrary and a collective phenomenon. Saussure's notion of 'system' was indeed like a Kantian category of 'community.' Community is founded on a temporally discrete judgment, as of a whole having many parts, which are thus comprehended as mutually determining: 'as coordinated with, not subordinated to each other, and so as determining each other, not in one direction only, as in a series, but reciprocally, as in an aggregate – if one member of the division [into parts] is posited, all the rest are excluded, and conversely' (Kant 1965:117). Any given element in such a community, say one of several distinguishable objects in a landscape, is comprehended as such by its existing relationships with the others: as a differential or positional value, conditioned by the presence of the others. The parts being thus constituted by reciprocal, contemporaneous relationships, time is ruled out of the intelligibility.

So it is, Saussure held, with language. The conceptual value of the sign is fixed by relationships with co-existing signs. By its contrasts with the other signs of its (systemic) environment, its own sense or conceptual value is sedimented. The value of 'green' is determined by the presence alongside it of 'blue,' and vice versa. If, as is true in many natural languages, there were no 'blue,' then 'green' would have greater conceptual and referential extension. Hence language can be analyzed as a structure only insofar as it is considered as a *state*, its elements standing in the temporal order of simultaneity. [. . .]

But if this language is indeed systematic and analyzable as such, its signs must also be arbitrary. As it were, language is a meaningful system in and for itself: its signs determined as values purely by reciprocal relationships with other signs, as distinct from any connection with the objects to which they may refer. For if a sign had some necessary or inherent link to its referent, its value would not result solely from relationships to other signs. The notion of language as an autonomous structure is then compromised. It loses coherence or systematicity, inasmuch as certain values are externally imposed and carry over through time [. . .]

A dilemma is posed to a general semiology, a cultural structuralism, by the distinction between language and speech. Speech likewise presents the sign in the form of a 'heterogeneous' object, subject to other considerations than the pure relationships among signs. For the expression of language in speech is notoriously imperfect and endlessly variable, conditioned by all sorts of biographical accidents of the speaker. This is once more to say that the determination of discourse goes quite beyond the relationships between the terms of a linguistic system, to facts of a different nature: sociological, psychological, even physiological. Hence the necessity, for Saussure, of constituting language in its collective dimension, apart from its individual implementations in discourse. It exists as a perfect semiotic system only in the community of speakers.

Yet consider what is then excluded from a meaningful *cum* structural analysis. In speech is History made. Here signs are set in various and contingent relationships according to people's instrumental purposes – purposes of course that are socially constituted even as they may be individually variable. Signs thus take on functional and implicational values in a project of action, not merely the mutual determinations of a synchronic state. They are subjected to analysis and recombination, from which arise unprecedented forms and meanings (metaphors, for example). Above all, in speech people bring signs into indexical relationships with the objects of their projects, as these objects form the perceived context for speech as a social activity. Such a context is indeed a signified context; the meanings of its objects may even be presupposed by the act of discourse. On the other hand, the world may not conform to the presuppositions by which some people talk about it. In the event, speech brings signs into 'new' contexts of use, entailing contradictions which must be in turn encompassed by the system. Value is truly constituted in a system of signs, but people use and experience signs as the names of things, hence they condition and potentially revise the general conceptual values of linguistic terms and relations by reference to a world. The encounter with the word is itself a valuation, and a potential revaluation, of signs.

If structural/semiotic analysis is to be extended to general anthropology on the model of its pertinence to 'language,' then what is lost is not merely history and change, but practice – human action in the world. Some might think that what is lost is what anthropology is all about. For them, the prospect is enough to reject such structuralism out of hand. On the other hand, it is possible that the sacrifices apparently attending structural analysis – history, event, action, the world – are not truly required. [. . .]

Hawaiian culture did not merely reproduce itself in the early years of European contact and the kingdom. In the course of reproducing that contact in its own image, the culture changed radically and decisively. The received system did enter into a dialectic with practice. The strong claim of a structuralist understanding does not consist in ignoring that dialectic. Rather, the interaction of system and event is itself susceptible of structural account, that is, as a meaningful process.

My aim is to demonstrate such historical uses of structural theory. I examine a certain interplay between pragmatic 'structures of the conjuncture' and the received cultural order, as mediated by the constituted interests of the historical actors. The exposition begins with a paradigmatic example, an incident again from the initial days of contact between Captain Cook and the Hawaiians. The first anchorage of the *Resolution* and *Discovery* in the Sandwich Islands was at Waimea Bay, Kauai, on 20 January 1778. On the 23rd, however, the *Resolution* under Cook lost her berth while trying to shift to a more sheltered location and was driven to sea, leaving the *Discovery*, Captain James Clerke, alone in the Bay. Next morning found the latter ship surrounded by a great many Hawaiian canoes, occupied by ordinary people engaged in a traffic of provisions for British iron, when abruptly the large double canoe of a chief appeared and ordered the others away. But 'without ceremony' or 'regard' for the smaller vessels that could not move off quickly enough, the chief's canoe 'ran against, or over them, without endeavoring in the least, to avoid them' (King Log: 29 January 1778; Cook and King 1784 v.2:245–6). The occupants of four canoes were left swimming in the wreckage.

The chief was Kaneoneo (known originally to the British as 'Kamahano'). Grandson of the ruling chief of Oahu, Kaneoneo was then, or had been shortly before, the consort of the ranking chiefess of Kauai. He was also at this moment competing for the supremacy of Kauai with another of the chiefess's husbands (Kaeo, half brother of the Maui paramount). But above all, Kaneoneo was a sacred chief of the highest tabus: offspring of a brother-sister union *(pi'o)*. Such a one is 'called divine, *akua*'; he is 'fire, heat and raging blazes'. When he goes abroad, the people must fall prostrate until he passes *(kapu moe)*, the posture also of human victims on the altars of sacrifice. Kaneoneo was one of the few chiefs of the time – Captain Cook also among them – entitled to this, the highest Hawaiian form of obeisance. Which was why he ran over the people's canoes. If Kaneoneo's action seems unnecessarily high-handed, still the people had been slow to move off as ordered. For they were caught in an Hawaiian double-bind: prostrating face down in their canoes for the passage of the sacred chief, they could not also get out of his way.

Kaneoneo's relation to Captain Clerke was no less contradictory – for reasons that can be judged equally traditional. If Clerke were a godlike being from Kahiki, descending upon the Islands with iron and other marvelous goods, he was as much a potential rival and danger to the Hawaiian chief as a source of desirable *mana*. Every action of Kaneoneo's attendants aboard the *Discovery* testified to the ambiguities. Nor would Clerke's behavior disconfirm them, since he managed at once to violate the chief's tabus and present him some remarkable things.

Kaneoneo was attended by a retinue of lesser chiefs and men, but distinguished from these by a feather cloak thrown over his shoulders, while they wore loin-cloths only. Clerke wrote that never in all his life had he seen 'a Person paid such abject Homage to; most of the Indians [i.e., Hawaiians] that were in the Vessel jumped overboard and hurried away in their Canoes when they saw him coming, the rest prostrated themselves before him, as soon as he got on board' (Clerke Log:24 January 1778). In fact he never exactly got on board. He was handed up the ship's side by his attendants who then immediately linked arms to form a protective circle around him on the gangway, and suffered no one but Clerke to approach him. Nothing could induce the chief's attendants to allow him to go below or even move from the spot, and after a short while he was carried down to his canoe by his people.

Clerke's reaction was friendly British gesture – which violated the strictest Hawaiian tabus on the person of a sacred chief. But then, Clerke was a down-to-earth man; unlike Cook, he could never tolerate the abject signs of homage the Hawaiians were always willing to give him. This time, 'I was very desirous of laughing them out of their ridiculous fears; I said all I could, then took him by the hand and clapp'd him on the shoulder; upon which they [Kaneoneo's attendants] gently took away my hand and beg'd I would not touch him. There were at least half a score of principle people about him, who took as much care in getting him in and out of their canoe, as tho' a drop of salt water would have destroyed him.' Kaneoneo presented a handsomely carved kava bowl and a large hog to Clerke, receiving in return a large cut-glass bowl, some red cloth and, 'what he prized more than all,' some very long nails (Clerke Log: 24 January 1778).

The point I make of this anecdote is that the relationships generated in practical action, although motivated by the traditional self-conceptions of the actors, may in fact functionally revalue those conceptions. Nothing guarantees that the situations encountered in practice will stereotypically follow from the cultural categories by which the circumstances are interpreted and acted upon. Practice, rather, has its own dynamics – a 'structure of the conjuncture' – which meaningfully defines the persons and the objects that are parties to it. And these contextual values, if unlike the definitions culturally presupposed, have the capacity then of working back on the conventional values. Entailing unprecedented relations between the acting subjects, mutually and by relation to objects, practice entails unprecedented objectifications of categories.

Everything that was done by the English and the Hawaiians was appropriately done, according to their own determinations of social persons, their interests and intentions. Yet the effect of thus putting culture into practice was to give some significance to the actors and actions that had not been traditionally envisioned. This functional effect is fairly self-evident in considering what (unintended) meaning a British gesture might have for an Hawaiian or vice versa. More radical are the effects on Hawaiian order itself, notably on the relations between chiefs and commoners. The arrival of the British occasioned an uncustomary violence between them. Hence even though, in proceeding upon their respective self-definitions, chiefs and commoners were reproducing the relationships that characterized them, they were also putting these relationships in jeopardy.

The difference in response of chiefs and people to the British presence is intel-ligible from the received structure. If the people unhesitatingly flocked to the ships and entered into commerce with them, such conduct is consistent with the Hawaiian notion of *'imi haki* 'seeking a lord'. We shall see that the same was an important motivation for the remarkable readiness – indeed the importunate demands – of ordinary Hawaiian women for sexual congress with European seamen. Behind this lay a system of landholding and personal security that depended, not on corporate lineage membership – for such was absent in Hawaii – but on the benevolent disposition of higher powers: chiefs and gods. On the other hand, the ambivalence of chiefs with regard to their divine visitors from Kahiki is also understandable from custom. Time and time again the chiefs approached European ships only several days after their arrival, and with a display at once of dignity, power and circumspection. The same kind of ambivalence, we already know, had its role in the death of Cook. But if the chiefs were hesitant, their own status *vis-à-vis* the people required a privileged access to the foreigners and their godly treasure. They would have to take priority in the mediation of foreign contact and exchange, whatever the risks of dealing with sharks that travel on land. Each party, chiefs and commoners, thus acted on interests pertinent to their social position, and in a way that would maintain the categorical difference between them.

Yet the effect was a degree and form of opposition that would not charac-terize relations between them in the normal cause. In fact, if not in myth, the advent of ultrahuman beings from Kahiki was not an ordinary occurrence. Ordinarily, in fact, there would be no occasion for a tabu chief to run down his people's canoes, since the rule is that when a fleet goes out no canoe should take the lead on the chief's – not to mention that chiefs of the greatest tabus (such as the *kapu moe* held by Kaneoneo) should normally go outdoors only at night, just to avoid, it is said, such general inconvenience or danger to the people. There is evidence even in the present instance of an attempt to avoid the problem. The log of Thomas Edgar, master of the *Discovery*, reads that on the morning of 24 January at first no canoes came off to the ship, to the surprise of the British, and Hawaiians on board said their King was coming. Occurrences of this sort are frequently remarked in later voyages: the waters are cleared by the imposition of a tabu, to make way for the privileged advent of the chief. It may be that we have here the first example of what is also documented for later voyages – that the tabu is violated by daring commoners. In any event, the attempt to clear failed, and chiefs and people, each following their rightful course and dispositions, down to the niceties of prostration that immobilized the people, came into collision.

I take this incident as a paradigm, not only of the unfolding relations between chiefs and commoners, but of the historical stress put upon the entire Hawaiian scheme of social distinctions, together with its cosmological values.

The categories were redefined by their differential relationships to the European presence. Men in opposition to women, priests to chiefs, *kaukau ali'i* 'lesser chiefs' to *ali'i nui* 'greater chiefs' – or, at other levels, the windward islands of Hawaii and Maui in contrast to Oahu, the exposed coasts vs. the sheltered ports, the valleys that support taro as opposed to those that grow yams, the pigs (which the Europeans would eat) by relation to the dogs (which they would not) – all these categorical distinctions proved vulnerable to a pragmatic revaluation. No matter that the motivation for the differential responses of men and women or commoners and chiefs to the foreigners was altogether Hawaiian. The content picked up in the experience meant that the relationships between them would never again be the same. Returning from ship to shore, especially from trade to domestic consumption – in short, from practice to structure – the effects become systemic. An alteration in the relationship between given categories affects their possible relationships to other categories. The structure, as a set of relationships among relationships, is transformed. [. . .]

Women had been transgressing ritual tabus from the time of Cook's voyage, if not before. I say possibly before, because the tabu did not sit upon Hawaiian women with the force it had for men. The sanction on women's violations, for one thing, was not a susceptibility to sacrifice, as it was for men. The sacrificial offering must be of the nature of the god to whom it is offered, and women as ritually unmarked (noa), descended rather from Earth than the gods, were not suitable as victims. For the same reason they were contaminating to everything that had to do with the gods: thus to men themselves when they were under tabu or inherently tabu by status, and to foods that were used in offerings, such as pig, certain turtles, certain bananas and coconuts. Moreover, as men ate in communion with the gods, every meal itself a sacrifice, women could not dine with them, nor could their own food be cooked in the same ovens as men's. Hence the tabu as it affected women was rather the negative image of the consecrated status of men and gods: functioning to protect the sanctity of divine beings and things rather than a positive condition, state or attribute of the women themselves. Nor was it at all certain that an act of transgression on her part would automatically afflict a woman (least of all a chiefly woman, whose status was ambivalent, being tabu as a chief if noa as a woman). In historic records, the sanctions of women's tabu violations were socially imposed; they depended on detection and punishment by men, not the malevolent visitation of a god. It is true that such punishments, even unto death, are attested as late as 1817; on the other hand, women had also been escaping the effects of their tabu violations since the time of Cook.

The Cook chronicles testify to two sorts of tabu transgressions by ordinary Hawaiian women. First, they ignored interdictions on the sea by swimming out to the ships at night while a tabu was on. On the 29th of January, 1779, Samwell reports, the British ships were put under tabu, and 'no Girls were suffered to come on board,' presumably because an important chief was scheduled to arrive, and the waters were to be cleared for his advent. In fact, the chief never materialized, but the women did. 'These tabus,' Samwell comments, 'are not so strictly observed but a few Girls can make shift to pay us a visit at night time' (in Beaglehole 1967:1171). Second, when women slept on board the ships, as on most nights, they did taste of forbidden fruits and pork, and in the company of men – the British seamen. The testimony of Messrs King, Ellis and Samwell is unequivocal on this, if varying in detail regarding the extent of women's transgressions. [. . .]

We shall see that both types of violation continued until the tabus were finally abrogated in 1819, as does a third sort, also first documented in 1779: defiance by commoner men of ritual or chiefly prohibitions on the sea or trade. Indeed, there is reason to believe that commoners were transgressing the Makahiki tabus during Cook's entire circumnavigation of Hawaii Island by putting off to trade with the British. Hawaiian traditions of the Cook sojourn say as much, explaining that since Lono was on the water at this time, the people thought they were free to do the same. In any event, a clearcut breach of tabu by commoner men is reported for January 1779 at Kealakekua. The Bay had been interdicted the day before in preparation for the arrival of the ruling chief, Kalaniopuu, from Maui. The tabu held on the 24th. But the next morning, the British 'endeavoured, both by threats and promises, to induce the natives to come along-side' (Cook and King 1784 v.3:16). The cessation of provisioning was not welcome to Cook's company, and their urging had the desired effect. However, as some canoes were putting off with pigs and vegetable produce, a chief intervened and attempted to drive them back to shore (or, by Mr. Law's version, to run them down). The British thereupon fired some small shot over the chief's canoe, chasing him off. The people's canoes subsequently came out 'and refreshments were soon purchased as usual,' evidently for the rest of the day (Cook and King 1784 v.3:16). Note the correlation of forces in this incident: a structure of conjuncture in which British power joins with the inclinations of Hawaiian commoners to set the latter against their own chiefs.

Something of the same can be said of Hawaiian women's eating aboard European ships. No doubt they were encouraged by their paramours to thus engage in what one later European visitor called 'social living' – by opposition presumably to 'natural.' Here, in the matter of co-dining and food restrictions on women, was one site in which European and Hawaiian opinions on the culture/nature distinction differed radically. [. . .] Townsend, along with many other visitors before and after, gave report of how the women continued to set both chiefs and priests at defiance by violating the food tabus: 'I found the women very glad to eat of these [forbidden] articles if they were out of reach of detection' (1888:64). That was 1798. A few years earlier, Manby of the Vancouver expedition observed, 'When on board the ships a few of them [i.e., the women] would shut themselves up in a cabin and regale most heartily on forbidden eatables' (1929 I(1):22). So [. . .] as Campbell says, women broke the ritual tabus that would confine them to shore, sometimes in open disregard of the chiefs or priests. Colnett describes a typical incident at Kauai in 1788: a priest came out to the *Prince of Wales* to call the women on shore because of a 'Taboo Boua' (probably *kapu pule*, a monthly tabu ritual); but few of them bothered to obey him (Journal: [no day] February 1788). On a similar occasion in 1793, the women were observed to comply – 'our female friends instantly left us' – but not without 'many invectives against the barbarous [n.b.] custom that would now confine them to their habitations for two nights and a day' (Manby 1929 I(1):42). Earlier the same month, the women had evaded the interdictions of the bonito tabu by swimming out to Vancouver's ships at night where, says Menzies, 'the sailors had the humanity and gallantry to take them in as they came alongside, & in the Society of the honest Tars they found an asylum of freedom more congenial to their disposition & native simplicity' (Menzies Journal: 14 February 1793).

As for the disposition of ordinary men to break through the ritual tabus to trade with European ships, it is equally well documented in the post-Cook period. [. . .]

The respective relations of chiefs and people to the European presence thus set them in practical opposition to one another. I reiterate that the engagement of different categories of Hawaiian society – women, men and chiefs – to the foreigners from Kahiki was traditionally motivated: the interests they severally displayed in the European shipping followed from their customary relationships to each other and to the world as Hawaiians conceived it. In this sense, Hawaiian culture would reproduce itself as history. Its tendency was to encompass the advent of Europeans within the system as constituted, thus to integrate circumstance as structure and make of the event a version of itself. But in the event, the project of cultural reproduction failed. For again, the pragmatics had its own dynamics: relationships that defeated both intention and convention. The complex of exchanges that developed between Hawaiians and Europeans, the structure of the conjuncture, brought the former into uncharacteristic conditions of internal conflict and contradiction. Their differential connections with Europeans thereby endowed their own relationships to each other with novel functional content. This is structural transformation. The values acquired in practice return to structure as new relationships between its categories.

Ordinary men and women developed a solidary interest in the acquisition of foreign *mana* and domestic utilities distinct from, and opposed to, the chiefly acquisition of power from the same source. The so-called prostitution of Hawaiian women is important here for several reasons: it involved the valorization of a local resource – in considerable demand, besides – other than the agricultural produce, especially pigs, over which chiefs would exert more direct claim and control; the exchange with common seamen bypassed the alliance between Hawaiian and European elites that otherwise regulated commercial intercourse; by its nature, the 'service' provided by women called for domestic returns, an exchange moreover that might be relatively concealed from chiefly view. The schismogenic cleavage thus opened between commoners and chiefs became manifest during the earliest encounters with Europeans. [. . .]

The full import of such divisions within Hawaiian society cannot be assessed without considering the implications of practice for the concepts of tabu – from which ensue certain implications of the tabu for the concepts of practice. I do not speak of a 'reflection' of social relations in ideological terms. [. . .]

I take notice of two structural effects that developed, in the decades following Cook, from violations of the tabus. The first concerns the cleavage among Hawaiians between commoner men and women on one side, their chiefs on the other. The second concerns the cultural and ethnic separation of Hawaiians and Europeans. The commensality of Hawaiian women and European seamen figures decisively in both processes. In both also, the historical changes consequent upon the transgression of the tabus were predicted on the logic of the tabus.

By eating with men – their sailor 'husbands' – and of foods reserved to the gods, Hawaiian women violated the sacred restrictions that had defined them as women. At the same time their menfolk acquired a substantial pragmatic interest in these transgressions, even as parallel breaches of tabu by commoner men were of benefit to their women. Developing in this way a collective and negative relation to the tabu, men and women of the underlying population overrode a distinction in ritual value that had differentially linked them to chiefs. [. . .]

Enter now the pragmatics of trade which, while unifying commoner men and women in unusual fashion and extent, counterpose them to the interests and tabus of the powers-that-be. Running thus in the same direction as the traditional differences in ritual participation – the exclusion of commoners from the temple cult – the pragmatics of trade would break apart the traditional series of proportions, men:women::chiefs:commoners::tabu:*noa*. For everything that sharpens the distinction between chiefs and commoners, or weakens the distinction between men and women, undermines the equivalence of these oppositions – most especially the complicity of men and women in tabu violations, which negates the entire proportional logic. The class distinction between chiefs and the underlying population was in this way foregrounded. It became more pertinent and consequential for social action than the tabu distinctions by gender that had before cut across it. Hence it is not simply that values of given relationships – as between men and women, chiefs and common people – were revised. The relationship between such relationships was revised. Structure is revised. [. . .]

# Chapter 4

# James Clifford

## ON ETHNOGRAPHIC ALLEGORY

[. . .]

**I**N A RECENT ESSAY on narrative Victor Turner argues that social performances enact powerful stories – mythic and commonsensical – that provide the
social process 'with a rhetoric, a mode of employment, and a meaning' (1980:
153). In what follows I treat ethnography itself as a performance emplotted by
powerful stories. Embodied in written reports, these stories simultaneously describe
real cultural events and make additional, moral, ideological, and even cosmological statements. Ethnographic writing is allegorical at the level both of its content
(what it says about cultures and their histories) and of its form (what is implied
by its mode of textualization).

 An apparently simple example will introduce my approach. Marjorie Shostak
begins her book *Nisa: The Life and Words of a !Kung Woman* with a story of childbirth
the !Kung way – outside the village, alone. Here are some excerpts:

> I lay there and felt the pains as they came, over and over again.
> Then I felt something wet, the beginning of the childbirth. I thought,
> 'Eh hey, maybe it is the child.' I got up, took a blanket and covered
> Tashay with it; he was still sleeping. Then I took another blanket and
> my smaller duiker skin covering and I left. Was I not the only one?
> The only other woman was Tashay's grandmother, and she was asleep
> in her hut. So, just as I was, I left. I walked a short distance from the
> village and sat down beside a tree. . . . After she was born, I sat there,
> I didn't know what to do. I had no sense. She lay there, moving her
> arms about, trying to suck her fingers. She started to cry. I just sat
> there, looking at her. I thought, 'Is this my child? Who gave birth to
> this child?' Then I thought, 'A big thing like that? How could it possibly

have come out from my genitals?' I sat there and looked at her, looked
and looked and looked.

(1981:1–3)

The story has great immediacy. Nisa's voice is unmistakable, the experience
sharply evoked: 'She lay there, moving her arms about, trying to suck her fingers.'
But as readers we do more than register a unique event. The story's unfolding
requires us, first, to imagine a different *cultural* norm (!Kung birth, alone in the
bush) and then to recognize a common *human* experience (the quiet heroism of
childbirth, feelings of postpartum wonder and doubt). The story of an occurrence
somewhere in the Kalahari Desert cannot remain just that. It implies both local
cultural meanings and a general story of birth. A difference is posited and transcended. Moreover, Nisa's story tells us (how could it not?) something basic about
woman's experience. Shostak's life of a !Kung individual inevitably becomes an allegory of (female) humanity.

I argue below that these kinds of transcendent meanings are not abstractions
or interpretations 'added' to the original 'simple' account. Rather, they are the
conditions of its meaningfulness. Ethnographic texts are inescapably allegorical, and
a serious acceptance of this fact changes the ways they can be written and read.
Using Shostak's experiment as a case study I examine a recent tendency to distinguish allegorical levels as specific 'voices' within the text. I argue, finally, that the
very activity of ethnographic *writing* – seen as inscription or textualization – enacts
a redemptive Western allegory. This pervasive structure needs to be perceived and
weighed against other possible emplotments for the performance of ethnography.

> *Literary description always opens onto another scene set, so to
> speak, 'behind' the this-worldly things it purports to depict.*
> Michel Beaujour, 'Some Paradoxes of Description'

Allegory (Gr. *allos*, 'other,' and *agoreuein*, 'to speak') usually denotes a practice in
which a narrative fiction continuously refers to another pattern of ideas or events.
It is a representation that 'interprets' itself. I am using the term allegory in the
expanded sense reclaimed for it by recent critical discussions, notably those of
Angus Fletcher (1964) and Paul De Man (1979). Any story has a propensity to
generate another story in the mind of its reader (or hearer), to repeat and displace
some prior story. To focus on ethnographic allegory in preference, say, to ethnographic 'ideology' – although the political dimensions are always present – draws
attention to aspects of cultural description that have until recently been minimized.
A recognition of allegory emphasizes the fact that realistic portraits, to the extent
that they are 'convincing' or 'rich,' are extended metaphors, patterns of associations that point to coherent (theoretical, esthetic, moral) additional meanings.
Allegory (more strongly than 'interpretation') calls to mind the poetic, traditional,
cosmological nature of such writing processes.

Allegory draws special attention to the *narrative* character of cultural representations, to the stories built into the representational process itself. It also breaks
down the seamless quality of cultural description by adding a temporal aspect to

the process of reading. One level of meaning in a text will always generate other levels. Thus the rhetoric of presence that has prevailed in much post-romantic literature (and in much 'symbolic anthropology') is interrupted. De Man's critique of the valorization of symbols over allegory in romantic esthetics also questions the project of realism (De Man 1969). The claim that nonallegorical description was possible – a position underlying both positivist literalism and realist synecdoche – the organic, functional, or 'typical' relationship of parts to wholes – was closely allied to the romantic search for unmediated meaning in the event. Positivism, realism, and romanticism – nineteenth-century ingredients of twentieth-century anthropology – all rejected the 'false' artifice of rhetoric along with allegory's supposed abstractness. Allegory violated the canons both of empirical science and of artistic spontaneity. It was too deductive, too much an open imposition of meaning on sensible evidence. The recent 'revival' of rhetoric by a diverse group of literary and cultural theorists (Roland Barthes, Kenneth Burke, Gerard Genette, Michel de Certeau, Hayden White, Paul De Man, and Michel Beaujour among others) has thrown serious doubt on the positivist-romantic-realist consensus. In ethnography the current turn to rhetoric coincides with a period of political and epistemological reevaluation in which the constructed, imposed nature of representational authority has become unusually visible and contested. Allegory prompts us to say of any cultural description not 'this represents, or symbolizes, that' but rather, 'this is a (morally charged) *story* about that.'

The specific accounts contained in ethnographies can never be limited to a project of scientific description so long as the guiding task of the work is to make the (often strange) behavior of a different way of life humanly comprehensible. To say that exotic behavior and symbols make sense either in 'human' or 'cultural' terms is to supply the same sorts of allegorical added meanings that appear in older narratives that saw actions as 'spiritually' significant. Culturalist and humanist allegories stand behind the controlled fictions of difference and similitude that we call ethnographic accounts. What is maintained in these texts is a double attention to the descriptive surface and to more abstract, comparative, and explanatory levels of meaning. This twofold structure is set out by Coleridge in a classic definition:

> We may then safely define allegorical writing as the employment of one set of agents and images with actions and accompaniments correspondent, so as to convey, while in disguise, either moral qualities or conceptions of the mind that are not in themselves objects of the senses, or other images, agents, fortunes, and circumstances so that the difference is everywhere presented to the eye or imagination, while the likeness is suggested to the mind; and this connectedly, so that the parts combine to form a consistent whole.
>
> (1936:30)

What one *sees* in a coherent ethnographic account, the imaged construct of the other, is connected in a continuous double structure with what one *understands*. At times, the structure is too blatant: 'During the ceramic manufacturing process, women converse gently, quietly, always without conflict, about ecosystem dynamics . . .' (Whitten 1978:847). Usually it is less obvious and thus more realistic. Adapting

Coleridge's formula, what appears descriptively to the senses (and primarily, as he suggests, to the observing eye) seems to the 'other,' while what is suggested by the coherent series of perceptions is an underlying similitude. Strange behavior is portrayed as meaningful within a common network of symbols – a common ground of understandable activity valid for both observer and observed, and by implication for all human groups. Thus ethnography's narrative of specific differences presupposes, and always refers to, an abstract plane of similarity.

It is worth noting, though I cannot pursue the theme here, that before the emergence of secular anthropology as a science of *human* and *cultural* phenomena, ethnographic accounts were connected to different allegorical referents. Father Lafitau's famous comparison (1724) of Native American customs with those of the ancient Hebrews and Egyptians exemplifies an earlier tendency to map descriptions of the other onto conceptions of the '*premiers temps.*' More or less explicit biblical or classical allegories abound in the early descriptions of the New World. For as Johannes Fabian (1983) argues, there has been a pervasive tendency to prefigure others in a temporally distinct, but locatable, space (earlier) within an assumed progress of Western history. Cultural anthropology in the twentieth century has tended to replace (though never completely) these historical allegories with humanist allegories. It has eschewed a search for origins in favor of seeking human similarities and cultural differences. But the representational process itself has not essentially changed. Most descriptions of others continue to assume and refer to elemental or transcendent levels of truth.

This conclusion emerges clearly from the recent Mead-Freeman controversy. Two competing portrayals of Samoan life are cast as scientific projects; but both configure the other as a morally charged alter ego. Mead claimed to be conducting a controlled 'experiment' in the field, 'testing' the universality of stressful adolescence by examining a counter instance empirically. But despite Boasian rhetoric about the 'laboratory' of fieldwork, Mead's experiment produced a message of broad ethical and political significance. Like Ruth Benedict in *Patterns of Culture* (1934), she held a liberal, pluralist vision, responding to the dilemmas of a 'complex' American society. The ethnographic stories Mead and Benedict told were manifestly linked to the situation of a culture struggling with diverse values, with an apparent breakdown of established traditions, with utopian visions of human malleability and fears of disaggregation. Their ethnographies were 'fables of identity,' to adapt Northrop Frye's title (1963). Their openly allegorical purpose was not a kind of moral or expository frame for empirical descriptions, something added on in prefaces and conclusions. The entire project of inventing and representing 'cultures' was, for Mead and Benedict, a pedagogical, ethical undertaking.

Mead's 'experiment' in controlled cultural variation now looks less like science than allegory – a too sharply focused story of Samoa suggesting a possible America. Derek Freeman's critique ignores any properly literary dimensions in ethnographic work, however, and instead applies its own brand of scientism, inspired by recent developments in sociobiology. As Freeman sees it, Mead was simply wrong about Samoans. They are not the casual, permissive people she made famous, but are beset by all the usual human tensions. They are violent. They get ulcers. The main body of his critique is a massing of counterexamples drawn from the historical record and from his own fieldwork. In 170 pages of empirical overkill, he successfully shows what was already explicit for an alert reader of *Coming of Age in Samoa*: that Mead constructed a foreshortened picture, designed to propose moral, practical lessons for American society. But as Freeman heaps up instances of Samoan anxiety and violence, the allegorical frame for his own undertaking begins to emerge. Clearly something more is getting expressed than simply the 'darker side,' as Freeman puts it of Samoan life. In a revealing final page he admits as much, countering Mead's 'Apollonian' sense of cultural balance with biology's 'Dionysian' human nature (essential, emotional, etc.) But what is the scientific status of a 'refutation' that can be subsumed so neatly by a Western mythic opposition? One is left with a stark contrast: Mead's attractive, sexually liberated, calm Pacific world, and now Freeman's Samoa of seething tensions, strict controls, and violent outbursts. Indeed Mead and Freeman form a kind of diptych, whose opposing panels signify a recurrent Western ambivalence about the 'primitive.' One is reminded of Melville's *Typee*, a sensuous paradise woven through with dread, the threat of violence.

> *Le transfert de l'Empire de la Chine à l'Empire de soi-même est constant.*
>
> Victor Segalen

A scientific ethnography normally establishes a privileged allegorical register it identifies as 'theory,' 'interpretation,' or 'explanation.' But once *all* meaningful levels in a text, including theories and interpretations, are recognized as allegorical, it becomes difficult to view one of them as privileged, accounting for the rest. Once this anchor is dislodged, the staging and valuing of multiple allegorical registers, or 'voices,' becomes an important area of concern for ethnographic writers. Recently this has sometimes meant giving indigenous discourse a semi-independent status in the textual whole, interrupting the privileged monotone of 'scientific' representation. Much ethnography, taking its distance from totalizing anthropology, seeks to evoke multiple (but not limitless) allegories.

Marjorie Shostak's *Nisa* exemplifies, and wrestles with, the problem of presenting and mediating multiple stories. I shall dwell on it at some length. Shostak explicitly stages three allegorical registers: (1) the representation of a coherent cultural subject as source of scientific knowledge (Nisa is a '!Kung woman'); (2) the construction of a gendered subject (Shostak asks: what is it to be a woman?); (3) the story of a mode of ethnographic production and relationship (an intimate dialogue). Nisa is the pseudonym of a fifty-year-old woman who has lived most of her life in semi-nomadic conditions. Marjorie Shostak belongs to a Harvard-based research group that has studied the '!Kung San hunter-gatherers since the 1950s. The complex truths that emerge from this 'life and words' are not limited to an individual or to her surrounding cultural world.

The book's three registers are in crucial respects discrepant. First, the autobiography, cross-checked against other '!Kung women's lives, is inserted within an ongoing cultural interpretation (to which it adds 'depth'). Second, this shaped experience soon becomes a story of 'women's' existence, a story that rhymes closely with many of the experiences and issues highlighted in recent feminist thought. Third, *Nisa* narrates an intercultural encounter in which two individuals collaborate to produce a specific domain of truth. The ethnographic encounter itself becomes, here, the subject of the book, a fable of communication, rapport, and, finally, a kind of fictional, but potent kinship. *Nisa* is thus manifestly an allegory of scientific comprehension, operating at the levels both of cultural description and of a search for human origins. Along with other students of gatherer-hunters, the Harvard project – Shostak included – tend to see in this longest stage of human cultural development a baseline for human nature. *Nisa* is a Western feminist allegory, part of the reinvention of the general category 'woman' in the 1970s and 80s. *Nisa* is an allegory of ethnography, of contact and comprehension. [. . .]

Anthropological fieldwork has been represented as both a scientific 'laboratory' and a personal 'rite of passage.' The two metaphors capture nicely the discipline's impossible attempt to fuse objective and subjective practices. Until recently, this impossibility was masked by marginalizing the intersubjective foundations of fieldwork, by excluding them from serious ethnographic texts, relegating them to prefaces, memoirs, anecdotes, confessions, and so forth. Lately this set of disciplinary rules is giving way. The new tendency to name and quote informants more fully and to introduce personal elements into the text is altering ethnography's discursive strategy and mode of authority. Much of our knowledge about other cultures must now be seen as contingent, the problematic outcome of intersubjective dialogue, translation, and projection. This poses fundamental problems for any science that moves predominantly from the particular to the general, that can make use of personal truths only as examples of typical phenomena or as exceptions to collective patterns.

Once the ethnographic process is accorded its full complexity of historicized dialogical relations, what formerly seemed to be empirical/interpretive accounts of generalized cultural facts (statements and attributions concerning 'the !Kung,' 'the Samoans,' etc.) now appear as just one level of allegory. Such accounts may be complex and truthful; and they are, in principle, susceptible to refutation, assuming access to the same pool of cultural facts. But as written versions based on fieldwork, these accounts are clearly no longer *the* story, but a story among other stories. *Nisa*'s discordant allegorical registers – the book's three, never quite manageable, 'voices' – reflect a troubled, inventive moment in the history of cross-cultural representation.

> Welcome of Tears *is a beautiful book, combining the stories of a vanishing people and the growth of an anthropologist.*
> Margaret Mead, blurb for the paperback edition
> of Charles Wagley's *Welcome of Tears*

Ethnographic texts are not only, or predominantly, allegories. Indeed, as we have seen, they struggle to limit the play of their 'extra' meanings, subordinating them to mimetic, referential functions. This struggle (which often involves disputes over what will count as 'scientific' theory and what as 'literary' invention or 'ideological' projection) maintains disciplinary and generic conventions. If ethnography as a tool for positive science is to be preserved, such conventions must mask, or direct, multiple allegorical processes. For may not every extended description, stylistic turn, story, or metaphor be read to mean something else? (Need we accept the three explicit levels of allegory in a book like *Nisa*? What about its photographs, which tell their own story?) Are not readings themselves undecidable? Critics like De Man (1979) rigorously adopt such a position, arguing that the choice of a dominant rhetoric, figure, or narrative mode in a text is always an imperfect attempt to impose a reading or range of readings on an interpretive process that is open-ended, a series of displaced 'meanings' with no full stop. But whereas the free play of readings may in theory be infinite, there are, at any historical moment, a limited range of canonical and emergent allegories available to the competent reader (the reader whose interpretation will be deemed plausible by a specific community). These structures of meaning are historically bounded and coercive. There is, in practice, no 'free play.'

Within this historical predicament, the critique of stories and patterns that persistently inform cross-cultural accounts remains an important political as well as scientific task. In the remainder of this essay I explore a broad, orienting allegory (or more accurately, a pattern of possible allegories) that has recently emerged as a contested area – a structure of retrospection that may be called 'ethnographic pastoral.' Shostak's book and the Harvard hunter-gatherer studies, to the extent that they engage in a search for fundamental, desirable human traits, are enmeshed in this structure.

In a trenchant article, 'The Use and Abuse of Anthropology: Reflections on Feminism and Cross-Cultural Understanding,' Michelle Rosaldo has questioned a persistent tendency to appropriate ethnographic data in the form of a search for origins. Analyses of social 'givens' such as gender and sexuality show an almost reflexive need for anthropological just-so-stories. Beginning with Simone de Beauvoir's founding question, 'What is woman?', scholarly discussions 'move . . . to a diagnosis of contemporary subordination and from then on the queries 'Were things always as they are today?' and then 'When did "it" start?' (1980: 391). Enter examples drawn from ethnography. In a practice not essentially different from that of Herbert Spencer, Henry Maine, Durkheim, Engels, or Freud, it is assumed that evidence from 'simple' societies will illuminate the origins and structure of contemporary cultural patterns. Rosaldo notes that most scientific anthropologists have, since the early twentieth century, abandoned the evolutionary search for origins, but her essay suggests that the reflex is pervasive and enduring. Moreover, even scientific ethnographers cannot fully control the meanings – readings – provoked by their accounts. This is especially true of representations that have not historicized their objects, portraying exotic societies in an 'ethnographic present' (which is always, in fact, a past). This synchronic suspension effectively textualizes the other, and gives the sense of a reality not in temporal flux, not in the same ambiguous moving *historical* present that includes and situates the other, the ethnographer, and the reader. 'Allochronic' representations, to use Johannes Fabian's term, have been pervasive in twentieth-century scientific ethnography. They invite allegorical appropriations in the mythologizing mode Rosaldo repudiates.

Even the most coolly analytic accounts may be built on this retrospective appropriation. E. E. Evans-Pritchard's *The Nuer* (1940) is a case in point, for it portrays an appealingly harmonious anarchy, a society uncorrupted by a Fall. Henrika Kuklick (1984) has analyzed *The Nuer* (in the context of a broad trend in British political anthropology concerned with acephalous 'tribal' societies) as a political allegory reinscribing a recurrent 'folk model' of Anglo-Saxon democracy. When Evans-Pritchard writes, 'The is no master and no servant in their society, but only equals who regard themselves as God's noblest creation,' it is not difficult to hear echoes of a long political tradition of nostalgia for 'an egalitarian, contractual union' of free individuals. Edenic overtones are occasionally underscored, as always with Evans-Pritchard, drily:

> Though I have spoken of time and units of time the Nuer have no expression equivalent to 'time' in our language, and they cannot, there-fore, as we can, speak of time as though it were something actual, which passes, can be wasted, can be saved, and so forth. I do not think that they ever experience the same feeling of fighting against time or of having to coordinate activities with an abstract passage of time, because their points of reference are mainly the activities themselves, which are generally of a leisurely character. Events follow a logical order, but they are not controlled by an abstract system, there being no autonomous points of reference to which activities have to conform with precision. Nuer are fortunate.
>
> (1940:103)

For a readership caught up in the post-Darwinian bourgeois experience of time — a linear, relentless progress leading nowhere certain and permitting no pause or cyclic return, the cultural islands out of time (or 'without history') described by many ethnographers have a persistent prelapsarian appeal. We note, however, the ironic structure (which need not imply an ironic tone) of such allegories. For they are presented through the detour of an ethnographic subjectivity whose attitude toward the other is one of participant-observation, or better perhaps, belief-skepticism. Nuer are fortunate. (We are unfortunate.) The appeal is fictional, the temporal ease and attractive anarchy of Nuer society are distant, irretrievable. They are lost qualities, textually recovered.

This ironic appeal belongs to a broad ideological pattern that has oriented much, perhaps, most, twentieth century cross-cultural representation. 'For us, primitive societies [Naturvölker] are ephemeral. . . . At the very instant they become known to us they are doomed.' Thus, Adolph Bastian in 1881 (quoted in Fabian 1983:122). In 1921, Bronislaw Malinowski: 'Ethnology is in the sadly ludicrous, not to say tragic position, that at the very moment when it begins to put its work-shop in order, to gorge its proper tools, to start ready for work on its appointed task, the material of its study melts away with hopeless rapidity' (1961:xv). Authentic Trobriand society, he implied, was not long for this world. Writing in the 1950s, Claude Lévi-Strauss saw a global process of entropy. Tristes Tropiques sadly portrays differentiated social structures disintegrating into global homogeneity under the shock of contact with a potent monoculture. A Rousseauian quest for 'elementary' forms of human collectivity leads Lévi-Strauss to the Nambikwara. But their world is falling apart. 'I had been looking for a society reduced to its simplest expression. That of the Nambikwara was so truly simple that all I could find in it was individual human beings' (1975:317).

The theme of the vanishing primitive, of the end of traditional society (the very act of naming it 'traditional' implies a rupture), is pervasive in ethnographic writing. It is, in Raymond Williams's phrase, a 'structure of feeling' (1973:12). Undeniably, ways of life can, in a meaningful sense, 'die'; populations are regularly violently disrupted, sometimes exterminated. Traditions are constantly being lost. But the persistent and repetitious 'disappearance' of social forms at the moment of their ethnographic representation demands analysis as a narrative structure. A few years ago the *American Ethnologist* printed an article based on recent fieldwork among the Nambikwara – who are still something more than 'individual human beings.' And living Trobriand culture has been the object of recent field study (Weiner 1976). The now-familiar film *Trobriand Cricket* shows a very distinct way of life, reinventing itself under the conditions of colonialism and early nationhood.

Ethnography's disappearing object is, then, in significant degree, a rhetorical construct legitimating a representational practice: 'salvage' ethnography in its widest sense. The other is lost, in disintegrating time and space, but saved in the text. The rationale for focusing one's attention on vanishing lore, for rescuing in writing the knowledge of old people, may be strong (though it depends on local circumstances and cannot any longer be generalized). I do not wish to deny specific cases of disappearing customs and languages, or to challenge the value of recording such phenomena. I do, however, question the assumption that with rapid change something essential ('culture'), a coherent differential identity, vanishes. And I question, too, the mode of scientific and moral authority associated with salvage, or redemptive, ethnography. It is assumed that the other society is weak and 'needs' to be represented by an outsider (and that what matters in its life is its past, not present or future). The recorder and interpreter of fragile custom is custodian of an essence, unimpeachable witness to an authenticity. (Moreover, since the 'true' culture has always vanished, the salvaged version cannot be easily refuted.)

Such attitudes, though they persist, are diminishing. Few anthropologists today would embrace the logic of ethnography in the terms in which it was enunciated in Franz Boas's time, as a last-chance rescue operation. But the allegory of salvage is deeply ingrained. Indeed, I shall argue in a moment that it is built into the conception and practice of ethnography as a process of writing, specifically of textualization. Every description or interpretation that conceives itself as 'bringing a culture into writing,' moving from oral-discursive experience (the 'native's,' the fieldworker's) to a written version of that experience (the ethnographic text) is enacting the structure of 'salvage.' To the extent that the ethnographic process is seen as inscription (rather than, for example, as transcription, or dialogue) the representation will continue to enact a potent, and questionable, allegorical structure.

This structure is appropriately located within a long Western tradition of pastoral [. . .] Raymond Williams's *The Country and the City* (1973), while drawing on an established tradition of scholarship on pastoral, strains toward a global scope wide enough to accommodate ethnographic writing. He shows how a fundamental contrast between city and country aligns itself with other pervasive oppositions: civilized and primitive, West and 'non-West,' future and past. He analyzes a complex, inventive, strongly patterned set of responses to social dislocation and change, stretching from classical antiquity to the present. Williams traces the constant reemergence of a conventionalized pattern of retrospection that laments the loss of a 'good' country, a place where authentic social and natural contacts were once possible. He soon, however, notes an unsettling regression. For each time one finds a writer looking back to a happier place, to a lost, 'organic' moment, one finds another writer of that earlier period lamenting a similar, previous disappearance. The ultimate referent is, of course, Eden (9–12).

Williams does not dismiss this structure as simply nostalgic, which it manifestly is; but rather follows out a very complex set of temporal, spatial, and moral positions. He notes that pastoral frequently involves a *critical nostalgia*, a way (as Diamond [1974] argues for a concept of the primitive) to break with the hegemonic, corrupt present by asserting the reality of a radical alternative. Edward Sapir's 'Culture, Genuine and Spurious' (1966) recapitulates these critical pastoral values. And indeed every imagined authenticity presupposes, and is produced by, a present circumstance of felt inauthenticity. But Williams's treatment suggests that such projections need not be consistently located in the past; or, what amounts to the same thing, that the 'genuine' elements of cultural life need not be repetitiously encoded as fragile, threatened, and transient. This sense of pervasive social fragmentation, of a constant disruption of 'natural' relations, is characteristic of a subjectivity Williams loosely connects with city life and with romanticism. The self, cut loose from viable collective ties, is an identity in search of wholeness, having internalized loss and embarked on an endless search for authenticity. Wholeness by definition becomes a thing of the past (rural, primitive, childlike) accessible only as a fiction, grasped from a stance of incomplete involvement. George Eliot's novels epitomize this situation of participant-observation in a 'common condition . . . a knowable community, belong[ing] ideally in the past.' *Middlemarch*, for example, is projected a generation back from the time of its writing to 1830. And this is approximately the temporal distance that many conventional ethnographies assume when they describe a passing reality, 'traditional' life, in the present tense. The fiction of a knowable community 'can be recreated there for a widely ranging moral action. But the real step that has been taken is withdrawal from any full response to an existing society. Value is in the past, as a general retrospective condition, and is in the present only as a particular and private sensibility, the individual moral action' (180).

In George Eliot we can see the development of a style of sociological writing that will describe whole cultures (knowable worlds) from a specific temporal distance and with a presumption of their transience. This will be accomplished from a loving, detailed, but ultimately disengaged, standpoint. Historical worlds will be salvaged as textual fabrications disconnected from ongoing lived milieux and suitable for moral, allegorical appropriation by individual readers. In properly *ethnographic* pastoral this textualizing structure is generalized beyond the dissociations of nineteenth-century England to a wider capitalist topography of Western/non-Western, city/country oppositions. 'Primitive,' nonliterate, underdeveloped, tribal societies are constantly yielding to progress, 'losing' their traditions. 'In the name of science, we anthropologists compose requiems,' writes Robert Murphy (1984). But the most problematic, and politically charged, aspect of this 'pastoral' encodation is its relentless placement of others in a present-becoming-past. What would it require, for example, consistently to associate the inventive, resilient, enormously varied societies of Melanesia with the cultural *future* of the planet?

How might ethnographies be differently conceived if this standpoint could be seriously adopted? Pastoral allegories of cultural loss and textual rescue would, in any event, have to be transformed.

Pervasive assumptions about ethnography as writing would also have to be altered. For allegories of salvage are implied by the very practice of textualization that is generally assumed to be at the core of cultural description. Whatever else an ethnography does, it translates experience into text. There are various ways of effecting this translation, ways that have significant ethical and political consequences. One can 'write up' the results of an individual experience of research. This may generate a realistic account of the unwritten experience of another group or person. One can present this textualization as the outcome of observation, of interpretation, of dialogue. One can construct an ethnography composed of dialogues. One can feature multiple voices, or a single voice. One can portray the other as a stable, essential whole, or one can show it to be the product of a narrative of discovery, in specific historical circumstances. I have discussed some of these choices elsewhere (1983a). What is irreducible, in all of them, is the assumption that ethnography brings experience and discourse into writing.

Though this is manifestly the case, and indeed reflects a kind of common sense, it is not an innocent common sense. Since antiquity the story of a passage from the oral/aural into writing has been a complex and charged one. Every ethnography enacts such a movement, and this is one source of the peculiar authority that finds both rescue and irretrievable loss — a kind of death in life — in the making of texts from events and dialogues. Words and deeds are transient (and authentic), writing endures (as supplementarity and artifice). The text embalms the event as it extends its 'meaning.' Since Socrates' refusal to write, itself powerfully written by Plato, a profound ambivalence toward the passage from oral to literate has characterized Western thinking. And much of the power and pathos of ethnography derives from the fact that it has situated its practice within this crucial transition. The fieldworker presides over, and controls in some degree, the making of a text out of life. His or her descriptions and interpretations become part of the 'consultable record of what man has said' (Geertz 1973:30). The text is a record of something enunciated, in a *past*. The structure, if not the thematic content, of pastoral is repeated. [. . .]

I have explored some important allegorical forms that express 'cosmological' patterns of order and disorder, fables of personal (gendered) identity, and politicized models of temporality. The future of these forms is uncertain; they are being rewritten and criticized in current practice. A few conclusions, or at least assertions, may be drawn from this exploration:

- There is no way definitely, surgically, to separate the factual from the allegorical in cultural accounts. The data of ethnography make sense only within patterned arrangements and narratives, and these are conventional, political, and meaningful in a more than referential sense. Cultural facts are not true and cultural allegories false. In the human sciences the relation of fact to allegory is a domain of struggle and institutional discipline.

- The meanings of an ethnographic account are uncontrollable. Neither an author's intention, nor disciplinary training, nor the rules of genre can limit the readings of a text that will emerge with new historical, scientific, or political projects. But if ethnographies are susceptible to multiple interpretations, these are not at any given moment infinite, or merely 'subjective' (in the pejorative sense). Reading is indeterminate only to the extent that history itself is open-ended. If there is a common resistance to the recognition of allegory, a fear that it leads to a nihilism of reading, this is not a realistic fear. It confuses contests for meaning with disorder. And often it reflects a wish to preserve an 'objective' rhetoric, refusing to locate its own mode of production within inventive culture and historical change.

- A recognition of allegory inescapably poses the political and ethical dimensions of ethnographic writing. It suggests that these be manifested, not hidden. In this light, the open allegorizing of a Mead or a Benedict enacts a certain probity – properly exposing itself to the accusation of having *used* tribal societies for pedagogical purposes. (Let those free of such purposes cast the first stone!) One need not, of course, purvey heavy-handed 'messages,' or twist cultural facts (as presently known) to a political purpose. I would suggest as a model of allegorical tact Marcel Mauss's *The Gift*. No one would deny its scientific importance or scholarly commitment. Yet from the outset, and especially in its concluding chapter, the work's aim is patent: 'to draw conclusions of a moral nature about some of the problems confronting us in our present economic crisis' (1967:2). The book was written in response to the breakdown of European reciprocity in World War I. The troubling proximity it shows between exchange and warfare, the image of the round table evoked at the end, these and other urgent resonances mark the work as a socialist-humanist allegory addressed to the political world of the twenties. This is not the work's only 'content.' The many rereadings *The Gift* has generated testify to its productivity as a text. It can even be read – in certain graduate seminars – as a classic comparative study of exchange, with admonitions to skim over the final chapter. This is a sad mistake. For it misses the opportunity to learn from an admirable example of science deploying itself *in* history.

- A recognition of allegory complicates the writing and reading of ethnographies in potentially fruitful ways. A tendency emerges to specify and separate different allegorical registers within the text. The marking off of extended indigenous discourses shows the ethnography to be a hierarchical structure of powerful stories that translate, encounter, and recontextualize other powerful stories. It is a palimpsest. Moreover, an awareness of allegory heightens awareness of the narratives, and other temporal setups, implicitly or explicitly at work. Is the redemptive structure of salvage-textualization being replaced? By what new allegories? Of conflict? Of emergence? Of syncretism?

- Finally, a recognition of allegory requires that as readers and writers of ethnographies, we struggle to confront and take responsibility for our systematic constructions of others and of ourselves through others. This recognition need not ultimately lead to an ironic position – though it must contend with profound ironies. If we are condemned to tell stories we cannot control, may we not, at least, tell stories we believe to be true.

# POSTSTRUCTURALISM

- Michel Foucault, Power/knowledge

- Ernesto Laclau and Chantal Mouffe, Hegemony: the genealogy of a concept

**Michel Foucault** was born in Poitiers, France on 15 October 1926. He taught at many universities in France, Europe, and the United States. In 1969 he was elected to the Collège de France as a professor of the History of Thought Systems. Foucault was the author of *Discipline and Punish* (1975) and *The History of Sexuality* (1976).

**Ernesto Laclau** studied both in Buenos Aires and at Oxford University. Since 1973, he has taught government at the University of Essex. **Chantal Mouffe** studied in Belgium, France and England. She has taught at the National University of Columbia, the University of London, Harvard, and Cornell. Laclau and Mouffe co-authored *Hegemony and Socialist Strategy* (1985).

# Chapter 5

# Michel Foucault

## POWER/KNOWLEDGE

[. . .]

I WOULD SAY, THEN, that what has emerged in the course of the last ten or fifteen years is a sense of the increasing vulnerability to criticism of things, institutions, practices, discourses. A certain fragility has been discovered in the very bedrock of existence – even, and perhaps above all, in those aspects of it that are most familiar, most solid and most intimately related to our bodies and to our everyday behaviour. But together with this sense of instability and this amazing efficacy of discontinuous, particular and local criticism, one in fact also discovers something that perhaps was not initially foreseen, something one might describe as precisely the inhibiting effect of global, *totalitarian theories*. It is not that these global theories have not provided nor continue to provide in a fairly consistent fashion useful tools for local research: Marxism and psychoanalysis are proofs of this. But I believe these tools have only been provided on the condition that the theoretical unity of these discourses was in some sense put in abeyance, or at least curtailed, divided, overthrown, caricatured, theatricalised, or what you will. In each case, the attempt to think in terms of a totality has in fact proved a hindrance to research.

So, the main point to be gleaned from these events of the last fifteen years, their predominant feature, is the *local* character of criticism. That should not, I believe, be taken to mean that its qualities are those of an obtuse, naïve or primitive empiricism; nor is it a soggy eclecticism, an opportunism that laps up any and every kind of theoretical approach; nor does it mean a self-imposed ascetism which taken by itself would reduce to the worst kind of theoretical impoverishment. I believe that what this essentially local character of criticism indicates in reality is an autonomous, non-centralised kind of theoretical production, one that is to say whose validity is not dependent on the approval of the established régimes of thought.

It is here that we touch upon another feature of these events that has been manifest for some time now: it seems to me that this local criticism has proceeded by means of what one might term 'a return of knowledge'. What I mean by that phrase is this: it is a fact that we have repeatedly encountered, at least at a superficial level, in the course of most recent times, an entire thematic to the effect that it is not theory but life that matters, not knowledge but reality, not books but money etc.; but it also seems to me that over and above, and arising out of this thematic, there is something else to which we are witness, and which we might describe as an *insurrection of subjugated knowledges*.

By subjugated knowledges I mean two things: on the one hand, I am referring to the historical contents that have been buried and disguised in a functionalist coherence or formal systemisation. Concretely, it is not a semiology of the life of the asylum, it is not even a sociology of delinquency, that has made it possible to produce an effective criticism of the asylum and likewise of the prison, but rather the immediate emergence of historical contents. And this is simply because only the historical contents allow us to rediscover the ruptural effects of conflict and struggle that the order imposed by functionalist or systematising thought is designed to mask. Subjugated knowledges are thus those blocs of historical knowledge which were present but disguised within the body of functionalist and systematising theory and which criticism – which obviously draws upon scholarship – has been able to reveal.

On the other hand, I believe that by subjugated knowledges one should understand something else, something which in a sense is altogether different, namely, a whole set of knowledges that have been disqualified as inadequate to their task or insufficiently elaborated: naïve knowledges, located low down on the hierarchy, beneath the required level of cognition or scientificity. I also believe that it is through the re-emergence of these low-ranking knowledges, these unqualified, even directly disqualified knowledges (such as that of the psychiatric patient, of the ill person, of the nurse, of the doctor – parallel and marginal as they are to the knowledge of medicine – that of the delinquent etc.), and which involve what I would call a popular knowledge (*le savoir des gens*) though it is far from being a general commonsense knowledge, a differential knowledge incapable of unanimity and which owes its force only to the harshness with which it is opposed by everything surrounding it – that it is through the re-appearance of this knowledge, of these local popular knowledges, these disqualified knowledges, that criticism performs its work.

However, there is a strange kind of paradox in the desire to assign to this same category of subjugated knowledges what are on the one hand the products of meticulous, erudite, exact historical knowledge, and on the other hand local and specific knowledges which have no common meaning and which are in some fashion allowed to fall into disuse whenever they are not effectively and explicitly maintained in themselves. Well, it seems to me that our critical discourses of the last fifteen years have in effect discovered their essential force in this association between the buried knowledges of erudition and those disqualified from the hierarchy of knowledges and sciences.

In the two cases – in the case of the erudite as in that of the disqualified knowledges – with what in fact were these buried, subjugated knowledges really concerned? They were concerned with a *historical knowledge of struggles*. In the specialised areas of erudition as in the disqualified popular knowledge there lay the memory of hostile encounters which even up to this day have been confined to the margins of knowledge.

What emerges out of this is something one might call a genealogy, or rather a multiplicity of genealogical researches, a painstaking rediscovery of struggles together with the rude memory of their conflicts. And these genealogies, that are the combined product of an erudite knowledge and a popular knowledge, were not possible and could not even have been attempted except on one condition, namely that the tyranny of globalising discourses with their hierarchy and all their privileges of a theoretical *avant-garde* was eliminated.

Let us give the term *genealogy* to the union of erudite knowledge and local memories which allows us to establish a historical knowledge of struggles and to make use of this knowledge tactically today. This then will be a provisional definition of the genealogies which I have attempted to compile with you over the last few years.

You are well aware that this research activity, which one can thus call genealogical, has nothing at all to do with an opposition between the abstract unity of theory and the concrete multiplicity of facts. It has nothing at all to do with a disqualification of the speculative dimension which opposes to it, in the name of some kind of scientism, the rigour of well established knowledges. It is not therefore via an empiricism that the genealogical project unfolds, nor even via a positivism in the ordinary sense of that term. What it really does is to entertain the claims to attention of local, discontinuous, disqualified, illegitimate knowledges against the claims of a unitary body of theory which would filter, hierarchise and order them in the name of some true knowledge and some arbitrary idea of what constitutes a science and its objects. Genealogies are therefore not positivistic returns to a more careful or exact form of science. They are precisely anti-sciences. Not that they vindicate a lyrical right to ignorance or non-knowledge: it is not that they are concerned to deny knowledge or that they esteem the virtues of direct cognition and base their practice upon an immediate experience that escapes encapsulation in knowledge. It is not that with which we are concerned. We are concerned, rather, with the insurrection of knowledges that are opposed primarily not to the contents, methods or concepts of a science, but to the effects of the centralising powers which are linked to the institution and functioning of an organised scientific discourse within a society such as ours. Nor does it basically matter all that much that this institutionalisation of scientific discourse is embodied in a university, or, more generally, in an educational apparatus, in a theoretical-commercial institution such as psychoanalysis or within the framework of reference that is provided by a political system such as Marxism; for it is really against the effects of the power of a discourse that is considered to be scientific that the genealogy must wage its struggle.

To be more precise, I would remind you how numerous have been those who for many years now, probably for more than half a century, have questioned whether Marxism was, or was not, a science. One might say that the same issue has been posed, and continues to be posed, in the case of psychoanalysis, or even worse, in that of the semiology of literary texts. But to all these demands of: 'Is it or is it not a science?', the genealogies or the genealogists would reply: 'If you really want to know, the fault lies in your very determination to make a science out of Marxism or psychoanalysis or this or that study'. If we have any objection against Marxism, it lies in the fact that it could effectively be a science. In more detailed terms, I would say that even before we can know the extent to which something such as Marxism or psychoanalysis can be compared to a scientific practice in its everyday functioning, its rules of construction, its working concepts, that even before we can pose the question of a formal and structural analogy between Marxist or psycho-analytic discourse, it is surely necessary to question ourselves about our aspirations to the kind of power that is presumed to accompany such a science. It is surely the following kinds of question that would need to be posed: What types of know-ledge do you want to disqualify in the very instant of your demand: 'Is it a science'? Which speaking, discoursing subjects – which subjects of experience and know-ledge – do you then want to 'diminish' when you say: 'I who conduct this discourse am conducting a scientific discourse, and I am a scientist'? Which theoretical-polit-ical *avant garde* do you want to enthrone in order to isolate it from all the discontinuous forms of knowledge that circulate about it? When I see you straining to establish the scientificity of Marxism I do not really think that you are demon-strating once and for all that Marxism has a rational structure and that therefore its propositions are the outcome of verifiable procedures; for me you are doing something altogether different, you are investing Marxist discourses and those who uphold them with the effects of a power which the West since Medieval times has attributed to science and has reserved for those engaged in scientific discourse.

By comparison, then, and in contrast to the various projects which aim to inscribe knowledges in the hierarchical order of power associated with science, a genealogy should be seen as a kind of attempt to emancipate historical knowledges from that subjection, to render them, that is, capable of opposition and of struggle against the coercion of a theoretical, unitary, formal and scientific discourse. It is based on a reac-tivation of local knowledges – of minor knowledges, as Deleuze might call them – in opposition to the scientific hierarchisation of knowledges and the effects intrinsic to their power: this, then, is the project of these disordered and fragmentary genealo-gies. If we were to characterise it in two terms, then 'archaeology' would be the appro-priate methodology of this analysis of local discursivities, and 'genealogy' would be the tactics whereby, on the basis of the descriptions of these local discursivities, the subjected knowledges which were thus released would be brought into play. [. . .]

The course of study that I have been following until now – roughly since 1970/71 – has been concerned with the *how* of power. [. . .] [I]n the seventeenth and eighteenth centuries, we have the production of an important phenomenon, the emergence, or rather the invention, of a new mechanism of power possessed of highly specific procedural techniques, completely novel instruments, quite different apparatuses, and which is also, I believe, absolutely incompatible with the relations of sovereignty.

This new mechanism of power is more dependent upon bodies and what they do than upon the Earth and its products. It is a mechanism of power which permits time and labour, rather than wealth and commodities, to be extracted from bodies. It is a type of power which is constantly exercised by means of surveillance rather

than in a discontinuous manner by means of a system of levies or obligations distributed over time. It presupposes a tightly knit grid of material coercions rather than
the physical existence of a sovereign. It is ultimately dependent upon the principle,
which introduces a genuinely new economy of power, that one must be able simultaneously both to increase the subjected forces and to improve the force and efficacy
of that which subjects them.

This type of power is in every aspect the antithesis of that mechanism of power
which the theory of sovereignty described or sought to transcribe. The latter is
linked to a form of power that is exercised over the Earth and its products, much
more than over human bodies and their operations. The theory of sovereignty is
something which refers to the displacement and appropriation on the part of power,
not of time and labour, but of goods and wealth. It allows discontinuous obligations distributed over time to be given legal expression but it does not allow for
the codification of a continuous surveillance. It enables power to be founded in
the physical existence of the sovereign, but not in continuous and permanent
systems of surveillance. The theory of sovereignty permits the foundation of an
absolute power in the absolute expenditure of power. It does not allow for a calculation of power in terms of the minimum expenditure for the maximum return.

This new type of power, which can no longer be formulated in terms of sovereignty, is, I believe, one of the great inventions of bourgeois society. It has been a
fundamental instrument in the constitution of industrial capitalism and of the type
of society that is its accompaniment. This non-sovereign power, which lies outside
the form of sovereignty, is disciplinary power. Impossible to describe in the terminology of the theory of sovereignty from which it differs so radically, this disciplinary
power ought by rights to have led to the disappearance of the grand juridical edifice
created by that theory. But in reality, the theory of sovereignty has continued not
only to exist as an ideology of right, but also to provide the organising principle
of the legal codes which Europe acquired in the nineteenth century, beginning with
the Napoleonic Code.

Why has the theory of sovereignty persisted in this fashion as an ideology
and an organising principle of these major legal codes? For two reasons, I believe.
On the one hand, it has been, in the eighteenth and again in the nineteenth century,
a permanent instrument of criticism of the monarchy and of all the obstacles that
can thwart the development of disciplinary society. But at the same time, the theory
of sovereignty, and the organisation of a legal code centred upon it, have allowed
a system of right to be superimposed upon the mechanisms of discipline in such
a way as to conceal its actual procedures, the element of domination inherent
in its techniques, and to guarantee to everyone, by virtue of the sovereignty of
the State, the exercise of his proper sovereign rights. The juridical systems –
and this applies both to their codification and to their theorisation – have enabled
sovereignty to be democratised through the constitution of a public right articulated upon collective sovereignty, while at the same time this democratisation
of sovereignty was fundamentally determined by and grounded in mechanisms of
disciplinary coercion.

To put this in more rigorous terms, one might say that once it became necessary for disciplinary constraints to be exercised through mechanisms of domination
and yet at the same time for their effective exercise of power to be disguised, a

theory of sovereignty was required to make an appearance at the level of the legal apparatus, and to re-emerge in its codes. Modern society, then, from the nineteenth century up to our own day, has been characterised on the one hand, by a legislation, a discourse, an organisation based on public right, whose principle of articulation is the social body and the delegative status of each citizen; and, on the other hand, by a closely linked grid of disciplinary coercions whose purpose is in fact to assure the cohesion of this same social body. Though a theory of right is a necessary companion to this grid, it cannot in any event provide the terms of its endorsement. Hence these two limits, a right of sovereignty and a mechanism of discipline, which define, I believe, the arena in which power is exercised. But these two limits are so heterogeneous that they cannot possibly be reduced to each other. The powers of modern society are exercised through, on the basis of, and by virtue of, this very heterogeneity between a public right of sovereignty and a polymorphous disciplinary mechanism. This is not to suggest that there is on the one hand an explicit and scholarly system of right which is that of sovereignty, and, on the other hand, obscure and unspoken disciplines which carry out their shadowy operations in the depths, and thus constitute the bedrock of the great mechanism of power. In reality, the disciplines have their own discourse. They engender, for the reasons of which we spoke earlier, apparatuses of knowledge (*savoir*) and a multiplicity of new domains of understanding. They are extraordinarily inventive participants in the order of these knowledge-producing apparatuses. Disciplines are the bearers of a discourse, but this cannot be the discourse of right. The discourse of discipline has nothing in common with that of law, rule, or sovereign will. The disciplines may well be the carriers of a discourse that speaks of a rule, but this is not the juridical rule deriving from sovereignty, but a natural rule, a norm. The code they come to define is not that of law but that of normalisation. Their reference is to a theoretical horizon which of necessity has nothing in common with the edifice of right. It is human science which constitutes their domain, and clinical knowledge their jurisprudence.

In short, what I have wanted to demonstrate in the course of the last few years is not the manner in which at the advance front of the exact sciences the uncertain, recalcitrant, confused dominion of human behaviour has little by little been annexed to science: it is not through some advancement in the rationality of the exact sciences that the human sciences are gradually constituted. I believe that the process which has really rendered the discourse of the human sciences possible is the juxtaposition, the encounter between two lines of approach, two mechanisms, two absolutely heterogeneous types of discourse: on the one hand there is the re-organisation of right that invests sovereignty, and on the other, the mechanics of the coercive forces whose exercise takes a disciplinary form. And I believe that in our own times power is exercised simultaneously through this right and these techniques and that these techniques and these discourses, to which the disciplines give rise invade the area of right so that the procedures of normalisation come to be ever more constantly engaged in the colonisation of those of law. I believe that all this can explain the global functioning of what I would call a *society of normalisation*. I mean, more precisely, that disciplinary normalisations come into ever greater conflict with the juridical systems of sovereignty: their incompatibility with each other is ever more acutely felt and apparent; some kind of arbitrating discourse is made ever more necessary, a type of power and of knowledge that the sanctity of science would render neutral. It is precisely in the extension of medicine that we see, in some sense, not so much the linking as the perpetual exchange or encounter of mechanisms of discipline with the principle of right. The developments of medicine, the general medicalisation of behaviours, conducts, discourses, desires etc., take place at the point of intersection between the two heterogeneous levels of discipline and sovereignty. For this reason, against these usurpations by the disciplinary mechanisms, against this ascent of a power that is tied to scientific knowledge, we find that there is no solid recourse available to us today, such being our situation, except that which lies precisely in the return to a theory of right organised around sovereignty and articulated upon its ancient principle. When today one wants to object in some way to the disciplines and all the effects of power and knowledge that are linked to them, what is it that one does, concretely, in real life, what do the Magistrates Union or other similar institutions do, if not precisely appeal to this canon of right, this famous, formal right, that is said to be bourgeois, and which in reality is the right of sovereignty? But I believe that we find ourselves here in a kind of blind alley: it is not through recourse to sovereignty against discipline that the effects of disciplinary power can be limited, because sovereignty and disciplinary mechanisms are two absolutely integral constituents of the general mechanism of power in our society.

If one wants to look for a non-disciplinary form of power, or rather, to struggle against disciplines and disciplinary power, it is not towards the ancient right of sovereignty that one should turn, but towards the possibility of a new form of right, one which must indeed be anti-disciplinarian, but at the same time liberated from the principle of sovereignty. It is at this point that we once more come up against the notion of repression, whose use in this context I believe to be doubly unfortunate. On the one hand, it contains an obscure reference to a certain theory of sovereignty, the sovereignty of the sovereign rights of the individual, and on the other hand, its usage introduces a system of psychological reference points borrowed from the human sciences, that is to say, from discourses and practices that belong to the disciplinary realm. I believe that the notion of repression remains a juridical-disciplinary notion whatever the critical use one would make of it. To this extent the critical application of the notion of repression is found to be vitiated and nullified from the outset by the two-fold juridical and disciplinary reference it contains to sovereignty on the one hand and to normalisation on the other.

# Chapter 6

# Ernesto Laclau and Chantal Mouffe

## HEGEMONY
## The genealogy of a concept

[. . .]

### Articulation and discourse

IN THE CONTEXT of this discussion, we will call *articulation* any practice
establishing a relation among elements such that their identity is modified as a
result of the articulatory practice, we will call *discourse*. The differential positions,
insofar as they appear articulated within a discourse, we will call *moments*. By
contrast, we will call *element* any difference that is not discursively articulated. In
order to be correctly understood, these distinctions require three main types of
specification: with regard to the dimensions and extensions of the discursive; and
with regard to the openness or closure exhibited by the discursive formation.

1. A discursive formation is not unified either in the logical coherence of its
elements, or in the a priori of a transcendental subject, or in a meaning–giving
subject à la Husserl, or in the unity of an experience. The type of coherence we
attribute to a discursive formation is – with the differences we will indicate later
– close to that which characterizes the concept of 'discursive formation' formulated by Foucault: regularity in dispersion. In the *Archaeology of Knowledge*, Foucault
rejects four hypotheses concerning the unifying principle of a discursive formation
– reference to the same object, a common style in the production of statements,
constancy of the concepts, and reference to a common theme. Instead, he makes
dispersion itself the principle of unity, insofar as it is governed by rules of formation, by the complex conditions of existence of the dispersed statements. A remark
is necessary at this point. A dispersion governed by rules may be seen from two
symmetrically opposed perspectives. In the first place, as *dispersions*: this requires
determination of the point of reference with respect to which the elements can

be thought of as dispersed. (In Foucault's case, one can evidently speak of dispersion only by reference to the type of absent unity constituted around the common object, the style, the concepts and the theme.) But the discursive formation can also be seen from the perspective of the *regularity* in dispersion, and be thought, in that sense, as an ensemble of differential positions. This ensemble is not the expression of any underlying principle external to itself – it cannot, for instance, be apprehended either by a hermeneutic reading or by a structuralist combinatory – but it constitutes a configuration, which in certain contexts of exteriority can be *signified* as a totality. Given that our principal concern is with articulatory practices, it is this second aspect which interests us in particular.

Now, in an articulated discursive totality, where every element occupies a differential position – in our terminology, where every *element* has been reduced to a *moment* of that totality – all identity is relational and all relations have a necessary character. Benveniste, for example, states with reference to Saussure's principle of value: 'To say that the values are 'relative' means that they are relative *to each other*. Now, is that not precisely the proof of their *necessity*? . . . Whoever says system says arrangement or conformity of parts in a structure which transcends and explains its elements. Everything is so *necessary* in it that modifications of the whole and of the details reciprocally condition one another. The relativity of values is the best proof that they depend closely upon one another in the synchrony of a system which is always being threatened, always being restored. The point is that all values are values of opposition and are defined only by their difference . . . If language is something other than a fortuitous conglomeration of erratic notions and sounds uttered at random, it is because necessity is inherent in its structure as in all structure. Necessity derives, therefore, not from an underlying intelligible principle but from the regularity of a system of structural positions. In this sense, no relation can be contingent or external, since the identity of its elements would then be specified outside the relation itself. But this is no more than to affirm that in a discursive–structural formation constituted in this way, the practice of articulation would be impossible: the latter involves working on *elements*, while here we would be confronted only with *moments* of a closed and fully constituted totality where every moment is subsumed from the beginning under the principle of repetition. As we shall see, if contingency and articulation are possible, this is because no discursive formation is a sutured totality and the transformation of the elements into moments is never complete.

2. Our analysis rejects the distinction between discursive and non-discursive practices. It affirms: a) that every object is constituted as an object of discourse, insofar as no object is given outside every discursive condition of emergence; and b) that any distinction between what are usually called the linguistic and behavioural aspects of a social practice, is either an incorrect distinction or ought to find its place as a differentiation within the social production of meaning, which is structured under the form of discursive totalities. Foucault, for example, who has maintained a distinction – in our opinion inconsistent – between discursive and non-discursive practices, attempts to determine the relational totality that founds the regularity of the dispersions of a discursive formation. But he is only capable of doing this in terms of a discursive practice: [Clinical medicine must be regarded] as the establishment of a relation, in medical discourse, between a number

of distinct elements, some of which concerned the status of doctors, others the institutional and technical site from which they spoke, others their position as subjects perceiving, observing, describing, teaching, etc. It can be said that this relation between different elements (some of which are new, while others were already in existence) is effected by clinical discourse: it is this, as a practice, that establishes between them all a system of relations that is not 'really' given or constituted *a priori*; and if there is a unity, if the modalities of enunciation that it uses, or to which it gives place, are not simply juxtaposed by a series of historical contingencies it is because it makes constant use of this group of relations. Two points have to be emphasized here. Firstly, if the so-called non-discursive complexes – institutions, techniques, productive organization, and so on – are analysed, we will only find more or less complex forms of differential positions among objects, which do not arise from a necessity external to the system structuring them and which can only therefore be conceived as discursive articulations. Secondly, the very logic of Foucault's argument concerning the articulatory nature of clinical discourse implies that the identity of the articulated elements must be at least partially modified by that articulation that is, the category of dispersion only partially permits us to think the specificity of the regularities. The status of the dispersed entities is constituted in some intermediate region between the elements and the moments.

We cannot enter here into all the complexities of a theory of discourse as we understand it, but we should at least indicate the following basic points in order to obviate the more common misunderstandings.

(a) The fact that every object is constituted as an object of discourse has *nothing to do* with whether there is a world external to thought, or with the realism/idealism opposition. An earthquake or the falling of a brick is an event that certainly exists, in the sense that it occurs here and now, independently of my will. But whether their specificity as objects is constructed in terms of 'natural phenomena' or 'expressions of the wrath of God', depends upon the structuring of a discursive field. What is denied is not that such objects exist externally to thought, but the rather different assertion that they could constitute themselves as objects outside any discursive condition of emergence.

(b) At the root of the previous prejudice lies an assumption of the *mental* character of discourse. Against this, we will affirm the *material* character of every discursive structure. To argue the opposite is to accept the very classical dichotomy between an objective field constituted outside of any discursive intervention, and a discourse consisting of the pure expression of thought. This is, precisely, the dichotomy which several currents of contemporary thought have tried to break. The theory of speech acts has, for example, underlined their performative character. Language games, in Wittgenstein, include within an indissoluble totality both language and the actions interconnected with it: 'A is building with building-stones: there are blocks, pillars, slabs, and beams. B has to pass the stones, and that in the order in which A needs them. For this purpose they use a language consisting of the words 'block', 'pillar', 'slab', 'beam'. A calls them out; B brings the stone which he has learnt to bring at such and such a call. The conclusion is inevitable: 'I shall also call the whole, consisting of language and the actions into which it is woven, the 'language-game'.' It is evident that the very material properties of objects are part of what Wittgenstein calls language game, which is an example of what we

have called discourse. What constitutes a differential position and therefore a relational identity with certain linguistic elements, is not the idea of building-stone
or slab, but the building-stone or the slab as such. (The connection with the idea
of 'building-stone' has not, as far as we know, been sufficient to construct any
building.) The linguistic and non-linguistic elements are not merely juxtaposed, but
constitute a differential and structured system of positions – that is, a discourse.
The differential positions include, therefore, a dispersion of very diverse material
elements.

It might be argued that, in this case, the discursive unity is the teleological
unity of a project; but this is not so. The objective world is structured in relational
sequences which do not necessarily have finalistic sense and which, in most cases,
do not actually require any meaning at all: it is sufficient that certain regularities
establish differential positions for us to be able to speak of a discursive formation.
Two important conclusions follow from this. The first is that the material character of discourse cannot be unified in the experience or consciousness of a founding
subject; on the contrary, diverse *subject positions* appear dispersed within a discursive formation. The second consequence is that the practice of articulation, as
fixation/dislocation of a system of differences, cannot consist of purely linguistic
phenomena; but must instead pierce the entire material density of the multifarious institutions, rituals and practices through which a discursive formation is
structured. The recognition of this complexity, and of its discursive character, began
to beat an obscure path in the terrain of Marxist theorization. Its characteristic
form was the progressive affirmation, from Gramsci to Althusser, of the material
character of *ideologies*, inasmuch as these are not simple systems of ideas but are
embodied in institutions, rituals and so forth. What did, however, become an
obstacle for the full theoretical unfolding of this intuition was that, in all cases, it
was referred to the field of *ideologies*: that is, to formations whose identity was
thought under the concept of 'superstructure'. It was an a priori unity vis-à-vis
the dispersion of its materiality, so that it required an appeal either to the unifying
role of a class (Gramsci), or to the functional requirements of the logic of reproduction (Althusser). But once this essentialist assumption is abandoned, the category
of articulation acquires a different theoretical status: articulation is now a discursive practice which does not have a plane of constitution prior to, or outside, the
dispersion of the articulated elements.

(c) Finally, we must consider the meaning and productivity of the centrality
we have assigned to the category of discourse. Through this centrality, we obtain
a considerable enlargement of the field of objectivity, and the conditions are created
which permit us to think numerous relations placed before us by the analysis of
the preceding chapters. Let us suppose that we attempted to analyse social relations on the basis of the type of objectivity constructed by the discourse of natural
sciences. This immediately sets strict limits both on the objects that it is possible
to construct within that discourse, and on the relations that can be established
among them. Certain relations and certain objects are excluded in advance.
Metaphor, for example, is impossible as an objective relation between two entities.
But this excludes the possibility of conceptually specifying a wide range of relations
among objects in the social and political field. What we characterized as 'communist enumeration', for example, is based on a relation of *equivalence* among different

class sectors within a social space divided into two antagonistic camps. But this equivalence supposes the operation of the principle of analogy among literally diverse contents — and what is this but a metaphorical transposition? It is important to observe that the equivalence constituted through communist enumeration is not the discursive *expression* of a real movement constituted outside discourse; on the contrary, this enumerative discourse *is* a real force which contributes to the moulding and constitution of social relations. Something similar occurs with a notion such as 'contradiction' — to which we will return below. If we consider social relations from the perspective of a naturalist paradigm, contradiction is excluded. But if we consider social relations as discursively constructed, contradiction becomes possible. For, whereas the classical notion of 'real object' excludes contradiction, a relation of contradiction can exist between two objects of discourse. The main consequence of a break with the discursive/extra-discursive dichotomy is the abandonment of the thought/reality opposition, and hence a major enlargement of the field of those categories which can account for social relations. Synonymy, metonymy, metaphor are not forms of thought that add a second sense to a primary, constitutive literality of social relations; instead, they are part of the primary terrain itself in which the social is constituted. Rejection of the thought/reality dichotomy must go together with a rethinking and interpenetration of the categories which have until now been considered exclusive of one or the other.

3. Now, the transition to the relational totality that we have called 'discourse', would hardly be able to solve our initial problems if the relational and differential logic of the discursive totality prevailed without any limitation. In that case, we would be faced with pure relations of necessity, and, as we earlier pointed out, any articulation would be impossible given that every 'element' would *ex definitione* be 'moment'. This conclusion can impose itself, however, only if we allow that the relational logic of discourse be carried through to its ultimate consequences, without limitation by any exterior. If we accept, on the contrary, that a discursive totality never exists in the form of a simply *given and delimited* positivity, the relational logic will be incomplete and pierced by contingency. The transition from the 'elements' to the 'moments' is never entirely fulfilled. A no-man's-land thus emerges, making the articulatory practice possible. In this case, there is no social identity fully protected from a discursive exterior that deforms it and prevents it becoming fully sutured. Both the identities and the relations lose their necessary character. As a systematic structural ensemble, the relations are unable to absorb the identities; but as the identities are purely relational, this is but another way of saying that there is no identity which can be fully constituted.

This being so, all discourse of fixation becomes metaphorical: literality is, in actual fact, the first of metaphors.

Here we arrive at a decisive point in our argument. The incomplete character of every totality necessarily leads us to abandon, as a terrain of analysis, the premise of *'society'* as a sutured and self-defined totality. 'Society' is not a valid object of discourse. There is no single underlying principle fixing — and hence constituting — the whole field of differences. The irresoluble interiority/exteriority tension is the condition of any social practice: necessity only exists as a partial limitation of the field of contingency. It is in this terrain, where neither a total interiority nor a total exteriority is possible, that the social is constituted. For the same reason that the social cannot be reduced to the interiority of a fixed system of differences, pure exteriority is also impossible. In order to be *totally* external to each other, the entities would have to be totally internal with regard to themselves: that is, to have a fully constituted identity which is not subverted by any exterior. But this is precisely what we have just rejected. *This field of identities which never manage to be fully fixed, is the field of overdetermination.*

Thus, neither absolute fixity nor absolute non-fixity is possible. We will now consider these two successive moments, beginning with non-fixity. We have referred to 'discourse' as a system of differential entities – that is, of moments. But we have just seen that such a system only exists as a partial limitation of a 'surplus of meaning' which subverts it. Being inherent in every discursive situation, this 'surplus' is the necessary terrain for the constitution of every social practice. We will call it the *field of discursivity*. This term indicates the form of its relation with every concrete discourse it determines at the same time the necessarily discursive character of any object, and the impossibility of any given discourse to implement a final suture. On this point, our analysis meets up with a number of contemporary currents of thought which – from Heidegger to Wittgenstein – have insisted on the impossibility of fixing ultimate meanings. Derrida, for example, starts from a radical break in the history of the concept of structure, occurring at the moment in which the centre – the *transcendental signified* in its multiple forms: eidos, arché, telos, energeia, ousia, alétheia, etc. – is abandoned, and with it the possibility of fixing a meaning which underlies the flow of differences. At this point, Derrida generalizes the concept of discourse in a sense coincident with that of our text.

> It became necessary to think both the law which somehow governed desire for a centre in the constitution of structure, and the process of signification which orders the displacements and substitutions for this law of central presence – but as a central presence which has never been itself, has always already been exiled from itself into its own substitute. The substitute does not substitute itself for anything which has somehow existed before it, henceforth, it was necessary to begin thinking that there was no centre, that the centre could not be thought in the form of a present-being, that the centre had no natural site, that it was not a fixed locus but a function, a sort of non-locus in which an infinite number of sign-substitutions came into play. This was the moment when language invaded the universal problematic, the moment when, in the absence of a centre or origin, everything became discourse – provided we can agree on this word – that is to say, a system in which the central signified, the original or transcendental signified, is never absolutely present outside a system of differences. The absence of the transcendental signified extends the domain and the play of signification infinitely.

Let us move on to our second dimension. The impossibility of an ultimate fixity of meaning implies that there have to be partial fixations – otherwise, the very flow of differences would be impossible. Even in order to differ, to subvert meaning, there has to be *a* meaning. If the social does not manage to fix itself in the intelligible and instituted forms of a *society*, the social only exists, however, as an effort to construct that impossible object. Any discourse is constituted as an attempt to dominate the field of discursivity, to arrest the flow of differences, to construct a centre. We will call the privileged discursive points of this partial fixation, *nodal points*. (Lacan has insisted on these partial fixations through his concept of *points de capiton*, that is, of privileged signifiers that fix the meaning of a signifying chain. This limitation of the productivity of the signifying chain establishes the positions that make predication possible – a discourse incapable of generating any fixity of meaning is the discourse of the psychotic.)

Saussure's analysis of language considered it as a system of differences without positive terms; the central concept was that of *value*, according to which the meaning of a term was purely relational and determined only by its opposition to all the others. But this shows us that we are presented with the conditions of possibility of a *closed* system: only within it is it possible to fix in such a manner the meaning of every element. When the linguistic model was introduced into the general field of human sciences, it was this effect of systematicity that predominated, so that structuralism became a new form of essentialism: a search for the underlying structures constituting the inherent law of any possible variation. The critique of structuralism involved a break with this view of a fully constituted structural space; but as it also rejected any return to a conception of unities whose demarcation was given, like a nomenclature, by its reference to an object, the resulting conception was of a relational space unable to constitute itself as such – of a field dominated by the name of a split, of an impossible suture between signified and signifier.

We now have all the necessary analytical elements to specify the concept of articulation. Since all identity is relational – even if the system of relations does not reach the point of being fixed as a stable system of differences – since, too, all discourse is subverted by a field of discursivity which overflows it, the transition from 'elements' to 'moments' can never be complete. The status of the 'elements' is that of floating signifiers, incapable of being wholly articulated to a discursive chain. And this floating character finally penetrates every discursive (i.e. social) identity. But if we accept the non-complete character of all discursive fixation and, at the same time, affirm the relational character of every identity, the ambiguous character of the signifier, its non-fixation to any signified, can only exist insofar as there is a proliferation of signifieds. It is not the poverty of signifieds but, on the contrary, polysemy that disarticulates a discursive structure. That is what establishes the overdetermined, symbolic dimension of every social identity. Society never manages to be identical to itself, as every nodal point is constituted within an intertextuality that overflows it. *The practice of articulation, therefore, consists in the construction of nodal points which partially fix meaning; and the partial character of this fixation proceeds from the openness of the social, a result, in its turn, of the constant overflowing of every discourse by the infinitude of the field of discursivity.*

Every social practice is therefore – in one of its dimensions – articulatory. As it is not the internal moment of a self-defined totality, it cannot simply be the expression of something already acquired, it cannot be *wholly* subsumed under the principle of repetition; rather, it always consists in the construction of new differences. The social *is* articulation insofar as 'society' is impossible. Earlier we said that, for the social, necessity only exists as a partial effort to limit contingency. This implies that the relations between 'necessity' and 'contingency' cannot be conceived as relations between two areas that are delimited and external to each other – as, for example, in Labriola's morphological prediction – because the contingent only exists within the necessary. This presence of the contingent in the necessary is what we earlier called *subversion*, and it manifests itself as symbolization, metaphorization, paradox, which deform and question the literal character of every necessity. Necessity, therefore, exists not under the form of an underlying principle, of a ground, but as an effort of literalization which fixes the differences of a relational system. The necessity of the social is the necessity proper to purely relational identities – as in the linguistic principle of value – not natural 'necessity' or the necessity of an analytical judgement. 'Necessity', in this sense, is simply equivalent to a 'system of differential positions in a sutured space'.

This way of approaching the problem of articulation would seem to contain all the necessary elements to resolve the apparent antinomies with which the logic of hegemony confronted us: on the one hand, the open and incomplete character of every social identity permits its articulation to different historico–discursive formations – that is, to 'blocs' in the sense of Sorel and Gramsci; on the other hand, the very identity of the articulatory force is constituted in the general field of discursivity – this eliminates any reference to a transcendental or originative subject. However, before formulating our concept of hegemony, we need to tackle two further questions. The first concerns the precise status in our analysis of the category of 'subject'; the second concerns the concept of *antagonism* whose importance stems from the fact that, in one of its key dimensions, the specificity of a *hegemonic* articulatory practice is given by its confrontation with other articulatory practices of an antagonistic character.

## The category of 'subject'

Discussion of this category requires us to distinguish two very different problems, which have frequently been confused in recent debates: the problem of the discursive or pre-discursive character of the category of subject; and the problem of the relationship among different subject positions.

The first problem has received more consistent attention, and has led to a growing questioning of the 'constitutive' role that both rationalism and empiricism attribute to 'human individuals'. This critique has essentially borne upon three conceptual targets: the view of the subject as an agent both rational and transparent to itself; the supposed unity and homogeneity of the ensemble of its positions; and the conception of the subject as origin and basis of social relations (the problem of constitutivity in the strict sense). We do not need to refer in detail to the main dimensions of this critique, as its classical moments – Nietzsche, Freud, Heidegger – are well enough known. More recently, Foucault has shown how the tensions of the 'analytic of finitude', characteristic of what he has called the 'Age of Man', are resolved into a set of oppositions – the empirical/the transcendental, the Cogito/the unthought, withdrawal/return of the origin – which are insurmountable insofar as the category of 'Man' is maintained as a unified subject. Other analyses have pointed out the difficulties in breaking with the category of 'originative subject', which continues to creep into the very conceptions that seek to implement the rupture with it.

With regard to this alternative, and to its diverse constitutive elements, our position is clear. Whenever we use the category of 'subject' in this text, we will do so in the sense of 'subject positions' within a discursive structure. Subjects cannot, therefore, be the origin of social relations – not even in the limited sense of being endowed with powers that render an experience possible – as all 'experience' depends on precise discursive conditions of possibility. This, however, is only an answer to our first problem which in no way anticipates the solution that will be given to the second. From the discursive character of all subject positions, nothing follows concerning the type of relation that could exist among them. As every subject position is a discursive position, it partakes of the open character of every discourse; consequently, the various positions cannot be totally fixed in a closed system of differences. We can see why these very different problems were confused. Since the affirmation of the discursive character of every subject position was linked to the rejection of the notion of subject as an originative and founding totality, the analytic moment that had to prevail was that of dispersion, detotalization or decentring of certain positions with regard to others. Every moment of articulation or relation among them broke the cognitive effects of the dispersion metaphor, and led to the suspicion of a retotalization which would surreptitiously reintroduce the category of subject as a unified and unifying essence. From here, it was but one step to transform that *dispersion* of subject positions into an effective *separation* among them. However, the transformation of dispersion into separation obviously creates all the analytical problems we signalled earlier – especially those inherent in the replacement of the essentialism of the totality with an essentialism of the elements. If every subject position is a discursive position, the analysis cannot dispense with the forms of overdetermination of some positions by others – of the contingent character of all necessity which, as we have seen, is inherent in any discursive difference.

Let us consider two cases which have recently given rise to important discussions: that relating to the status of apparently abstract categories (above all, 'Man'); and that relating to the 'subject' of feminism. The first is at the centre of the entire recent debate on humanism. If the status of 'Man' were that of an *essence*, its location with regard to other characteristics of 'human beings' would be inscribed on a logical scale proceeding from the abstract to the concrete. This would open the way for all the familiar tricks of an analysis of concrete situations in terms of 'alienation' and 'misrecognition'. But if, on the contrary, 'Man' is a discursively constructed subject position, its presumed abstract character in no way anticipates the form of its articulation with other subject positions. (The range is here infinite, and it challenges the imagination of any 'humanist'. For example, it is known how, in the colonial countries, the equivalence between 'rights of Man' and 'European values' was a frequent and effective form of discursively constructing the acceptability of imperialist domination.) The confusion created by E.P. Thompson in his attack on Althusser, rests precisely on this point. When referring to 'humanism', Thompson believes that if humanist values are denied the status of an essence, then they are deprived of all historical validity. In reality, however, what is important is to try to show how 'Man' has been produced in modern times, how the 'human' subject – that is, the bearer of a human identity without distinctions – appears in certain religious discourses, is embodied in juridical practices and is diversely constructed in other spheres. An understanding of this dispersion can help us to grasp the fragility of 'humanist' values themselves, the possibility of their perversion through equivalential articulation with other values, and their restriction to certain categories of the population – the property-owning class, for example, or the male population. Far from considering that 'Man' has the status of an essence – presumably a gift from heaven – such an analysis can show us the historical conditions of its emergence and the reasons for its current vulnerability, thus enabling us to struggle more efficiently, and without illusions, in defence of humanist values. But it is equally evident that the analysis cannot simply remain at the moment of *dispersion*, given that 'human identity' involves not merely an ensemble of dispersed positions but also the forms of overdetermination existing among them. 'Man' is a fundamental nodal point from which it has been possible to proceed, since the eighteenth century, to the 'humanization' of a number of social practices. To insist on the dispersion of the positions from which 'Man' has been produced, constitutes only a first moment; in a second stage, it is necessary to show the relations of overdetermination and totalization that are established among these. The non-fixation or openness of the system of discursive differences is what makes possible these effects of analogy and interpenetration.

Something similar may be said about the 'subject' of feminism. The critique of feminist essentialism has been carried out in particular by the English journal *m/f*: a number of important studies have rejected the notion of a preconstituted category 'women's oppression' – whether its cause is located in the family, the mode of production or elsewhere – and have attempted to study 'the particular historical moment, the institutions and practices through which the category of woman is produced'. Once it is denied that there is a single mechanism of women's oppression, an immense field of action opens up for feminist politics. One can then perceive the importance of punctual struggles against any oppressive form of constructing sexual differences, be it at the level of law, of the family, of social policy, or of the multiple cultural forms through which the category of 'the feminine' is constantly produced. We are, therefore, in the field of a dispersion of subject positions. The difficulty with this approach, however, arises from the one-sided emphasis given to the moment of dispersion – so one-sided that we are left with only a heterogeneous set of sexual differences constructed through practices which have no relation to one another. Now, while it is absolutely correct to question the idea of an original sexual division represented a posteriori in social practices, it is also necessary to recognize that overdetermination among the diverse sexual differences produces a systematic effect of sexual *division*. Every construction of sexual differences, whatever their multiplicity and heterogeneity, invariably constructs the feminine as a pole subordinated to the masculine. It is for this reason that it is possible to speak of a sex/gender system. The ensemble of social practices, of institutions and discourses which produce woman as a category, are not completely isolated but mutually reinforce and act upon one another. This does not mean that there is a single cause of feminine subordination. It is our view that once female sex has come to connote a feminine gender with specific characteristics, this 'imaginary signification' produces concrete effects in the diverse social practices. Thus, there is a close correlation between 'subordination', as a general category informing the ensemble of significations constituting 'femininity', and the autonomy and uneven development of the diverse practices which construct the concrete forms of subordination. These latter are not the *expression* of an immutable feminine essence; in their construction, however, the symbolism which is linked to the feminine condition in a given society, plays a primordial role. The diverse forms of concrete subordination react, in turn, by contributing to the maintenance and reproduction of this symbolism. It is therefore possible to criticize the idea of an original antagonism between men and women, constitutive of the sexual division, without denying that in the various forms of construction of 'femininity', there is a common element which has strong overdetermining effects in terms of the sexual division. [. . .]

All this shows us that the specificity of the category of subject cannot be established either through the absolutization of a dispersion of 'subject positions', or through the equally absolutist unification of these around a 'transcendental subject'. The category of subject is penetrated by the same ambiguous, incomplete and polysemical character which overdetermination assigns to every discursive identity. For this reason, the moment of closure of a discursive totality, which is not given at the 'objective' level of that totality, cannot be established at the level of a 'meaning–giving subject', since the subjectivity of the agent is penetrated by the same precariousness and absence of suture apparent at any other point of the discursive totality of which it is part. 'Objectivism' and 'subjectivism'; 'holism' and 'individualism' are symmetrical expressions of the *desire* for a fullness that is permanently deferred. Owing to this very absence of a final suture, the dispersion of subject positions cannot constitute a solution: given that none of them manages ultimately to consolidate itself as a *separate position*, there is a game of overdetermination among them that reintroduces the horizon of an impossible totality. It is this game which makes hegemonic articulation possible. [. . .]

# CULTURAL STUDIES

■ Stuart Hall, Cultural studies

■ Fredric Jameson, The political unconscious: narrative as a socially symbolic act

**Stuart Hall** was born in 1932 in Jamaica. In 1951, he went to Oxford University as a Rhodes Scholar. Hall has been professor of Sociology at the Open University in the United Kingdom since 1979. He was the director of the Centre for Cultural Studies at Birmingham in the 1970s. Much of Hall's work is collaborative. His major works include *Resistance Through Rituals* (1974) and *Policing the Crisis* (1978).

**Fredric Jameson** was born on 14 April 1934 in the United States. He taught at various universities in the United States, including, most recently, Duke University. Jameson is the author of *The Political Unconscious* (1981) and *Postmodernism, or, the Cultural Logic of Late Capitalism* (1991).

# Chapter 7

# Stuart Hall

## CULTURAL STUDIES

[. . .]

### New dimensions of culture and the impact of the 'structuralisms'

FROM THIS POINT ONWARDS, Cultural Studies is no longer a dependent intellectual colony. It has a direction, an object of study, a set of themes and issues, a distinctive problematic of its own.

First, there was the move away from older definitions of culture to new formulations. Culture no longer meant a set of texts and artefacts. Even less did it mean the 'selective tradition' in which those texts and artefacts had been arranged, studied and appreciated. Particularly it did not mean the values and ideals, which were supposed to be expressed *through* those texts – especially when these were projected out of definite societies in historical time – and deployed as an 'ideal order' (what Williams called a 'court of appeal'), against which the (widely assumed) inevitable process of cultural decline could be measured. These constituted very much the going 'Humanities' definition of culture. It seemed to us to ascribe a general and universal function to values in the abstract which could only be understood in terms of their specific social and historical contexts: in short, an ideological definition, as important for what it obscured as for what it revealed. This definition had to be, to use an ugly neologism, 'problematized'.

The abstraction of texts from the social practices which produced them and the institutional sites where they were elaborated was a fetishization – even if it had pertinent societal effects. This obscured how a particular ordering of culture came to be produced and sustained: the circumstances and conditions of cultural reproduction which the operations of the 'selective tradition' rendered natural, 'taken for granted'. But the process of ordering (arrangement, regulation) is always the result of concrete sets of practices and relations. In constituting a particular cultural order as 'dominant', it implied (though this was rarely examined) the active subordination of alternatives – their marginalization and incorporation into a dominant structure: hence, also, the resistances, antagonisms and struggles which result from regulation. Strikingly, these concepts were altogether absent: they had been 'naturalized' out of existence. Making culture problematic meant therefore raising these absences to visibility. What were the processes by means of which a dominant cultural order came to be 'preferred'? Who preferred *this* order rather than that? What were the effects of a particular ordering of the cultures of a social formation on the other hierarchized social arrangements? How did the preferred cultural order help to sustain 'definite forms of life' in particular social formations? How and why did societies come to be culturally 'structured in dominance'? Broadly speaking, two steps were involved here: First, the move (to give it a too condensed specification) to an 'anthropological' definition of culture practices: questioning the anthropological meaning and interrogating its universality by means of the concepts of social formation, cultural power, domination and regulation, resistance and struggle. These moves did not exclude the analysis of texts, but it treated them as archives, decentring their assumed privileged status – one kind of evidence, among others.

Second, the question of the relation between cultural practices and other practices in definite social formations. Here we posed the issue of the relation of the 'cultural' to what we may call – again, for shorthand purposes – the economic, political ideological instances. This was part of the project to develop a materialist definition of culture. It referenced, immediately, the problems of 'base'/'super-structure' and the question of determination. But the classical terms of that metaphor were now clearly inadequate. The work of revision had indeed already commenced.

Thompson had called attention to the

> dialectical interaction between culture and something that is not culture.
> We must suppose the raw material of life experience to be at one pole,
> and all the infinitely complex human disciplines and systems, articulate
> and inarticulate, formalized in institutions or dispersed in the least
> formal ways, which 'handle', transmit or distort this raw material to
> be at the other. It is the active process – which is at the same time the
> process through which men make their history – that I am insisting
> upon.

In the effort to give culture its own specificity, place and determinate effect, *The Long Revolution* had also proposed a radical revision to the 'base/superstructure' metaphor. It said, in effect, all the practices – economic, political, ideological, cultural – interact with effect on each other. This rescued culture from its residual status as the mere expression of other forces: but at the expense of a radical relativism, skirting the problem of determination. Other related traditions (Williams at this stage noted the convergences between his own work and that of Goldmann and Lukács) retained the old 'base'/'superstructure' distinction but expanded the complexity and 'reciprocal effect' of the latter (in which culture–ideology was firmly located) on the former. This retained the determinacy – but in an elongated, 'last instance only' fashion. Did it go far enough? Sartre attempted to go behind this formulation by isolating the aspect of *signification* as the specifically cultural element:

> Because we are men and because we live in the world of men, of work and of conflicts, all the objects which surround us are signs. By themselves they scarcely mask the real project of those who have made them thus for us and who address us through them. Thus significations come from man and his project but they are inscribed everywhere in things and in the order of things. . . .

These reworkings all tended to bring together again things which had been dispersed into the binary poles of the 'base' / 'superstructure' metaphor, on the ground of a common, general *praxis*: human activity, 'the process through which men made history', with none of that false abstraction which their assignment to different levels of effective determinacy seemed to imply. This was close to the position taken by Marx in *The German Ideology*, with its 'consciousness/being' dialectic, and its affirmation that all abstractions could be resolved into the general historical process itself – 'which is nothing but the activity of men'. This had a radically historicized philosophical anthropology as its basis. It entailed a very specific way of conceptualizing the totality: a 'whole', in which each social practice mediated every other practice, or, to adopt Williams's distinctive gloss, conceiving *praxis* as the essential forms of human energy. It also entailed thinking of society as an 'expressive totality'.

The major phase of theoretical development which followed must therefore be broadly identified with all those influences which interrupted this search for unities and underlying 'totalities'. These were linked with a different conception of a social totality – as a necessarily 'complex structure', which does not express a unity but is 'structured in dominance'. Here, as Marx argued in the 1857 *Introduction*, unity is the 'result of many determinations', the product of a particular articulation of distinctions and differences rather than of similarity and correspondence. Determinacy had to be thought not as emanating from one level of the social totality – for example, 'the base' – in a unilinear fashion but as an 'over-determination'. The problematic of Cultural Studies thus became closely identified with the problem of the 'relative autonomy' of cultural practices. This was a radical break. It goes far beyond the impact of the 'structuralisms' – though they were instrumental in a major way in bringing this question to the fore. But, actually, the strongest thrust in 'structuralism' as a mode of thought is towards a radical diversity – the heterogeneity of discourses, the autonomization of instances, the effective dispersal of *any* unity or ensemble, even that of a 'relatively autonomous' one. So the problematic of 'relative autonomy' is more accurately characterized as the site where 'structuralism' and Marxism confront each other at their theoretical limits. It was precisely at this juncture that Engels began his long, difficult and seminal 'correction' of the economistic and mechanical applications of Marxism which had become orthodox in his time. It is now commonly agreed that what

Engels did was to identify the core problem of a non-reductionist Marxism, and to provide the elements only of a possible 'solution': the solutions he offered remain (as, surprisingly, both Althusser and Thompson have recently acknowledged) unsatisfactory. 'Relative autonomy' is/was therefore not an accomplished position, theoretically secure against all comers. If anything, its inadequacies only reinforced a general recognition of the major *lacunae* in classical Marxist theory in relation to the whole problem of the 'superstructures'. It signalled work to be done, knowledge to be produced – an open Marxism – rather than the application of ready-made schema.

If structuralism forced on us this question in a peculiarly urgent form, it was certainly not alone in this respect. And its 'solutions' were also, themselves, open to serious question. Its formalism and rationalism, its privileging of the highest levels of abstraction as the exclusive mode of operation of 'Theory' with a capital 'T', its obsession with epistemological issues, themselves constituted formidable barriers to the solution of problems which structuralism itself posed. In noting the impact of structuralism, therefore, we are signalling a formative intervention which coloured and influenced everything that followed. But we are *not* charting a fixed orthodoxy to which we subscribed uncritically. Indeed, here we have not a single influence but a succession, a series. Critiques and rejections of structuralism are as significant in this part of the story as influences absorbed and positions affirmed. We attempt to assess this formative phase and to indicate something of its complexity, in a shorthand way, by taking four representative instances, which reinforce the point.

The first can be identified with the initial impact of the early work of Lévi-Strauss and Barthes. Both deployed the models of structural linguistics as a paradigm (some would say, infinitely expandable) for the scientific study of culture. Indeed, then and since language has been used as a paradigm figure through which all social practices could potentially be analysed, in effect holding out the promise – which long eluded the 'human sciences' – of a mode of analysis at one and the same time rigorous, scientific and non-reductionist, non-positivist. Language, which is the medium for the production of meaning, is both an ordered or 'structured' system and a means of 'expression'. It could be rigorously and systematically studied – but not within the framework of a set of simple determinacies. Rather, it had to be analysed as a structure of variant possibilities, the arrangement of elements in a signifying chain, as a practice not 'expressing' the world (that is, reflecting it in words) but articulating it, articulated upon it. Lévi-Strauss employed this model to decipher the languages (myths, culinary practices and so on) of so-called 'primitive' societies. Barthes offered a more informal 'semiotics', studying the systems of signs and representations in an array of languages, codes and everyday practices in contemporary societies. Both brought the term 'culture' down from its abstract heights to the level of the 'anthropological', the everyday.

If the weakness of the positions outlined earlier was their tendency to *dissolve* the cultural back into society and history, structuralism's main emphasis was on the specificity, the irreducibility, of the cultural. Culture no longer simply reflected other practices in the realm of ideas. It was itself a practice – a *signifying* practice – and had its own determinate product: meaning. To think of the specificity of the cultural was to come to terms with what defined it, in structuralism's view, as a practice: its internal forms and relations, its internal structuration. It was – following Saussure, Jakobsen and the other structural linguists – the way elements were selected, combined and articulated in language which 'signified'. The stress therefore shifted from the substantive contents of different cultures to their forms of arrangement – from the *what* to the *how* of cultural systems.

This was a radical departure. In Sartre, the link between signification and praxis had been founded theoretically on the intentional and expressive project of men (fetishized, masked by their objectivated, alienated appearance in 'the order of things': see above). Modern structuralism proposed instead to think of men as spoken by, as well as speaking, their culture: spoken through its codes and systems. The latter aspect (the linguistic system, the social part of language, the *langue*) rather than individual utterances (*paroles*) was what could be studied systematically. In this, as in much else, Lévi-Strauss recapitulated, within structuralism, many of the conditions of a 'science of society' first proposed in Durkheim's *Rules of Sociological Method* (for instance, the suicide rate, not individual suicides, was for Durkheim the properly constituted 'social fact'). In the same way Lévi-Strauss established the 'rule' as central in the construction of all ordered human systems. He imposed 'difference' and 'distinction' where previously there had been correspondences and unities (compare Goldmann's protocol for a sociology of literature in *The Hidden God*).

Structuralism thus constituted a fundamental *decentring* of cultural processes from their authorial centre in 'man's project'. Culture was as much constituted by its conditions of existence as it constituted them. It established constraint and regulation alongside expression and agency in the analysis of structured practices. Structuralism thus marked a radical break with the dominant forms of theoretical humanism. It bracketed the terms 'consciousness' and 'intention'. Culture was better understood as the inventories, the folk taxonomies, through which social life is 'classified out' in different societies. It was not so much the product of 'consciousness' as the unconscious forms and categories through which historically definite forms of consciousness were produced. This brought the term 'culture' closer to an expanded definition of ideology – though now without the connotations of 'false consciousness' which the term had previously carried.

Lévi-Strauss helped to rehabilitate the work of Durkheim and to demonstrate his varied lineage: where Parsons had worked towards the structural-functionalist synthesis via the Durkheim of *Suicide*, Lévi-Strauss directed attention to Durkheim and Mauss's *Primitive Classification*, which he identified as an integral part of structuralism's 'uncompleted programme'. In polemical fashion, Lévi-Strauss privileged the synchronic level of analysis over the diachronic – an anti-historical inversion with which, from the outset, we were far from happy. For, while it powerfully moved the level of analysis back to that of 'system' and 'structure', this was at the cost (never fully reckoned with by its devotees) of reconstituting some of the fundamental positions of structural-functionalism (for example, society as a 'system of systems') which earlier positions had correctly contested. With these costs Cultural Studies had at once to reckon. In a wider sense, Lévi-Strauss tilted the intellectual pendulum sharply from German to French influences and models, and from a neo-Hegelianism to a distinctive variant of neo-Kantianism. Yet the impact of structuralism, one must repeat, does not consist of positions unqualifiedly subscribed to. We must acknowledge a major theoretical intervention. Whatever else it could not do, structuralism displaced 'man in general' from the full intentional centre of the cultural project. It thus ended a certain theoretical innocence, whatever the critiques of structuralist theories which had then to be made. It made culture, in its expressive sense, conditional – because conditioned. It obliged us really to rethink the 'cultural' as a set of practices: to think of the material conditions of signification and its necessary determinateness.

This may seem strange since Lévi-Strauss, by concentrating so absolutely on the *internal* relations of 'the cultural', effectively side-stepped the issue of determinacy. He resolved the problem cognitively by reference to a set of universal elements and rules common to *all* cultural practices, which he ascribed to the structure of the human mind as such – *l'esprit humain*. In this sense – as Ricoeur observed and Lévi-Strauss acknowledged – he remained a 'Kantian without the transcendental imperative' (that is, God). He was also, if only in a deep sense, a 'Durkheimean', founding culture at the level of reciprocal exchange rather than on production. His work also exemplified a sustained formalism – the price of his proper attention to forms. Nevertheless, a conception of determinate practice lay somewhere near the centre of his work. It could not be constrained for long inside its Kantian and Durkheimean brackets, the limits of his structuralism.

This is clearly demonstrated by what rapidly succeeded it – the work of the Marxist structuralists, here personified in the example of Althusser. Marxist structuralism looked initially like a take-over bid; but it is important to see the internal logic which drove structuralism from its Durkheimean to its Marxian inflexion. If language is a social practice, it can be adequately reduced neither to the mere sum of the individual speakers nor to the individual utterances spoken in it. It must be defined in terms of the 'systems of relations' which make these individual interventions possible and which structure, determine and limit them. There is, despite all their radical differences, a common starting-point here between Durkheim and Marx – in Marx's insistence that we must start with relations, and Durkheim's insistence that the object of social science is 'the social *sui generis*'. On the irreducibility of a 'structure' to the conscious intentions of its individual elements *both* agree – at least as to this necessary level of abstraction. There the salient compatibilities end. For where Durkheim isolated 'the social' (as Lévi-Strauss, following him, abstracted 'the cultural'), Marx insisted on the relations *between* material relations – thinking of 'societies' as ensembles. And where Lévi-Strauss centred his analysis on the 'rule', the codes and formal oppositions, Marx worked from relations and contradictions. Nevertheless, the manner in which Althusser attempted to rethink structuralism on Marxist foundations owed much more to Lévi-Strauss (and through him, inevitably, to Durkheim) than he or his followers have been willing to acknowledge.

Althusser's impact is harder to detail satisfactorily. Here one can only select certain key themes. The first is the break (powerfully established in the early *For Marx* essays) with expressive and totalizing ways of thinking about the relationships between different practices in a social formation. It is well known that there are more ways than one in which this rethinking appears in his work. There is a notion of societies as necessarily complex, unevenly determining and determinate practices, caught in his concepts of 'relative autonomy' and 'over-determination'. There is the full-blown 'structural causality' of *Reading Capital*, where each practice is only the condensed effect of the structure as a whole. The differences between these positions cannot be commented on further here. Crudely, the important innovation was the attempt to think the 'unity' of a social formation in terms of an articulation. This posed the issues of the 'relative autonomy' of the cultural–ideological level and a new concept of social totality: totalities as complex structures.

Second, but closely related, was Althusser's attempt to reformulate the problem of determination in a non-reductionist way (or ways). Third, there were the varied, sometimes internally inconsistent, ways in which he defined *ideology*. This work on ideology was of special relevance to Cultural Studies. It revived two earlier stresses and added two new ones. It reasserted the conception of ideologies as practices rather than as systems of ideas. It defined ideologies as providing the frameworks of understanding through which men interpret, make sense of, experience and 'live' the material conditions in which they find themselves. This second emphasis was very close to the 'culture' of Lévi-Strauss; but it employed a more Marxist connotation, stressing the degrees of mis-recognition involved in these framings and classifications of social existence. Thus, for Althusser, ideologies were those images, representations, categories through which men 'live', in an imaginary way, their real relation to their conditions of existence. To these, Althusser added two further, more controversial, propositions. Ideologies were materially located and were therefore best examined, in their practico-social effect, in the institutional sites and apparatuses (the ISAs) which elaborated them. But also ideologies worked by constituting or interpellating 'subjects'. The 'I', the seat of consciousness and the foundation of ideological discourses, was not the integral Cartesian centre of thought but a contradictory discursive category constituted by ideological discourse itself. Here Althusser, whose borrowings from Freud were already strategic (for example, the concept of 'over-determination'), now ambiguously made another, more tactical, 'loan' from the psychoanalytic work of Lacan.

The problems with the Althusserean formulations on these key theoretical issues (and on the related epistemological questions concerning the relation between science and ideology, knowledge and the 'real') are well rehearsed and cannot be resumed here. We must include in any such account a substantive critique made from within the Centre itself. Basically, the concepts of 'relative autonomy' and 'over-determination' proved fruitful and have been developed – even though they are by no means theoretically secure (what is relative? how autonomous is 'autonomy'?). 'Structuralist causality' has been amply shown to be just another, larger, self-sufficient and self-generating 'expressive totality': all its effects are given in the structure which is itself the sum of all the practices – even if this is a totality of a Spinozean rather than a Hegelian variety. Ultimately, it proved both formalist and functionalist in character, giving a basis for Thompson's subsequent caricature of Althusser's 'structure' as a sort of self-generating machine. Althusser's later work – critical of both the formalism and the theoreticism of his earlier efforts – returns us to more acceptable positions, but these are descriptively rather than theoretically established.

In its integral form, then, 'Althussereanism' remained an internally inconsistent position. In its fully orthodox form it never really existed for the Centre. Few people swallowed *Reading Capital* whole – though elsewhere it did, for a time, acquire doctrinal status. But again the impact was not a matter of mere subscription. Althusser interrupted certain previous lines of thinking in a decisive way. Those who have gone on to further developments nevertheless continue to work and think in his shadow, after his 'break'. Many who have definitively criticized him are still standing on his shoulders.

One last aspect of his influence must be noted. This concerns the ways in which Althusser himself, and those influenced by him, reshaped the central issue of the relationship between ideologies/culture and class formations. Cultures as the lived practices of social groups in definite societies produced, inevitably, a focus on the major social formations of industrial capitalist societies: class formations. In many ways the earlier Marxist tradition – Lukács and Goldmann are good exemplifications here – conducted the analysis of specific cultural formations largely by conceiving them as the products or expressions, at the cultural–ideological level, of the 'world outlooks' or *visions du monde* of particular classes. Class structures, class domination and class contradictions also constituted, at the level of cultures and ideologies, parallel formations – class ideologies. Althusser not only challenged any attempt to reduce the specificity of the 'ideological instance' to the simple effect of the economic base (hence, 'over-determination' and uneven relations and relative autonomy): he also challenged the expressive notion of a simple correspondence between class formations (mainly determined by economic relations) and cultural formations. He did not deny mutual and reciprocal effects between them within the structured complexity of social formations, but he refused any simple transparencies and correspondences. Two related steps were involved here. First, the argument that classes were not simple 'economic' structures but formations constituted by *all* the different practices – economic, political and ideological – and their effects on each other. ('Contradiction' and 'over-determination' were, indeed, Althusser's attempt to 'think' this proposition, which he derived from Engels's letters, against a reductionist Marxist economism, on what he conceived as a more theoretically adequate basis.) Secondly, classes were not integral formations and did not, as Poulantzas put it, carry their ideologies already prescribed and prearranged like number plates on their backs. The manner in which Althusser tried to reformulate this relationship has been the subject of extended critiques. But as a general protocol for the field of study, the force with which it posed the cultures/classes question cannot be overestimated. He asked, to put it simply, how the relationship of cultures/ideologies to classes could be conceived, if one were to avoid reducing the former to the latter.

In sum, one might say that structuralism posed, rather than answered satisfactorily, certain absolutely critical questions for Cultural Studies. This summary proposition could, of course, be divided into many more subdivisions than we have space for here. It offered the challenge of further work on the problem of a materialist, non-reductionist theory of culture.

We have noted the importance of Althusser's 'Ideological state apparatuses' essay. This influential paper was important because its definition of ideologies embraced many of the wider ways in which we had come to define culture – also, because of its stress on 'practices' rather than merely on 'ideas'. It was influential, too, because it retained a classical Marxist emphasis on the 'function' which ideology performed in reproducing the conditions and relations necessary to the mode of production of class societies. This third emphasis was important because it initiated ways of thinking about the relationship of ideologies to class-structured social formations (that is, through reproduction), without reducing the former to classes. It related the production of ideologies to 'dominant ideologies' and to all those apparatuses which produce and reproduce the ideological structures of society, located in the state and in the institutions of civil society (churches, trade unions, the family, the social, cultural apparatuses and so on). But it tended to conceptualize these relations as 'functional supports' for a given system of dominant social arrangements. Thus it consistently down-played the notion of cultural contradiction and struggle. For all practical purposes, the domain of ideology was, for Althusser, the domain of the '*dominant* ideologies'. Althusser attempted to redress the functionalist balance of this essay in a footnote on ideology as 'struggle' – but, so far as the theoretical structure of his argument was concerned, this eleventh-hour revision was merely 'gestural'. This was a critique of his work which the Centre began to develop from its first encounter. And the importance of this critique may be indicated by naming another influential figure – Antonio Gramsci – who provided, for us, very much the 'limit case' of Marxist structuralism and whose work has therefore been widely influential, in a different way, for the Centre.

Like the structuralists, Gramsci steadfastly resists any attempt neatly to align cultural and ideological questions with class and economic ones. His work stands as a prolonged repudiation of any form of reductionism – especially that of 'economism': 'It is the problem of the relations between structure and superstructure which must be accurately posed and resolved if the forces which are active in the history of a particular period are to be correctly analysed and the relation between them determined. This connection and specificity is elaborated in Gramsci through his extended work on the nature of the state and civil society in developed capitalist societies; in his discussion of 'the specificity of the political'; in his work on 'national–popular' cultures and the role and formation of intellectuals; in his analysis of 'common sense' as the ground on which different organized ideologies intervene; in his emphasis on the practico–social role which ideologies have in organizing and mobilizing masses of people; and in the complex notion which he has of what constitutes a 'class' formation and the complex role of class alliances within a historical bloc.

Gramsci brings these ideas together within the framework of the concept of 'hegemony', which has placed a seminal role in Cultural Studies. This is an enlarged and complex idea. In essence, it refers to all those processes whereby a fundamental social group (Gramsci speaks of alliances of class strata, not of a unitary and unproblematic 'ruling class'), which has achieved direction over the 'decisive economic nucleus', is able to expand this into a moment of social, political and cultural leadership and authority throughout civil society and the state attempting to unify and reconstruct the social formation around an organic tendency through a series of 'national tasks'. Gramsci speaks of this elaboration of a tendency into a civilization as the 'passage from the structure to the complex superstructure' – a formative and connective moment, requiring new kinds and levels of intervention, in which previously germinated ideologies become 'party', come into confrontation and conflict, until one of them or at least a combination of them tends to prevail, to gain the upper hand, to propagate itself throughout society – bringing about not only a unison of economic and political aims, but also intellectual and moral unity, posing all the questions around which the struggle rages, not on a corporate but on a 'universal' plane, and thus creating the hegemony of a fundamental group over a series of subordinate groups.

Here one finds Gramsci thinking of complex social formations and the relations between their different aspects in a connective but non-reductionist way. 'Hegemony' retains its base in the way the productive life of societies is organized. But it raises as critical the formative and educative tasks which are required if this is to become the basis of a profound revision of the whole social formation – the structures of civil and political life, culture and ideologies. The important point is that such 'moments' assume a different character, have different degrees of success and provoke qualitative challenges of different kinds at different times, depending on the definite forms of society, the balance of contending forces and the historical conjuncture. In this respect Gramsci massively corrects the ahistorical, highly abstract, formal and theoreticist level at which structuralist theories tend to operate. His thinking is always historically specific and 'conjunctural'. It is conjunctural in two senses. It is always made specific to a particular historical phase in specific national societies; but, further, the concept of hegemony is elaborated specifically in relation to those advanced capitalist societies in which the institutions of state and civil society have reached a stage of great complexity, in which the mobilization and consent of the popular masses is required to secure the ascendancy of a particular tendency and in which 'reform' requires an extended and complex process of struggle, mastery, compromise and transformation to reshape society to new goals and purposes. Gramsci's thinking is thus peculiarly relevant to societies like ours, in which political and cultural power has been established through the parliamentary and representative political system, with a complex state structure and a massive development of the cultural institutions of civil society.

For Gramsci, 'hegemony' is never a permanent state of affairs and never uncontested. He distances himself from both the 'ruling class/ruling ideas' propositions of *The German Ideology* and the functionalist conception of 'dominant ideology' in Althusser's essay. 'Hegemony' is always the (temporary) mastery of a particular theatre of struggle. It marks a shift in the dispositions of contending forces in a field of struggle and the articulation of that field into a tendency. Such tendencies do not immediately 'profit' a ruling class or a fraction of capital, but they create the conditions whereby society and the state may be conformed in a larger sense to certain formative national–historical tasks. Thus particular outcomes always depend on the balance in the relations of force in any theatre of struggle and reform. This rids Gramsci's thinking of any trace of a necessitarian logic and any temptation to 'read off' political and ideological outcomes from some hypostatized economic base. Its effect is to show how cultural questions can be linked, in a non-reductionist manner, to other levels: it enables us to think of societies as complex formations, necessarily contradictory, always historically specific.

Gramsci, of course, remains within the basic terms of a materialist theory. But there have been other influences which, in certain areas of our work, have taken the line of thinking beyond these terms of reference. One may think here of the difficult but important work stemming from the critique of earlier semiotic models of language, and of parallel developments based on an appropriation of psychoanalytic theories. These tendencies may be conveniently represented by Foucault, in whose work one finds an even more radical attempt to break with any model of a hierarchy of determining factors through the concept of 'discursive practices'. Foucault's name must be taken here as 'personifying' a whole set of theoretical developments based on the critique of the early models of language promulgated in the first phase of semiotic theory and structural linguistics. In his notion of 'discourse' Foucault goes some way to breaking down the dichotomy, which most other positions appear to retain in some form, between the signifying ('discursive') and the 'extra-discursive' aspects of any practice. This work privileges, but in a new way, the study of textual archives and the sites through which the 'discursive' practices of a society are constructed. His analysis of the practices of sexuality or of punishment examines the rules and regularities through which, at different moments, the objects of these practices are formulated and elaborated. Foucault, following the lead of Lévi-Strauss, though in a very different way, directs attention to the *internal* relations and regularities of any field of knowledge. He remains agnostic about their general determining conditions and about their 'truth'. He examines them largely from a 'topographical' or genealogical vantage point – studying their arrangement, their disposition, their interventions on each other, their articulation and transformation. This, once again, skirts the difficult question of determination, but it has provided the basis for extensive, concrete studies of different fields of knowledge and practice. He has helped further to break down that dichotomy between social practices and the ways they are represented in ideologies, in discourse and in particular regimes of knowledge. He has opened up again the problem of 'representation' itself, on which so many theories of ideology and symbolic representation have been based.

We have deliberately not attempted here to resume the entire theoretical spectrum of the Centre's recent work in this period. We have referenced some major turning-points through a selection of representative instances. This abbreviated account should not be taken as marking a steady and unified 'long march' through the theoretical continents. Different theorists and positions outlined above have been more or less influential in different areas of the Centre's work. While maintaining a consistent level of debate and discussion about and between them, a certain theoretical 'pluralism' has been both necessary and inevitable. Thus, to give an example: the Centre's work on language [. . .] explored very fully the post-Saussure critique of semiotic models and has worked fairly consistently on terrain staked out by Derrida, Foucault, Kristeva, the 'Tel Quel' group and Lacanian psychoanalysis (the contribution to this volume amply demonstrates this in detail). By contrast the media group has been critical of the 'autonomy' it saw implied in those positions and the universalism entailed by the revisions of psychoanalysis advanced by Lacan. Despite these real differences in theoretical perspective, the two groups have learned much from each other. Another example: analysis in the Work Group has always retained an earlier stress on the importance of observational methods and the accounts actors give of their experience: nevertheless, this work has moved progressively towards its own distinctive ways of conceptualizing the structural conditions of the labour process (for example, Part 2 of Paul Willis's *Learning to Labour*). Much of this research now relates to women's work, reflecting a more developed feminist perspective, but within this work *both* kinds of emphases are present. (This is discussed in *Women Take Issue*.) In feminist research more generally the emphasis on experience and consciousness (in, for example, Sheila Rowbotham's work) sharply contrasts with 'Althusserean' and Lévi-Straussean emphases (for example, Juliet Mitchell's *Psychoanalysis and Feminism* or the Lacanian positions of the journal, *m/f*). Yet another example: the Centre's History Group, which pursued the rationalist position on history and theory as far as it could be taken, then went on to provide one of the most developed and formative critiques of this position. Theoretical openness has by no means been easy to sustain within the Centre, but the Centre has consciously attempted to undercut any attempts to establish an 'orthodoxy' (in the sense of a set of prescribed positions to which everyone had to adhere).

## The impact of the feminisms

We have traced the complex and uneven impact of 'the structuralisms'. The most profound challenge to any attempt to establish a Cultural Studies 'orthodoxy' has, however, undoubtedly arisen from the emergence of feminism within the Centre's work. In challenging the male-oriented models and assumptions and the heavily masculine subject-matter and topics which for long constituted the assumed terrain of Cultural Studies (in a profoundly unconscious and unreflexive way), feminism has had an obvious impact on Cultural Studies. It has forced a major rethink in every substantive area of work. But its impact can in no sense be limited to these substantive reworkings. It is impossible, from a vantage point inside feminism, to retain a reductionist theory of culture. In posing all those areas and sites in any social formation which need to be rethought from the perspective of the position and the oppression of women and the centrality of patriarchal relations, feminism has provoked a break with any residual attempt to give the term 'material conditions' an exclusively economistic or 'productivist' meaning. In raising the question of how to think of both the causes and the effects of the contradictions of gender, it has displaced forever any exclusive reference to class contradictions as the stable point of reference for cultural analysis. All that is involved in thinking about the specificity of 'gender' – distinct from, even though it can be shown to be articulated with, 'class' – has moved Cultural Studies away from its tendency to a complex class reductionism. We have seen that the question of 'determination' has been one of the principal theoretical motors of work in this area. But the attention to the structuring principle of gender and to questions of sexual difference and patriarchal relations has rendered it impossible to fall back behind the intrinsic heterogeneity and necessary complexity of different kinds of contradiction, attributable in neither a 'first' or 'last' sense to the 'economic' in its simple designation.

Feminism has thus been responsible not only for setting 'reproduction', alongside 'production', as a key site for the elaboration of cultural structures, but also for profoundly rethinking the concept of 'production' itself. Both Gramsci and Althusser cited the school and the family as key instances in the construction of 'hegemony'. But neither school nor family can be seriously considered outside the sexual division of labour, the construction of gender roles, identities and relations and the principle of sexual difference. The institutions of state and civil society are both 'capitalist' and 'patriarchal' in character, in their very mode of operation: but capitalism and patriarchy have distinct histories, different conditions of existence, different cross-cutting effects and consequences, which make impossible any neat alignment or correspondences between them. A theory of culture which cannot account for patriarchal structures of dominance and oppression is, in the wake of feminism, a non-starter. But patriarchal relations are not amenable to simple extensions, marginal qualifications or emendations to other theories which – but for this question – retain their general validity. The problematics of these theories have had to be profoundly recast, their premises brought into radical question, because of the absence, in their very theoretical structure, of the question of sexual difference.

Feminism has therefore radically altered the terrain of Cultural Studies. It has, of course, brought whole new concrete areas of inquiry, new sites of investigation into being within the Cultural Studies agenda, as well as reshaping existing ones. But its larger impact has been theoretical and organizational – all that has been required to think the whole field anew from the site of a different contradiction and all that this has meant, in its consequences, both for what is studied in the Centre and for how it is studied: the organization of a new intellectual practice. The attempt really to take these questions into account – not simply to nod, generally, in their direction – has been a painful exercise at times (as those who have read the account by women in the Centre in *Women Take Issue* will readily understand): not so much a crisis of intent – which was subscribed to at an early stage, though not without resistance – but rather of bringing about a deep change in practice and in the modes of intellectual work in the Centre. The resistances have been all the stronger because of the depth and extent of what had been repressed, the hard-won certainties which, rightly and necessarily, were challenged and undermined. In one area after another of the Centre's work feminism has sent certainties and orthodoxies back to the drawing-board. It has redrawn the map of Cultural Studies, as it is slowly redesigning every area of critical intellectual life. The transformations it has provoked are profound and unstoppable. [. . .]

# Chapter 8

# Fredric Jameson

## THE POLITICAL UNCONSCIOUS
## Narrative as a socially symbolic act

[. . .]

**A**LWAYS HISTORICIZE! This slogan – the one absolute and we may even say 'transhistorical' imperative of all dialectical thought – will unsurprisingly turn out to be the moral of *The Political Unconscious* as well. But, as the traditional dialectic teaches us, the historicizing operation can follow two distinct paths, which only ultimately meet in the same place: the path of object and the path of subject, the historical origins of the things themselves and that more intangible historicity of the concepts and categories by which we attempt to understand those things. In the area of culture, which is the central field of the present book, we are thus confronted with a choice between study of the nature of the 'objective' structures of a given cultural text (the historicity of its forms and of its content, the historical moment of emergence of its linguistic possibilities, the situation–specific function of its aesthetic) and something rather different which would instead foreground the interpretive categories or codes through which we read and receive the text in question. For better or for worse, it is this second path we have chosen to follow here: *The Political Unconscious* accordingly turns on the dynamics of the act of interpretation and presupposes, as its organizational fiction, that we never really confront a text immediately, in all its freshness as a thing-in-itself. Rather, texts come before us as the always-already-read; we apprehend them through sedimented layers of previous interpretations, or – if the text is brand-new – through the sedimented reading habits and categories developed by those inherited interpretive traditions. This presupposition then dictates the use of a method (which I have elsewhere termed the 'metacommentary') according to which our object of study is less the text itself than the interpretations through which we attempt to confront and to appropriate it. Interpretation is here construed as an essentially allegorical act, which consists in rewriting a given text in terms of a particular interpretive master code. The identification of the latter will then lead to an evaluation of such codes or, in other words, of the 'methods' or approaches current in American literary and cultural study today. Their juxtaposition with a dialectical or totalizing, properly Marxist ideal of understanding will be used to demonstrate the structural limitations of the other interpretive codes, and in particular to show the 'local' ways in which they construct their objects of study and the 'strategies of containment' whereby they are able to project the illusion that their readings are somehow complete and self-sufficient. [. . .]

[T]he convenient working distinction between cultural texts that are social and political and those that are not becomes something worse than an error: namely, a symptom and a reinforcement of the reification and privatization of contemporary life. Such a distinction reconfirms that structural, experiential, and conceptual gap between the public and the private, between the social and the psychological, or the political and the poetic, between history or society and the 'individual,' which — the tendential law of social life under capitalism — maims our existence as individual subjects and paralyzes our thinking about time and change just as surely as it alienates us from our speech itself. To imagine that, sheltered from the omnipresence of history and the implacable influence of the social, there already exists a realm of freedom — whether it be that of the microscopic experience of words in a text or the ecstasies and intensities of the various private religions — is only to strengthen the grip of Necessity over all such blind zones in which the individual subject seeks refuge, in pursuit of a purely individual, a merely psychological, project of salvation. The only effective liberation from such constraint begins with the recognition that there is nothing that is not social and historical — indeed, that everything is 'in the last analysis' political.

The assertion of a political unconscious proposes that we undertake just such a final analysis and explore the multiple paths that lead to the unmasking of cultural artifacts as socially symbolic acts. It projects a rival hermeneutic to those already enumerated; but it does so, as we shall see, not so much by repudiating their findings as by arguing its ultimate philosophical and methodological priority over more specialized interpretive codes whose insights are strategically limited as much by their own situational origins as by the narrow or local ways in which they construe or construct their objects of study. [. . .]

[T]he ideal of an immanent analysis of the text, of a dismantling or deconstruction of its parts and a description of its functioning and malfunctioning, amounts less to a wholesale nullification of all interpretive activity than to a demand for the construction of some new and more adequate, immanent or antitranscendent hermeneutic model, which it will be the task of the following pages to propose. [. . .]

[I]f interpretation in terms of expressive causality or of allegorical master narratives remains a constant temptation, this is because such master narratives have inscribed themselves in the texts as well as in our thinking about them; such allegorical narrative signifieds are a persistent dimension of literary and cultural texts precisely because they reflect a fundamental dimension of our collective thinking and our collective fantasies about history and reality. [. . .] We would therefore propose the following revised formulation: that history is *not* a text, not a narrative, master or otherwise, but that, as an absent cause, it is inaccessible to us except in textual form, and that our approach to it and to the Real itself necessarily passes through its prior textualization, its narrativization in the political uncon-scious. [. . .]

[I]deology leaves its mark on myth criticism insofar as the latter proposes an unbroken continuity between the social relations and narrative forms of primitive society and the cultural objects of our own. For Marxism, on the contrary, it is the radical break between the two social formations which must be stressed, if we are to begin to grasp the degree to which capitalism has effectively dissolved all the older forms of collective relations, leaving their cultural expressions and their myths as incomprehensible to us as so many dead languages or undecipherable codices. [. . .]

The Marxian vision of history outlined in the previous chapter has sometimes, as we have observed, been described as a 'comic' archetype or a 'romance' paradigm. What is meant thereby is the salvational or redemptive perspective of some secure future, from which, with William Morris' Time Traveller, we can have our 'fill of the pleasure of the eyes without any of that sense of incongruity, that dread of approaching ruin, which had always beset me hitherto when I had been among the beautiful works of art of the past.' In such a future, indeed, or from its perspec-tive, our own cultural tradition – the monuments of power societies (for Goethe, the *Iliad* was a glimpse into hell) as well as the stories of fierce market competi-tion and the expressions of commodity lust and of the triumph of the commodity form – will be read as children's books, recapitulating the barely comprehensible memory of ancient dangers.

Even from the standpoint of an ideal of realism (traditionally in one form or another the central model of Marxist aesthetics as a narrative discourse which unites the experience of daily life with a properly cognitive, mapping, or well-nigh 'scientific' perspective) this apparently contradictory valorization of romance has much to be said for it. Let Scott, Balzac, and Dreiser serve as the non-chrono-logical markers of the emergence of realism in its modern form; these first great realisms are characterized by a fundamental and exhilarating heterogeneity in their raw materials and by a corresponding versatility in their narrative apparatus. In such moments, a generic confinement to the existent has a paradoxically liberating effect on the registers of the text, and releases a set of heterogeneous historical perspectives – the past for Scott, the future for Balzac, the process of commodi-fication for Dreiser – normally felt to be inconsistent with a focus on the historical present. Indeed, this multiple temporality tends to be sealed off and recontained again in 'high' realism and naturalism, where a perfected narrative apparatus (in particular the threefold imperatives of authorial depersonalization, unity of point of view, and restriction to scenic representation) begins to confer on the 'realistic' option the appearance of an asphyxiating, self-imposed penance. It is in the context of the gradual reification of realism in late capitalism that romance once again comes to be felt as the place of narrative heterogeneity and of freedom from that reality principle to which a now oppressive realistic representation is the hostage. Romance now again seems to offer the possibility of sensing other historical rhythms, and of demonic or Utopian transformations of a real now unshakably set in place; and Frye is surely not wrong to assimilate the salvational perspective of romance to a reexpression of Utopian longings, a renewed meditation on the

Utopian community, a reconquest (but at what price?) of some feeling for a salvational future.

The association of Marxism and romance therefore does not discredit the former so much as it explains the persistence and vitality of the latter, which Frye takes to be the ultimate source and paradigm of all storytelling. On this view, the oral tales of tribal society, the fairy tales that are the irrepressible voice and expression of the underclasses of the great systems of domination, adventure stories and melodrama, and the popular or mass culture of our own time are all syllables and broken fragments of some single immense story.

Yet Frye's identification of narrative in general with the particular narrative genre of romance raises the apparently unrelated issue of genre criticism, which, though thoroughly discredited by modern literary theory and practice, has in fact always entertained a privileged relationship with historical materialism. The first extended exercise in Marxist literary criticism – the letters of Marx and Engels to Lassalle about the latter's verse tragedy, *Franz von Sickingen* – was indeed essentially generic; while the most developed corpus of Marxist literary analysis in our own time, the work of Georg Lukács, spanning some sixty years, is dominated by concepts of genre from beginning to end. I take it, indeed, as one of the moments of 'high seriousness' in the history of recent Marxist thought that when the aging Lukács felt the urgency of supporting Solzhenitsyn's denunciation of Stalinism but also of responding to the religious and antisocialist propaganda to which the latter lent his talent and the authority of his personal suffering, he did so by sitting down at his desk and producing a piece of genre criticism. The strategic value of generic concepts for Marxism clearly lies in the mediatory function of the notion of a genre, which allows the coordination of immanent formal analysis of the individual text with the twin diachronic perspective of the history of forms and the evolution of social life.

Meanwhile, in the other traditions of contemporary literary criticism, generic perspectives live something like a 'return of the repressed.' Frye's own work, so resolutely organized around narrative, owed its widespread influence to the New Critical context in which it first appeared, and in which the fundamental object of literary study had been only too narrowly construed as the lyric, or poetic language. Contemporary structural and semiotic methods also, with their rigorous self-imposed restriction to discrete individual texts, have known the reemergence of a meditation on hitherto marginalized types of discourse: legal language, the fragment, the anecdote, autobiography, Utopian discourse; the fantastic, novelistic description (or *ekphrasis*), the preface, the scientific treatise, which are increasingly conceived as so many distinct generic modes.

What literary criticism seems unable to do without completely, however, literary production has in modern times ceaselessly and systematically undermined. The emancipation of the 'realistic novel' from its generic restrictions (in the tale, the letter, the framed *récit*), the emergence, first of modernism, with its Joycean or Mallarmean ideal of a single Book of the world, then of the post-modernist aesthetic of the text or of *écriture*, of 'textual productivity' or schizophrenic writing – all seem rigorously to exclude traditional notions of the literary kinds, or of systems of the fine arts, as much by their practice as by their theory.

Nor is it difficult to see why this has been so. Genres are essentially literary *institutions*, or social contracts between a writer and a specific public, whose function is to specify the proper use of a particular cultural artifact. The speech acts of daily life are themselves marked with indications and signals (intonation, gesturality, contextual deictics and pragmatics) which ensure their appropriate reception. In the mediated situations of a more complicated social life – and the emergence of writing has often been taken as paradigmatic of such situations – perceptual signals must be replaced by conventions if the text in question is not to be abandoned to a drifting multiplicity of uses (as *meanings* must, according to Wittgenstein, be described). Still, as texts free themselves more and more from an immediate performance situation, it becomes ever more difficult to enforce a given generic rule on their readers. No small part of the art of writing, indeed, is absorbed by this (impossible) attempt to devise a foolproof mechanism for the automatic exclusion of undesirable responses to a given literary utterance.

It is not merely the performance situation, but the generic contract and institution itself, which, along with so many other institutions and traditional practices, falls casualty to the gradual penetration of a market system and a money economy. With the elimination of an instititionalized social status for the cultural producer and the opening of the work of art itself to commodification, the older generic specifications are transformed into a brand-name system against which any authentic artistic expression must necessarily struggle. The older generic categories do not, for all that, die out, but persist in the half-life of the subliterary genres of mass culture, transformed into the drugstore and airport paperback lines of gothics, mysteries, romances, bestsellers, and popular biographies, where they await the resurrection of their immemorial, archetypal resonance at the hands of a Frye or a Bloch. Meanwhile, it would seem necessary to invent a new, historically reflexive, way of using categories, such as those of genre, which are so clearly implicated in the literary history and the formal production they were traditionally supposed to classify and neutrally to describe. [. . .]

A first specification of romance would then be achieved if we could account for the way in which, in contrast to realism, its inner-worldly objects such as landscape or village, forest or mansion – mere temporary stopping places on the lumbering coach or express-train itinerary of realistic representation – are somehow transformed into folds in space, into discontinuous pockets of homogeneous time and of heightened symbolic closure, such that they become tangible analoga or perceptual vehicles for *world* in its larger phenomenological sense. Heidegger's account goes on to supply the key to this enigma, and we may borrow his cumbersome formula to suggest that romance is precisely that form in which the *worldness* of *world* reveals or manifests itself, in which, in other words, *world* in the technical sense of the transcendental horizon of our experience becomes visible in an inner-worldly sense. Frye is therefore not wrong to evoke the intimate connection between romance as a mode and the 'natural' imagery of the earthly paradise or the waste land, of the bower of bliss or the enchanted wood. What is misleading is the implication that this 'nature' is in any sense itself a 'natural' rather than a very peculiar and specialized social and historical phenomenon. [. . .]

[T]he driving force of Frye's system is the idea of historical *identity*: his identification of mythic patterns in modern texts aims at reinforcing our sense of the
affinity between the cultural present of capitalism and the distant mythical past of
tribal societies, and at awakening a sense of the continuity between our psychic
life and that of primitive peoples. Frye's is in this sense a 'positive' hermeneutic,
which tends to filter out historical difference and the radical discontinuity of modes
of production and of their cultural expressions. A negative hermeneutic, then,
would on the contrary wish to use the narrative raw material shared by myth and
'historical' literatures to sharpen our sense of historical difference, and to stimu-
late an increasingly vivid apprehension of what happens when plot falls into history,
so to speak, and enters the force fields of the modern societies.

From this point of view, then, the problem raised by the persistence of romance
as a mode is that of substitutions, adaptations, and appropriations, and raises the
question of what, under wholly altered historical circumstances, can have been
found to replace the raw materials of magic and Otherness which medieval romance
found ready to hand in its socioeconomic environment. A history of romance as a
mode becomes possible, in other words, when we explore the substitute codes and
raw materials, which, in the increasingly secularized and rationalized world that
emerges from the collapse of feudalism, are pressed into service to replace the
older magical categories of Otherness which have now become so many dead
languages. [. . .]

[P]recisely to the degree to which it suggests that in the secularized and
reified world of modern capitalism, epiphany is possible as a positive event, as the
revelation of presence. But if epiphany itself is a mirage, then the most authentic
vocation of romance in our time would not be that reinvention of the providential
vision invoked and foretold by Frye, but rather its capacity, by absence and by
the silence of the form itself, to express that ideology of desacralization by which
modern thinkers from Weber to the Frankfurt School have sought to convey
their sense of the radical impoverishment and constriction of modern life. So
the great expressions of the modern fantastic, the last unrecognizable avatars of
romance as a mode, draw their magical power from an unsentimental loyalty
to those henceforth abandoned clearings across which higher and lower worlds
once passed. [. . .]

[I]t would seem that its ultimate condition of figuration, on which the other
preconditions we have already mentioned are dependent – the category of worldness, the ideologeme of good and evil felt as magical forces, a salvational historicity
– is to be found in a transitional moment in which two distinct modes of production, or moments of socioeconomic development, coexist. Their antagonism is not
yet articulated in terms of the struggle of social classes, so that its resolution can
be projected in the form of a nostalgic (or less often, a Utopian) harmony. Our
principal experience of such transitional moments is evidently that of an organic
social order in the process of penetration and subversion, reorganization and rationalization, by nascent capitalism, yet still, for another long moment, coexisting
with the latter. So Shakespearean romance (like its falling cadence in Eichendorff)
opposes the phantasmagoria of 'imagination' to the bustling commercial activity at
work all around it, while the great art-romances of the early nineteenth century
take their variously reactive stances against the new and unglamorous social

institutions emerging from the political triumph of the bourgeoisie and the setting in place of the market system. But this romance does its work well; under the spell of this wondrous text, the French Revolution proves to be an illusion, and the grisly class conflict of decades of Napoleonic world war fades into the mere stuff of bad dreams.

# PART TWO

# The normative turn

# JUSTICE

- Michael Walzer, A defense of pluralism and equality

- John Rawls, Political liberalism

**Michael Walzer** was born in New York, New York on 3 March 1935. He has taught in the United States at universities including Princeton and Harvard. Walzer has written numerous books, including *Spheres of Justice* (1985) and *What it Means to be American* (1992).

**John Rawls** was born on 21 February 1921 in Baltimore, Maryland. He has taught at various universities in the United States, including Princeton, Cornell and Harvard. Rawls is the author of *A Theory of Justice* (1971) and *Political Liberalism* (1993).

# Chapter 9

# Michael Walzer

# A DEFENSE OF PLURALISM
# AND EQUALITY

## Complex equality

### Pluralism

**D**ISTRIBUTIVE JUSTICE IS a large idea. It draws the entire world of goods within the reach of philosophical reflection. Nothing can be omitted; no feature of our common life can escape scrutiny. Human society is a distributive community. That's not all it is, but it is importantly that: we come together to share, divide, and exchange. We also come together to make the things that are shared, divided, and exchanged; but that very making – work itself – is distributed among us in a division of labor. My place in the economy, my standing in the political order, my reputation among my fellows, my material holdings: all these come to me from other men and women. It can be said that I have what I have rightly or wrongly, justly or unjustly; but given the range of distributions and the number of participants, such judgments are never easy.

The idea of distributive justice has as much to do with being and doing as with having, as much to do with production as with consumption, as much to do with identify and status as with land, capital, or personal possessions. Different political arrangements enforce, and different ideologies justify, different distributions of membership, power, honor, ritual eminence, divine grace, kinship and love, knowledge, wealth, physical security, work and leisure, rewards and punishments, and a host of goods more narrowly and materially conceived – food, shelter, clothing, transportation, medical care, commodities of every sort, and all the old things (paintings, rare books, postage stamps) that human beings collect. And this multiplicity of goods is matched by a multiplicity of distributive procedures, agents, and criteria. There are such things as simple distributive systems – slave galleys, monasteries, insane asylums, kindergartens (though each of these, looked at closely, might show unexpected complexities); but no full-fledged human society has ever avoided the multiplicity. We must study it all, the goods and the distributions, in many different times and places.

There is, however, no single point of access to this world of distributive arrangements and ideologies. There has never been a universal medium of exchange. Since the decline of the barter economy, money has been the most common medium. But the old maxim according to which there are some things that money can't buy is not only normatively but also factually true. What should and should not be up for sale is something men and women always have to decide and have decided in many different ways. Throughout history, the market has been one of the most important mechanisms for the distribution of social goods; but it has never been, it nowhere is today, a complete distributive system.

Similarly, there has never been either a single decision point from which all distributions are controlled or a single set of agents making decisions. No state power has ever been so pervasive as to regulate all the patterns of sharing, dividing, and exchanging out of which a society takes shape. Things slip away from the state's grasp; new patterns are worked out — familial networks, black markets, bureaucratic alliances, clandestine political and religious organizations. State officials can tax, conscript, allocate, regulate, appoint, reward, punish, but they cannot capture the full range of goods or substitute themselves for every other agent of distribution. Nor can anyone else do that: there are market coups and cornerings, but there has never been a fully successful distributive conspiracy.

And finally, there has never been a single criterion, or a single set of interconnected criteria, for all distributions. Desert, qualification, birth and blood, friendship, need, free exchange, political loyalty, democratic decision: each has had its place, along with many others, uneasily coexisting, invoked by competing groups, confused with one another.

In the matter of distributive justice, history displays a great variety of arrangements and ideologies. But the first impulse of the philosopher is to resist the displays of history, the world of appearances, and to search for some underlying unity: a short list of basic goods, quickly abstracted to a single good; a single distributive criterion or an interconnected set; and the philosopher himself standing, symbolically at least, at a single decision point. I shall argue that to search for unity is to misunderstand the subject matter of distributive justice. Nevertheless, in some sense the philosophical impulse is unavoidable. Even if we choose pluralism, as I shall do, that choice still requires a coherent defense. There must be principles that justify the choice and set limits to it, for pluralism does not require us to endorse every proposed distributive criteria or to accept every would-be agent. Conceivably, there is a single principle and a single legitimate kind of pluralism. But this would still be a pluralism that encompassed a wide range of distributions. By contrast, the deepest assumption of most of the philosophers who have written about justice, from Plato onward, is that there is one, and only one, distributive system that philosophy can rightly encompass.

Today this system is commonly described as the one that ideally rational men and women would choose if they were forced to choose impartially, knowing nothing of their own situation, barred from making particularist claims, confronting an abstract set of goods. If these constraints on knowing and claiming are suitably shaped, and if the goods are suitably defined, it is probably true that a singular conclusion can be produced. Rational men and women, constrained this way or that, will choose one, and only one, distributive system. But the force of that singular conclusion is not easy to measure. It is surely doubtful that those same men and women, if they were transformed into ordinary people, with a firm sense of their own identity, with their own goods in their hands, caught up in everyday troubles, would reiterate their hypothetical choice or even recognize it as their own. The problem is not, most importantly, with the particularism of interest, which philosophers have always assumed they could safely – that is, uncontroversially – set aside. Ordinary people can do that too, for the sake, say, of the public interest. The greater problem is with the particularism of history, culture, and membership. Even if they are committed to impartiality, the question most likely to arise in the minds of the members of a political community is not, What would rational individuals choose under universalizing conditions of such-and-such a sort? But rather, What would individuals like us choose, who are situated as we are, who share a culture and are determined to go on sharing it? And this is a question that is readily transformed into, What choices have we already made in the course of our common life? What understandings do we (really) share?

Justice is a human construction, and it is doubtful that it can be made in only one way. At any rate, I shall begin by doubting, and more than doubting, that standard philosophical assumption. The questions posed by the theory of distributive justice admit of a range of answers, and there is room within the range for cultural diversity and political choice. It's not only a matter of implementing some singular principle or set of principles in different historical settings. No one would deny that there is a range of morally permissible implementations. I want to argue for more than this: that the principles of justice are themselves pluralistic in form; that different social goods ought to be distributed for different reasons, in accordance with different procedures, by different agents; and that all these differences derive from different understandings of the social goods themselves – the inevitable product of historical and cultural particularism.

## A theory of goods

Theories of distributive justice focus on a social process commonly described as if it had this form:

*People distribute goods to (other) people.*

Here, 'distribute' means give, allocate, exchange, and so on, and the focus is on the individuals who stand at either end of these actions: not on producers and consumers, but on distributive agents and recipients of goods. We are as always interested in ourselves, but, in this case, in a special and limited version of ourselves, as people who give and take. What is our nature? What are our rights? What do we need, want, deserve? What are we entitled to? What would we accept under ideal conditions? Answers to these questions are turned into distributive principles, which are supposed to control the movement of goods. The goods, defined by abstraction, are taken to be movable in any direction.

But this is too simple an understanding of what actually happens, and it forces us too quickly to make large assertions about human nature and moral agency – assertions unlikely, ever, to command general agreement. I want to propose a more precise and complex description of the central process:

*People conceive and create goods, which they then distribute among themselves.*

Here, the conception and creation precede and control the distribution. Goods don't just appear in the hands of distributive agents who do with them as they like or give them out in accordance with some general principle. Rather, goods with their meanings – because of their meanings – are the crucial medium of social relations; they come into people's minds before they come into their hands; distributions are patterned in accordance with shared conceptions of what the goods are for. Distributive agents are constrained by the goods they hold; one might almost say that goods distribute themselves among people.

Things are in the saddle
And ride mankind.

But these are always particular things and particular groups of men and women. And, of course, we make the things – even the saddle. I don't want to deny the importance of human agency, only to shift our attention from distribution itself to conception and creation: the naming of the goods, and the giving of meaning, and the collective making. What we need to explain and limit the pluralism of distributive possibilities is a theory of goods. For our immediate purposes, that theory can be summed up in six propositions.

1.  All the goods with which distributive justice is concerned are social goods. They are not and they cannot be idiosyncratically valued. I am not sure that there are any other kinds of goods; I mean to leave the question open. Some domestic objects are cherished for private and sentimental reasons, but only in cultures where sentiment regularly attaches to such objects. A beautiful sunset, the smell of new-mown hay, the excitement of an urban vista: these perhaps are privately valued goods, though they are also, and more obviously, the objects of cultural assessment. Even new inventions are not valued in accordance with the ideas of their inventors; they are subject to a wider process of conception and creation. God's goods, to be sure, are exempt from this rule – as in the first chapter of Genesis: 'and God saw every thing that He had made, and, behold, it was very good' (1: 31). That evaluation doesn't require the agreement of mankind (who might be doubtful), or of a majority of men and women, or of any group of men and women meeting under ideal conditions (though Adam and Eve in Eden would probably endorse it). But I can't think of any other exemptions. Goods in the world have shared means because conception and creation are social processes. For the same reason, goods have different meanings in different societies. The same 'thing' is valued for different reasons, or it is valued here and disvalued there. John Stuart Mill once complained that 'people like in crowds,' but I know of no other way to like or to dislike social goods. A solitary person could hardly

understand the meaning of the goods or figure out the reasons for taking them as likable or dislikable. Once people like in crowds, it becomes possible for individuals to break away, pointing to latent or subversive meanings, aiming at alternative values – including the values, for example, of notoriety and eccentricity. An easy eccentricity has sometimes been one of the privileges of the aristocracy: it is a social good like any other.

2. Men and women take on concrete identities because of the way they conceive and create, and then possess and employ social goods. 'The line between what is me and mine,' wrote William James, 'is very hard to draw.' Distributions cannot be understood as the acts of men and women who do not yet have particular goods in their minds or in their hands. In fact, people already stand in a relation to a set of goods; they have a history of transactions, not only with one another but also with the moral and material world in which they live. Without such a history, which begins at birth, they wouldn't be men and women in any recognizable sense, and they wouldn't have the first notion of how to go about the business of giving, allocating, and exchanging goods.

3. There is no single set of primary or basic goods conceivable across all moral and material worlds – or, any such set would have to be conceived in terms so abstract that they would be of little use in thinking about particular distributions. Even the range of necessities, if we take into account moral as well as physical necessities, is very wide, and the rank orderings are very different. A single necessary good, and one that is always necessary – food, for example – carries different meanings in different places. Bread is the staff of life, the body of Christ, the symbol of the Sabbath, the means of hospitality, and so on. Conceivably, there is a limited sense in which the first of these is primary, so that if there were twenty people in the world and just enough bread to feed the twenty, the primacy of bread-as-staff-of-life would yield a sufficient distributive principle. But that is the only circumstance in which it would do so; and even there, we can't be sure. If the religious uses of bread were to conflict with its nutritional uses – if the gods demanded that bread be baked and burned rather than eaten – it is by no means clear which use would be primary. How, then, is bread to be incorporated into the universal list? The question is even harder to answer, the conventional answers less plausible, as we pass from necessities to opportunities, powers, reputations, and so on. These can be incorporated only if they are abstracted from every particular meaning – hence, for all practical purposes, rendered meaningless.

4. But it is the meaning of goods that determines their movement. Distributive criteria and arrangements are intrinsic not to the good-in-itself but to the social good. If we understand what it is, what it means to those for whom it is a good, we understand how, by whom, and for what reasons it ought to be distributed. All distributions are just or unjust relative to the social meanings of the goods at stake. This is in obvious ways a principle of legitimation, but it is also a critical principle. When medieval Christians, for example, condemned the sin of simony, they were claiming that the meaning of a particular social good, ecclesiastical office, excluded its sale and purchase. Given the Christian understanding of office, it followed – I am inclined to say, it necessarily followed – that office holders should be chosen for their knowledge and piety and not for their wealth. There are presumably things that money can buy, but not this thing. Similarly, the words *prostitution*

and *bribery*, like *simony*, describe the sale and purchase of goods that, given certain understandings of their meaning, ought never to be sold or purchased.

5. Social meanings are historical in character; and so distributions, and just and unjust distributions, change over time. To be sure, certain key goods have what we might think of as characteristic normative structures, reiterated across the lines (but not all the lines) of time and space. It is because of this reiteration that the British philosopher Bernard Williams is able to argue that goods should always be distributed for 'relevant reasons' – where relevance seems to connect to essential rather than to social meanings. The idea that offices, for example, should go to qualified candidates – though not the only idea that has been held about offices – is plainly visible in very different societies where simony and nepotism, under different names, have similarly been thought sinful or unjust. (But there has been a wide divergence of views about what sorts of position and place are properly called 'offices.') Again, punishment has been widely understood as a negative good that ought to go to people who are judged to deserve it on the basis of a verdict, not of a political decision. (But what constitutes a verdict? Who is to deliver it? How, in short, is justice to be done to accused men and women? About these questions there has been significant disagreement.) These examples invite empirical investigation. There is no merely intuitive or speculative procedure for seizing upon relevant reasons.

6. When meanings are distinct, distributions must be autonomous. Every social good or set of goods constitutes, as it were, a distributive sphere within which only certain criteria and arrangements are appropriate. Money is inappropriate in the sphere of ecclesiastical office; it is an intrusion from another sphere. And piety should make for no advantage in the marketplace, as the marketplace has commonly been understood. Whatever can rightly be sold ought to be sold to pious men and women and also to profane, heretical, and sinful men and women (else no one would do much business). The market is open to all comers; the church is not. In no society, of course, are social meanings entirely distinct. What happens in one distributive sphere affects what happens in the others; we can look, at most, for relative autonomy. But relative autonomy, like social meaning, is a critical principle – indeed, as I shall be arguing throughout this book, a radical principle. It is radical even though it doesn't point to a single standard against which all distributions are to be measured. There is no single standard. But there are standards (roughly knowable even when they are also controversial) for every social good and every distributive sphere in every particular society; and these standards are often violated, the goods usurped, the spheres invaded, by powerful men and women.

## Dominance and monopoly

In fact, the violations are systematic. Autonomy is a matter of social meaning and shared values, but it is more likely to make for occasional reformation and rebellion than for everyday enforcement. For all the complexity of their distributive arrangements, most societies are organized on what we might think of as a social version of the gold standard: one good or one set of goods is dominant and determinative of value in all the spheres of distributions. And that good or set of goods is commonly monopolized whenever a single man or woman, a monarch in the world of value – or a group of men and women, oligarchs – successfully hold it against all rivals. Dominance describes a way of using social goods that isn't limited by their intrinsic meanings or that shapes those meanings in its own image. Monopoly describes a way of owning or controlling social goods in order to exploit their dominance. When goods are scarce and widely needed, like water in the desert, monopoly itself will make them dominant. Mostly, however, dominance is a more elaborate social creation, the work of many hands, mixing reality and symbol. Physical strength, familial reputation, religious or political office, landed wealth, capital, technical knowledge: each of these, in different historical periods, has been dominant; and each of them has been monopolized by some group of men and women. And then all good things come to those who have the one best thing. Possess that one, and the others come in train. Or, to change the metaphor, a dominant good is converted into another good, into many others, in accordance with what often appears to be a natural process but is in fact magical, a kind of social alchemy.

No social good ever entirely dominates the range of goods; no monopoly is ever perfect. I mean to describe tendencies only, but crucial tendencies. For we can characterize whole societies in terms of the patterns of conversion that are established within them. Some characterizations are simple: in a capitalist society, capital is dominant and readily converted into prestige and power; in a technocracy, technical knowledge plays the same part. But it isn't difficult to imagine, or to find, more complex social arrangements. Indeed, capitalism and technocracy are more complex than their names imply, even if the names do convey real information about the most important forms of sharing, dividing, and exchanging. Monopolistic control of a dominant good makes a ruling class, whose members stand atop the distributive system – much as philosophers, claiming to have the wisdom they love, might like to do. But since dominance is always incomplete and monopoly imperfect, the rule of every ruling class is unstable. It is continually challenged by other groups in the name of alternative patterns of conversion.

Distribution is what social conflict is all about. Marx's heavy emphasis on productive processes should not conceal from us the simple truth that the struggle for control of the means of production is a distributive struggle. Land and capital are at stake, and these are goods that can be shared, divided, exchanged, and endlessly converted. But land and capital are not the only dominant goods; it is possible (it has historically been possible) to come to them by way of other goods – military or political power, religious office and charisma, and so on. History reveals no single dominant good and no naturally dominant good, but only different kinds of magic and competing bands of magicians.

The claim to monopolize a dominant good – when worked up for public purposes – constitutes an ideology. Its standard form is to connect legitimate possession with some set of personal qualities through the medium of a philosophical principle. So aristocracy, or the rule of the best, is the principle of those who lay claim to breeding and intelligence: they are commonly the monopolists of landed wealth and familial reputation. Divine supremacy is the principle of those who claim to know the word of God: they are the monopolists of grace and office. Meritocracy, or the career open to talents, is the principle of those who claim to be talented: they are most often the monopolists of education. Free exchange is the principle of those who are ready, or who tell us they are ready, to put their money at risk: they are the monopolists of movable wealth. These groups – and others, too, similarly marked off by their principles and possessions – complete with one another, struggling for supremacy. One group wins, and then a different one; or coalitions are worked out, and supremacy is uneasily shared. There is no final victory, nor should there be. But that is not to say that the claims of the different groups are necessarily wrong, or that the principles they invoke are of no value as distributive criteria; the principles are often exactly right within the limits of a particular sphere. Ideologies are readily corrupted, but their corruption is not the most interesting thing about them.

It is in the study of these struggles that I have sought the guiding thread of my own argument. The struggles have, I think, a paradigmatic form. Some group of men and women – class, caste, strata, estate, alliance, or social formation – comes to enjoy a monopoly or a near monopoly of some dominant good; or, a coalition of groups comes to enjoy, and so on. This dominant good is more or less systematically converted into all sorts of other things – opportunities, powers, and reputations. So wealth is seized by the strong, honor by the wellborn, office by the well educated. Perhaps the ideology that justifies the seizure is widely believed to be true. But resentment and resistance are (almost) as pervasive as belief. There are always some people, and after a time there are a great many, who think the seizure is not justice but usurpation. The ruling group does not possess, or does not uniquely possess, the qualities it claims; the conversion process violates the common understanding of the goods at stake. [. . .]

## Tyranny and complex equality

I want to argue that we should focus on the reduction of dominance – not, or not primarily, on the break-up or the constraint of monopoly. We should consider what it might mean to narrow the range within which particular goods are convertible and to vindicate the autonomy of distributive spheres. But this line of argument, thought it is not uncommon historically, has never fully emerged in philosophical writing. Philosophers have tended to criticize (or to justify) existing or emerging monopolies of wealth, power, and education. Or, they have criticized (or justified) particular conversions – of wealth into education or of office into wealth. And all this, most often, in the name of some radically simplified distributive system. The critique of dominance will suggest instead a way of reshaping and then living with the actual complexity of distributions.

Imagine now a society in which different social goods are monopolistically held – as they are in fact and always will be, barring continual state intervention – but in which no particular good is generally convertible. As I go along, I shall try to define the precise limits on convertibility, but for now the general description will suffice. This is a complex egalitarian society. Though there will be many small inequalities, inequality will not be multiplied through the conversion process. Nor will it be summed across different goods, because the autonomy of distributions will tend to produce a variety of local monopolies, held by different groups of men and women. I don't want to claim that complex equality would necessarily be more stable than simple equality, but I am inclined to think that it would open the way for more diffused and particularized forms of social conflict. And the resistance to convertibility would be maintained, in large degree, by ordinary men and women within their own spheres of competence and control, without large-scale state action.

This is, I think, an attractive picture, but I have not yet explained just why it is attractive. The argument for complex equality begins from our understanding – I mean, our actual, concrete, positive, and particular understanding – of the various social goods. And then it moves on to an account of the way we relate to one another through those goods. Simple equality is a simple distributive condition, so that if I have fourteen hats and you have fourteen hats, we are equal. And it is all to the good if hats are dominant, for then our equality is extended through all the spheres of social life. On the view that I shall take here, however, we simply have the same number of hats, and it is unlikely that hats will be dominant for long. Equality is a complex relation of persons, mediated by the goods we make, share, and divide among ourselves; it is not an identity of possessions. It requires then, a diversity of distributive criteria that mirrors the diversity of social goods.

The argument for complex equality has been beautifully put by Pascal in one of his *Pensées*.

> The nature of tyranny is to desire power over the whole world and outside its own sphere.
>
> There are different companies – the strong, the handsome, the intelligent, the devout – and each man reigns in his own, not elsewhere. But sometimes they meet, and the strong and the handsome fight for mastery – foolishly, for their mastery is of different kinds. They misunderstand one another, and make the mistake of each aiming at universal dominion. Nothing can win this, not even strength, for it is powerless in the kingdom of the wise. . . .
>
> *Tyranny.* The following statements, therefore, are false and tyrannical: 'Because I am handsome, so I should command respect.' 'I am strong, therefore men should love me. . . .' 'I am . . . et cetera.'
>
> Tyranny is the wish to obtain by one means what can only be had by another. We owe different duties to different qualities: love is the proper response to charm, fear to strength, and belief to learning.

Marx made a similar argument in his early manuscripts; perhaps he had this *pensée* in mind:

> Let us assume man to be man, and his relation to the world to be a human one. Then love can only be exchanged for love, trust for trust, etc. If you wish to enjoy art you must be an artistically cultivated person; if you wish to influence other people, you must be a person who really has a stimulating and encouraging effect upon others. . . . If you love without evoking love in return, i.e., if you are not able, by the manifestation of yourself as a loving person, to make yourself a beloved person – then your love is impotent and a misfortune.

These are not easy arguments, and most of my book is simply an exposition of their meaning. But here I shall attempt something more simple and schematic: a translation of the arguments into the terms I already been using.

The first claim of Pascal and Marx is that personal qualities and social goods have their own spheres of operation, where they work their effects freely, spontaneously, and legitimately. There are ready or natural conversions that follow from, and are intuitively plausible because of, the social meaning of particular goods. The appeal is to our ordinary understanding and, at the same time, against our common acquiesence in illegitimate conversion patterns. Or, it is an appeal from our acquiesence to our resentment. There is something wrong, Pascal suggests, with the conversion of strength into belief. In political terms, Pascal means that no ruler can rightly command my opinions merely because of the power he wields. Nor can he, Marx adds, rightly claim to influence my actions: if a ruler wants to do that, he must be persuasive, helpful, encouraging, and so on. These arguments depend for their force on some shared understanding of knowledge, influence, and power. Social goods have social means, and we find our way to distributive justice through an interpretation of those meanings. We search for principles internal to each distributive sphere.

The second claim is that the disregard of these principles is tyranny. To convert one good into another, when there is no intrinsic connection between the two, is to invade the sphere where another company of men and women properly rules. Monopoly is not inappropriate within the spheres. There is nothing wrong, for example, with the grip that persuasive and helpful men and women (politicians) establish on political power. But the use of political power to gain access to other goods is a tyrannical use. Thus, an old description of tyranny is generalized: princes become tyrants, according to medieval writers, when they seize the property or invade the family of their subjects. In political life – but more widely, too – the dominance of goods makes for the domination of people.

The regime of complex equality is the opposite of tyranny. It establishes a set of relationships such that domination is impossible. In formal terms, complex equality means that no citizen's standing in one sphere or with regard to one social good can be undercut by his standing in some other sphere, with regard to some other good. Thus, citizen X may be chosen over citizen Y for political office, and then the two of them will be unequal in the sphere of politics. But they will not be unequal generally so long as X's office gives him no advantages over Y in any other sphere – superior medical care, access to better schools for his children, entrepreneurial opportunities, and so on. So long as office is not a dominant good, is not generally convertible, office holders will stand, or at least can stand, in a relation of equality to the men and women they govern. [. . .]

The critique of dominance and domination points toward an open-ended distributive principle. *No social good* x *should be distributed to men and women who possess some other good* y *merely because they possess* y *and without regarding to the meaning of* x. This is a principle that has probably been reiterated, at one time or another, for every y that has ever been dominant. But it has not often been stated in general terms. Pascal and Marx have suggested the application of the principle against all possible y's, and I shall attempt to work out that application. I shall be looking, then, not at the members of Pascal's companies – the strong or the weak, the handsome or the plain – but at the goods they share and divide. The purpose of the principle is to focus our attention; it doesn't determine the shares or the division. The principle directs us to study the meaning of social goods, to examine the different distributive spheres from the inside. [. . .]

## Equality and social change

Complex equality might look more secure if we could describe it in terms of the harmony, rather than the autonomy, of spheres. But social meanings and distributions are harmonious only in this respect: that when we see why one good has a certain form and is distributed in a certain way, we also see why another must be different. Precisely because of these differences, however, boundary conflict is endemic. The principles appropriate to the different spheres are not harmonious with one another; nor are the patterns of conduct and feeling they generate. Welfare systems and markets, offices and families, schools and states are run on different principles: so they should be. The principles must somehow fit together within a single culture; they must be comprehensible across the different companies of men and women. But this doesn't rule out deep strains and odd juxtapositions. Ancient China was ruled by a hereditary divine-right emperor and a meritocratic bureaucracy. One has to tell a complex story to explain that sort of coexistence. A community's culture is the story its members tell so as to make sense of all the different pieces of their social life – and justice is the doctrine that distinguishes the pieces. In any differentiated society, justice will make for harmony only if it first makes for separation. Good fences make just societies.

We never know exactly where to put the fences; they have no natural location. The goods they distinguish are artifacts; as they were made, so they can be remade. Boundaries, then, are vulnerable to shifts in social meaning, and we have no choice but to live with the continual probes and incursions through which these shifts are worked out [. . .]

# Chapter 10

# John Rawls

## POLITICAL LIBERALISM

[. . .]

**T**HE POLITICAL CULTURE of a democratic society is always marked by a diversity of opposing and irreconcilable religious, philosophical, and moral doctrines. Some of these are perfectly reasonable, and this diversity among reasonable doctrines political liberalism sees as the inevitable long-run result of the powers of human reason at work within the background of enduring free institutions. Thus, the second question is what are the grounds of toleration so understood and given the fact of reasonable pluralism as the inevitable outcome of free institutions? Combining both questions we have: how is it possible for there to exist over time a just and stable society of free and equal citizens, who remain profoundly divided by reasonable religious, philosophical, and moral doctrines?

The most intractable struggles, political liberalism assumes, are confessedly for the sake of the highest things: for religion, for philosophical views of the world, and for different moral conceptions of the good. We should find it remarkable that, so deeply opposed in these ways, just cooperation among free and equal citizens is possible at all. In fact, historical experience suggests that it rarely is [. . .]

[. . .] How might political philosophy find a shared basis for settling such a fundamental question as that of the most appropriate family of institutions to secure democratic liberty and equality? Perhaps the most that can be done is to narrow the range of disagreement. Yet even firmly held convictions gradually change: religious toleration is now accepted, and arguments for persecution are no longer openly professed; similarly, slavery, which caused our Civil War, is rejected as inherently unjust, and however much the aftermath of slavery may persist in social policies and unavowed attitudes, no one is willing to defend it. We collect such settled convictions as the belief in religious toleration and the rejection of slavery and try to organize the basic ideas and principles implicit in these convictions into a coherent political conception of justice. These convictions are provisional fixed points that it seems any reasonable conception must account for. We start, then, by looking to the public culture itself as the shared fund of implicitly recognized basic ideas and principles. We hope to formulate these ideas and principles clearly enough to be combined into a political conception of justice congenial to our most firmly held convictions. We express this by saying that a political conception of justice, to be acceptable, must accord with our considered convictions, at all levels of generality, on due reflection, or in what I have called elsewhere 'reflective equilibrium.'

The public political culture may be of two minds at a very deep level. Indeed, this must be so with such an enduring controversy as that concerning the most appropriate understanding of liberty and equality. This suggests that if we are to succeed in finding a basis of public agreement, we must find a way of organizing familiar ideas and principles into a conception of political justice that expresses those ideas and principles in a somewhat different way than before. Justice as fairness tries to do this by using a fundamental organizing idea within which all ideas and principles can be systematically connected and related. This organizing idea is that of society as a fair system of social cooperation between free and equal persons viewed as fully cooperating members of society over a complete life. It lays a basis for answering the first fundamental question [. . .]

Now suppose justice as fairness were to achieve its aims and a publicly acceptable political conception were found. Then this conception provides a publicly recognized point of view from which all citizens can examine before one another whether their political and social institutions are just. It enables them to do this by citing what are publicly recognized among them as valid and sufficient reasons singled out by that conception itself. Society's main institutions and how they fit together into one system of social cooperation can be assessed in the same way by each citizen, whatever that citizen's social position or more particular interests.

The aim of justice as fairness, then, is practical: it presents itself as a conception of justice that may be shared by citizens as a basis of a reasoned, informed, and willing political agreement. It expresses their shared and public political reason. But to attain such a shared reason, the conception of justice should be, as far as possible, independent of the opposing and conflicting philosophical and religious doctrines that citizens affirm. In formulating such a conception, political liberalism applies the principle of toleration to philosophy itself. The religious doctrines that in previous centuries were the professed basis of society have gradually given way to principles of constitutional government that all citizens, whatever their religious view, can endorse. Comprehensive philosophical and moral doctrines likewise cannot be endorsed by citizens generally, and they also no longer can, if they ever could, serve as the professed basis of society.

Thus, political liberalism looks for a political conception of justice that we hope can gain the support of an overlapping consensus of reasonable religious, philosophical, and moral doctrines in a society regulated by it. Gaining this support of reasonable doctrines lays the basis for answering our second fundamental question as to how citizens, who remain deeply divided on religious, philosophical, and moral doctrines, can still maintain a just and stable democratic society. To this end, it is normally desirable that the comprehensive philosophical and moral views we are wont to use in debating fundamental political issues should give way in public life. Public reasons – citizens' reasoning in the public forum about constitutional essentials and basic questions of justice – is now best guided by a political conception, the principles and values of which all citizens can endorse. That political conception is to be, so to speak, political and not metaphysical.

Political liberalism, then, aims for a political conception of justice as a free-standing view. It offers no specific metaphysical or epistemological doctrine beyond what is implied by the political conception itself. As an account of political values, a free-standing political conception does not deny there being other values that apply, say, to the personal, the familial, and the associational; nor does it say that political values are separate from, or discontinuous with, other values. One aim, as I have said, is to specify the political domain and its conception of justice in such a way that its institutions can gain the support of an overlapping consensus. In this case, citizens themselves, within the exercise of their liberty of thought and conscience, and looking to their comprehensive doctrines, view the political conception as derived from, or congruent with, or at least not in conflict with, their other values.

To this point I have used the idea of a political conception of justice without explaining its meaning. From what I have said, one can perhaps gather what I mean by it and why political liberalism uses that idea. Yet we need an explicit statement thus: a political conception of justice has three characteristic features, each of which is exemplified by justice as fairness. I assume some but not much acquaintance with that view.

The first concerns the subject of a political conception. While such a conception is, of course, a moral conception, it is a moral conception worked out for a specific kind of subject, namely, for political, social, and economic institutions. In particular, it applies to what I shall call the 'basic structure' of society, which for our present purposes I take to be a modern constitutional democracy. (I use 'constitutional democracy' and 'democratic regime,' and similar phrases interchangeably unless otherwise stated.) By the basic structure I mean a society's main political, social, and economic institutions, and how they fit together into one unified system of social cooperation from one generation to the next. [. . .]

The second feature concerns the mode of presentation: a political conception of justice is presented as a freestanding view. While we want a political conception to have a justification by reference to one or more comprehensive doctrines, it is neither presented as, nor is derived from such a doctrine applied to the basic structure of society, as if this structure were simply another subject to which that doctrine applied. It is important to stress this point: it means that we must distinguish between how a political conception is presented and its being part of, or as derivable within, a comprehensive doctrine. I assume all citizens to affirm a comprehensive doctrine to which the political conception they accept is in some way related. But a distinguishing feature of a political conception is that it is presented as free-standing and expounded apart from, or without reference to, any such wider background. To use a current phrase, the political conception is a module, an essential constituent part, that fits into and can be supported by various reasonable comprehensive doctrines that endure in the society regulated by it. This means that it can be presented without saying, or knowing, or hazarding a conjecture about, what such doctrines it may belong to, or be supported by.

In this respect a political conception of justice differs from many moral doctrines, for these are widely regarded as general and comprehensive views. Utilitarianism is a familiar example: the principle of utility, however understood, is usually said to hold for all kinds of subjects ranging from the conduct of individuals and personal relations to the organization of society as a whole as well as to the law of peoples. By contrast, a political conception tries to elaborate a reasonable conception for the basic structure alone and involves, so far as possible, no wider commitment to any other doctrine.

This contrast will be clearer if we observe that the distinction between a political conception of justice and other moral conceptions is a matter of scope: that is, the range of subjects to which a conception applies and the content a wider range requires. A moral conception is general if it applies to a wide range of subjects, and in the limit to all subjects universally. It is comprehensive when it includes conceptions of what is of value in human life, and ideals of personal character, as well as ideals of friendship and of familial and associational relationships, and much else that is to inform our conduct, and in the limit to our life as a whole. A conception is fully comprehensive if it covers all recognized values and virtues within one rather precisely articulated system; whereas a conception is only partially comprehensive when it comprises a number of, but by no means all, nonpolitical values and virtues and is rather loosely articulated. Many religious and philosophical doctrines aspire to be both general and comprehensive.

The third feature of a political conception of justice is that its content is expressed in terms of certain fundamental ideas seen as implicit in the public political culture of a democratic society. This public culture comprises the political institutions of a constitutional regime and the public traditions of their interpretation (including those of the judiciary), as well as historic texts and documents that are common knowledge. Comprehensive doctrines of all kinds – religious, philosophical, and moral – belong to what we may call the 'background culture' of civil society. This is the culture of the social, not of the political. It is the culture of daily life, of its many associations: churches and universities, learned and scientific societies, and clubs and teams, to mention a few. In a democratic society there is a tradition of democratic thought, the content of which is at least familiar and intelligible to the educated common sense of citizens generally. Society's main institutions, and their accepted forms of interpretation, are seen as a fund of implicitly shared ideas and principles.

Thus, justice as fairness starts from within a certain political tradition. [. . .]

[W]e must find some point of view, removed from and not distorted by the particular features and circumstances of the all-encompassing background framework, from which a fair agreement between persons regarded as free and equal can be reached.

The original position, with the features I have called 'the veil of ignorance,' is this point of view. [. . .]

[O]ne of our considered convictions, I assume, is this: the fact that we occupy a particular social position is not a good reason for us to propose, or to expect others to accept, a conception of justice that favors those in this position. Similarly, the fact that we affirm a particular religious, philosophical, or moral comprehensive doctrine with its associated conception of the good is not a reason for us to propose, or to expect others to accept, a conception of justice that favors those of that persuasion. To model this conviction in the original position, the parties are not allowed to know the social position of those they represent, or the particular comprehensive doctrine of the person each represents. The same idea is extended to information about people's race and ethnic group, sex and gender, and their various native endowments such as strength and intelligence, all within the normal range. We express these limits on information figuratively by saying the parties are behind a veil of ignorance. Thus, the original position is simply a device of representation: it describes the parties, each of whom is responsible for the essential interests of a free and equal citizen, as fairly situated and as reaching an agreement subject to conditions that appropriately limit what they can put forward as good reasons. [. . .]

As a device of representation the idea of the original position serves as a means of public reflection and self-clarification. It helps us work out what we now think, once we are able to take a clear and uncluttered view of what justice requires when society is conceived as a scheme of cooperation between free and equal citizens from one generation to the next. The original position serves as a mediating idea by which all our considered convictions, whatever their level of generality – whether they concern fair conditions for situating the parties or reasonable constraints on reasons, or first principles and precepts, or judgements about particular institutions and actions – can be brought to bear on one another. [. . .]

We can imagine a society (history offers many examples) in which basic rights and recognized claims depend on religious affiliation and social class. Such a society has a different political conception of the person. It lacks a conception of equal citizenship, for this conception goes with that of a democratic society of free and equal citizens.

There is a second sense of identity specified by reference to citizens' deeper aims and commitments. Let's call it their noninstitutional or moral identity. Citizens usually have both political and nonpolitical aims and commitments. They affirm the values of political justice and want to see them embodied in political institutions and social policies. They also work for the other values in nonpublic life and for the ends of the associations to which they belong. These two aspects of their moral identity citizens must adjust and reconcile. It can happen that in their personal affairs, or in the internal life of associations, citizens may regard their final ends and attachments very differently from the way the political conception supposes. They may have, and often do have at any given time, affections, devotions, and loyalties that they believe they would not, indeed could and should not, stand apart from and evaluate objectively. They may regard it as simply unthinkable to view themselves apart from certain religious, philosophical, and moral convictions, or from certain enduring attachments and loyalties.

These two kinds of commitments and attachments – political and nonpolitical – specify moral identity and give shape to a person's way of life, what one sees oneself as doing and trying to accomplish in the social world. If we suddenly lost them, we would be disoriented and unable to carry on. In fact, there would be, we might think, no point in carrying on. But our conceptions of the good may and often do change over time, usually slowly but sometimes rather suddenly. When these changes are sudden, we are likely to say that we are no longer the same person. We know what this means: we refer to a profound and pervasive shift, or reversal, in our final ends and commitments; we refer to our different moral (which includes our religious) identity. On the road to Damascus Saul of Tarsus becomes Paul the Apostle. Yet such a conversion implies no change in our public or institutional identity, nor in our personal identity as this concept is understood by some writers in the philosophy of mind. Moreover, in a well-ordered society supported by an overlapping consensus, citizens (more general) political values and commitments, as part of their noninstitutional or moral identity, are roughly the same. [. . .]

# ETHICS

- Alasdair MacIntyre, Whose justice? Which rationality?

- Zygmunt Bauman, Postmodern ethics

**Alasdair MacIntyre** was born 12 January 1929 in Glasgow, Scotland. He has taught at various universities in Great Britain and the United States, including Oxford, Princeton and Boston. He is the author of numerous books, among them *After Virtue* (1981) and *Whose Justice? Which Rationality?* (1988).

**Zygmunt Bauman** was born in Poland in 1925. He was educated at the University of Warsaw. He has taught in Israel and more recently at Leeds University in England. Among his books are *Intimations of Postmodernity* (1992) and *Post-modern Ethics* (1993).

# Chapter 11

# Alasdair MacIntyre

## WHOSE JUSTICE?
## WHICH RATIONALITY?

### Rival justices, competing rationalities

Begin by considering the intimidating range of questions about what justice requires
and permits, to which alternative and incompatible answers are offered by contending individuals and groups within contemporary societies. Does justice permit
gross inequality of income and ownership? Does justice require compensatory action
to remedy inequalities which are the result of past injustice, even if those who pay
the costs of such compensation had no part in that injustice? Does justice permit
or require the imposition of the death penalty and, if so, for what offences? Is it
just to permit legalized abortion? When is it just to go to war? The list of such
questions is a long one.

Attention to the reasons which are adduced for offering different and rival
answers to such questions makes it clear that underlying this wide diversity of
judgments upon particular types of issue are a set of conflicting conceptions
of justice, conceptions which are strikingly at odds with one another in a number
of ways. Some conceptions of justice make the concept of desert central, while
others deny it any relevance at all. Some conceptions appeal to inalienable human
rights, others to some notion of social contract, and others again to a standard of
utility. Moreover, the rival theories of justice which embody these rival conceptions also give expression to disagreements about the relationship of justice to other
human goods, about the kind of equality which justice requires, about the range
of transactions and persons to which considerations of justice are relevant, and
about whether or not a knowledge of justice is possible without a knowledge of
God's law.

So those who had hoped to discover good reasons for making this rather than
that judgment on some particular type of issue – by moving from the arenas in
which in everyday social life groups and individuals quarrel about what it is just

to do in particular cases over to the realm of theoretical enquiry, where systematic conceptions of justice are elaborated and debated – will find that once again they have entered upon a scene of radical conflict. What this may disclose to them is not only that our society is one not of consensus, but of division and conflict, at least so far as the nature of justice is concerned, but also that to some degree that division and conflict is within themselves. For what many of us are educated into is, not a coherent way of thinking and judging, but one constructed out of an amalgam of social and cultural fragments inherited both from different traditions from which our culture was originally derived (Puritan, Catholic, Jewish) and from different stages in and aspects of the development of modernity (the French Enlightenment, the Scottish Enlightenment, nineteenth-century economic liberalism, twentieth-century political liberalism). So often enough in the disagreements which emerge within ourselves, as well as in those which are matters of conflict between ourselves and others, we are forced to confront the question: How ought we to decide among the claims of rival and incompatible accounts of justice competing for our moral, social, and political allegiance?

It would be natural enough to attempt to reply to this question by asking which systematic account of justice we would accept if the standards by which our actions were guided were the standards of rationality. To know what justice is, so it may seem, we must first learn what rationality in practice requires of us. Yet someone who tries to learn this at once encounters the fact that disputes about the nature of rationality in general and about practical rationality in particular are apparently as manifold and as intractable as disputes about justice. To be practically rational, so one contending party holds, is to act on the basis of calculations of the costs and benefits to oneself of each possible alternative course of action and its consequences. To be practically rational, affirms a rival party, is to act under those constraints which any rational person, capable of an impartiality which accords no particular privileges to one's own interests, would agree should be imposed. To be practically rational, so a third party contends, is to act in such a way as to achieve the ultimate and true good of human beings. So a third level of difference and conflict appear.

One of the most striking facts about modern political orders is that they lack institutionalized forums within which fundamental disagreements can be systematically explored and charted, let alone there being any attempt made to resolve them. The facts of disagreement themselves frequently go unacknowledged, disguised by a rhetoric of consensus. And when on some single, if complex issue, as in the struggles over the Vietnam war or in the debates over abortion, the illusions of consensus on questions of justice and practical disagreement is institutionalized in such a way as to abstract that single issue from those background contexts of different and incompatible beliefs from which such disagreements arise. This serves to prevent, so far as is possible, debate extending to the fundamental principles which inform those background beliefs.

Private citizens are thus for the most part left to their own devices in these matters. Those of them who do not, very understandably, abandon any attempt to think through such issues systematically are generally able to discover only two major types of resource: those provided by the enquiries and discussions of modern academic philosophy and those provided by more or less organized communities of shared belief, such as churches or sects, religious and nonreligious, or certain kinds of political association. What do these resources in fact afford?

Modern academic philosophy turns out by and large to provide means for a more accurate and informed definition of disagreement rather than for progress toward its resolution. Professors of philosophy who concern themselves with questions of justice and of practical rationality turn out to disagree with each other as sharply, as variously, and, so it seems, as irremediably upon how such questions are to be answered as anyone else. They do indeed succeed in articulating the rival standpoints with greater clarity, greater fluency, and a wider range of arguments than do most others, but apparently little more than this. And, upon reflection, we should perhaps not be surprised.

Consider, for example, one at first sight very plausible philosophical thesis about how we ought to proceed in these matters if we are to be rational. Rationality requires, so it has been argued by a number of academic philosophers, that we first divest ourselves of allegiance to any one of the contending theories and also abstract ourselves from all those particularities of social relationship in terms of which we have been accustomed to understand our responsibilities and our interests. Only by so doing, it has been suggested, shall we arrive at a genuinely neutral, impartial, and, in this way, universal point of view, freed from the partisanship and the partiality and onesidedness that otherwise affect us. And only by so doing shall we be able to evaluate the contending accounts of justice rationally.

One problem is that those who agree about this procedure then proceed to disagree about what precise conception of justice it is which is as a result to be accounted rationally acceptable. But even before *that* problem arises, the question has to be asked whether, by adopting this procedure, key questions have not been begged. For it can be argued and it has been argued that this account of rationality is itself contentious in two related ways: its requirement of disinterestedness in fact covertly presupposes one particular partisan type of account of justice, that of liberal individualism, which it is later to be used to justify, so that its apparent neutrality is no more than an appearance, while its conception of ideal rationality as consisting in the principles which a socially disembodied being would arrive at illegitimately ignores the inescapably historically and socially context-bound character which any substantive set of principles of rationality, whether theoretical or practical, is bound to have.

Fundamental disagreements about the character of rationality are bound to be peculiarly difficult to resolve. For already in initially proceeding in one way rather than another to approach the disputed questions, those who so proceed will have had to assume that these particular procedures are the ones which it is rational to follow. A certain degree of circularity is ineliminable. And so when disagreements between contending views are sufficiently fundamental, as they are in the case of these disagreements about practical rationality in which the nature of justice is at stake, those disagreements will extend even to the answers to the question of how to proceed in order to resolve those same disagreements.

Aristotle argued in Book Gamma of the *Metaphysics* that anyone who denies that basic law of logic, the law of noncontradiction, and who is prepared to defend his or her position by entering into argumentative debate, will in fact be unable to avoid relying upon the very law which he or she purports to reject. And it may be that for other laws of logic parallel defenses can be constructed. But even if Aristotle was successful, and I believe that he was, in showing that no one who understands the laws of logic can remain rational while rejecting them, observance of the laws of logic is only a necessary and not a sufficient condition for rationality, whether theoretical or practical. It is on what has to be added to observance of the laws of logic to justify ascriptions of rationality – whether to oneself or to others, whether to modes of enquiry or to justifications of belief, or to courses of action and their justification – that disagreement arises concerning the fundamental nature of rationality and extends into disagreement over how it is rationally appropriate to proceed in the face of these disagreements. So the resources provided by modern academic philosophy enable us to redefine, but do not themselves seem to resolve the problems of those confronting the rival claims upon their allegiance that are made by protagonists of conflicting accounts of justice and of practical rationality.

The only other type of resource generally available in our society to such persons is that which is supplied by participation in the life of one of those groups whose thought and action are informed by some distinctive profession of settled conviction with regard to justice and to practical rationality. Those who resorted or resort to academic philosophy hoped or hope to acquire thereby a set of sound arguments by means of which they could assure themselves and others of the rational justification for their views. Those who resort instead to a set of beliefs embodied in the life of a group put their trust in persons rather than in arguments. In doing so they cannot escape the charge of a certain arbitrariness in their commitments, a charge, however, which tends to carry little weight with those against whom it is directed. Why does that charge carry so little weight?

Partly it is a matter of a general cynicism in our culture about the power or even the relevance of rational argument to matters sufficiently fundamental. Fideism has a large, not always articulate, body of adherents, and not only among the members of those Protestant churches and movements which openly proclaim it; there are plenty of secular fideists. And partly it is because of a strong and sometimes justified suspicion by those against whom the charge is leveled that those who level it do so, not so much because they themselves are genuinely moved by rational argument, as because by appealing to argument they are able to exercise a kind of power which favors their own interests and privileges, the interests and privileges of a class which has arrogated the rhetorically effective use of argument to itself for its own purposes.

Arguments, that is to say, have come to be understood in some circles not as expressions of rationality, but as weapons, the techniques for deploying which furnish a key part of the professional skills of lawyers, academics, economists, and journalists who thereby dominate the dialectically unfluent and inarticulate. There is thus a remarkable concordance in the way in which apparently very different types of social and cultural groups envisage each other's commitments. To the readership of the *New York Times*, or at least to that part of it which shares the presuppositions of those who write that parish magazine of affluent and self-congratulatory liberal enlightenment, the congregations of evangelical fundamentalism appear unfashionably unenlightened. But to the members of those congregations that readership appears to be just as much a community of prerational faith as they themselves are but one whose members, unlike themselves, fail to recognize themselves for what they are, and hence are in no position to level charges of irrationality at them or anyone else.

We thus inhabit a culture in which an inability to arrive at agreed rationally justifiable conclusions on the nature of justice and practical rationality coexists with appeals by contending social groups to sets of rival and conflicting convictions unsupported by rational justification. Neither the voices of academic philosophy, nor for that matter of any other academic discipline, nor those of the partisan subcultures, have been able to provide for ordinary citizens a way of uniting conviction of such matters with rational justification. Disputed questions concerning justice and practical rationality are thus treated in the public realm, not as matter for rational enquiry, but rather for the assertion and counterassertion of alternative and incompatible sets of premises.

How did this come to be the case? The answer falls into two parts, each having to do with the Enlightenment and with its subsequent history. It was a central aspiration of the Enlightenment, an aspiration the formulation of which was itself a great achievement, to provide for debate in the public realm standards and methods of rational justification by which alternative courses of action in every sphere of life could be adjudged just or unjust, rational or irrational, enlightened or unenlightened. So, it was hoped, reason would displace authority and tradition. Rational justification was to appeal to principles undeniable by any rational person and therefore independent of all those social and cultural particularities which the Enlightenment thinkers took to be the mere accidental clothing of reason in particular times and places. And that rational justification could be nothing other than what the thinkers of the Enlightenment had said that it was came to be accepted, at least by the vast majority of educated people, in post-Enlightenment cultural and social orders.

Yet both the thinkers of the Enlightenment and their successors proved unable to agree as to what precisely those principles were which would be found undeniable by all rational persons. One kind of answer was given by the authors of the *Encyclopédie*, a second by Rousseau, a third by Bentham, a fourth by Kant, a fifth by the Scottish philosophers of common sense and their French and American disciples. Nor has subsequent history diminished the extent of such disagreement. It has rather enlarged it. Consequently, the legacy of the Enlightenment has been the provision of an ideal of rational justification which it has proved impossible to attain. And hence in key part derives the inability within our culture to unite conviction and rational justification. Within that kind of academic philosophy which is the heir to the philosophies of the Enlightenment enquiry into the nature of rational justification has continued with ever-increasing refinement and undiminishing disagreement. In cultural, political, moral, and religious life post-Enlightenment conviction effectively has acquired a life of its own, independent of rational enquiry.

It is therefore worth asking whether the Enlightenment may not have contributed to our present condition in a second way, not only by what its achievements in propagating its distinctive doctrines led to, but also by what it succeeded in excluding from view. Is there some mode of understanding which could find no placement in the Enlightenment's vision of the world by means of which the conceptual and theoretical resources can be provided for reuniting conviction concerning such matters as justice on the one hand and rational enquiry and justification on the other? It will be important in trying to answer this question not to trap ourselves by, perhaps inadvertently, continuing to accept the standards of the Enlightenment. We already have the best of reasons for supposing that those standards cannot be met, and we know in advance, therefore, that from the standpoint of the Enlightenment and its successors any account of an alternative mode of understanding will inescapably be treated as one more contending view, unable to vindicate itself conclusively against its Enlightenment rivals. Any attempt to provide a radically different alternative standpoint is bound to be found rationally unsatisfactory in a variety of ways from the standpoint of the Enlightenment itself. Hence it is inevitable that such an attempt should be unacceptable to and rejected by those whose allegiance is to the dominant intellectual and cultural modes of the present order. At the same time, since what will be introduced will be a set of claims concerning rational justification and its requirements, those whose nonrational convictions flout any such requirement will be equally apt to be offended.

Is there, then, such an alternative mode of understanding? Of what did the Enlightenment deprive us? What the Enlightenment made us for the most part blind to and what we now need to recover is, so I shall argue, a conception of rational enquiry as embodied in a tradition, a conception according to which the standards of rational justification themselves emerge from and are part of a history in which they are vindicated by the way in which they transcend the limitations of and provide remedies for the defects of their predecessors within the history of that same tradition. [. . .]

It is not then that competing traditions do not share some standards. All the traditions with which we have been concerned agree in according a certain authority to logic both in their theory and in their practice. Were it not so, their adherents would be unable to disagree [. . .] It may therefore seem to be the case that we are confronted with the rival and competing claims of a number of traditions to our allegiance in respect of our understanding of practical rationality and justice, among which we can have no good reason to decide in favor of any one rather than of the others. Each has its own standards of reasoning; each provides its own background beliefs. To offer one kind of reason, to appeal to one set of background beliefs, will already be to have assumed the standpoint of one particular tradition. But if we make no such assumption, then we can have no good reason to give more weight to the contentions advanced by one particular tradition than to those advanced by its rivals.

Argument along these lines has been adduced in support of a conclusion that if the only available standards of rationality are those made available by and within traditions, then no issue between contending traditions is rationally decidable. To assert or to conclude this rather than that can be rational relative to the standards of some particular tradition, but not rational as such. There can be no rationality as such. Every set of standards, every tradition incorporating a set of standards, has as much and as little claim to our allegiance as any other. Let us call this the relativist challenge [. . .]

What I have to do, then, is to provide an account of the rationality presupposed by and implicit in the practice of those enquiry-bearing traditions with whose history I have been concerned [. . .]

The rationality of a tradition-constituted and tradition-constitutive enquiry is in key and essential part a matter of the kind of progress which it makes through a number of well-defined types of stage. Every such form of enquiry begins in and from some condition of pure historical contingency, from the beliefs, institutions, and practices of some particular community which constitute a given. Within such a community authority will have been conferred upon certain texts and certain voices. Bards, priests, prophets, kings, and, on occasion, fools and jesters will all be heard [. . .]

What takes a given community from a first stage in which the beliefs, utterances, texts, and persons taken to be authoritative are deferred to unquestioningly, or at least without systematic questioning, may be one or more of several types of occurrence. Authoritative texts or utterances may be shown to be susceptible to, by actually receiving, alternative and incompatible interpretations, enjoining perhaps alternative and incompatible courses of action. Incoherences in the established system of beliefs may become evident. Confrontation by new situations, engendering new questions, may reveal within established practices and beliefs a lack of resources for offering or for justifying answers to these new questions. The coming together of two previously separate communities, each with its own well-established institutions, practices, and beliefs, either by migration or by conquest, may open up new alternative possibilities and require more than the existing means of evaluation are able to provide.

What responses the inhabitants of a particular community make in the face of such stimuli toward the reformulation of their beliefs or the remaking of their practices or both will depend not only upon what stock of reasons and of questioning and reasoning abilities they already possess but also upon their inventiveness. And these in turn will determine the possible range of outcomes in the rejection, emendation, and reformulation of beliefs, the revaluation of authorities, the reinterpretation of new texts [. . .]

Those members of a community who have accepted the beliefs of the tradition in their new form – and those beliefs may inform only a limited part of the whole community's life or be such as concern its overall structure and indeed its relationship to the universe – become able to contrast their new beliefs with the old. Between those older beliefs and the worlds as they now understand it there is a radical discrepancy to be perceived. It is this lack of correspondence, between what the mind then judged and believed and reality as now perceived, classified, and understood, which is ascribed then to those earlier judgments and beliefs that are called *false*. [. . .]

[C]entral to a tradition-constituted enquiry at each stage in its development will be its current problematic, that agenda of unsolved problems and unresolved issues by reference to which its success or lack of it in making rational progress toward some further stage of development will be evaluated. At any point it may happen to any tradition-constituted enquiry that by its own standards of progress it ceases to make progress. Its hitherto trusted methods of enquiry have become sterile. Conflicts over rival answers to key questions can no longer be settled rationally. Moreover, it may indeed happen that the use of the methods of enquiry and of the forms of argument, by means of which rational progress had been achieved so far, begins to have the effect of increasingly disclosing new inadequacies, hitherto unrecognized incoherences, and new problems for the solution of which there seem to be insufficient or no resources within the established fabric of belief.

This kind of dissolution of historically founded certitudes is the mark of an epistemological crisis. The solution to a genuine epistemological crisis requires the invention or discovery of new concepts and the framing of some new type or types of theory which meet three highly exacting requirements. First, this in some ways radically new and conceptually enriched scheme, if it is to put an end to epistemological crisis, must furnish a solution to the problems which had previously proved intractable in a systematic and coherent way. Second, it must also provide an explanation of just what it was which rendered the tradition, before it had acquired these new resources, sterile or incoherent or both. And third, these first two tasks must be carried out in a way which exhibits some fundamental continuity of the new conceptual and theoretical structures with the shared beliefs in terms of which the tradition of enquiry had been defined up to this point. [. . .]

Every tradition, whether it recognizes the fact or not, confronts the possibility that at some future time it will fall into a state of epistemological crisis, recognizable as such by its own standards of rational justification, which have themselves been vindicated up to that time as the best to emerge from the history of that particular tradition. All attempts to deploy the imaginative and inventive resources which the adherents of the tradition can provide may founder, either merely by doing nothing to remedy the condition of sterility and incoherence into which the enquiry has fallen or by also revealing or creating new problems, and revealing new flaws and new limitations. Time may elapse, and no further resources or solutions emerge.

For the adherents of a tradition which is now in this state of fundamental and radical crisis may at this point encounter in a new way the claims of some particular rival tradition, perhaps one with which they have for some time coexisted, perhaps one which they are now encountering for the first time. They now come or had already come to understand the beliefs and way of life of this other alien tradition, and to do so they have or have had to learn (as we shall see when we go on to discuss the linguistic characteristics of tradition) the language of the alien tradition as a new and second first language.

When they have understood the beliefs of the alien tradition, they may find themselves compelled to recognize that within this other tradition it is possible to construct from the concepts and theories peculiar to it what they were unable to provide from their own conceptual and theoretical resources, a cogent and illuminating explanation – cogent and illuminating, that is, by their own standards – of why their own intellectual tradition had been unable to solve its problems or restore its coherence. The standards by which they judge this explanation to be cogent and illuminating will be the very same standards by which they have found their tradition wanting in the face of epistemological crisis. [. . .]

Thus a tradition can be rationally discredited by and in the light of appeal to its very own standards of rationality in more than one way. These are the possibilities which the relativist challenge has failed to envisage. [. . .]

# Chapter 12

# Zygmunt Bauman

## POSTMODERN ETHICS

[. . .]

**P**OSTMODERNITY, ONE MAY SAY as well, brings 're-enchantment' of the world after the protracted and earnest, though in the end inconclusive, modern struggle to dis-enchant it (or, more exactly, the resistance to dis-enchantment, hardly ever put to sleep, was all along the 'postmodern thorn' in the body of modernity). The mistrust of human spontaneity, of drives, impulses and inclinations resistant to prediction and rational justification, has been all but replaced by the mistrust of unemotional, calculating reason. Dignity has been returned to emotions; legitimacy to the 'inexplicable', nay *irrational*, sympathies and loyalties which cannot 'explain themselves' in terms of their usefulness and purpose.[. . .] We accept that not all actions, and particularly not all among the most important of actions, need to justify and explain themselves to be worthy of our esteem. [. . .]

To let morality out of the stiff armour of the artificially constructed ethical codes (or abandoning the ambition to keep it there), means to *re-personalize* it. Human passions used to be considered too errant and fickle, and the task to make human cohabitation secure too serious, to entrust the fate of human coexistence to moral capacities of human persons. What we come to understand now is that that fate may not be taken proper care of (that is, all the care offered or contemplated would prove unrealistic or, worse still, counter-productive) unless the fashion in which we go about caring takes cognizance of personal morality and its stubborn presence. What we are learning, and learning the hard way, is that it is the personal morality that makes ethical negotiation and consensus possible, not the other way round. To be sure, personal morality would not guarantee the success of such negotiations. It may even make them harder and add quite a few obstacles to the course: no more will the roads be blazed by bulldozing. Most likely, it would make any agreement that may be reached inconclusive, temporary and short of universal acceptance. Yet we know now that this is precisely where things stand, where we stand, and that we could pretend otherwise only at the peril to our upright posture.

Re-personalizing morality means returning moral responsibility from the finishing line (to which it was exiled) to the starting point (where it is at home) of the ethical process. We realize now – with a mixture of apprehension and hope – that unless moral responsibility was 'from the start', somehow rooted in the very way we humans are – it would never be conjured up at a later stage by no matter how high-minded or high-handed an effort. [. . .]

The postulate of universality was always a demand with an address; or, somewhat more concretely, a sword with the edge aimed against a selected target. The *postulate* was a reflection on the modern *practice* of *universalization* – in a way similar to that of the related concepts of 'one human nature' or 'human essence', which reflected the *intention* to substitute the *citizen* (the person with only such attributes as have been assigned by the laws of the single and uncontested authority acting on behalf of the unified and sovereign state) for the motley collection of parishioners, kinsmen and other locals. The theoretical postulate squared well with the uniformizing ambitions and practices of the modern state, with the war it declared on *les pouvoirs intermédiaires*, with its cultural crusades against local customs redefined as superstitions and condemned to death for the crime of resisting centralized management. The 'universal man', pared to the bare bones of 'human nature', was to be – in Alasdair MacIntyre's expression – an 'unencumbered self'; not necessarily unaffected by the communally inspired particularisms, yet capable of cutting himself loose from the communal roots and loyalties; of lifting himself, so to speak, onto a higher plane and taking from there a long, detached and critical view of communal demands and pressures.

The requisite of recognizing as moral only such rules as pass the test of some universal, extemporal and exterritorial principles, meant first and foremost the disavowal of the temporal and territorially bound, communal pretences to make moral judgements with authority. The sword used for the purpose, however, was soon found to be what it had been from the start – double-edged. True, it cut deep into the flesh of the named adversaries of the state-disapproved parochialism, but it also hurt where it was not meant to, seriously damaging the state's own sovereignty it was hoped to defend. Indeed, why should the 'unencumbered self' admit the right of the Law of the State, this state here and now, to spell out its essence? Why should it accept the call to confine itself to the state-shaped mould of citizenship?

When taken up seriously (that is, the way it is taken by philosophers, not the practitioners of legislating powers), the postulate of universality not only saps the moral prerogatives of communities now transformed into administrative units of the homogeneous nation-state, but renders the state's bid for supreme moral authority all but unsustainable. The logic of the postulate is dissonant with the practice of *any* self-confined political community; it opposes not just the specific counter-power currently in the dock on the charge of obstructing the movement toward universality, but the very Aristotelian principle of the polity as the ultimate fount and the guardian of humanity. It militates against any theory, like those of Michael Walzer or Michael Oakeshott, contemporary Aristotelians, who conceive of 'moral reasoning as an appeal of meanings internal to a political community, not an appeal to abstract principles', regardless of the level at which the political community in question has been located.

Any *polis* separates, sets apart, 'particularizes' its members from members of other communities, as much as it unites them and makes alike inside its own boundaries. The 'situated' self (in MacIntyre's terms, the opposite of the 'unencumbered' one) is always set against a self *differently* situated – rooted in another *polis*. For this reason, the universalistic demand tends to turn round against the *polis*, which wished to domesticate it and deploy in the war against its own rebels; at its logical limits, this demand cannot but incessantly gestate the opposition against *all* moral dictate, and thus spawn a radically *individualistic* stance. While promoting ostensibly universal, yet by necessity home-grown and home-bound standards, the polity finds itself opposed and resisted in the name of the selfsame principle of universalism which enlightens and/or ennobles its purpose. Promotion of universal standards then looks suspiciously like suppression of human nature and tends to be censured as *intolerance*.

To the defenders of the 'situated' self ('communitarians', as they came to be known) universalistic ambitions and universalizing practices are, of course, an outrage – vehicles of oppression, an act of violence perpetrated upon human freedom. They are, however, unacceptable also to the *bona fide*, earnest and consistent liberal universalists who are wary of any narrower-than-universal powers claiming to be the promoters of allegedly universal standards. As consistent liberals see it, morality may only be rooted in qualities and capacities possessed by individuals *qua* human persons. [. . .]

However powerful these constraints and profound the innate contradictions of the universalistic project, modernity treated all relativity as a nuisance and a challenge – above all, as a temporary irritant, shortly to be cured. However difficult the practising of moral universality proved to be, no practical difficulty was allowed to cast doubt on universality as an ideal and the horizon of history. Relativism was always merely 'current'; its persistence in spite of present efforts tended to be played down as merely a momentary hitch in an otherwise unstoppable movement toward the ideal. The dream of universality as the *ultimate destination of human kind*, and the determination to bring it forth, took refuge in the *processual* concept of *universalization*. There it was secure – as long as it could be reasonably believed that the process of universalization does take place, that the 'march of time' might be credibly viewed as unstoppable, and that it will lead to the progressive trimming down, and eventually to the smothering, of present differences. The trust in the wondrous healing skills of time – and especially its not-yet part, a part one could freely fantasize about and assign magical powers without fear of empirical test – was, after all, a most conspicuous feature of the modern mind. Diderot called modern man 'postéromane' – in love with posterity; and, as Alan Finkielkraut recently put it,

> Modern man counted on the competence of the future to correct the injustices of the present. He envisaged humanity as a whole as a move-

ment of qualities which would defy humans taken separately. He vested
with the time that will arrive the confidence he had in Eternity . . .
Modern man marches toward posterity.

It is that belief, so characteristic of modern mentality, which has been undermined
and cast out of fashion at the postmodern stage (together with the powers whose
ambitions kept it alive). The postmodern version of the historiosophy of universalization is the perspective of 'globalization' – the vision of a global spread of
information, technology and economic interdependency that conspicuously does
not include the ecumenization of political, cultural and moral authorities (factors
supposed to 'globalize' are seen as *non*-national, rather than *inter*- or *supra*-national).
If anything, the new historiosophy renders the prospects of moral universality
achieved by the spread of the 'civilizing process' distant and dim. [. . .]

The moment one accepts the likelihood that the plurality of cultural/moral
sovereignties (as distinct from political/economic ones) will persist for an indefinite time, perhaps forever – one finds the retreat from the cold and abstract
territory of universal moral values into the cosy and homely shelter of 'native
community' exceedingly tempting; many would find the seduction irresistible.
Hence the 'community first' vision of the human world, which for the better part
of modern times was exiled to the seldom visited periphery of philosophical and
political reflection, disdainfully rejected as 'conservative', 'nostalgic', or 'romantic'
and consigned to oblivion by the dominant thought which proudly described itself
as 'marching with time', scientific and 'progressive' – is now back with a vengeance;
indeed, it comes quite close to being elevated to the canon and uncontested 'good
sense' of human sciences. [. . .]

[A] community truly able to 'situate' its members with any degree of lasting consequence appears to be more a methodological postulate than a fact of life. Whenever
one descends from the relatively secure realm of concepts to the description of
any concrete object the concepts are supposed to stand for – one finds merely a
fluid collection of men and women acting at cross-purposes, fraught with inner
controversy and conspicuously short of the means to arbitrate between conflicting
ethical propositions. The moral community proves to be not so much *imagined* as
*postulated*, and postulated *contentiously*. It is always the matter of one postulate set
against other postulates; a *programme*, a bid to bind the future, rather than to defend
or vindicate the past; above all, a bid to bind a certain number of men and women
and subordinate their actions to certain choices made preferable by the effort to
make the postulated existence of community real. What is described as 'moral' in
the moral community are the desired effects of such subordination – the limiting
and the streamlining of individual choices obtained through the demand to cooperate in making the group real, disguised as a demand to keep the group alive
(the demand often expressed bluntly, and duplicitously, as the need to sacrifice
individual, selfish interests for the – always putative – interest of all). [. . .]

What is demanded is a kind of loyalty that should marginalize or render null
and void the competitive demands of obedience, anchored in other aspects of the
multi-faceted identity. The self needs to be first lopped and trimmed, dissected,
and then reassembled, in order to become truly 'situated'. The theory of the situated

self, and an ideology serving the community-construction which that theory reflects [. . .] the enmity towards 'spontaneous' and autonomous, individually begotten morality is, in the case of postulated communities, much more vigilant, intense and pugnacious than in the case of a well-entrenched, secure and self-confident state. Militant intolerance stems from insecurity, which in the case of the postulated communities is endemic and incurable. [. . .]

In the same way as the clarion call of 'unencumbered' self served all too often to silence the protest against the suppression of moral autonomy by the unitary nation-state, the image of 'situated' self tends to cover up the 'communitarian' practices of similar suppression. Neither of the two is immune to misuse; neither is properly protected against being harnessed to the promotion of moral heteronomy and the expropriation of the individual's right to moral judgement.

What makes both concepts eminently usable for the promotion of ethical heteronomy is the fact that what any vision of group-universal morality tacitly assumes (whether the group in question is co-terminous with the human species as a whole, or a nation-state, or a postulated community), is that moral conduct may indeed be expressed in rules which can be given universal form. That is, that moral selves may be dissolved in the all-embracing 'we' – the moral 'I' being just a singular form of the ethical 'us'. And that within this ethical 'we', 'I' is exchangeable with 's/he'; whatever is moral when stated in the first person remains moral when stated in the second or third. As a matter of fact, only such rules as withstand this 'depersonalization' are seen as meeting the conditions set for *ethical* norms. That morality can be only *collective* in one way or another – as an outcome of either the authoritative legislation or of the allegedly non-deliberate, yet equally powerful *a priori* communal 'situating' – is hence tautologically 'evident'. Its truth has been guaranteed in advance by the way moral phenomena have been defined and singled out.

And yet the premises can survive only as long as they remain tacit, and thus uncontrolled. At a closer look, they do not appear either immediately obvious or even safe to accept.

Take the first premise – that when considering moral phenomena, we are free to follow the grammatical injunction to treat the 'we' as the plural form of 'I'. This is, however, a travesty of morality – objects Emmanuel Lévinas. He explains:

> To show respect cannot mean to subject oneself; yet the other does command me. I am commanded, that is recognized as someone capable of realizing a work. To show respect is to bow down not before the law, but before a being who commands a work from me. But for this command to not involve humiliation – which would take from me the very possibility of showing respect – the command I receive must also be a command to command him who commands me. I consists in commanding a being to command me. This reference from a command to command is the fact of saying 'we', of constituting a party. By reason of this reference of one command to another, 'we' is not the plural of 'I' (Nous n'est pas le pluriel de Je).

There would be a smooth way leading from many 'I's to the collective 'we' only if one could posit all 'I's as by and large identical, at least in respect of an attribute which assigns the units as members of one set (like 'we, the blond-haired', or 'we, the graduates of X University', or 'we, the supporters of Leeds United') – and therefore, again in this respect, exchangeable; 'we' becomes a plural of 'I' only at the cost of glossing over I's multi-dimensionality. 'We' is then a sum, a result of counting – an aggregate of ciphers, not an organic whole. This is not, however, the case of the 'moral party'. If the idea of supra-individual totality may at all apply to the world of morality, it may only refer to a whole knit together, and continuously knit together, out of the commands that are given and received and followed by the selves which are oral subjects precisely *because each one of them is irreplaceable*, and because their relations are *asymmetrical*.

Attitude *before* the relations; one-sidedness, *not* reciprocity; a relation that cannot be reversed: these are the indispensable, defining traits of a moral stance. 'In the relation to the Face, what is affirmed is asymmetry; in the beginning, it does not matter who the Other is in relation to me – that is his business.' This sentence of Lévinas can be read as a definition of the Face: Face is encountered if, and only if, my relation to the Other is *programmatically* non-symmetrical; that is, not dependent on the Other's past, present, anticipated or hoped-for *reciprocation*. And morality is the encounter with the Other as Face. Moral stance begets an essentially *unequal* relationship; this inequality, non-equity, this non-asking-for-reciprocation, this disinterest in mutuality, this indifference to the 'balancing up' of gains or rewards – in short, this organically 'unbalanced' and hence non-reversible character of 'I versus the Other' relationship is what makes the encounter a moral event.

Lévinas draws a most radical conclusion from Kant's solution to the mysteries of 'moral law inside me', but only such radicalism may give justice to Kant's conception of morality as a posture guided solely by the concern for the Other *for the Other's sake*, and the respect for the Other as a free subject and the 'end in itself'. Other, milder versions of post-Kantian ethical theory can hardly match the enormity of the moral demand which Kant's conception entails. For Martin Buber, for instance, what sets the I–Thou relationship apart from the I–it (one in which the Other does not appear as a moral subject) is from the start the *dialogical* character of the encounter, or the anticipation of a dialogue; I–Thou has an 'address and response' structure, a structure of ongoing conversation, in the course of which the partners incessantly exchange the roles, address each other and respond to each other in kind. It is the symmetry of attitudes and responsibilities that gives the relation its I–Thou character, being present in it from the start, as a postulate or categorical expectation; if I treat you as Thou rather than It, it is precisely because I stipulate (expect, work towards) being also treated by you as your Thou. [. . .]

I am for the Other whether the Other is for me or not; his being for me is, so to speak, his problem, and whether or how he 'handles' that problem does not in the least affect my being-for-Him (as far as my being-for-the-Other includes respect for the Other's autonomy, which in its turn includes my consent not to blackmail the Other into being-for-me, nor interfere in any other way with the Other's freedom). Whatever else 'I-for-you' may contain, it does not contain a demand to be repayed, mirrored or 'balanced out' in the 'you-for-me'. My rela-tion to the Other is not reversible; if it happens to be reciprocated, the reciprocation is but an accident from the point of view of my being-for.

The 'we' that stands for a 'moral party' is not, therefore, a plural of 'I' – but a term which connotes a complex structure that ties together units of sharply unequal standing. In a moral relationship, I and the Other are not exchangeable, and thus cannot be 'added up' to form a plural 'we'. In a moral relationship, all the 'duties' and 'rules' that may be conceived are addressed solely to me, bind only me, constitute me and me alone as an 'I'. When addressed to me, responsibility is moral. It may well lose its moral content completely the moment I try to turn it around to bind the Other. [. . .]

The readiness to sacrifice for the sake of the other burdens me with the respon-sibility which is *moral* precisely for my acceptance that the command to sacrifice applies to me and me only, that the sacrifice is not a matter of exchange or reci-procation of services, that the command is *not universalizable* and thus cannot be shrugged off my shoulders so that it falls on someone else's. Being a moral person means that I *am* my brother's keeper. But this also means that *I* am my brother's keeper whether or not my brother sees his own brotherly duties the same way I do; and that I am my brother's keeper whatever other brothers, real or putative, do or may do. At least, I can be properly his keeper only if I act *as if* I was the only one *obliged*, or even likely, to act this way. I am always the one who carries that straw which will break the back of the camel of moral indifference. It is this uniqueness (not 'generalizability'!), and this non-reversibility of my responsi-bility, which puts me in the moral relationship. This is what counts, whether or not all brothers of the world would do for their own brothers what I am about to do. [. . .]

[C]onverting the object of responsibility to my standard, taking him or her into my possession, putting under my command, making identical with myself in this or any other respect, and thus stripping him or her of *their* responsibility, which constitutes *their* alterity, their *uniqueness* – is most certainly not the outcome my responsibility may pursue or contemplate without denying itself, without ceasing to be a moral stance. Our 'moral party' is not one of fusion, of identity, of joint submission to a 'third term' (that is, to neither I nor Thou, but certain impersonal principles which everyone must needs obey), of dissolving my saintliness and your alterity in a common standard that obliterates the individuality of us both (and that includes the standard of reciprocity, of equal treatment, of balanced exchange). [. . .]

No universal standards, then. No looking over one's shoulders, to take a glimpse of what other people 'like me' do. No listening to what they say they do or ought to be doing – and then following their example, absolving myself for not doing anything else, nothing that others would not do, and enjoying a clear conscience at the end of the day. We do look and listen, but it does not help – at least does not help *radically*. Pointing my finger away from myself – 'this is what people do, this is how things are' – does not save me from sleepless nights and days full of self-depreciation. 'I have done my duty' may perhaps get the judges off my back, but won't disband the jury of what I, for not being able to point my finger at anybody, call 'conscience'. '*The duty of us all*' which I *know*, does not seem to be the same thing as *my responsibility* which I *feel*. [. . .]

Only rules can be universal. One may legislate universal rule-dictated *duties*, but moral *responsibility* exists solely in interpellating the individual and being carried individually. Duties tend to make humans alike; responsibility is what makes them into individuals. Humanity is not captured in common denominators – it sinks and vanishes there. The morality of the moral subject does not, therefore, have the character of a rule. One may say that the moral is what *resists* codification, formalization, socialization, universalization. [. . .]

[M]orality is endemically and irredeemably *non-rational* – in the sense of not being calculable, hence not being presentable as following impersonal rules, hence not being describable as following rules that are in principle universalizable. [. . .]

# TRUTH

- Richard Rorty, Pragmatism, relativism, and irrationalism

- Seyla Benhabib, Feminism and the question of postmodernism

**Richard Rorty** was born in New York on 4 October 1931. He has taught at several universities in the United States, among them Yale, Princeton and Stanford. His writings include *Philosophy and the Mirror of Nature* (1979) and *The Consequences of Pragmatism* (1982).

**Seyla Benhabib** was born in Istanbul, Turkey. She received her PhD in Philosophy at Yale University. Since 1993, Benhabib has been Professor of Government and Senior Research Fellow at the Center for European Studies at Harvard University. She is the author of *Critique, Norm and Utopia* (1986) and *Situating the Self* (1992).

# Chapter 13

# Richard Rorty

## PRAGMATISM, RELATIVISM, AND IRRATIONALISM

### Part I: Pragmatism

'**PRAGMATISM**' **IS A VAGUE**, ambiguous, and overworked word. Nevertheless, it names the chief glory of our country's intellectual tradition.

My first characterization of pragmatism is that it is simply anti-essentialism applied to notions like 'truth,' 'knowledge,' 'language,' 'morality,' and similar objects of philosophical theorizing. Let me illustrate this by James's definition of 'the true' as 'what is good in the way of belief.' This has struck his critics as not to the point, as unphilosophical, as like the suggestion that the essence of aspirin is that it is good for headaches. James's point, however, was that there *is* nothing deeper to be said: truth is not the sort of thing which *has* an essence. More specifically, his point was that it is no use being told that truth is 'correspondence to reality.' Given a language and a view of what the world is like, one can, to be sure, pair off bits of the language with bits of what one takes the world to be in such a way that the sentences one believes true have internal structures isomorphic to relations between things in the world. When we rap out routine undeliberated reports like 'This is water,' 'That's read,' 'That's ugly,' 'That's immoral,' our short categorical sentences can easily be thought of as pictures, or as symbols which fit together to make a map. Such·reports do indeed pair little bits of language with little bits of the world. Once one gets to negative universal hypotheticals, and the like, such pairing will become messy and *ad hoc*, but perhaps it can be done. James's point was that carrying out this exercise will not enlighten us about why truths are good to believe, or offer any clues as to why or whether our present view of the world is, roughly, the one we should hold. Yet nobody would have asked for a 'theory' of truth if they had not wanted answers to these latter questions. Those who want truth to have an essence want knowledge, or rationality, or inquiry, or the relation between thought and its object, to have an essence. Further, they want to be able to use their knowledge of such essences to criticize views they take to be false, and to point the direction of progress toward the discovery of more truths. James thinks these hopes are vain. There are no essences anywhere in the area. There is no wholesale, epistemological way to direct, or criticize, or underwrite, the course of inquiry.

Rather, the pragmatists tell us, it is the vocabulary of practise rather than of theory, of action rather than contemplation, in which one can say something useful about truth. Nobody engages in epistemology or semantics because he wants to know how 'This is red' pictures the world. Rather, we want to know in what sense Pasteur's views of disease picture the world accurately and Paracelsus' inaccurately, or what exactly it is that Marx pictured more accurately than Machiavelli. But just here the vocabulary of 'picturing' fails us. When we turn from individual sentences to vocabularies and theories, critical terminology naturally shifts from metaphors of isomorphism, symbolism, and mapping to talk of utility, convenience, and like-lihood of getting what we want. To say that the parts of properly analyzed true sentences are arranged in a way isomorphic to the parts of the world paired with them sounds plausible if one thinks of a sentence like 'Jupiter has moons.' It sounds slightly less plausible for 'The earth goes round the sun,' less still for 'There is no such thing as natural motion,' and not plausible at all for 'The universe is infinite.' When we want to praise or blame assertions of the latter sort of sentence, we show how the decision to assert them fits into a whole complex of decisions about what terminology to use, what books to read, what projects to engage in, what life to live. In this respect they resemble such sentences as 'Love is the only law' and 'History is the story of class struggle.' The whole vocabulary of isomorphism, picturing, and mapping is out of place here, as indeed is the notion of being true *of objects*. If we ask what objects these sentences claim to be true of, we get only unhelpful repetitions of the subject terms – 'the universe,' 'the law,' 'history.' Or, even less helpfully, we get talk about 'the facts,' or 'the way the world is.' The natural approach to such sentences, Dewey tells us, is not 'Do they get it right?', but more like 'What would it be like to believe that? What would happen if I did? What would I be committing myself to?' The vocabulary of contemplation, looking, *theoria*, deserts us just when we deal with theory rather than observation, with programming rather than input. When the contemplative mind, isolated from the stimuli of the moment, takes large views, its activity is more like deciding what to *do* than deciding that a representation is accurate. James's dictum about truth says that the vocabulary of practice is uneliminable, that no distinction of kind sepa-rates the sciences from the crafts, from moral reflection, or from art.

So a second characterization of pragmatism might go like this: there is no epis-temological difference between truth about what ought to be and truth about what is, nor any metaphysical difference between facts and values, nor any method-ological difference between morality and science. Even nonpragmatists think Plato was wrong to think of moral philosophy as discovering the essence of goodness, and Mill and Kant wrong in trying to reduce moral choice to rule. But every reason for saying that they were wrong is a reason for thinking the epistemolog-ical tradition wrong in looking for the essence of science, and in trying to reduce rationality to rule. For the pragmatists the pattern of all inquiry – scientific as well as moral – is deliberation concerning the relative attractions of various concrete alternatives. The idea that in science or philosophy we can substitute 'method' for deliberation between alternative results of speculation is just wishful thinking. It is like the idea that the morally wise man resolves his dilemmas by consulting his memory of the Idea of the Good, or by looking up the relevant article of the moral law. It is the myth that rationality consists in being constrained by rule. According to this Platonic myth, the life of reason is not the life of Socratic conversation but an illuminated state of consciousness in which one never needs to ask if one has exhausted the possible descriptions of, or explanations for, the situation. One simply arrives at true beliefs by obeying mechanical procedures.

Traditional, Platonic, epistemologically-centred philosophy is the search for such procedures. It is the search for a way in which one can avoid the need for conversation and deliberation and simply tick off the way things are. The idea is to acquire beliefs about interesting and important matters in a way as much like visual perception as possible – by confronting an object and responding to it as programmed. This urge to substitute *theoria* for *phronesis* is what lies behind the attempt to say that 'There is no such thing as natural motion' pictures objects in the same way as does 'The cat is on the mat.' It also lies behind the hope that some arrangement of objects may be found which is pictured by the sentence 'Love is better than hate,' and the frustration which ensues when it is realized that there may be no such objects. The great fallacy of the tradition, the pragmatists tell us, is to think that the metaphors of vision, correspondence, mapping, picturing, and representation which apply to small, routine assertions will apply to large and debatable ones. This basic error begets the notion that where there are no objects to correspond to we have no hope of rationality, but only taste, passion, and will. When the pragmatist attacks the notion of truth as accuracy of representation he is thus attacking the traditional distinctions between reason and desire, reason and appetite, reason and will. For none of these distinctions make sense unless reason is thought of on the model of vision, unless we persist in what Dewey called 'the spectator theory of knowledge.'

The pragmatist tells us that once we get rid of this model we see that the Platonic idea of the life of reason is impossible. A life spent representing objects accurately would be spent recording the results of calculations, reasoning through sorites, calling off the observable properties of things, construing cases according to unambiguous criteria, getting things right. Within what Kuhn calls 'normal science,' or any similar social context, one can, indeed, live such a life. But conformity to *social* norms is not good enough for the Platonist. He wants to be constrained not merely by the disciplines of the day, but by the ahistorical and nonhuman nature of reality itself. This impulse takes two forms – the original Platonic strategy of postulating novel *objects* for treasured propositions to correspond to, and the Kantian strategy of finding *principles* which are definatory of the essence of knowledge, or representation, or morality, or rationality. But this difference is unimportant compared to the common urge to escape the vocabulary and practices of one's own time and find something ahistorical and necessary to cling to. It is the urge to answer questions like 'Why believe what I take to be true?' 'Why do what I take to be right?' by appealing to something *more* than the ordinary, retail, detailed, concrete reasons which have brought one to one's present view. This urge is common to nineteenth-century idealists and contemporary scientific realists, to Russell and to Husserl; it is definatory of the Western philosophical tradition, and of the culture for which that tradition speaks. James and Dewey stand with Nietzsche and Heidegger in asking us to abandon that tradition, and that culture.

Let me sum up by offering a third and final characterization of pragmatism: it is the doctrine that there are no constraints on inquiry save conversational ones – no wholesale constraints derived from the nature of the objects, or of the mind, or of language, but only those retail constraints provided by the remarks of our fellow-inquirers. The way in which the properly-programmed speaker cannot help believing that the patch before him is red has *no* analogy for the more interesting and controversial beliefs which provoke epistemological reflection. The pragmatist tells us that it is useless to hope that objects will constrain us to believe the truth about them, if only they are approached with an unclouded mental eye, or a rigorous method, or a perspicuous language. He wants us to give up the notion that God, or evolution, or some other underwriter of our present world-picture, has programmed us as machines for accurate verbal picturing, and that philosophy brings self-knowledge by letting us read our own program. The only sense in which we are constrained to truth is that, as Peirce suggested, we can make no sense of the notion that the view which can survive all objections might be false. But objections – conversational constraints – cannot be anticipated. There is no method for knowing *when* one has reached the truth, or when one is closer to it than before.

I prefer this third way of characterizing pragmatism because it seems to me to focus on a fundamental choice which confronts the reflective mind: that between accepting the contingent character of starting-points, and attempting to evade this contingency. To accept the contingency of starting-points is to accept our inheritance from, and our conversation with, our fellow-humans as our only source of guidance. To attempt to evade this contingency is to hope to become a properly-programmed machine. This was the hope which Plato thought might be fulfilled at the top of the divided line, when we passed beyond hypotheses. Christians have hoped it might be attained by becoming attuned to the voice of God in the heart, and Cartesians that it might be fulfilled by emptying the mind and seeking the indubitable. Since Kant, philosophers have hoped that it might be fulfilled by finding the a priori structure of any possible inquiry, or language, or form of social life. If we give up this hope, we shall lose what Nietzsche called 'metaphysical comfort,' but we may gain a renewed sense of community. Our identification with our community – our society, our political tradition, our intellectual heritage – is heightened when we see this community as *ours* rather than *nature's, shaped* rather than *found*, one among many which men have made. In the end, the pragmatists tell us, what matters is our loyalty to our human beings clinging together against the dark, not our hope of getting things right. James, in arguing against realists and idealists that 'the trail of the human serpent is over all,' was reminding us that our glory is in our participation in fallible and transitory human projects, not in our obedience to permanent nonhuman constraints.

## Part II: Relativism

'Relativism' is the view that every belief on a certain topic, or perhaps about *any* topic, is as good as every other. No one holds this view. Except for the occasional cooperative freshman, one cannot find anybody who says that two incompatible opinions on an important topic are equally good. The philosophers who get *called* 'relativists' are those who say that the grounds for choosing between such opinions are less algorithmic than had been thought. Thus one may be attacked as a relativist for holding that familiarity of terminology is a criterion of theory-choice in physical science, or that coherence with the institutions of the surviving parliamentary democracies is a criterion in social philosophy. When such criteria are invoked, critics say that the resulting philosophical position assumes an unjustified primacy for 'our conceptual framework,' or our purposes, or our institutions. The position in question is criticized for not having done what philosophers are employed to do: explain why our framework, or culture, or interests, or language, or whatever, is at last on the right track – in touch with physical reality, or the moral law, or the real numbers, or some other sort of object patiently waiting about to be copied. So the real issue is not between people who think one view as good as another and people who do not. It is between those who think our culture, or purpose, or intuitions cannot be supported except conversationally, and people who still hope for other sorts of support.

If there *were* any relativists, they would, of course, be easy to refute. One would merely use some variant of the self-referential arguments Socrates used against Protagoras. But such neat little dialectical strategies only work against lightly-sketched fictional characters. The relativist who says that we can break ties among serious and in compatible candidates for belief only by 'nonrational' or 'noncognitive' considerations is just one of the Platonist or Kantian philosopher's imaginary playmates, inhabiting the same realm of fantasy as the solipsist, the skeptic, and the moral nihilist. Disillusioned, or whimsical, Platonists and Kantians occasionally play at being one or another of these characters. But when they do they are never offering relativism or skepticism or nihilism as a serious suggestion about how we might do things differently. These positions are adopted to make *philosophical* points – that is, moves in a game played with fictitious opponents, rather than fellow-participants in a common project.

The association of pragmatism with relativism is a result of a confusion between the pragmatist's attitude toward *philosophical* theories with his attitude towards *real* theories. James and Dewey are, to be sure, metaphilosophical relativists, in a certain limited sense. Namely: they think there is no way to choose, and no point in choosing, between incompatible philosophical theories of the typical Platonic or Kantian type. Such theories are attempts to ground some element of our practices on something external to these practices. Pragmatists think that any such philosophical grounding is, apart from elegance of execution, pretty much as good or as bad as the practice it purports to ground. They regard the project of grounding as a wheel that plays no part in the mechanism. In this, I think, they are quite right. No sooner does one discover the categories of the pure understanding for a Newtonian age than somebody draws up another list that would do nicely for an Aristotelian or an Einsteinian one. No sooner does one draw up a categorical imperative for Christians than somebody draws up one which works for cannibals. No sooner does one develop an evolutionary epistemology which explains why our science is so good than somebody writes a science-fiction story about bug-eyed and monstrous evolutionary epistemologists praising bug-eyed and monstrous evolutionary epistemologists praising bug-eyed and monstrous scientists for the survival value of their monstrous theories. The reason this game is so easy to play is that none of these philosophical theories have to do much hard work. The real work has been done by the scientists who developed the explanatory theories by patience and genius, or the societies which developed the moralities and institutions in struggle and pain. All the Platonic or Kantian philosopher does is to take the finished first-level product, jack it up a few levels of abstraction, invent a metaphysical or epistemological or semantical vocabulary into which to translate it, and announce that he has *grounded* it.

'Relativism' only seems to refer to a disturbing view, worthy of being refuted, if it concerns *real* theories, not just philosophical theories. Nobody really cares if there are incompatible alternative formulations of a categorical imperative, or incompatible sets of categories of the pure understanding. We *do* care about alternative, concrete, detailed cosmologies, or alternative concrete, detailed proposals for political change. When such an alternative is proposed, we debate it, not in terms of categories or principles but in terms of the various concrete advantages and disadvantages it has. The reason relativism is talked about so much among Platonic and Kantian philosophers is that they think being relativistic about philosophical theories – attempts to 'ground' first-level theories – leads to being relativistic about the first-level theories themselves. If anyone really believed that the worth of a theory depends upon the worth of its philosophical grounding, then indeed they would be dubious about physics, or democracy, until relativism in respect to philosophical theories had been overcome. Fortunately, almost nobody believes anything of the sort.

What people do believe is that it would be good to hook up our views about democracy, mathematics, physics, God, and everything else, into a coherent story about how everything hangs together. Getting such a synoptic view often does require us to change radically our views on particular subjects. But this holistic process of readjustment is just muddling through on a large scale. It has nothing to do with the Platonic-Kantian notion of grounding. That notion involves finding constraints, demonstrating necessities, finding immutable principles to which to subordinate oneself. When it turns out that suggested constraints, necessities, and principles are as plentiful as blackberries, nothing changes except the attitude of the rest of culture towards the philosophers. Since the time of Kant, it has become more and more apparent to nonphilosophers that a really professional philosopher can supply a philosophical foundation for just about anything. This is one reason why philosophers have, in the course of our century, become increasingly isolated from the rest of culture. Our proposals to guarantee this and clarify that have come to strike our fellow-intellectuals as merely comic.

## Part III: Irrationalism

[. . .]

Questions about irrationalism have become acute in our century because the sullen resentment which sins against Socrates, which withdraws from conversation and community, has recently become articulate. Our European intellectual tradition is now abused as 'merely conceptual' or 'merely ontic' or as 'committed to abstractions.' Irrationalists propose such rubbishy pseudo-epistemological notions as 'intuition' or 'an inarticulate sense of tradition' or 'thinking with the blood' or 'expressing the will of the oppressed classes.' Our tyrants and bandits are more hateful than those of earlier times because, invoking such self-deceptive rhetoric, they pose as intellectuals. Our tyrants write philosophy in the morning and torture in the afternoon; our bandits alternately read Hölderlin and bomb people into bloody scraps. So our culture clings, more than ever, to the hope of the Enlightenment, the hope that drove Kant to make philosophy formal and rigorous and professional. We hope that by formulating the *right* conceptions of reason, of science, of thought, of knowledge, of morality, the conceptions which express their *essence*, we shall have a shield against irrationalist resentment and hatred.

Pragmatists tell us that this hope is vain. On their view, the Socratic virtues – willingness to talk, to listen to other people, to weigh the consequences of our actions upon other people – are *simply* moral virtues. They cannot be inculcated nor fortified by theoretical research into essence. Irrationalists who tell us to think with our blood cannot be rebutted by better accounts of the nature of thought, or knowledge, or logic. The pragmatists tell us that the conversation which it is our moral duty to continue is *merely* our project, the European intellectual's form of life. It has no metaphysical nor epistemological guarantee of success. Further (and this is the crucial point) *we do not know what 'success' would mean except simply 'continuance.'* We are not conversing because we have a goal, but because Socratic conversation is an activity which is its *own* end. The anti-pragmatist who insists that agreement is its goal is like the basketball player who thinks that the reason for playing the game is to make baskets. He mistakes an essential moment in the course of an activity for the end of the activity. Worse yet, he is like a basketball fan who argues that all men by nature desire to play basketball, or that the nature of things is such that balls can go through hoops.

For the traditional, Platonic or Kantian philosopher, on the other hand, the possibility of *grounding* the European form of life – of showing it to be more than European, more than a contingent human project – seems the central task of philosophy. He wants to show that sinning against Socrates is sinning against our nature, not just against our community. So he sees the pragmatist as an irrationalist. The charge that pragmatism is 'relativistic' is simply his first unthinking expression of disgust at a teaching which seems cynical about our deepest hopes. If the traditional philosopher gets beyond such epithets, however, he raises a question which the pragmatist must face up to: the *practical* question of whether the notion of 'conversation' *can* substitute for that of 'reason.' 'Reason,' as the term is used in the Platonic and Kantian traditions, is interlocked with the notions of truth as correspondence, of knowledge as discovery of essence, or morality as obedience to principle, all the notions which the pragmatist tries to deconstruct. For better or worse, the Platonic and Kantian vocabularies are the ones in which Europe has described and praised the Socratic virtues. It is not clear that we know how to describe these virtues without those vocabularies. So the deep suspicion which the pragmatist inspires is that, like Alcibiades, he is essentially frivolous – that he is commending uncontroversial common goods while refusing to participate in the only activity which can preserve those goods. He seems to be sacrificing our common European project to the delights of purely negative criticism.

The issue about irrationalism can be sharpened by noting that when the pragmatist says 'All that can be done to explicate "truth", "knowledge", "morality", "virtue" is to refer us back to the concrete details of the culture in which these terms grew up and developed,' the defender of the Enlightenment takes him to be saying 'Truth and virtue are simply what a community agrees that they are.' When the pragmatist says 'We have to take truth and virtue as whatever emerges from the conversation of Europe,' the traditional philosopher wants to know what is so special about Europe. Isn't the pragmatist saying, like the irrationalist, that *we* are in a privileged situation simply by being *us*? Further, isn't there something terribly dangerous about the notion that truth can only be characterized as 'the outcome of doing more of what we are doing now'? What if the 'we' is the Orwellian state? When tyrants employ Lenin's blood-curdling sense of 'objective' to describe their lies as 'objectively true,' what is to prevent them from citing Peirce in Lenin's defense?

The pragmatist's first line of defense against this criticism has been created by Habermas, who says that such a definition of truth works only for the outcome of *undistorted* conversation, and that the Orwellian state is the paradigm of distortion. But this is *only* a first line, for we need to know more about what counts as 'undistorted.' Here Habermas goes transcendental and offers principles. The pragmatist, however, must remain ethnocentric and offer examples. He can only say: 'undistorted' means employing *our* criteria of relevance, where *we* are the people who have read and pondered Plato, Newton, Kant, Marx, Darwin, Freud, Dewey, etc. Milton's 'free and open encounter,' in which truth is bound to prevail, must itself be described in terms of examples rather than principles – it is to be more like the Athenian market-place than the council-chamber of the Great King, more like the twentieth century than the twelfth, more like the Prussian Academy in 1925 than in 1935. The pragmatist must avoid saying, with Peirce, that truth is *fated* to win. He must even avoid saying that truth *will* win. He can only say, with Hegel, that truth and justice lie in the direction marked by the successive stages of European thought. This is not because he knows some 'necessary truths' and cites these examples as a result of this knowledge. It is simply that the pragmatist knows no better way to explain his convictions than to remind his interlocutor of the position they both are in, the contingent starting points they both share, the floating, ungrounded conversations of which they are both members. This means that the pragmatist cannot answer the question 'What is so special about Europe?' save by saying 'Do you have anything non-European to suggest which meets *our* European purposes better?' He cannot answer the question 'What is so good about the Socratic virtues, about Miltonic free encounters, about undistorted communication?' save by saying 'What else would better fulfill the purposes *we* share with Socrates, Milton, and Habermas?'

To decide whether this obviously circular response is enough is to decide whether Hegel or Plato had the proper picture of the progress of thought. Pragmatists follow Hegel in saying that 'philosophy is its time grasped in thought.' Anti-pragmatists follow Plato in striving for an escape from conversation to something atemporal which lies in the background of all possible conversations. I do not think one can decide between Hegel and Plato save by meditating on the past efforts of the philosophical tradition to escape from time and history. One can see these efforts as worthwhile, getting better, worth continuing. Or one can see them as doomed and perverse. I do not know what would count as a noncircular metaphysical or epistemological or semantical argument for seeing them in either way. So I think that the decision has to be made simply by reading the history of philosophy and drawing a moral.

Nothing that I have said, therefore, is an argument in favor of pragmatism. At best, I have merely answered various superficial criticisms which have been made of it. Nor have I dealt with the central issue about irrationalism. I have not answered the deep criticism of pragmatism which I mentioned a few minutes ago: the criticism that the Socratic virtues cannot, as a practical matter, be defended save by Platonic means, that without some sort of metaphysical comfort nobody will be able *not* to sin against Socrates. William James himself was not sure whether this criticism could be answered. Exercising his own right to believe, James wrote: 'If this life be not a real fight in which something is eternally gained for the universe by success, it is no better than a game of private theatricals from which we may withdraw at will.' 'It *feels*,' he said, 'like a fight.'

For us, footnotes to Plato that we are, it *does* feel that way. But if James's own pragmatism were taken seriously, if pragmatism became central to our culture and our self-image, then it would no longer feel that way. We do not know how it *would* feel. We do not even know whether, given such a change in tone, the conversation of Europe might not falter and die away. We just do not know. James and Dewey offered us no guarantees. They simply pointed to the situation we stand in, now that both the Age of Faith and the Enlightenment seem beyond recovery. They grasped our time in thought. We did not change the course of the conversation in the way they suggested we might. Perhaps we are still unable to do so; perhaps we never shall be able to. But we can nevertheless honor James and Dewey for having offered what very few philosophers have succeeded in giving us: a hint of how our lives might be changed.

# Chapter 14

# Seyla Benhabib

## FEMINISM AND THE QUESTION
## OF POSTMODERNISM

[. . .]

**T**HIS CHAPTER WILL CONSIDER the contemporary alliance between feminism and postmodernism. Viewed from within the intellectual and academic culture of western capitalist democracies, feminism and postmodernism have emerged as two leading currents of our time, and each is in its own way profoundly critical of the principles and meta-narratives of western Enlightenment and modernity. Although exactly what constitutes such Enlightenment and modernity, and what those principles and meta-narratives are to which we should bid farewell is by no means clear. Feminism and postmodernism are often mentioned as if they were allies; yet certain other characterizations of postmodernism should make us rather ask 'feminism or postmodernism?' At issue, of course, are not merely terminological quibbles. Both feminism and postmodernism are not merely descriptive categories: they are constitutive and evaluative terms, informing and helping define the very practices which they attempt to describe. As categories of the present, they project modes of thinking about the future and evaluating the past. Here I will consider the complex relationship between feminism and postmodernism with an eye to one issue in particular: are the meta-philosophical premises of the positions referred to as 'post-modernism' compatible with the normative content of feminism, not just as a theoretical position but as a theory of women's struggle for emancipation? [. . .]

Let me articulate strong and weak versions of the 'death of metaphysics' thesis. In considering this point it would be important to note right at the outset that much of the postmodernist critique of western metaphysics itself proceeds under the spell of a meta-narrative, namely, the narrative first articulated by Heidegger and then developed by Derrida that 'Western metaphysics has been under the spell of the "metaphysics of presence" at least since Plato . . .' This characterization of the philosophical tradition allows postmodernists the rhetorical advantage of presenting what they are arguing against in its least defensible versions: listen again to Flax's words: 'For postmodernists this quest for the Real conceals the philosophers' desire, which is to master the world' or 'Just as the Real is the ground of Truth, so too philosophy as the privileged representative of the Real . . .' etc. But is the philosophical tradition so monolithic and so essentialist as postmodernists would like to claim? Would not even Thomas Hobbes shudder at the suggestion that the 'Real is the ground of Truth'? What would Kant say when confronted with the claim that 'philosophy is the privileged representative of the Real'? Would not Hegel consider the view that concepts and language are one sphere and the 'real' yet another merely a version of a naïve correspondence theory of truth which the chapter on 'Sense Certainty' in the *Phenomenology of Spirit* so eloquently dispensed with? In its strong version, the 'death of metaphysics' thesis suffers not only from a subscription to a grandiose meta-narrative, but more significantly, this grandiose meta-narrative flattens out the history of modern philosophy and the competing conceptual schemes it contains to the point of unrecognizability. Once this history is rendered unrecognizable then the conceptual and philosophical problems involved in this bravado proclamation of the 'death of metaphysics' can be neglected.

The weak version of the 'death of metaphysics' thesis which is today more influential than the strong Heidegger–Derrida thesis about the 'metaphysics of presence' is Richard Rorty's account. In *Philosophy and the Mirror of Nature* Rorty has shown in a subtle and convincing manner that empiricist as well as rationalist projects in the modern period presupposed that philosophy, in contradistinction from the developing natural sciences in this period, could articulate the basis of validity of right knowledge and correct action. Rorty names this the project of 'epistemology;' this is the view that philosophy is a metadiscourse of legitimation, articulating the criteria of validity presupposed by all other discourses. Once it ceases to be a discourse of justification, philosophy loses its raison d'être. This is indeed the crux of the matter. Once we have detranscendentalized, contextualized, historicized, genderized the subject of knowledge, the context of inquiry, and even the methods of justification, what remains of philosophy? Does not philosophy become a form of genealogical critique of regimes of discourse and power as they succeed each other in their endless historical monotony? Or maybe philosophy becomes a form of thick cultural narration of the sort that hitherto only poets had provided us with? Or maybe all that remains of philosophy is a form of sociology of knowledge, which instead of investigating the conditions of the validity of knowledge and action, investigates the empirical conditions under which communities of interpretation generate such validity claims?

Why is this question concerning the identity and future and maybe the possibility of philosophy of interest to feminists? Can feminist theory not flourish without getting embroiled in the arcane debates about the end or transformation of philosophy? The inclination of the majority of feminist theorists at the present is to argue that we can side-step this question; even if we do not want to ignore it, we must not be committed to answer it one way or another. Fraser and Nicholson ask: 'How can we conceive a version of criticism without philosophy which is robust enough to handle the tough job of analyzing sexism in all its endless variety and monotonous similarity?' My answer is that we cannot, and it is this which makes me doubt that as feminists we can adopt postmodernism as a theoretical ally. Social criticism without some form of philosophy is not possible, and without social criticism the project of a feminist theory which is at once committed to knowledge and to the emancipatory interests of women is inconceivable. Sabina Lovibond has articulated the dilemma of postmodernists quite well:

> I think we have reason to be wary, not only of the unqualified Nietzschean vision of an end of legitimation, but also of the suggestion that it would somehow be 'better' if legitimation exercises were carried out in a self-consciously parochial spirit. For if feminism aspires to be something more than a reformist movement, then it is bound sooner or later to find itself calling the parish boundaries into question.
>
> [. . .]
>
> So postmodernism seems to face a dilemma: either it can concede the necessity, in terms of the aims of feminism, of 'turning the world upside down' in the way just outlined – thereby opening a door once again to the Enlightenment idea of a total reconstruction of society on rational lines; or it can dogmatically reaffirm the arguments already marshalled against that idea – thereby licensing the cynical thought that, here as elsewhere, 'who will do what to whom under the new pluralism is depressingly predictable.'

Faced with this objection, the answer of postmodernists committed both to the project of social criticism and to the thesis of the death of philosophy as a meta-narrative of legitimation will be that the 'local narratives,' 'les petits récits,' which constitute our everyday social practices or language games, are themselves reflexive and self-critical enough to pass judgments on themselves. The Enlightenment fiction of philosophical reflection, of *episteme* juxtaposed to the non-critical practice of everyday *doxa*, is precisely that, a fiction of legitimation which ignores that everyday practices and traditions also have their own criteria of legit-imation and criticism. The question then would be if among the criteria made available to us by various practices, language games and cultural traditions we could not find some which would serve feminists in their task of social criticism and radical political transformation. Following Michael Walzer, such postmodernists might wish to maintain that the view of the social critic is never 'the view from nowhere,' but always the view of the one situated somewhere, in some culture, society and tradition.

## Feminism as situated criticism

The initial answer to any defender of the view of 'situated criticism' is that cultures, societies and traditions are not monolithic, univocal and homogeneous fields of meaning. However one wishes to characterize the relevant context to which one is appealing for example as 'the Anglo-American liberal tradition of thought,' 'the

tradition of progressive and interventionist jurisprudence,' 'the Judeo-Christian tradition,' 'the culture of the West,' 'the legacy of the Suffragettes,' 'the tradition of
courtly love,' 'Old Testament views of justice,' 'the political culture of democratic
welfare states,' etc., all these characterizations are themselves 'ideal types' in some
Weberian sense. They are constructed out of the tapestry of meaning and interpretation which constitutes the horizon of our social lifeworld. The social critic does
not find criteria of legitimation and self-criticism to be given in the culture as one
might find, say, apples on a tree and goldfish in an aquarium; she no less than
social actors is in the position of constantly interpreting, appropriating, reconstructing and constituting the norms, principles and values which are an aspect of
the lifeworld. There is never a single set of constitutive criteria to appeal to in characterizing complex social practices. Complex social practices, like constitutional traditions, ethical and political views, religious beliefs, scientific institutions are not like
games of chess. The social critic cannot assume that when she turns to an immanent
analysis and characterization of these practices that she will find a single set of criteria on which there is such universal consensus that one can simply assume that by
juxtaposing these criteria to the actual carrying out of the practice one has accomplished the task of immanent social criticism. So the first defect of situated criticism
is a kind of 'hermeneutic monism of meaning,' the assumption namely that the
narratives of our culture are so univocal and uncontroversial that in appealing to
them one could simply be exempt from the task of evaluative, ideal-typical reconstruction. Social criticism needs philosophy precisely because the narratives of our
cultures are so conflictual and irreconcilable that, even when one appeals to them,
a certain ordering of one's normative priorities, a statement of the methodological
assumptions guiding one's choice of narratives, and a clarification of those principles
in the name of which one speaks is unavoidable.

The second defect of 'situated criticism' is to assume that the constitutive
norms of a given culture, society and tradition will be sufficient to enable one to
exercise criticism in the name of a desirable future. There certainly may be times
when one's own culture, society and tradition are so reified, dominated by such
brutal forces, when debate and conversation are so dried up or simply made impossible that the social critic becomes the social exile. Not only social critics in
modernity from Thoreau to the Frankfurt School, from Albert Camus to the dissidents of Eastern Europe have exemplified this gesture. Antiquity as well as the
Middle Ages have had philosophers in exile, chiliastic sects, mystical brotherhoods
and sisterhoods, and Prophets who have abandoned their cities. Certainly the social
critic need not be the social exile; however, insofar as criticism presupposes a
necessary distantiation of oneself from one's everyday certitudes, maybe eventually
to return to them and to reaffirm them at a higher level of analysis and justification, to this extent the vocation of the social critic is more like the vocation of
the social exile and the expatriate than the vocation of the one who never left
home, who never had to challenge the certitude of her own way of life. And to
leave home is not to end up nowhere; it is to occupy a space outside the walls of
the city, in a host country, in a different social reality. Is this not in effect the quintessential postmodern condition in the twentieth century? Maybe the nostalgia for
situated criticism is itself a nostalgia for home, for the certitudes of one's own
culture and society in a world in which no tradition, no culture and no society

can exist any more without interaction and collaboration, confrontation and exchange. When cultures and societies clash, where do we stand as feminists, as social critics and political activists?

Finally, let me remark upon an ambiguity which may surround the term 'situated criticism' itself. Very often in recent discussions this concept has come to signify the practice of 'local narratives' or 'les petits récits' as opposed to grand theories or narratives of legitimation. Certainly, theorists as divergent as Michael Walzer and Jean-François Lyotard as well as Richard Rorty have this usage in mind. There is also a second tradition of 'situated criticism' deriving from the work of the early Marx (the practice of immanent critique of capitalism) and transformed in this century into an extremely powerful tool of social and cultural reflection by Theodor Adorno through his method of practicing 'determinate negation.' I have explored the strengths and difficulties of this latter tradition elsewhere. In the present context, it is not this second tradition which has concerned me but rather the first. My objections to the practice of situated criticism, as understood by this group of contemporary authors (Walzer, Lyotard, Rorty), does not assume however that there can be 'transcendent criticism' or an 'Archimedean point of view.' The standpoint of 'interactive universalism' defended in this book is itself very much situated within the hermeneutic horizon of modernity. *Au fond*, all criticism is situated, but differences arise regarding the construction of the context within which the thinker considers her own thought to be situated. As opposed to the retreat to small narratives and local knowledge, I see even this postmodern moment as being situated within the larger processes of modernization and rationalization which have been proceeding on a world scale since the seventeenth century, and which have truly become global realities in our own. In this sense, interactive universalism is the practice of situated criticism for a global community that does not shy away from knocking down the 'parish walls.'

Are we closer to resolving the question posed at the end of the previous section as to whether feminist social criticism without philosophy was possible? In considering the postmodernists' thesis of the 'death of metaphysics' I suggested that the weak version of this thesis would identify the end of metaphysics with the end of philosophy as a metadiscourse of legitimation, transcending local narratives, while the strong version of the thesis would eliminate, I argued, not only meta-narratives of legitimation but the practice of context-transcending legitimation and criticism altogether. Postmodernists could then respond that this need not be the case, and that there were internal criteria of legitimation and criticism in our culture which the social critic could turn to such that social criticism without philosophy would be possible. I am now arguing that the practice of situated social criticism has two defects: first, the turn to internal criteria of legitimation appears to exempt one from the task of philosophical justification only because the postmodernists assume, inter alia, that there is one obvious set of such criteria to appeal to. But if cultures and traditions are more like competing sets of narratives and incoherent tapestries of meaning, then the social critic must herself construct out of these conflictual and incoherent accounts the set of criteria in the name of which she speaks. The 'hermeneutic monism of meaning' brings no exemption from the responsibility of normative justification.

In the second place I have argued that the vocation of social criticism might require social exile, for there might be times when the immanent norms and values of a culture are so reified, dead or petrified that one can no longer speak in their name. The social critic who is in exile does not adopt the 'view from nowhere' but the 'view from outside the walls of the city,' wherever those walls and those boundaries might be. It may indeed be no coincidence that from Hypatia to Diotima to Olympe de Gouges and to Rosa Luxemburg, the vocation of the feminist thinker and critic has led her to leave home and the city walls.

## Feminism and the postmodernist retreat from utopia

In the previous sections of this chapter I have disagreed with the view of some feminist theorists that feminism and postmodernism are conceptual and political allies. A certain version of postmodernism is not only incompatible with but would undermine the very possibility of feminism as the theoretical articulation of the emancipatory aspirations of women. This undermining occurs because in its strong version postmodernism is committed to three theses: the death of man understood as the death of the autonomous, self-reflective subject, capable of acting on principle; the death of history, understood as the severance of the epistemic interest in history of struggling groups in constructing their past narratives; the death of metaphysics, understood as the impossibility of criticizing or legitimizing institutions, practices and traditions other than through the immanent appeal to the self-legitimation of 'small narratives.' Interpreted thus, postmodernism undermines the feminist commitment to women's agency and sense of selfhood, to the reappropriation of women's own history in the name of an emancipated future, and to the exercise of radical social criticism which uncovers gender 'in all its endless variety and monotonous similarity.'

I dare suggest in these concluding considerations that postmodernism has produced a 'retreat from utopia' within feminism. By 'utopia' I do not mean the modernist vision of a wholesale restructuring of our social and political universe according to some rationally worked-out plan. These utopias of the Enlightenment have not only ceased to convince but with the self-initiated exit of previously existing 'socialist utopias' from their state of grace, one of the greatest rationalist utopias of mankind, the utopia of a rationally planned economy leading to human emancipation, has come to an end. The end of these rationalistic visions of social engineering cannot dry up the sources of utopia in humanity. As the longing for the 'wholly other' (*das ganz Andere*), for that which is not yet, such utopian thinking is a practical-moral imperative. Without such a regulative principle of hope, not only morality but also radical transformation is unthinkable. What scares the opponents of utopia, like Lyotard for example, is that in the name of such future utopia the present in its multiple ambiguity, plurality and contradiction will be reduced to a flat grand narrative. I share some of Lyotard's concerns insofar as utopian thinking becomes an excuse either for the crassest instrumentalism in the present – the end justifies the means – or to the extent that the coming utopia exempts the undemocratic and authoritarian practices of the present from critique. Yet we cannot deal with these political concerns by rejecting the ethical impulse of utopia but only by articulating the normative principles of democratic action and organization in the present. Will the postmodernists join us in this task or will they be content with singing the swan-song of normative thinking in general?

# Postdisciplinary debates: societies

# POSTMODERNITY

- Jean-François Lyotard, The postmodern condition

- David Harvey, The condition of postmodernity

**Jean-François Lyotard** was born in France in 1924. He earned a doctorate in 1971, after teaching for many years in a secondary school in Algeria. He has taught at the Sorbonne, Nanterre, and Vincennes University in Paris. He is the author of, among other books, *The Postmodern Condition* (1984) and *The Differend* (1988).

**David Harvey** has been a Professor of Geography at Oxford University. Among his writings are *The Limits of Capital* (1982) and *The Condition of Postmodernity* (1990).

# Chapter 15

# Jean-François Lyotard

## THE POSTMODERN
## CONDITION

I DEFINE POSTMODERN as incredulity toward metanarratives. This incredulity is undoubtedly a product of progress in the sciences: But that progress
in turn presupposes it. To the obsolescence of the metanarrative apparatus of legitimation corresponds, most notably, the crisis of metaphysical philosophy and of the
university institution which in the past relied on it. The narrative function is losing
its functors, its great hero, its great dangers, its great voyages, its great goal. It is
being dispersed in clouds of narrative language elements – narrative, but also denotative, prescriptive, descriptive, and so on. Conveyed within each cloud are pragmatic valencies specific to its kind. Each of us lives at the intersection of many of
these. However, we do not necessarily establish stable language combinations, and
the properties of the ones we do establish are not necessarily communicable.

Thus the society of the future falls less within the province of a Newtonian
anthropology (such as structuralism or systems theory) than a pragmatics of
language particles. There are many different language games – a heterogeneity
of elements. They only give rise to institutions in patches – local determinism.

The decision makers, however, attempt to manage these clouds of sociality
according to input/output matrices, following a logic which implies that their
elements are commensurable and that the whole is determinable. They allocate our
lives for the growth of power. In matters of social justice and of scientific truth
alike, the legitimation of that power is based on its optimizing the system's performance – efficiency. The application of this criterion to all of our games necessarily
entails a certain level of terror, whether soft or hard: be operational (that is,
commensurable) or disappear.

The logic of maximum performance is no doubt inconsistent in many ways,
particularly with respect to contradiction in the socio-economic field: It demands

both less work (to lower production costs) and more (to lessen the social burden of the idle population). But our incredulity is now such that we no longer expect salvation to rise from these inconsistencies, as did Marx.

Still, the postmodern condition is as much a stranger to disenchantment as it is to the blind positivity of delegitimation. Where, after the metanarratives, can legitimacy reside? The operativity criterion is technological; it has no relevance for judging what is true or just. Is legitimacy to be found in consensus obtaining through discussion, as Jürgen Habermas thinks? Such consensus does violence to the heterogeneity of language games. And invention is always born of dissension. Postmodern knowledge is not simply a tool of the authorities; it refines our sensitivity to differences and reinforces our ability to tolerate the incommensurable. Its principle is not the expert's homology, but the inventor's paralogy. [. . .]

In contemporary society and culture – postindustrial society, postmodern culture – the question of the legitimation of knowledge is formulated in different terms. The grand narrative has lost its credibility, regardless of what mode of unification it uses, regardless of whether it is a speculative narrative or a narrative of emancipation.

The decline of narrative can be seen as an effect of the blossoming of techniques and technologies since the Second World War, which has shifted emphasis from the ends of action to its means; it can also be seen as an effect of the redeployment of advanced liberal capitalism after its retreat under the protection of Keynesianism during the period 1930–60, a renewal that has eliminated the communist alternative and valorized the individual enjoyment of goods and services.

Anytime we go searching for causes in this way we are bound to be disappointed. Even if we adopted one or the other of these hypotheses, we would still have to detail the correlation between the tendencies mentioned and the decline of the unifying and legitimating power of the grand narratives of speculation and emancipation.

It is, of course, understandable that both capitalist renewal and prosperity and the disorienting upsurge of technology would have an impact on the status of knowledge. But in order to understand how contemporary science could have been susceptible to those effects long before they took place, we must first locate the seeds of 'delegitimation' and nihilism that were inherent in the grand narratives of the nineteenth century.

First of all, the speculative apparatus maintains an ambiguous relation to knowledge. It show that knowledge is only worthy of that name to the extent that it reduplicates itself ('lifts itself up,' *heht sich auf*; is sublated) by citing its own statements in a second-level discourse (autonomy) that functions to legitimate them. This is as much as to say that, in its immediacy, denotative discourse bearing on a certain referent (a living organism, a chemical property, a physical phenomenon, etc.) does not really know what it thinks it knows. Positive science is not a form of knowledge. And speculation feeds on its suppression. The Hegelian speculative narrative thus harbors a certain skepticism toward positive learning, as Hegel himself admits.

A science that has not legitimated itself is not a true science; if the discourse that was meant to legitimate it seems to belong to a prescientific form of knowledge, like a 'vulgar' narrative, it is demoted to the lowest rank, that of an ideology or instrument of power. And this always happens if the rules of the science game that discourse denounces as empirical are applied to science itself.

Take for example the speculative statement: 'A scientific statement is know-ledge if and only if it can take its place in a universal process of engendering.' The question is: Is this statement knowledge as it itself defines it? Only if it can take its place in a universal process of engendering. Which it can. All it has to do is to presuppose that such a process exists (the Life of spirit) and that it is itself an expression of that process. This presupposition, in fact, is indispensable to the spec-ulative language game. Without it, the language of legitimation would not be legitimate; it would accompany science in a nosedive into nonsense, at least if we take idealism's word for it.

But this presupposition can also be understood in a totally different sense, one which takes us in the direction of postmodern culture: We could say, in keeping with the perspective we adopted earlier, that this presupposition defines the set of rules one must accept in order to play the speculative game. Such an appraisal assumes first that we accept that the 'positive' sciences represent the general mode of knowledge and second that we understand this language to imply certain formal and axiomatic presuppositions that it must always make explicit. This is exactly what Nietzsche is doing, though with a different terminology, when he shows that 'European nihilism' resulted from the truth requirement of science being turned back against itself.

There thus arises an idea of perspective that is not far removed, at least in this respect, from the idea of language games. What we have here is a process of dele-gitimation fueled by the demand for legitimation itself. The 'crisis' of scientific knowledge, signs of which have been accumulating since the end of the nineteenth century, is not born of a chance proliferation of sciences, itself an effect of progress in technology and the expansion of capitalism. It represents, rather, an internal erosion of the legitimacy principle of knowledge. There is erosion at work inside the speculative game, and by loosening the weave of the encyclopedic net in which each science was to find its place, it eventually sets them free.

The classical dividing lines between the various fields of science are thus called into question – disciplines disappear, overlappings occur at the borders between sciences, and from these new territories are born. The speculative hierarchy of learning gives way to an immanent and, as it were, 'flat' network of areas of inquiry, the respective frontiers of which are in constant flux. The old 'faculties' splinter into institutes and foundations of all kinds, and the universities lose their function of speculative legitimation. Stripped of the responsibility for research (which was stifled by the speculative narrative), they limit themselves to the transmission of what is judged to be established knowledge, and through didactics they guarantee the replication of teachers rather than the production of researchers. This is the state in which Nietzsche finds and condemns them.

The potential for erosion intrinsic to the other legitimation procedure, the emancipation apparatus flowing from the *Aufklarung*, is no less extensive than the one at work within speculative discourse. But it touches a different aspect. Its distinguishing characteristic is that it grounds the legitimation of science and truth in the autonomy of interlocutors involved in ethical, social, and political praxis.

As we have seen, there are immediate problems with this form of legitimation: The difference between a denotative statement with cognitive value and a prescriptive statement with practice value is one of relevance, therefore of competence. There is nothing to prove that if a statement describing a real situation is true, it follows that a prescriptive statement based upon it (the effect of which will necessarily be a modification of that reality) will be just.

Take, for example, a closed door. Between 'The door is closed' and 'Open the door' there is no relation of consequence as defined in propositional logic. The two statements belong to two autonomous sets of rules defining different kinds of relevance, and therefore of competence. Here, the effect of dividing reason into cognitive or theoretical reason on the one hand, and practical reason on the other, is to attack the legitimacy of the discourse of science; not directly, but indirectly, by revealing that it is a language game with its own rules (of which the a priori conditions of knowledge in Kant provide a first glimpse) and that it has no special calling to supervise the game of praxis (nor the game of aesthetics, for that matter). The game of science is thus put on a par with the others.

If this 'delegitimation' is pursued in the slightest and if its scope is widened (as Wittgenstein does in his own way, and thinkers such as Martin Buber and Emmanuel Levinas in theirs) the road is then open for an important current of postmodernity: Science plays its own game; it is incapable of legitimating the other language games. The game of prescription, for example, escapes it. But above all, it is incapable of legitimating itself, as speculation assumed it could.

The social subject itself seems to dissolve in this dissemination of language games. The social bond is linguistic, but is not woven with a single thread. It is a fabric formed by the intersection of at least two (and in reality an indeterminate number of) language games, obeying different rules. Wittgenstein writes: 'Our language can be seen as an ancient city: a maze of little streets and squares, of old and new houses, and of houses with additions from various periods; and this surrounded by a multitude of new boroughs with straight regular streets and uniform houses.' And to drive home that the principle of unitotality – or synthesis under the authority of a metadiscourse of knowledge – is inapplicable, he subjects the 'town' of language to the old sorites paradox by asking: 'how many houses or streets does it take before a town begins to be a town?'

New languages are added to the olds ones, forming suburbs of the old town: 'the symbolism of chemistry and the notation of the infinitesimal calculus.' Thirty-five years later we can add to the list: machine languages, the matrices of game theory, new systems of musical notation, systems of notation for nondenotative forms of logic (temporal logics, deontic logics, modal logics), the language of the genetic code, graphs of phonological structures, and so on.

We may form a pessimistic impression of this splintering: Nobody speaks all of those languages, they have no universal metalanguage, the project of the system-subject is a failure, the goal of emancipation has nothing to do with science, we are all stuck in the positivism of this or that discipline of learning, the learned scholars have turned into scientists, the diminished tasks of research have become compartmentalized and no one can master them all. Speculative or humanistic philosophy is forced to relinquish its legitimation duties, which explains why philosophy is facing a crisis wherever it persists in arrogating such functions and is reduced to the study of systems of logic or the history of ideas where it has been realistic enough to surrender them.

Turn-of-the-century Vienna has weaned on this pessimism: not just artists such as Musil, Kraus, Hofmannsthal, Loos, Schonberg, and Broch, but also the philosophers Mach and Wittgenstein. They carried awareness of and theoretical and artistic responsibility for delegitimation as far as it could be taken. We can say today that the mourning process has been completed. There is no need to start all over again. Wittgenstein's strength is that he did not opt for the positivism that was being developed by the Vienna Circle, but outlined in his investigation of language games a kind of legitimation not based on performativity. This is what the postmodern world is all about. Most people have lost the nostalgia for the lost narrative. It in no way follows that they are reduced to barbarity. What saves them from it is their knowledge that legitimation can only spring from their own linguistic practice and communicational interaction. Science 'smiling into its beard' at every other belief has taught them the harsh austerity of realism. . . .

## Legitimation by paralogy

Let us say at this point that the facts we have presented concerning the problem of the legitimation of knowledge today are sufficient for our purposes. We no longer have recourse to the grant narratives – we can resort neither to the dialectic of Spirit nor even to the emancipation of humanity as a validation for postmodern scientific discourse. But as we have just seen, the little narrative [*petit récit*] remains the quintessential form of imaginative invention, most particularly in science. In addition, the principle of consensus as a criterion of validation seems to be inadequate. It has two formulations. In the first consensus is an agreement between men, defined as knowing intellects and free wills, and is obtained through dialogue. This is the form elaborated by Habermas, but his conception is based on the validity of the narrative of emancipation. In the second, consensus is a component of the system, which manipulates it in order to maintain and improve its performance. It is the object of administrative procedures, in Luhmann's sense. In this case, its only validity is as an instrument to be used toward achieving the real goal, which is what legitimates the system – power.

The problem is therefore to determine whether it is possible to have a form of legitimation based solely on paralogy. Paralogy must be distinguished from innovation: The latter is under the command of the system, or at least used by it to improve its efficiency; the former is a move (the importance of which is often not recognized until later) played in the pragmatics of knowledge. The fact that it is in reality frequently, but not necessarily, the case that one is transformed into the other presents no difficulties for the hypothesis.

Returning to the description of scientific pragmatics [. . .] it is now dissension that much be emphasized. Consensus is a horizon that is never reached. Research that takes place under the aegis of a paradigm tends to stabilize; it is like the exploitation of a technological, economic, or artistic 'idea.' It cannot be discounted. But what is striking is that someone always comes along to disturb the order of 'reason.' It is necessary to posit the existence of a power that destabilizes the

capacity for explanation, manifested in the promulgation of new norms for understanding or, if one prefers, in a proposal to establish new rules circumscribing a
new field of research for the language of science. This, in the context of scientific
discussion, is the same process Thom calls morphogenesis. It is not without rules
(there are classes of catastrophes), but is always locally determined. Applied to
scientific discussion and placed in temporal framework, this property implies that
'discoveries' are unpredictable. In terms of the idea of transparency, it is a factor
that generates blind spots and defers consensus.

This summary makes it easy to see that systems theory and the kind of legitimation it proposes have no scientific basis whatsoever; science itself does not
function according to this theory's paradigm of the system, and contemporary
science excludes the possibility of using such a paradigm to describe society.

In this context, let us examine two important points in Luhmann's argument.
On the one hand, the system can only function by reducing complexity, and on
the other, it must induce the adaptation of individual aspirations to its own ends.
The reduction in complexity is required to maintain the system's power capability.
If all messages could circulate freely among all individuals, the quantity of the
information that would have to be taken into account before making the correct
choice would delay decisions considerably, thereby lowering performativity. Speed,
in effect, is a power component of the system.

The objection will be made that these molecular opinions must indeed be taken
into account if the risk of serious disturbances is to be avoided. Luhmann replies
– and this is the second point – that it is possible to guide individual aspirations
through a process of 'quasi-apprenticeship,' 'free of all disturbance,' in order to
make them compatible with the system's decisions. The decisions do not have to
respect individuals' aspirations: The aspirations have to aspire to the decisions, or
at least to their effects. Administrative procedures should make individuals 'want'
what the system needs in order to perform well. It is easy to see what role telematics technology could play in this.

It cannot be denied that there is persuasive force in the idea that context
control and domination are inherently better than their absence. The performativity criterion has its 'advantages.' It excludes in principle adherence to a
metaphysical discourse; it requires the renunciation of fables; it demands clear
minds and cold wills; it replaces the definition of essences with the calculation of
interactions; it makes the 'players' assume responsibility not only for the statements they propose, but also for the rules to which they submit those statements
in order to render them acceptable. It brings the pragmatic functions of knowledge clearly to light, to the extent that they seem to relate to the criterion of
efficiency: the pragmatics of argumentation, of the production of proof, of the
transmission of learning, and of the apprenticeship of the imagination.

It also contributes to elevating all language games to self-knowledge, even those
not within the realm of canonical knowledge. It tends to jolt everyday discourse
into a kind of metadiscourse: Ordinary statements are now displaying a propensity for self-citation, and the various pragmatic posts are tending to make an indirect
connection even to current messages concerning them. Finally, it suggests that the
problems of internal communication experience by the scientific community in the
course of its work of dismantling and remounting it languages are comparable in

nature to the problems experienced by the social collectivity when, deprived of its narrative culture, it must reexamine its own internal communication and in the process question the nature of the legitimacy of the decision made in its name.

At [the] risk of scandalizing the reader, I would also say that the system can count severity among its advantages. Within the framework of the power criterion, a request (that is, a form of prescription) gains nothing in legitimacy by virtue of being based on the hardship of an unmet need. Rights do not flow from hardship, but from the fact that the alleviation of hardship improves the system's perform-ance. The needs of the most underprivileged should not be used as a system regulator as a matter of principle: Since the means of satisfying them is already known, their actual satisfaction will not improve the system's performance, but only increase its expenditures. The only counterindication is that not satisfying them can destablize the whole. It is against the nature of force to be ruled by weakness. But it is in its nature to induce new requests meant to lead to a redefinition of the norms of 'life.' In this sense, the system seems to be a vanguard machine drag-ging humanity after it, dehumanizing it in order to rehumanize it at a different level of normative capacity. The technocrats declare that they cannot trust what society designates as its needs; they 'know' that society cannot know its own needs since they are not variables independent of the new technologies. Such is the arro-gance of the decision makers – and their blindness.

What their 'arrogance' means is that they identify themselves with the social system conceived as a totality in quest of its most performative unity possible. If we look at the pragmatics of science, we learn that such an identification is impos-sible: In principle, no scientist embodies knowledge or neglects the 'needs' of a research project, or the aspirations of a researcher, on the pretext that they do not add to the performance of 'science' as a whole. The response a researcher usually makes to a request is: 'We'll have to see, tell me your story.' In principle, he does not prejudge that a case has already been closed or that the power of 'science' will suffer if it is reopened. In fact, the opposite is true.

Of course, it does not always happen like this in reality. Countless scientists have seen their 'move' ignored or repressed, sometimes for decades, because it too abruptly destabilized the accepted positions, not only in the university and scien-tific hierarchy, but also in the problematic. The stronger the 'move,' the more likely it is to be denied the minimum consensus, precisely because it changes the rules of the game upon which consensus had been based. But when the institution of knowledge functions in this manner, it is acting like an ordinary power center whose behavior is governed by a principle of homeostasis.

Such behavior is terrorist, as is the behavior of the system described by Luhmann. By terror I mean the efficiency gained by eliminating, or threatening to eliminate, a player from the language game one shares with him. He is silenced or consents, not because he has been refuted, but because his ability to participate has been threatened (there are many ways to prevent someone from playing). The decision makers' arrogance, which in principle has no equivalent in the sciences, consists in the exercise of terror. It says: 'Adapt your aspirations to our ends – or else.'

Even permissiveness toward the various games is made conditional on perfor-mativity. The redefinition of the norms of life consists in enhancing the system's

competence for power. That this is the case is particularly evident in the introduction of telematics technology: The technocrats see in telematics a promise of
liberalization and enrichment in the interactions between interlocutors; but what
makes this process attractive for them is that it will result in new tensions in the
system, and these will lead to an improvement in its performativity.

To the extent that science is differential, its pragmatics provides the antimodel
of a stable system. A statement is deemed worth retaining the moment it marks
a difference from what is already known, and after an argument and proof in
support of it has been found. Science is a model of an 'open system,' in which a
statement becomes relevant if it 'generates ideas,' that is, if it generates other statements and other game rules. Science possesses no general metalanguage into which
all other languages can be transcribed and evaluated. This is what prevents its identification with the system and, all things considered, with terror. If the division
between decision makers and executors exists in the scientific community (and it
does), it is a fact of the socioeconomic system and not of the pragmatics of science
itself. It is in fact one of the major obstacles to the imaginative development of
knowledge.

The general question of legitimation becomes: What is the relationship between
the antimodel of the pragmatics of science and society? Is it applicable to the vast
clouds of language material constituting a society? Or is it limited to the game of
learning? And if so, what role does it play with respect to the social bond? Is it an
impossible ideal of an open community? Is it an essential component for the subset
of decision makers, who force on society the performance criterion they reject for
themselves? Or, conversely, is it a refusal to cooperate with the authorities, a move
in the direction of counterculture, with the attendant risk that all possibility for
research will be foreclosed due to lack of funding?

From the beginning of this study, I have emphasized the differences (not only
formal, but also pragmatic) between the various language games, especially between
denotative, or knowledge, games and prescriptive, or action, games. The pragmatics
of science is centered on denotative utterances, which are the foundation upon
which it builds institutions of learning (institutes, centers, universities, etc.). But
its postmodern development brings a decisive 'fact' to the fore: Even discussions
of denotative statements need to have rules. Rules are not denotative but prescriptive utterances, which we are better off calling metaprescriptive utterances to avoid
confusion (they prescribe what the moves of language games must be in order to
be admissible). The function of the differential or imaginative or paralogical activity
of the current pragmatics of science is to point out these metaprescriptives (science's
'presuppositions') and to petition the players to accept different ones. The only
legitimation that can make this kind of request admissible is that it will generate
ideas, in other words, new statements.

Social pragmatics does not have the 'simplicity' of scientific pragmatics. It is a
monster formed by the interweaving of various networks of heteromorphous classes
of utterances (denotative, prescriptive, performative, technical, evaluative, etc.).
There is no reason to think that it would be possible to determine metaprescriptives common to all of these language games or that a revisable consensus like
the one in force at a given moment in the scientific community could embrace the
totality of metaprescriptions regulating the totality of statements circulating in

the social collectivity. As a matter of fact, the contemporary decline of narratives of legitimation – be they traditional or 'modern' (the emancipation of humanity, the realization of the Idea) – is tied to the abandonment of this belief. It is its absence for which the ideology of the 'system,' with its pretensions to totality, tries to compensate and which it expresses in the cynicism of its criterion of performance.

For this reason, it seems neither possible, nor even prudent, to follow Habermas in orienting our treatment of the problem of legitimation in the direction of a search for universal consensus through what he calls *Diskurs*, in other words, a dialogue of argumentation.

This would be to make two assumptions. The first is that it is possible for all speakers to come to agreement on which rules or metaprescriptions are universally valid for language games, when it is clear that language games are heteromorphous, subject to heterogenous sets of pragmatic rules.

The second assumption is that the goal of dialogue is consensus. But as I have shown in the analysis of the pragmatics of science, consensus is only a particular state of discussion, not its end. Its end, on the contrary, is paralogy. This double observation (the heterogeneity of the rules and the search for dissent) destroys a belief that still underlies Habermas's research, namely, that humanity as a collective (universal) subject seeks its common emancipation through the regularization of the 'moves' permitted in all language games and that the legitimacy of any statement resides in its contributing to that emancipation.

It is easy to see what function this recourse plays in Habermas's argument against Luhmann. *Diskurs* is his ultimate weapon against the theory of the stable system. The cause is good, but the argument is not. Consensus has become an outmoded and suspect value. But justice as a value is neither outmoded nor suspect. We must thus arrive at an idea and practice of justice that is not linked to that of consensus.

A recognition of the heteromorphous nature of language games is a first step in that direction. This obviously implies a renunciation of terror, which assumes that they are isomorphic and tries to make them so. The second step is the principle that any consensus on the rules defining a game and the 'moves' playable within it *must* be local, in other words, agreed on by its present players and subject to eventual cancellation. The orientation then favors a multiplicity and finite meta-arguments, by which I mean argumentation that concerns metaprescriptives and is limited in space and time.

This orientation corresponds to the course that the evolution of social interaction is currently taking; the temporary contract is in practice supplanting permanent institutions in the professional, emotional, sexual, cultural, family, and international domains, as well as in political affairs. This evolution is of course ambiguous: The temporary contract is favored by the system due to its greater flexibility, lower cost, and the creative turmoil of its accompanying motivations – all of these factors contribute to increased operativity. In any case, there is no question here of proposing a 'pure' alternative to the system: We all now know, as the 1970s come to a close, that an attempt at an alternative of that kind would end up resembling the system it was meant to replace. We should be happy that the tendency toward the temporary contract is ambiguous: It is not totally subordinated to the goal of the system, yet the system tolerates it. This bears witness to the existence of another goal within the system: knowledge of language games as such and the decision to assume responsibility for their rules and effects. Their most significant effect is precisely what validates the adoption of rules – the quest for paralogy.

We are finally in a position to understand how the computerization of society affects this problematic. It could become the 'dream' instrument for controlling and regulating the market system, extended to include knowledge itself and governed exclusively by the performativity principle. In that case, it would inevitably involve the use of terror. But it could also aid groups discussing metaprescriptives by supplying them with the information they usually lack for making knowledge-able decisions. The line to follow for computerization to take the second of these two paths is, in principle, quite simple: Give the public free access to the memory and data banks. Language games would then be games of perfect information at any given moment. But they would also be non-zero-sum games, and by virtue of that fact discussion would never risk fixating in a position of minimax equilibrium because it had exhausted its stakes. For the stakes would be knowledge (or infor-mation, if you will), and the reserve of knowledge – language's reserve of possible utterances – is inexhaustible. This sketches the outline of a politics that would respect both the desire for justice and the desire for the unknown.

# Chapter 16

# David Harvey

# THE CONDITION OF
# POSTMODERNITY

T HERE HAS BEEN A SEA-CHANGE in cultural as well as in political–economic practices since around 1972.

This sea-change is bound up with the emergence of new dominant ways in which we experience space and time.

While simultaneity in the shifting dimensions of time and space is no proof of necessary or causal connection, strong a priori grounds an be adduced for the proposition that there is some kind of necessary relation between the rise of post-modernist cultural forms, the emergence of more flexible modes of capital accumulation, and a new round of 'time–space compression' in the organization of capitalism.

But these changes, when set against the basic rules of capitalistic accumulation, appear more as shifts in surface appearance rather than as signs of the emergence of some entirely new postcapitalist or even postindustrial society. [. . .]

How, then, should postmodernism in general be evaluated? My preliminary assessment would be this. That in its concern for difference, for the difficulties of communication, for the complexity and nuances of interests, cultures, places, and the like, it exercises a positive influence. The meta-languages, meta-theories, and meta-narratives of modernism (particularly in its later manifestations) did tend to gloss over important differences, and failed to pay attention to important disjunctions and details. Postmodernism has been particularly important in acknowledging 'the multiple forms of otherness as they emerge from differences in subjectivity, gender and sexuality, race and class, temporal (configurations of sensibility) and spatial geographic locations and dislocations' (Huyssens 1984, 50). It is this aspect of postmodernist thought that gives it a radical edge, so much so that traditional neo-conservatives, such as Daniel Bell, fear rather than welcome its accommo-dations with individualism, commercialism, and entrepreneuralism. Such neo-conservatives would, after all, hardly welcome Lyotard's (1980, 66) assertion that 'the temporary contract is in practice supplanting permanent institutions in the professional, emotional, sexual, cultural, family, and international domains, as well as in political affairs. Daniel Bell plainly regrets the collapse of solid bourgeois values, the erosion of the work ethic in the working class, and sees contemporary trends less as a turn towards a vibrant postmodernist future and more as an exhaustion of modernism that surely harbingers a social and political crisis in years to come.

Postmodernism also ought to be looked at as mimetic of the social, economic, and political practices in society. But since it is mimetic of different facets of those practices it appears in very different guises. The superimposition of different worlds in many a postmodern novel, worlds between which an uncommunicative 'otherness' prevails in a space of coexistence, bears an uncanny relationship to the increasing ghettoization, disempowerment, and isolation of poverty and minority populations in the inner cities of both Britain and the United States. It is not hard to read a postmodern novel as a metaphorical transect across the fragmenting social landscape, the sub-cultures and local modes of communication, in London, Chicago, New York, or Los Angeles. Since most social indicators suggest a strong increase in actual ghettoization since 1970, it is useful to think of postmodern fiction as perhaps mimetic of that fact.

But the increasing affluence, power, and authority emerging at the other end of the social scale produces an entirely different ethos. For while it is hard to see that working in the postmodern AT&T building by Philip Johnson is any different from working in the modernist Seagram building by Mies van der Rohe, the image projected to the outside is different. 'AT&T insisted they wanted something other than just another glass box,' said the architect. 'We were looking for something that projected the company's image of nobility and strength. No material does that better than granite' (even though it was double the cost of glass). With luxury housing and corporate headquarters, aesthetic twists become an expression of class power. Crimp (1987) takes it further:

> The present condition of architecture is one in which architects debate academic, abstract aesthetics while they are in fact in the thrall of the real-estate developers who are ruining our cities and turning working class people out of their homes. [. . .] Philip Johnson's new skyscraper [. . .] is a developer building, with a few applied geegaws, thrust upon a neighborhood that is not particularly in need of another skyscraper.

Invoking the memory of Hitler's architect Albert Speer, Crimp goes on to attack the postmodernist mask of what he sees as a new authoritarianism in the direction of city forms.

I have chosen these two examples to illustrate how important it is to think through exactly what kinds of social practice, what sets of social relations, are being reflected in different aesthetic movements. Yet this account is surely incomplete because we have yet to establish [. . .] exactly what postmodernism might be mimetic of. Furthermore, it is just as surely dangerous to presuppose that postmodernism is solely mimetic rather than an aesthetic intervention in politics, economy, and social life in its own right. The strong injection of *fiction* as well as *function* into common sensibility, for example, must have consequences, perhaps unforeseen, for social action. Even Marx insisted, after all, that what distinguishes the worst of architects from the best of bees is that the architect erects structures in the imagination before giving them material form. Changes in the way we imagine, think, plan, and rationalize are bound to have material consequences. Only in these very broad terms of the conjoining of mimesis and aesthetic intervention can the broad range of postmodernism make sense.

Yet postmodernism sees itself rather more simply: for the most part as a wilful and rather chaotic movement to overcome all the supposed ills of modernism. But in this regard I think postmodernists exaggerate when they depict the modern as grossly as they do, either caricaturing the whole modernist movement to the point where, as even Jencks admits, 'modern architecture bashing has become a form of sadism that is getting far too easy,' or isolating one wing of modernism for criticism (Althusserianism, modern brutalism, or whatever) as if that was all there was. There were, after all, many cross-currents within modernism, and postmodernists echo some of them quite explicitly (Jencks, for example, looks back to the period 1870–1914, even to the confusions of the 1920s, while including Le Corbusier's monastery at Ronchamp as an important precursor of one aspect of postmodernism). The meta-narratives that the postmodernists decry (Marx, Freud, and even later figures like Althusser) were much more open, nuanced, and sophisticated than the critics admit. Marx and many of the Marxists (I think of Benjamin, Thompson, Anderson, as diverse examples) have an eye for detail, fragmentation, and disjunction that is often caricatured out of existence in postmodern polemics. Marx's account of modernization is exceedingly rich in insights into the roots of modernist as well as postmodernist sensibility.

It is equally wrong to write off the material achievements of modernist practices so easily. Modernists found a way to control and contain an explosive capitalist condition. They were effective for example, in the organization of urban life and the capacity to build space in such a way as to contain the intersecting processes that have made for a rapid urban change in twentieth-century capitalism. If there is a crisis implicit in all of that, it is by no means clear that it is the modernists, rather than the capitalists, who are to blame. There are, indeed, some extraordinary successes in the modernist pantheon (I note the British school building and design programme in the early 1960s that solved some of the acute housing problems of education within tight budget constraints). While some housing projects were indeed dismal failures, others were not, particularly when compared with the slum conditions from which many people came. And it turns out that the social conditions in Pruitt–Igoe – that great symbol of modernist failure – were much more at the heart of the problem than pure architectural form. The blaming of physical form for social ills has to rest on the most vulgar kind of environmental determinism that few would be prepared to accept in other circumstances (though I note with distress that another member of Prince Charles's 'kitchen cabinet' is the geographer Alice Coleman, who regularly mistakes correlation between bad design and anti-social behaviour with causation). It is interesting to note, therefore, how the tenant population in Le Corbusier's 'habitat for living' at Firminy-le-Vert has organized into a social movement to prevent its destruction (not, I should add, out of any particular loyalty to Le Corbusier but more simply because it happens to be their home). As even Jencks admits, postmodernists have taken over all of the great achievements of the modernists in architectural design, though they have certainly altered aesthetics and appearances in at least superficial ways.

I also conclude that there is much more continuity than difference between the broad history of modernism and the movement called postmodernism. It seems more sensible to me to see the latter as a particular kind of crisis within the former, one that emphasizes the fragmentary, the ephemeral, and the chaotic side of Baudelaire's formulation (that side which Marx so admirably dissects as integral to the capitalist mode of production) while expressing a deep scepticism as to any particular prescriptions as to how the eternal and immutable should be conceived of, represented, or expressed.

But postmodernism, with its emphasis upon the ephemerality of *jouissance*, its insistence upon the impenetrability of the other, its concentration on the text rather than the work, its penchant for deconstruction bordering on nihilism, its preference for aesthetics over ethics, takes matters too far. It takes them beyond the point where any coherent politics are left, while that wing of it that seeks a shameless accommodation with the market puts it firmly in the tracks of an entrepreneurial culture that is the hallmark of reactionary neoconservativism. Postmodernist philosophers tell us not only to accept but even to revel in the fragmentations and the cacophony of voices through which the dilemmas of the modern world are understood. Obsessed with deconstructing and delegitimating every form of argument they encounter, they can end only in condemning their own validity claims to the point where nothing remains of any basis for reasoned action. Postmodernism has us accepting the reifications and partitionings, actually celebrating the activity of masking and cover-up, all the fetishisms of locality, place, or social grouping, while denying that kind of meta-theory which can grasp the political–economic processes (money flows, international divisions of labour, financial markets, and the like) that are becoming ever more universalizing in their depth, intensity, reach and power over daily life.

Worst of all, while it opens up a radical prospect by acknowledging the authenticity of other voices, postmodernist thinking immediately shuts off those other voices from access to more universal sources of power by ghettoizing them within an opaque otherness, the specificity of this or that language game. It thereby disempowers those voices (of women, ethnic and racial minorities, colonized peoples, the unemployed, youth, etc.) in a world of lop-sided power relations. The language game of a cabal of international bankers may be impenetrable to us, but that does not put it on a par with the equally impenetrable language of inner-city blacks from the standpoint of power relations.

The rhetoric of postmodernism is dangerous for it avoids confronting the realities of political economy and the circumstances of global power. The silliness of Lyotard's 'radical proposal' that opening up the data banks to everyone as a prologue to radical reform (as if we would all have equal power to use that opportunity) is instructive, because it indicates how even the most resolute of postmodernists is faced in the end with either making some universalizing gesture (like Lyotard's appeal to some pristine concept of justice) or lapsing, like Derrida, into total political silence. Meta-theory cannot be dispensed with. The postmodernists simply

push it underground where it continues to function as a 'now unconscious effectivity' (Jameson 1984).

I find myself agreeing, therefore, with Eagleton's repudiation of Lyotard, for
whom 'there can be no difference between truth, authority and rhetorical seduc-
tiveness; he who has the smoothest tongue or the raciest story has the power.' The
eight-year reign of a charismatic story-teller in the White House suggests that there
is more than a little continuity to that political problem, and that postmodernism
comes dangerously close to complicity with the aestheticizing of politics upon which
it is based. This takes us back to a very basic question. If both modernity and post-
modernity derive their aesthetic from some kind of struggle with the *fact* of
fragmentation, ephemerality, and chaotic flux, it is, I would suggest, very important to establish why such a fact should have been so pervasive an aspect of modern
experience for so long a period of time, and why the intensity of that experience
seems to have picked up so powerfully since 1970. If the only thing certain about
modernity is uncertainty, then we should, surely, pay considerable attention to the
social forces that produce such a condition. [. . .]

[. . .] Down the left-hand side [of Table 16.1] are ranged a series of intersecting
terms to describe the condition of 'Fordist modernity,' while the right-hand column
represent 'Flexible postmodernism.' The table suggests amusing associations. But it
also indicates how two rather different regimes of accumulation and their associated modes of regulation (including the materializations of cultural habits,
motivations, and styles of representation) might hang together, each as a distinctive and relatively coherent kind of social formation. Two reservations to that idea
immediately come to mind. First, the oppositions, highlighted for didactic purposes,
are never so clear-cut, and the 'structure of feeling' in any society is always a
synthetic moment somewhere between the two. Second, associations are no proof
of historical causation or even of necessary or integral relations. Even if the associations look plausible – and many of them do – some other way has to be found
to establish that they form a meaningful configuration.

The oppositions within each profile are noteworthy. Fordist modernity is far
from homogeneous. There is much here that is about relative fixity and permanence – fixed capital in mass production, stable, standardized, and homogeneous
markets, a fixed configuration of political–economic influence and power, easily
identifiable authority and meta-theories, secure grounding in materiality and
technical–scientific rationality, and the like. But all of this is ranged around a social
and economic project of Becoming, of growth and transformation of social relations, of auratic art and originality, of renewal and avant-gardism. Postmodernist
flexibility, on the other hand, is dominated by fiction, fantasy, the immaterial (particularly of money), fictitious capital, images, ephemerality, chance, and flexibility in
production techniques, labour markets and consumption niches; yet it also embodies
strong commitments to Being and place, a penchant for charismatic politics,
concerns for ontology, and the stable institutions favoured by neo-conservatism.
Habermas's judgement that the value placed on the transitory and the ephemeral
'discloses a longing for an undefiled, immaculate and stable present' is everywhere
in evidence. It seems as if postmodernist flexibility merely reverses the dominant
order to be found in Fordist modernity. The latter achieved relative stability in its

*Table 16.1  Fordist modernity versus flexible postmodernity, or the interpenetration of opposed tendencies in capitalist society as a whole*

| Fordist modernity | Flexible postmodernity |
|---|---|
| economies of scale/master code/hierarchy homogeneity/detail division of labour | economies of scope/idiolect/anarchy diversity/social division of labour |
| paranoia/alienation/symptom public housing/monopoly capital | schizophrenia/decentering/desire homelessness/entrepreneurialism |
| purpose/design/mastery/determinacy production capital/universalism | play/chance/exhaustion/indeterminacy fictitious capital/localism |
| state power/trade unions state welfarism/metropolis | financial power/individualism neo-conservatism/counterurbanization |
| ethics/money commodity God the Father/materiality | aesthetics/moneys of account The Holy Ghost/immateriality |
| production/originality/authority blue collar/avant-gardism interest group politics/semantics | reproduction/pastiche/eclecticism white collar/commercialism charismatic politics/rhetoric |
| centralization/totalization synthesis/collective bargaining | decentralization/deconstruction antithesis/local contracts |
| operational management/master code phallic/single task/origin | strategic management/idiolect androgynous/multiple tasks/trace |
| metatheory/narrative/depth mass production/class politics technical-scientific rationality | language games/image/surface small-batch production/social movements/pluralistic otherness |
| utopia/redemptive art/concentration specialized work/collective consumption | heterotopias/spectacle/dispersal flexible worker/symbolic capital |
| function/representation/signified industry/protestant work ethic mechanical reproduction | fiction/self-reference/signifier services/temporary contract electronic reproduction |
| becoming/epistemology/regulation urban renewal/relative space | being/ontology/deregulation urban revitalization/place |
| state interventionism/industrialization internationalism/permanence/time | laissez-faire/deindustrialization geopolitics/ephemerality/space |

political–economic apparatus in order to produce strong social and material change, whereas the former has been dogged by disruptive instability in its political–economic apparatus, but sought compensation in stable places of being and in charismatic geopolitics.

But what if the table as a whole itself constitutes a structural description of the totality of political–economic and cultural–ideological relations within capitalism? To view it this way requires that we see the oppositions across as well as within the profiles as internal relations within a structured whole. That idea, outrageous by postmodernism's own standards (because it resurrects the ghost of Marxist thinkers like Lukács and appeals to a theory of internal relations of the sort that Bertell Ollman advances) makes more than a little sense. It helps explain how it is that Marx's *Capital* is so rich in insights into what the current status of thinking is all about. It also helps us understand how the cultural forces at work in, say, *fin de siècle* Vienna constituted such a complex mix that it is almost impossible to tell where the modernist impulse begins or ends. It helps us dissolve the categories of both modernism and postmodernism into a complex of oppositions expressive of the cultural contradictions of capitalism. We then get to see the categories of both modernism and postmodernism as static reifications imposed upon the fluid interpenetration of dynamic oppositions. Within this matrix of internal relations, there is never one fixed configuration, but a swaying back and forth between centralization and decentralization, between authority and deconstruction, between hierarchy and anarchy, between permanence and flexibility, between the detail and the social division of labour (to list but a few of the many oppositions that can be identified). The sharp categorical distinction between modernism and postmodernism disappears, to be replaced by an examination of the flux of internal relations within capitalism as a whole.

But why the flux? This brings us back to the problem of causation and historical trajectory. [. . .]

The oppositional relations depicted in table 16.1 are always subject to the restless transformative activity of capital accumulation and speculative change. Exact configurations cannot be predicted in advance, even though the law-like behaviour of the transformative force can. Put more concretely, the degree of Fordism and modernism, or of flexibility and postmodernism, is bound to vary from time to time and from place to place, depending on which configuration is profitable and which is not. Behind all the ferment of modernity and postmodernity, we can discern some simple generative principles that shape an immense diversity of outcomes. Yet the latter strikingly fail (as in the case of the serially produced downtown renewals) to create unpredictable novelty, even though the seemingly infinite capacity to engender products feeds all the illusions of freedom and of open paths for personal fulfilment. Wherever capitalism goes, its illusory apparatus, its fetishisms, and its system of mirrors come not far behind.

It is here that we can invoke, once more, Bourdieu's thesis [. . .] that we each of us possess powers of regulated improvisation, shaped by experience, which allow us 'an endless capacity to engender products – thoughts, perceptions, expressions, actions – whose limits are set by the historically situated conditions' of their production; the 'conditioned and conditional freedom' this secures 'is as remote from the creation of unpredictable novelty as it is from simple mechanical reproduction of the initial conditionings.' It is, Bourdieu suggests, through mechanisms of this sort that every established order tends to produce 'the naturalization of its own arbitrariness' expressed in the 'sense of limits' and the 'sense of reality' which in turn form the basis for an 'ineradicable adherence to the established order.' The reproduction of the social and symbolic order through the exploration of difference and 'otherness' is all too evident in the climate of postmodernism.

So where, then, can real change come from? To begin with, the contradictory experiences acquired under capitalism – many of which are set out in Table 16.1 – render the novelty a little less thoroughly predictable than was the case in Bourdieu's encounter with the Kabyles. Mechanical reproduction of value systems, beliefs, cultural preferences, and the like is impossible, not in spite of but precisely because of the speculative grounding of capitalism's inner logic. The exploration of contradictions always lies at the heart of original thought. But it is also evident that the expression of such contradictions in the form of objective and materialized crises plays a key role in breaking the powerful link 'between the subjective structures and the objective structures' and thereby lay the groundwork for a critique that 'brings the undiscussed into discussion and the unformulated into formulation'. While crises in the experience of space and time, in the financial system, or in the economy at large, may form a necessary condition for cultural and political changes, the sufficient conditions lie more deeply embedded in the internalized dialectics of thought and knowledge production. For it is ever the case that, as Marx (1967, 178) has it, 'we erect our structure in imagination before we erect it in reality'.

# CIVIL SOCIETY

- Jean L. Cohen and Andrew Arato, The utopia of civil society

- Jeffrey C. Alexander, The binary discourse of civil society

**Jean L. Cohen** was born in New York on 28 November 1946. Educated at the New School, she has recently been a professor of Political Science at Columbia University. **Andrew Arato** is a professor of Sociology and a member of the Program on East Central Europe of the Graduate Faculty, New School for Social Research, in New York City. Cohen and Arato are co-authors of *Civil Society and Political Theory*.

**Jeffrey C. Alexander** was educated at Harvard (BA) and the University of California, Berkeley (Ph. D). He is Professor of Sociology at Yale University and is the author of, among other books, *Theoretical Logic in Sociology* (1982–3) and *Fin de Siècle Social Theory* (1995).

# Chapter 17

# Jean L. Cohen and Andrew Arato

## THE UTOPIA OF CIVIL SOCIETY

**W**E ARE ON THE THRESHOLD of yet another great transformation of the self-understanding of modern societies. There have been many attempts from various points of view to label this process: the ambiguous terms 'postindustrial' and 'postmodern' reflect the vantage points of economic and cultural concerns. Our interest is in politics. But from this standpoint, the changes occurring in political culture and social conflicts are poorly characterized by terms whose prefix implies 'after' or 'beyond.' To be sure, for a variety of empirical and theoretical reasons the old hegemonic paradigms have disintegrated, as have the certainties and guarantees that went with them. Indeed we are in the midst of a remarkable revival of political and social thought that has been going on for the last two decades.

One response to the collapse of the two dominant paradigms of the previous period – pluralism and neo-Marxism – has been the attempt to revive political theory by 'bringing the state back in.' While this approach has led to interesting theoretical and empirical analyses, its state-centered perspective has obscured an important dimension of what is new in the political debates and in the stakes of social contestation. The focus on the state is a useful antidote to the reductionist functionalism of many neo-Marxian and pluralist paradigms that would make the political system an extension, reflex, or functional organ of economic (class) or social (group) structures of selectivity and domination. In this respect the theoretical move served the cause of a more differentiated analysis. But with respect to all that is nonstate, the new paradigm continues the reductionist tendency of Marxism and neo-Marxism by identifying class relations and interests as the key to contemporary forms of collective action. Moreover, the legal, associational, cultural, and public spheres of society have no theoretical place in this analysis. It thereby loses sight of a great deal of interesting and normatively instructive forms of social conflict today.

The current 'discourse of civil society,' on the other hand, focuses precisely on new, generally non class-based forms of collective action oriented and linked to the legal, associational, and public institutions of society. These are differentiated not only from the state but also from the capitalist market economy. Although we cannot leave the state and the economy out of consideration if we are to understand the dramatic changes occurring in Latin America and Eastern Europe in particular, the concept of civil society is indispensable if we are to understand the stakes of these 'transitions to democracy' as well as the self-understanding of the relevant actors. It is also indispensable to any analysis that seeks to grasp the import of such changes for the West, as well as indigenous contemporary forms and stakes of conflict. In order to discover, after the demise of Marxism, if not a common normative project between the 'transitions' and radical social initiatives under established liberal democracies, then at least the conditions of possibility of fruitful dialogue between them, we must inquire into the meaning and possible shapes of the concept of civil society. [. . .]

Phrases involving the *resurrection, reemergence, rebirth, reconstruction*, or *renaissance* of civil society are heard repeatedly today. These terms, indicating the continuity of an emerging political paradigm with essential trends of early modernity, are misleading in one important respect: They refer not only to something *modern* but also to something significantly *new*. [. . .] For a period of more than a decade and a half now, citizen initiatives, associations, and movements have increasingly oriented themselves toward the defense and expansion of a variously described societal realm, the forms and projects of which are clearly distinguished from statism.

Two crucial ambiguities remain from the orientation 'society against the state.' First, while increasingly significant groupings of collective actors reject any representation of their program in terms of communitarianism, others continue to defend an idealized *Gemeinschaft* or premodern network of communities, traditional solidarities, and collectives against modernity itself. Second, there are various neoconservative, neoliberal, and libertarian initiatives (rarely movements, but with significant force behind them) that identify 'society' with market economy. Both of these trends are regressive versions of antistatism. The first wishes to retreat behind the modern state, thus eliminating an essential precondition of modernity itself; the second wishes to repeat the already failed experiment with the fully self-regulated market economy of classical capitalism. There is no chance of the first trend registering even temporary successes, although it will continue to have a role within most social movements. The second trend, wherever successful, threatens to transform history into oscillation between economic liberalism and paternalist statism.

We believe there are today important elements of a third project for retrieving the category of *civil society* from the tradition of classical political theory. These involve attempts to thematize a program that seeks to represent the values and interests of social autonomy in face of *both* the modern state and the capitalist economy, without falling into a new traditionalism. Beyond the antinomies of state and market, public and private, *Gesellschaft* and *Gemeinschaft*, and, as we shall show, reform and revolution, the idea of the defense *and* the democratization of civil society is the best way to characterize the really new, common strand of contemporary forms of self-organization and self-constitution. [. . .]

In an age when totalizing revolutionary utopias have been discredited, the dualistic model of civil society we have reconstructed avoids 'soulless' reformism by allowing us to thematize a self-reflective and self-limiting utopia of civil society. We can thereby link the project of radical democracy, reinterpreted in terms of our notion of 'the plurality of democracies,' to some key institutional premises of modernity.

The slogan 'society against the state' has often been understood as a funda-mentalist call for generalizing participatory democratic decision making, as a coordinating principle, to all spheres of social life, including the state and the economy. Indeed, the ideal of free voluntary association, democratically structured and communicatively coordinated, has always informed the utopia of civil (polit-ical) society, from Aristotle to the young Marx in 1843. But such a 'democratic' utopia, if totally generalized, threatens the differentiation of society that forms the basis of modernity. Moreover, from a normative point of view, any project of dedif-ferentiation is contradictory, because it would involve such an overburdening of the democratic process that it would discredit democracy by associating it with political disintegration or by opening it to subversion through covert, unregulated strategic action.

As opposed to this, the self-limiting utopia of radical democracy based on the dualistic model of civil society would open up 'the utopian horizon of a civil society.' To quote Habermas: The rationalization of the lifeworld allows, on the one hand, the differentiation of independent subsystems and opens up, on the other hand, the utopian horizon of a civil society in which the formally organized spheres of action of the bourgeois (economy and state apparatus) constitute the foundations for the posttraditional lifeworld of *l'homme* (private sphere) and *citoyen* (public sphere).

This utopia is one of differentiation rather than unification. Of course, the idea of differentiation is in itself not utopian. It involves a normatively desirable model of an alternative society, one that is 'regulative' for critical thought (and thus a 'utopia') only through its link with another idea: the creation of institutions capable of fully realizing the potentials of the communicative reproduction of a modern lifeworld. In particular, the development of postconventional structures of culture would allow the projection of interconnected institutions of intimacy and publicity, which would replace unexamined traditional relations of domination with uncon-strained forms of solidarity produced and reproduced through free, voluntary interaction. This second, genuinely utopian idea is linked to a theory of differen-tiation involving processes of self-reflection and self-limitation.

Given the experience of the liberal utopia of the self-regulating market, on the one hand, and of socialism, with its synthetic utopia of a rationally organized (planned) society of free producers (or creative, working individuals), on the other, it is clear that utopian thought can be saved only if critical self-reflection can be built into it. One element the two failed utopias have in common is their attempt to totalize a single model of a 'rational' society, rooted in one or both of the subsys-tems, each linked to a single value: negative freedom in one case, substantive equality in the other. Today we know that the very plausibility of these utopias, and what linked them with the logic of history itself, lay in the dynamism of an economy-centered instrumental reason in one case and of state-centered functional reason in the other. We should now be aware of the negative consequences of either

type of subsumption. While each of these utopias made greater or lesser conces-
sions to democratic models of social organization, the stress on a fully autonomous
market rationality or on a form of power capable of coordinating a nonmarket but
nevertheless modern economy was incompatible with the reproduction of the lifeworld substratum of democratic coordination of action. That this was not a
fundamental internal dilemma for either model is shown by the existence of authoritarian versions of the utopias of both market and planning. From the point of view
of democratic politics, both utopias had to and did become suspect even before
the disastrous consequences were manifested in practice.

Since its emergence around 1919, the tradition of Western Marxism has always
been aware of the dangers of the productivist utopias of classical socialism: The
alternatives of Lukács, Bloch, and Marcuse had little to do with a laboring society.
Instead, these thinkers developed some of the inherent teleologies of the modern
spheres of aesthetic culture (the young Lukács, Bloch) and personality (the later
Marcuse) in utopian and totalizing directions. Their affinities with Leninist avant-
gardism – explicit for Lukács and Bloch, implicit for Marcuse – indicate, however,
that they could not really free themselves from the utopia of power. It certainly
seems to be the case that primarily cultural utopias, to the extent that they are
fundamentalist and revolutionary, implicitly base their promise of social transformation on the dynamic potential of the medium of power. Within the Marxist
tradition, only Adorno and Horkheimer were able to escape the charms of power,
at the price, however, of developing a utopia of solidarity whose terms could not
be linked to any politics or even explicitly articulated.

Admittedly, democratic utopias drawing on the resource of solidarity and
projecting the vast expansion of communicative processes of will formation can
also be, and have often been, totalizing. This feature of democratic fundamentalism, whenever present, has tended to make anarchist utopias either transparent
covers for projects of power or projects for the primitivist dedifferentiation
of society. While totalization led to the destruction of democracy in the case of
utopias of market and power, in each versions of the utopia of communication
the result was self-destruction. The reason for this difference is that, in the case
of the utopia of communication, totalization represents a contradiction in principle. The lifeworld is dissimilar to money and power; even its associationally
organized institutions cannot easily or spontaneously invade and subsume the differentiated subsystems. Even more important, its own modernization depends on the
differentiation of modern economy and state; their dedifferentiation would deprive
civil society of time resources for democratic deliberation and decision making.
Thus, the totalization of the (communicative) logic of democratic association is not
only conducive to short- and long-term dysfunctional side effects and pathologies;
it is in principle self-contradictory. It is evident, therefore, that the self-reflection
of utopian thought leads both to the idea of the limitation of the logics of power
and money, 'pulling the emergency brake' with respect to their dynamism, and to
the idea of the self-limitation of radical democracy. This double setting of limits
requires differentiation.

There is yet another reason for the self-limitation of democratic utopianism,
and this is the link, admittedly contingent, between many historical utopias and
the idea of revolutionary rupture. Irrespective of their projects, revolutions in the

modern sense are carried out, or at least won, by organizations of power that, in a genuine rupture with the old society and in the inevitable chaos and power vacuum that follow, are driven to increase rather than limit sovereign power. It is this constellation, for example, that led to the difference in spirit between the American constitution and Bill of Rights and the French Declaration of the Rights of Man. While the utopias of power have an elective affinity with total rupture, the utopia of democratic communication is threatened by revolution despite its own revolutionary origins. Obviously, the issue of the desirability of revolution in a given context cannot be decided from the point of view of utopian projects alone, especially when the overthrow of an oppressive system is involved. But it is important to note the dangers of revolutionary rupture for democracy, and also to note an indispensable precondition for its legitimacy: Democracy's only possible legitimation lies in a principle contrary to revolutionary logic, namely, the lasting institutionalization of a new power accompanied by limits to even the new forms of power in terms of rights.

Even a democratic revolution must be limited by rights. Such is the consequence of the utopia of differentiation. This is equivalent to saying that democratic revolutions can remain democratic in the modern world only if they institutionalize civil society. This is in fact never possible on the basis of abolishing even imperfect models of civil society. And yet the utopia of communication, the plurality of democracies, cannot simply be a project of establishing *any* kind of civil society or any model of rights. The utopia of civil society that we have in mind is not identical to the models of civil society discussed so far, and the structure of rights implied is not equivalent to any found in today's constitutions. The legitimating principles of democracy and rights are compatible only with a model of civil society that institutionalizes democratic communication in a multiplicity of publics and defends the conditions of individual autonomy by liberating the intimate sphere from all traditional as well as modern forms of inequality and unfreedom. The model of rights we require would put the rights of communication (the public sphere) and the rights of the intimate (or 'private') sphere into the center of the catalogue of constitutional freedoms. These would have priority over all political, economic, and social rights, which would constitute only their prerequisites. The establishment of such a catalogue would indeed signify the institutionalization of a new model of civil society. [. . .]

Totalizing utopias, especially those linked to the idea of revolutionary rupture, aim for a constitutive rather than a regulative relation to politics. The rationally constructed model is to be actualized in practice. Such utopias can rely entirely on a transcendent critique of existing reality, with a revolutionary movement as a kind of deus ex machina obliterating existing structures and creating entirely new ones. Revolutionary utopias can use versions of genuine immanent criticism, relying on the contradictions between counterfactual norms and actual institutions, only inconsistently, since the idea of rupture excludes the notion that something is intrinsically worth saving. From such a point of view, however, the norms of a society become nothing but a transparent subterfuge for strategic action, and this is an attitude incompatible with immanent criticism.

The proper relationship of self-limiting utopias to reality should be a regulative one. Projects of reconstruction ought to be guided by normative principles that determine only the legitimate procedures but not the actual contents of new institutional life. Above all, such utopias do not aim at imposing a single form of life beyond all conflict. Like all utopias, the one we have in mind has an element of transcendence with respect to existing reality. But self-limiting utopianism has an intrinsic relation with immanent criticism, since it cannot and ought not construct the new society, even ideally, from its own substance. Thus, the utopia we advocate must combine, as Adorno foresaw, transcendent and immanent forms of social criticism.

All the more serious, then, is Adorno's own suspicion, echoed by Marcuse, that in both the West and the East, one-dimensional and totally administered societies, characterized by the reification of all spheres of life, have become dominant. In such societies, ideologies in the true sense disappear, carrying with them the only possible object of immanent criticism. This radical judgment, seemingly resting on an implausible identification of capitalist liberal democracies with totalitarian societies, was in fact backed up by the whole tradition of Frankfurt School analyses of economy, politics, culture, family, and personality.

The utopia of civil society starts out from the obviously plausible counterthesis according to which the Western liberal democracies, unlike Soviet-type societies, are civil societies, however imperfect. If true, this claim would validate the self-limiting and regulative status of this utopia and give it a potential link to politics by a refurbished immanent critique. [. . .]

This represents the best point of view from which to explore the institutional domains of family, culture, and associations, as well as the domain of legality that is so important for the modern subsystems. Those aspects of contemporary institutions that contribute to the autonomy and further rationalization of civil society constitute the positive side; the reified structures that promote colonization, the negative. Here we can only indicate the outlines of the conception that would have to be developed for a theory of the institutional dynamics of contemporary civil society. Our evidence is constituted at this stage only by the tradition of social and political theory that seeks to contest the opposing theses of one dimensionality and system integration. Even from such a preliminary point of view, we believe that it is possible to claim that the institutional developments of the modern family, of political and cultural public spheres, and of associations are all similarly dualistic.

1. With respect to the family, we support Habermas's challenge to the old Frankfurt thesis (which he used to share) that the assumption of socialization by the schools and the mass media and the loss of the property base of the middle-class patriarchal family entails, along with the abolition of the father's authority, the end of ego autonomy. From the standpoint of the system/lifeworld distinction, the picture looks rather different. The freeing of the family from many economic functions and the diversification of the agencies of socialization create a potential for egalitarian interfamilial relations and liberalized socialization processes. The rationality potential of communicative interaction in this sphere is thereby released. Of course, new types of conflicts and even pathologies appear when these potentials are blocked and when the demands of the formally organized subsystems in which the adult must participate conflict with the capacities and expectations of those who have experienced these emancipatory socialization processes.

2. The principles of democratic legitimacy and representation imply the free discussion of all interests within institutionalized public spheres (parliaments) and the primacy of the lifeworld with respect to the two subsystems [. . .] the bureaucratic catch-all party form presupposed by elite theorists does not seem to provide sufficient centers of social identification, nor is it able to respond well to the emergence of new issues of great urgency. Thus, some countries have experienced the emergence of extraparliamentary oppositions or parties with a new type of relation to movements. These phenomena have affected the structure of the political public sphere as well. While the central political public sphere, constituted by parliaments and the major media, remains rather (but not everywhere equally!) closed and inaccessible, a plurality of alternative publics, differentiated but interrelated, time and again revives the processes and the quality of political communication. With the emergence of new types of political organizations, even the public discussion in parliaments and party conventions tends to be affected, as has been the case in West Germany. It seems, therefore, that along with the elite democratic, oligarchic tendencies toward the drying up of political public life, we should postulate a contrary, if weaker, trend of redemocratization, based on the new cultural (practical, aesthetic, and cognitive) potentials of the lifeworld.

3. Nor can one construe the development of the mass media as a purely negative sign of the commodification or administrative distortion of communication. This point is especially important because, in Habermas's early thesis on the public sphere, the fusion argument, implying the obliteration of the bridges between state and civil society, works only if the cultural substance of mediation is 'commodified' and 'industrialized.' There is little reason to deny the immense role in our societies of a top-to-bottom, center-to-periphery model of mass communication. Yet generalized forms of communication also deprovincialize, expand, and create new publics. In the area of general communications, what we said about the differentiation and pluralization of political publics is even more true. From subcultures to great educational institutions, from political to scientific publics, from social movements to microinstitutions, the spaces for consequential, critical communication have immensely expanded along with the growth of the commercialized and manipulated frameworks of public relations, advertising, and industrial culture. Since the project of an enlightened public sphere was first articulated, we have had neither a single history of decline (the rise of mass culture) nor a process of 'democratization,' but two simultaneous histories made possible by democratization: one of the penetration of culture through money and power, and another of the renewal of a more universal, inclusive, and pluralistic public life made possible by the modernization of the lifeworld. While the first of these processes often seems to be dominant, this is not due to an inevitability latent in the technical means of communication. The technical development of the electronic media does not necessarily lead to centralization; it can involve horizontal, creative, autonomous forms of media pluralism.

4. The problem of associations, which is excluded from Habermas's analysis, is parallel to that of culture, to which it is linked through the structures of the public sphere. As Durkheim and Gramsci realized, the hostility of the modern state and economy to corporate bodies and associations could not block their reemergence and modernization. In this context, the bureaucratization of associations

and the emergence of pseudo-pluralist and corporatist forms of interest representation and aggregation, a key dimension of the fusion argument, cannot be considered the only tendency in contemporary associational life. The existence of an immense number of voluntary associations in all liberal democracies, the emergence of new ones in the context of corporatist bargaining, and their role in citizen initiatives and social movements may not demonstrate the somewhat one-sided Parsonian point that ours is the age of association and not bureaucracy; but it is clear that legitimate left criticisms of a pluralist thesis that occludes the highly differential access of various types of associations to the political system should not close our eyes to the validity of this thesis against all claims of atomization and massification in our societies. The resilience of associations and the periodic revival of their dynamism can be explained through the modernization of the lifeworld and its normative contribution to the scarce resource of solidarity.

5. Finally, the development of legality up to the contemporary democratic welfare state involves both the modernization of civil society and its penetration by administrative agencies. It is, moreover, in the double nature of law itself that one must locate the ambiguous character of the contemporary juridification of society. According to Habermas, as a 'medium,' law functions as an organizational means together with money and/or power to *constitute* the structure of economy and administration in such a way that they can be coordinated independently of direct communication. As an 'institution,' on the other hand, law is 'a societal component of the lifeworld [. . .] embedded in a broader political, cultural, and social context [. . .] in a continuum with moral norms and superimposed communicatively structured areas of action'. Juridification in this sense plays a regulative rather than a constitutive role, expanding and giving a binding form to (the ethical principles of) communicatively coordinated areas of action. This empowering dimension of at least some types of legal regulation is fostered by juridification itself. Foucault's error in this regard, typical of all anarchist postures, is to have focused exclusively on the role of law as medium, while dismissing the freedom-securing, empowering institutional moment as mere show. [. . .]

# Chapter 18

# Jeffrey C. Alexander

## THE BINARY DISCOURSE
## OF CIVIL SOCIETY

SOCIOLOGISTS HAVE WRITTEN MUCH about the social forces that create conflict and polarize society, about interests and structures of political, economic, racial, ethnic, religious, and gender groups. But they have said very little about the construction, destruction, and deconstruction of civic solidarity itself. They are generally silent about the sphere of fellow feeling that makes society into society and about the processes that fragment it.

I would like to approach this sphere of fellow feeling from the concept of 'civil society.' Civil society, of course, has been a topic of enormous discussion and dispute throughout the history of social thought. Marx and critical theory have employed the concept to theorize the very lack of community, the world of egoistic, self-regulating individuals produced by capitalist production. I am relying for my understanding of the term of a different tradition, on the line of democratic, liberal thought that extended from the seventeenth century to the early nineteenth, an age of democratic theorizing that was supplanted by industrial capitalism and the concern with 'the social question' [. . .]

I will define *civil society* as a sphere or subsystem of society that is analytically and, to various degrees, empirically separated from the spheres of political, economic, and religious life. Civil society is a sphere of solidarity in which abstract universalism and particularistic versions of community are tensely intertwined. It is both a normative and real concept. It allows the relation between universal individual rights and particularistic restrictions on these rights to be studied empirically, as the conditions that determine the status of civil society itself.

Civil society depends on resources, or inputs, from these other spheres, from political life, from economic institutions, from broad cultural discussion, from territorial organization, and from primordiality. In a causal sense, civil society is dependent on these spheres, but only by what Parsons called a 'combinatorial logic.' Civil society – and the groups, individuals, and actors who represent their interests in this system's terms – pulls together these inputs according to the logic and demands of its particular situation. This is to say that the solidary sphere that we call civil society has relative autonomy and can be studied in its own right. [. . .]

Against the new utilitarianism [. . .] and critical theory [. . .] alike, therefore, I wish to defend the position that there is, indeed, a *society* that can be defined in moral terms. The stipulations of this moral community articulate with (not determine) organizations and the exercise of power via institutions like constitutions and legal codes, on the one hand, and 'office,' on the other. Civil society also has organizations of its own: the courts, institutions of mass communication, and public opinion polls are all significant examples. Civil society is constituted by its own distinctive structure of elites, not only by functional oligarchies that control the legal and communications systems, but by those that exercise power and identity through voluntary organizations ('dignitaries' or 'public servants') and social movements ('mouvements intellectuels' [. . .]).

But civil society is not merely an institutional realm. It is also a realm of structured, socially established consciousness, a network of understandings that operates beneath and above explicit institutions and the self-conscious interests of elites. To study this subjective dimension of civil society we must recognize and focus on the distinctive symbolic codes that are critically important in constituting the very sense of society for those who are within and without it. These codes are so sociologically important, I would argue, that every study of social/sectional/subsystem conflict must be complemented by reference to this civil symbolic sphere.

The codes supply the structured categories of pure and impure into which every member, or potential member, of civil society is made to fit. It is in terms of symbolic purity and impurity that centrality is defined, that marginal demographic status is made meaningful and high position understood as deserved or illegitimate. Pollution is a threat to any allocative system; its sources must either be kept at bay or transformed by communicative actions, like rituals and social movements, into a pure form.

Despite their enormous behavioral impact, however, pure and impure categories do not develop merely as generalizations or inductions from structural position or individual behavior. They are imputations that are induced, via analogy and metaphor, from the internal logic of symbolic code. For this reason, the internal structure of the civil code must become an object of study in itself. Just as there is no developed religion that does not divide the world into the saved and the damned, there is no civil discourse that does not conceptualize the world into those who deserve inclusion and those who do not. Members of national communities firmly believe that 'the world,' and this notably includes their own nation, is filled with people who either do not deserve freedom and communal support or are not capable of sustaining them (in part because they are immoral egoists). Members of national communities do not want to 'save' such persons. They do not wish to include them, protect them, or offer them rights because they conceive them as being unworthy and amoral, as in some sense 'uncivilized.'

This distinction is not 'real.' Actors are not intrinsically either worthy or moral: they are determined to be so by being placed in certain positions on the grid of civil culture. When citizens make judgments about who should be included in civil society and who should not, about who is a friend and who is an enemy, they draw on a systematic, highly elaborated symbolic code. This symbolic structure was already clearly implied in the very first philosophical thinking about democratic societies that emerged in ancient Greece. Since the Renaissance it has permeated popular thinking and behavior, even while its centrality in philosophical thinking has continued to be sustained. The symbolic structure takes different forms in different nations, and it is the historical residue of diverse movements in social, intellectual, and religious life – of classical ideas, republicanism and Protestanism, Enlightenment and liberal thought, of the revolutionary and common law traditions. The cultural implications of these variegated movements, however, have been drawn into a highly generalized symbolic system that divides civic virtue from civic vice in a remarkably stable and consistent way. It is for this reason that, despite divergent historical roots and variations in national elaborations, the language that forms the cultural core of civil society can be isolated as a general structure and studied as a relatively autonomous symbolic form.

The basic elements of this structure can be understood semiotically – they are sets of homologies, which create likeness between various terms of social description and prescription, and antipathies, which establish antagonisms between these terms and other sets of symbols. Those who consider themselves worthy members of a national community (as most persons do, of course) define themselves in terms of the positive side of this symbolic set; they define those who are not deemed worthy in terms of the bad. It is fair to say, indeed, that members of a community 'believe in' both the positive and the negative sides, that they employ both as viable normative evaluations of political communities. For the members of every democratic society, both the positive and the negative symbolic sets are thought to be realistic descriptions of individual and social life.

The binary discourse occurs at three levels: motives, relations, and institutions. The motives of political actors are clearly conceptualized (What kind of people are they?) along with the social relations and institutions they are capable of sustaining.

Let us first discuss motives. Code and countercode posit human nature in diametrically opposed ways. Because democracy depends on self-control and individual initiatives, the people who compose it are described as being capable of activism and autonomy rather than as being passive and dependent. They are seen as rational and reasonable rather than as irrational and hysterical, as calm rather than excited, as controlled rather than passionate, as sane and realistic, not as given to fantasy or as mad. Democratic discourse, then, posits the following qualities as axiomatic: activism, autonomy, rationality, reasonableness, calm, control, realism, and sanity. The nature of the countercode, the discourse that justifies the restriction of civil society, is already clearly implied. If actors are passive and dependent, irrational and hysterical, excitable, passionate, unrealistic, or made, they cannot be allowed the freedom that democracy allows. On the contrary, these persons deserve to be repressed, not only for the sake of civil society, but for their own sakes as well. (These qualities are schematized in table 18.1).

On the basis of such contradictory codes about human motives, distinctive representations of social relationships can be built. Democratically motivated persons – persons who are active, autonomous, rational, reasonable, calm, and realistic – will be capable of forming open social relationships rather than secretive ones; they

*Table 18.1 The discursive structure of social motives*

| Democratic Code | Counterdemocratic Code |
| --- | --- |
| Activism | Passivity |
| Autonomy | Dependence |
| Rationality | Irrationality |
| Reasonableness | Hysteria |
| Calm | Excitable |
| Self-control | Passionate |
| Realistic | Unrealistic |
| Sane | Mad |

will be trusting rather than suspicious, straightforward rather than calculating, truthful rather than deceitful. Their decisions will be based on open deliberation rather than conspiracy, and their attitude toward authority will be critical rather than deferential. In their behavior toward other community members they will be bound by conscience and honor rather than by greed and self-interest, and they will treat their fellows as friends rather than enemies.

If actors are irrational, dependent, passive, passionate, and unrealistic, on the other hand, the social relationships they form will be characterized by the second side of these fateful dichotomies. Rather than open and trusting relationships, they will form secret societies that are premised on their suspicion they will be deferential, but to those outside their tiny group they will behave in a greedy and self-interested way. They will be conspiratorial, deceitful toward others, and calculating in their behavior, conceiving of those outside their group as enemies. If the positive side of this second discourse set describes the symbolic qualities necessary to sustain civil society, the negative side describes a solidary structure in which mutual respect and expansive social integration has been broken down (see table 18.2).

*Table 18.2 Discursive structure of social relationships*

| Democratic Code | Counterdemocratic Code |
| --- | --- |
| Open | Secret |
| Trusting | Suspicious |
| Critical | Deferential |
| Honorable | Self interested |
| Conscience | Greed |
| Truthful | Deceitful |
| Straightforward | Calculating |
| Deliberative | Conspiratorial |
| Friend | Enemy |

*Table 18.3 The discursive structure of social institutions*

| Democratic Code | Counterdemocratic Code |
| --- | --- |
| Rule regulated | Arbitrary |
| Law | Power |
| Equality | Hierarchy |
| Inclusive | Exclusive |
| Impersonal | Personal |
| Contractual | Ascriptive loyalty |
| Social groups | Factions |
| Office | Personality |

Given the discursive structure of motives and civic relationships, it should not be surprising that this set of homologies and antipathies extends to the social understanding of political and legal institutions themselves. If members of a national community are irrational in motive and distrusting in social relationships, they will naturally create institutions that are arbitrary rather than rule regulated, that emphasize brute power rather than law and hierarchy rather than equality, that are exclusive rather than inclusive and promote personal loyalty over impersonal and contractual obligation, that are regulated by personalities rather than by office obligations, and that are organized by faction rather than by groups that are responsible to the needs of the community as a whole (see table 18.3).

These three sets of discursive structures are tied together. Indeed, every element in any one of the sets can be linked via anological relations – homologous relations of likeness – to any element in another set on the same side. 'Rule regulated,' for example, a key element in the symbolic understanding of democratic social institutions, is considered homologous – synonymous or mutually reinforcing in a cultural sense – with 'truthful' and 'open,' terms that define social relationships, and with 'reasonable' and 'autonomous,' elements from the symbolic set that stipulates democratic motives. In the same manner, any element from any set on one side is taken to be antithetical to any element from any set on the other. According to the rules of this broader cultural formation, for example, 'hierarchy' is thought to be inimical to 'critical' and 'open' and also to 'activistic' and 'self-controlled.'

When they are presented in their simple binary forms, these cultural codes appear merely schematic. In fact, however, they reveal the skeletal structures on which social communities build the familiar stories, the rich narrative forms, that guide their everyday, taken-for-granted political life. The positive side of these structured sets provides the elements for the comforting and inspiring story of a democratic, free, and spontaneously integrated social order, a civil society in an ideal-typical sense. People are rational, can process information intelligently and independently, know the truth when they see it, do not need strong leaders, can engage in criticism, and easily coordinate their own society. Law is not an external mechanism that coerces people but an expression of their innate rationality, mediating between truth and mundane events. Office is an institutional mechanism that mediates between law and action. It is a calling, a vocation to which persons adhere because of their trust and reason. Those who know the truth do not defer to authorities, nor are they loyal to particular persons. They obey their conscience rather than follow their vulgar interest; they speak plainly rather than conceal their ideas; they are open, idealistic, and friendly toward their fellow human beings.

The structure and narrative of political virtue form the discourse of liberty. This discourse is embodied in the founding documents of democratic societies. In America, for example, the Bill of Rights postulates 'the right of people to be secure against unreasonable searches' and guarantees that 'no person shall be deprived of liberty without due process of law.' In so doing it ties rights to reasons and liberty to law. The discourse is also embodied in the great and the little stories that democratic nations tell about themselves, for example, in the American story about George Washington and the cherry tree, which highlights honesty and virtue, or in English accounts of the Battle of Britain, which reveal the courage, self-sufficiency, and spontaneous cooperation of the British in contrast to the villainous forces of Hitlerian Germany.

Whatever institutional or narrative form it assumes, the discourse of liberty centers on the capacity for voluntarism. Action is voluntary if it is intended by rational actors who are in full control of body and mind. If action is not voluntary, it is deemed to be worthless. If laws do not facilitate the achievement of freely intended action, they are discriminatory. If confessions of guilt are coerced rather than freely given, they are polluted. If a social group is constituted under the discourse of liberty, it must be given social rights because the members of this group are conceived of as possessing the capacity for voluntary action. Political struggles over the status of lower-class groups, racial and ethnic minorities, women, children, criminals, and the mentally, emotionally, and physically handicapped have always involved discursive struggles over whether the discourse of liberty can be extended and applied. Insofar as the founding constitutional documents of democratic societies are universalistic, they implicitly stipulate that the discourse can and must be.

The elements on the negative side of these symbolic sets are also tightly intertwined. They provide the elements for the plethora of taken-for-granted stories that permeate democratic understanding of the negative and repugnant sides of community life. Taken together, these negative structures and narratives form the 'discourse of repression.' If people do not have the capacity for reason, if they cannot rationally process information and cannot tell truth from falseness, then they will be loyal to leaders for purely personal reasons and will be easily manipulated by them in turn. Because such persons are ruled by calculation rather than by conscience, they are without the honor that is critical in democratic affairs. Since they have no honor, they do not have the capacity to regulate their own affairs. It is because of this situation that such persons subject themselves to hierarchical authority. These anticivil qualities make it necessary to deny such persons access to rights and the protection of law. Indeed, because they lack the capacity for both voluntary and responsible behavior, these marginal members of the national community – those who are unfortunate enough to be constructed under the counterdemocratic code – must ultimately be repressed. They cannot be regulated by law, nor will they accept the discipline of office. Their loyalties can be only familial and particularistic. The institutional and legal boundaries of civil society, it is widely believed, can provide no bulwark against their lust for personal power.

The positive side of this discursive formation is viewed by the members of democratic communities as a source not only of purity but also of purification. The discourse of liberty is taken to sum up 'the best' in a civil community, and its tenets are considered to be sacred. The objects that the discourse creates seem to possess an awesome power that places them at the 'center' of society, a location – sometimes geographic, often stratificational, always symbolic – that compels their defense at almost any cost. The negative side of this symbolic formation is viewed as profane. Representing the 'worst' in the national community, it embodies evil. The objects it identifies threaten the core community from somewhere outside it. From this marginal position, they present a powerful source of pollution. To be close to these polluted objects – the actors, structures, and processes that are constituted by this repressive discourse – is dangerous. Not only can one's reputation be sullied and one's status endangered, but one's very security can be threatened as well. To have one's self or movement be identified in terms of these objects causes anguish, disgust, and alarm. This code is taken to be a threat to the very center of civil society itself.

Public figures and events must be categorized in terms of one side of this discursive formation or the other, although, when politics functions routinely, such classifications are neither explicit nor subject to extended public debate. Even in routine periods, however, it is their specification within the codes of this underlying discourse that gives political things meaning and allows them to assume the role they seem 'naturally' to have. Even when they are aware that they are struggling over these classifications, moreover, most political actors do not recognize that it is they who are creating them. Such knowledge would relativize reality, creating an uncertainty that could undermine not only the cultural core but also the institutional boundaries and solidarity of civil society itself. Social events and actors seem to 'be' these qualities, not to be labeled by them.

The discourse of civil society, in other words, is concrete, not abstract. It is elaborated by narrative accounts that are believed to describe not only the present but also the past faithfully. Every nation has a myth of origin, for example, that anchors this discourse in an account of the historical events involved in its early formation. Like their English compatriots, early Americans believed their rights to have emerged from the ancient constitution of eleventh-century Anglo-Saxons. The specially American discourse of liberty was first elaborated in accounts of Puritan saints and later in stories about revolutionary heroes. It was woven into the myth of the yeoman farmer and then into tales about cowboys and still later into pulp stories about detectives and the malcontents they hoped to ferret out. The discourse of repression was made palpable through early religious accounts of miscreants and stories about loyalists and aristocrats in the Revolutionary War. Later it was elaborated in accounts of wild Indians and 'popist' immigrants and then in regional myths about treason during the Civil War.

For contemporary Americans, the categories of the pure and the polluted discourses seem to exist in just as natural and fully historical a way. Democratic law and procedures are seen as having been won by the voluntary struggles of the founding fathers and guaranteed by historical documents like the Bill of Rights and the Constitution. The qualities of the repressive code are embodied in the dark visions of tyranny and lawlessness, whether those of eighteenth-century British monarchs or Soviet Communists. Pulp fiction and highbrow drama seek to counterpose these dangers with compelling images of the good. When works of the imagination represent the discursive formation in a paradigmatic way, they become contemporary classics. For the generation that matured during World War II, for example, George Orwell's *1984* made the discourse of repression emblematic of the struggles of their time.

Within the confines of a particular national community, the binary codes and concrete representations that make up the discourse of civil society are not usually divided up between different social groups. To the contrary, even in societies that are rent by intensive social conflict, the constructions of both civic virtue and civic vice are in most cases widely accepted. What is contested in the course of civic life, what is not at all consensual, is how the antithetical sides of this discourse, its two symbolic sets, will be applied to particular actors and groups. If most of the members of democratic society accepted the 'validity' and 'reality' of *1984*, they disagreed fundamentally over its relevant social application. Radicals and liberals were inclined to see the book as describing the already repressive or at least imminent tendencies of their own capitalist societies; conservatives understood the work as referring to Communism alone.

Of course, some events are so gross or so sublime that they generate almost immediate consensus about how the symbolic sets should be applied. For most members of a national community, great national wars clearly demarcate the good and the bad. The nation's soldiers are taken to be courageous embodiments of the discourse of liberty; the foreign nations and soldiers who oppose them are deemed to represent some potent combination of the counterdemocratic code. In the course of American history, this negative code has, in fact, been extended to a vast and variegated group, to the British, native peoples, pirates, the South and the North, Africans, old European nations, fascists, Communists, Germans, and Japanese. Identification in terms of the discourse of repression is essential if vengeful combat is to be pursued. Once this polluting discourse is applied, it becomes impossible for good people to treat and reason with those on the other side. If one's opponents are beyond reason, deceived by leaders who operate in secret, the only option is to read them out of the human race. When great wars are successful, they provide powerful narratives that dominate the nation's postwar life. Hitler and Nazism formed the backbone of a huge array of Western myth and stories, providing master metaphors for everything from profound discussions about the 'final solution' to the good guy/bad guy plots of television dramas and situation comedies.

For most events, however, discursive identity is contested. Political fights are, in part, about how to distribute actors across the structure of discourse, for there is no determined relation between any event or group and either side of the cultural scheme. Actors struggle to taint one another with the brush of repression and to wrap themselves in the rhetoric of liberty. In periods of tension and crisis, political struggle becomes a matter of how far and to whom the discourses of liberty and repression apply. The effective cause of victory and defeat, imprisonment and freedom, sometimes even of life and death, is often discursive domination, which depends on just how popular narratives about good and evil are extended. Is it protesting students who are like Nazis or the conservatives who are pursuing them? Are members of the Community party to be understood as fascistic or the members of the House Un-American Activities Committee who interrogate them? When Watergate began, only the actual burglars were called conspirators and polluted by the discourse of repression. George McGovern and his fellow Democrats were unsuccessful in their efforts to apply this discourse to the White House, executive staff, and Republican party, elements of civil society that succeeded in maintaining their identity in liberal terms. At a later point in the crisis, such a reassuring relation to the culture structure no longer held.

The general discursive structure, in other words, is used to legitimate friends and delegitimate opponents in the course of real historical time. If an independent civil society were to be fully maintained, of course, the discourse of repression would be applied only in highly circumscribed ways, to groups like children and criminals who are not usually taken to be in sufficient possession of their rational or moral faculties. It is often the case, indeed, that individuals and groups within civil society will be able to sustain the discourse of liberty over a significant period of time. They will be able to understand their opponents as other rational individuals without indulging in moral annihilation.

Over an extended historical period, however, it is impossible for the discourse of repression not to be brought into significant play and for opponents to be understood as enemies of the most threatened kind. It may be the case, of course, that the opponents are, in fact, ruthless enemies of the public good. The Nazis were moral idiots, and it was wrong to deal with them as potential civic participants, as Chamberlain and the other appeasers did. The discourse of repression is applied, however, whether its objects are really evil or not, eventually creating an objective reality where none had existed before. The symbolism of evil that had been applied by the Allies in an overzealous way to the German nation in World War I was extended indiscriminately to the German people and governments of the postwar period. It produced the debilitating reparations policy that helped establish the economic and social receptiveness to Nazism.

This points to the fact that the social application of polarizing symbolic identifications must also be understood in terms of the internal structure of the discourse itself. Rational, individualistic, and self-critical societies are vulnerable because these very qualities make them open and trusting, and if the other side is devoid of redeeming social qualities, then trust will be abused in the most merciless terms. The potential for dependent and irrational behavior, moreover, can be found even in good citizens themselves, for deceptive information can be provided that might lead them, on what would seem to be rational grounds, to turn away from the structures or processes of democratic society itself. In other words, the very qualities that allow civil societies to be internally democratic – qualities that include the symbolic oppositions that allow liberty to be defined in any meaningful way – mean that the members of civil society do not feel confident that they can deal effectively with their opponents, from either within or without. The discourse of repression is inherent in the discourse of liberty. This is the irony at the heart of the discourse of civil society.

# MULTICULTURALISM

- Iris Marion Young, Justice and the politics of difference

- Will Kymlicka, Multicultural citizenship

**Iris Marion Young** is a Professor of Political Science at the University of Chicago. Young has written extensively in the areas of justice, democratic theory, feminist social theory and female body experience. Her major work is *Justice and the Politics of Difference* (1990).

**Will Kymlicka** has taught philosophy at the University of Ottawa and Carleton University in Canada. He is the author of *Multicultural Citizenship* (1995) and *Liberalism, Community, and Culture* (1989).

# Chapter 19

# Iris Marion Young

## JUSTICE AND THE POLITICS
## OF DIFFERENCE

[. . .]

**T**HE IDEAL OF UNIVERSAL HUMANITY that denies natural differences has been a crucial historical development in the struggle against exclusion and status differentiation. It has made possible the assertion of the equal moral worth of all persons, and thus the right of all to participate and be included in all institutions and positions of power and privilege. The assimilationist ideal retains significant rhetorical power in the face of continued beliefs in the essentially different and inferior natures of women, Blacks, and other groups.

The power of this assimilationist ideal has inspired the struggle of oppressed groups and the supporters against the exclusion and denigration of these groups, and continues to inspire many. Periodically in American history, however, movements of the oppressed have questioned and rejected this 'path to belonging'. [. . .] Instead they have seen self-organization and the assertion of a positive group cultural identity as a better strategy for achieving power and participation in dominant institutions. Recent decades have witnessed a resurgence of this 'politics of difference' not only among racial and ethnic groups, but also among women, gay men and lesbians, old people, and the disabled.

Not long after the passage of the Civil Rights Act and the Voting Rights Act, many white and Black supporters of the Black civil rights movement were surprised, confused, and angered by the emergence of the Black Power movement. Black Power advocates criticized the integrationist goal and reliance on the support of white liberals that characterized the civil rights movement. They encouraged Blacks to break their alliance with whites and assert the specificity of their own culture, political organization, and goals. Instead of integration, they encouraged Blacks to seek economic and political empowerment in their separate neighborhoods [. . .]. Since the late 1960s many Blacks have claimed that the integration successes of the civil rights movement have had the effect of dismantling the bases of Black-organized social and economic institutions at least as much as they have lessened Black–white animosity and opened doors of opportunity. While some individual Blacks may be better off than they would have been if these changes had not occurred, as a group, Blacks are no better off and may be worse off, because the Blacks who have succeeded in assimilating into the American middle class no longer associate as closely with lower-class Blacks [. . .].

While much Black politics has questioned the ideal of assimilation in economic and political terms, the past twenty years have also seen the assertion and cele-bration by Blacks of a distinct Afro-American culture, both as a recovery and revaluation of an Afro-American history and in the creation of new cultural forms. The slogan 'Black is beautiful' pierced American consciousness, deeply unsettling the received body aesthetic which [. . .] continues to be a powerful reproducer of racism. Afro-American hairstyles pronounced themselves differently stylish, not less stylish. Linguistic theorists asserted that Black English is English differently constructed, not bad English, and Black poets and novelists exploited and explored its particular nuances.

In the late 1960s Red Power came fast on the heels of Black Power. The American Indian Movement and other radical organizations of American Indians rejected perhaps even more vehemently than Blacks the goal of assimilation which has dominated white–Indian relations for most of the twentieth century. They asserted a right to self-government on Indian lands and fought to gain and main-tain a dominant Indian voice in the Bureau of Indian Affairs. American Indians have sought to recover and preserve their language, rituals, and crafts, and this renewal of pride in traditional culture has also fostered a separatist political movement. The desire to pursue land rights claims and to fight for control over resources on reser-vations arises from what has become a fierce commitment to tribal self-determination, the desire to develop and maintain Indian political and economic bases in but not of white society [. . .].

These are but two examples of a widespread tendency in the politics of the 1970s and 1980s for oppressed, disadvantaged, or specially marked groups to orga-nize autonomously and assert a positive sense of their cultural and experiential specificity. Many Spanish-speaking Americans have rejected the traditional assump-tion that full participation in American society requires linguistic and cultural assimilation. In the last twenty years many have developed a renewed interest and pride in their Puerto Rican, Chicano, Mexican, or other Latin American heritage. They have asserted the right to maintain their specific culture and speak their language and still receive the benefits of citizenship, such as voting rights, decent education, and job opportunities. Many Jewish Americans have similarly rejected the ideal of assimilation, instead asserting the specificity and positive meaning of Jewish identity, often insisting publicly that Christian culture cease to be taken as the norm.

Since the late 1960s the blossoming of gay cultural expression, gay organiza-tion, and the public presence of gays in marches and other forums have radically altered the environment in which young people come to sexual identity, and changed many people's perceptions of homosexuality. Early gay rights advocacy had a distinctly assimilationist and universalist orientation. The goal was to remove the stigma of being homosexual, to prevent institutional discrimination, and to achieve societal recognition that gay people are 'no different' from anyone else. The very process of political organization against discrimination and police harassment and for the achievement of civil rights, however, fostered the development of gay and lesbian communities and cultural expression, which by the mid 1970s flowered in meeting places, organizations, literature, music, and massive street celebrations [. . .].

Today most gay and lesbian liberation advocates seek not merely civil rights, but the affirmation of gay men and lesbians as social groups with specific experiences and perspectives. Refusing to accept the dominant culture's definition of healthy sexuality and respectable family life and social practices, gay and lesbian liberation movements have proudly created and displayed a distinctive self-definition and culture. For gay men and lesbians the analogue to racial integration is the typical liberal approach to sexuality, which tolerates any behavior as long as it is kept private. Gay pride asserts that sexual identity is a matter of culture and politics, and not merely 'behavior' to be tolerated or forbidden.

The women's movement has also generated its own versions of a politics of difference. Humanist feminism, which predominated in the nineteenth century and in the contemporary women's movement until the late 1970s, finds in any assertion of difference between women and men only a legacy of female oppression and an ideology to legitimate continued exclusion of women from socially valued human activity. Humanist feminism is thus analogous to an ideal of assimilation in identifying sexual equality with gender blindness, with measuring women and men according to the same standards and treating them in the same way. Indeed, for many feminists, androgny names the ideal of sexual liberation – a society in which gender difference itself would be eliminated. Given the strength and plausibility of this vision of sexual equality, it was confusing when feminists too began taking the turn to difference, asserting the positivity and specificity of female experience and values [. . .].

Feminist separatism was the earliest expression of such gynocentric feminism. Feminist separatism rejected wholly or partly the goal of entering the male-dominated world, because it requires playing according to rules that men have made and that have been used against women, and because trying to measure up to male-defined standards inevitably involves accommodating or pleasing the men who continue to dominate socially valued institutions and activities. Separatism promoted the empowerment of women through self-organization, the creation of separate and safe spaces where women could share and analyze their experiences, voice their anger, play with and create bonds with one another, and develop new and better institutions and practices.

Most elements of the contemporary women's movement have been separatist to some degree. Separatists seeking to live as much of their lives as possible in women-only institutions were largely responsible for the creation of the women's culture that burst forth all over the United States by the mid 1970s, and continues to claim the loyalty of millions of women – in the form of music, poetry, spirituality, literature, celebrations, festivals, and dances [. . .]. Whether drawing on images of Amazonian grandeur, recovering and revaluing traditional women's arts, like quilting and weaving, or inventing new rituals based on medieval witchcraft, the development of such expressions of women's culture gave many feminists images of a female-centered beauty and strength entirely outside capitalist patriarchal definitions of feminine pulchritude. The separatist impulse also fostered the development of the many autonomous women's institutions and services that have concretely improved the lives of many women, whether feminists or not – such as health clinics, battered women's shelters, rape crisis centers, and women's coffeehouses and bookstores.

Beginning in the late 1970s much feminist theory and political analysis also took a turn away from humanist feminism, to question the assumption that traditional female activity expresses primarily the victimization of women and the distortion of their human potential and that the goal of women's liberation is the participation of women as equals in public institutions now dominated by men. Instead of understanding the activities and values associated with traditional femininity as largely distortions and inhibitions of women's truly human potentialities, this gynocentric analysis sought to revalue the caring, nurturing, and cooperative approach to social relations they found associated with feminine socialization, and sought in women's specific experiences the bases for an attitude toward the body and nature healthier than that predominant in male-dominated Western capitalist culture.

None of the social movements asserting positive group specificity is in fact a unity. All have group differences within them. The Black movement, for example, includes middle-class Blacks and working-class Blacks, gays and straight people, men and women, and so it is with any other group. The implications of group differences within a social group have been most systematically discussed in the women's movement. Feminist conferences and publications have generated particularly fruitful, though often emotionally wrenching, discussions of the oppression of racial and ethnic blindness and the importance of attending to group differences among women [. . .]. From such discussions emerged principled efforts to provide autonomously organized forums of Black women, Latinas, Jewish women, lesbians, differently abled women, old women, and any other women who see reason for claiming that they have as a group a distinctive voice that might be silenced in a general feminist discourse. Those discussions, along with the practices feminists instituted to structure discussion and interaction among differently identifying groups of women, offer some beginning models for the development of a heterogeneous public. Each of the other social movements has also generated discussion of group differences that cut across their identities, leading to other possibilities of coalition and alliance.

## Emancipation through the politics of difference

Implicit in emancipatory movements asserting a positive sense of group difference is a different ideal of liberation, which might be called democratic cultural pluralism [. . .]. In this vision the good society does not eliminate or transcend group difference. Rather, there is equality among socially and culturally differentiated groups, who mutually respect one another and affirm one another in their differences. What are the reasons for rejecting the assimilationist ideal and promoting a politics of difference?

Some deny the reality of social groups. For them, group difference is an invidious fiction produced and perpetuated in order to preserve the privilege of the few. Others [. . .] may agree that social groups do now exist and have real social consequences for the way people identify themselves and one another, but assert that such social group differences are undesirable. The assimilationist ideal involves denying either the reality or the desirability of social groups.

Those promoting a politics of difference doubt that a society without group differences is either possible or desirable. Contrary to the assumption of modernization theory, increased urbanization and the extension of equal formal rights to all groups has not led to a decline in particularist affiliations. If anything, the urban concentration and interactions among groups that modernizing social processes introduce tend to reinforce group solidarity and differentiation [. . .]. Attachment to specific traditions, practices, language, and other culturally specific forms is a crucial aspect of social existence. People do not usually give up their social group identifications, even when they are oppressed.

Whether eliminating social group difference is possible or desirable in the long run, however, is an academic issue. Today and for the foreseeable future societies are certainly structured by groups, and some are privileged while others are oppressed. New social movements of group specificity do not deny the official story's claim that the ideal of liberation as eliminating difference and treating everyone the same has brought significant improvement in the status of excluded groups. Its main quarrel is with the story's conclusion, namely, that since we have achieved formal equality, only vestiges and holdovers of differential privilege remain, which will die out with the continued persistent assertion of an ideal of social relations that make differences irrelevant to a person's life prospects. The achievement of formal equality does not eliminate social differences, and rhetorical commitment to the sameness of persons makes it impossible even to name how those differences presently structure privilege and oppression.

Though in many respects the law is now blind to group differences, some groups continue to be marked as deviant, as the Other. In everyday interactions, images, and decisions, assumptions about women, Blacks, Hispanics, gay men and lesbians, old people, and other marked groups continue to justify exclusion, avoidance, paternalism, and authoritarian treatment. Continued racist, sexist, homophobic, ageist, and ableist institutions and behavior create particular circumstances for these groups usually disadvantaging them in their opportunity to develop their capacities. Finally, in part because they have been segregated from one another, and in part because they have particular histories and traditions, there are cultural differences among social groups – differences in language, style of living, body comportment and gestures, values, and perspectives on society.

Today in American society, as in many other societies, there is widespread agreement that no person should be excluded from political and economic activities because of ascribed characteristics. Group differences nevertheless continue to exist, and certain groups continue to be privileged. Under these circumstances, insisting that equality and liberation entail ignoring difference has oppressive consequences in three respects.

First, blindness to difference disadvantages groups whose experience, culture, and socialized capacities differ from those of privileged groups. The strategy of assimilation aims to bring formerly excluded groups into the mainstream. So assimilation always implies coming into the game after it is already begun, after the rules and standards have already been set, and having to prove oneself according to those rules and standards. In the assimilationist strategy, the privileged groups implicitly define the standards according to which all will be measured. Because their privilege involves not recognizing these standards as culturally and experientially specific, the ideal of a common humanity in which all can participate without regard to race, gender, religion, or sexuality poses as neutral and universal. The real differences between oppressed groups and the dominant norm, however, tend to put them at a disadvantage in measuring up to these standards, and for that reason assimilationist policies perpetuate their disadvantage. [. . .]

Second, the ideal of a universal humanity without social group differences allows privileged groups to ignore their own group specificity. Blindness to difference perpetuates cultural imperialism by allowing norms expressing the point of view and experience of privileged groups to appear neutral and universal. The assimilationist ideal presumes that there is a humanity in general, an unsituated group-neutral human capacity for self-making that left to itself would make individuality flower, thus guaranteeing that each individual will be different. [. . .] Because there is no such unsituated group-neutral point of view, the situation and experience of dominant groups tend to define the norms of such a humanity in general. Against such a supposedly neutral humanist ideal, only the oppressed groups come to be marked with particularity; they, and not the privileged groups, are marked, objectified as the Others.

Thus, third, this denigration of groups that deviate from an allegedly neutral standard often produces an internalized devaluation by members of those groups themselves. When there is an ideal of general human standards according to which everyone should be evaluated equally, then Puerto Ricans or Chinese Americans are ashamed of their accents or their parents, Black children despise the female-dominated kith and kin networks of their neighborhoods, and feminists seek to root out their tendency to cry, or to feel compassion for a frustrated stranger. The aspiration to assimilate helps produce the self-loathing and double consciousness characteristic of oppression. The goal of assimilation holds up to people a demand that they 'fit,' be like the mainstream, in behavior, values, and goals. At the same time, as long as group differences exist, group members will be marked as different – as Black, Jewish, gay – and thus as unable simply to fit. When participation is taken to imply assimilation the oppressed person is caught in an irresolvable dilemma: to participate means to accept and adopt an identity one is not, and to try to participate means to be reminded by oneself and others of the identity one is.

A more subtle analysis of the assimilationist ideal might distinguish between a conformist and a transformational ideal of assimilation. In the conformist ideal, status quo institutions and norms are assumed as given, and disadvantaged groups who differ from those norms are expected to conform to them. A transformational ideal of assimilation, on the other hand, recognizes that institutions as given express the interests and perspective of the dominant groups. Achieving assimilation therefore requires altering many institutions and practices in accordance with neutral rules that truly do not disadvantage or stigmatize any person, so that group membership really is irrelevant to how persons are treated. Wasserstrom's ideal fits a transformational assimilation, as does the group-neutral ideal advocated by some feminists [. . .]. Unlike the conformist assimilationist, the transformational assimilationist may allow that group-specific policies, such as affirmative action, are necessary and appropriate means for transforming institutions to fit the assimilationist ideal. Whether conformist or transformational, however, the assimilationist ideal still denies that group difference can be positive and desirable; thus any form of the ideal of assimilation constructs group difference as a liability or disadvantage.

Under these circumstances, a politics that asserts the positivity of group difference is liberating and empowering. In the act of reclaiming the identity the dominant culture has taught them to despise [. . .], and affirming it as an identity to celebrate, the oppressed remove double consciousness. I am just what they say I am – a Jewboy, a colored girl, a fag, a dyke, or a hag – and proud of it. No longer does one have the impossible project of trying to become something one is not under circumstances where the very trying reminds one of who one is. This politics asserts that oppressed groups have distinct cultures, experiences, and perspectives on social life with humanly positive meaning, some of which may even be superior to the culture and perspective of mainstream society. The rejection and devaluation of one's culture and perspective should not be a condition of full participation in social life.

Asserting the value and specificity of the culture and attributes of oppressed groups, moreover, results in a relativizing of the dominant culture. When feminists assert the validity of feminine sensitivity and the positive value of nurturing behavior, when gays describe the prejudice of heterosexuals as homophobic and their own sexuality as positive and self-developing, when Blacks affirm a distinct Afro-American tradition, then the dominant culture is forced to discover itself for the first time as specific: as Anglo, European, Christian, masculine, straight. In a political struggle where oppressed groups insist on the positive value of their specific culture and experience, it becomes increasingly difficult for dominant groups to parade their norms as neutral and universal, and to construct the values and behavior of the oppressed as deviant, perverted, or inferior. By puncturing the universalist claim to unity that expels some groups and turns them into the Other, the assertion of positive group specificity introduces the possibility of understanding the relation between groups as merely difference, instead of exclusion, opposition, or dominance.

The politics of difference also promotes a notion of group solidarity against the individualism of liberal humanism. Liberal humanism treats each person as an individual, ignoring differences of race, sex, religion, and ethnicity. Each person should be evaluated only according to her or his individual efforts and achievements. With the institutionalization of formal equality some members of formerly excluded groups have indeed succeeded, by mainstream standards. Structural patterns of group privilege and oppression nevertheless remain. When political leaders of oppressed groups reject assimilation they are often affirming group solidarity. Where the dominant culture refuses to see anything but the achievement of autonomous individuals, the oppressed assert that we shall not separate from the people with whom we identify in order to 'make it' in a white Anglo male world.

The politics of difference insists on liberation of the whole group of Blacks, women, American Indians, and that this can be accomplished only through basic institutional changes. These changes must include group representation in policymaking and an elimination of the hierarchy of rewards that forces everyone to compete for scarce positions at the top.

Thus the assertion of a positive sense of group difference provides a standpoint from which to criticize prevailing institutions and norms. Black Americans find in their traditional communities, which refer to their members as 'brother' and 'sister,' a sense of solidarity absent from the calculating individualism of white professional capitalist society. Feminists find in the traditional female values of nurturing a challenge to a militarist world-view, and lesbians find in their relationships a confrontation with the assumption of complementary gender roles in sexual relationships. From their experience of a culture tied to the land American Indians formulate a critique of the instrumental rationality of European culture that results in pollution and ecological destruction. Having revealed the specificity of the dominant norms which claim universality and neutrality, social movements of the oppressed are in a position to inquire how the dominant institutions must be changed so that they will no longer reproduce the patterns of privilege and oppression.

From the assertion of positive difference the self-organization of oppressed groups follows. Both liberal humanist and leftist political organizations and movements have found it difficult to accept this principle of group autonomy. In a humanist emancipatory politics, if a group is subject to injustice, then all those interested in a just society should unite to combat the powers that perpetuate that injustice. If many groups are subject to injustice, moreover, then they should unite to work for a just society. The politics of difference is certainly not against coalition, nor does it hold that, for example, white should not work against racial injustice or men against sexist injustice. This politics of group assertion, however, takes as a basic principle that members of oppressed groups need separate organizations that exclude others, especially those from more privileged groups. Separate organization is probably necessary in order for these groups to discover and reinforce the positivity of their specific experience, to collapse and eliminate double consciousness. In discussions within autonomous organizations, group members can determine their specific needs and interests. Separation and self-organization risk creating pressures toward homogenization of the groups themselves, creating new privileges and exclusions [. . .]. But contemporary emancipatory social movements have found group autonomy an important vehicle for empowerment and the development of a group-specific voice and perspective.

Integration into the full life of the society should not have to imply assimilation to dominant norms and abandonment of groups affiliation and culture [. . .]. If the only alternative to the oppressive exclusion of some groups defined as Other by dominant ideologies is the assertion that they are the same as everybody else, then they will continue to be excluded because they are not the same.

Some might object to the way I have drawn the distinction between an assimilationist ideal of liberation and a radical democratic pluralism. They might claim that I have not painted the ideal of a society that transcends group differences fairly, representing it as homogeneous and conformist. The free society envisaged by liberalism, they might say, is certainly pluralistic. In it persons can affiliate with whomever they choose; liberty encourages a proliferation of life styles, activities, and associations. While I have no quarrel with social diversity in this sense, this vision of liberal pluralism does not touch on the primary issues that give rise to the politics of difference. The vision of liberation as the transcendence of group difference seeks to abolish the public and political significance of group difference, while retaining and promoting both individual and group diversity in private, or nonpolitical, social contexts. [. . .] I argued that this way of distinguishing public and private spheres, where the public represents universal citizenship and the private individual differences, tends to result in group exclusion from the public. Radical democratic pluralism acknowledges and affirms the public and political significance of social group differences as a means of ensuring the participation and inclusion of everyone in social and political institutions. [. . .]

# Chapter 20

# Will Kymlicka

# MULTICULTURAL CITIZENSHIP

## The politics of multiculturalism

**M**ODERN SOCIETIES ARE increasingly confronted with minority groups demanding recognition of their identity, and accommodation of their cultural differences. This is often phrased as the challenge of 'multiculturalism'. But the term 'multicultural' covers many different forms of cultural pluralism, each of which raises its own challenges. There are a variety of ways in which minorities become incorporated into political communities, from the conquest and colonization of previously self-governing societies to the voluntary immigration of individuals and families. These differences in the mode of incorporation affect the nature of minority groups, and the sort of relationship they desire with the larger society.

Generalizations about the goals or consequences of multiculturalism can therefore be very misleading. Indeed, much of the public debate over multiculturalism suffers from this flaw. For example, opponents of multiculturalism often say that it ghettoizes minorities, and impedes their integration into mainstream society; proponents respond that this concern for integration reflects cultural imperialism. Both of these charges are over-generalizations which ignore differences amongst minority groups, and misinterpret their actual motivations. [. . .]

I focus on two broad patterns of cultural diversity. In the first case, cultural diversity arises from the incorporation of previously self-governing, territorially concentrated cultures into a larger state. These incorporated cultures, which I call 'national minorities', typically wish to maintain themselves as distinct societies alongside the majority culture, and demand various forms of autonomy or self-government to ensure their survival as distinct societies.

In the second case, cultural diversity arises from individual and familial immigration. Such immigrants often coalesce into loose associations which I call 'ethnic groups'. They typically wish to integrate into the larger society, and to be accepted as full members of it. While they often seek greater recognition of their ethnic identity, their aim is not to become a separate and self-governing nation alongside the larger society, but to modify the institutions and laws of the mainstream society to make them more accommodating of cultural differences. [. . .]

One source of cultural diversity is the coexistence within a given state of more than one nation, where 'nation' means a historical community, more or less institutionally complete, occupying a given territory or homeland, sharing a distinct language and culture. A 'nation' in this sociological sense is closely related to the idea of a 'people' or a 'culture' – indeed, these concepts are often defined in terms of each other. A country which contains more than one nation is, therefore, not a nation-state but a multination state, and the smaller cultures form 'national minorities'. The incorporation of different nations into a single state may be involuntary, as occurs when one cultural community is invaded and conquered by another, or is ceded from one imperial power to another, or when its homeland is overrun by colonizing settlers. But the formation of a multination state may also arise voluntarily, when different cultures agree to form a federation for their mutual benefit.

Many Western democracies are multinational. For example, there are a number of national minorities in the United States, including the American Indians, Puerto Ricans, the descendants of Mexicans (Chicanos) living in the south-west when the United States annexed Texas, New Mexico, and California after the Mexican War of 1846–8, native Hawaiians, the Chamorros of Guam, and various other Pacific Islanders. These groups were all involuntarily incorporated into the United States, through conquest or colonization. Had a different balance of power existed, these groups might have retained or established their own sovereign governments. And talk of independence occasionally surfaces in Puerto Rico or the larger Indian tribes. However, the historical preference of these groups has not been to leave the United States, but to seek autonomy within it.

As they were incorporated, most of these groups acquired a special political status. For example, Indian tribes are recognized as 'domestic dependent nations' with their governments, courts, and treaty rights; Puerto Rico is a 'Commonwealth'; and Guam is a 'Protectorate'. Each of these peoples is federated to the American polity with special powers of self-government. [. . .]

The second source of cultural pluralism is immigration. A country will exhibit cultural pluralism if it accepts large numbers of individuals and families from other cultures as immigrants, and allows them to maintain some of their ethnic particularity. This has always been a vital part of life in Australia, Canada, and the United States; which have the three highest per capita rates of immigration in the world. Indeed, well over half of all legal immigration in the world goes into one of these three countries.

Prior to the 1960s, immigrants to these countries were expected to shed their distinctive heritage and assimilate entirely to existing cultural norms. This is known as the 'Anglo-conformity' model of immigration. Indeed, some groups were denied entry if they were seen as unassimilable (e.g. restrictions on Chinese immigration in Canada and the United States, the 'white-only' immigration policy in

Australia). Assimilation was seen as essential for political stability, and was further rationalized through ethnocentric denigration of other cultures.

This shared commitment to Anglo-conformity is obscured by the popular but misleading contrast between the American 'melting-pot' and the Canadian 'ethnic mosaic'. While 'ethnic mosaic' carries the connotation of respect for the integrity of immigrant cultures, in practice it simply meant that immigrants to Canada had a choice of two dominant cultures to assimilate to. While Canada is binational, the 'uneasy tolerance which French and English were to show towards each other was not extended to foreigners who resisted assimilation or were believed to be unassimilable'.[1]

However, beginning in the 1970s, under pressure from immigrant groups, all three countries rejected the assimilationist model, and adopted a more tolerant and pluralistic policy which allows and indeed encourages immigrants to maintain various aspects of their ethnic heritage. It is now widely (though far from unanimously) accepted that immigrants should be free to maintain some of their old customs regarding food, dress, religion, and to associate with each other to maintain these practices. This is no longer seen as unpatriotic or 'unamerican'.

But it is important to distinguish this sort of cultural diversity from that of national minorities. Immigrant groups are not 'nations', and do not occupy homelands. Their distinctiveness is manifested primarily in their family lives and in voluntary associations, and is not inconsistent with their institutional integration. They still participate within the public institutions of the dominant culture(s) and speak the dominant language(s). For example, immigrants (except for the elderly) must learn English to acquire citizenship in Australia and the United States, and learning English is a mandatory part of children's education. In Canada, they must learn either of the two official languages (French or English). [. . .]

So while immigrant groups have increasingly asserted their right to express their ethnic particularity, they typically wish to do so within the public institutions of the English-speaking society (or French-speaking in Canada). In rejecting assimilation, they are not asking to set up a parallel society, as is typically demanded by national minorities. The United States and Australia, therefore, have a number of 'ethnic groups' as loosely aggregated subcultures within the larger English-speaking society, and so exhibit what I will call 'polyethnicity'. Similarly in Canada there are ethnic subcultures within both the English- and French-speaking societies. [. . .]

Obviously, a single country may be both multinational (as a result of the colonizing, conquest, or confederation of national communities) and polyethnic (as a result of individual and familial immigration). Indeed, all of these patterns are present in Canada – the Indians were overrun by French settlers, the French were conquered by the English, although the current relationship between the two can be seen as a voluntary federation, and both the English and French have accepted immigrants who are allowed to maintain their ethnic identity. So Canada is both multinational and polyethnic, as is the United States.

Those labels are less popular than the term 'multicultural'. But that term can be confusing, precisely because it is ambiguous between multinational and polyethnic. This ambiguity has led to unwarranted criticisms of the Canadian government's 'multiculturalism' policy, which is the term the government uses for its post-1970 policy of promoting polyethnicity rather than assimilation for immigrants. Some French Canadians have opposed the 'multiculturalism' policy because they think it reduces their claims of nationhood to the level of immigrant ethnicity.[2] Other people had the opposite fear that the policy was intended to treat immigrant groups as nations, and hence support the development of institutionally complete cultures alongside the French and English. In fact, neither fear was justified, since 'multiculturalism' is a policy of supporting polyethnicity within the national institutions of the English and French cultures [. . .]. Since 'multicultural' invites this sort of confusion, I will use the terms 'multinational' and 'polyethnic' to refer to the two main forms of cultural pluralism.

Some people use 'multicultural' in an even broader way, to encompass a wide range of non-ethnic social groups which have, for various reasons, been excluded or marginalized from the mainstream of society. This usage is particularly common in the United States, where advocates of a 'multicultural' curriculum are often referring to efforts to reverse the historical exclusion of groups such as the disabled, gays and lesbians, women, the working class, atheists, and Communists.[3]

This points out the complexity of the term 'culture'. Many of these groups do have a distinct culture in one common sense of that word – that is, where 'culture' refers to the distinct customs, perspectives, or ethos of a group or association, as when we talk about a 'gay culture', or even a 'bureaucratic culture'. This is perhaps the most localized meaning of 'a culture'. At the other extreme, using 'culture' in the widest sense, we can say that all of the Western democracies share a common 'culture' – that is, they all share a modern, urban, secular industrialized civilization, in contrast to the feudal, agricultural, and theocratic world of our ancestors.

These two non-ethnic senses of culture are captured by the OED's definition of culture as the 'customs' or 'civilization' of a group or people. If culture refers to the 'customs' of a group, then the various lifestyle enclaves, social movements, and voluntary associations which can be found in any modern society all have their own 'cultures'. Defined this way, even the most ethnically homogeneous state, like Iceland, would none the less be 'multicultural', since it contains a diverse array of associations and groups based on class, gender, sexual orientation, religion, moral belief, and political ideology.

If culture refers to the 'civilization' of a people, then virtually all modern societies share the same culture. Defined this way, even the most multinational country like Switzerland, or the most polyethnic country like Switzerland, or the most polyethnic country like Australia, is not very 'multicultural', in so far as the various national and ethnic groups all participate in the same modern industrialized form of social life.

I am using culture (and 'multicultural') in a different sense. My focus will be on the sort of 'multiculturalism' which arises from national and ethnic differences. As I said earlier, I am using 'a culture' as synonymous with 'a nation' or 'a people' – that is, as an intergenerational community, more or less institutionally complete, occupying a given territory or homeland, sharing a distinct language and history. And a state is multicultural if its members either belong to different nations (a multination state), or have emigrated from different nations (a polyethnic state), and if this fact is an important aspect of personal identity and political life.

This is simply my stipulative definition of 'culture' and 'multicultural', although I think it corresponds with one common usage of these terms. I am not including the sorts of lifestyle enclaves, social movements, and voluntary associations which others include within the ambit of multiculturalism. This is not because I think the issues raised by these groups and movements are unimportant. On the contrary, I take it as given that accommodating ethnic and national differences is only part of a larger struggle to make a more tolerant and inclusive democracy.

The marginalization of women, gays and lesbians, and the disabled cuts across ethnic and national lines – it is found in majority cultures and homogeneous nation-states as well as national minorities and ethnic groups – and it must be fought in all these places. An adequate theory of the rights of cultural minorities must there-fore be compatible with the just demands of disadvantaged social groups, and I hope to show that my theory meets this test. Moreover, as I will discuss, there are important analogies between the claims of justice made by these social movements and the claims of ethnic groups, since both have been excluded and marginalized in virtue of their 'difference'.

Given these analogies, some people are tempted to say that these social groups form distinct 'cultures' or 'subcultures', and that the struggle against their oppres-sion is a struggle for 'multiculturalism'.[4] And there is a sense in which gays and lesbians, women, and the disabled form separate cultures within the larger society. But this is very different from the sense in which the Québécois form a separate culture within Canada, and it is important to keep these different senses of cultures (and 'multiculturalism') in mind.

[. . .] I will not describe all of these groups as 'cultures' or 'subcultures'; nor will I use 'multiculturalism' as an umbrella term for every group-related differ-ence in moral perspective or personal identity, although I recognize that this may be an appropriate usage in other contexts. What matters is not the terminology we use, but that we keep certain distinctions in mind. I believe, as I will argue throughout the book, that it is important to distinguish national minorities (distinct and potentially self-governing societies incorporated into a larger state) from ethnic groups (immigrants who have left their national community to enter another society). We can distinguish both of these from what are often called 'new social movements' – that is, associations and movements of gays, women, the poor, the disabled – who have been marginalized within their own national society or ethnic group. Each raises its own distinctive issues, and must be examined on its own merits. My focus [. . .] will be on the first two [. . .].

Virtually all liberal democracies are either multinational or polyethnic, or both. The 'challenge of multiculturalism' is to accommodate these national and ethnic differences in a stable and morally defensible way [. . .]. In this section, I will discuss some of the most important ways in which democracies have responded to the demands of national minorities and ethnic groups.

In all liberal democracies, one of the major mechanisms for accommodating cultural differences is the protection of the civil and political rights of individuals. It is impossible to overstate the importance of freedom of association, religion, speech, mobility, and political organization for protecting group difference. These rights enable individuals to form and maintain the various groups and associations which constitute civil society, to adapt these groups to changing circumstances, and to promote their views and interests to the wider population. The protection afforded by these common rights of citizenship is sufficient for many of the legitimate forms of diversity in society.

Various critics of liberalism – including some Marxists, communitarians, and feminists – have argued that the liberal focus on individual rights reflects an atomistic, materialistic, instrumental, or conflictual view of human relationships. I believe that this criticism is profoundly mistaken, and that individual rights can be and typically are used to sustain a wide range of social relationships. Indeed, the most basic liberal right – freedom of conscience – is primarily valuable for the protection it gives to intrinsically social (and non-instrumental) activities.

However, it is increasingly accepted in many countries that some forms of cultural difference can only be accommodated through special legal or constitutional measures, above and beyond the common rights of citizenship. Some forms of group difference can only be accommodated if their members have certain group-specific rights – what Iris Young calls 'differentiated citizenship' [. . .].

## Individual rights and collective rights

Many liberals fear that the 'collective rights' demanded by ethnic and national groups are, by definition, inimical to individual rights. This view has been popularized in Canada by former Prime Minister Pierre Trudeau, who explained his opposition to self-government rights for Quebec by saying that he believed in 'the primacy of the individual', and that 'only the individual is the possessor of rights' [. . .].

However, this rhetoric about individual versus collective rights is unhelpful. We need to distinguish two kinds of claims that an ethnic or national group might make. The first involves the claim of a group against its own members; the second involves the claim of a group against the larger society. Both kinds of claims can be seen as protecting the stability of national or ethnic communities, but they respond to different sources of instability. The first kind is intended to protect the group from the destabilizing impact of *internal dissent* (e.g. the decision of individual members not to follow traditional practices or customs), whereas the second is intended to protect the group from the impact of *external decisions* (e.g. the economic or political decisions of the larger society). To distinguish these two kinds of claims, I will call the first 'internal restrictions', and the second 'external protections'.

Both of these get labelled as 'collective rights', but they raise very different issues. Internal restrictions involve *intra-group* relations – the ethnic or national group may seek the use of state power to restrict the liberty of its own members in the name of group solidarity. This raises the danger of individual oppression. Critics of 'collective rights' in this sense often invoke the image of theocratic and patriarchal cultures where women are oppressed and religious orthodoxy legally enforced as an example of what can happen when the alleged rights of the collectivity are given precedence over the rights of the individual.

Of course, all forms of government and all exercises of political authority involve restricting the liberty of those subject to the authority. In all countries, no matter how liberal and democratic, people are required to pay taxes to support public goods. Most democracies also require people to undertake jury duty, or to perform some amount of military or community service, and a few countries require people to vote (e.g. Australia). All governments expect and sometimes require a minimal level of civic responsibility and participation from their citizens.

But some groups seek to impose much greater restrictions on the liberty of their members. It is one thing to require people to do jury duty or to vote, and quite another to compel people to attend a particular church or to follow traditional gender roles. The former are intended to uphold liberal rights and democratic institutions, the latter restrict these rights in the name of cultural tradition or religious orthodoxy. For the purposes of this discussion, I will use 'internal restrictions' to refer only to the latter sort of case, where the basic civil and political liberties of group members are being restricted.[5] [. . .]

The two kinds of claims need not go together. Some ethnic or national groups seek external protections against the larger society without seeking to impose legally enforceable internal restrictions on their own members. Other groups do not claim any external protection against the larger community, but seek wide powers over the behaviour of their own members. Yet other groups make both kinds of claims. These variations lead to fundamentally different conceptions of minority rights, and it is important to determine what sort of claim a group is making. [. . .] I will argue that liberals can and should endorse certain external protections, where they promote fairness between groups, but should reject internal restrictions which limit the right of group members to question and revise traditional authorities and practices. [. . .]

It is often difficult for outsiders to assess the likelihood that self-government for an indigenous or national minority will lead to the suppression of basic individual rights. The identification of oppression requires sensitivity to the specific situation, particularly when dealing with other cultures. [. . .]

It is also possible for polyethnic rights to be used to impose internal restrictions. Immigrant groups and religious minorities could, in principle, seek the legal power to impose traditional cultural practices on their members. Ethnic groups could demand the right to take their children out of school before the legally prescribed age, so as to reduce the chances that the child will leave the community; or the right to continue traditional customs such as clitoridectomy or compulsory arranged marriages that violate existing laws regarding informed consent. There have been cases of husbands who have beaten their wives because they took a job outside the home, and who have then used the fact that wife assault is acceptable practice in their original homeland as a legal defence. More generally, there are fears that 'multiculturalism taken to its logical extreme' could justify allowing each ethnic group to impose its own legal traditions on its members, even when these traditions conflict with basic human rights and constitutional principles. [. . .]

The threat to individual rights from such internal restrictions is real enough. But it is a mistake to suggest that allowing such oppressive practices is the 'logical' extension of current 'multiculturalism' policies in the major immigrant countries. Existing policies are intended to enable immigrants to express their ethnic identity, if they so desire, and to reduce some of the external pressures on them to assimilate. It is perfectly logical to accept that aim, while denying that groups are entitled to impose practices on members who do not wish to maintain them. The model of polyethnicity underlying public policy in Canada, Australia, and the United States supports the ability of immigrants to choose for themselves whether to maintain their ethnic identity. There is no suggestion that ethnic groups should have any ability to regulate individuals' freedom to accept or reject that identity. As such, public policy (quite consistently) endorses some external protections, while rejecting internal restrictions [. . .].

Moreover, there is little support for the imposition of internal restrictions amongst the members of minority groups themselves. Very few of the mainstream immigrant organizations within Western democracies have sought such policies.[6] Most demands for polyethnic rights are defended in terms of, and take the form of, external protections against the larger community.

Of course, some groups do demand internal restrictions. This is particularly true of religious communities, rather than immigrant groups *per se*. [. . .]

For example, the Salman Rushdie affair has led some British Muslims to propose group-libel laws that would provide the same protection to religious groups that hate-speech laws provide to racial groups. In the case of hate-speech laws, the motivation was to provide a form of external protection – that is, to protect blacks and Jews from racist elements in the larger society. Group-libel laws are often similarly defended as a way of protecting Muslims from the virulent 'Islamophobia' of Western countries. But group-libel laws can also be used to restrict the spread of blasphemy or apostasy within a religious community. Indeed, as the example of Rushdie himself suggests, there is reason to think that some Muslim leaders seek such laws primarily to control apostasy within the Muslim community, rather than to control the expression of non-Muslims. Laws that are justified in terms of external protection can open the door to internal restrictions. [. . .]

In so far as internal restrictions are present, they are often defended in this way as unavoidable by-products of external protections, rather than as desirable in and of themselves.[7] There is little enthusiasm for what we might call 'pure' internal restrictions – that is, protecting the historical customs or religious character of an ethnic or national group through limitations on the basic civil liberties of its members.

This distinction between internal restrictions and external protections is often ignored by both proponents and critics of group-differentiated rights. Thus we find liberal critics who assume that all forms of group-differentiated citizenship are 'affected by an inherent deficiency in that they place the group over and above the individual' [. . .]. While this is a relevant objection to internal restrictions, it is not valid for external protections, which do not 'place the group over and above the individual'.

The same mistake is also made by proponents of group-differentiated citizenship. For example, some Aboriginals in Canada have argued that their right to external protections against the larger society entails the right to limit the basic liberties of their own members. This was evident in two recent court cases in Canada. The first case involved the special fishing rights of Aboriginal peoples, which are a form of external protection. Fishing is an important aspect of some Aboriginal cultures, and guaranteed fishing rights ensure that they are not outbid or outvoted by the larger society on decisions regarding access to fishing. These external protections were upheld by the Canadian Supreme Court. [. . .]

We can now see why the term 'collective rights' is so unhelpful as a label for the various forms of group-differentiated citizenship. The problem is partly that the term is too broad, and partly that it fails to distinguish internal restrictions from external protections. But a deeper problem is that it suggests a false dichotomy with individual rights. [. . .]

So describing group-differentiated citizenship in the language of collective rights is doubly misleading. Some group-differentiated rights are in fact exercised by individuals, and in any event the question of whether the rights are exercised by individuals or collectives is not the fundamental issue. The important issue is why certain rights are group-differentiated – that is, why the members of certain groups should have rights regarding land, language, representation, etc. that the members of other groups do not have.[8]

This conflation of group-differentiated citizenship with collective rights has had a disastrous effect on the philosophical and popular debate. Because they view the debate in terms of collective rights, many people assume that the debate over group-differentiated citizenship is essentially equivalent to the debate between individualists and collectivists over the relative priority of the individual and the community. Individualists argue that the individual is morally prior to the community: the community matters only because it contributes to the well-being of the individuals who compose it. If those individuals no longer find it worthwhile to maintain existing cultural practices, then the community has no independent interest in preserving those practices, and no right to prevent individuals from modifying or rejecting them. Hence individualists reject the idea that ethnic and national groups have any collective rights.

Collectivists, by contrast, deny that a community's interests are reducible to the interests of the members who compose it. They put collective rights on a par with individual rights, and defend them in a parallel way. Theories of individual rights begin by explaining what an individual is, what interests she has *qua* individual, and then derive a set of individual rights that protect those interests. Similarly, collectivists begin by explaining what a community is, what interests it has *qua* community, and then derive a set of community rights that protect those interests. Just as certain individual rights flow from each individual's interest in personal liberty, so certain community rights flow from each community's interest in self-preservation. These community rights must then be weighed against the right of the individuals who compose the community. [. . .]

## Notes

1    [. . .] In so far as immigrant groups seem more cohesive in Canada, this is probably due to the fact that they contain a higher proportion of recent migrants than US ethnic groups, which in turn is due to Canada's higher immigration rate. In 1981, 16.1% of Canadian residents were foreign-born, compared to 6.2% of Americans [. . .]. However, the process of integration for settled immigrants and their children is similar in both counties. The term 'melting-pot' is also somewhat misleading. It referred primarily to the biological fusing of various (white) ethnic groups through intermarriage, more than the fusing of their

cultural practices. According to Theodore Roosevelt, the 'representatives of many old-world races are being fused together into a new type', but 'the crucible into which all the new types are melted into one was shaped from 1776 to 1789, and our nationality was definitely fixed in all its essentials by the men of Washington's day' [. . .]. This was particularly true of language [. . .].

2  As René Lévesque, former premier of Quebec, put it, multiculturalism 'is a "Red Herring". The notion was devised to obscure "the Quebec business", to give an impression that we are all ethnics and do not have to worry about special status for Quebec' [. . .]. Similar concerns have been raised by the Maori in New Zealand – i.e. that the rhetoric of 'multiculturalism' is a way of denying their national claims, by lumping them in with the polyethnic claims of non-British immigrants [. . .].

I should note that many writers use the term 'ethnic group' to refer, not to immigrant groups, but to national minorities which have not mobilized politically. On this usage, ethnic groups are pre-political national groups [. . .]. Obviously, I am using 'ethnic' and 'national' in a different way, to refer to a group's mode of incorporation into a larger society, not its level of political mobilization. On my usage there can be quiescent national minorities, and highly mobilized immigrant groups. [. . .]

3  These various senses of culture are reflected in the different meanings attached to the term 'multiculturalism' in different countries. In Canada, it typically refers to the right of immigrants to express their ethnic identity without fear of prejudice or discrimination; in Europe, it often refers to the sharing of powers between national communities; in the USA, it is often used to include the demand of marginalized social groups.

4  Part of the motivation for this approach is that many illiberal accounts of the value of national and ethnic differences end up rationalizing oppression within the minority group in the name of respect for traditions, or protecting the 'authenticity' or 'integrity' of cultures [. . .]. One way to defend against this danger is to insist that gays or women form their own cultures, and that the integrity of their cultures also deserves respect. [. . .] I will take a more direct line of attack, however, by severing the defence of cultural rights from any illiberal hallowing of 'tradition' and 'authenticity', and instead connecting it to a liberal theory of justice that is committed to individual autonomy and social equality [. . .]. A related concern is that defining multiculturalism in terms of ethnic and national differences may lead to a neglect of disadvantaged groups, whose demands get obscured beneath the fashionable concern for multiculturalism. This is a legitimate concern, but it is worth noting that the danger runs in both directions. That is, some advocates of a 'politics of difference', whose focus is primarily on disadvantaged groups, obscure the distinctive demands of national groups. I think this is true, for example, of Iris Young's influential work on the 'politics of difference'. While she ostensibly includes the demands of American Indians and New Zealand Maori in her account of group-differentiated citizenship, she in fact misinterprets their demands by treating them as a marginalized group, rather than as self-governing nations [. . .]. The best way to ensure that neither sort of group is made invisible is to keep them clearly distinguished.

5  Obviously, groups are free to require such actions as terms of membership in private, voluntary associations. A Catholic organization can insist that its members attend church. The problem arises when a group seeks to use governmental

power to restrict the liberty of members. Liberals insist that whoever exercises political power within a community must respect the civil and political rights of its members, and any attempt to impose internal restrictions which violate this condition is illegitimate.

6   E.g., while the practices of suttee and female infanticide are still defended in parts of India, no Hindu immigrant organization in a Western democracy has sought the freedom to continue them. These are extreme cases, but they reflect a general trend. Internal restrictions which are deeply rooted in the immigrant's homeland often become undesired – even unthinkable – in the new country. [. . .]

7   [. . .] Another example of the way that internal restrictions and external protections are combined is the language laws in Quebec. This example is complex, since the laws distinguish between various kinds of language use (government services, education, workplace, and commercial signs), and various groups (resident anglophones, anglophones who move to Quebec from other provinces, francophones, and immigrants). The primary justification for these laws is to ensure equal opportunity for francophones against the economic and political pressure of the anglophone majority in Canada (and North America). As such, they have been quite successful, particularly in enabling francophones to use French in the workplace. However, some aspects of these laws involve internal restrictions. For example, the law not only guarantees that commercial signs are available in French, it also restricts the availability of signs in English, thereby preventing francophones from voluntarily choosing to use English. This is partly an internal restriction, since it is partly designed to protect the stability of Québécois society from the choices of its own members. It is also partly an over-restrictive external protection, since it unnecessarily restricts the freedom of anglophones to use their own language [. . .].

8   The same problem arises with other popular terms used to describe these policies: e.g. some people refer to the various forms of group-differentiated rights as 'community rights' or 'group rights'. However, these terms also imply a false contrast with individual rights. Moreover, 'community rights' gives a misleading sense of the homogeneity of the cultural group. Ethnic and national groups are not 'communities' if that means a group of people united by a common set of beliefs or values, or even a sense of solidarity. As I discuss later, ethnic and national groups can be deeply divided in terms of their political, religious, or lifestyle commitments, and the term 'community' can serve to obscure these divisions (see I. Young 1990: ch. 8).

The term 'minority rights' is somewhat better, since it does not imply an artificial contrast between individual and group-specific rights. However, it is potentially misleading in another way, since it has historically been used to refer to any constitutional restrictions on the scope of majority rule, including restrictions protecting the common rights of citizenship. Hence guarantees of freedom of conscience have often been seen as a 'minority right', since they have protected religious minorities from persecution by the majority. Moreover, all these terms suffer from the fact that many of the claims made by ethnic and national groups do not in fact take the form of *rights*, in the strict legal sense of that term. They may instead take the form of legislative powers or legal immunities. To avoid ambiguity, I should perhaps talk about 'the claims of the members of ethnic and national groups for group-differentiated rights, powers, status or immunities, beyond the common rights of citizenship'. To save space, however, I will use 'group-differentiated rights' or 'minority rights' as the best available shorthand.

# NATIONALISM

- Benedict Anderson, Imagined communities: reflections on the origin and spread of nationalism

- Rogers Brubaker, Nationalism reframed: nationhood and the national question in the new Europe

**Benedict Anderson** was born in Kunming, Yunnan, China on 26 August 1936. He has taught at Cornell University. His books include *Imagined Communities* (1983) and *In the Mirror* (1985).

**Rogers Brubaker** is currently a Professor of Sociology at the University of California, Los Angeles. He is the author of *Nationalism Reframed* (1998) and *Citizenship and Nationhood in France and Germany* (1992).

# Chapter 21

# Benedict Anderson

## IMAGINED COMMUNITIES
## Reflections on the origin and spread of nationalism

### Introduction

PERHAPS WITHOUT BEING MUCH noticed yet, a fundamental transformation in the history of Marxism and Marxist movements is upon us. Its most visible signs are the recent wars between Vietnam, Cambodia and China. These wars are of world-historical importance because they are the first to occur between regimes whose independence and revolutionary credentials are undeniable, and because none of the belligerents has made more than the most perfunctory attempts to justify the bloodshed in terms of a recognizable *Marxist* theoretical perspective. While it was still just possible to interpret the Sino-Soviet border clashes of 1969, and the Soviet military interventions in Germany (1953), Hungary (1956), Czechoslovakia (1968), and Afghanistan (1980) in terms of – according to taste – 'social imperialism,' 'defending socialism,' etc., no one, I imagine, seriously believes that such vocabularies have much bearing on what has occurred in Indochina.

If the Vietnamese invasion and occupation of Cambodia in December 1978 and January 1979 represented the first *large-scale conventional war* waged by one revolutionary Marxist regime against another, China's assault on Vietnam in February rapidly confirmed the precedent. Only the most trusting would dare wager that in the declining years of this century any significant outbreak of inter-state hostilities will necessarily find the USSR and the PRC – let alone the smaller socialist states – supporting, or fighting on, the same side. Who can be confident that Yugoslavia and Albania will not one day come to blows? Those variegated groups who seek a withdrawal of the Red Army from its encampments in Eastern Europe should remind themselves of the degree to which its overwhelming presence has, since 1945, ruled out armed conflict between the region's Marxist regimes.

Such considerations serve to underline the fact that since World War II every successful revolution has defined itself in *national* terms – the People's Republic of

China, the Socialist Republic of Vietnam, and so forth – and, in so doing, has grounded itself firmly in a territorial and social space inherited from the prerevolutionary past.

Almost every year the United Nations admits new members. And many 'old nations,' once thought fully consolidated, find themselves challenged by 'sub'-nationalisms within their borders – nationalisms which, naturally, dream of shedding this subness one happy day. The reality is quite plain: the 'end of the era of nationalism,' so long prophesied, is not remotely in sight. Indeed, nation-ness is the most universally legitimate value in the political life of our time.

But if the facts are clear, their explanation remains a matter of long-standing dispute. Nation, nationality, nationalism – all have proved notoriously difficult to define, let alone to analyse. In contrast to the immense influence that nationalism has exerted on the modern world, plausible theory about it is conspicuously meagre.. . .

I propose the following definition of the nation: it is an imagined political community – and imagined as both inherently limited and sovereign.

It is *imagined* because the members of even the smallest nation will never know most of their fellow-members, meet them, or even hear of them, yet in the minds of each lives the image of their communion.. . .

The nation is imagined as *limited* because even the largest of them, encompassing perhaps a billion living human beings, has finite, if elastic, boundaries, beyond which lie other nations. No nation imagines itself coterminous with mankind. The most messianic nationalists do not dream of a day when all the members of the human race will join their nation in the way that it was possible, in certain epochs, for, say, Christians to dream of a wholly Christian planet.

It is imagined as *sovereign* because the concept was born in an age in which Enlightenment and Revolution were destroying the legitimacy of the divinely-ordained, hierarchical dynastic realm. Coming to maturity at a stage of human history when even the most devout adherents of any universal religion were inescapably confronted with the living *pluralism* of such religions, and the allomorphism between each faith's ontological claims and territorial stretch, nations dream of being free, and, if under God, directly so. The gage and emblem of this freedom is the sovereign state.

Finally, it is imagined as a *community*, because, regardless of the actual inequality and exploitation that may prevail in each, the nation is always conceived as a deep, horizontal comradeship. Ultimately it is this fraternity that makes it possible, over the past two centuries, for so many millions of people, not so much to kill, as willingly to die for such limited imaginings.

These deaths bring us abruptly face to face with the central problem posed by nationalism: what makes the shrunken imaginings of recent history (scarcely more than two centuries) generate such colossal sacrifices? I believe that the beginnings of an answer lie in the cultural roots of nationalism.

## Cultural roots

No more arresting emblems of the modern culture of nationalism exist than cenotaphs and tombs of Unknown Soldiers. The public ceremonial reverence accorded these monuments precisely *because* they are either deliberately empty or no one knows who lies inside them, has no true precedents in earlier times. To feel the force of this modernity one has only to imagine the general reaction to the busy-body who 'discovered' the Unknown Soldier's name or insisted on filling the cenotaph with some real bones. Sacrilege of a strange, contemporary kind! Yet void as these tombs are of identifiable mortal remains or immortal souls, they are nonetheless saturated with ghostly *national* imaginings. (This is why so many different nations have such tombs without feeling any need to specify the nation-ality of their absent occupants. What else could they be *but* Germans, Americans, Argentinians . . .?)

The cultural significance of such monuments becomes even clearer if one tries to imagine, say, a Tomb of the Unknown Marxist or a cenotaph for fallen Liberals. Is a sense of absurdity avoidable? The reason is that neither Marxism nor Liberalism are much concerned with death and immortality. If the nationalist imagining is so concerned, this suggests a strong affinity with religious imaginings. As this affinity is by no means fortuitous, it may be useful to begin a consideration of the cultural roots of nationalism with death, as the last of a whole gamut of fatalities. [. . .]

With the ebbing of religious belief, the suffering which belief in part composed did not disappear. Disintegration of paradise: nothing makes fatality more arbitrary. Absurdity of salvation: nothing makes another style of continuity more necessary. What then was required was a secular transformation of fatality into continuity, contingency into meaning. As we shall see, few things were (are) better suited to this end than an idea of nation. If nation-states are widely conceded to be 'new' and 'historical,' the nations to which they give political expression always loom out of an immemorial past, and, still more important, glide into a limitless future. It is the magic of nationalism to turn chance into destiny. With Debray we might say, 'Yes, it is quite accidental that I am born French; but after all, France is eternal.'

Needless to say, I am not claiming that the appearance of nationalism towards the end of the eighteenth century was 'produced' by the erosion of religious certainties, or that this erosion does not itself require a complex explanation. Nor am I suggesting that somehow nationalism historically 'supersedes' religion. What I am proposing is that nationalism has to be understood by aligning it, not with self-consciously held political ideologies, but with the large cultural systems that preceded it, out of which – as well as against which – it came into being. [. . .]

Our [. . .] conception of simultaneity has been a long time in the making, and its emergence is certainly connected, in ways that have yet to be well studied, with the development of the secular sciences. But it is a conception of such fundamental importance that, without taking it fully into account, we will find it difficult to probe the obscure genesis of nationalism. What has come to take the place of the mediaeval conception of simultaneity-along-time is, to borrow again from Benjamin, an idea of 'homogeneous, empty time,' in which simultaneity is, as it were, trans-verse, cross-time, marked not by prefiguring and fulfilment, but by temporal coincidence, and measured by clock and calendar.

Why this transformation should be so important for the birth of the imagined community of the nation can best be seen if we consider the basic structure of two forms of imagining which first flowered in Europe in the eighteenth century:

the novel and the newspaper. For these forms provided the technical means for 're-presenting' the *kind* of imagined community that is the nation.

Consider first the structure of the old-fashioned novel, a structure typical not only of the masterpieces of Balzac but also of any contemporary dollar-dreadful. It is clearly a device for the presentation of simultaneity in 'homogeneous, empty time,' or a complex gloss upon the word 'meanwhile'. Take, for illustrative purposes, a segment of a simple novel-plot, in which a man (A) has a wife (B) and a mistress (C), who in turn has a lover (D). We might imagine a sort of time-chart for this segment as follows:

| Time: | I | II | III |
| --- | --- | --- | --- |
| Events: | A quarrels with B | A telephones C | D gets drunk in a bar |
|  | C and D make love | B shops | A dines at home with B |
|  |  | D plays pool | C has an ominous dream |

Notice that during this sequence A and D never meet, indeed may not even be aware of each other's existence if C has played her cards right. What then actually links A to D? Two complementary conceptions: First, that they are embedded in 'societies' (Wessex, Lübeck, Los Angeles). These societies are sociological entities of such firm and stable reality that their members (A and D) can even be described as passing each other on the street, without ever becoming acquainted, and still be connected. Second, that A and D are embedded in the minds of the omniscient readers. Only they, like God, watch A telephoning C, B shopping, and D playing pool all *at once*. That all these acts are performed at the same clocked, calendrical time, but by actors who may be largely unaware of one another, shows the novelty of this imagined world conjured up by the author in his readers' minds.

The idea of a sociological organism moving calendrically through homogeneous, empty time is a precise analogue of the idea of the nation, which also is conceived as a solid community moving steadily down (or up) history. An American will never meet, or even know the names of more than a handful of his 240,000-odd fellow-Americans. He has no idea of what they are up to at any one time. But he has complete confidence in their steady, anonymous, simultaneous activity. [. . .]

[I]f we now turn to the newspaper as cultural product, we will be struck by its profound fictiveness. What is the essential literary convention of the newspaper? If we were to look at a sample front page of, say, *The New York Times*, we might find there stories about Soviet dissidents, famine in Mali, a gruesome murder, a coup in Iraq, the discovery of a rare fossil in Zimbabwe, and a speech by Mitterrand. Why are these events so juxtaposed? What connects them to each other? Not sheer caprice. Yet obviously most of them happen independently, without the actors being aware of each other or of what the others are up to. The arbitrariness of their inclusion and juxtaposition (a later edition will substitute a baseball triumph for Mitterrand) shows that the linkage between them is imagined.

This imagined linkage derives from two obliquely related sources. The first is simply calendrical coincidence. The date at the top of the newspaper, the single most important emblem on it, provides the essential connection – the steady onward clocking of homogeneous, empty time. Within that time, 'the world' ambles sturdily ahead. The sign for this: if Mali disappears from the pages of *The New York Times* after two days of famine reportage, for months on end, readers do not for a moment imagine that Mali has disappeared or that famine has wiped out all its citizens. The novelistic format of the newspaper assures them that somewhere out there the 'character' Mali moves along quietly, awaiting its next reappearance in the plot.

The second source of imagined linkage lies in the relationship between the newspaper, as a form of book, and the market. It has been estimated that in the 40-odd years between the publication of the Gutenberg Bible and the close of the fifteenth century, more than 20,000,000 printed volumes were produced in Europe. Between 1500 and 1600, the number manufactured had reached between 150,000,000 and 200,000,000. 'From early on [. . .] the printing shops looked more like modern workshops than the monastic workrooms of the Middle Ages. In 1455, Fust and Schoeffer were already running a business geared to standardised production, and twenty years later large printing concerns were operating everywhere in all [sic] Europe.' In a rather special sense, the book was the first modern-style mass-produced industrial commodity. The sense I have in mind can be shown if we compare the book to other early industrial products, such as textiles, bricks, or sugar. For these commodities are *measured* in mathematical amounts (pounds or loads or pieces). A pound of sugar is simply a quantity, a convenient load, not an object in itself. The book, however – and here it prefigures the durables of our time – is a distinct, self-contained object, exactly reproduced on a large scale. One pound of sugar flows into the next; each book has its own eremitic self-sufficiency. (Small wonder that libraries, personal collections of mass-produced commodities, were already a familiar sight, in urban centres like Paris, by the sixteenth century.)

In this perspective, the newspaper is merely an 'extreme form' of the book, a book sold on a colossal scale, but of ephemeral popularity. Might we say: one-day best-sellers? The obsolescence of the newspaper on the morrow of its printing – curious that one of the earlier mass-produced commodities should so prefigure the inbuilt obsolescence of modern durables – nonetheless, for just this reason, creates this extraordinary mass ceremony: the almost precisely simultaneous consumption ('imagining') of the newspaper-as-fiction. We know that particular morning and evening editions will overwhelmingly be consumed between this hour and that, only on this day, not that. (Contrast sugar, the use of which proceeds in an unclocked, continuous flow; it may go bad, but it does not go out of date.) The significance of this mass ceremony – Hegel observed that newspapers serve modern man as a substitute for morning prayers – is paradoxical. It is performed in silent privacy, in the lair of the skull. Yet each communicant is well aware that the ceremony he performs is being replicated simultaneously by thousands (or millions) of others of whose existence he is confident, yet of whose identity he has not the slightest notion. Furthermore, this ceremony is incessantly repeated at daily or half-daily intervals throughout the calendar. What more vivid figure for the secular, historically clocked, imagined community can be envisioned? At the same time, the newspaper reader, observing exact replicas of his own paper being consumed by his subway, barbershop, or residential neighbours, is continually reassured that the imagined world is visibly rooted in everyday life.[. . .]

## Patriotism and racism

In the preceding chapters I have tried to delineate the processes by which the nation came to be imagined, and, once imagined, modelled, adapted and transformed. Such an analysis has necessarily been concerned primarily with social change and different forms of consciousness. But it is doubtful whether either social change or transformed consciousnesses, in themselves, do much to explain the *attachment* that people feel for the inventions of their imaginations – or, to revive a question raised at the beginning of this text – why people are ready to die for these inventions.

In an age when it is so common for progressive, cosmopolitan intellectuals (particularly in Europe?) to insist on the near-pathological character of nationalism, its roots in fear and hatred of the Other, and its affinities with racism, it is useful to remind ourselves that nations inspire love, and often profoundly self-sacrificing love. The cultural products of nationalism – poetry, prose fiction, music, plastic arts – show this love very clearly in thousands of different forms and styles. On the other hand, how truly rare it is to find *analogous* nationalist products expressing fear and loathing. Even in the case of colonized peoples, who have every reason to feel hatred for their imperialist rulers, it is astonishing how insignificant the element of hatred is in these expressions of national feeling [. . .]

Something of the nature of this political love can be deciphered from the ways in which languages describe its object: either in the vocabulary of kinship (motherland, *Vaterland, patria*) or that of home (*heimat* or *tanah air* [earth and water, the phrase for the Indonesians' native archipelago]). Both idioms denote something to which one is naturally tied. As we have seen earlier, in everything 'natural' there is always something unchosen. In this way, nation-ness is assimilated to skin-colour, gender, parentage and birth-era – all those things one can not help. And in these 'natural ties' one senses what one might call 'the beauty of *gemeinschaft*'. To put it another way, precisely because such ties are not chosen, they have about them a halo of disinterestedness. [. . .]

[F]or most ordinary people of whatever class the whole point of the nation is that it is interestless. Just for that reason, it can ask for sacrifices.

As noted earlier, the great wars of this century are extraordinary not so much in the unprecedented scale on which they permitted people to kill, as in the colossal numbers persuaded to lay down their lives. Is it not certain that the numbers of those killed vastly exceeded those who killed? The idea of the ultimate sacrifice comes only with an idea of purity, through fatality.

Dying for one's country, which usually one does not choose, assumes a moral grandeur which dying for the Labour Party, the American Medical Association, or perhaps even Amnesty International cannot rival, for these are all bodies one can join or leave at easy will. Dying for the revolution also draws its grandeur from the degree to which it is felt to be something fundamentally pure. (If people imagined the proletariat *merely* as a group in hot pursuit of refrigerators, holidays, or power, how far would they, including members of the proletariat, be willing to die for it?). Ironically enough, it may be that to the extent that Marxist interpretations of history are felt (rather than intellected) as representations of ineluctable necessity, they also acquire an aura of purity and disinterestedness.

Here we may usefully return once more to language. First, one notes the primordialness of languages, even those known to be modern. No one can give the date for the birth of any language. Each looms up imperceptibly out of a horizonless past. (Insofar as *homo sapiens* is *homo dicens*, it can seem difficult to imagine an origin of language newer than the species itself.) Languages thus appear rooted beyond almost anything else in contemporary societies. At the same time, nothing connects us affectively to the dead more than language. If English-speakers hear the words 'Earth to earth, ashes to ashes, dust to dust' – created almost four-and-a-half centuries ago – they get a ghostly intimation of simultaneity across homogeneous, empty time. The weight of the words derives only in part from their solemn meaning; it comes also from an as-it-were ancestral 'Englishness'.

Second, there is a special kind of contemporaneous community which language alone suggests – above all in the form of poetry and songs. Take national anthems, for example, sung on national holidays. No matter how banal the words and mediocre the tunes, there is in this singing an experience of simultaneity. At precisely such moments, people wholly unknown to each other utter the same verses to the same melody. The image: unisonance. Singing the Marseillaise, Waltzing Matilda, and Indonesia Raya provide occasions for unisonality, for the echoed physical realization of the imagined community. (So does listening to [and maybe silently chiming in with] the recitation of ceremonial poetry, such as sections of *The Book of Common Prayer*.) How selfless this unisonance feels! If we are aware that others are singing these songs precisely when and as we are, we have no idea who they may be, or even where, out of earshot, they are singing. Nothing connects us all but imagined sound.

Yet such choruses are joinable in time. If I am a Lett, my daughter may be an Australian. The son of an Italian immigrant to New York will find ancestors in the Pilgrim Fathers. If nationalness has about it an aura of fatality, it is nonetheless a fatality embedded in *history*. Here San Martín's edict baptizing Quechua-speaking Indians as 'Peruvians' – a movement that has affinities with religious conversion – is exemplary. For it shows that from the start the nation was conceived in language, not in blood, and that one could be 'invited into' the imagined community [. . .]

## Note

Reading a newspaper is like reading a novel whose author has abandoned any thought of a coherent plot.

# Chapter 22

# Rogers Brubaker

## NATIONALISM REFRAMED
## Nationhood and the national question
## in the new Europe

M OST DISCUSSIONS OF NATIONHOOD are discussions of
*nations*. Nations are understood as real entities, as communities, as substantial, enduring collectivities. *That* they exist is taken for granted, although *how* they
exist – and how they came to exist – is much disputed.

A similar realism of the group long prevailed in many areas of sociology and
kindred disciplines. Yet in the last decade or so, at least four developments in social
theory have combined to undermine the treatment of groups as real, substantial
entities. The first is the growing interest in network forms, the flourishing of
network theory, and the increasing use of network as an overall orienting image
or metaphor in social theory. Second, there is the challenge posed by theories of
rational action, with their relentless methodological individualism, to realist understandings of groupness. The third development is a shift from broadly structuralist
to a variety of more 'constructivist' theoretical stances; while the former envisioned
groups as enduring components of social structure, the later see groupness as
constructed, contingent, and fluctuating. Finally, an emergent postmodernist theoretical sensibility emphasizes the fragmentary, the ephemeral, and the erosion of
fixed forms and clear boundaries. These developments are disparate, even contradictory. But they have converged in problematizing groupness, and in undermining
axioms of stable group being.

Yet this movement away from the realism of the group has been uneven. It
has been striking, to take just one example, in the study of class, especially in the
study of the working class – a term that is hard to use today without quotation
marks or some other distancing device. Indeed *the* working class – understood as
a real entity or substantial community – has largely dissolved as an object of analysis.
It has been challenged both by theoretical statements and by detailed empirical
research in social history, labor history, and the history of popular discourse and
mobilizaton.[1] The study of class as a cultural and political idiom, as a mode of

conflict, and as an underlying abstract dimension of economic structure remains vital; but it is no longer encumbered by an understanding of *classes* as real, enduring entities.

At the same time, an understanding of *nations* as real entities continues to inform the study of nationhood and nationalism. This realist, substantialist understanding of nations is shared by those who hold otherwise widely diverging views of nationhood and nationalism.

At one pole, it informs the view of nationalism held by nationalists themselves and by nationally minded scholars. On this view, nationalism presupposes the existence of nations, and expresses their strivings for autonomy and independence. Nations are conceived as collective individuals, capable of coherent, purposeful collective action. Nationalism is a drama in which nations are the key actors. One might think that this sociologically naïve view has no place in recent scholarship. But it has in fact flourished in recent years in interpretations of the national uprisings in the former Soviet Union.[2]

But the realist ontology of nations informs more sober and less celebratory scholarship as well. Consider just one indicator of this. Countless discussions of nationhood and nationalism begin with the question: what is a nation? This question is not as theoretically innocent as it seems: the very terms in which it is framed presuppose the existence of the entity that is to be defined. The question itself reflects the realist, substantialist belief that 'a nation' is a real entity of some kind, though perhaps one that is elusive and difficult to define.

The treatment of nations as real entities and substantial collectivities is not confined to so-called primordialists, meaning those who emphasize the deep roots, ancient origins, and emotive power of national attachments.[3] This view is also held by many 'modernists' and 'constructivists,' who see nations as shaped by such forces as industrialization, uneven development, the growth of communication and transportation networks, and the powerfully integrative and homogenizing forces of the modern state. Nor is the substantialist approach confined to those who define nations 'objectively,' that is in terms of shared objective characteristics such as language, religion, etc.; it is equally characteristic of those who emphasize subjective factors such as shared myths, memories, of self-understandings.

Paradoxically, the realist and substantialist approach informs even accounts that seek to debunk and demystify nationalism by denying the real existence of nations. On this view, if the nation is an illusory or spurious community, an ideological smokescreen, then nationalism must be a case of false consciousness, of mistaken identity. This approach reduces the question of the reality or real efficacy of nationhood or nationness to the question of the reality of nations as concrete communities or collectivities, thereby foreclosing alternative and more theoretically promising ways of conceiving nationhood and nationness.

The problem with this substantialist treatment of nations as real entities is that it adopts *categories of practice as categories of analysis*. It takes a conception inherent in the *practice* of nationalism and in the workings of the modern state and state-system – namely the realist, reifying conception of nations as real communities – and it makes this conception central to the *theory* of nationalism. Reification is a social process, not only an intellectual practice. As such, it is central to the phenomenon of nationalism, as we have seen all too clearly in the last few years.[4]

As analysts of nationalism, we should certainly try to *account* for this social process of reification – this process through which the political fiction of the nation becomes momentarily yet powerfully realized in practice. This may be one of the most important tasks of the theory of nationalism. But we should avoid unintentionally *reproducing* or *reinforcing* this reification of nations in practice with a reification of nations in theory.

To argue against the realist and substantialist way of thinking about nations is not to dispute the reality of nationhood.[5] It is rather to reconceptualize that reality. It is to decouple the study of nationhood and nationness from the study of nations as substantial entities, collectivities, or communities. It is a focus on nationness as conceptual variable, to adopt J. P. Nettl's phrase,[6] not on nations as real collectivities. It is to treat nation not as substance but as institutionalized form; not as collectivity but as practical category; not as entity but as contingent event. Only in this way can we capture the reality of nationhood and the real power of nationalism without invoking in our theories the very 'political fiction' of 'the nation' whose potency in practice we wish to explain.[7]

We should not ask 'what is a nation' but rather: how is nationhood as a political and cultural form institutionalized within and among states? How does nation work as practical category, as classificatory scheme, as cognitive frame? What makes the use of that category by or against states more or less resonant or effective? What makes the nation-evoking, nation-invoking efforts of political entrepreneurs more or less likely to succeed?[8]

This might seem an unpropitious moment for such an argument. The collapse of the Soviet Union, the national conflicts in the successor states, the ethnonational wars in Transcaucasia and the North Caucasus, the carnage in the former Yugoslavia: doesn't all this – it might be asked – vividly demonstrate the reality and power of nations? Doesn't it show that nations could survive as solidary groups, as foci of identity and loyalty and bases of collective action, despite the efforts of the Soviet and Yugoslav states to crush them?

In a context of rampant ethnonationalism, the temptation to adopt a nation-centred perspective is understandable. But the temptation should be resisted. Nationalism is not engendered by nations. It is produced – or better, it is induced – by *political fields* of particular kinds.[9] Its dynamics are governed by the properties of political fields, not by the properties of collectivities.

Take for example the case of Soviet and post-Soviet nationalisms. To see these as the struggles of nations, of real, solidary groups who somehow survived despite Soviet attempts to crush them – to suggest that nations and nationalism flourish today *despite* the Soviet regime's ruthlessly antinational policies – is to get things exactly backwards. Nationhood and nationalism flourish today largely *because of* the regime's policies. Although antinational*ist*, those policies were anything but anti-*national*. Far from ruthlessly suppressing nationhood, the Soviet regime pervasively institutionalized it. The regime repressed *nationalism*, of course; but at the same time [. . .] it went further than any other state before or since in institutionalizing territorial *nationhood* and ethnic *nationality* as fundamental social categories. In doing so it inadvertently created a political field supremely conducive to nationalism.

The regime did this in two days. On the one hand, it carved up the Soviet state into more than fifty national territories, each expressly defined as the homeland of and for a particular ethnonational group. The top-level national territories – those that are today the independent successor states – were defined as quasi-nation states, complete with their own territories, names, constitutions, legislatures, administrative staffs, cultural and scientific institutions, and so on.

On the other hand, the regime divided the citizenry into a set of exhaustive and mutually exclusive ethnic nationalities, over a hundred in all. Thus codified, ethnic nationality served not only as a *statistical category*, a fundamental unit of social accounting, but also, and more distinctively, as an *obligatory ascribed status*. It was assigned by the state at birth on the basis of descent. It was registered in personal identity documents. It was recorded in almost all bureaucratic encounters and official transactions. And it was used to control access to higher education and to certain desirable jobs, restricting the opportunities of some nationalities, especially Jews, and promoting others through preferential treatment policies for so-called 'titular' nationalities in 'their own' republics.

Long before Gorbachev, then, territorial nationhood and ethnic nationality were pervasively institutionalized social and cultural forms. These forms were by no means empty. They were scorned by Sovietologists – no doubt because the regime consistently and effectively repressed all signs of overt political nationalism, and sometimes even cultural nationalism. Yet the repression of nationalism went hand in hand with the establishment and consolidation of nationhood and nationality as fundamental cognitive and social forms. Under glasnost, these already pervasively institutionalized forms were readily politicized. They constituted elementary forms of political understanding, political rhetoric, political interest, and political identity. In the terms of Max Weber's 'switchman' metaphor, they determined the tracks, the cognitive frame, along which action was pushed by the dynamic of material and ideal interests. In so doing, they contributed powerfully to the breakup of the Soviet Union and to the structuring of nationalist politics in its aftermath.

I have argued that we should think about nation not as substance but as institutionalized form, not as collectivity but as practical category, not as entity but as contingent event. Having talked about nationhood as institutionalized form, and as cognitive and sociopolitical category, I want to say a few words in conclusion about nationness as event. Here my remarks will be even more sketchy and programmatic. I want simply to point to a gap in the literature, and to suggest one potentially fruitful line of work.

In speaking of nationness as event, I signal a double contrast. The first is between nation as entity and nationness as a variable property of groups, of relationships, and of what Margaret Somers has recently called 'relational settings.'[10] The second contrast is between thinking of nationhood or nationness as something that *develops*, and thinking of it as something that *happens*. Here I want to focus on this second contrast, between developmentalist and eventful perspectives. I borrow the latter term from a recent paper by William Sewell, Jr.[11]

We have a large and mature developmentalist literature on nationhood and nationalism. This literature traces the long-term political, economic, and cultural changes that led, over centuries, to the gradual emergence of nations or, as I would prefer to put it, of nationness. The major works of the last decade on nationhood and nationalism – notably by Ernest Gellner, Benedict Anderson, Anthony Smith, and Eric Hobsbawm[12] – are all developmentalist in this sense.

By contrast, we lack theoretically sophisticated eventful analyses of nationness and nationalism. There are of course many studies of particular nationalisms geared to much shorter time spans than the decades or centuries characteristic of the developmentalist literature. But those conducted by sociologists and political scientists have tended to abstract from events in their search for generalized structural or cultural explanations, while historians, taking for granted the significance of contingent events, have not been inclined to theorize them.[13]

I know of no sustained analytical discussions of nationness as an event, as something that suddenly crystallizes rather than gradually develops, as a contingent, conjuncturally fluctuating, and precarious frame of vision and basis for individual and collective action, rather than as a relatively stable product of deep developmental trends in economy, polity, or culture. Yet a strong theoretical case can be made for an eventful approach to nationness. As Craig Calhoun has recently argued, in a paper on the Chinese student protest movement of 1989, identity should be understood as a 'changeable product of collective action,' not as its stable underlying cause.[14] Much the same thing could be said about nationness.

A theoretically sophisticated eventful perspective on nationness and nationalism is today urgently needed. To make sense of the Soviet and Yugoslav collapse and their aftermaths, we need – among other things – to think theoretically about relatively sudden fluctuations in the 'nationness' of groups and relational settings. We need to think theoretically about the process of being 'overcome by nationhood,' to use the poignant phrase of the Croatian writer Slavenka Drakulic. Drakulic was characterizing her own situation. Like many of her postwar generation, she was largely indifferent to nationality. Yet she came – against her will – to be defined by her nationality alone, imprisoned by an all-too-successfully reified category.[15] As predicaments go, in the former Yugoslavia, this one is not especially grave. But it illustrates in personal terms a more general and fateful occurrence – the relatively sudden and pervasive 'nationalization' of public and even private life. This has involved the nationalization of narrative and interpretative frames, of perception and evaluation, of thinking and feeling. It has involved the silencing or marginalization of alternative, non-nationalist political languages. It has involved the nullification of complex identities by the terrible categorical simplicity of ascribed nationality. It has involved essentialist, demonizing characterizations of the national 'other,' characterizations that transform Serbs into Chetniks, Croats into Ustashas, Muslims into Fundamentalists.

We know well from a variety of appalling testimony *that* this has happened; but we know too little about *how* it happened. This is where we need an eventful perspective. Following the lead of such thinkers as Marshall Sahlins, Andrew Abbott, and William Sewell, Jr., we must give serious theoretical attention to contingent events and to their transformative consequences.[16] Only in this way can we hope to understand the processual dynamics of nationalism. And it is the close study of such processual dynamics, I think, that will yield the most original and significant work on nationalism in the coming years, work that promises theoretical advances as well as a richer understanding of particular cases.[17]

I began with the question: how should we think about nationhood and nationness, and how are they implicated in nationalism? Reduced to a formula, my argument is that we should focus on nation as a category of practice, nationhood as an institutionalized cultural and political form, and nationness as a contingent event or happening, and refrain from using the analytically dubious notion of 'nations' as substantial, enduring collectivities. A recent book by Julia Kristeva bears the English title *Nations without Nationalism*; but the analytical task at hand, I submit, is to think about nationalism without nations.

Ours is not, as is often asserted, even by as sophisticated a thinker as Anthony Smith, 'a world of nations.'[18] It is a world in which nationhood is pervasively institutionalized in the practice of states and the workings of the state system. It is a world in which nation is widely, if unevenly, available and resonant as a category of social vision and division. It is a world in which nationness may suddenly, and powerfully, 'happen.'[. . .]

[. . .] I would like to conclude with a more concrete illustrative discussion. Volumes have been written about the collapse of Yugoslavia, and many more are sure to follow. My aim here is not to provide even a summary account of the collapse, but rather to highlight [. . .] how the [. . .] approach outlined above might illuminate its bloody dynamics. I limit my attention here to the first phase of the breakup, involving Croatian and Slovenian moves toward independence and culminating in the war in Croatia; I do not discuss the war in Bosnia.

The first phase of the Yugoslav collapse was presented in the American press as a dyadic struggle. On one side stood Serbia, determined to reassert centralized control (and therefore Serb hegemony) over Yugoslavia as a whole, or, failing that, to carve out a 'greater Serbia' from the ruins of the state. On the other side stood Slovenia and Croatia, seeking autonomy and ultimately independence in the face of the Serbian push for hegemony.[19] Yet while the Slovenian issue was indeed dyadic, the Croatian conflict was, from the beginning, fundamentally triadic, involving a tension-fraught dynamic interplay between an incipient national minority (Serbs in Croatia), an incipient nationalizing state (Croatia), and an incipient external national homeland (Serbia).

Seeing the core dynamic in this way is not simply a matter of 'adding' the Croatian Serbs to the equation. Rather, it directs our attention to differing underlying processes. The dyadic view of the Serb–Croat conflict construes it as involving a push for Serb hegemony, a responsive Croatian secessionist movement, and a subsequent war of aggression against independent Croatia. The triadic view, by contrast, focuses on the complex interplay of three overlapping and mutually intensifying processes: the nationalization of the Croatian incipient state (both before and after independence was formally declared); the increasing disaffection, and nationalist mobilization, of Serbs in the ethnic borderlands of Croatia; and the development of a radical and belligerent 'homeland' stance in the incipient Serbian state, leading eventually to the intervention of the increasingly Serb-dominated Yugoslav army in Croatia on the side of plans to salvage a 'Greater Serbia' from the rubble of the federation.

The dyadic view rightly sees the Croatian drive for autonomy and independence as responding, in significant part, to Serbian nationalist assertiveness. Milošević's use of nationalist rhetoric to usurp leadership of the Serbian Communist Party in September 1987 and to mobilize mass support thereafter – especially his emphasis on Serb victimization in overwhelmingly Albanian Kosovo and on the need to reassert Serbian control over it by curtailing its constitutionally guaranteed autonomy – represented a fundamental and destabilizing challenge to the precarious national equilibrium constructed by Tito. The key to that equilibrium lay in the institutional restraints on the power of Serbia, preventing the Serbs from reacquiring the political dominance they had exercised, to disastrous effect, in the interwar Yugoslav state. The Serbian push to reassert control of Kosovo (and of the likewise formally autonomous Serbian province of Vojvodina) directly challenged those constraints and the fragile equilibrium built on them. While the resurgent Croatian nationalism of the late 1980s certainly had deep historical roots, and in many respects could be seen as reenacting (though going beyond) the Croatian nationalist movement of 1967–71, it was in crucial part a response to this destabilizing Serbian bid for hegemony within Yugoslavia.[20]

While the dyadic view illuminates the causes and antecedents of the Croat drive for autonomy and independence, it obscures the nature and consequences of that drive. Construing it as a *secessionist* movement, the dyadic view obscures the extent to which it was also, and inseparably, a *nationalizing* movement – a movement to assert Croat 'ownership' and control over the territory and institutions of Croatia, to make Croatia the state of and for the Croatian nation.

This was evident in the campaign rhetoric with which Franjo Tudjman, with strong financial backing from nationalist Croat émigrés, swept to victory in the spring 1990 elections, especially in his stress on the deep cultural differences between Serbs and Croats and the need to replace Serbs, heretofore overrepresented in key cultural, economic, and administrative positions in the republic, with Croats. It was evident in the iconography of the new regime, notably in the ubiquitous display of the red-and-white checkered armorial shield that had been an emblem of the medieval Croatian state but also of the murderous wartime Ustasha state (which the new leadership failed categorically and publicly to denounce). It was evident in the official, and ludicrous, 'Croatization' of language. It was evident in the rhetoric of the new Croatian constitution, which claimed 'full state sovereignty' as the 'historical right of the Croatian nation' and symbolically demoted Serbs from their previous status as co-'owners' of the Republic. And it was evident, perhaps most significantly, in substantial purges, concentrated in the state administration but extending beyond it as well, in which many Serbs lost their jobs.[21]

The significance of these and similar events, discourses, and practices lay not in themselves but in the representations and reactions they evoked among Croatian Serbs – especially village and small-town Serbs of the Krajina region – and in Serbia. The dynamic of nationalization, though partial and incipient, was real – and troubling – enough. But through varying mixes of selective appropriation, exaggeration, distortion, and outright fabrication, Serb nationalist politicians in Croatia and in Serbia proper represented these nationalizing moves in a sinister light as heralding the establishment of an ultranationalist regime that threatened the liberties, livelihoods, and – if Croatia were to opt for full independence – even the lives of Croatian Serbs.

The cynical and opportunistic manipulation involved in the more extreme of these representations and misrepresentations, irresponsibly evoking the specter of the Ustasha regime to discredit every manifestation of Croatian nationalism, is often stressed. But the emphasis on elite manipulation cannot explain why

representations of a prospectively independent Croatia as a dangerously nationalizing state were sufficiently resonant, and sufficiently plausible, among certain
segments of the Krajina Serb population, to inspire genuine fear and induce militant mobilization, and eventually armed rebellion, against the Croatian regime.[22]

While the dyadic view treats Croatian and particularly Krajina Serbs as passive
dupes, vehicles, or objects of manipulative designs originating in Serbia, the triadic
view sees them as active participants in the intensifying conflict and as political
subjects in their own right, construing (and misconstruing) the dangers of the
present in the light of the atrocities of the past. The complex process through
which representations of Croatia as a dangerously nationalizing, even protofascist,
state emerged, took root, and became hegemonic among Serbs in certain parts of
Croatia's ethnic borderlands cannot be reduced to a story of outside manipulation.
Efforts by nationalist radicals in Serbia to mobilize grievances and fears among
Croatian Serbs were indeed an important part of the process. But the bulk of the
work of mobilizing grievances and fears was undertaken locally by Croatian Serbs.
And the grievances and fears were there to be mobilized. Although representations
of wartime atrocities – often greatly exaggerated – were indeed widely propagated
from Belgrade, memories of and stories about the murderous wartime Independent
State of Croatia, and especially about the gruesome fate of many Croatian and
Bosnian Serbs (Bosnia having been incorporated into the wartime Croatian state),
were not imports. They were locally rooted, sustained within family and village
circles, and transmitted to the postwar generations, especially in the ethnically
mixed and partly Serb-majority borderland regions where (outside of Bosnia)
most atrocities against Serb civilians had occurred, and where (again excluding
Bosnia) the main Partisan as well as the few Chetnik strongholds in Croatia had
been located. It was among village and small-town Serbs in just these regions –
and not, for example, among the cosmopolitan Serbs of Zagreb – that encounters
with the incipient Croatian nationalizing state, interpreted through the prism of
revived representations of wartime trauma, generated intransigent opposition to
Croatian independence.[23]

These mutually alienating encounters between the nationalizing and increasingly independent Croatian state and the fearful and increasingly radicalized Serb
borderland minority thus had their own destabilizing logic; they were not orchestrated from Belgrade. But Serbian 'homeland politics' was crucial to the overall
relational nexus. Homeland stances – involving identification with, assertions of
responsibility for, and demands to support or even 'redeem' and incorporate ethnic
Serbs outside Serbian state territory – have a long tradition in Serbian politics.[24]
The relation between the expansionist 'small Serbia' (established as an independent
kingdom, though still under nominal Ottoman suzerainty, in 1829 and recognized
as fully independent in 1878) and the large Serb communities in the Ottoman and
Austro-Hungarian empires was a burning issue in the decades before World War
I, and one that touched off the war when a Bosnian Serb nationalist revolutionary
assassinated Archduke Francis Ferdinand, heir to the Habsburg throne, in Sarajevo.
With the formation of a Serb-dominated South Slav state after the war, incorporating the great majority of former Habsburg and Ottoman Serbs, the problematic
of homeland politics receded. Nor did it reemerge openly after World War II in
Tito's reconstructed (and more nationally equilibrated) Yugoslavia. Just as Russians

viewed the Soviet Union as a whole (and not just the Russian republic) as 'their' state, so Serbs viewed the Yugoslav state as a whole (and not just Serbia) as their own, regarding internal boundaries as insignificant or 'merely administrative.' Yet homeland politics revived in Serbia, and emerged in Russia, when the 'national-ization' of constituent units of Yugoslavia and the Soviet Union eroded Serbs' and Russians' sense of being 'at home' throughout the state.

The revival of Serbian homeland politics – of politicized concern with Serbs outside Serbia – centred initially on Kosovo. Although it was formerly part of the Serbian Republic, its constitutional promotion to near-republic status in 1974, together with its gradual but thoroughgoing 'Albanianization' (through differential fertility, Serb out-migration, and preferential treatment in cultural and adminis-trative positions), were perceived by Serb intellectuals as a 'quiet secession' that had, in practice, stripped Serbia of its historic heartland.[25] The dwindling Serb community in Kosovo was represented as a physically and psychologically harassed national minority, forced increasingly to emigrate, subject to 'genocide,' in the scan-dalously hyperbolic language of the first major statement of the Serb nationalist revival.[26] Having again been 'lost,' Kosovo was in need of redemption, of reincor-poration into a restored, strengthened, unitary Serbia – a program taken up, with great mobilizational success, by Milošević.

As Slovenia, Croatia, and later Bosnia-Hercegovina moved toward indepen-dence, Serbian homeland politics – as articulated by Milošević, by his even more radically nationalist opponents, and by the state-controlled broadcast media – was extended to, and came to focus increasingly on, Serb minorities in Croatia and Bosnia. Through the prevalence in the media and public discourse of what one anthropologist has called 'narratives of victimization and of threat, linking the present with the past and projecting onto the future,'[27] the plight of Kosovo Serbs was represented in generalized terms as a threat to Serbs in minority positions everywhere. After the election of Tudjman, this threat was seen as particularly acute in Croatia, which was increasingly represented as a protofascist successor to the wartime Ustasha state. Croatian claims to self-determination and sovereign statehood were met with counterclaims that Serbs, too, had the right to self-deter-mination, the right to a state of their own – if not Yugoslavia, then an enlarged Serbia. The secession of Croatia, Milošević bluntly warned throughout 1990 and the first half of 1991, would require the redrawing of its boundaries. Croatia's borderland Serbs were encouraged to take a stand of intransigent opposition to the new Croatian regime and to its bid for independence, and, as the crisis intensified, were provided with arms and logistical support.

The increasingly ominous tenor of Serbian homeland politics was doubly desta-bilizing, provoking both the Croatian government and Croatian Serbs to adopt more intransigent stances. Just as the reassertion of central Serbian control over Kosovo, by upsetting the precarious national equilibrium in Yugoslavia, helped spark Croa-tian secessionism, so Serbian claims to speak for Croatian Serbs, by challenging Croatian sovereignty and reinforcing representations and fears of aggressive Serb hegemony, helped push the Croatian government toward a more uncompromising stance – toward the pursuit of full independence (rather than a restructured federal or confederal arrangement) and toward the more vigorous assertion of its authority in the rebellious borderlands (which occasioned armed clashes that led to the intervention of the army, initially as a peacekeeping force, but increasingly as an ally of local Serb forces). At the same time, the pan-Serb rhetoric, anti-Croat propaganda, and talk of border revisions emanating from Belgrade, together with the more uncompromising Croatian government stance, pushed Croatia's borderland Serbs toward greater intransigence – toward such steps as the formation of a 'Serbian National Council' (July 1990), the holding of a referendum on autonomy for Croatian Serbs despite its prohibition by Croatian authorities (August 1990), the establishment of the 'Serbian Autonomous Region of Krajina' (December 1990), and the proclamation of that region's 'separation' from Croatia (February 1991).

It is not possible here to discuss in detail the interactive dynamic that led to the outbreak of a war pitting the heavily Serbianized 'Yugoslav People's Army' and various Croatian Serb militias against the overmatched Croatian army, resulting in the occupation for several years of nearly a third of Croatian territory (including parts in which Serbs had been only a small minority) and sealing the final dissolution of Yugoslavia before spreading, with still more devastating consequences, to Bosnia-Hercegovina. I have had to limit my discussion to a general sketch of the interplay between the incipient Serb national minority in Croatia, the incipient Croatian nationalizing state, and the incipient Serbian homeland, locked in an intensifying spiral of mistrust, misrepresentation, and mutual fear. I have had to ignore not only the detailed interactive sequence of that interplay, but also the struggles among competing stances internal to the minority, nationalizing state, and homeland. Enough has perhaps been said, however, to suggest the potential fruitfulness of a relational, dynamic, interactive approach to nationalist conflict. [. . .]

## Notes

1   The great book of E. P. Thompson on *The Making of the English Working Class* (New York: Vintage, 1963) marked the beginning of this process. While stressing on the one hand that class is not a thing, that '"it" [i.e. class understood as a thing] does not exist,' that class is rather 'something [. . .] which happens,' a 'fluency,' a 'relationship' (pp. 9–11), Thompson nonetheless ends up treating the working class as a real entity, a community, an historical individual, characterizing his book as a 'biography of the English working class from its adolescence until its early manhood,' and summing up his findings as follows: 'When every caution has been made, the outstanding fact of the period from 1790 to 1830 is the formation of the working class' (pp. 9–11, 194).

2   It mars even the work of so eminent a specialist on Soviet nationality affairs as Hélène Carrère d'Encausse. See *The End of the Soviet Empire: The Triumph of the Nations* (New York: Basic Books, 1993).

3   I stress that I am not simply criticizing primordialism – long-dead horse that writers on ethnicity and nationalism continue to flog. No serious scholar today holds the view that is routinely attributed to primordialists in straw-man setups, namely that nations or ethnic groups are primordial, unchanging entities. Everyone agrees that nations are historically formed constructs, although there is disagreement about the relative weight of premodern traditions and modern transformations, of ancient memories and recent mobilizations, of 'authentic' and 'artificial' group feeling. What I am criticizing is not the straw

man of primordialism, but the more pervasive substantialist, realist cast of mind that attributes real, enduring existence to nations as collectivities, however those collectivities are conceived.

4   As Pierre Bourdieu's work on the symbolic dimensions of group-making suggests, reification is central to the quasi-performative discourse of nationalist politicians which, at certain moments, can succeed in creating what it seems to presuppose – namely, the existence of nations as real, mobilized or mobilizable groups. Bourdieu has not written specifically on nationalism, but this theme is developed in his essay on regionalism, 'L'identité et la représentation: éléments pour une réflexion critique sur l'idée de région,' *Actes de la recherche en sciences sociales* 35 (November 1980), part of which is reprinted in Bourdieu, *Language and Symbolic Power* (Cambridge, Mass.: Harvard University Press, 1991), pp. 220–8; see also the conclusion to 'Social Space and the Genesis of Classes' in that same collection (pp. 248–51).

5   Here I differ from those who, finding 'nation' inadequate or hopelessly muddled as a designator of a putative real entity or collectivity, avoid engaging the phenomenon of nationhood or nationness altogether. This was the case notably for the influential work of Charles Tilly and his collaborators, *The Formation of National States in Western Europe* (Princeton: Princeton University Press, 1975). As Tilly wrote in the introductory essay to that volume, '"nation" remains one of the most puzzling and tendentious items in the political lexicon' (p. 6). Tilly shifted the focus of analysis from nation to state, marking a deliberate break with the older literature on nation-building. The adjective 'national' appears throughout the book; yet it is strictly a term of scale and scope, meaning essentially 'statewide'; it has nothing to do with the phenomenon of nationhood or nationness.

6   See J. P. Nettl, 'The State as a Conceptual Variable,' *World Politics* 20 (1968).

7   On nation as political fiction, see Louis Pinto, 'Une fiction politique: la nation,' *Actes de la recherche en sciences sociales* 64 (1986), a Bourdieuian appreciation of the studies of nationalism carried out by the eminent Hungarian historian Jenö Szücs.

8   For suggestive recent discussions of nationalism that avoid treating 'the nation' as a real entity, see Richard Handler, 'Is "Identity" a Useful Cross-Cultural Concept?,' in John Gillis, ed., *Commemorations: The Politics of National Identity* (Princeton: Princeton University Press, 1994); Katherine Verdery, 'Whither "Nation" and "Nationalism"?,' *Daedalus* 122, no. 3 (1993), and Craig Calhoun, 'Nationalism and Ethnicity,' *Annual Review of Sociology* 19 (1993).

9   Not only political fields but economic and cultural fields too can generate nationalism. See for example Katherine Verdery, 'Nationalism and National Sentiment in Post-Socialist Romania,' *Slavic Review* 52 (1993) for an argument about the nationalism-generating power of post-socialist economic restructuring.

10  Margaret R. Somers, 'Narrativity, Narrative Identity, and Social Action: Rethinking English Working-Class Formation,' *Social Science History* 16 (1992), 608ff. For an anthropological approach to the study of nationness as something produced and reproduced in everyday relationships, see John Borneman, *Belonging in the Two Berlins* (New York: Cambridge University Press, 1992); see also Verdery, 'Whither "Nation" and "Nationalism"?,' 41.

11  William Sewell, Jr., 'Three Temporalities: Toward an Eventful Sociology,' forthcoming in Terrence J. McDonald, ed., *The Historic Turn in the Human Sciences* (Ann Arbor: University of Michigan Press).

12    Ernest Gellner, *Nations and Nationalism* (Ithaca, NY: Cornell University Press, 1983); Benedict Anderson, *Imagined Communities: Reflections on the Origin and Spread of Nationalism* (London: Verso, revised edn. 1991); Anthony Smith, *The Ethnic Origins of Nations* (Oxford: Basil Blackwell, 1986); Eric Hobsbawm, *Nations and Nationalism since 1780* (Cambridge: Cambridge University Press, 1990).

13    Sewell, 'Three Temporalities'; cf. Marshall Sahlins, 'The Return of the Event, Again: With Reflections on the Beginnings of the Great Fijian War of 1843 to 1855 between the Kingdoms of Bau and Rewa,' in Aletta Biersack, ed., *Clio in Oceania: Toward a Historical Anthropology* (Washington and London: Smithsonian Institution Press, 1991), p. 38.

14    Craig Calhoun, 'The Problem of Identity in Collective Action,' in Joan Huber, ed., *Macro-Micro Linkages in Sociology* (Newbury Park, Calif.: Sage, 1991), p. 59.

15    'Being Croat has become my destiny [. . .] I am defined by my nationality, and by it alone [. . .] Along with millions of other Croats, I was pinned to the wall of nationhood – not only by outside pressure from Serbia and the Federal Army but by national homogenization within Croatia itself. That is what the war is doing to us, reducing us to one dimension: the Nation. The trouble with this nationhood, however, is that whereas before, I was defined by my education, my job, my ideas, my character – and, yes, my nationality too – now I feel stripped of all that. I am nobody because I am not a person any more. I am one of 4.5 million Croats [. . .] I am not in a position to choose any longer. Nor, I think, is anyone else [. . .] something people cherished as a part of their cultural iden-tity – an alternative to the all-embracing communism [. . .] – has become their political identity and turned into something like an ill-fitting shirt. You may feel the sleeves are too short, the collar too tight. You might not like the colour, and the cloth might itch. But there is no escape; there is nothing else to wear. One doesn't have to succumb voluntarily to this ideology of the nation – one is sucked into it. So right now, in the new state of Croatia, no one is allowed not to be a Croat' (Slavenka Drakulic, *The Balkan Express: Fragments from the Other Side of War* [New York: W. W. Norton, 1993], pp. 50–2).

16    Sahlins, 'The Return of the Event, Again'; Andrew Abbott, 'From Causes to Events: Notes on Narrative Postivism,' *Sociological Methods and Research* 20 (1992); Sewell, 'Three Temporalities.'

17    Here the study of nationalism might fruitfully draw on the recent literature on revolution, with its attention to transformative events and processual dynamics. See for example the debate in *Contention* between Nikki Keddie, 'Can Revolutions be Predicted? Can their Causes be Understood?' (1, no. 2 [1992]) and Jack Goldstone, 'Predicting Revolutions: Why We Could (and Should) have Foreseen the Revolutions of 1989–1991 in the U.S.S.R. and Eastern Europe' (2, no. 2 [1993]). Although Keddie and Goldstone disagree about the predictability of revo-lution, they agree about the importance of transformative events, complex interactions, and rapid changes in ideas, stances, and behavior.

18    Anthony Smith, *National Identity* (London: Penguin, 1991), p. 176.

19    For a sophisticated statement of this view, see Branka Magaš, *The Destruction of Yugoslavia* (London: Verso, 1993).

20    For a lucid and sustained analysis of the resurgent Serbian nationalism of the 1980s, see Veljko Vujacic, 'Communism and Nationalism in Russia and Serbia,' Ph.D. dissertation, University of California at Berkeley, 1995.

21    See Misha Glenny, *The Fall of Yugoslavia: The Third Balkan War* (London: Penguin,

1992), esp. pp. 12–13, 77, 81–2; Leonard J. Cohen, *Broken Bonds: The Disintegration of Yugoslavia* (Boulder, Colo.: Westview Press, 1993), pp. 96–8, 208; Bette Denich, 'Dismembering Yugoslavia: Nationalist Ideologies and the Symbolic Revival of Genocide,' *American Ethnologist* 21, no. 2 (1994), 377–81; Robert Hayden, 'Constitutional Nationalism in the Formerly Yugoslav Republics,' *Slavic Review* 51, no. 4 (1992); Eugene A. Hammel, 'The Yugoslav Labyrinth,' in Eugene Hammel, Irwin Wall, and Benjamin Ward, *Crisis in the Balkans* (Berkeley: Institute of International Studies, University of California, 1993), pp. 16–17; and Bogdan Denitch, *Ethnic Nationalism: The Tragic Death of Yugoslavia* (Minneapolis: University of Minnesota Press, 1994), p. 45.

22   Glenny, *The Fall of Yugoslavia*, p. 11; and Denich, 'Dismembering Yugoslavia,' 381.

23   Denich, 'Dismembering Yugoslavia'; Glenny, *The Fall of Yugoslavia*; and Denitch, *Ethnic Nationalism*, p. 33.

24   Ivo Lederer, 'Nationalism and the Yugoslavs,' in Peter F. Sugar and Ivo John Lederer, eds., *Nationalism in Eastern Europe* (Seattle: University of Washington Press, 1994 [1969]).

25   Dennison Rusinow, 'Nationalities Policy and the "National Question,"' in Pedro Ramet, ed., *Yugoslavia in the 1980s* (Boulder, Colo.: Westview Press, 1985), pp. 146–7. On the background to Serb concern about Kosovo, see Vujacic, 'Communism and Nationalism,' pp. 204–30.

26   This was the 'Memorandum' of the Serbian Academy of Arts and Sciences, prepared in 1986. A French version has been published in Mirko Grmek *et al.*, eds., *Le nettoyage ethnique: documents historiques sur une idélogie serbe* (Paris: Fayard, 1993). On the memorandum, see Vujacic, *Communism and Nationalism*, pp. 257–67.

27   Bette Denich, 'Unmaking Multi-Ethnicity in Yugoslavia: Metamorphosis Observed,' *Anthropology of East Europe Review* 11, nos. 1–2 (1993), 51.

# GLOBALISATION

- Anthony Giddens, Dimensions of globalisation

- Arjun Appadurai, Disjuncture and difference in the global cultural economy

**Anthony Giddens** was born in 1938 and was educated at the London School of Economics. He has been a Professor of Sociology at Cambridge University and is currently the Director of the London School of Economics. Among his books are *The Constitution of Society* (1984) and *The Consequences of Modernity* (1990).

**Arjun Appadurai** is Professor of Anthropology at the University of Pennsylvania, where he is co-director of the Center for Transnational Cultural Studies and associate editor of Public Culture. He is the author *of Worship and Conflict Under Colonial Rule* (1981) and *Modernity at Large (1998).*

# Chapter 23

# Anthony Giddens

## DIMENSIONS OF GLOBALISATION

### The globalising of modernity

**M**ODERNITY IS INHERENTLY GLOBALISING — this is evident in some of the most basic characteristics of modern institutions, including partially their disembeddedness and reflexivity. But what exactly is globalisation, and how might we best conceptualise the phenomenon? I shall consider these questions at some length here, since the central importance of globalising processes today has scarcely been matched by extended discussions of the concept in the sociological literature. We can begin by recalling some points made earlier. The undue reliance which sociologists have placed upon the idea of 'society,' where this means a bounded system, should be replaced by a starting point that concentrates upon analysing how social life is ordered across time and space – the problematic of time–space distanciation. The conceptual framework of time–space distanciation directs our attention to the complex relations between *local involvements* (circumstances of co-presence) and *interaction across distance* (the connections of presence and absence). In the modern era, the level of time–space distanciation is much higher than in any previous period, and the relations between local and distant social forms and events become correspondingly 'stretched.' Globalisation refers essentially to that stretching process, in so far as the modes of connection between different social contexts or regions become networked across the earth's surface as a whole.

Globalisation can thus be defined as the intensification of worldwide social relations which link distant localities in such a way that local happenings are shaped by events occurring many miles away and vice versa. This is the dialectical process because such local happenings may move in an obverse direction from the very distanciated relations that shape them. *Local transformation* is as much a part of globalisation as the lateral extension of social connections across time and space. Thus whoever studies cities today, in any part of the world, is aware that what happens in a local neighbourhood is likely to be influenced by factors – such as world money and commodity markets – operating at an indefinite distance away from that neighbourhood itself. The outcome is not necessarily, or even usually, a generalised set of changes acting in a uniform direction, but consists in mutually opposed tendencies. The increasing prosperity of an urban area in Singapore might be causally related, via a complicated network of global economic ties, to the impoverishment of a neighbourhood in Pittsburgh whose local products are uncompetitive in world markets.

Another example from the very many that could be offered is the rise of local nationalisms in Europe and elsewhere. The development of globalised social relations probably serves to diminish some aspects of nationalist feeling linked to nation-states (or some states) but may be causally involved with the intensifying of more localised nationalist sentiments. In circumstances of accelerating globalisation, the nation-state has become 'too small for the big problems of life, and too big for the small problems of life.' At the same time as social relations become laterally stretched and as part of the same process, we see the strengthening of pressures for local autonomy and regional cultural identity.

## Two theoretical perspectives

Apart from the work of Marshall McLuhan and a few other individual authors, discussions of globalisation tend to appear in two bodies of literature, which are largely distinct from one another. One is the literature of international relations, the other that of 'world-system theory,' particularly as associated with Immanuel Wallerstein, which stands fairly close to a Marxist position.

Theorists of international relations characteristically focus upon the development of the nation-state system, analysing its origins in Europe and its subsequent worldwide spread. Nation-states are treated as actors, engaging with one another in the international arena – and with other organisations of a transnational kind (intergovernmental organisations or non-state actors). Although various theoretical positions are represented in this literature, most authors paint a rather similar picture in analysing the growth of globalisation. Sovereign states, it is presumed, first emerge largely as separately entities, having more or less complete administrative control within their borders. As the European state system matures and later becomes a global nation-state system, patterns of interdependence become increasingly developed. These are not only expressed in the ties states form with one another in the international arena, but in the burgeoning of intergovernmental organisations. These processes mark an overall movement towards 'one world,' although they are continually fractured by war. Nation-states, it is held, are becoming progressively less sovereign than they used to be in terms of control over their own affairs – although few today anticipate in the near future the emergence of the 'world-state' which many in the early part of this century foresaw as a real prospect.

While this view is not altogether wrong, some major reservations have to be expressed. For one thing, it again covers only one overall dimension of globalisation as I wish to utilise the concept here – the international coordination of states. Regarding states as actors has its uses and makes sense in some contexts. However, most theorists of international relations do not explain *why* this usage makes sense; for it does so only in the case of nation-states, not in that of pre-modern states. The reason has to do with a theme discussed earlier – there is a far greater concentration of administrative power in nation-states than in their precursors, in which it would be relatively meaningless to speak of 'governments' who negotiate with other 'governments' in the name of their respective nations. Moreover, treating states as actors having connections with each other and with other organisations in the international arena makes it difficult to deal with social relations that are not between or outside states, but simply crosscut state divisions.

A further shortcoming of this type of approach concerns its portrayal of the increasing unification of the nation-state system. The sovereign power of modern states was not formed prior to their involvement in the nation-state system, even in the European state system, but developed in conjunction with it. Indeed, the sovereignty of the modern state was from the first *dependent upon the relations between states*, in terms of which each state (in principle if by no means always in practice) recognised the autonomy of others within their own borders. No state, however powerful, held as much sovereign control in practice as was enshrined in legal principle. The history of the past two centuries is thus not one of the progressive loss of sovereignty on the part of the nation-state. Here again we must recognise the dialectical character of globalisation and also the influence of processes of uneven development. Loss of autonomy on the part of some states or groups of states has often gone along with an *increase* in that of others, as a result of alliances, wars, or political and economic changes of various sorts. For instance, although the sovereign control of some of the 'classical' Western nations may have diminished as a result of the acceleration of the global division of labour over the past thirty years, that of some Far Eastern countries – in some respects at least – has grown.

Since the stance of world-system theory differs so much from international relations, it is not surprising to find that the two literatures are at arm's distance from one another. Wallerstein's account of the world system makes many contributions, in both theory and empirical analysis. Not least important is the fact that he skirts the sociologists' usual preoccupation with 'societies' in favour of a much more embracing conception of globalised relationships. He also makes a clear differentiation between the modern era and preceding ages in terms of the phenomena with which he is concerned. What he refers to as 'world economies' – networks of economic connections of a geographically extensive sort – have existed prior to modern times, but these were notably different from the world system that has developed over the past three or four centuries. Earlier world economies were usually centred upon large imperial states and never covered more than certain regions in which the power of these states was concentrated. The emergence of capitalism, as Wallerstein analyses it, ushers in a quite different type of order, for the first time genuinely global in its span and based more on economic than political power – the 'world capitalist economy.' The world capitalist economy, which has its origins in the sixteenth and seventeenth centuries, is integrated through commercial and manufacturing connections, not by a political centre. Indeed, there exists a multiplicity of political centres, the nation-states. The modern world system is divided into three components, the core, the semi-periphery, and the periphery, although where these are located regionally shifts over time.

According to Wallerstein, the worldwide reach of capitalism was established quite early on in the modern period: 'Capitalism was from the beginning an affair of the world economy and not of nation-states. [. . .] Capital has never allowed its aspirations to be determined by national boundaries.' Capitalism has been such a fundamental globalising influence precisely because it is an economic rather than a political order; it has been able to penetrate far-flung areas of the world which the states of its origin could not have brought wholly under their political sway. The colonial administration of distant lands may in some situations have helped to consolidate economic expansion, but it was never the main basis of the spread of capitalistic enterprise globally. In the late twentieth century, where colonialism in its original form has all but disappeared, the world capitalist economy continues to involve massive imbalances between core, semi-periphery, and periphery.

Wallerstein successfully breaks away from some of the limitations of much orthodox sociological thought, most notably the strongly defined tendency to focus upon 'endogenous models' of social change. But his work has its own shortcomings. He continues to see only one dominant institutional nexus (capitalism) as responsible for modern transformations. World-system theory thus concentrates heavily upon economic influences and finds it difficult satisfactorily to account for just those phenomena made central by the theorists of international relations: the rise of the nation-state and the nation-state system. Moreover, the distinctions between core, semi-periphery, and periphery (themselves perhaps of questionable value), based upon economic criteria, do not allow us to illuminate political or military concentrations of power, which do not align in an exact way to economic differentiations.

I shall, in contrast, regard the world capitalist economy as one of four dimensions of globalisation, following the four-fold classification of the institutions of modernity mentioned above (see Figure 23.1). The nation-state system is a second dimension; as the discussion above indicated, although these are connected in various ways, neither can be explained exhaustively in terms of the other.

If we consider the present day, in what sense can world economic organisation be said to be dominated by capitalistic economic mechanisms? A number of considerations are relevant to answering this question. The main centres of power in the world economy are capitalist states – states in which capitalist economic enterprise (with the class relations that this implies) is the chief form of production. The domestic and international economic policies of these states involve many forms of regulation of economic activity, but, as noted, their institutional organisation maintains an 'insulation' of the economic from the political. This allows wide scope for the global activities of business corporations, which always have a home base within a particular state but may develop many other regional involvements elsewhere.

Business firms, especially the transnational corporations, may wield immense economic power, and have the capacity to influence political policies in their home bases and elsewhere. The biggest transnational companies today have budgets larger than those of all but a few nations. But there are some key respects in which their power cannot rival that of states – especially important here are the factors of

*Figure 23.1    The dimensions of globalisation*

territoriality and control of the means of violence. There is no area on the earth's surface, with the partial exception of the polar regions, which is not claimed as the legitimate sphere of control of one state or another. All modern states have a more or less successful monopoly of control of the means of violence within their own territories. No matter how great their economic power, industrial corporations are not military organisations (as some of them were during the colonial period), and they cannot establish themselves as political/legal entities which rule a given territorial area.

If nation-states are the principal 'actors' within the global political order, corporations are the dominant agents within the world economy. In their trading relations with one another, and with states and consumers, companies (manufacturing corporations, financial firms, and banks) depend upon production for profit. Hence the spread of their influence brings in its train a global extension of commodity markets, including money markets. However, even in its beginnings, the capitalist world economy was never just a market for the trading of goods and services. It involved, and involves today, the commodifying of labour power in class relations which separate workers from control of their means of production. This process, of course, is fraught with implications for global inequalities.

All nation-states, capitalist and state socialist, within the 'developed' sectors of the world, are primarily reliant upon industrial production for the generation of the wealth upon which their tax revenues are based. The socialist countries form something of an enclave within the capitalist world economy as a whole, industry being more directly subject to political imperatives. These states are scarcely post-capitalist, but the influence of capitalistic markets upon the distribution of goods and labour power is substantially muted. The pursuit of growth by both Western and East European societies inevitably pushes economic interests to the forefront of the policies which states pursue in the international arena. But it is surely plain to all, save those under the sway of historical materialism, that the material involvements of nation-states are not governed purely by economic considerations, real or perceived. The influence of any particular state within the global political order is strongly conditioned by the level of its wealth (and the connection between this and military strength). However, states derive their power from their sovereign capabilities, as Hans J. Morgenthau emphasises. They do not operate as economic machines, but as 'actors' jealous of their territorial rights, concerned with the fostering of national cultures, and having strategic geopolitical involvements with other states or alliances of states.

The nation-state system has long participated in that reflexivity characteristic of modernity as a whole. The very existence of sovereignty should be understood as something that is reflexively monitored, for reasons already indicated. Sovereignty is linked to the replacement of 'frontiers' by 'borders' in the early development of the nation-state system: autonomy inside the territory claimed by the state is sanctioned by the recognition of borders by other states. As noted, this is one of the major factors distinguishing the nation-state system from systems and states in the pre-modern era, where few reflexively ordered relations of this kind existed and where the notion of 'international relations' made no sense.

One aspect of the dialectical nature of globalisation is the 'push and pull' between tendencies towards centralisation inherent in the reflexivity of the system of states on the one hand and the sovereignty of particular states on the other. Thus, concerted action between countries in some respects diminishes the individual sovereignty of the nations involved, yet by combining their power in other ways, it increases their influence within the state system. The same is true of the early congresses, which, in conjunction with war, defined and redefined states' borders – and of truly global agencies such as the United Nations. The global influence of the U.N. (still decisively limited by the fact that it is not territorial and does not have significant access to the means of violence) is not purchased solely by means of a diminution of the sovereignty of nation-states – things are more complicated than this. An obvious example is that of the 'new nations' – autonomous nation-states set up in erstwhile colonised areas. Armed struggle against the colonising countries was very generally a major factor in persuading the colonisers to retreat. But discussion in the U.N. played a key role in setting up ex-colonial areas as states with internationally recognised borders. However weak some of the new nations may be economically and militarily, their emergence *as* nation-states (or, in many cases, 'state-nations') marks a net gain in terms of sovereignty, as compared to their previous circumstances.

The third dimension of globalisation is the world military order. In specifying its nature, we have to analyse the connections between the industrialisation of war, the flow of weaponry and techniques of military organisation from some parts of the world to others, and the alliances which states build with one another. Military alliances do not necessarily compromise the monopoly over the means of violence held by a state within its territories, although in some circumstances they certainly can do so.

In tracing the overlaps between military power and the sovereignty of states, we find the same push-and-pull between opposing tendencies noted previously. In the current period, the two most military developed states, the United States and the Soviet Union, have built a bipolar system of military alliances of truly global scope. The countries involved in these alliances necessarily accept limitations over their opportunities to forge independent military strategies externally. They may also forfeit complete monopoly of military control within their own territories, in so far as American or Soviet forces stationed there take their orders from abroad. Yet, as a result of the massive destructive power of modern weaponry, almost all states possess military strength far in excess of that of even the largest of pre-modern civilisations. Many economically weak Third World countries are militarily powerful. In an important sense there is no 'Third World' in respect of weaponry, only a 'First World,' since most countries maintain stocks of technologically advanced armaments and have modernised the military in a thoroughgoing way. Even the possession of unclear weaponry is not confined to the economically advanced states.

The globalising of military power obviously is not confined to weaponry and alliances between the armed forces of different states – it also concerns war itself. Two world wars attest to the way in which local conflicts became matters of global involvement. In both wars, the participants were drawn from virtually all regions (although the Second World War was a more truly worldwide phenomenon). In an era of nuclear weaponry, the industrialisation of war has proceeded to a point at which, as was mentioned earlier, the obsolescence of Clausewitz's main doctrine has become apparent to everyone. The only point of holding nuclear weapons – apart from their possible symbolic value in world politics – is to deter others from using them.

While this situation may lead to a suspension of war between the nuclear powers (or so we all must hope), it scarcely prevents them from engaging in military adventures outside their own territorial domains. The two superpowers in particular engage in what might be called 'orchestrated wars' in peripheral areas of military strength. By these I mean military encounters, with the governments of other states or with guerrilla movements or both, in which the troops of the superpower are not necessarily even engaged at all, but where the power is a prime organising influence.

The fourth dimension of globalisation concerns industrial development. The most obvious aspect of this is the expansion of the global division of labour, which includes the differentiations between more and less industrialised areas in the world. Modern industry is intrinsically based on divisions of labour, not only on the level of job tasks but on that of regional specialisation in terms of type of industry, skills, and the production of raw materials. There has undoubtedly taken place a major expansion of global interdependence in the division of labour since the Second World War. This has helped to bring about shifts in the worldwide distribution of production, including the deindustrialisation of some regions in the developed countries and the emergence of the 'Newly Industrialising Countries' in the Third World. It has also undoubtedly served to reduce the internal economic hegemony of many states, particularly those with a high level of industrialisation. It is more difficult for the capitalist countries to manage their economies than formerly was the case, given accelerating global economic interdependence. This is almost certainly one of the major reasons for the declining impact of Keynesian economic policies, as applied at the level of the national economy, in current times.

One of the main features of the globalising implications of industrialism is the worldwide diffusion of machine technologies. The impact of industrialism is plainly not limited to the sphere of production, but affects many aspects of day-to-day life, as well as influencing the generic character of human interaction with the material environment.

Even in states which remain primarily agricultural, modern technology is often applied in such a way as to alter substantially preexisting relations between human social organisation and the environment. This is true, for example, of the use of fertilisers or other artificial farming methods, the introduction of modern farming machinery, and so forth. The diffusion of industrialism has created 'one world' in a more negative and threatening sense than that just mentioned – a world in which there are actual or potential ecological changes of a harmful sort that affect everyone on the planet. Yet industrialism has also decisively conditioned our very sense of living in 'one world.' For one of the most important effects of industrialism has been the transformation of technologies of communication.

This comment leads on to a further and quite fundamental aspect of globalisation, which lies behind each of the various institutional dimensions that have been mentioned and which might be referred to as cultural globalisation. Mechanised technologies of communication have dramatically influenced all aspects of globalisation since the first introduction of mechanical printing into Europe. They form an essential element of the reflexivity of modernity and of the discontinuities which have torn the modern away from the traditional.

The globalising impact of media was noted by numerous authors during the period of the early growth of mass circulation newspapers. Thus one commentator in 1892 wrote that, as a result of modern newspapers, the inhabitant of a local village has a broader understanding of contemporary events than the prime minister of a hundred years before. The villager who reads a paper 'interests himself simultaneously in the issue of a revolution in Chile, a bush-war in East Africa, a massacre in North China, a famine in Russia.'

The point here is not that people are contingently aware of many events, from all over the world, of which previously they would have remained ignorant. It is that the global extension of the institutions of modernity would be impossible were it not for the pooling of knowledge which is represented by the 'news.' This is perhaps less obvious on the level of general cultural awareness than in more specific contexts. For example, the global money markets of today involve direct and simultaneous access to pooled information on the part of individuals spatially widely separated from one another.

# Chapter 24

# Arjun Appadurai

## DISJUNCTURE AND DIFFERENCE IN THE GLOBAL CULTURAL ECONOMY

IT TAKES ONLY THE merest acquaintance with the facts of the modern world to note that it is now an interactive system in a sense that is strikingly new. Historians and sociologists, especially those concerned with translocal processes [. . .] and the world systems associated with capitalism [. . .] have long been aware that the world has been a congeries of large-scale interactions for so many centuries. Yet today's world involves interactions of a new order and intensity. Cultural transactions between social groups in the past have generally been restricted, sometimes by the facts of geography and ecology, and at other times by active resistance to interactions with the Other (as in China for much of its history and in Japan before the Meiji Restoration). Where there have been sustained cultural transactions across large parts of the globe, they have usually involved the long-distance journey of commodities (and of the merchants most concerned with them) and of travelers and explorers of every type [. . .]. The two main forces for sustained cultural interaction before this century have been warfare (and the large-scale political systems sometimes generated by it) and religions of conversion, which have sometimes, as in the case of Islam, taken warfare as one of the legitimate instruments of their expansion. Thus, between travelers and merchants, pilgrims and conquerors, the world has seen much long-distance (and long term) cultural traffic. This much seems self-evident.

But few will deny that given the problems of time, distance, and limited technologies for the command of resources across vast spaces, cultural dealings between socially and spatially separated groups have, until the past few centuries, been bridged at great cost and sustained over time only with great effort. The forces of cultural gravity seemed always to pull away from the formation of large-scale ecumenes, whether religious, commercial, or political, toward smaller-scale accretions of intimacy and interest.

Sometime in the past few centuries, the nature of this gravitational field seems to have changed. Partly because of the spirit of the expansion of Western maritime interests after 1500, and partly because of the relatively autonomous developments of large and aggressive social formations in the Americas (such as the Aztecs and the Incas), in Eurasia (such as the Mongols and their descendants, the Mughals and Ottomans), in island Southeast Asia (such as the Buginese), and in the kingdoms of precolonial Africa (such as Dahomey), an overlapping set of ecumenes began to emerge, in which congeries of money, commerce, conquest, and migration began to create durable cross-societal bonds. This process was accelerated by the technology transfers and innovations of the late eighteenth and nineteenth centuries [. . .], which created complex colonial orders centred on European capitals and spread throughout the non-European world. This intricate and overlapping set of Eurocolonial worlds (first Spanish and Portuguese, later principally English, French, and Dutch) set the basis for a permanent traffic in ideas of peoplehood and self-hood, which created the imagined communities [. . .] of recent nationalisms throughout the world.

With what Benedict Anderson has called 'print capitalism,' new power was unleashed in the world, the power of mass literacy and its attendant large-scale production of projects of ethnic affinity that were remarkably free of the need for face-to-face communication or even of indirect communication between persons and groups. The act of reading things together set the stage for movements based on a paradox – the paradox of constructed primordialism. There is, of course, a great deal else that is involved in the story of colonialism and its dialectically generated nationalisms [. . .], but the issue of constructed ethnicities is surely a crucial strand in this tale.

But the revolution of print capitalism and the cultural affinities and dialogues unleashed by it were only modest precursors to the world we live in now. For in the past century, there has been a technological explosion, largely in the domain of transportation and information, that makes the interactions of a print-dominated world seem as hard-won and as easily erased as the print revolution made earlier forms of cultural traffic appear. For with the advent of the steamship, the automobile, the airplane, the camera, the computer, and the telephone, we have entered into an altogether new condition of neighborliness, even with those most distant from ourselves. Marshall McLuhan, among others, sought to theorize about this world as a 'global village,' but theories such as McLuhan's appear to have overestimated the communitarian implications of the new media order. We are now aware that with media, each time we are tempted to speak of the global village, we must be reminded that media create communities with 'no sense of place' [. . .]. The world we live in now seems rhizomic [. . .], even schizophrenic, calling for theories of rootlessness, alienation, and psychological distance between individuals and groups on the one hand, and fantasies (or nightmares) of electronic propinquity on the other. Here, we are close to the central problematic of cultural processes in today's world.

Thus, the curiosity that recently drove Pico Iyer to Asia [. . .] is in some ways the product of a confusion between some ineffable McDonalidization of the world and the much subtler play of indigenous trajectories of desire and fear with global flows of people and things. Indeed, Iyer's own impressions are testimony to the

fact that, if a global cultural system is emerging, it is filled with ironies and resistances, sometimes camouflaged as passivity and a bottomless appetite in the Asian
world for things Western.

Iyer's own account of the uncanny Philippine affinity for American popular
music is rich testimony to the global culture of the hyperreal, for somehow
Philippine renditions of American popular songs are both more widespread in the
Philippines, and more disturbingly faithful to their originals, than they are in the
United States today. An entire nation seems to have learned to mimic Kenny Rogers
and the Lennon sisters, like a vast Asian Motown chorus. But *Americanization* is
certainly a pallid term to apply to such a situation, for not only are there more
Filipinos singing perfect renditions of some American songs (often from the
American past) than there are Americans doing so, there is also, of course, the fact
that the rest of their lives is not in complete synchrony with the referential world
that first gave birth to these songs.

In a further globalizing twist on what Fredric Jameson has recently called
nostalgia for the present [. . .], these Filipinos look back to a world they have never
lost. This is one of the central ironies of the politics of global cultural flows, especially in the arena of entertainment and leisure. It plays havoc with the hegemony
of Eurochronology. American nostalgia feeds on Filipino desire represented as a
hypercompetent reproduction. Here, we have nostalgia without memory. The
paradox, of course, has its explanations, and they are historical, unpacked, they lay
bare the story of the American missionization and political rape of the Philippines,
one result of which has been the creation of a nation of makebelieve Americans,
who tolerated for so long a leading lady who played the piano while the slums of
Manila expanded and decayed. Perhaps the most radical postmodernists would
argue that this is hardly surprising because in the peculiar chronicities of late capitalism, pastiche and nostalgia are central modes of image production and reception.
Americans themselves are hardly in the present anymore as they stumble into the
mega-technologies of the twenty-first century garbed in the film-noir scenarios of
sixties' chills, fifties' diners, forties' clothing, thirties' houses, twenties' dances, and
so on ad infinitum.

As far as the United States is concerned, one might suggest that the issue
is no longer one of nostalgia but of a social *imaginaire* built largely around
reruns. Jameson was bold to link the politics of nostalgia to the postmodern
commodity sensibility, and surely he was right [. . .]. The drug wars in Colombia
recapitulate the tropical sweat of Vietnam, with Ollie North and his succession
of masks – Jimmy Stewart concealing John Wayne concealing Spiro Agnew and
all of them transmogrifying into Sylvester Stallone, who wins in Afghanistan – thus
simultaneously fulfilling the secret American envy of Soviet imperialism and
the rerun (this time with a happy ending) of the Vietnam War. The Rolling
Stones, approaching their fifties, gyrate before eighteen-year-olds who do not
appear to need the machinery of nostalgia to be sold on their parents' heroes.
Paul McCartney is selling the Beatles to a new audience by hitching his oblique
nostalgia to their desire for the new that smacks of the old. *Dragnet* is back
in nineties' drag, and so is *Adam-12*, not to speak of *Batman* and *Mission Impossible*,
all dressed up technologically but remarkably faithful to the atmospherics of their
originals.

The past is now not a land to return to in a simple politics of memory. It has become a synchronic warehouse of cultural scenarios, a kind of temporal central casting, to which recourse can be taken as appropriate, depending on the movie to be made, the scene to be enacted, the hostages to be rescued. All this is par for the course, if you follow Jean Baudrillard or Jean-Francois Lyotard into a world of signs wholly unmoored from their social signifiers (all the world's a Disneyland). But I would like to suggest that the apparent increasing substitutability of whole periods and postures for one another, in the cultural styles of advanced capitalism, is tied to larger global forces, which have done much to show Americans that the past is usually another country. If your present is their future (as in much modernization theory and in many self-satisfied tourist fantasies), and their future is your past (as in the case of the Filipino virtuosos of American popular music), then your own past can be made to appear as simply a normalized modality of your present. Thus, although some anthropologists may continue to relegate their Others to temporal spaces that they do not themselves occupy [. . .], postindustrial cultural productions have entered a postnostalgic phase.

The crucial point, however, is that the United States is no longer the puppeteer of a world system of images but is only one node of a complex transnational construction of imaginary landscapes. The world we live in today is characterized by a new role for the imagination in social life. To grasp this new role, we need to bring together the old idea of images, especially mechanically produced images (in the Frankfurt School sense); the idea of the imagined community (in Anderson's sense); and the French idea of the imaginary (*imaginaire*) as a constructed landscape of collective aspirations, which is no more and no less real than the collective representations of Émile Durkheim, now mediated through the complex prism of modern media.

The image, the imagined, the imaginary – these are all terms that direct us to something critical and new in global cultural processes: *the imagination as a social practice*. No longer mere fantasy (opium for the masses whose real work is elsewhere), no longer simple escape (from a world defined principally by more concrete purposes and structures), no longer elite pastime (thus not relevant to the lives of ordinary people), and no longer mere contemplation (irrelevant for new forms of desire and subjectivity), the imagination has become an organized field of social practices, a form of work (in the sense of both labor and culturally organized practice), and a form of negotiation between sites of agency (individuals) and globally defined fields of possibility. This unleashing of the imagination links the play of pastiche (in some settings) to the terror and coercion of states and their competitors. The imagination is now central to all forms of agency, is itself a social fact, and is the key component of the new global order. But to make this claim meaningful, we must address some other issues.

The central problem of today's global interactions is the tension between cultural homogenization and cultural heterogenization. A vast array of empirical facts could be brought to bear on the side of the homogenization argument, and much of it has come from the left end of the spectrum of media studies [. . .], and some from other perspectives [. . .]. Most often, the homogenization argument subspeciates into either an argument about Americanization or an argument about commoditization, and very often the two arguments are closely linked. What these arguments fail to consider is that at least as rapidly as forces from various metropolises are brought into new societies they tend to become indigenized in one or another way: this is true of music and housing styles as much as it is true of science and terrorism, spectacles and constitutions. The dynamics of such indigenization have just begun to be explored systematically [. . .], and much more needs to be done. But it is worth noticing that for the people of Irian Jaya, Indonesianization may be more worrisome than Americanization, as Japanization may be for Koreans, Indianization for Sri Lankans, Vietnamization for the Cambodians, and Russianization for the people of Soviet Armenia and the Baltic republics. Such a list of alternative fears to Americanization could be greatly expanded, but it is not a shapeless inventory: for polities of smaller scale, there is always a fear of cultural absorption by polities of larger scale, especially those that are nearby. One man's imagined community is another man's political prison.

This scalar dynamic, which has widespread global manifestations, is also tied to the relationship between nations and states, to which I shall return later. For the moment let us note that the simplification of these many forces (and fears) of homogenization can also be exploited by nation-states in relation to their own minorities, by posing global commoditization (or capitalism, or some other such external enemy) as more real than the threat of its own hegemonic strategies.

The new global cultural economy has to be seen as a complex, overlapping, disjunctive order that cannot any longer be understood in terms of existing center–periphery models (even those that might account for multiple centers and peripheries). Nor is it susceptible to simple models of push and pull (in terms of migration theory), or of surpluses and deficits (as in traditional models of balance of trade), or of consumers and producers (as in most neo-Marxist theories of development). Even the most complex and flexible theories of global development that have come out of the Marxist tradition [. . .] are inadequately quirky and have failed to come to terms with what Scott Lash and John Urry have called disorganized capitalism [. . .]. The complexity of the current global economy has to do with certain fundamental disjunctures between economy, culture, and politics that we have only begun to theorize.

I propose that an elementary framework for exploring such disjunctures is to look at the relationship among five dimensions of global cultural flows that can be termed (a) *ethnoscapes*, (b) *mediascapes*, (c) *technoscapes*, (d) *financescapes*, and (e) *ideoscapes*. The suffix *-scape* allows us to point to the fluid, irregular shapes of these landscapes, shapes that characterize international capital as deeply as they do international clothing styles. These terms with the common suffix *-scape* also indicate that these are not objectively given relations that look the same from every angle of vision but, rather, that they are deeply perspectival constructs, inflected by the historical, linguistic, and political situatedness of different sorts of actors: nation-states, multinationals, diasporic communities, as well as subnational groupings and movements (whether religious, political, or economic), and even intimate face-to-face groups, such as villages, neighborhoods, and families. Indeed, the individual actor is the last locus of this perspectival set of landscapes, for these landscapes are eventually navigated by agents who both experience and constitute larger formations, in part from their own sense of what these landscapes offer.

These landscapes thus are the building blocks of what (extending Benedict Anderson) I would like to call *imagined worlds*, that is, the multiple worlds that are constituted by the historically situated imaginations of persons and groups spread around the globe [. . .]. An important fact of the world we live in today is that many persons on the globe live in such imagined worlds (and not just in imagined communities) and thus are able to contest and sometimes even subvert the imagined worlds of the official mind and of the entrepreneurial mentality that surround them.

By *ethnoscape*, I mean the landscape of persons who constitute the shifting world in which we live: tourists, immigrants, refugees, exiles, guest workers, and other moving groups and individuals constitute an essential feature of the world and appear to affect the politics of (and between) nations to a hitherto unprecedented degree. This is not to say that there are no relatively stable communities and networks of kinship, friendship, work, and leisure, as well as of birth, residence, and other filial forms. But it is to say that the warp of these stabilities is everywhere shot through with the woof of human motion, as more persons and groups deal with the realities of having to move or the fantasies of wanting to move. What is more, both these realities and fantasies now function on larger scales, as men and women from villages in India think not just of moving to Poona or Madras but of moving to Dubai and Houston, and refugees from Sri Lanka find themselves in South India as well as in Switzerland, just as the Hmong are driven to London as well as to Philadelphia. And as international capital shifts its needs, as production and technology generate different needs, as nation-states shift their policies on refugee populations, these moving groups can never afford to let their imaginations rest too long, even if they wish to.

By *technoscape*, I mean the global configuration, also ever fluid, of technology and the fact that technology, both high and low, both mechanical and informational, now moves at high speeds across various kinds of previously impervious boundaries. Many countries now are the roots of multinational enterprise: a huge steel complex in Libya may involve interests from India, China, Russia, and Japan, providing different components of new technological configurations. The odd distribution of technologies, and thus the peculiarities of these technoscapes, are increasingly driven not by any obvious economies of scale, of political control, or of market rationality but by increasingly complex relationships among money flows, political possibilities, and the availability of both un- and highly skilled labor. So, while India exports waiters and chauffeurs to Dubai and Sharjah, it also exports software engineers to the United States — indentured briefly to Tata-Burroughs or the World Bank, then laundered through the State Department to become wealthy resident aliens, who are in turn objects of seductive messages to invest their money and know-how in federal and state projects in India.

The global economy can still be described in terms of traditional indicators (as the World Bank continues to do) and studied in terms of traditional comparisons (as in Project Link at the University of Pennsylvania), but the complicated technoscapes (and the shifting ethnoscapes) that underlie these indicators and comparisons are further out of the reach of the queen of social sciences than ever before. How is one to make a meaningful comparison of wages in Japan and the United States or of real-estate costs in New York and Tokyo, without taking sophisticated account of the very complex fiscal and investment flows that link the two economies through a global grid of currency speculation and capital transfer?

Thus it is useful to speak as well of *financescapes*, as the disposition of global capital is now a more mysterious, rapid, and difficult landscape to follow than ever before, as currency markets, national stock exchanges, and commodity speculations move megamonies through national turnstiles at blinding speed, with vast, absolute implications for small differences in percentage points and time units. But the critical point is that the global relationship among ethnoscapes, technoscapes, and financescapes is deeply disjunctive and profoundly unpredictable because each of these landscapes is subject to its own constraints and incentives (some political, some informational, and some technoenvironmental), at the same time as each acts as a constraint and a parameter for movements in the others. Thus, even an elementary model of global political economy must take into account the deeply disjunctive relationships among human movement, technological flow, and financial transfers.

Further refracting these disjunctures (which hardly form a simple, mechanical global infrastructure in any case) are what I call *mediascapes* and *ideoscapes*, which are closely related landscapes of images. *Mediascapes* refer both to the distribution of the electronic capabilities to produce and disseminate information (newspapers, magazines, television stations, and film-production studios), which are now available to a growing number of private and public interests throughout the world, and to the images of the world created by these media. These images involve many complicated inflections, depending on their mode (documentary or entertainment), their hardware (electronic or preelectronic), their audiences (local, national, or transnational), and the interests of those who own and control them. What is most important about these mediascapes is that they provide (especially in their television, film, and cassette forms) large and complex repertoires of images, narratives, and ethnoscapes to viewers throughout the world, in which the world of commodities and the world of news and politics are profoundly mixed. What this means is that many audiences around the world experience the media themselves as a complicated and interconnected repertoire of print, celluloid, electronic screens, and billboards. The lines between the realistic and the fictional landscape they see are blurred, so that the farther away these audiences are from the experiences of metropolitan life, the more likely they are to construct imagined worlds that are chimerical, aesthetic, even fantastic objects, particularly if assessed by the criteria of some other perspective, some other imagined world.

Mediascapes, whether produced by private or state interests, tend to be image-centred, narrative-based accounts of strips of reality, and what they offer to those who experience and transform them is a series of elements (such as characters, plots, and textual forms) out of which scripts can be formed of imagined lives, their own as well as those of others living in other places. These scripts can and do get disaggregated into complex sets of metaphors by which people live [. . .] as they help to constitute narratives of the Other and protonarratives of possible lives, fantasies that could become prolegomena to the desire for acquisition and movement.

*Ideoscapes* are also concatenations of images, but they are often directly political and frequently have to do with the ideologies of states and the counterideologies of movements explicitly oriented to capturing state power or a piece of it. These ideoscapes are composed of elements of the Enlightenment worldview, which consists of a chain of ideas, terms, and images, including *freedom, welfare, rights, sovereignty, representation*, and the master term *democracy*. The master narrative of the Enlightenment (and its many variants in Britain, France, and the United States) was constructed with a certain internal logic and presupposed a certain relationship between reading, representation, and the public sphere. [. . .] But the diaspora of these terms and images across the world, especially since the nineteenth century, has loosened the internal coherence that held them together in a Euro-American master narrative and provided instead a loosely structured synopticon of politics, in which different nation-states, as part of their evolution, have organized their political cultures around different keywords [. . .].

As a result of the differential diaspora of these keywords, the political narratives that govern communication between elites and followers in different parts of the world involve problems of both a semantic and pragmatic nature: semantic to the extent that words (and their lexical equivalents) require careful translation from context to context in their global movements, and pragmatic to the extent that the use of these words by political actors and their audiences may be subject to very different sets of contextual conventions that mediate their translation into public politics. Such conventions are not only matters of the nature of political rhetoric: for example, what does the aging Chinese leadership mean when it refers to the dangers of hooliganism? What does the South Korean leadership mean when it speaks of discipline as the key to democratic industrial growth?

These conventions also involve the far more subtle question of what sets of communicative genres are valued in what way (newspapers versus cinema, for example) and what sorts of pragmatic genre conventions govern the collective readings of different kinds of text. So, while an Indian audience may be attentive to the resonances of a political speech in terms of some keywords and phrases reminiscent of Hindi cinema, a Korean audience may respond to the subtle codings of Buddhist or neo-Confucian rhetoric encoded in a political document. The very relationship of reading to hearing and seeing may vary in important ways that determine the morphology of these different ideoscapes as they shape themselves in different national and transnational contexts. This globally variable synaesthesia has hardly even been noted, but it demands urgent analysis. Thus *democracy* has clearly become a master term, with powerful echoes from Haiti and Poland to the former Soviet Union and China, but it sits at the center of a variety of ideoscapes, composed of distinctive pragmatic configurations of rough translations of other central terms from the vocabulary of the Enlightenment. This creates ever new terminological kaleidoscopes, as states (and the groups that seek to capture them) seek to pacify populations whose own ethnoscapes are in motion and whose mediascapes may create severe problems for the ideoscapes with which they are presented. The fluidity of ideoscapes is complicated in particular by the growing diasporas (both voluntary and involuntary) of intellectuals who continuously inject new meaning-streams into the discourse of democracy in different parts of the world.

This extended terminological discussion of the five terms I have coined sets the basis for a tentative formulation about the conditions under which current global flows occur: they occur in and through the growing disjunctures among ethnoscapes, technoscapes, financescapes, mediascapes, and ideoscapes. This formulation, the core of my model of global cultural flow, needs some explanation. First, people, machinery, money, images, and ideas now follow increasingly non-isomorphic paths; of course, at all periods in human history, there have been some disjunctures in the flows of these things, but the sheer speed, scale, and volume of each of these flows are now so great that the disjunctures have become central to the politics of global culture. The Japanese are notoriously hospitable to ideas and are stereotyped as inclined to export (all) and import (some) goods, but they are also notoriously closed to immigration, like the Swiss, the Swedes, and the Saudis. Yet the Swiss and the Saudis accept populations of guest workers, thus creating labor diasporas of Turks, Italians, and other circum-Mediterranean groups. Some such guest-worker groups maintain continuous contact with their home nations, like the Turks, but others, like high-level South Asian migrants, tend to desire lives in their new homes, raising anew the problem of reproduction in a deterritorialized context.

Deterritorialization, in general, is one of the central forces of the modern world because it brings laboring populations into the lower-class sectors and spaces of relatively wealthy societies, while sometimes creating exaggerated and intensified senses of criticism or attachment to politics in the home state. Deterritorialization, whether of Hindus, Sikhs, Palestinians, or Ukrainians, is now at the core of a variety of global fundamentalisms, including Islamic and Hindu fundamentalism. In the Hindu case, for example, it is clear that the overseas movement of Indians has been exploited by a variety of interests both within and outside India to create a complicated network of finances and religious identifications, by which the problem of cultural reproduction for Hindus abroad has become tied to the politics of Hindu fundamentalism at home.

At the same time, deterritorialization creates new markets for film companies, art impresarios, and travel agencies, which thrive on the need of the deterritorialized population for contact with its homeland. Naturally, these invented homelands, which constitute the mediascapes of deterritorialized groups, can often become sufficiently fantastic and one-sided that they provide the material for new ideoscapes in which ethnic conflicts can begin to erupt. The creation of Khalistan, an invented homeland of the deterritorialized Sikh population of England, Canada, and the United States, is one example of the bloody potential in such mediascapes as they interact with the internal colonialisms of the nation-state [. . .]. The West Bank, Namibia, and Eritrea are other theaters for the enactment of the bloody negotiation between existing nation-states and various deterritorialized groupings.

It is in the fertile ground of deterritorialization, in which money, commodities, and persons are involved in ceaselessly chasing each other around the world, that the mediascapes and ideoscapes of the modern world find their fractured and fragmented counterpart. For the ideas and images produced by mass media often are only partial guides to the goods and experiences that deterritorialized populations transfer to one another. In Mira Nair's brilliant film *India Cabaret*, we see the multiple loops of this fractured deterritorialization as young women, barely competent in Bombay's metropolitan glitz, come to seek their fortunes as cabaret dancers and prostitutes in Bombay, entertaining men in clubs with dance formats derived wholly from the prurient dance sequences of Hindi films. These scenes in turn cater to ideas about Western and foreign women and their looseness, while they provide tawdry career alibis for these women. Some of these women come from Kerala, where cabaret clubs and the pornographic film industry have blossomed, partly in response to the purses and tastes of Keralites returned from the Middle East, where their diasporic lives away from women distort their very sense of what the relations between men and women might be. These tragedies of displacement could certainly be replayed in a more detailed analysis of the relations between the Japanese and German sex tours to Thailand and the tragedies of the sex trade in Bangkok, and in other similar loops that tie together fantasies about the Other, the conveniences and seductions of travel, the economics of global trade, and the brutal mobility fantasies that dominate gender politics in many parts of Asia and the world at large.

While far more could be said about the cultural politics of deterritorialization and the larger sociology of displacement that it expresses, it is appropriate at this juncture to bring in the role of the nation-state in the disjunctive global economy of culture today. The relationship between states and nations is everywhere an embattled one. It is possible to say that in many societies the nation and the state have become one another's projects. That is, while nations (or more properly groups with ideas about nationhood) seek to capture or co-opt states and state power, states simultaneously seek to capture and monopolize ideas about nationhood [. . .]. In general, separatist transnational movements, including those that have included terror in their methods, exemplify nations in search of states. Sikhs, Tamil Sri Lankans, Basques, Moros, Quebecois – each of these represents imagined communities that seek to create states of their own or carve pieces out of existing states. States, on the other hand, are everywhere seeking to monopolize the moral resources of community, either by flatly claiming perfect coevality between nation and state, or by systematically museumizing and representing all the groups within them in a variety of heritage politics that seems remarkably uniform throughout the world [. . .].

Here, national and international mediascapes are exploited by nation-states to pacify separatists or even the potential fissiparousness of all ideas of difference. Typically, contemporary nation-states do this by exercising taxonomic control over difference, by creating various kinds of international spectacle to domesticate difference and by seducing small groups with the fantasy of self-display on some sort of global or cosmopolitan stage. One important new feature of global cultural politics, tied to the disjunctive relationships among the various landscapes discussed earlier, is that state and nation are at each other's throats, and the hyphen that links them is now less an icon of conjuncture than an index of disjuncture. This disjunctive relationship between nation and state has two levels: at the level of any given nation-state, it means that there is a battle of the imagination, with state and nation seeking to cannibalize one another. Here is the seedbed of brutal separatisms – majoritarianisms that seem to have appeared from nowhere and microidentities that have become political projects within the nation-state. At another level, this disjunctive relationship is deeply entangled with the global disjunctures discussed throughout this chapter: ideas of nationhood appear to be steadily increasing in scale and regularly crossing existing state boundaries, sometimes, as with the Kurds, because previous identities stretched across vast national spaces or, as with the Tamils in Sri Lanka, the dormant threads of a transnational diaspora have been activated to ignite the micropolitics of a nation-state.

In discussing the cultural politics that have subverted the hyphen that links the nation to the state, it is especially important not to forget the mooring of such politics in the irregularities that now characterize disorganized capital [. . .]. Because labor, finance, and technology are now so widely separated, the volatilities that underlie movements for nationhood (as large as transnational Islam on the one hand, or as small as the movement of the Gurkhas for a separate state in Northeast India) grind against the vulnerabilities that characterize the relationships between states. States find themselves pressed to stay open by the forces of media, technology, and travel that have fueled consumerism throughout the world and have increased the craving, even in the non-Western world, for new commodities and spectacles. On the other hand, these very cravings can become caught up in new ethnoscapes, mediascapes, and, eventually, ideoscapes, such as democracy in China, that the state cannot tolerate as threats to its own control over ideas of nationhood and peoplehood. States throughout the world are under siege, especially where contests over the ideoscapes of democracy are fierce and fundamental, and where there are radical disjunctures between ideoscapes and technoscapes (as in the case of very small countries that lack contemporary technologies or production and information); or between ideoscapes and financescapes (as in countries such as Mexico or Brazil, where international lending influences national politics to a very large degree); or between ideoscapes and ethnoscapes (as in Beirut, where diasporic, local, and translocal filiations are suicidally at battle); or between ideoscapes and mediascapes (as in many countries in the Middle East and Asia) where the lifestyles represented on both national and international TV and cinema completely overwhelm and undermine the rhetoric of national politics. In the Indian case, the myth of the law-breaking hero has emerged to mediate this naked struggle between the pieties and realities of Indian politics, which has grown increasingly brutalized and corrupt[. . .].

The transnational movement of the martial arts, particularly through Asia, as mediated by the Hollywood and Hong Kong film industries [. . .] is a rich illustration of the ways in which long-standing martial arts traditions, reformulated to meet the fantasies of contemporary (sometimes lumpen) youth populations, create new cultures of masculinity and violence, which are in turn the fuel for increased violence in national and international politics. Such violence is in turn the spur to an increasingly rapid and amoral arms trade that penetrates the entire world. The worldwide spread of the AK-47 and the Uzi, in films, in corporate and state security, in terror, and in police and military activity, is a reminder that apparently simple technical uniformities often conceal an increasingly complex set of loops, linking images of violence to aspirations for community in some imagined world.

Returning then to the ethnoscapes with which I began, the central paradox of ethnic politics in today's world is that primordia (whether of language or skin color or neighborhood or kinship) have become globalized. That is, sentiments, whose greatest force is in their ability to ignite intimacy into a political state and turn locality into a staging ground for identity, have become spread over vast and irregular spaces as groups move yet stay linked to one another through sophisticated media capabilities. This is not to deny that such primordia are often the product of invented traditions [. . .] or retrospective affiliations, but to emphasize that because of the disjunctive and unstable interplay of commerce, media, national policies, and consumer fantasies, ethnicity, once a genie contained in the bottle of some sort of locality (however large), has now become a global force, forever slipping in and through the cracks between states and borders.

But the relationship between the cultural and economic levels of this new set of global disjunctures is not a simple one-way street in which the terms of global cultural politics are set wholly by, or confined wholly within, the vicissitudes of international flows of technology, labor, and finance, demanding only a modest modification of existing neo-Marxist models of uneven development and state formation. There is a deeper change, itself driven by the disjunctures among all the landscapes I have discussed and constituted by their continuously fluid and uncertain interplay, that concerns the relationship between production and consumption in today's global economy. Here, I begin with Marx's famous (and often mined) view of the fetishism of the commodity and suggest that this fetishism has been replaced in the world at large (now seeing the world as one large, interactive system, composed of many complex subsystems) by two mutually supportive descendants, the first of which I call production fetishism and the second, the fetishism of the consumer.

By *production fetishism* I mean an illusion created by contemporary transnational production loci that masks translocal capital, transnational earning flows, global management, and often faraway workers (engaged in various kinds of high-tech putting-out operations) in the idiom and spectacle of local (sometimes even worker) control, national productivity, and territorial sovereignty. To the extent that various kinds of free-trade zones have become the models for production at large, especially of high-tech commodities, production has itself become a fetish, obscuring not social relations as such but the relations of production, which are increasingly transnational. The locality (both in the sense of the local factory or site of production and in the extended sense of the nation-state) becomes a fetish that disguises the globally dispersed forces that actually drive the production process. This generates alienation (in Marx's sense) twice intensified, for its social sense is not compounded by a complicated spatial dynamic that is increasingly global.

As for the *fetishism of the consumer*, I mean to indicate here that the consumer has been transformed through commodity flows (and the media-scapes, especially of advertising, that accompany them) into a sign, both in Baudrillard's sense of a simulacrum that only asymptomatically approaches the form of a real social agent, and in the sense of a mask for the real seat of agency, which is not the consumer but the producer and the many forces that constitute production. Global advertising is the key technology for the worldwide dissemination of a plethora of creative and culturally well-chosen ideas of consumer agency. These images of agency are increasingly distortions of a world of merchandising so subtle that the consumer is consistently helped to believe that he or she is an actor, where in fact he or she is at best a chooser.

The globalization of culture is not the same as its homogenization, but globalization involves the use of a variety of instruments of homogenization (armaments, advertising techniques, language hegemonies, and clothing styles) that are absorbed into local political and cultural economies, only to be repatriated as heterogeneous dialogues of national sovereignty, free enterprise, and fundamentalism in which the state plays an increasingly delicate role: too much openness to global flows, and the nation-state is threatened by revolt, as in the China syndrome; too little, and the state exits the international stage, as Burma, Albania, and North Korea in various ways have done. In general, the state has become the arbitrageur of this *repatriation of difference* (in the form of goods, signs, slogans, and styles). But this repatriation or export of the designs and commodities of difference continuously exacerbates the internal politics of majoritarianism and homogenization, which is most frequently played out in debates over heritage.

Thus the central feature of global culture today is the politics of the mutual effort of sameness and difference to cannibalize one another and thereby proclaim their successful hijacking of the twin Enlightenment ideas of the triumphantly universal and the resiliently particular. This mutual cannibalization shows its ugly face in riots, refugee flows, state-sponsored torture, and ethnocide (with or without state support). Its brighter side is in the expansion of many individual horizons of hope and fantasy, in the global spread of oral rehydration therapy and other low-tech instruments of well-being, in the susceptibility even of South Africa to the force of global opinion, in the inability of the Polish state to repress its own working classes, and in the growth of a wide range of progressive, transnational alliances. Examples of both sorts could be multiplied. The critical point is that both sides of the coin of global cultural process today are products of the infinitely varied mutual contest of sameness and difference on a stage characterized by radical disjunctures between different sorts of global flows and the uncertain landscapes created in and through these disjunctures. [. . .]

# NATURE

- Ulrich Beck, Ecological questions in a framework of manufactured uncertainties

- Donna Haraway, The biopolitics of postmodern bodies

**Ulrich Beck** was born in 1944 in Germany. He has taught sociology at the University of Munich. Among his chief works are *Risk Society* (1986) and *Ecological Enlightenment* (1992).

**Donna Haraway** was trained in the history and philosophy of science. She holds a PhD in biology from Yale. Haraway teaches in the History of Consciousness Program at the University of California at Santa Cruz. Her writings include *Primate Visions* (1989) and *Simians, Cyborgs, and Women* (1991).

# Chapter 25

# Ulrich Beck

## ECOLOGICAL QUESTIONS IN A FRAMEWORK OF MANUFACTURED UNCERTAINTIES

R ISK SOCIETY, FULLY thought through, means world risk society. For its axial principle, its challenges, are dangers produced by civilization which cannot be socially delimited in either space or time. In this way the basic conditions and principles of the first, industrial modernity – class antagonism, national statehood, as well as the images of linear, technical-economic rationality and control – are circumvented and annulled [. . .].

It is clear, then, which concepts will *not* be employed here. The focus will not be on 'nature' or the 'destruction of nature', nor on 'ecological' or 'environmental problems'. Does this have to do with a systematic setting of goals? Yes, it does – as we shall see. In fact, we shall propose – for the sociological analysis of ecological questions – a conceptual framework which allows us to grasp as problems not of the *environ*ment or surrounding world, but of the *inner* world of society. In place of the seemingly self-evident key concepts of 'nature', 'ecology' and 'environment', which have their ground in an opposition to the social, this framework starts beyond the dualism of society and nature. Its central themes and perspectives have to do with *fabricated uncertainty* within our civilization: risk, danger, side-effects, insurability, individualization and globalization.

It has often been objected that such talk of a world risk society encourages a kind of neo-Spenglerism and blocks any political action. We shall see, however, that the opposite is also the case. In the self-understanding of world risk society, society becomes *reflexive* in three sense [. . .]. First, it becomes an issue and problem for itself: global dangers set up global mutualities, and indeed the contours of a (potential) world public sphere begin to take shape. Second, the perceived globality of the self-endangerment of civilization triggers a politically mouldable impulse towards the development of co-operative international institutions. Third, the boundaries of the political come to be removed: constellations appear of a sub-politics at once global and direct, which relativizes or circumvents the co-ordinates

and coalitions of nation-state politics and may lead to worldwide 'alliances of mutually exclusive beliefs'. In other words, 'cosmopolitan society' (Kant) can take shape
in the perceived necessity of world risk society.

## I  Elements of a theory of world risk society

### The indeterminacy of the concepts of 'nature' and ecology

The concept of 'ecology' has had quite a success story. Today, responsibility for the
condition of nature is laid at the door of ministers and managers. Evidence that
the 'side-effects' of products or industrial processes are endangering the basic conditions of life can cause markets to collapse, destroying political confidence as well
as economic capital and belief in the superior rationality of experts. This success,
in many respects thoroughly subversive, disguises the fact that 'ecology' is a quite
vague concept; everyone gives a different answer to the question of what should
be preserved. [. . .]

  If someone uses the word 'nature', the question immediately arises: what *cultural
model* of 'nature' is being taken for granted? Nature 'in hand', driven to exhaustion by industry? Or the country life of the 1950s (as it appears today in retrospect
or as it appeared then to people living in the country)? Mountain solitude before
there was a book called *Wandering in the Solitary Mountains*? The nature of the natural
sciences? Or as it is sold in the tourist supermarket brochures of world solitude?
The 'hard-headed' view of businessmen that industrial operations on nature can
always be fully compensated? Or the view of 'sensitive' people stirred by nature,
who consider that even small-scale operations may cause irreparable damage?

  So, nature itself is not nature: it is a concept, a norm, a recollection, a utopia,
an alternative plan. Today more than ever. Nature is being rediscovered, pampered,
at a time when it is no longer there. The ecological movement is reacting to the
global state of a contradictory fusion of nature and society, which has superseded
both concepts in a relationship of mutual linkages and injuries of which we do not
yet have any idea, let alone any concept. In the ecological debate, attempts to use
nature as a standard against its own destruction rest upon a *naturalistic misunder-
standing*. For the nature invoked is no longer there [. . .]. What is there, and what
creates such a political stir, are different forms of socialization and different symbolic
mediations of nature (and the destruction of nature). It is these *cultural concepts* of
nature, these opposing views of nature and their (national) cultural traditions which,
behind the disputes among experts and the technical formulae and dangers, have
a determining influence on ecological conflicts in Europe, as well as between Europe
and 'Third World' countries and within those countries themselves.

  But if nature 'in itself' cannot be the analytic reference for the ecological crisis
and for a critique of the industrial system, what can play this role? A number of
answers are possible. The most common is: the *science* of nature. Technical formulae
– toxicity of air, water and food, climatological models, or feedback loops of
the ecosystem conceived along cybernetic lines – are supposed to be decisive
for whether damage and destruction are tolerable. This approach, however, has at
least three drawbacks. First, it leads straight towards 'ecocracy', which differs from

technocracy through its greater extent of power (global management), crowned with a distinctively good conscience.

Second, it ignores the significance of cultural perceptions and of intercultural conflict and dialogue. For the same dangers appear to one person as dragons, and to another as earthworms. The best example of this is the assessment of the hazards of atomic energy. For our French neighbours, nuclear power stations symbolize the pinnacle of modernity; adults take their children to them on bank-holiday pilgrimages of awe. Nothing has changed as a result of Chernobyl, or of the realization that even today, ten years later, all the dead and injured from that 'accident' have not yet been *born*.

Third, natural-science approaches to ecological questions again imply hidden cultural models of nature (e.g. the model characteristic of scientific systems, which clearly differs from the earlier one of natural conservation).

Of course, everyone has to think in the concepts of natural science, simply to perceive the world as ecologically threatened. Everyday ecological consciousness is thus the exact opposite of some 'natural' consciousness: it is a totally scientific view of the world, in which chemical formulae determine everyday behaviour.

And yet, all manner of experts can never answer the question: how do we want to live? What people are and are not prepared to go on accepting, does not follow from any technical or ecological diagnosis of dangers. This must rather become the object of a global dialogue between cultures. And it is precisely that which appears as the aim in a second perspective, associated with the science of *culture*. Here, the scale and urgency of the ecological crisis vary according to intra-cultural and intercultural perceptions and evaluations.

What kind of truth is it – we might ask with Montaigne – which ends on the border with France and is then regarded as pure illusion? Dangers, it would seem, do not exist 'in themselves', independently of our perceptions. They become a political issue only when people are generally aware of them; they are social constructs which are strategically defined, covered up or dramatized in the public sphere with the help of scientific material supplied for the purpose. Not by chance, two Anglo-Saxon social anthropologists – Mary Douglas and Aaron Wildavsky – have been developing this analysis since their book *Risk and Culture* was published in 1983. Douglas and her co-author argue there (as an affront to the rising ecological consciousness) that there is no substantive difference between the dangers posed in early history and in developed civilization – except in the mode of cultural perception and the way in which it is organized in world society.

True and important though this view may be, it is still not satisfactory. For, among other things, we know that people in the Stone Age did not have the capacity for nuclear ecological annihilation, and that the dangers posed by lurking demons did not have the same political dynamic as the man-made hazards of ecological self-destruction. [. . .]

## Beyond insurability

With these points in mind, the theory of world risk society can be made somewhat more concrete. It shares in the farewell to the society–nature dualism that Bruno Latour, Donna Haraway and Barbara Adams conduct with such intellectual flair. The only question is: how do we handle nature *after* it ends? This question, which both eco-feminism and the crisis theory of social-natural relations attempt to illuminate in various ways, is further developed in the theory of world risk society [. . .] in the direction of *institutional constructivism*. 'Nature' and the 'destruction of nature' are institutionally produced and defined (in 'lay–expert conflicts') within industrially internalized nature. Their essential content correlates with institutional power to act and to mould. Production and definition are thus two aspects of the material *and* symbolic 'production' of 'nature and the destruction of nature'; they refer, one might say, to discourse coalitions within and between quite different, ultimately world-wide action networks. It will be the task of future research to examine in detail *how* – and with what discursive and industrial resources and strategies – these differences in the naturalness of nature, in its 'destruction' and 'renaturalization', are produced, suppressed, normalized and integrated within institutions and in the conflict between cognitive actors.

The theory of world risk society translates the question of the destruction of nature into another question. How does modern society deal with self-generated manufactured uncertainties? The point of this formulation is to distinguish between decision-department *risks* that can in principle be brought under control, and *dangers* that have escaped or neutralized the control requirements of industrial society. This latter process may take at least two forms.

First, there may be a failure of the norms and institutions developed within industrial society: risk calculation, insurance principle, the concept of an accident, disaster prevention, prophylactic aftercare. Is there a ready indicator of this? Yes, there is. Controversial industries and technologies are often those which not only do not have private insurance but are completely cut off from it. This is true of atomic energy, genetic engineering (including research), and even high-risk sectors of chemical production. What goes without saying for motorists – not to use their car without insurance cover – seems to have been quietly dropped for whole industrial branches and sunrise technologies, where the dangers simply present too many problems. In other words, there are highly reliable 'technological pessimists' who do not agree with the judgement of technicians and relevant authorities about the harmlessness of their product or technology. These pessimists are the insurance actuaries and insurance companies, whose economic realism prevents them from having anything to do with a supposed 'nil risk'. World risk society, then, balances its way along *beyond the limits of insurability*.. Or, conversely, the criteria that industrial modernity uses in making provision for its self-generated dangers can be turned around into yardsticks of criticism.

Second, the pattern of decisions in industrial society, and the globality of their aggregate consequences, vary between two distinct epochs. To the extent that the decision bound up with the scientific, technical-economic dynamic are still organized at the level of the nation-state and the individual enterprise, the resulting threats make us all members of a world risk society. To assure the health and safety of citizens, no task can be performed at national level in the developed system of danger-industrialism. This is one of the essential lessons of the ecological crisis. With the appearance of ecological discourse, there is talk every day about the end of 'foreign politics', the end of 'internal affairs of another country', the end of the national state. Here we can see immediately a central strategy in the production of difference and lack of difference. The established rules of allocation and responsibility – causality and guilt – break down. This means that their undaunted application in administration, management and legal terminology now produces the opposite result: dangers grow *through* being made anonymous. The old routines of decision, control and production (in law, science, administration, industry and politics) effect the material destruction of nature *and* its symbolic normalization. The two complement and accentuate each other. Concretely, it is not rule-breaking but the rules themselves which 'normalize' the death of species, rivers or lakes.

This circular movement between symbolic normalization and permanent material threats and destruction is indicated by the concept of 'organized irresponsibility'. The state administration, politics, industrial management and research negotiate the criteria of what is 'rational and safe' – with the result that the ozone hole grows bigger, allergies spread on a mass scale and so on.

Alongside (and independently of) physical explosiveness discourse-strategic action tends to make *politically* explosive the dangers normalized in the legitimation circle of administration, politics, law and management, which spread uncontrollably to assume global dimensions. We might say, both with and against Max Weber, that purposive-rational bureaucracy transforms all-round guilt into acquittal – and thereby, as an unintended consequence, threatens the very basis of its claim to rational control.

The theory of world risk society thus replaces talk of the 'destruction of nature' with the following key idea. The conversion of the unseen side-effects of industrial production into global ecological flashpoints is not strictly a problem of the world surrounding us – not a so-called 'environmental problem' – but rather a *deep institutional crisis of the first (national) phase of industrial modernity* ('reflexive modernization'). So long as these new developments are grasped within the conceptual horizon of industrial society, they continue to be seen as negative side-effects of seemingly accountable and calculable action ('residual risks'), rather than as trends which are eroding the system and delegitimating the bases of rationality. Their central political and cultural significance becomes clear only in the concept and vantage-point of world risk society, where they draw attention to the need for reflexive self-definition (and redefinition) of the Western model of modernity.

In the phase of discourse about world risk society, it may become accepted that the threats generated through technological-industrial development – as measured by the existing institutional yardsticks – are neither calculable nor controllable. This forces people to reflect on the bases of the democratic, national, economic model of the first modernity, and to examine prevailing institutions (the externalization of effects in economics, law, science, etc.) and their historical devaluation of the bases of rationality. Here arises a truly global challenge, out of which new world flashpoints and even wars – but also supranational institutions of co-operation, conflict regulation and consensus-building – can be 'forged' [. . .].

The situation of the economy also undergoes radical change. Once upon a time – in the early-capitalist entrepreneurial paradise – industry could launch projects *without* submitting to special checks and provisions. Then came the period of state regulation, when economic activity was possible only in the framework of labour legislation, safety ordinances, tariff agreement and so on. In the world risk society

– and this is a decisive change – all these agencies and regulations can play their role, and all the valid agreements can be honoured, without this resulting in any security. Even though it respects the norms, a management team may suddenly find itself put into the dock by world public opinion and treated as 'environmental pigs'. Markets for goods and services become in principle unstable – that is, out of the control of firms using household remedies. Manufactured insecurity thus appears in the core areas of action and management based upon economic ratio-nality. The normal reactions to this are the blocking of demands for serious thought, and the condemnation as 'irrational' or 'hysterical' of the storm of protest that breaks out *in spite of* official agreements. The way is now open to a series of errors. Filled with pride at representing Reason itself in a sea of irrationalism, people stumble into the trap of risk conflicts that are hard to bring under control [. . .].

In world risk society, industrial projects become a *political* venture, in the sense that large investments presuppose long-term consensus. Such consensus, however, is no longer guaranteed – but rather jeopardized – with the old routines of simple modernization. What could previously be negotiated and implemented behind closed doors, through the force of practical constraints (e.g. waste disposal prob-lems, and even production methods or product design) are now potentially exposed to the crossfire of public criticism.

For there is probably no longer any incentive for the old 'progress coalition' of state, economy and science; industry certainly raises productivity, but at the same time it is at risk of losing legitimacy. The legal order no longer guarantees social peace, because it generalizes and legitimizes the threats to life. Consequently, there is a reversal of what is politics and what is not politics. The political is becoming non-political, and the non-political political. The hour of *subpolitics* is sounding. [. . .]

## A typology of global threats

Three types of global threat may be distinguished in the application of this theory.

First, there are conflicts over what we might call 'bads' (as opposed to 'goods'): that is, *wealth-driven* ecological destruction and technological-industrial dangers, such as the hole in the ozone layer, the greenhouse effect or regional water short-ages, as well as the unpredictable risks involved in the genetic engineering of plants and humans.

A second category, however, comprises risks that are directly related to poverty. The Brundtland Commission was the first to point out that not only is environ-mental destruction the danger shadowing growth-based modernity, but the exact opposite is also the case: a close association exists between poverty and environ-mental destruction. 'This inequality is the planet's main "environmental" problem; it is also its main "development" problem' [. . .]. Accordingly, an integrated analysis of habitation and food, loss of species and genetic resources, energy, industry and human population, shows that all these things are connected with one another and cannot be treated separately. [. . .]

Wealth-driven or poverty-driven dangers are, as it were, 'normal': they usually arise in conformity with the rules, through the application of safety norms that have been introduced precisely because they offer no protection at all or are full of loopholes. The *third* threat, however, from NBC (nuclear, biological, chemical) *weapons of mass destruction*, is actually deployed (rather than used for the purposes of terror) in the exceptional situation of war. Even after the end of the East–West confrontation, the danger of regional or global self-destruction through NBC weapons has by no means been exorcised – on the contrary, it has broken out of the control structure of the 'atomic pact' between the superpowers. To the threat of military conflict between states is now added the (looming) threat of fundamentalist or private terrorism. It can less and less be ruled out that the private possession of weapons of mass destruction, and the potential they provide for political terror, will become a new source of dangers in the world risk society.

These various global threats may very well complement and accentuate one another: that is, it will be necessary to consider the interaction between ecological destruction, wars and the consequences of uncompleted modernization. Thus, ecological destruction may promote war, either in the form of armed conflict over vitally necessary resources such as water, or because eco-fundamentalists in the West call for the use of military force to stop destruction already under way (such as the clearing of tropical forests). It is easy to imagine that a country which lives in growing poverty will exploit the environment to the hilt. In desperation (or as political cover for desperation), a military attempt might be made to grab resources vital to another country's existence. Or, ecological destruction (e.g. the flooding of Bangladesh) might trigger mass emigration which in turn leads to war. Or, again, states threatened with defeat in war might turn to the 'ultimate weapon' of blowing up their own or other countries' nuclear or chemical plants, in order to threaten nearby regions or cities with annihilation. There are no limits in our imagination to the horror scenarios that could bring the various threats into relationship with one another. [. . .]

All this confirms the diagnosis of a world risk society. For the so-called global threats have together led to a world where the basis of established risk-logic has been whittled away, and where hard-to-manage dangers prevail instead of quantifiable risks. The new dangers are removing the conventional pillars of safety calculation. Damage loses its spatio-temporal limits and becomes global and lasting. It is hardly possible any more to blame definite individuals for such damage: the principle of a guilty party has been losing its cutting edge. Often, too, financial compensation cannot be awarded for the damage done; it has no meaning to insure oneself against the worst-case effects of spiralling global threats. Hence there are no plans for aftercare if the worst should happen. [. . .]

## II The emergence of a world public and a global subpolitics

When we speak of a world risk *society*, it is also necessary to say that global threats cause, or will cause, people to act. Two distinct perspectives – arenas or actors – are possible here: in the first, globalization *from above* (e.g. through international treaties and institutions), in the second, globalization *from below* (e.g. through new transnational actors operating beyond the system of parliamentary politics and challenging established political organizations and interest groups). There is weighty evidence for both kinds of globalization. [. . .]

Richard Falk identifies a number of political arenas in which globalization from above is negotiated and pushed through.

> The response to threats against strategic oil reserves in the Middle East, the efforts to expand the GATT framework, the coercive implementation of the nuclear nonproliferation regime, the containment of South-North migration and refugee flows. [. . .] The legal implications of globalization-from-above would tend to supplant interstate law with a species of global law, but one at odds in most respects with 'the law of humanity'.

There is hardly need of further proof that, in the field of global environmental politics, it has long been a question (at best) of proverbial drops in the ocean. At the same time, however, a number of spectacular boycott movements operating world-wide across cultures have made it clear that the impotence of official politics in dealing with the industrial bloc is impotence with regard to the classical stage-setting. For powerful actors of a globalization *from below* have also appeared on the scene, especially Non-Governmental Organizations (NGOs) such as Robin Wood, Greenpeace, Amnesty International or Terre des Hommes. The UN estimates that there are now some 50,000 such groups in the world, but that does not mean much because each one, or almost each, is different. *Die Zeit* speaks of the 'New International' (article by Martin Merz and Christian Wernicke, *Die Zeit*, 25 Aug. 1995:-9ff.), which by definition falls between two stools, market and state, but which, as a third force, is gaining more and more influence and displaying its political muscle-power in relation to governments, international corporations and authorities. Here we can see the first outlines of a 'global citizenship' [. . .] – or, as we would put it, the new constellation of a global subpolitics. We must now examine how this has become possible and how it is now actually emerging.

With the victory march of industrial modernity, a purposive-rational system of politics is everywhere asserting itself. The common sense of this epoch is drawn from an everything-under-control mentality, which applies even to the uncontrollability that it itself produces. However, the accomplishment of this form of order and control brings about its opposite – the return of uncertainty and insecurity. 'Second-order dangers' [. . .] then appear as the other side of any attempt to 'get on top' of this. Unintentionally, in the shadow of the 'side-effects' of global dangers, society thus opens out into the (sub)political. In every sphere – the economy as well as science, private life and the family as well as politics – the bases of action reach a decisive turning-point: they have to be rejustified, renegotiated, rebalanced. How is this to be conceptualized?

'Crisis' is not the right concept, any more than 'dysfunction' or 'disintegration', for it is precisely the *victories* of unbridled industrial modernization that call it into question. This is just what is meant by the term '*reflexive* modernization': theoretically, application to itself; empirically, self-transformation (through individualization and globalization processes, for example); politically, loss of legitimacy and a vacuum of power. What this means may be clarified by Thomas Hobbes, the theorist of the state. As is well known, he argued for a strong, authoritarian state, but he also mentioned *one* individual right of civil resistance. If a state brings about conditions threatening to life, or if it commands a citizen 'to abstain from the use of food, ayre, medicine, or any other thing, without which he cannot live', then, according to Hobbes [. . .], 'hath that man the Liberty to disobey'.

In terms of social politics, then, the ecological crisis involves a *systematic violation of basic rights*, a crisis of basic rights whose long-term effect in weakening society can scarcely be underestimated. For dangers are being produced by industry, externalized by economics, individualized by the legal system, legitimized by the natural sciences and made to appear harmless by politics. That this is breaking down the power and credibility of institutions only becomes clear when the system is put on the spot, as Greenpeace, for example, has tried to do. The result is the subpoliticization of world society.

The concept of 'subpolitics' refers to politics outside and beyond the representative institutions of the political system of nation-states. It focuses attention on signs of an (ultimately global) self-organization of politics, which tends to set all areas of society in motion. Subpolitics means *'direct'* politics – that is, *ad hoc* individual participation in political decisions, bypassing the institutions of representative opinion-formation (political parties, parliaments) and often even lacking the protection of the law. In other words, subpolitics means the shaping of society from below. Economy, science, career, everyday existence, private life, all become caught up in the storms of political debate. But these do not fit into the traditional spectrum of party-political differences. What is characteristic of the subpolitics of world society are precisely *ad hoc 'coalitions of opposites'* (of parties, nations, regions, religions, governments, rebels, classes). Crucially, however, subpolitics sets politics free by changing the rules and boundaries of the political so that it becomes more open and susceptible to new linkages – as well as capable of being negotiated and reshaped. [. . .]

# Chapter 26

# Donna Haraway

## THE BIOPOLITICS OF
## POSTMODERN BODIES

### Lumpy discourses and the denatured bodies of biology and medicine

It has become commonplace to emphasize the multiple and specific cultural dialects interlaced in any social negotiation of disease and sickness in the contemporary worlds marked by biological research, biotechnology, and scientific medicine. The language of biomedicine is never alone in the field of empowering meanings, and its power does not flow from a consensus about symbols and actions in the face of suffering. [. . .] The power of biomedical language – with its stunning artefacts, images, architectures, social forms, and technologies – for shaping the unequal experience of sickness and death for millions is a social fact deriving from ongoing heterogeneous social processes. The power of biomedicine and biotechnology is constantly re-produced, or it would cease. This power is not a thing fixed and permanent, embedded in plastic and ready to section for microscopic observation by the historian or critic. The cultural and material authority of biomedicine's productions of bodies and selves is more vulnerable, more dynamic, more elusive, and more powerful than that.

But if there has been recognition of the many non-, para-, anti-, or extra-scientific languages in company with biomedicine that structure the embodied semiosis of mortality in the industrialized world, it is much less common to find emphasis on the multiple languages *within* the territory that is often so glibly marked scientific. 'Science says' is represented as a univocal language. Yet even the spliced character of the potent words in 'science' hints at a barely contained and inharmonious heterogeneity. The words for the overlapping discourses and their objects of knowledge, and for the abstract corporate names for the concrete places where the discourse-building work is done, suggest both the blunt foreshortening of technicist approaches to communication and the uncontainable pressures and confusions at the boundaries of meanings within 'science' – biotechnology, biomedicine, psychoneuroimmunology, immunogenetics, immunoendocrinology, neuroendocrinology, monoclonal antibodies, hybridomas, interleukines, Genentech, Embrex, Immunetech, Biogen.

This chapter explores some of the contending popular and technical languages constructing biomedical, biotechnical bodies and selves in postmodern scientific culture in the United States in the 1980s. Scientific discourses are 'lumpy'; they contain and enact condensed contestations for meanings and practices. The chief object of my attention will be the potent and polymorphous object of belief, knowledge, and practice called the immune system. My thesis is that the immune system is an elaborate icon for principal systems of symbolic and material 'difference' in late capitalism. Pre-eminently a twentieth-century object, the immune system is a map drawn to guide recognition and misrecognition of self and other in the dialectics of Western biopolitics. That is, the immune system is a plan for meaningful action to construct and maintain the boundaries for what may count as self and other in the crucial realms of the normal and the pathological. The immune system is a historically specific terrain, where global and local politics; Nobel Prize-winning research; heteroglossic cultural productions, from popular dietary practices, feminist science fiction, religious imagery, and children's games, to photographic techniques and military strategic theory; clinical medical practice; venture capital investment strategies; world-changing developments in business and technology; and the deepest personal and collective experiences of embodiment, vulnerability, power, and mortality interact with an intensity matched perhaps only in the biopolitics of sex and reproduction.

The immune system is both an iconic mythic object in high-technology culture and a subject of research and clinical practice of the first importance. Myth, laboratory, and clinic are intimately interwoven. This mundane point was fortuitously captured in the title listings in the 1986–87 *Books in Print*, where I was searching for a particular undergraduate textbook on immunology. The several pages of entries beginning with the prefix 'immuno-' were bounded, according to the English rules of alphabetical listing, by a volume called *Immortals of Science Fiction*, near one end, and by *The Immutability of God*, at the other. Examining the last section of the textbook to which *Books in Print* led me, *Immunology: A Synthesis* (Golub, 1987), I found what I was looking for: a historical progression of diagrams of theories of immunological regulation and an obituary for their draftsman, an important immunologist, Richard K. Gershon, who 'discovered' the suppressor T cell. The standard obituary tropes for the scientist, who 'must have had what the earliest explorers had, an insatiable desire to be the first person to see something, to know that you are where no man has been before', set the tone. The hero-scientist 'gloried in the layer upon interconnected layer of [the immune response's] complexity. He thrilled at seeing a layer of that complexity which no one had seen before' [. . .]. It is reasonable to suppose that all the likely readers of this textbook have been reared within hearing range of the ringing tones of the introduction to the voyages of the federation starship *Enterprise* in *Star Trek* – to boldly go where no man has gone before. Science remains an important genre of Western exploration and travel literature. Similarly, no reader, no matter how literal-minded, could be innocent of the gendered erotic trope that figures the hero's probing into nature's laminated secrets, glorying simultaneously in the layered complexity and in his own techno-erotic touch that goes ever deeper. Science as heroic quest and as erotic technique applied to the body of nature are utterly conventional figures. They take on a particular edge in late twentieth-century immune system discourse, where themes of nuclear exterminism, space adventure, extra-terrestrialism, exotic invaders, and military high-technology are pervasive.

But Golub's and Gershon's intended and explicit text is not about space invaders and the immune system as a Star Wars prototype. Their theme is the love of complexity and the intimate natural bodily technologies for generating the harmonies of organic life. In four illustrations – dated 1968, 1974, 1977, and 1982 – Gershon sketched his conception of 'the immunological orchestra' (Golub, 1987, pp. 533–6). This orchestra is a wonderful picture of the mythic and technical dimensions of the immune system [. . .]. All the illustrations are about co-operation and control, the major themes of organismic biology since the late eighteenth century. From his commanding position in the root of a lymph node, the G.O.D. of the first illustration conducts the orchestra of T and B cells and macrophages as they march about the body and play their specific parts [. . .]. The lymphocytes all look like Casper the ghost with the appropriate distinguishing nuclear morphologies drawn in the centre of their shapeless bodies. Baton in hand, G.O.D.'s arms are raised in quotation of a symphonic conductor. G.O.D. recalls the other 1960s bioreligious, Nobel Prize-winning 'joke' about the coded bodily text of post-DNA biology and medicine – the Central Dogma of molecular biology, specifying that 'information' flows only from DNA to RNA to protein. These three were called the Blessed Trinity of the secularized sacred body, and histories of the great adventures of molecular biology could be titled *The Eighth Day of Creation* [. . .], an image that takes on a certain irony in the venture capital and political environments of current biotechnology companies, like Genetech. In t he technical-mythic systems of molecular biology, code rules embodied structure and function, never the reverse. Genesis is a serious joke, when the body is theorized as a coded text whose secrets yield only to the proper reading conventions, and when the laboratory seems best characterized as a vast assemblage of technological and organic inscription devices. The Central Dogma was about a master control system for information flow in the codes that determine meaning in the great technological communication systems that organisms progressively have become after the Second World War. The body is an artificial intelligence system, and the relation of copy and original is reversed and then exploded.

G.O.D. is the Generator of Diversity, the source of the awe-inspiring multiple specificities of the polymorphous system of recognition and misrecognition we call the immune system. By the second illustration [. . .], G.O.D. is no longer in front of the immune orchestra, but is standing, arms folded, looking authoritative but not very busy, at the top of the lymph node, surrounded by the musical lymphocytes [. . .]. A special cell, the T suppressor cell, has taken over the role of conductor. By 1977, the illustration [. . .] no longer has a single conductor, but is 'led' by three mysterious subsets of T cells, who hold a total of twelve batons signifying their direction-giving surface identity markers; and G.O.D. scratches his head in patent confusion. But the immune band plays on. In the final illustration, from 1982, [. . .] 'the generator of diversity seems resigned to the conflicting calls of the angels of help and suppression', who perch above his left and right shoulders

(Golub, 1987, p. 536). Besides G.O.D. and the two angels, there is a T cell conductor and two conflicting prompters, 'each urging its own interpretation'. The joke of single masterly control of organismic harmony in the symphonic system responsible for the integrity of 'self' has become a kind of postmodern pastiche of multiple centres and peripheries, where the immune music that the page suggests would surely sound like nursery school space music. All the actors that used to be on the stage-set for the unambiguous and coherent biopolitic subject are still present, but their harmonies are definitely a bit problematic.

By the 1980s, the immune system is unambiguously a postmodern object – symbolically, technically, and politically. Katherine Hayles [. . .] characterizes postmodernism in terms of 'three waves of developments occurring at multiple sites within the culture, including literature and science'. Her archaeology begins with Saussurean linguistics, through which symbol systems were 'denaturalized'. Internally generated relational difference, rather than mimesis, ruled signification. Hayles sees the culmination of this approach in Claude Shannon's mid-century statistical theory of information, developed for packing the largest number of signals on a transmission line for the Bell Telephone Company and extended to cover communication acts in general, including those directed by the codes of bodily semiosis in ethology or molecular biology. 'Information' generating and processing systems, therefore, are postmodern objects, embedded in a theory of internally differentiated signifiers and remote from doctrines of representation as mimesis. A history-changing artefact, 'information' exists only in very specific kinds of universes. Progressively, the world and the sign seemed to exist in incommensurable universes – there was literally no *measure* linking them, and the reading conventions for all texts came to resemble those required for science fiction. What emerged was a global technology that 'made the separation of text from context an everyday experience'. Hayles's second wave, 'energized by the rapid development of information technology, made the disappearance of stable, reproducible context an international phenomenon . . . Context was no longer a natural part of every experience, but an artifact that could be altered at will.' Hayles's third wave of denaturalization concerned time. 'Beginning with the Special Theory of Relativity, time increasingly came to be seen not as an inevitable progression along a linear scale to which all humans were subject, but as a construct that could be conceived in different ways.'

Language is no longer an echo of the *verbum dei*, but a technical construct working on principles of internally generated difference. If the early modern natural philosopher or Renaissance physician conducted an exegesis of the text of nature written in the language of geometry or of cosmic correspondences, and postmodern scientist still reads for a living, but has as a text the coded systems of recognition – prone to the pathologies of mis-recognition – embodied in objects like computer networks and immune systems. The extraordinarily close tie of language and technology could hardly be overstressed in postmodernism. The 'construct' is at the centre of attention; making, reading, writing, and meaning seem to be very close to the same thing. This near-identity between technology, body, and semiosis suggests a particular edge to the mutually constitutive relations of political economy, symbol, and science that 'inform' contemporary research trends in medical anthropology.

## The apparatus of bodily production: the techno biopolitics of engagement

Bodies, then, are not born; they are made [. . .]. Bodies have been as thoroughly denaturalized as sign, context, and time. Late twentieth-century bodies do not grow from internal harmonic principles theorized within Romanticism. Neither are they discovered in the domains of realism and modernism. One is not born a woman, Simone de Beauvoir correctly insisted. It took the political-epistemological terrain of postmodernism to be able to insist on a co-text to de Beauvoir's: one is not born an organism. Organisms are made; they are constructs of a world-changing kind. The constructions of an organism's boundaries, the job of the discourses of immunology, are particularly potent mediators of the experiences of sickness and death for industrial and post-industrial people.

In this over-determined context, I will ironically – and inescapably – invoke a constructionist concept as an analytic device to pursue an understanding of what kinds of units, selves, and individuals inhabit the universe structured by immune system discourse [. . .]. Scientific bodies are not *ideological* constructions. Always radically historically specific, bodies have a different kind of specificity and effectivity, and so they invite a different kind of engagement and intervention. The notion of a 'material-semiotic actor' is intended to highlight the object of knowledge as an active part of the apparatus of bodily production, without *ever* implying immediate presence of such objects or, what is the same thing, their final or unique determination of what can count as objective knowledge of a biomedical body at a particular historical juncture. Bodies as objects of knowledge are material-semiotic generative nodes. Their boundaries materialize in social interaction; 'objects' like bodies do not pre-exist as such. Scientific objectivity (the siting/sighting of objects) is not about dis-engaged discovery, but about mutual and usually unequal structuring, about taking risks. The various contending biological bodies emerge at the intersection of biological research, writing, and publishing; medical and other business practices; cultural productions of all kinds, including available metaphors and narratives; and technology, such as the visualization technologies that bring colour-enhanced killer T cells and intimate photographs of the developing foetus into high-gloss art books for every middle-class home. [. . .]

But also invited into that node of intersection is the analogue to the lively languages that actively intertwine in the production of literary value: the coyote and protean embodiments of a world as witty agent and actor. Perhaps our hopes for accountability in the techno-biopolitics in postmodern frames turn on revisioning the world as coding trickster with whom we must learn to converse. Like a protein subjected to stress, the world for us may be thoroughly denatured, but it is not any less consequential. So while the late twentieth-century immune system is a construct of an elaborate apparatus of bodily production, neither the immune system nor any other of bio-medicine's world-changing bodies – like a virus – is a ghostly fantasy. Coyote is not a ghost, merely a protean trickster.

The following chart abstracts and dichotomizes two historical moments in the biomedical production of bodies from the late nineteenth century to the 1980s. The chart highlights epistemological, cultural, and political aspects of possible contestations for constructions of scientific bodies in this century. The chart itself is a traditional little machine for making particular meanings. Not a description, it must be read as an argument, and one which relies on a suspect technology for the production of meanings – binary dichotomization.

| | |
|---|---|
| Representation | Simulation |
| Bourgeois novel | Science fiction |
| Realism and modernism | Postmodernism |
| Organism | Biotic component, code |
| Work | Text |
| Mimesis | Play of signifiers |
| Depth, integrity | Surface, boundary |
| Heat | Noise |
| Biology as clinical practice | Biology as inscription |
| Physiology | Communications engineering |
| Microbiology, tuberculosis | Immunology, AIDS |
| Magic bullet | Immunomodulation |
| Small group | Subsystem |
| Perfection | Optimization |
| Eugenics | Genetic engineering |
| Decadence | Obsolescence |
| Hygiene | Stress management |
| Organic division of labour | Ergonomics, cybernetics |
| Functional specialization | Modular construction |
| Biological determinism | System constraints |
| Reproduction | Replication |
| Individual | Replicon |
| Community ecology | Ecosystem |
| Racial chain of being | United Nations humanism |
| Colonialism | Transnational capitalism |
| Nature/culture | Fields of difference |
| Co-operation | Communications enhancement |
| Freud | Lacan |
| Sex | Surrogacy |
| Labour | Robotics |
| Mind | Artificial intelligence |
| Second World War | Star Wars |
| White capitalist patriarchy | Informatics of domination |

It is impossible to see the entries in the right-hand column as 'natural', a realization that subverts naturalistic status for the left-hand column as well. From the eighteenth to the mid-twentieth centuries, the great historical constructions of gender, race, and class were embedded in the organically marked bodies of woman, the colonized or enslaved, and the worker. Those inhabiting these marked bodies have been symbolically other to the fictive rational self of universal, and so unmarked, species man, a coherent subject. The marked organic body has been a critical locus of cultural and political contestation, crucial both to the language of the liberatory politics of identity and to systems of domination drawing on widely shared languages of nature as resource for the appropriations of culture. For example, the sexualized bodies of nineteenth-century middle-class medical advice literature in England and the United States, in their female form organized around the maternal function and the physical site of the uterus and in their male form ordered by the spermatic economy tied closely to the nervous system, were part of an elaborate discourse of organic economy. The narrative field in which these bodies moved generated accounts of rational citizenship, bourgeois family life, and prophylaxis against sexual pollution and inefficiency, such as prostitution, criminality, or race suicide. Some feminist politics argued for the full inclusion of women in the body politic on grounds of maternal functions in the domestic economy extended to a public world. Late into the twentieth century, gay and lesbian politics have ironically and critically embraced the marked bodies constructed in nineteenth- and twentieth-century sexologies and gender identity medicines to create a complex humanist discourse of sexual liberation. Negritude, feminine writing, various separatisms, and other recent cultural movements have both drawn on and subverted the logics of naturalization central to biomedical discourse on race and gender in the histories of colonization and male supremacy. In all of these various, oppositionally interlinked, political and biomedical accounts, the body remained a relatively unambiguous locus of identity, agency, labour, and hierarchicalized function. Both scientific humanisms and biological determinisms could be authorized and contested in terms of the biological organism crafted in post-eighteenth-century life sciences.

But how do narratives of the normal and the pathological work when the biological and medical body is symbolized and operated upon, not as a system of work, organized by the hierarchical division of labour, ordered by a privileged dialectic between highly localized nervous and reproductive functions, but instead as a coded text, organized as an engineered communications system, ordered by a fluid and dispersed command-control-intelligence network? From the mid-twentieth century, biomedical discourses have been progressively organized around a very different set of technologies and practices, which have destabilized the symbolic privilege of the hierarchical, localized, organic body. Concurrently – and out of some of the same historical matrices of decolonization, multinational capitalism, world-wide high-tech militarization, and the emergence of new collective political actors in local and global politics from among those persons previously consigned to labour in silence – the question of 'differences' has destabilized humanist discourses of liberation based on a politics of identity and substantive unity. Feminist theory as a self-conscious discursive practice has been generated in this post-Second World War period characterized by the translation of Western scientific and political languages of nature from those based on work, localization, and the marked body to those based on codes, dispersal and networking, and the fragmented postmodern subject. An account of the biomedical, biotechnical body must start from the multiple molecular interfacings of genetic, nervous, endocrine, and immune systems. Biology is about recognition and misrecognition, coding errors, the body's reading practices (for example, frameshift mutations), and billion-dollar projects to sequence the human genome to be published and stored in a national genetic 'library'. The body is conceived as a strategic system, highly militarized in key arenas of imagery and practice. Sex, sexuality, and reproduction are theorized in terms of local investment strategies; the body ceases to be a stable spatial map of normalized functions and instead emerges as a highly mobile field of strategic differences. The biomedical-biotechnical body is a semiotic system, a complex meaning-producing field, for which the discourse of immunology, that is, the central biomedical discourse on recognition/misrecognition, has become a high-stakes practice in many senses.

In relation to objects like biotic components and codes, one must think, not in terms of laws of growth and essential properties, but rather in terms of costs of lowering constraints. Sexual reproduction becomes one possible strategy among many, with costs and benefits theorized as a function of the system environment. Disease is a subspecies of information malfunction or communications pathology; disease is a process of misrecognition or transgression of the boundaries of a strategic assemblage called self. Ideologies of sexual reproduction can no longer easily call upon the notions of unproblematic sex and sex role as organic aspects in 'healthy' natural objects like organisms and families. Likewise for race, ideologies of human diversity have to be developed in terms of frequencies of parameters and fields of power-charged differences, not essences and natural origins or homes. Race and sex, like individuals, are artefacts sustained or undermined by the discursive nexus of knowledge and power. Any objects or persons can be reasonably thought of in terms of disassembly and reassembly; no 'natural' architectures constrain system design. Design is none the less highly constrained. What counts as a 'unit', a one, is highly problematic, not a permanent given. Individuality is a strategic defence problem.

One should expect control strategies to concentrate on boundary conditions and interfaces, on rates of flow across boundaries, not on the integrity of natural objects. 'Integrity' or 'sincerity' of the Western self gives way to decision procedures, expert systems, and resource investment strategies. 'Degrees of freedom' becomes a very powerful metaphor for politics. Human beings, like any other component or subsystem, must be localized in a system architecture whose basic modes of operation are probabilistic. No objects, spaces, or bodies are sacred in themselves; any component can be interfaced with any other if the proper standard, the proper code, can be constructed for processing signals in a common language. In particular, there is no ground for ontologically opposing the organic, the technical, and the textual. But neither is there any ground for opposing the *mythical* to the organic, textual, and technical. Their convergences are more important than their residual oppositions. The privileged pathology affecting all kinds of components in this universe is stress – communications breakdown. In the body stress is theorized to operate by 'depressing' the immune system. Bodies have become cyborgs – cybernetic organisms – compounds of hybrid techno-organic embodiment and textuality [. . .]. The cyborg is text, machine, body, and metaphor – all theorized and engaged in practice in terms of communications. [. . .]

# DOMINATION/LIBERATION

- ■ Nancy Fraser, From redistribution to recognition? Dilemmas of justice in a 'postsocialist' age

- ■ David Halperin, Queer politics

**Nancy Fraser** is a Professor of Political Science at the New School for Social Research. She received her PhD in philosophy from the City University of New York. Fraser is the author of *Unruly Practices* (1989) and *Justice Interruptus* (1997).

**David Halperin** has taught at MIT and the University of Michigan. Among his writings are *One Hundred Years of Homosexuality and Other Essays on Greek Love* (1990) and *Saint Foucault* (1995).

# Chapter 29

# Nancy Fraser

## FROM REDISTRIBUTION TO RECOGNITION?
## Dilemmas of justice in a 'postsocialist' age

T HE 'STRUGGLE FOR RECOGNITION' is fast becoming the paradigmatic form of political conflict in the late twentieth century. Demands for 'recognition of difference' fuel struggles of groups mobilized under the banners of nationality, ethnicity, 'race,' gender, and sexuality. In these 'postsocialist' conflicts, group identity supplants class interest as the chief medium of political mobilization. Cultural domination supplants exploitation as the fundamental injustice. And cultural recognition displaces socioeconomic redistribution as the remedy for injustice and the goal of political struggle.

This is not, of course, the whole story. Struggles for recognition occur in a world of exacerbated material inequality – in income and property ownership; in access to paid work, education, health care, and leisure time; but also, more starkly, in caloric intake and exposure to environmental toxicity, and hence in life expectancy and rates of morbidity and mortality. Material inequality is on the rise in most of the world's countries – in the United States in China, in Sweden and in India, in Russia and in Brazil. It is also increasing globally, most dramatically across the line that divides North from South.

How, then, should we view the eclipse of a socialist imaginary centered on terms such as 'interest,' 'exploitation,' and 'redistribution'? And what should we make of the rise of a new political imaginary centered on notions of 'identity,' 'difference,' 'cultural domination,' and 'recognition'? Does this shift represent a lapse into 'false consciousness'? Or does it, rather, redress the culture-blindness of a materialist paradigm rightfully discredited by the collapse of Soviet communism?

Neither of those two stances is adequate, in my view. Both are too wholesale and unnuanced. Instead of simply endorsing or rejecting all of identity politics *simpliciter*, we should see ourselves as presented with a new intellectual and practical task: that of developing a *critical* theory of recognition, one that identifies and defends only whose versions of the cultural politics of difference that can be coherently combined with the social politics of equality.

In formulating this project, I assume that justice today requires *both* redistribution *and* recognition. And I propose to examine the relation between them. In part, this means figuring out how to conceptualize cultural recognition and social equality in forms that support rather than undermine one another. (For there are many competing conceptions of both!) It also means theorizing the ways in which economic disadvantage and cultural disrespect are currently entwined with and support one another. Then, too, it requires clarifying the political dilemmas that arise when we try to combat both those injustices simultaneously.

My larger aim is to connect two political problematics that are currently dissociated from each other, for only by integrating recognition and redistribution can we arrive at a framework that is adequate to the demands of our age [. . .]

To help clarify this situation and the political prospects it presents, I propose to distinguish two broadly conceived, analytically distinct understandings of injustice. The first is socioeconomic injustice, which is rooted in the political-economic structure of society. Examples include exploitation (having the fruits of one's labor appropriated for the benefit of others); economic marginalization (being confined to undesirable or poorly paid work or being denied access to income-generating labor altogether), and deprivation (being denied an adequate material standard of living).

Egalitarian theorists have long sought to conceptualize the nature of these socioeconomic injustices. Their accounts include Marx's theory of capitalist exploitation, John Rawls's account of justice as fairness in the choice of principles governing the distribution of 'primary goods,' Amartya Sen's view that justice requires ensuring that people have equal 'capabilities to function,' and Ronald Dworkin's view that it requires 'equality of resources.' For my purposes here, however, we need not commit ourselves to any one particular theoretical account. We need only subscribe to a rough and general understanding of socioeconomic injustice informed by a commitment to egalitarianism.

The second understanding of injustice is cultural or symbolic. Here injustice is rooted in social patterns of representation, interpretation, and communication. Examples include cultural domination (being subjected to patterns of interpretation and communication that are associated with another culture and are alien and/or hostile to one's own); nonrecognition (being rendered invisible by means of the authoritative representational, communicative, and interpretative practices of one's culture); and disrespect (being routinely maligned or disparaged in stereotyping public cultural representations and/or in everyday life interactions. [. . .]

Despite these mutual entwinements, I shall continue to distinguish economic injustice and cultural injustice analytically. The remedy for economic injustice is political-economic restructuring of some sort. This might involve redistributing income, reorganizing the division of labor, subjecting investment to democratic decision making, or transforming other basic economic structures. Although these various remedies differ importantly from one another, I shall henceforth refer to the whole group of them by the generic term 'redistribution.' The remedy for cultural injustice, in contrast, is some sort of cultural or symbolic change. This could involve upwardly revaluing disrespected identities and the cultural products of maligned groups. It could also involve recognizing and positively valorizing cultural diversity. More radically still, it could involve the wholesale transformation of societal patterns of representation, interpretation, and communication in ways that would change *everybody's* sense of self. Although these remedies differ importantly from one another, I shall henceforth refer to the whole group of them by the generic term 'recognition.'[. . .]

With these distinctions in place, I can now post the following questions: What is the relation between claims for recognition, aimed at remedying cultural injustice, and claims for redistribution, aimed at redressing economic injustice? And what sorts of mutual interferences can arise when both kinds of claims are made simultaneously?

There are good reasons to worry about such mutual interferences. Recognition claims often take the form of calling attention to, if not performatively creating, the putative specificity of some group and then of affirming its value. Thus, they tend to promote group differentiation. Redistribution claims, in contrast, often call for abolishing economic arrangements that underpin group specificity. (An example would be feminist demands to abolish the gender division of labor.) Thus, they tend to promote group dedifferentiation. The upshot is that the politics of recognition and the politics of redistribution often appear to have mutually contradictory aims. Whereas the first tends to promote group differentiation, the second tends to undermine it. Thus, the two kinds of claim stand in tension with each other; they can interfere with, or even work against each other.

Here, then, is a difficult dilemma. I shall henceforth call it the redistribution-recognition dilemma. People who are subject to both cultural injustice and economic injustice need both recognition and redistribution. They need both to claim and to deny their specificity. How, if at all, is this possible? [. . .]

Matters are thus fairly straightforward at the two extremes of our conceptual spectrum. When we deal with collectivities that approach the ideal type of the exploited working class, we face distributive injustices requiring redistributive remedies. When we deal with collectivities that approach the ideal type of the despised sexuality, in contrast, we face injustices of misrecognition requiring remedies of recognition. In the first case, the logic of the remedy is to put the group out of business as a group. In a second case, on the contrary, it is to valorize the group's 'groupness' by recognizing its specificity.

Matters become murkier, however, once we move away from these extremes. When we consider collectivities located in the middle of the conceptual spectrum, we encounter hybrid modes that combine features of the exploited class with features of the despised sexuality. These collectivities are 'bivalent.' They are differentiated as collectivities by virtue of *both* the political-economic structure *and* the cultural-valuational structure of society. When oppressed or subordinated, therefore, they suffer injustices that are traceable to both political economy and culture simultaneously. Bivalent collectivities, in sum, may suffer both socioeconomic maldistribution and cultural misrecognition in forms where neither of these injustices is an indirect effect of the other, but where both are primary and co-original. In that case, neither redistributive remedies alone nor recognition remedies alone will suffice. Bivalent collectivities need both.

Both gender and 'race' are paradigmatic bivalent collectivities. Although each has peculiarities not shared by the other, both encompass political-economic dimensions and cultural-valuation dimensions. Gender and 'race,' therefore, implicate both redistribution and recognition.

Gender, for example, has political-economic dimensions because it is a basic structuring principle of the political economy. On the one hand, gender structures the fundamental division between paid 'productive' labor and unpaid 'reproductive' and domestic labor, assigning women primary responsibility for the latter. On the other hand, gender also structures the division within paid labor between higher-paid, male-dominated, manufacturing and professional occupations and lower-paid, female-dominated 'pink-collar' and domestic service occupations. The result is a political-economic structure that generates gender-specific modes of exploitation, marginalization, and deprivation. This structure constitutes gender as a political-economic differentiation endowed with certain classlike characteristics. When viewed under this aspect, gender injustice appears as a species of distributive injustice that cries out for redistributive redress. Much like class, gender justice requires transforming the political economy so as to eliminate its gender structuring. Eliminating gender-specific exploitation, marginalization, and deprivation requires abolishing the gender division of labor – both the gendered division between paid and unpaid labor and the gender division within paid labor. The logic of the remedy is akin to the logic with respect to class: it is to put gender out of business as such. If gender were nothing but a political-economic differentiation, in sum, justice would require its abolition.

That, however, is only half the story. In fact, gender is not only a political-economic differentiation but a cultural-valuation differentiation as well. As such, it also encompasses elements that are more like sexuality than class and that bring it squarely within the problematic of recognition. Certainly, a major feature of gender injustice is androcentrism: the authoritative construction of norms that privilege traits associated with masculinity. Along with this goes cultural sexism: the pervasive devaluation and disparagement of things coded as 'feminine,' paradigmatically – but not only – women. This devaluation is expressed in a range of harms suffered by women, including sexual assault, sexual exploitation, and pervasive domestic violence; trivializing, objectifying, and demeaning stereotypical depictions in the media; harassment and disparagement in all spheres of everyday life; subjection to androcentric norms in relation to which women appear lesser or deviant and that work to disadvantage them, even in the absence of any intention to discriminate; attitudinal discrimination; exclusion or marginalization in public spheres and deliberative bodies; and denial of full legal rights and equal protections. These harms are injustices of recognition. They are relatively independent of political economy and are not merely 'superstructural.' Thus, they cannot be remedied by political-economic redistribution alone but require additional independent remedies of recognition. Overcoming androcentrism and sexism requires changing the cultural valuations (as well as their legal and practical expressions) that privilege masculinity and deny equal respect to women. It requires decentering androcentric norms and revaluing a despised gender. The logic of the remedy is akin to the logic with respect to sexuality: it is to accord positive recognition to a devalued group specificity.

Gender, in sum, is a bivalent mode of collectivity. It contains a political economic face that brings it within the ambit of redistribution. Yet it also contains a cultural-valuational face that brings it simultaneously within the ambit of recognition. Of course, the two faces are not neatly separated from each other. Rather, they intertwine to reinforce each other dialectically because sexist and androcentric cultural norms are institutionalized in the state and the economy, and women's economic disadvantage restricts women's 'voice,' impeding equal participation in the making of culture, in public spheres and in everyday life. The result is a vicious circle of cultural and economic subordination. Redressing gender injustice, therefore, requires changing both political economy and culture.

But the bivalent character of gender is the source of a dilemma. Insofar as women suffer at least two analytically distinct kinds of injustice, they necessarily require at least two analytically distinct kinds of remedy: both redistribution and recognition. The two remedies pull in opposite directions, however, and are not easily pursued simultaneously. Whereas the logic of redistribution is to put gender out of business as such, the logic of recognition is to valorize gender specificity. Here, then, is the feminist version of the redistribution-recognition dilemma: How can feminists fight simultaneously to abolish gender differentiation and to valorize gender specificity?

An analogous dilemma arises in the struggle against racism. 'Race,' like gender, is a bivalent mode of collectivity. On the one hand, it resembles class in being a structural principle of political economy. In this aspect, 'race' structures the capitalist division of labor. It structures the division within paid work between low-paid, low-status, menial, dirty, and domestic occupations held disproportionately by people of color, and higher-paid, higher-status, white-collar, professional, technical, and managerial occupations held disproportionately by 'whites.' Today's racial division of paid labor is part of the historic legacy of colonialism and slavery, which elaborated racial categorization to justify brutal new forms of appropriation and exploitation, effectively constituting 'blacks' as a political-economic caste. Currently, moreover, 'race' also structures access to official labor markets, constituting large segments of the population of color as a 'superfluous,' degraded subproletariat or underclass, unworthy even of exploitation and excluded from the productive system altogether. The result is a political-economic structure that generates 'race'-specific modes of exploitation, marginalization, and deprivation. This structure constitutes 'race' as a political-economic differentiation endowed with certain classlike characteristics. When viewed under this aspect, racial injustice appears as a species of distributive injustice that cries out for redistributive redress. Much like class, racial justice requires transforming the political economy so as to eliminate its racialization. Eliminating 'race'-specific exploitation, marginalization, and deprivation requires abolishing the racial division of labor — both the racial division between exploitable and superfluous labor and the racial division within paid labour. The logic of the remedy is like the logic with respect to class: it is to put 'race' out of business as such. If 'race' were nothing but a political-economic differentiation, in sum, justice would require its abolition.

Yet 'race,' like gender, is not only political-economic. It also has cultural-valuational dimensions, which bring it into the universe of recognition. Thus, 'race' too encompasses elements that are more like sexuality than class. A major aspect of racism is Eurocentrism: the authoritative construction of norms that privilege traits associated with 'whiteness.' Along with this goes cultural racism: the pervasive devaluation and disparagement of things coded as 'black,' 'brown,' and 'yellow,' paradigmatically – but not only – people of color. This depreciation is expressed in a range of harms suffered by people of color, including demeaning stereotypical depictions in the media as criminal, bestial, primitive, stupid, and so on; violence, harassment, and 'dissing' in all spheres of everyday life; subjection to Eurocentric norms in relation to which people of color appear lesser or deviant and that work to disadvantage them, even in the absence of any intention to discriminate; attitudinal discrimination; exclusion from and/or marginalization in public spheres and deliberative bodies; and denial of full legal rights and equal protections. As in the case of gender, these harms are injustices of recognition. Thus, the logic of their remedy, too, is to accord positive recognition to devalued group specificity.

'Race,' too, therefore, is a bivalent mode of collectivity with both a political-economic face and a cultural-valuational face. Its two faces intertwine to reinforce each other dialectically, moreover, because racist and Eurocentric cultural norms are institutionalized in the state and the economy, and the economic disadvantage suffered by people of color restricts their 'voice.' Redressing racial injustice, therefore, requires changing both political economy and culture. But as with gender, the bivalent character of 'race' is the source of a dilemma. Insofar as people of color suffer at least two analytically distinct kinds of injustice, they necessarily require at least two analytically distinct kinds of remedy, redistribution and recognition, which are not easily pursued simultaneously. Whereas the logic of redistribution is to put 'race' out of business as such, the logic of recognition is to valorize group specificity. Here, then, is the antiracist version of the redistribution-recognition dilemma: How can antiracists fight simultaneously to abolish 'race' and to valorize the cultural specificity of subordinated racialized groups?

Both gender and 'race,' in sum, are dilemmatic modes of collectivity. Unlike class, which occupies one end of the conceptual spectrum, and unlike sexuality, which occupies the other, gender and 'race' are bivalent, implicated simultaneously in both the politics of redistribution and the politics of recognition. Both, consequently, face the redistribution-recognition dilemma. Feminists must pursue political-economic remedies that would undermine gender differentiation, while also pursuing cultural-valuation remedies that valorize the specificity of a despised collectivity. Antiracists, likewise, must pursue political-economic remedies that would undermine 'racial' differentiation, while also pursuing cultural-valuation remedies that valorize the specificity of despised collectivities. How can they do both things at once?

So far I have posed the redistribution–recognition dilemma in a form that appears quite intractable. I have assumed that redistributive remedies for political-economic injustice always dedifferentiate social groups. Likewise, I have assumed that recognition remedies for cultural-valuational injustice always enhance social group differentiation. Given these assumptions, it is difficult to see how feminists and antiracists can pursue redistribution and recognition simultaneously.

Now, however, I want to complicate these assumptions. In this section, I shall examine alternative conceptions of redistribution, on the one hand, and alternative conceptions of recognition, on the other. My aim is to distinguish two broad approaches to remedying injustice that cut across the redistribution-recognition divide. I shall call them 'affirmation' and 'transformation' respectively. After sketching each of them generically, I shall show how each operates in regard to both redistribution and recognition. On this basis, finally, I shall reformulate the redistribution-recognition dilemma in a form that is more amenable to resolution.

Let me begin by briefly distinguishing affirmation and transformation. By affirmative remedies for injustice I mean remedies aimed at correcting inequitable outcomes of social arrangements without disturbing the underlying framework that generates them. By transformative remedies, in contrast, I mean remedies aimed at correcting inequitable outcomes precisely by restructuring the underlying generative framework. The crux of the contrast is end-state outcomes versus the processes that produce them. It is *not* gradual versus apocalyptic change.

This distinction can be applied, first of all, to remedies for cultural injustice. Affirmative remedies for such injustices are currently associated with what I shall call 'mainstream multiculturalism.' This sort of multiculturalism proposes to redress disrespect by revaluing unjustly devalued group identities, while leaving intact both the contents of those identities and the group differentiations that underlie them. Transformative remedies, by contrast, are currently associated with deconstruction. They would redress disrespect by transforming the underlying cultural-valuational structure. By destabilizing existing group identities and differentiations, these remedies would not only raise the self-esteem of members of currently disrespected groups; they would change *everyone's* sense of self.

To illustrate the distinction, let us consider, once again, the case of the despised sexuality. Affirmative remedies for homophobia and heterosexism are currently associated with gay-identity politics, which aims to revalue gay and lesbian identity. Transformative remedies, in contrast, are associated with queer politics, which would deconstruct the homo–hetero dichotomy. Gay-identity politics treats homosexuality as a cultural positivity with its own substantive content, much like (the commonsense view of) an ethnicity. This positivity is assumed to subsist in and of itself and to need only additional recognition. Queer politics, in contrast, treats homosexuality as the constructed and devalued correlate of heterosexuality; both are reifications of sexual ambiguity and are codefined only in virtue of each other. The transformative aim is not to solidify a gay identity but to deconstruct the homo–hetero dichotomy so as to destabilize all fixed sexual identities. The point is not to dissolve all sexual difference in a single, universal human identity; it is, rather, to sustain a sexual field of multiple, debinarized, fluid, ever-shifting differences.

Both these approaches have considerable interest as remedies for misrecognition. But there is one crucial difference between them. Whereas gay-identity politics tends to enhance existing sexual group differentiation, queer politics tends to destabilize it — at least ostensibly and in the long run. The point holds for recognition remedies more generally. Whereas affirmative recognition remedies tend to promote existing group differentiations, transformative recognition remedies tend, in the long run, to destabilize them so as to make room for future regroupments. [. . .]

Analogous distinctions hold for the remedies for economic injustice. Affirmative remedies for such injustices have been associated historically with the liberal welfare state. They seek to redress end-state maldistribution, while leaving intact much of the underlying political-economic structure. Thus, they would increase the consumption share of economically disadvantaged groups, without otherwise restructuring the system of production. Transformative remedies, in contrast, have been historically associated with socialism. They would redress unjust distribution by transforming the underlying political-economic structure. By restructuring the relations of production, these remedies would not only alter the end-state distribution of consumption shares; they would also change the social division of labor and thus the conditions of existence for everyone.

To illustrate the distinction, let us consider, once again, the case of the exploited class. Affirmative redistribution remedies for class injustices typically include income transfers of two distinct kinds: social insurance programs share some of the costs of social reproduction for the stably employed, the so-called primary sectors of the working class; public assistance programs provide means-tested, 'targeted' aid to the 'reserve army' of the unemployed and underemployed. Far from abolishing class differentiation per se, these affirmative remedies support it and shape it. Their general effect is to shift attention from the class division between workers and capitalists to the division between employed and nonemployed fractions of the working class. Public assistance programs 'target' the poor, not only for aid but for hostility. Such remedies, to be sure, provide needed material aid. But they also create strongly cathected, antagonistic group differentiations.

The logic here applies to affirmative redistribution in general. Although this approach aims to redress economic injustice, it leaves intact the deep structures that generate class disadvantage. Thus, it must make surface reallocations again and again. The result is to mark the most disadvantaged class as inherently deficient and insatiable, as always needing more and more. In time such a class can even come to appear privileged, the recipient of special treatment and undeserved largesse. Thus, an approach aimed at redressing injustices of distribution can end up creating injustices of recognition.

In a sense, this approach is self-contradictory. Affirmative redistribution generally presupposes a universalist conception of recognition, the equal moral worth of persons. Let us call this its 'official recognition commitment.' Yet the practice of affirmative redistribution, as iterated over time, tends to set in motion a second–stigmatizing–recognition dynamic, which contradicts its official commitment to universalism. This second, stigmatizing, dynamic can be understood as the 'practical recognition-effect' of affirmative redistribution.

Now contrast this logic with transformative remedies for distributive injustices of class. Transformative remedies typically combine universalist social-welfare programs, steeply progressive taxation, macroeconomic policies aimed at creating full employment, a large nonmarket public sector, significant public and/or collective ownership, and democratic decision making about basic socioeconomic priorities. They try to assure access to employment for all, while also tending to delink basic consumption shares from employment. Hence, their tendency is to undermine class differentiation. Transformative remedies reduce social inequality without, however, creating stigmatized classes of vulnerable people perceived as beneficiaries of special largesse. They tend therefore to promote reciprocity and solidarity in the relations of recognition. Thus, an approach aimed at redressing injustices of distribution can help redress (some) injustices of recognition as well.

This approach is self-consistent. Like affirmative redistribution, transformative redistribution generally presupposes a universalist conception of recognition, the equal moral worth of persons. Unlike affirmative redistribution, however, its practice tends not to undermine this conception. Thus, the two approaches generate different logics of group differentiation. Whereas affirmative remedies can have the perverse effect of promoting class differentiation, transformative remedies tend to blur it. In addition, the two approaches generate different subliminal dynamics of recognition. Affirmative redistribution can stigmatize the disadvantaged, adding the insult of misrecognition to the injury of deprivation. Transformative redistribution, in contrast, can promote solidarity, helping to redress some forms of misrecognition.

What, then, should we conclude from this discussion? In this section, we have considered only the 'pure' ideal-typical cases at the two extremes of the conceptual spectrum. We have contrasted the divergent effects of affirmative and transformative remedies for the economically rooted distributive injustices of class, on the one hand, and for the culturally rooted recognition injustices of sexuality, on the other. We saw that affirmative remedies tend generally to promote group differentiation, while transformative remedies tend to destabilize or blur it. We also saw that affirmative redistribution remedies can generate a backlash of misrecognition, while transformative redistribution remedies can help redress some forms of misrecognition.

All this suggests a way of reformulating the redistribution–recognition dilemma. We might ask: For groups who are subject to injustices of both types, what combinations of remedies work best to minimize, if not altogether to eliminate, the mutual interferences that can arise when both redistribution and recognition are pursued simultaneously? [. . .]

# Chapter 28

# David Halperin

## QUEER POLITICS

[. . .]

**T**HE HISTORY OF THE ONGOING struggles for homosexual emancipation and gay liberation has consisted largely in the story of how lesbians
and gay men fought to wrest from non-gay-identified people control over such
matters as who gets to speak for us, who gets to represent our experience, who
is authorized to pronounce knowledgeably about our lives. It has been the story
of one long struggle to reverse the discursive positioning of homosexuality and
heterosexuality: to shift heterosexuality from the position of a universal subject of
discourse to an object of interrogation and critique, and to shift homosexuality
from the position of an object of power/knowledge to a position of legitimate
subjective agency – from the status of that which is spoken about while remaining
silent to the status of that which speaks. The possibility of producing such a shift
in the status of homosexuality from object to subject illustrates what Foucault has
called in *The History of Sexuality, Volume I*, 'the tactical polyvalence of discourses':
'We must not imagine,' he insists, 'a world of discourse divided between accepted
discourse and excluded discourse, or between the dominant discourse and the
dominated one. [. . .] Discourses are not once and for all subservient to power or
raised up against it, any more than silences are. We must make allowance for the
complex and unstable process whereby discourse can be both an instrument and
an effect of power, but also a hindrance, a stumbling-block, a point of resistance
and a starting point for an opposing strategy.'
It is precisely because the characteristic and defining political strategy of gay
liberation is one of discursive reversal that Foucault situates his sole theoretical
analysis of the gay liberation movement in the context of his discussion of 'the
tactical polyvalence of discourses' in *The History of Sexuality, Volume I*.

There is no question that the appearance in nineteenth-century psychiatry, jurisprudence, and literature of a whole series of discourses on
the species and subspecies of homosexuality, inversion, pederasty, and
'psychic hermaphrodism' made possible a strong advance of social
controls into this area of 'perversity'; but it also made possible the
formation of a 'reverse' discourse: homosexuality began to speak in its
own behalf, to demand that its legitimacy or 'naturality' be acknowledged, often in the same vocabulary, using the same categories by which
it was medically disqualified.

To the extent that the 'reverse discourse' produced by the early homosexual emancipationists as well as by recent gay liberationists recapitulates (albeit in a positive
mode) the sexual terms, categories, and concepts of the pathologizing medical and
psychological discourses to which it opposes itself – and to the extent that it
thereby extends, prolongs, and fortifies the regime of power/knowledge responsible for constructing the homosexual/heterosexual binarism in the first place –
Foucault remains critical of sexual liberation discourse in particular, and of discursive reversal in general, as a political strategy. Nonetheless, Foucault made it very
clear on a number of occasions that he considered the early homosexual emancipation movement's discursive reversal of medical discourse to have been in its time,
an absolutely necessary strategic move, and therefore an important, politically
progressive development. 'I believe that the movements labeled "sexual liberation"
ought to be understood as movements of affirmation "starting with" sexuality,'
Foucault explained to an interviewer in 1977.

Which means two things: they are movements that start with sexuality,
with the apparatus of sexuality inside of which we're caught, and that
make it function right up to the limit; but, at the same time, they are
in motion relative to it, disengaging themselves and surmounting it.
Take the case of homosexuality. Psychiatrists began a medical analysis
of it around the 1870s – a point of departure for a whole series of new
interventions and controls. [. . .] But [we see homosexuals] taking such
discourses literally, and thereby turning them about; we see responses
arising in the form of defiance: 'All right, we are what you say we are
– by nature, disease, or pervasion, as you like. Well, if that's what we
are, let's be it, and if you want to know what we are, we can tell you
ourselves better than you can.'[. . .] It is the strategic turnabout of one
and the 'same' will to truth.

By putting 'the "same"' in quotation marks, Foucault scoffs at the hostile liberal
reading of *The History of Sexuality, Volume I*, that understands it to be making the
implausible and odious claim that there is no difference between repression and
liberation, or that a 'reverse discourse' is one and the same as the discourse it
reverses. On the contrary: to recapitulate in an affirmative vein, as the nineteenth-
century homosexual emancipationists did, the oppressive, medicalizing discourse
to which they were subjected, while strategically reversing the object-and subject-

positions assigned by it to themselves and to the medical authorities, respectively, is, in Foucault's eyes, to perform a significant act of political resistance.

If Foucault did indeed find fault with the modern project of liberating a supposedly repressed sexuality, then, the reason was not that 'the repressive hypothesis' was *wrong* but that it was politically bankrupt: '[W]e had arrived at a situation in which notions of sexual repression found themselves overburdened, worn out, and it was a matter of asking oneself how to make those notions function at the interior of a struggle, a battle, a debate.' Foucault's explanation for his emphasis on resistance rather than liberation indicates that his critique of liberation in *The History of Sexuality, Volume I*, should not be read as a blanket condemnation or disqualification of it. Foucault's objection to liberation as the goal of sexual politics does not express his theoretical position on the issue – it is not an enunciation of some cardinal principle or abstract law – but reflects his understanding of a specific historical situation, of concrete political realities and techniques of power: 'a complex strategic situation in a particular society.'

In any case, to conceive gay politics as a reverse discourse and a form of resistance is not to assign to it an entirely reactive, or negative character – to deny it a claim to independence or creativity. After all, a reverse discourse, as Foucault describes it, does not simply produce a mirror reversal – a pure, one-to-one inversion of the existing terms of the discourse it reverses. Gay liberation is not the upside-down reflection of medical pathologization, nor is it the exact opposite of homophobic stigmatization and oppression. Gay liberation, rather, is a surprising, unexpected, dynamic, and open-ended movement whose ultimate effects extend beyond its immediate tactics. Gay politics is not a politics of pure reactivity, then, even though its conditions of possibility are admittedly rooted in an oppressive regime of power/knowledge. It is a reversal that takes us in a new direction. To quote a formulation with which Foucault registered strong agreement when it was put to him some years later, once again in reference to the lesbian and gay movement, 'To resist is not simply a negation but a creative process.'

Similarly, the project of shifting the discursive position of homosexuality from that of object to subject does not constitute a mere attempt to *reform* sexual discourses. It is not an exercise in restraining the supposed 'excesses' of homophobic bigotry, eliminating the supposed 'distortions' produced by homophobic 'prejudice,' and reasserting a new and more rigorous standard of unbiased sexual knowing, available in principle to 'everyone' (meaning nongay people). The aim is not to produce a supposedly kinder, gentler, more objective, less tendentious form of expertise about homosexuality, to be licensed presumably by non-gay-identified authorities – or by lesbians and gay men accredited by straight institutions; it is not to reconstitute homosexuality as a real object to be studied and understood, definitively if sympathetically, by those in a legitimate position to know. The aim, rather, is to treat homosexuality as a position from which one *can* know, to treat it as a legitimate *condition* of knowledge. Homosexuality, according to this Foucauldian vision of *un gai savoir*, 'a gay science,' is not something to be got right but an eccentric positionality to be exploited and explored: a potentially privileged site for the criticism and analysis of cultural discourses.

In order to reverse the discourses of contemporary homophobia, then, it is not enough to attempt to reclaim and transvalue homosexuality. The most radical reversal of homophobic discourses consists not in asserting, with the Gay Liberation Front of 1968, that 'gay is good' (on the analogy with 'black is beautiful') but in assuming and empowering a marginal positionality – not in rehabilitating an already demarcated, if devalued, identity but in taking advantage of the purely oppositional location homosexuality has been made to occupy by the logic of the supplement and by the fantasmatic character of homophobic discourse. 'The homosexual' constituted by that discourse is, as we have seen, an impossibly contradictory creature, not a natural reality but a fantasmatic projection, an incoherent construction that functions to stabilize and to consolidate the cultural meaning of heterosexuality by encapsulating everything that is 'other' than or 'different' from it. 'The homosexual' is defined by negation and opposition as everything the heterosexual is not. In short, 'the homosexual' is an identity without an essence.

To shift the position of 'the homosexual' from that of object to subject is therefore to make available to lesbians and gay men a new kind of sexual identity, one characterized by its lack of a clear definitional content. The homosexual subject can now claim an identity without an essence. To do so is to reverse the logic of the supplement and to make use of the vacancy left by the evacuation of the contradictory and incoherent definitional content of 'the homosexual' in order to take up instead a position that is (and always had been) defined wholly relationally, by its distance to and difference from the normative. (Homo)sexual identity can now be constituted not substantively but oppositionally, not by *what* it is but by *where* it is and *how* it operates. [. . .]

Unlike gay identity, which, though deliberately proclaimed in an act of affirmation, is nonetheless rooted in the positive fact of homosexual object-choice, queer identity need not be grounded in any positive truth or in any stable reality. As the very word implies 'queer' does not name some natural kind or refer to some determinate object; it acquires its meaning from its oppositional relation to the norm. Queer is by definition *whatever* is at odds with the normal, the legitimate, the dominant. *There is nothing in particular to which it necessarily refers.* It is an identity without an essence. 'Queer,' then, demarcates not a positivity but a positionality vis-à-vis the normative – a positionality that is not restricted to lesbians and gay men but is in fact available to anyone who is or who feels marginalized because of her or his sexual practices: it could include some married couples without children, for example, or even (who knows?) some married couples *with* children – with, perhaps, *very naughty* children. 'Queer,' in any case, does not designate a class of already objectified pathologies or perversions; rather, it describes a horizon of possibility whose precise extent and heterogeneous scope cannot in principle be delimited in advance. It is from the eccentric positionality occupied by the queer subject that it may become possible to envision a variety of possibilities for reordering the relations among sexual behaviors, erotic identities, constructions of gender, forms of knowledge, regimes of enunciation, logics of representation, modes of self-constitution, and practices of community – for restructuring, that is, the relations among power, truth, and desire. [. . .]

Foucault insisted that homosexuality did not name an already existing form of desire but was rather '*something to be desired.*' Our task is therefore 'to *become* homosexual, not to persist in acknowledging that we *are*.' Or, to put it more precisely, what Foucault meant is that our task is to become queer. For his remarks make sense only if he understood his term 'homosexual' according to my defini- tion of 'queer' – as an identity without an essence, not a given condition but a horizon of possibility, an opportunity for self-transformation, a queer potential. Because one can't *become* homosexual, strictly speaking: either one is or one isn't. But one can marginalize oneself; one can transform oneself; one can become queer. Indeed, 'queer' marks the very site of gay becoming.

It was on the basis of such a queer ethic, of such a vision of gay becoming, that Foucault argued against concentrating too much political energy on the struggle to obtain specific juridical 'rights' for lesbians and gay men.

> I think we should consider the battle for gay rights as an episode that cannot be the final stage. For two reasons: first because a right, in its real effects, is much more linked to attitudes and patterns of behavior than to legal formulations. There can be discrimination against homo- sexuals even if such discriminations are prohibited by law. It is therefore necessary to establish homosexual lifestyles, existential choices in which sexual relations with people of the same sex will be important. It's not enough as part of a more general way of life, or in addition to it, to be permitted to make love with someone of the same sex. The fact of making love with someone of the same sex can very naturally involve a whole series of choices, a whole series of other values and choices for which there are not yet real possibilities. It's not only a matter of integrating this strange little practice of making love with someone of the same sex into pre-existing cultures; it's a matter of constructing cultural forms.

And Foucault went on to add, '[I]f what we want to do is create a new way of life, then the question of individual rights is not pertinent.' The point is not to disparage the struggle for gay rights, which Foucault himself supported ('It is impor- tant [. . .] to have the possibility – and the right – to choose your own sexuality. Human rights regarding sexuality are important. [. . .]'), but to look beyond that struggle to something else, to the possibility of inventing new rights and estab- lishing new kinds of relationships that might entail their own privileges, duties, and rights.

That queerness constitutes not just a resistance to social norms or a negation of established values but a positive and creative construction of different ways of life seemed self-evident to Foucault. 'As far back as I can remember,' he told an interviewing for *Gai pied*,

> to desire boys meant to desire relationships with boys. That has always been, for me, something important. Not necessarily in the form of the couple, but as a question of existence: How is it possible for men to be together? to live together, to share their time, their meals, their room, their leisure, their sorrows, their knowledge, their confidences? What exactly is this thing – to be among men, 'stripped down,' outside

institutionalized relationships, family, profession, obligatory forms of association?

The problem of inventing queer relationships can be further complicated by additional factors, such as differences between the partners in age or race or class or nationality: there exist no readily available social formulas for mediating and negotiating those differences. 'Two men of notably different ages – what rule will they be able to use in order to communicate?' Foucault asked; 'they are face to face with one another, without armor, without conventional phrases, without anything to stabilize the meaning of the movement which takes them one toward the other. They have to invent from A to Z a relationship without form [. . .].' Self-invention is not a luxury or a pastime for lesbians and gay men: it is a necessity. And it is therefore part of the acquired practice of what Foucault called 'becoming homosexual.'

What, specifically, might constitute a queer way of life? What might some of the new relationships of which Foucault spoke look like? Foucault gave a few hints about what he had in mind in some of his interviews with the gay press. The first challenge he saw was 'to make ourselves infinitely more susceptible to pleasures' and, accordingly, to devise relationships that might offer strategies for enhancing pleasure and might enable us to escape the ready-made formulas already available to us – formulas which offer no alternative to purely sexual encounters, on the one hand, and the merging of identities in love, on the other. [. . .] [S]ome of Foucault's clearest indications of what might count as *queer praxis* occur in the context of his discussions of S/M. It is also in those discussions that Foucault's belief in the transformative potential of queer sex emerges most eloquently, if still somewhat sketchily.

First of all, Foucault emphasizes that what goes by the name of 'domination' in S/M is a strategy for creating pleasure, not a form of personal or political subjugation.

> What strikes me with regard to S/M is how it differs from social power. What characterizes power is the fact that it is a strategic relation that has been stabilized through institutions. So the mobility in power relations is limited, and there are strongholds that are very, very difficult to suppress because they have been institutionalized and are now very pervasive in courts, codes and so on. All that means that the strategic relations of people are made rigid.
>
> On this point, the S/M game is very interesting because it is a strategic relation, but it is always fluid. Of course, there are roles, but everyone knows very well that those roles can be reversed. [. . .] Or, even when the roles are stabilized, you know very well that it is always a game. Either the rules are transgressed, or there is an agreement, either explicit or tacit, that makes [the participants] aware of certain boundaries. This strategic game as a source of bodily pleasure is very interesting. But I wouldn't say that it is a reproduction, inside the erotic relationship, of the structure of power. It is an acting out of power

structures by a strategic game that is able to give sexual pleasure or
bodily pleasure.

The practice of S/M is the creation of pleasure, and there is an identity with [i.e., a personal identity attached to] that creation. And that's
why S/M is really a subculture. It's a process of invention. S/M is *the use*
of a strategic relationship as a source of pleasure (physical pleasure).
[. . .] What is interesting, is that in [. . .] heterosexual life those strategic
relations [e.g., pursuit and flight] come before sex. It's a strategic relation
in order to obtain sex. And in S/M those strategic relations are inside
sex, as a convention of pleasure within a particular situation.

So S/M is a game in which power differentials are subordinated to the overall
strategic purpose of producing human pleasure; it is not a form of domination in
which human beings are subordinated to the functioning of rigidly structured power
differentials.

Next, Foucault saw S/M, especially as it was cultivated and elaborated in gay
male urban enclaves in the United States as part of a wider practice of subcultural
community formation, not as the expression of a deep psychological impulse which
a permissive society had finally enabled people to indulge but rather as something
new that modern subjects could *do* with the sexuality to which their identities had
become so closely attached. S/M represented to Foucault 'a process of invention,'
insofar as it detaches sexual pleasure from sexuality (in an S/M scene, the precise
gender and sexual orientation of one's sexual partner may lose some of their importance as prerequisites of sexual excitement) and insofar as it frees bodily pleasure
from organ specificity, from exclusive localization in the genitals. S/M thereby
makes possible a new relation between the body and pleasure, and one effect of
continued S/M practice is to alter one's relation to one's own body.

I don't think that this movement of sexual practices has anything to do
with the disclosure or the uncovering of S/M tendencies deep within our
unconscious, and so on. I think that S/M is much more than that; it's the
real creation of new possibilities of pleasure, which people had no idea
about previously. The idea that S/M is related to a deep violence, that
S/M practice is a way of liberating this violence, this aggression, is stupid.
We know very well what all those people are doing is not aggressive;
they are inventing new possibilities of pleasure with strange parts of their
body – through the eroticization of the body. I think it's a kind of creation, a creative enterprise, which has as one of its main features what I
call the desexualization [i.e., the 'degenitalization'] of pleasure. The idea
that bodily pleasure should always come from sexual pleasure, and the
idea that sexual pleasure is the root of *all* our possible pleasure – I think
*that's* something quite wrong. These practices are insisting that we can
produce pleasure with very odd things, very strange parts of our bodies,
in very unusual situations, and so on.

The notion of 'desexualization' is a key one for Foucault, and it has been much
misunderstood. When he speaks of 'desexualization,' Foucault is drawing on the

meaning of the French word *sexe* in the sense of sexual organ. What he means by S/M's 'desexualization of pleasure' is not that S/M detaches pleasure from all acts of a conceivably sexual nature (even if it does destroy the absolute dependence of sexual pleasure on sexual intercourse narrowly defined) but that S/M detaches sexual pleasure from genital specificity, from localization in or dependence on the genitals. S/M, along with various related (though often quite distinct) practices of bondage, shaving, tit torture, cock and ball torture, piercing, humiliation, flagellation, and fist-fucking, produces intense pleasures while bypassing, to a greater or lesser extent, the genitals themselves; it involves the eroticization of nongenital regions of the body, such as the nipples, the anus, the skin, and the entire surface of the body. And it finds other erotic uses for the genitals than that of stimulation to the point of orgasm. S/M therefore represents a remapping of the body's erotic sites, a redistribution of its so-called erogenous zones, a breakup of the erotic monopoly traditionally held by the genitals, and even a re-eroticization of the male genitals as sites of vulnerability instead of as objects of veneration. In all of those respects, S/M represents an encounter between the modern subject of sexuality and the otherness of his or her body. Insofar as that encounter produces changes in the relations among subjectivity, sexuality, pleasure, and the body, S/M qualifies as a potentially self-transformative practice [. . .].

If we are to prevent personal identity from becoming 'the law, the principle, the rule' of individual existence, then it is ultimately sexuality itself that will have to be resisted, for it is sexuality that amalgamates desire and identity into a unitary and stable feature of the individual person and thereby imparts to the subject a 'true self' – a 'self' that constitutes the 'truth' of the person and functions as an object both of social regulation and of personal administration. Modern techniques of power make use of sexuality in order to attach to us a personal identity, defined in part by our sexual identity; by attaching that identity to us, they attach us to themselves. 'Just because this notion of sexuality has enabled us to fight [on behalf of our own homosexuality] doesn't mean that it doesn't carry with it a certain number of dangers,' Foucault remarked to Jean Le Bitoux. 'There is an entire biologism of sexuality and therefore an entire hold over it by doctors and psychologists – in short, by the agencies of normalization. We have over us doctors, pedagogues, law-makers, adults, parents who talk of sexuality! [. . .] It is not enough to liberate sexuality; we also have to liberate ourselves [. . .] from the very notion of sexuality.' And in an interview given a few years earlier, Foucault made a number of positive recommendations. 'We have to invent with our bodies – with their elements, their surfaces, their masses, their volumes – a non-disciplinary eroticism: an eroticism of the body in its volatile and diffuse potentialities, its chance encounters and uncalculated pleasures. [. . .]' Foucault's famous and rather cryptic remarks, at the end of *The History of Sexuality, Volume I*, about the political importance of attacking sexuality itself and promoting pleasures at the expense of sex make a great deal more sense when they are set in the context of his insistent distinction between pleasure and desire, and his tendency to champion bodies and pleasures, on the one hand, at the expense of desire, identity, and sexuality, on the other. 'We must not believe that by saying yes to sex, one says no to power,' Foucault wrote;

on the contrary, one thereby follows in the track of the entire apparatus of sexuality. It is from the agency of sex that one has to free oneself if one wishes, through a tactical reversal of the various mechanisms of sexuality, to assert, against the hold of power, the claims of bodies, pleasures, and knowledges in their multiplicity and their possibility of resistance. The rallying point for the counterattack against the apparatus of sexuality ought not to be sex-desire, but bodies and pleasures.

The transformative power of the queer sexual practices that gay men have invented reveals in this context something of its political efficacy: through the invention of novel, intense, and scattered bodily pleasures, queer culture brings about a tactical reversal of the mechanisms of sexuality, making strategic use of power differentials, physical sensations, and sexual identity-categories in order to create a queer praxis that ultimately dispenses with 'sexuality' and destabilizes the very constitution of identity itself. As Leo Bersani summarizes Foucault's position, 'The most effective resistance to this disciplinary productivity [of power in the guise of sexuality] should, Foucault suggests, take the form not of a struggle against prohibition, but rather of a kind of counter-productivity. It is not a question of lifting the barriers to seething repressed drives, but of consciously, deliberately playing on the surfaces of our bodies with forms or intensities of pleasure not covered, so to speak, by the disciplinary classifications that have until now taught us what sex is.' Fist-fucking and sadomasochism appear in this light as utopian political practices, insofar as they disrupt normative sexual identities and thereby generate – of their own accord, and despite being indulged in *not* for the sake of politics but purely for the sake of pleasure – a means of resistance to the discipline of sexuality, a form of counterdiscipline – in short, a technique of ascesis. The shattering force of intense bodily pleasure, detached from its exclusive localization in the genitals and regionalized throughout various zones of the body, decenters the subject and disarticulates the psychic and bodily integrity of the sale to which a sexual identity has become attached. By shattering the subject of sexuality, queer sex opens up the possibility for the cultivation of a more impersonal self, a self that can function as the substance of ongoing ethical elaboration – and thus as the site of future transformation. [. . .]

# Reference

Foucault, M. (1978) *History of Sexuality*, vol. 1, New York: Pantheon Books.

# PART FOUR

# Postdisciplinary debates: identities

# SELF

- Robert N. Bellah *et al.*, Individualism and commitment in American life

- Charles Taylor, The making of modern identity

**Robert N. Bellah** was born in Altus, Oklahoma on 23 February 1927. He has taught Sociology and Comparative Studies at the University of California, Berkeley. His writings include *Beyond Belief* (1970) and (as co-author) *Habits of the Heart* (1985).

**Charles Taylor** was born on 5 November 1931 in Montreal, Quebec, Canada. He has taught at universities at Montreal and Quebec and at Oxford University. His writings include *Hegel and Modern Society* (1979) and *The Ethics of Authenticity* (1991).

# Robert N. Bellah, Richard Madsen, William M. Sullivan, Ann Swidler and Steven M. Tipton

## INDIVIDUALISM AND COMMITMENT IN AMERICAN LIFE

[. . .]

**H**OW ARE WE AMERICANS to think about the nature of success, the meaning of freedom, and the requirements of justice in the modern world? Our conversations with our fellow citizens have deepened our conviction that although we have to rely on our traditions to answer those questions, we will have to probe those traditions much more critically than we are used to doing if we are going to make sense of the challenges posed by the rapidly changing world in which we live.

[. . .] Americans tend to think of the ultimate goals of a good life as matters of personal choice. The means to achieve individual choice, they tend to think, depend on economic progress. This dominant American tradition of thinking about success does not, however, help very much in relating economic success to our ultimate success as persons and our ultimate success as a society.

A century and a half ago, when most Americans still lived in small towns and worked in small businesses or on family-owned farms, the requirements of economic success were perhaps more easily reconciled with understandings of success in family and civic life. In that context, running a profitable farm or business would often have required a reputation for being a good family person and a public-spirited citizen, the meanings of which would be defined in terms of the conventions of one's local community. In Joe Gorman's story, we can see a relic of the way in which the requirements of success in one's job might have encouraged one to define the success of one's life in accordance with the conventional wisdom of one's small town.

But only a small percentage of Americans now work in small businesses in small towns. Most of us work in large public or private bureaucracies. To be a success at work means to advance up the hierarchy of such corporations by helping the corporation make a good profit. But how is this kind of success related to a more fundamental kind of success in life? Even Joe Gorman now works for a large national manufacturing corporation; and he can play such an extraordinarily active part in his community because it fits in with his job as a public relations man for his corporation. If Joe's corporation should ever decide to move its Suffolk factory away from New England to a cheaper labor market, or if the company should offer Gorman an exceptionally good promotion to work at its Houston headquarters, Joe may yet face serious difficulties reconciling the requirements of economic success with his loyalties to his home town.

Someone like Brian Palmer has, of course, already encountered such difficulties. We have seen him wrestle with the question of how to integrate his ambitions to climb the corporate ladder with his desire to have a good family life. This caused him problems, not only because the pressures of work sometimes kept him from spending adequate time with his family, but, even more subtly, because the way of thinking about success that helped him move up the corporate ladder was inappropriate for adequately comprehending the goals of a good family life. And although Brian at least recognizes the problems of integrating a successful work life with a good family life, he seems blithely unconcerned with the wider political and social implications of his work.

Throughout this book, we will be wrestling, together with Brian Palmer and many others, with this question of how to think about the relationship between economic success in our centralized, bureaucratized economy and the ultimate goals of a successful private and public life.

Freedom is perhaps the most resonant, deeply held American value. In some ways, it defines the good in both personal and political life. Yet freedom turns out to mean being left alone by others, not having other people's values, ideas, or styles of life forced upon one, being free of arbitrary authority in work, family, and political life. What it is that one might do with that freedom is much more difficult for Americans to define. And if the entire social world is made up of individuals, each endowed with the right to be free of others' demands, it becomes hard to forge bonds of attachment to, or cooperation with, other people, since such bonds would imply obligations that necessarily impinge on one's freedom. Thus Margaret Oldham, for example, sets great store on becoming an autonomous person, responsible for her own life, and she recognizes that other people, like herself, are free to have their own values and to lead their lives the way they choose. But then, by the same token, if she doesn't like what they do or the way they live, her only right is the right to walk away. In some sense, for her, freedom to be left alone is freedom that implies being alone.

For Margaret, as for others influenced by modern psychological ideals, to be free is not simply to be left alone by others; it is also somehow to be your own person in the sense that you have defined who you are, decided for yourself what you want out of life, free as much as possible from the demands of conformity to family, friends, or community. From this point of view, to be free psychologically is to succeed in separating oneself from the values imposed by one's past or by conformity to one's social milieu, so that one can discover what one really wants.

This was precisely the transformation Brian Palmer experienced. He came to feel that the success he had been seeking was a false goal that didn't meet his own needs, so he pushed it aside, feeling it an assertion of freedom to be able to step back from the demands of his company and fulfill his own vision of happiness. The difficulty, of course, is that this vision of freedom as freedom *from* the demands of others provides no vocabulary in which Brian, Margaret, or other Americans can easily address common conceptions of the ends of a good life or ways to coordinate cooperative action with others. Indeed, Brian points out that one thing he likes in California is the freedom people have to do what they want as long as they stay within the walls of their own houses and do not impinge on others. Implicit here, of course, is an image of self-sufficiency, as if Brian will, on his own in the context of his own small family, be able to imbue his children with 'values' independently of what his neighbors are doing behind the walls of their own homes. The larger hope that his freedom might encompass an ability to share a vision of a good life or a good society with others, to debate that vision, and come to some sort of consensus, is precluded in part by the very definition of freedom Brian holds.

Joe Gorman and Wayne Bauer both value democratic as well as personal freedom. But even their more political and social definition of freedom – not freedom to be your own person so much as the freedom cherished in a democracy, freedom to speak out, to participate freely in a community, and to have one's rights respected, is highly individualistic. As a traditional American patriot, Joe Gorman deeply cherishes the American ideal of freedom, even though in many ways it is precisely the ideal of freedom that makes his dream of a united Suffolk family impossible to achieve. The success of Suffolk's family spirit depends, as he has discovered, on the willingness of a few people like himself to volunteer freely to sustain community life with their own efforts. Yet he recognizes that very few people in Suffolk are willing to undertake the burdens of shaping community life, and that a man like himself is therefore likely to become exhausted, repeatedly finding himself the only volunteer.

Even more, it is the freedom Joe Gorman values – freedom of each person to live where he wants, do what he wants, believe what he wants, and, certainly, do what he can to improve his material circumstances – that makes community ties so fragile. The freedom of free enterprise makes Suffolk a bedroom community to which the residents are attached mainly by housing prices, while economic opportunities tempt most of its native sons and daughters away. The ideal of freedom Joe Gorman holds most dear makes it difficult even to discuss the question of how a just economy or a good society might best be developed in modern circumstances. For Joe, freedom and community can be reconciled only in the nostalgic dream of an idealized past.

While Wayne Bauer holds what he would conceive to be social and political ideals radically different to those of Joe Gorman, he is if anything even more committed to the American ideal of freedom. He would, of course, be willing to limit the freedom of large corporations, but his guiding ideal is simply to restore what he sees as the lost freedom of everyone else. He wants to help give people back a sense that they are effective and can exercise some control over their own lives. But his passionate commitment to economic and political democracy turns out to be strangely without content. He can envision freedom from what he sees as current forms of economic exploitation, but that freedom is, for him, a virtual end in itself. The legacy of freedom is still the right of each person to feel powerful, to be free to strive after whatever he or she happens to want. Wayne's political vocabulary, despite its social-ist patina, is forged from authentically American ore. He waxes passionate about how the freedom of individuals is limited by current economic and political arrangements, but he, too, has difficulty finding a way to think about what a more cooperative, just, and equal social order might look like. Like other Americans, he thinks of freedom very much as freedom *from* – from people who have economic power over you, from people who try to limit what you can do or say. This ideal of freedom has histori-cally given Americans a respect for individuals; it has, no doubt, stimulated their ini-tiative and creativity; it has sometimes even made them tolerant of differences in a diverse society and resistant to overt forms of political oppression. But it is an ideal of freedom that leaves Americans with a stubborn fear of acknowledging structures of power and interdependence in a technologically complex society dominated by giant corporations and an increasingly powerful state. The ideal of freedom makes Americans nostalgic for their past, but provides few resources for talking about their collective future.

Our American traditions encourage us to think of justice as a matter of equal opportunities for every individual to pursue whatever he or she understands by happiness. Equal opportunities are guaranteed by fair laws and political procedures – laws and procedures applied in the same way to everyone. But this way of thinking about justice does not in itself contain a vision of what the distribution of goods in a society would end up looking like if individuals had an equal chance to pursue their interests. Thus, there could be great disparities in the income given to people in different occupations in a just society so long as everyone had an equal chance of getting a well-paid job. But if, as is now becoming painfully apparent, there are more qualified applicants than openings for the interesting jobs, is equal opportu-nity enough to assure justice? What of the socially disadvantaged for whom a fair race is to no avail since they are left well short of the starting line?

Our society has tried to establish a floor below which no one will be allowed to fall, but we have not thought effectively about how to include the deprived more actively in occupational and civic life. Nor have we thought whether it is healthy for our society to give inordinate rewards to relatively few. We need to reach common understandings about distributive justice – an appropriate sharing of economic resources – which must in turn be based on conceptions of a substan-tively just society. Unfortunately, our available moral traditions do not give us nearly as many resources for thinking about distributive justice as about procedural justice, and even fewer for thinking about substantive justice.

Even a self-styled radical such as Wayne Bauer has a difficult time going beyond notions of procedural justice. He is outraged because in Santa Monica the polit-ical cards have been stacked against poor tenants in favor of wealthy landlords. He wants to liberate tenants from this unfair system, to give them the same oppor-tunities as rich people to exercise their wills individually. But he becomes confused when asked what kind of society, with what kind of distribution of wealth, the tenants should try to create once they have achieved a fair chance. There is, after all, not enough land near the coast in Southern California to accommodate everyone who would want to live there. If the mechanisms of the free market are not to determine who should live in places like Santa Monica, how should that determination be made? How, in short, should scarce resources be distributed in the new social order created by liberated tenants? What would a just society really look like? To answer such questions, Wayne would have to do more than think about the fair procedures that should be created to give individuals the ability to exercise power over their own lives. He would need some sense of substantive goals, some way to think about distributive justice. But here his cultural resources fail him, as they do most of us. [. . .]

Breaking with the past is part of our past. Leaving tradition behind runs all the way through our tradition. But how is such a separate self to be shaped and grounded? Do we have answers today that correspond to those provided by Winthrop's God, Jefferson's nature, Franklin's progress, and Whitman's poetic feeling? Almost everyone who talked with us spoke of 'values' in reply. Some of them, like Joe Gorman, make no bones about what those values 'really' are and should be for everyone. Those who don't know better need to be told, like children, 'Shut up and listen!' Those who do know need to pitch in to stem the chaos and 'cooperate with each other for the good of the community.' Others, like Wayne Bauer, return repeatedly to 'this value question' to emphasize that we should be 'helping one another and working together' instead of seeking our own success. Margaret Oldham is more conscious of the fragile basis of her 'values.' 'It really sort of comes down to the authority I say I give my values [. . .] all those sorts of goals I've set up for myself, that kind of motivate me and tell me which way to go, what to avoid.'

If the self is defined by its ability to choose its own values, on what grounds are those choices themselves based? For Margaret and many others, there is simply no objectifiable criterion for choosing one value or course of action over another. One's own idiosyncratic preferences are their own justification, because they define the true self. Brian Palmer explains his drastic shift from obsession with work to devotion to family by saying that he just got more personal satisfaction from course *B* than from course *A*. The right act is simply the one that yields the agent the most exciting challenge or the most good feeling about himself.

Now if selves are defined by their preferences, but those preferences are arbitrary, then each self constitutes its own moral universe, and there is finally no way to reconcile conflicting claims about what is good in itself. All we can do is refer to chains of consequences and ask if our actions prove useful or consistent in light of our own 'value-systems.' All we can appeal to in relationships with others is their self-interest, likewise enlightened, or their intuitive sympathies. In therapy, for example, Margaret would 'try to get them to come to the realization that they're probably causing the other person a whole lot of pain and then ask, "Do you think you ought to do anything about that?"' If confronted with a person whose values 'I really couldn't tolerate,' Margaret concludes, 'I wouldn't see them in therapy.' Where sympathy or already-congruent values are not enough to resolve moral disagreements between ourselves and others, we have no resource except to withdraw from them.

In the absence of any objectifiable criteria of right and wrong, good or evil, the self and its feelings become our only moral guide. What kind of world is inhabited by this self, perpetually in progress, yet without any fixed moral end? There each individual is entitled to his or her own 'bit of space' and is utterly free within its boundaries. In theory, at least, this civil and psychic right is extended to everyone, regardless of their race, ethnicity, or value system, insofar as their exercise of this right does not infringe on the right of others to do likewise.

But while everyone may be entitled to his or her own private space, only those who have enough money can, in fact, afford to purchase the private property required to do their own thing. As a consequence, economic inequalities necessarily delimit our individual 'rights' to self-fulfillment – or unjustly violate those rights, as Wayne Bauer argues in his political struggle to control the free-market explosion of rents in affluent Santa Monica. The tolerance for various values and 'lifestyles' so notable in Brian Palmer's suburban Silicon Valley is helped along by real estate prices (averaging well over $100,000 per house in the early 1980s) that exclude all but the upper middle class from buying homes there. Their livelihood does not hinge on their communal loyalties or local respectability, but on their technical skills, certified by university degrees and measured by the profit-accounting of corporations such as Brian's. Brian's separate self, in short, is socially located on private property that is marked off from the public sphere but depends entirely on the institutional structure of the society at large for its apparent freedoms.

Ted Oster, a lawyer without institutionalized religious or political commitments, who also lives in Silicon Valley, brings the world of the separate self into more extreme relief. He argues that 'rigid' moral standards interfere with one's freedom and enjoyment of life, since 'life is a big pinball game and you have to be able to move and adjust yourself to situations if you're going to enjoy it. You got to be able to realize that most things are not absolute. Very little is, other than life and death.' If the self is to be free, it must also be fluid, moving easily from one social situation and role to another without trying to fit life into any one set of values and norms, even one's own. In fact, one's values are not really a single 'system,' since they vary from one social situation and relationship to the next. Life conceived as a 'pinball game' has its rules, but they are all instrumental, meaningful not in themselves but only as a means to the player's enjoyment. Bending the rules makes sense if it enhances the player's satisfaction. Accordingly, with a good friend 'who is dishonest with some people in a pretty fundamental way,' says Ted Oster, 'to enjoy him I make certain compromises in the way I look at things in order to get into him and to be able to enjoy him.' 'I don't think I change basically who I am. I change what I am doing, perhaps the things I say. That's another aspect of not being totally honest all the time. I won't be totally honest with somebody so that I can enjoy them a little bit more. I put some of my feelings aside. I try to adjust to their way of looking at things without changing myself.'

A self free of absolute values or 'rigid' moral obligations can alter its behavior to adapt to others and to various social roles. It can play all of them as a game, keeping particular social identities at arm's length, yet never changing its own 'basic' identity, because that identity depends only on discovering and pursuing its own personal wants and inner impulses.

If the individual self must be its own source of moral guidance, then each individual must always know what he wants and desires or intuit what he feels. He must act so as to produce the greatest satisfaction of his wants or to express the fullest range of his impulses. The objectified moral goodness of Winthrop obeying God's will or Jefferson following nature's laws turns into the subjective goodness of getting what you want and enjoying it. Utility replaces duty; self-expression unseats authority. 'Being good' becomes 'feeling good.' 'I've always loved that thing that Mark Twain said about something moral is something you feel good after,' Ted Oster remarks, 'and something immoral is something you feel bad after. Which implies that you got to try everything at least once. I guess I'm pretty result-oriented, and whatever produces a good result must be right, and whatever produces a bad result must be wrong.' Acts, then, are not right or wrong in themselves, but only because of the results they produce, the good feelings they engender or express.

Given this individualistic moral framework, the self becomes a crucial site for the comparative examination and probing of feelings that result from utilitarian acts and inspire expressive ones. It is to enhance the efficiency and range of such examination that Oster suggests the need to 'try everything at least once.' The self must be maintained as the intuitive center of the wants and impulses that define right action, and as the unimpeachable evaluator of the good or bad feelings by which the utility of our acts can be calculated and the depth of their self-expression intuited. At first glance, this picture of the self seems common-sensically obvious and problem-free. A humanistic therapist comments, 'It's not so hard for people to figure out what they want. It's just they're afraid that going and getting it is going to deprive them of other things they also want. And they're not sure how to juggle everything at once. But I think people seem to by and large have an amazingly good sense somewhere in there of what makes them feel good.' Individuals can easily figure out what they want, since they intuitively know, 'somewhere in there,' what makes them feel good. The moral problems of a predominantly utilitarian self are simply strategic or technical problems: satisfying one want may obstruct our efforts to do likewise with another, requiring us to do some juggling.

But another difficulty arises to dim the possibility of individualistic self-knowledge. How can we be sure our own feelings and wants are uncompromised by those of others and truly independent of their values? 'The evaluations of others are those internalized ideas of being good, as opposed to feeling good. And they often clash,' explains the therapist. 'Even though I couldn't tell you what feeling good is, and some people don't ever experience it much, I think again people know when they feel good, but they may be confused about and distracted by all those other things. It's like being in love. It's so highly subjective and experienced so differently that I can't tell you what it is. But I can tell you when I feel it.' Feeling good oneself now stands in opposition to 'being good,' seen not as some objective state of virtue, but as conformity to the evaluations of others – doing what satisfies *them* or what defers to convention. For all its unmistakable presence and intensity on occasion, the experience of feeling good, like being in love, is so highly subjective that its distinguishing characteristics remain ineffable. The touchstone of individualistic self-knowledge turns out to be shaky in the end, and its guide to action proves elusive.

Separated from family, religion, and calling as sources of authority, duty, and moral example, the self first seeks to work out its own form of action by autonomously pursuing happiness and satisfying its wants. But what are the wants of the self? By what measure or faculty does it identify its happiness? In the face of these questions, the predominant ethos of American individualism seems more than ever determined to press ahead with the task of letting go of all criteria other than radical private validation. [. . .]

The two traditions of individualism offer us only the cost-benefit analysis of external success and the intuition of feeling inwardly more or less free, comfortable, and authentic on which to ground our self-approval. Ideas of the self's inner expansion reveal nothing of the shape moral character should take, the limits it should respect, and the community it should serve. Ideas of potentiality (for what?) tell us nothing of which tasks and purposes are worth pursuing and are blind, for example, to the differences between a job, career, and calling. Why should we do one thing rather than another, especially when we don't happen to feel like it or don't find it profitable?

It should be clear by now that 'values,' a term we heard constantly from almost everyone to whom we talked, are in themselves no answer. 'Values' turn out to be the incomprehensible, rationally indefensible thing that the individual chooses when he or she has thrown off the last vestige of external influence and reached pure, contentless freedom. The ideal self in its absolute freedom is completely 'unencumbered,' to borrow a term from Michael Sandel. The improvisational self chooses values to express itself; but it is not constituted by them as from a pre-existing source. This notion of an unencumbered self is derived not only from psychotherapy, but much more fundamentally from modern philosophy from Descartes, Locke, and Hume, who affect us more than we imagine. Locke was one of the first to discuss identity in the modern sense of the term when he said, 'The identity of the same man consists, viz., in nothing but a participation of the same continued life, by constantly fleeting particles of matter, in succession vitally united to the same organized body.'

There are a number of problems with this notion of the self that have bedeviled modern thought for a long time, and the people we talked to were at least partly conscious of them. For one thing, what guarantees the autonomy of so radically empty a self against invasion from outside? Radical empiricism starts with the autonomy of the self. But, as Locke argued, what can the self be but a success of experiences imprinted on a 'blank slate'? Psychological notions of socialization and conditioning come to the same thing. Thus Margaret, who proclaims the autonomy and final aloneness of the self, nonetheless believes that 'values are shaped by the way you're brought up,' the 'background and experiences that you've had when you were young.' The extreme of this point of view, sometimes expressed in the work of Erving Goffman, is that there is no self at all. What seems to be a self is merely a series of social masks that change with each successive situation. An absolutely autonomous self and a self determined completely by the social situation do not, then, turn out to be opposites. Many of those to whom we talked can switch from one vocabulary to the other, hardly noticing the difference.

The language of 'values' as commonly used is self-contradictory precisely because it is not a language of value, or moral choice. It presumes the existence of an absolutely empty unencumbered and improvisational self. It obscures personal reality, social reality, and particularly the moral reality that links person and society. [. . .]

Chapter 30

_____

# Charles Taylor

## THE MAKING OF MODERN
## IDENTITY

[. . .]

**T**HE MORAL WORLD of moderns is significantly different from that of previous civilizations. This becomes clear, among other places, when we look at the sense that human beings command our respect. In one form or another, this seems to be a human universal; that is, in every society, there seems to be some such sense. The boundary around those beings worthy of respect may be drawn parochially in earlier cultures, but there always is such a class. And among what we recognize as higher civilizations, this always includes the whole human species.

What is peculiar to the modern West among such higher civilizations is that its favoured formulation for this principle of respect has come to be in terms of rights. This has become central to our legal systems – and in this form has spread around the world. But in addition, something analogous has become central to our moral thinking.

The notion of a right, also called a 'subjective right', as this developed in the Western legal tradition, is that of a legal privilege which is seen as a quasi-possession of the agent to whom it is attributed. At first such rights were differential possessions: some people had the right to participate in certain assemblies, or to give counsel, or to collect tolls on this river, and so on. The revolution in natural law theory in the seventeenth century partly consisted in using this language of rights to express the universal moral norms. We began to speak of 'natural' rights, and now to such things as life and liberty which supposedly everyone has.

In one way, to speak of a universal, natural right to life doesn't seem much of an innovation. The change seems to be one of form. The earlier way of putting it was that there was a natural law against taking innocent life. Both formulations seem to prohibit the same things. But the difference lies not in what is forbidden but in the place of the subject. Law is what I must obey. It may confer on me benefits, here the immunity that my life, too, is to be respected; but fundamentally I am *under* law. By contrast, a subjective right is something which the possessor can and ought to act on to put it into effect. To accord you an immunity, formerly given you by natural law, in the form of a natural right is to give you a role in establishing and enforcing this immunity. Your concurrence is now necessary, and your degrees of freedom are correspondingly greater. At the extreme limit of these, you can even waive a right, thus defeating the immunity. This is why Locke, in order to close off this possibility in the case of his three basic rights, had to introduce the notion of 'inalienability'. Nothing like this was necessary on the earlier natural law formulation, because that language by its very nature excludes the power of waiver.

To talk of universal, natural, or human rights is to connect respect for human life and integrity with the notion of autonomy. It is to conceive people as active cooperators in establishing and ensuring the respect which is due them. And this expresses a central feature of the modern Western moral outlook. This change of form naturally goes along with one in content, with the conception of what it is to respect someone. Autonomy is now central to this. So the Lockean trinity of natural rights includes that to liberty. And for us respecting personality involves as a crucial feature respecting the person's moral autonomy. With the development of the post-Romantic notion of individual difference, this expands to the demand that we give people the freedom to develop their personality in their own way, however repugnant to ourselves and even to our moral sense [. . .].

Alongside ethics of fame, of rational mastery and control, of the transformation of the will, there has grown up in the last two centuries a distinction based on vision and expressive power. There is a set of ideas and intuitions, still inadequately understood, which makes us admire the artist and the creator more than any other civilization ever has; which convinces us that a life spent in artistic creation or performance is eminently worthwhile. This complex of ideas itself has Platonic roots. We are taking up a semi-suppressed side of Plato's thought which emerges, for instance, in the *Phaedrus*, where he seems to think of the poet, inspired by mania, as capable of seeing what sober people are not. The widespread belief today that the artist sees farther than the rest of us, attested by our willingness to take seriously the opinions about politics expressed by painters or singers, even though they may have no more special expertise in public affairs than the next person, seems to spring from the same roots. But there is also something quintessentially modern in this outlook. It depends on the modern sense, invoked in the previous section, that what meaning there is for us depends in part on our powers of expression, that discovering a framework is interwoven with inventing. [. . .]

[I]t has to do with our identity. In fact, our visions of the good are tied up with our understandings of the self. [. . .] We have a sense of who we are through our sense of where we stand to the good. But this will also mean, as we shall see in detail later, that radically different senses of what the good is go along with quite different conceptions of what a human agent is, different notions of the self. To trace the development of our modern visions of the good, which are in some respects unprecedented in human culture, is also to follow the evolution of unprecedented new understandings of agency and selfhood. [. . .]

My claim is rather that the picture of nature as a source was a crucial part of the conceptual armoury in which Romanticism arose and conquered European culture and sensibility.

[. . .] This places a value on our sentiments for themselves, as it were. Unlike the Aristotelian ethic it doesn't define certain motivations as virtuous in terms of the actions they move us to. It is more directly concerned with how we feel about the world and our lives in general. This makes the analogy with Plato's love of the Good. But unlike this, what is required is not the love of some transcendent object but rather a certain way of experiencing our lives, our ordinary desires and fulfilments, and the larger natural order in which we are set. To be in tune with nature is to experience these desires as rich, as full, as significant – to respond to the current of life in nature. It really is a matter of having certain *sentiments* as well as of aiming at or doing certain things. [. . .]

If our access to nature is through an inner voice or impulse, then we can only fully know this nature through articulating what we find within us. This connects to another crucial feature of this new philosophy of nature, the idea that its realization in each of us is also a form of expression. This is the view that I have called elsewhere 'expressivism'. I am focussing on particular features of expression in using this term. To express something is to make it manifest in a given medium. I express my feelings in my face; I express my thoughts in the words I speak or write. I express my vision of things in some work of art, perhaps a novel or a play. In all these cases, we have the notion of making something manifest, and in each case in the medium with certain specific properties. [. . .]

And so for this kind of expressive object, we think of its 'creation' as not only a making manifest but also a making, a bringing of something to be. This notion of expression is itself modern. It grows at the same time as the understanding of human life that I am trying to formulate. Indeed, it is one facet of it. I use it only because it is more generally recognizable to us in this field of artistic works. [. . .]

Fulfilling my nature means espousing the inner élan, the voice or impulse. And this makes what was hidden manifest for both myself and others. But this manifestation also helps to define what is to be realized. The direction of this élan wasn't and couldn't be clear prior to this manifestation. In realizing my nature, I have to define it in the sense of giving it some formulation; but this is also a definition in a stronger sense: I am realizing this formulation and thus giving my life a definitive shape. A human life is seen as manifesting a potential which is also being shaped by this manifestation; it is not just a matter of copying an external model or carrying out an already determinate formulation. [. . .]

Expressivism was the basis for a new and fuller individuation. This is the idea which grows in the late eighteenth century that each individual is different and original, and that this originality determines how he or she ought to live. Just the notion of individual difference is, of course, not new. Nothing is more evident, or more banal. What is new is the idea that this really makes a difference to how we're called on to live. The differences are not just unimportant variations within the same basic human nature; or else moral differences between good and bad individuals. Rather they entail that each one of us has an original path which we ought to tread; they lay the obligation on each of us to live up to our originality.

Herder formulated this idea in a telling image: 'Jeder Mensch hat ein eignes Mass, gleichsam eine eigne Stimmung aller seiner sinnlichen Gefühle zu einander' ('Each human being has his own measure, as it were an accord peculiar to him of all his feelings to each other'). Each person is to be measured by a different yardstick, one which is properly his or her own.

We can see ideas in the tradition which prepared the way for this – for instance, the Christian notion of a variety of gifts which is correlative to the variety of vocations, which we see expressed in St. Paul, and then taken up again by the Puritans. Here we have the notion that the good life for you is not the same as the good life for me; each of us has our own calling, and we shouldn't exchange them. Following you may be betraying my own calling, even though you are being faithful to yours. What the late eighteenth century adds is the notion of originality. It goes beyond a fixed set of callings to the notion that each human being has some original and unrepeatable 'measure'. We are all called to live up to our originality.

This radical individuation was obviously facilitated by expressivism and the notion of nature as a source. What the voice of nature calls us to cannot be fully known outside of and prior to our articulation/definition of it. We can only know what realizing our deep nature is when we have done it. But if this is true for human beings in general, why should it not also be true for each human being in particular? Just as the manifestations of the great current of life in the rest of nature can't be the same as its realization in human life, so its realization in you may be different from its realization in me. If nature is an intrinsic source, then each of us has to follow what is within; and this may be without precedent. We should not hope to find our models without.

This has been a tremendously influential idea. Expressive individuation has become one of the cornerstones of modern culture. So much so that we barely notice it, and we find it hard to accept that it is such a recent idea in human history and would have been incomprehensible in earlier times. In addition, this notion of originality as a vocation holds not only between individuals. Herder also used it to formulate a notion of national culture. Different *Völker* have their own way of being human, and shouldn't betray it by aping others. (In particular, Germans shouldn't ape Frenchmen. But Herder was also a passionate, and early, anti-colonialist.) This is one of the originating ideas of modern nationalism. [. . .]

[A]mong the great aspirations which come down to us from the Romantic era are those towards reunification: bringing us back in contact with nature, healing the divisions within between reason and sensibility, overcoming the divisions between people, and creating community. These aspirations are still alive: although the Romantic religions of nature have died away, the idea of our being open to nature within us and without is still a very powerful one. [. . .]

[T]he view of nature as a source can't ignore the point that mere sinking into unity with nature would be a negation of human autonomy. That is why the great thinkers who emerged out of the expressivist stream in this period all strove to unite radical autonomy and expressive unity, as we see with Schiller, Hölderlin, and Hegel, for instance. [. . .]

The expressivist theories of nature as source thus develop their own conceptions of history and of the narrative forms of human life, both in how an individual life unfolds towards self-discovery and in how this life fits into the whole human story. One such form is the spiral I've just been describing. But the critique of modern Enlightenment civilization as fragmented and dessicated could also generate a pessimistic sense that the world had declined, perhaps irreversibly, from an earlier, richer time. It could inspire a nostalgia for a past age of integrity – often identified with the Middle Ages.

Both forms broke with Enlightenment narrations. Even the 'optimistic' spiral view, in some ways similar to the extent that it points towards a higher, better future; but very different in its polarization, in the drama of separation and reunion. The linear picture of progress that Condorcet offers is utterly denied. Those things that can progress in a linear fashion – scientific knowledge, technological know-how, riches – are far from being accepted as unadulterated goods.

And the picture of the growth of a life is utterly different in the central place it gives to self-discovery. The expressivist revolution constituted a prodigious development of modern post-Augustinian inwardness, in its self-explanatory branch. [. . .] But only with the expressivist idea of articulating our inner nature do we see the grounds for construing this inner domain which reaches farther than we can ever articulate, which still stretches beyond our furthest point of clear expression.

That examining the soul should involve the exploration of a vast domain is not, of course, a new idea. The Platonic tradition would concur. But this domain is not an 'inner' one. To understand the soul, we are led to contemplate the order in which it is set, the public order of things. What is new in the post-expressivist era is that the domain is within, that is, it is only open to a mode of exploration which involves the first-person stance. That is what it means to define the voice or impulse as 'inner'.

Of course, Augustine had a notion of something 'inner' which similarly stretched beyond our powers of vision: our 'memory'. But at the base of this is God; to penetrate to the depths of our memory would be to be taken outside ourselves. And this is where we achieve our ultimate integrity as persons, in the eye of God, from the outside. Augustine's inwardness leads to the higher, as we said. In the philosophy of nature as source, the inexhaustible domain is properly within. To the extent that digging to the roots of our being takes us beyond ourselves, it is to the larger nature from which we emerge. But this we only gain access to through its voice in us. This nature, unlike Augustine's God, cannot offer us a higher view on ourselves from beyond our own self-exploration. The modern, post-expressivist subject really has, unlike the denizens of any earlier culture, 'inner depths'.

This concept of an inexhaustible inner domain is the correlative of the power of expressive self-articulation. The sense of depth in inner space is bound up with the sense that we can move into it and bring things to the fore. This we do when we articulate. The inescapable feeling of depth comes from the realization that whatever we bring up, there is always more down there. Depth lies in there being always, inescapably, something beyond our articulative power. This notion of inner depths is therefore intrinsically linked to our understanding of ourselves as expressive, as articulating an inner source.

The subject with depth is therefore a subject with this expressive power. Something fundamental changes in the late eighteenth century. The modern subject is no longer defined just by the power of disengaged rational control but by this new power of expressive self-articulation as well – the power which has been ascribed since the Romantic period to the creative imagination. This works in some ways in the same direction as the earlier power: it intensifies the sense of inwardness and leads to an even more radical subjectivism and an internalization of moral sources. But in other respects these powers are in tension. To follow the first all the way is to adopt a stance of disengagement from one's own nature and feelings, which renders impossible the exercise of the second. A modern who recognizes both these powers is constitutionally in tension. [. . .]

Bellah and his collaborators [. . .] see the threat that first utilitarian, and now also expressive individualism pose for our public life. They search for ways to recover a language of commitment to the greater whole. But without ever saying so, they write as though there were not really an independent problem of the loss of meaning in our culture, as though the recovery of a Tocquevillian commitment would somehow also fully resolve our problems of meaning, of expressive unity, of the loss of substance and resonance in our man-made environment, of a disenchanted universe. A crucial area of modern search and concern has been elided. [. . .]

The sympathies of this type of outlook tend to be rather narrow, and their reading of the varied facets of the modern identity unsympathetic. The deeper moral vision, the genuine moral sources invoked in the aspiration to disengaged reason or expressive fulfilment tend to be overlooked, and the less impressive motives – pride, self-satisfaction, liberation from demanding standards – brought to the fore. Modernity is often read through its least impressive, most trivializing offshoots.

But this distorts. The most frivolous and self-indulgent forms of the human potential movement in the United States today can't give us the measure of the aspiration to expressive fulfilment as we find it, for instance, in Goethe or Arnold. And even the most frivolous manifestation may reflect more than we can see at a glance. Above all, we have to avoid the error of declaring those goods invalid whose exclusive pursuit leads to contemptible or disastrous consequences. The search for pure subjective expressive fulfilment may make life thin and insubstantial, may ultimately undercut itself [. . .]. But that by itself does nothing to show that subjective fulfilment is not a good. It shows only that it needs to be part of a 'package', to be sought within a life which is also aimed at other goods. This can be the basis, of course, for a cruel dilemma, in which the demands of fulfilment run against these other goods – one which thousands of divorcing or near-divorcing couples are living through in our time, for instance. But a dilemma doesn't invalidate the rival goods. On the contrary, it presupposes them. [. . .]

# GENDER

- Norma Alarcón, The theoretical subject(s) of *This Bridge Called My Back* and Anglo-American feminism

- Judith Butler, Imitation and gender insubordination

**Norma Alarcón** is a native Mexican. She has taught at Purdue University and at the University of California, Berkeley. She was a founding editor of the Third Woman Press and is the author of *La Poetica feminista de Rosario Castellanos* (1992) and many essays.

**Judith Butler** was born in 1957. She took a doctorate in philosophy at Yale University. She is currently teaching at the University of California at Berkeley. Butler is the author of, among other books, *Gender Trouble* (1990) and *Bodies That Matter* (1993).

# Chapter 31

# Norma Alarcón

## THE THEORETICAL SUBJECT(S) OF
## *THIS BRIDGE CALLED MY BACK* AND
## ANGLO-AMERICAN FEMINISM

**T**HIS BRIDGE CALLED MY BACK: *Writings by Radical Women of Color*, edited by Chicana writers Cherríe Moraga and Gloria Anzaldúa,* was intended as a collection of essays, poems, tales and testimonials that would give voice to the contradictory experiences of 'women of color.' In fact, the editors state:

> We are the colored in a white feminist movement.
> We are the feminists among the people of our culture.
> We are often the lesbians among the straight.[1]

By giving voice to such experiences, each according to her style, the editors and contributors believed they were developing a theory of subjectivity and culture that would demonstrate the considerable differences between them and Anglo-American women, as well as between them and Anglo-European men and men of their own culture. As speaking subjects of a new discursive formation, many of *Bridge*'s writers were aware of the displacement of their subjectivity across a multiplicity of discourses: feminist/lesbian, nationalist, racial, socioeconomic, historical, etc. The peculiarity of their displacement implies a multiplicity of positions from which they are driven to grasp or understand themselves and their relations with the real, in the Althusserian sense of the word.[2] *Bridge* writers, in part, were aware that these positions are often incompatible or contradictory, and others did not have access to the maze of discourses competing for their body and voice. The self-conscious effort to reflect on their 'flesh and blood experiences to concretize a vision that can begin to heal our "wounded knee"'[3] led many *Bridge* speakers to take a position in conflict with multiple intercultural and intracultural discursive interpretations in an effort to come to grips with 'the many-headed demon of oppression.'[4]

Since its publication in 1981, *Bridge* has had a diverse impact on Anglo American feminist writings in the United States. Teresa de Lauretis, for example, claims that *Bridge* has contributed to a 'shift in feminist consciousness,'[5] yet her explanation fails to clarify what the shift consists of and for whom. There is little doubt, however, that *Bridge*, along with the 1980s writings by many women of color in the United States, has problematized many aversion of Anglo-American feminism, and has helped open the way for alternative feminist discourses and theories. Presently, however, the impact among most Anglo American theorists appears to be more cosmetic than not because, as Jane Flax has recently noted, 'The modal "person" in feminist theory still appears to be a self-sufficient individual adult.'[6] This particular 'modal person' corresponds to the female subject most admired in literature which Gayatri Chakravorty Spivak had characterized as one who 'articulates herself in shirting relationship to [. . .] the constitution and 'interpellation' of the subject not only as individual but as "individualist."'[7] Consequently, the 'native female' – object of colonialism and racism – is excluded because, in Flax's terms, white feminists have not 'explored how our understanding of gender relations, self, and theory are partially constituted in and through experiences of living in a culture in which a symmetric race relations are a central organizing principle of society.'[8] Thus, 'the most popular subject of Anglo American feminist is an autonomous, self-making, self determining subject who first proceeds according to the *logic of identification* with regard to the subject of consciousness, a notion usually viewed as the purview of man, but now claimed for women.'[9] Believing that in this respect she is the same as man, she now claims the right to pursue her own identity, to name herself, to pursue self-knowledge, and, in the words of Adrienne Rich, to effect 'a change in the concept of sexual identity.'[10]

Though feminism has problematized gender relations, indeed, as Flax observes, gender is 'the single most important advance in feminist theory,'[11] it has not problematized the subject of knowledge and her complicity with the notion of consciousness as 'synthetic unifactory power, the centre and active point of organization of representations determining their concatenation.'[12] The subject (and object) of knowledge is now a woman, but the inherited view of consciousness has not been questioned at all. As a result, some Anglo-American feminist subjects of consciousness have tended to become a parody of the masculine subject of consciousness, thus revealing their ethnocentric liberal underpinnings. In 1982, Jean Bethke Elshtain had noted the 'masculine cast' of radical feminist language, for example, noting the terms of 'raw power, brute force, martial discipline, law and order with a feminist face – and voice.'[13] Also in critiquing liberal feminism and its language, she notes that 'no vision of the political community that might serve as the ground work of a life in common is possible within a political life dominated by a self-interested, predatory individualism.'[14] Althusser argues that this tradition 'has privileged the category of the "subject" as Origin, Essence and Cause, responsible in its internality for all determinations of the external object. In other words, this tradition has promoted Man, in his ideas and experience, as the source of knowledge, morals and history.'[15] By identifying in this way with this tradition standpoint epistemologists have substituted, ironically, woman for man. This 'logic of identification' as a first step in constructing the theoretical subject of feminism is often veiled from standpoint epistemologists because greater attention is given to naming female identity, and describing women's ways of knowing as being considerably different than men's.[16] By emphasizing 'sexual difference,' the second step takes place, often called oppositional thinking (counteridentifying). However, this gendered standpoint epistemology leads to feminism's bizarre position with regard to other liberation movements, working inherently against the interests of non-white women and no one else. For example, Sandra Harding argues that oppositional thinking (counteridentification) with white men should be retained even though '[t]here are suggestions in the literature of Native Americans, Africans, and Asians that what feminists call feminine versus masculine personalities, ontologies, ethics, epistemologies, and world views may be what these other liberation movements call Non-Western versus Western personalities and world views. [. . .] I set aside the crucial and fatal complication for this way of thinking – the fact that one half of these people are women and that most women are not Western.'[17] She further suggests that feminists respond by relinquishing the totalizing 'master theory' character of our theory-making: 'This response to the issue [will manage] to retain the categories of feminist theory [. . .] and simply set them alongside the categories of the theory making of other subjugated groups. [. . .] Of course, it leave bifurcated (and perhaps even more finely divided) the identities of all except ruling-class white Western women.'[18] The apperception of this situation is precisely what led to the choice of title for the book *All The Women Are White, All The Blacks Are Men, But Some of Us Are Brave*, edited by Gloria T. Hull, Patricia Bell Scott and Barbara Smith.[19]

Notwithstanding the power of *Bridge* to affect the personal lives of its readers, *Bridge's* challenge to the Anglo-American subject of feminism has yet to effect a newer discourse. Women of color often recognize themselves in the pages of *Bridge*, and write to say, 'The women writers seemed to be speaking to me, and they actually understood what I was going through. Many of you put into words feelings I have had that I had no way of expressing. [. . .] The writings justified some of my thoughts telling me I had a right to feel as I did.'[20] On the other hand, Anglo-feminist readers of *Bridge* tend to appropriate it, cite it as an instance of difference by subsuming women of color into the unitary category of woman/women. The latter is often viewed as the 'common denominator' in an oppositional (counteridentifying) discourse with some white men, that leaves us unable to explore relationships among women.

*Bridge's* writers did not see the so-called 'common denominator' as the solution for the construction of the theoretical feminist subject. In the call for submissions the editors clearly stated: 'We want to express to all women – especially to white middle class women – the experiences which divide us as feminists; we want to explore the causes, and sources of, and solutions to these divisions. We want to create a definition that expands what 'feminist' means to us.'[21] Thus, the female subject of *Bridge* is highly complex. She is and has been constructed in a crisis of meaning situation which includes racial and cultural divisions and conflicts. The psychic and material violence that gives shape to that subjectivity cannot be underestimated nor passed over lightly. The fact that not all of this violence comes from men in general but also from women renders the notion of 'common denominator' problematic.

It is clear, however, that even as *Bridge* becomes a resource for the Anglo-American feminist theory classroom and syllabus, there's a tendency to deny differences if those differences pose a threat to the 'common denominator' category. That is, unity would be purchased with silence, putting aside the conflictive history of groups' interrelations and interdependence. In the words of Paula Treichler, '[h]ow do we address the issues and concerns raised by women of color, who may themselves be even more excluded from theoretical feminist discourse than from the women's studies curriculum? [. . .] Can we explore our 'common differences' without overemphasizing the division that currently seems to characterize the feminist of the United States and the world?[22] Clearly, this exploration appears impossible without a reconfiguration of the subject of feminist theory, and her relational position to a multiplicity of others, not just white men.

Some recent critics of the 'exclusionary practices in Women's Studies' have noted that its gender standpoint epistemology leads to a 'tacking on' of 'material about minority women' without any note of its 'significance for feminist knowledge.'[23] The common approaches noted were the tendency to 1) treat race and class as secondary features in social organization (as well as representation) with primacy given to female subordination; 2) acknowledge that inequalities of race, class and gender generate different experiences and then set race and class inequalities aside on the grounds that information was lacking to allow incorporation into an analysis; 3) focus on descriptive aspects of the ways of life, values, customs and problems of women in subordinate race and class categories with little attempt to explain their source or their broader meaning. In fact, it may be impossible for gender standpoint epistemology to ever do more than a 'pretheoretical presentation of concrete problems.'[24] Since the subject of feminist theory and its single theme – gender – go largely unquestioned, its point of view tends to suppress and repress voices that question its authority, and as Jane Flax remarks, 'The suppression of these voices seems to be a necessary condition for the (apparent) authority, coherence, and universality of our own.'[25] This may account for the inability to include the voices of 'women of color' into feminist discourse, though they are not necessarily under-represented in the reading list.

For the standpoint epistemologists, the desire to construct a feminist theory based solely on gender, on the one hand, and the knowledge or implicit recognition that such an account might distort the representation of many women and/or correspond to that of some men, on the other, gives rise to anxiety and ambivalence with respect to the future of that feminism, especially in Anglo-America. At the core of that attitude is the often unstated recognition that if the pervasiveness of women's oppression is virtually 'universal' on some level, it is also highly diverse from group to group and that women themselves may become complicitous with that oppression. 'Complicity arises,' says Macdonell, 'where through lack of a positive starting point either a practice is driven to make use of prevailing values or a critique becomes the basis for a new theory.'[26] Standpoint epistemologists have made use of the now gendered and feminist notion of consciousness, without too much question. (This notion, of course, represents the highest value of European culture since the Enlightenment.) The inclusion of other analytical categories such as race and class becomes impossible for a subject whose consciousness refuses to acknowledge that 'one becomes a woman' in ways that are much more complex than in a simple opposition to men. In cultures in which 'asymmetric race and class relations are a central organizing principle of society,' one may also 'become a woman' in opposition to other women. In other words, the whole category of women may also need to be problematized, a point that I shall take up later. In any case, one should not step into that category nor that of man that easily or simply.

Simone de Beauvoir and her key work *The Second Sex* have been most influential in the development of feminist standpoint epistemology. She may even be responsible for the creation of Anglo-American feminist theory's 'episteme': a highly self-conscious ruling class white Western female male subject locked in a struggle to the death with 'Man.' De Beauvoir has shaken the world of women, most especially with the ramification of her phrase, 'One is not born, but rather becomes, a woman.'[27] For over 400 pages of text after that statement, de Beauvoir demonstrates how a female is constituted as a 'woman' by society as her freedom is curtailed from childhood. The curtailment of freedom incapacitates her from affirming 'herself as a subject.'[28] Very few women, indeed, can escape the cycle of indocrination except perhaps the writer/intellectual because '[s]he knows that she is a conscious being, a subject.'[29] This particular kind of woman can perhaps make of her gender a project and transform her sexual identity.[30] But what of those women who are not so privileged, who neither have the political freedom nor the education? Do they now, then, occupy the place of the Other (the 'Brave') while some women become subjects? Or do we have to make a subject of the whole world?

Regardless of our point of view in this matter, the way to becoming a female subject has been effected through consciousness-raising. In 1982, in a major theoretical essay, 'Feminism, Method and the State: An Agenda for Theory,' Catharine A. MacKinnon cited *Bridge* as a book that explored the relationship between sex and race and argued that 'consciousness-raising' was *the* feminist method.[31] The reference to *Bridge* was brief. It served as an example, along with other texts, of the challenge that race and nationalism have posed for Marxism. According to her, Marxism has been unable to account for the appearance of these emancipatory discourses nor has it been able to assimilate them. Nevertheless, MacKinnon's major point was to demonstrate the epistemological challenge that feminism and its primary method, 'consciousness-raising,' posed for Marxism. Within Marxism, class as a method of analysis has failed to reckon with the historical force of sexism. Through 'consciousness-raising' (from women's point of view), women are led to know the world in a different way. Women's experience of politics, of life as sex objects, gives rise to its own method of appropriating that reality: feminist method. It challenges the objectivity of the 'empirical gaze' and 'rejects the distinction between knowing subject and known object.'[32] By having women be the subject of knowledge, the so-called 'objectivity' of men is brought into question. Often, this leads to privileging women's way of knowing in opposition to men's way of knowing, thus sustaining the very binary opposition that feminism would like to change or transform. Admittedly, this is only one of the many paradoxical procedures in feminist thinking, as Nancy Cott confirms: 'It acknowledges diversity among women while positing that women recognize their unity. It requires gender consciousness for its basis, yet calls for the elimination of prescribed gender roles.'[33]

However, I suspect that these contradictions or paradoxes have more profound implications than is readily apparent. Part of the problem may be that as feminist practice and theory recuperate their sexual differential, through 'consciousness-raising,' women reinscribe such a differential as feminist epistemology or theory. With gender as the central concept in feminist thinking, epistemology is flattened out in such a way that we lose sight of the complex and multiple ways in which the subject and object of possible experience are constituted. The flattening effect is multiplied when one considers that gender is often solely related to white men. There's no inquiry into the knowing subject beyond the fact of being a 'woman.' But what is a 'woman,' or a 'man' for that matter? If we refuse to define either term according to some 'essence,' then we are left with having to specify their conventional significance in time and space, which is liable to change as knowledge increases or interests change. The fact that Anglo American feminism has appropriated the generic term for itself leaves many a woman in this country having to call herself otherwise, i.e., 'woman of color,' which is equally 'meaningless' without further specification. It also gives rise to the tautology 'Chicana women.' Needless to say, the requirement of gender consciousness only in relationship to man leaves us in the dark about a good many things, including interracial and intercultural relations. It may be that the only purpose this type of differential has is as a political strategy. It does not help us envision a world beyond binary restrictions, nor does it help us to reconfigure feminist theory to include the 'native female.' It does, however, help us grasp the paradox that within this cultural context one cannot be a feminist without becoming a gendered subject of knowledge, which makes it very difficult to transcend gender at all and to imagine relations between women.

In *Feminist Politics and Human Nature*, Alison M. Jaggar, speaking as a socialist feminist, refers repeatedly to *Bridge* and other works by women of color. In that work, Jaggar states that subordinated women are unrepresented in feminist theory. Jaggar claims that socialist feminism is inspired by Marxist and radical feminist politics though the latter has failed to be scientific about its insights. *Bridge* is cited various times to counter the racist and classist position of radical feminists.[34] Jaggar charges that '[r]adical feminism has encouraged women to name their own experience but it has not recognized explicitly that this experience must be analyzed, explained and theoretically transcended.'[35] In a sense, Jaggar's charge amounts to the notion that radical feminists were flattening out their knowledge by an inadequate methodology, i.e. gender consciousness raising. Many of Jaggar's observations are a restatement of *Bridge*'s challenge to Anglo-American feminists of all persuasions, be it Liberal, Radical, Marxist, and Socialist, the types sketched out by Jaggar. For example, '[a] representation of reality from the standpoint of women must draw on the variety of all women's experience'[36] may be compared to Barbara Smith's view in *Bridge* that 'Feminism is the political theory and practice to free *all* women: women of color, working-class women, poor women, physically challenged women, lesbians, old women, as well as white economically privileged heterosexual women.'[37] Jaggar continues, 'Since historically diverse groups of women, such as working class women, women of color, and others have been excluded from intellectual work, they somehow must be enabled to participate as subjects as well as objects of feminist theorizing.'[38] Writers in *Bridge* did appear to think that 'consciousness-raising' and the naming of one's experience would deliver some theory and yield a notion of 'what "feminist" means to us.'[39] Except for Smith's statement, there is no overarching view that would guide us as to 'what "feminist" means to us.' Though there is a tacit political identity gender/class/race-encapsulated in the phrase 'women of color' that connects the pieces – they tend to split apart into 'vertical relations' between the culture of resistance and the culture resisted or from which excluded. Thus, the binary restrictions become as prevalent between race/ethnicity of oppressed versus oppressor as between the sexes. The problems inherent in Anglo-American feminism and race relations are so locked into the 'Self/Other' theme that it is no surprise that *Bridge*'s co-editor Moraga would remark, 'In the last three years I have learned that Third World feminism does not provide the kind of easy political framework that women of color are running to in droves. The *idea* of Third World feminism has proved to be much easier between the covers of a book than between real live women.'[40] She refers to the United States, of course, because feminism is alive and well throughout the Third World largely within the purview of women's rights, or as a class struggle.[41]

The appropriation of *Bridge*'s observations in Jaggar's work differs slightly from the others in its view of linguistic use, implying to a limited extent that language is also reflective of material existence. The crucial question is how, indeed, can women of color be subjects as well as objects of feminist theorizing? Jaggar cites María Lugones' doubts: 'We cannot talk to you in our language because you do not understand it. [. . .] The power of white Anglo women vis-à-vis Hispanas and Black women is in inverse proportion to their working knowledge of each other. [. . .] Because of their ignorance, white Anglo women who try to do theory with women of color inevitably disrupt the dialogue. Before they can contribute to collective dialogue, they need to 'know the text,' to have become familiar with an alternative way of viewing the world. [. . .] You need to learn to become un-intrusive, unimportant, patient to the point of tears, while at the same time open to learning any possible lessons. You will have to come to terms with the sense of alienation, of not belonging, of having your world thoroughly disrupted, having it criticized and scrutinized from the point of view of those who have been harmed by it, having important concepts central to it dismissed, being viewed with mistrust.'[42] One of *Bridge*'s breaks with prevailing conventions is linguistic. Lugones' advice to Anglo women to listen was post *Bridge*. If prevailing conventions of speaking/writing had been observed, many a contributor would have been censored or silenced. So would have many a major document or writing of minorities. *Bridge* leads us to understand that the silence and silencing of people begins with the dominating enforcement of linguistic conventions, the resistance to relational dialogues, as well as the disenablement of peoples by outlawing their forms of speech. Anglo-American feminist theory assumes a speaking subject who is an autonomous, self-conscious individual woman. Such theory does not discuss the linguistic status of the person. It takes for granted the linguistic status which founds subjectivity. In this way it appropriates woman/women for itself, and turns its work into a theoretical project within which the rest of us are compelled to 'fit.' By 'forgetting' or refusing to take into account that we are culturally consti-tuted in and through language in complex ways and not just engendered in a homogeneous situation, the Anglo-American subject of consciousness cannot come to terms with her (his) own class-biased ethnocentrism. She is blinded to her own construction not just as a woman but as an Anglo-American one. Such a subject creates a theoretical subject that could not possibly include all women just because we are women. It is against this feminist backdrop that many 'women of color' have struggled to give voice to their subjectivity and which effected the publication of the writings collected in *Bridge*. However, the freedom of women of color to posit themselves as multiple-voiced subjects is constantly in peril of repression precisely at that point where our constituted contradictions put us at odds with women different from ourselves.

The pursuit of a 'politics of unity' solely based on gender forecloses the 'pursuit of solidarity' through different political formations and the exploration of alternative theories of the subject of consciousness. There is a tendency in more sophisticated and elaborate gender standpoint epistemologists to affirm 'an identity made up of heterogeneous and heteronomous representations of gender, race, and class, and often indeed across languages and cultures'[43] with one breath, and with the next to refuse to explore how that identity may be theorized or analyzed, by reconfirming a unified subjectivity or 'shared consciousness' through gender. The difference is handed over with one hand and taken away with the other. If it be true, as Teresa de Lauretis has observed, that '[s]elf and identity [. . .] are always grasped and understood within particular discursive configurations,'[44] it does not necessarily follow that one can easily and self-consciously decide 'to reclaim [an identity] from a history of multiple assimilations,'[45] and still retain a 'shared consciousness.' Such a practice goes counter to the homogenizing tendency of the subject of consciousness in the United States. To be oppressed means to be disenabled not only from grasping an 'identity,' but also from reclaiming it. In this culture, to grasp or reclaim an identity means always already to have become a subject of consciousness. The theory of the subject of consciousness as a unitary and synthesizing agent of knowledge is always already posture of domination. One only has to think of Gloria Anzaldúa's essay in *Bridge*, 'Speaking in Tongues: A Letter to Third World Women Writers.'[46] Though de Lauretis concedes that a racial 'shared consciousness' may have prior claims than gender, she still insists on unity through gender: 'the female subject is always constructed and defined in gender, starting from gender.'[47] One is interested in having more than an account of gender, there are other relations to be accounted for. De Lauretis insists, in most of her work, that 'the differences among women may be better understood as differences with women.'[48] This position returns us all to our solitary, though different, consciousness, without noting that some differences are (have been) a result of relations of domination of women by women; that differences may be purposefully constituted for the purpose of domination or exclusion, especially in oppositional thinking. Difference, whether it be sexual, racial, social, have to be conceptualized within a political and ideological domain.[49] In *Bridge*, for example, Mirtha Quintanales points out that 'in this country, in this world, racism is used *both* to create false differences among us and to mask very significant ones – cultural, economic, political.'[50]

One of the most remarkable tendencies in the work reviewed is the implicit or explicit acknowledgement that women of color are excluded from feminist theory, on the one hand, and on the other the remainder that though excluded from theory, their books are read in the classroom and/or duly footnoted. It is clear that some of the writers in *Bridge* thought at some point in the seventies that feminism could be the ideal answer to their hope for liberation. Chrystos, for example, states her disillusionment as follows: 'I no longer believe that feminism is a tool which can eliminate racism or even promote better understanding between different races and kinds of women.'[51] The disillusionment is eloquently reformulated in the theme poem by Donna Kate Ruchin, 'The Bridge Poem.'[52] The dream of helping the people who surround her to reach an interconnectedness that would change society is given up in favor of self-translation into a 'true self.' In my view, the speaker's refusal to play 'bridge,' an enablement to others as well as self, is the acceptance of defeat at the hands of political groups whose self-definition follows the view of self as unitary, capable of being defined by a single 'theme.' The speaker's perception that the 'self' is multiple ('I'm sick of mediating with your worst self/on behalf on your better selves,'[53]) and its reduction harmful, gives emphasis to the relationality between one's selves and those of others as an ongoing process of struggle, effort and tension. Indeed, in this poem the better 'bridging self' of the speaker is defeated by the overriding notion of the unitary subject of knowledge and consciousness so prevalent in Anglo-American culture. Consciousness as a site of multiple voicings is the theoretical subject, par excellence, of *Bridge*. Concomitantly, these voicings (or thematic threads) are not viewed as necessarily originating with the subject, but as discourses that transverse consciousness and which the subject must struggle with constantly. Rosario Morales, for example, says 'I want to be whole. I want to claim myself to be Puertorican, and U. S. American, working class and middle class, housewife and intellectual, feminist, marxist and anti-imperialist.'[54] Gloria Anzaldúa observes, 'What am I? *A third world lesbian feminist with marxist and mystic learnings*. They would chop me up into little fragments and rag each piece with a label.'[55] The need to assign multiple registers of existence is an effect of the belief that knowledge of one's subjectivity cannot be arrived at through a single discursive 'theme.' Indeed, the multiple-voiced subjectivity is lived in resistance to competing notions for one's allegiance or self-identification. It is a process of disidentification[56] with prevalent formulations of the most forcefully theoretical subject of feminism. The choice of one or many themes is both theoretical and a political decision. Like gender epistemologists and other emancipatory movements, the theoretical subject of *Bridge* gives credit to the subject of consciousness as the site of knowledge but problematizes it by representing it as a weave. In Anzaldúa's terms, the woman of color has a 'plural personality.' Speaking of the new mestiza in *Borderlands/La Frontera*, she says, '[s]he learns to juggle cultures. [. . .] [the] juncture where the mestiza stands is where phenomena tend to collide.'[57] As an object of multiple indocrinations that heretofore have collided upon her, their new recognition as products of the oppositional thinking of others can help her come to terms with the politics of varied discourses and their antagonistic relations.

Thus, current political practices in the United States make it almost impossible to go beyond an oppositional theory of the subject, which is the prevailing feminist strategy and that of others; however, it is not the theory that will help us grasp the subjectivity of women of color. Socially and historically, women of color have been now central, now outside antagonistic relations between races, classes, and gender(s); this struggle of multiple antagonisms, almost always in relation to culturally different groups and not just genders, gives configuration to the theoretical subject of *Bridge*. It must be noted, however, that each woman of color cited here, even in her positing of a 'plurality of self,' is already privileged enough to reach the moment of cognition of a situation for herself. This should suggest that to privilege the subject, even if multiple-voiced, is not enough.

## Notes

* Hereafter cited as *Bridge*, the book has two editions. I used the second edition published by Kitchen Table Press, 1983. The first edition was published by Persephone Press, 1981.

1   Moraga and Anzaldúa, 2–3.
2   Louis Althusser, *Lenin and Philosophy and Other Essays*, Ben Brewster, tr. (London: New Left Books, 1971).
3   Moraga and Anzaldúa, 23.
4   Moraga and Anzaldúa, 195.
5   Teresa de Lauretis, *Technologies of Gender* (Bloomington: Indiana University Press, 1987), 10.
6   Jane Flax, 'Postmodernism and Gender Relations in Feminist Theory,' *Signs* 12:4 (Summer 1987), 640.
7   Gayatri Chakravorty Spivak, 'Three Women's Texts and a Critique of Imperialism,' *Critical Inquiry* 12:1 (Autumn 1985), 243–44.
8   Flax, 640.
9   Julia Kristeva. 'Women's Time,' *Signs* 7:1 (Autumn 1981), 19.
10   Adrienne Rich, *On Lies, Secrets and Silence* (New York: W. W. Norton, 1979), 35.
11   Flax, 627.
12   Michel Pecheux, *Language, Semantics and Ideology* (New York: St. Martin's Press, 1981), 122.
13   Jean Bethke Elshtain, 'Feminist Discourse and Its Discontents: Language, Power, and Meaning,' *Signs* 7:3 (Spring 1981), 611.
14   Elshtain, 617.
15   Diane Macdonell, *Theories of Discourses: An Introduction* (New York: Basil Blackwell, 1986), 76.
16   For an intriguing demonstration of these operations, see Seyla Benhabib, 'The Generalized and the Concrete Other: The Kohlberg–Gilligan Controversy and Feminist Theory' in Seyla Benhabib and Drucilla Cornell, *Feminism as Critique* (Minneapolis: University of Minnesota Press, 1987), 77–95.
17   Sandra Harding, 'The Instability of the Analytical Categories of Feminist Theory,' *Signs* 11:4 (Summer 1986), 659.
18   Harding, 660.
19   Gloria T. Hull, Patricia B. Scott and Barbara Smith, eds., *All The Women Are White, All The Blacks Are Men, But Some of Us Are Brave* (Westbury, N. Y.: Feminist Press, 1982).
20   Moraga and Anzaldúa, Foreword to the Second Edition, n.p.
21   Moraga and Anzaldúa, Introduction to the First Edition, xxiii.

22    Paula Treichler, 'Teaching Feminist Theory,' *Theory in the Classroom*, Cary Nelsen, ed. (Urbana: University of Illinois Press, 1986), 79.
23    Maxine Baca Zinn, Lynn Weber Cannon, Elizabeth Higginbotham and Bonnie Thronton Dill, 'The Cost of Exclusionary Practices in Women's Studies,' *Signs* 11:4 (Summer 1986), 296.
24    Baca Zinn *et al.*, 296–97.
25    Flax, 633.
26    Macdonell, 62.
27    Simone de Beauvoir, *The Second Sex* (New York: Vintage Books, 1974), 301.
28    de Beauvoir, 316.
29    de Beauvoir, 761.
30    For a detailed discussion of this theme, see Judith Butler, 'Variations on Sex and Gender: Beauvoir, Wittig, and Foucault' in Benhabib and Cornell, 128–42.
31    Catharine MacKinnon, 'Feminism, Marxism, Method and the State: An Agenda for Theory,' *Signs* 7:3 (Spring 1982), 536–38.
32    MacKinnon, 536.
33    Nancy F. Cott, 'Feminist Theory and Feminist Movements: The Past Before Us,' In *What Is Feminism: A Re-Examination*, Juliet Mitchell and Ann Oakley, eds. (New York: Pantheon Books, 1986), 49.
34    Alison M. Jaggar, *Feminist Politics and Human Nature* (Totowa, N. J.,: Rowman & Allanheld, 1983), 249–50; 295–96.
35    Jaggar, 381.
36    Jaggar, 386.
37    Moraga and Anzaldúa, 61.
38    Jaggar, 386.
39    Moraga and Anzaldúa, Introduction, xxiii.
40    Moraga and Anzaldúa, Foreword to the Second Edition, n.p.
41    Miranda Davies, *Third World: Second Sex* (London: Zed Books, 1987).
42    Jaggar, 386.
43    Teresa de Lauretis, 'Feminist Studies/Critical Studies: Issues, Terms, and Contexts,' *Feminist Studies/Critical Studies*, Teresa de Lauretis, ed. (Bloomington: Indiana University Press 1986), 9.
44    de Lauretis, *Feminist Studies*, 8.
45    de Lauretis, *Feminist Studies*, 9.
46    Moraga and Anzaldúa, 165–74.
47    de Lauretis, *Feminist Studies*, 14.
48    de Lauretis, *Feminist Studies*, 14.
49    Monique Wittig, cited in Elizabeth Meese. *Crossing the Double-Cross: The Practice of Feminist Criticism* (Chapel Hill: University of North Carolina Press, 1986), 74.
50    Moraga and Anzaldúa, 153.
51    Moraga and Anzaldúa, 69.
52    Moraga and Anzaldúa, xxi–xxii.
53    Moraga and Anzaldúa, xxii.
54    Moraga and Anzaldúa, 91.
55    Moraga and Anzaldúa, 205.
56    Pecheux, 158–59.
47    Gloria Anzaldúa, *Borderlands/La Frontera: The New Mestiza* (San Francisco: Spinsters/Aunt Lute, 1987), 79.

# Chapter 32

# Judith Butler

## IMITATION AND GENDER INSUBORDINATION

### To theorize as a lesbian?

At first I considered writing a different sort of essay, one with a philosophical tone: the 'being' of homosexual. The prospect of *being* anything, even for pay, has always produced in me a certain anxiety, for 'to be' gay, 'to be' lesbian seems to be more than a simple injunction to become who or what I already am. And in no way does it settle the anxiety for me to say that this is 'part' of what I am. To write or speak *as a lesbian* appears a paradoxical appearance of this 'I', one which feels neither true nor false. For it is a production, usually in response to a request, to come out or write in the name of an identity which, once produced, sometimes functions as a politically efficacious phantasm. I'm not at ease with 'lesbian theories, gay theories,' for as I've argued elsewhere, identity categories tend to be instruments of regulatory regimes, whether as the normalizing categories of oppressive structures or as the rallying points for a liberatory contestation of that very oppression. This is not to say that I will not appear at political occasions under the sign of a lesbian, but that I would like to have it permanently unclear what precisely that sign signifies. So it is unclear how it is that I can contribute to this book and appear under its title, for it announces a set of terms that I propose to contest. One risk I take is to be recolonized by the sign under which I write, and so it is this risk that I seek to thematize. To propose that the invocation of identity is always a risk does not imply that a resistance to it is always or only symptomatic of a self-inflicted homophobia. Indeed, a Foucaultian perspective might argue that the affirmation of 'homosexuality' is itself an extension of a homophobic discourse. And yet 'discourse,' he writes on the same page, 'can be both an instrument and an effect of power, but also a hindrance, a stumbling-block, a point of resistance and a starting point for an opposing strategy.'

So I am skeptical about how the 'I' is determined as it operates under the title of the lesbian sign, and I am no more comfortable with its homophobic determination than with those normative definitions offered by other members of the 'gay or lesbian community.' I'm permanently troubled by identity categories, consider them to be invariable stumbling blocks, and understand them, even promote them, as sites of necessary trouble. In fact, if the category were to offer no trouble, it would cease to be interesting to me: it is precisely the *pleasure* produced by the instability of those categories to begin with. To install myself within the terms of an identity category would be to turn against the sexuality that the category purports to describe; and this might be true for any identity category which seeks to control the very eroticism that it claims to describe and authorize, much less 'liberate.'

And what's worse, I do not understand the notion of 'theory,' and am hardly interested in being cast as its defender, much less in being signified as part of an elite gay/lesbian theory crowd that seeks to establish the legitimacy and domestication of gay/lesbian studies within the academy. Is there a pregiven distinction between theory, politics, culture, media? How do those divisions operate to quell a certain intertextual writing that might well generate wholly different epistemic maps? But I am writing here now: is it too late? Can this writing, can any writing, refuse the terms by which it is appropriated even as, to some extent, that very colonizing discourse enables or produces this stumbling block, this resistance? How do I relate the paradoxical situation of this dependency and refusal?

If the potential task is to show that theory is never merely *theoria*, in the sense of disengaged contemplation, and to insist that it is fully political (*phronesis or even praxis*), then why not simply call this operation *politics*, or some necessary permutation of it?

I have begun with confession of trepidation and a series of disclaimers, but perhaps it will become clear that *disclaiming*, which is no simple activity, will be what I have to offer as a form of affirmative resistance to a certain regulatory operation of homophobia. The discourse of 'coming out' has clearly served its purposes, but what are its risks? And here I am not speaking of unemployment or public attack or violence, which are quite clearly and widely on the increase against those who are perceived as 'out' whether or not of their own design. Is the 'subject' who is 'out' free of its subjection and finally in the clear? Or could it be that the subjection that subjectivates the gay or lesbian subject in some ways continues to oppress, or oppresses most insidiously, once 'outness' is claimed? What or who is it that is 'out,' made manifest and fully disclosed, when and if I reveal myself as lesbian? What is it that is now known, anything? What remains permanently concealed by the very linguistic act that offers up the promise of a transparent revelation of sexuality? Can sexuality even remain sexuality once it submits to a criterion of transparency and disclosure, or does it perhaps cease to be sexuality precisely when the semblance of full explicitness is achieved? Is sexuality of any kind even possible without that opacity designated by the unconscious, which means simply that the conscious 'I' who would reveal its sexuality is perhaps the last to know the meaning of what it says?

To claim that this is what I *am* is to suggest a provisional totalization of this 'I'. But if the I can so determine itself, then that which it excludes in order to make the determination remains constitutive of the determination itself. In other words, such a statement presupposes that the 'I' exceeds its determination, and even produces that very excess in and by the act which seeks to exhaust the semantic field of that 'I'. In the act which would disclose the true and full content of that 'I', a certain radical *concealment* is thereby produced. For it is always finally unclear what is meant by involving the lesbian-signifier, since its significantion is always to some degree out of one's control, but also because its *specificity* can only be demarcated by exclusions that return to disrupt its claim to coherence. What, if anything, can lesbians be said to share? And who will decide this question, and in the name of whom? If I claim to be a lesbian, I 'come out' only to produce a new and different 'closet.' The 'you' to whom I come out now has access to a different region of opacity. Indeed, the locus of opacity has simply shifted: before, you did not know whether I 'am,' but now you do not know what that means, which is to say that the copula is empty, that it cannot be substituted for with a set of descriptions.[7] And perhaps that is a situation to be valued. Conventionally, one comes out of the closet (and yet, how often is it the case that we are 'outted' when we are young and without resources?); so we are out of the closet, but into what? what new unbounded spatiality? the room, the den, the attic, the basement, the house, the bar, the university, some new enclosure whose door, like Kafka's door, produces the expectation of a fresh air and a light of illumination that never arrives? Curiously, it is the figure of the closet that produces this expectation, and which guarantees its dissatisfaction. For being 'out' always depends to some extent on being 'in'; it gains its meaning only within that polarity. Hence, being 'out' must produce the closet again and again in order to maintain itself as 'out'. In this sense, *outness* can only produce a new opacity; and *the closet* produces the promise of a disclosure that can, by definition, never come. Is this infinite postponement of the disclosure of 'gayness,' produced by the very act of 'coming out,' to be lamented? Or is this very deferral of the signified *to be valued*, a site for the production of values, precisely because the term now takes on a life that cannot be, can never be, permanently controlled?

It is possible to argue that whereas no transparent or full revelation is afforded by 'lesbian' and 'gay,' there remains a political imperative to use these necessary errors or category mistakes, as it were (what Gayatri Spivak might call 'catachrestic' operations: to use a proper name improperly), to rally and represent an oppressed political constituency. Clearly, I am not legislating against the use of the term. My question is simply: which use will be legislated, and what play will there be between legislation and use such that the instrumental uses of 'identity' do not become regulatory imperatives? If it is already true that 'lesbians' and 'gay men' have been traditionally designated as impossible identities, errors of classification, unnatural disasters within juridico-medical discourses, or, what perhaps amounts to the same, the very paradigm of what calls to be classified, regulated, and controlled, then perhaps these sites of disruption, error, confusion, and trouble can be the very rallying points for a certain resistance to classification and to identify as such.

The question is not one of *avowing* or *disavowing* the category of lesbian or gay, but, rather, why it is that the category becomes the site of this 'ethical' choice? What does it mean to *avow* a category that can only maintain its specificity and coherence by performing a prior set of *disavowals*? Does this make 'coming out' into the avoal of disavowal, that is, a return to the closet under the guise of an escape? And it is not something like heterosexuality or bisexuality that is disavowed by the category, but a set of identificatory and practical crossings between these categories that renders the discreteness of each equally suspect. It is not possible to maintain and pursue heterosexual identifications and aims within homosexual practice, and homosexual identifications and aims within heterosexual practices? If a sexuality is to be disclosed, what will be taken as the true determinant of its meaning: the phantasy structure, the act, the orifice, the gender, the anatomy? And if the practice engages a complex interplay of all of those, which one of those, which one of this erotic dimensions will come to stand for the sexuality that requires them all? Is it the *specificity* of a lesbian experience or lesbian desire or lesbian sexuality that lesbian theory needs to elucidate? Those efforts have only and always produced a set of contests and refusals which should by now make it clear that there is no necessarily common element among lesbians, except perhaps that we all know something about how homophobia works against women – although, even then, the language and the analysis we use will differ.

To argue that there might be a *specificity* to lesbian sexuality has seemed a necessary counterpoint to the claim that lesbian sexuality is just heterosexuality once removed, or that it is derived, or that it does not exist. But perhaps the claim of specificity, on the one hand, and the claim of derivativeness or non-existence, on the other, are not as contradictory as they seem. Is it not possible that lesbian sexuality is a process that reinscribes the power domains that it resists, that it is constituted in part from the very heterosexual matrix that it seeks to displace, and that its specificity is to be established, not *outside* or *beyond* that reinscription or reiteration, but in the very modality and effects of that reinscription. In other words, the negative constructions of lesbianism as a fake or a bad copy can be occupied and reworked to call into question the claims of heterosexual priority. In a sense I hope to make clear in what follows, lesbian sexuality can be understood to redeploy its 'derivativeness' in the service of displacing hegemonic heterosexual norms. Understood in this way, the political problem is not to establish the specificity of lesbian sexuality over and against its derivativeness, but to turn the homophobic construction of the bad copy against the framework that privileges heterosexuality as origin, and so 'derive' the former from the latter. This description requires a reconsideration of imitation, drag, and other forms of sexual crossing that affirm the internal complexity of a lesbian sexuality constituted in part within the very matrix of power that it is compelled both to reiterate and to oppose.

## On the being of gayness as necessary drag

The professionalization of gayness requires a certain performance and production of a 'self' which is the *constituted effect* of a discourse that nevertheless claims to 'represent' that self as a prior truth. When I spoke at the conference on homosexuality in 1989, I found myself telling my friends beforehand that I was off to Yale to be a lesbian, which of course didn't mean that I wasn't one before, but that somehow then, as I spoke in that context, I *was* one in some more thorough and totalizing way, at least for the time being. So I *am* one, and my qualifications are even fairly unambiguous. Since I was sixteen, being a lesbian is what I've been. So what's the anxiety, the discomfort? Well, it has something to do with that redoubling, the way I can say, I'm going to Yale to be a lesbian: a lesbian is what I've been for so long. How is it that I can both 'be' one, and yet endeavor to be one at the same time? When and where does my being a lesbian come into play, when and where does this playing a lesbian constitute something like what I am? To say that I 'play' at being one is not to say that I am not one 'really'; rather, how and where I play at being one is the way in which that 'being' gets established, instituted, circulated, and confirmed. This is not a performance from which I can take radical distance, for this is deep-seated play, psychically entrenched play, *and this 'I' does not play its lesbianism as a role.* Rather, it is through the repeated play of this sexuality that the 'I' is insistently reconstituted as a lesbian 'I'; paradoxically, it is precisely the *repetition* of that play that established as well the *instability* of the very category that it constitutes. For if the 'I' is a site of repetition, that is, if the 'I' only achieves the semblance of identity through a certain repetition of itself, then the I is always displaced by the very repetition that sustains it. In other words, does or can the 'I' ever repeat itself, cites itself, faithfully, or is there always a displacement from its former moment that establishes the permanently non-self-identical status of that 'I' or its 'being lesbian'? What 'performs' does not exhaust the 'I'; it does not lay out in visible terms the comprehensive content of that 'I', for if the performance is 'repeated,' there is always the question of what differentiates from each other the moments of identity that are repeated. And if the 'I' is the effect of a certain repetition, one which produces the semblance of a continuity or coherence, then there is no 'I' that precedes the gender that it is said to perform; the repetition, and the failure to repeat, produce a string of performances that constitute and contest the coherence of that 'I'.

But, *politically*, we might argue, isn't it quite crucial to insist on lesbian and gay identities precisely because they are being threatened with erasure and obliteration from homophobic quarters? Isn't the above theory *complicitous* with those political forces that would obliterate the possibility of gay and lesbian identity? Isn't it 'no accident' that such theoretical contestations of identity emerge within a political climate that is performing a set of similar obliterations of homosexual identities through legal and political means?

The question I want to raise in return is this: ought such threats of obliteration dictate the terms of the political resistance to them, and if they do, do such homophobic efforts to that extent win the battle from the start? There is no question that gays and lesbians are threatened by the violence of public erasure, but the decision to counter that violence must be careful not to reinstall another in its place. Which version of lesbian or gay ought to be rendered visible, and which internal exclusions will that rendering visible institute? Can the visibility of identity *suffice* as a political strategy, or can it only be the starting point for a strategic intervention which calls for a transformation of policy? Is it not a sign of despair over public politics when identity becomes its own policy, bringing with it those who would 'police' it from various sides? And this is not a call to return to silence or invisibility, but, rather, to make use of a category that can be called into question, made to account for what it excludes. That any consolidation of identity requires some set of differentiations and exclusions seems clear. But which ones ought to be valorized? That the identity-sign I use now has its purposes seems right, but there is no way to predict or control the political uses to which that sign will be put in the future. And perhaps this is a kind of openness, regardless of its risks, that ought to be safeguarded for political reasons. If the rendering visible of lesbian/gay identity now presupposes a set of exclusions, then perhaps part of what is necessarily excluded is the *future uses of the sign*. There is a political necessity to use some sign now, and we do, but how to use it in such a way that its futural significations are not *foreclosed*. How to use the sign and avow its temporal contingency at once?

In avowing the sign's provisionality (rather than its strategic essentialism), that identity can become a site of contest and revision, indeed, take on a future set of significations that those of us who use it now may not be able to foresee. It is in the safeguarding of the future of the political signifiers-preserving the signifier as a site of rearticulation that Laclau and Mouffe discern its democratic promise.

Within contemporary U.S. politics, there are a vast number of ways in which lesbianism in particular is understood as precisely that which cannot or dare not *be*. In a sense, Jesse Helms's attack on the NEA for sanctioning representations of 'homoeroticism' focuses various homophobic fantasies of what gay men are and do on the work of Robert Mapplethorpe. In a sense, for Helms, gay men exist as objects of prohibition; they are, in his twisted fantasy, sadomasochistic exploiters of children, the paradigmatic exemplars of 'obscenity'; in a sense, the lesbian is not even produced within this discourse as a prohibited object. Here it becomes important to recognize that oppression works not merely through acts of overt prohibition, but covertly, through the constitution of viable subjects and through the corollary constitution of a domain of unviable (un)subjects – *abjects*, we might call them – who are neither names nor prohibited within the economy of the law. Here oppression works through the production of a domain of unthinkability and unnameability. Lesbianism is not explicitly prohibited in part because it has not even made its way into the thinkable, the imaginable, that grid of cultural intelligibility that regulates the real and the nameable. How, then, to 'be' a lesbian in a political context in which the lesbian does not exist, that is, in a political discourse that wages its violence against lesbianism in part be excluding lesbianism from discourse itself? To be prohibited explicitly is to occupy a discursive site from which something like a reverse-discourse can be articulated; to be implicitly proscribed is not even to qualify as an object of prohibition. And though homosexualities of all kinds in this present climate are being erased, reduced, and (then) reconstituted as sites of radical homophobic fantasy, it is important to retrace the different routes by which the unthinkability of homosexuality is being constituted time and again.

It is one thing to be erased from discourse, and yet another to be present within discourse as an abiding falsehood. Hence, there is a political imperative to render lesbianism visible, but how is that to be done outside or through existing regulatory regimes? Can the exclusion from ontology itself become a rallying point for resistance?

Here is something like a confession which is meant merely to thematize the impossibility of confession: As a young person, I suffered for a long time, and I suspect many people have, from being told, explicitly or implicitly, that what I 'am' is a copy, an imitation, a derivative example, a shadow of the real. Compulsory heterosexuality sets itself up as the original, the true, the authentic; the norm that determines the real implies that 'being' lesbian is always a kind of miming, a vain effort to participate in the phantasmatic plenitude of naturalized heterosexuality which will always and only fail. And yet, I remember quite distinctly when I first read in Esther Newton's *Mother Camp: Female Impersonators in America* that drag is not an imitation or a copy of some prior and true gender; according to Newton, drag enacts the very structure of impersonation by which *any gender* is assumed. Drag is not the putting on of a gender that belongs properly to some other group, i.e. an ace of *ex*propriation or *ap*propriation that assumes that gender is the rightful property of sex, that 'masculine' belongs to 'male' and 'feminine' belongs to 'female.' There is no 'proper' gender, a gender proper to one sex rather than another, which is in some sense that sex's cultural property. Where that notion of the 'proper' operates, it is always and only *improperly* installed as the effect of a compulsory system. Drag constituted the mundane way in which genders are appropriated, theatricalized, worn, and done; it implies that all gendering is a kind of impersonation and approximation. If this is true, it seems, there is no original or primary gender that drag imitates, but *gender is a kind of imitation for which there is no original*; in fact, it is a kind of imitation that produces the very notion of the original as an *effect* and consequence of the imitation itself. In other words the naturalistic effects of heterosexualized genders are produced through imitative strategies; what they imitate is a phantasmatic ideal of heterosexual identity, one that is produced by the imitation as its effect. In this sense, the 'reality' of heterosexual identities is performatively constituted through an imitation that sets itself up as the origin and the ground of all imitations. In other words, heterosexuality is always in the process of imitating and approximating its own phantasmatic idealization of itself – *and failing*. Precisely because it is bound to fail, and yet endeavors to succeed, the project of heterosexual identity is propelled into an endless repetition of itself. Indeed, in its efforts to naturalize itself as the original, heterosexuality must be understood as a compulsive and compulsory repetition that can only produce the *effect* of its own originality; in other words, compulsory heterosexual identities, those ontologically consolidated phantasms of 'man' and 'woman,' are theatrically produced effects that posture as grounds, origins, the normative measure of the real.

Reconsider then the homophobic charge that queens and butches and femmes are imitations of the heterosexual real. Here 'imitation' carries the meaning of 'derivative' or 'secondary,' a copy of an origin which is itself the ground of all copies, but which is itself a copy of nothing. Logically, this notion of an 'origin' is suspect, for how can something operate as an origin if there are no secondary consequences which retrospectively confirm the originality of that origin? The origin requires its derivations in order to affirm itself as an origin, for origins only make sense to the extent that they are differentiated from that which they produce as derivatives. Hence, if it were not for the notion of the homosexual *as* copy, there would be no construct of heterosexuality *as* origin. Heterosexuality here presupposes homosexuality. And if the homosexual *as* copy *precedes* the heterosexual as *origin*, then it seems only fair to concede that the copy comes before the origin, and that homo-sexuality is thus the origin, and heterosexuality the copy.

But simple inversions are not really possible. For it is only *as* copy that homo-sexuality can be argued to *precede* heterosexuality as the origin. In other words, the entire framework of copy and origin proves radically unstable as each position inverts into the other and confounds the possibility of any stable way to locate the temporal or logical priority of either term.

But let us then consider this problematic inversion from a psychic/political perspective. If the structure of gender imitation is such that the imitat*ed* is to some degree produced – or, rather, *re*produced – by imitation (see again Derrida's inver-sion and displacement of mimesis in 'The Double Session'), then to claim that gay and lesbian identities are implicated in heterosexual norms or in hegemonic culture generally is not to *derive* gayness from straightness. On the contrary, *imitation* does not copy that which is prior, but produces and *inverts* the very terms of priority and derivativeness. Hence, if gay identities are implicated in heterosexuality, that is not the same as claiming that they are determined or derived from hetero-sexuality, and it is not the same as claiming that that heterosexuality is the only cultural network in which they are implicated. These are, quite literally, *inverted* imitations, ones which invert the order of imitated and imitation, and which, in the process, expose the fundamental dependency of 'the origin' on that which it claims to produce as its secondary effect.

What follows if we concede from the start that gay identities as derivative inversions are in part defined in terms of the very heterosexual identities from which they are differentiated? If heterosexuality is an impossible imitation of itself, an imitation that performatively constitutes itself as the original, then the imita-tive parody of 'heterosexuality' – when and where it exists in gay cultures – is always and only an imitation of an imitation, a copy of a copy, for which there is no original. Put in yet a different way, the parodic or imitative effect of gay iden-tities works neither to copy nor to emulate heterosexuality, but rather, to expose heterosexuality as an incessant and *panicked* imitation of its own naturalized ideal-ization. That heterosexuality is always in the act of elaborating itself is evidence that it is perpetually at risk, that is, that it 'knows' its own possibility of becoming undone: hence, its compulsion to repeat which is at once a foreclosure of that which threatens its coherence. That it can never eradicate that risk attests to its profound dependency upon the homosexuality that it seeks fully to eradicate and never can or that it seeks to make second, but which is always already there as a prior possibility.[15] Although this failure of naturalized heterosexuality might consti-tute a source of pathos for heterosexuality itself – what its theorists often refer to as its constitutive malaise – it can become an occasion for a subversive and prolif-erating parody of gender norms in which the very claim to originality and to the real is shown to be the effect of a certain kind of naturalized gender mime.

It is important to recognize the ways in which heterosexual norms reappear within gay identities, to affirm that gay and lesbian identities are not only structured in part by dominant heterosexual frames, but that they are *not* for that reason *determined* by them. They are running commentaries on those naturalized positions as well, parodic replays and resignifications of precisely those heterosexual structures that would consign gay life to discursive domains of unreality and unthinkability.

But to be constituted or structured in part by the very heterosexual norms by which gay people are oppressed is not, I repeat, to be claimed or determined by those structures. And it is not necessary to think of such heterosexual constructs as the pernicious intrusion of 'the straight mind,' one that must be rooted out in its entirety. In a way, the presence of heterosexual constructs and positionalities in whatever form in gay and lesbian identities presupposes that there is a gay and lesbian repetition of straightness, a recapitulation of its own ideality – within its own terms, a site in which all sorts of resignifying and parodic repetitions become possible. The parodic replication and resignification of heterosexual constructs within the non-heterosexual frames brings into relief the utterly constructed status of the so-called original, but it shows that heterosexuality only constitutes itself as the original through a convincing act of repetition. The more that 'act' is expropriated, the more the heterosexual claim to originality is exposed as illusory.

Although I have concentrated in the above on the reality-effects of gender practices, performances, repetitions, and mimes, I do not mean to suggest that drag is a 'role' that can be taken on or taken off at will. There is no volitional subject behind the mime who decides, as it were, which gender it will be today. On the contrary, the very possibility of becoming a viable subject requires that a certain gender mime be already underway. The 'being' of the subject is no more self-identical than the 'being' of any gender; in fact, coherent gender, achieved through an apparent repetition of the same, produces as its *effect* the illusion of a prior and volitional subject. In this sense, gender is not a performance that a prior subject elects to do, but gender is *performative* in the sense that it constitutes as an effect the very subject it appears to express. It is a *compulsory* performance in the sense that acting out of line with heterosexual norms brings with it ostracism, punishment, and violence, not to mention the transgressive pleasures produced by those very prohibitions.

To claim that there is no performer prior to the performed, that the performance is performative, that the performance constitutes the appearance of a 'subject' as its effect is difficult to accept. This difficulty is the result of a predisposition to think of sexuality and gender as 'expressing' in some indirect or direct way a psychic reality that precedes it. The denial of the *priority* of the subject, however, is not the denial of the subject: in fact, the refusal to conflate the subject with the psyche marks the psychic as that which exceeds the domain of the conscious subject. This psychic excess is precisely what is being systematically denied by the notion of a volitional 'subject' who elects at will which gender and/or sexuality to be at any given time and place, it is this excess which erupts within the intervals of those repeated gestures and acts that construct the apparent uniformity of heterosexual economy, implicitly includes homosexuality, that perpetual threat of a disruption which is quelled through a reinforced repetition of the same. And yet, if repetition is the way in which power works to construct the illusion of a seamless heterosexual identity, if heterosexuality is compelled to *repeat itself* in order to establish the illusion of its own uniformity and identity, then this is an identity permanently at risk, for what if it fails to repeat, or if the very exercise of repetition is redeployed for a very different performative purpose? If there is, as it were, always a compulsion to repeat, repetition never fully accomplishes identity. That there is a need for a repetition at all is a sign that identity is not self-identical. It requires to be instituted again and again, which is to say that it runs the risk of becoming *de*-instituted at every interval.

So what is this psychic excess, and what will constitute a subversive or *de*-instituting repetition? First, it is necessary to consider that sexuality always exceeds any given performance, presentation, or narrative which is why it is not possible to derive or read off a sexuality from any given gender presentation. And sexuality may be said to exceed any definitive narrativization. Sexuality is never fully 'expressed' in a performance or practice; there will be passive and butchy femmes, femmy and aggressive butches, and both of those, and more, will turn out to describe more or less anatomically stable 'males' and 'females.' There are no direct expressive or causal lines between sex, gender, gender presentation, sexual practice, fantasy and sexuality. None of those terms captures or determines the rest. Part of what constitutes sexuality is precisely that which does not appear and that which, to some degree, can never appear. This is perhaps the most fundamental reason why sexuality is to some degree always closeted, especially to the one who would express it through acts of self-disclosure. That which is excluded for a given gender presentation to 'succeed' may be precisely what is played out sexually, that is, an 'inverted' relation, as it were, between gender and gender presentation, and gender presentation and sexuality. On the other hand, both gender presentation and sexual practices may corollate such that it appears that the former 'expressed' the latter, and yet both are jointly constituted by the very sexual possibilities that they exclude.

This logic of inversion gets played out interestingly in versions of lesbian butch and femme gender stylization. For a butch can present herself as capable, forceful, and all-providing, and a stone butch may well seek to constitute her lover as the exclusive site of erotic attention and pleasure. And yet, this 'providing' butch who seems *at first* to replicate a certain husband-like role, can find herself caught in a logic of inversion whereby that 'providingness' turns to a self-sacrifice, which implicates here in the most ancient trap of feminine self-abnegation. She may well find herself in a situation of radical need, which is precisely what she sought to locate, find, and fulfill in her femme lover. In effect, the butch inverts into the femme or remains caught up in the specter of that inversion, or takes pleasure in it. On the other hand, the femme who, as Amber Hollibaugh has argued, 'orchestrates' sexual exchange, may well eroticize a certain dependency only to learn that the very power to orchestrate that dependency exposes her own incontrovertible power, at which point she inverts into a butch or becomes caught up in the specter of that inversion, or perhaps delights in it.

## Psychic memesis

What stylizes or forms an erotic style and/or a gender presentation – and that which makes such categories inherently unstable – is a set of *psychic identifications* that are not simple to describe. Some psychoanalytic theories tend to construe identification and desire as two mutually exclusive relations to love objects that have been lost through prohibition and/or separation. Any intense emotional attachment thus divides into either wanting to have someone or wanting to be that someone, but never both at once. It is important to consider that identification and desire can coexist, and that their formulation in terms of mutually exclusive oppositions serves a heterosexual matrix, but I would like to focus attention on yet a different construal of that scenario, namely that 'wanting to be' and 'wanting to have' can operate to differentiate mutually exclusive positionalities internal to lesbian erotic exchange. Consider that identifications are always made in response to loss of some kind, and that they involve a certain *mimetic practice* that seeks to incorporate the lost love within the very 'identity' of the one who remains. This was Freud's thesis in 'Mourning and Melancholia' in 1917 and continues to inform contemporary psychoanalytic discussions of identification.

For psychoanalytic theorists Mikkel Borch-Jacobsen and Ruth Leys, however, identification and, in particular, identificatory mimetism, *precedes* 'identity' and constitutes identity as that which is fundamentally 'other to itself.' The notion of this Other *in* the self, as it were, implies that the self/Other distinction is *not* primarily external (a powerful critique of ego psychology follows from this); the self is from the start radically implicated in the 'Other.' This theory of primary mimetism differs from Freud's account of melancholic incorporation. In Freud's view, which I continue to find useful, incorporation – a kind of psychic miming – is a response to, and refusal of, *loss*. Gender as the site of such psychic mimes is thus constituted by the variously gendered Others who have been loved and lost, where the loss is suspended through a melancholic and imaginary incorporation (and preservation) of those Others into the psyche. Over and against this account of psychic memesis by way of incorporation and melancholy, the theory of primary mimetism argues an even stronger position in favor of the non-self-identity of the psychic subject. Mimetism is not motivated by a drama of loss and wishful recovery, but appears to precede and constitute desire (and motivation) itself; in this sense, mimetism would be prior to the possibility of loss and the disappointments of love.

Whether loss or mimetism is primary (perhaps an undecidable problem), the psychic subject is nevertheless constituted internally by differentially gendered Others and is, therefore, never, as a gender, self-identical.

In my view, the self only becomes a self on the condition that it has suffered a separation (grammar fails us here, for the 'it' only becomes differentiated through that separation), a loss which is suspended and provisionally resolved through a melancholic incorporation of some 'Other.' That 'Other' installed in the self thus establishes the permanent incapacity of that 'self' to achieve self-identity; it is as it were always already disrupted by that Other: the disruption of the Other at the heart of the self is the very condition of that self's possibility.

Such a consideration of psychic identification would vitiate the possibility of any stable set of typologies that explain or describe something like gay or lesbian identities. And any effort to supply one – as evidenced in Kaja Silverman's recent inquiries into male homosexuality – suffer from simplification, and conform, with alarming ease, to the regulatory requirements of diagnostic epistemic regimes. If incorporation in Freud's sense in 1914 is an effort to *preserve* a lost and loved object and to refuse or postpone the recognition of loss and, hence, of grief, then to become *like* one's mother or father or sibling or other early 'lovers' may be an act of love and/or a hateful effort to replace or displace. How would we 'typolgize' the ambivalence at the heart of mimetic incorporations such as these?

How does this consideration of psychic identification return us to the question, what constitutes a subversive repetition? How are troublesome identifications apparent in cultural practices? Well, consider the way in which heterosexuality naturalizes itself through setting up certain illusions of continuity between sex, gender, and desire. When Aretha Franklin sings, 'you make me feel like a natural woman,' she seems at first to suggest that some natural potential of her biological sex is actualized by her participation in the cultural position of 'woman' as object of heterosexual recognition. Something in her 'sex' is thus expressed by her 'gender' which is then fully known and consecrated within the heterosexual scene. There is no breakage, no discontinuity between 'sex' as biological facticity and essence, or between gender and sexuality. Although Aretha appears to be all too glad to have her naturalness confirmed, she also seems fully and paradoxically mindful that that confirmation is never guaranteed, that the effect of naturalness is only achieved as a consequence of that moment of heterosexual recognition. After all, Aretha sings, you make me feel *like* a natural woman, suggesting that this is a kind of metaphorical substitution, an act of imposture, a kind of sublime and momentary participation in an ontological illusion produced by the mundane operation of heterosexual drag.

But what if Aretha were singing to me? Or what if she were singing to a drag queen whose performance somehow confirmed her own?

How do we take account of these kinds of identifications? It's not that there is some kind of *sex* that exists in hazy biological form that is somehow *expressed* in the gait, the posture, the gesture; and that some sexuality than expresses both that apparent gender or that more or less magical sex. If gender is drag, and if it is an imitation that regularly produces the ideal it attempts to approximate, then gender is a performance that *produces* the illusion of an inner sex or essence or psychic gender core; it *produces* on the skin, through the gesture, the move, the gait (that array of corporeal theatrics understood as gender presentation), the illusion of an inner depth. In effect, one way that gender gets naturalized is through being constructed as an inner psychic or physical *necessity*. And yet, it is always a surface sign, a signification on and with the public body that produces this illusion of an inner depth, necessity or essence that is somehow magically, causally expressed.

To dispute the psyche as *inner depth*, however, is not to refuse the psyche altogether. On the contrary, the psyche calls to be rethought precisely as a compulsive repetition, as that which conditions and disables the repetitive performance of identity. If every performance repeats itself to institute the effect of identity, then every repetition requires an interval between the acts, as it were, in which risk and excess threaten to disrupt the identity being constituted. The unconscious is this excess that enables and contests every performance, and which never fully appears within the performance itself. The psyche is not 'in' the body, but in the very signifying process through which that body comes to appear; it is the lapse in repetition as well as its compulsion, precisely what the performance seeks to deny, and that which compels it from the start.

To locate the psyche within this signifying chain as the instability of all iterability is not the same as claiming that it is inner core that is awaiting its full and liberatory expression. On the contrary, the psyche is the permanent failure of expression, a failure that has its values, for it impels repetition and so reinstates the possibility of disruption. What then does it mean to pursue disruptive repetition within compulsory heterosexuality?

Although compulsory heterosexuality often presumes that there is first a sex that is expressed through a gender and then through a sexuality, it may how be necessary fully to invert and displace that operation of thought. If a regime of sexuality mandates a compulsory performance of sex, then it may be only through that performance that the binary system of gender and the binary system of sex come to have intelligibility at all. It may be that the very categories of sex, of sexual identity, of gender are produced or maintained in the *effects* of this compulsory performance, effects which are disingenuously renamed as causes, origins, disingenuously lined up within a causal or expressive sequence that the heterosexual norm produces to legitimate itself as the origin of all sex. How then to expose the causal lines as retrospectively and performatively produced fabrications, and to engage gender itself as an inevitable fabrication, to fabricate gender in terms which reveal every claim to the origin, the inner, the true, and the real as nothing other than the effects of *drag*, whose subversive possibilities ought to be played and replayed to make the 'sex' of gender into a site of insistent political play? Perhaps this will be a matter of working sexuality *against* identity, even against gender, and of letting that which cannot fully appear in any performance persist in its disruptive promise.

# SEXUALITY

- Diana Fuss, Theorizing hetero- and homosexuality

- Steven Seidman, From identity to queer politics: shifts in normative heterosexuality

**Diana Fuss** teaches English and Women's Studies at Princeton University. She is the author of *Essentially Speaking* (1989) and editor of *Inside/Out* (1991).

**Steven Seidman** studied at the New School for Social Research and the University of Virginia. He is currently a Professor of Sociology at the State University of New York at Albany. He has written *Contested Knowledge* (1998) and *Difference Troubles* (1997).

# Chapter 33

# Diana Fuss

## THEORIZING HETERO- AND HOMOSEXUALITY

T HE PHILOSOPHICAL OPPOSITION between 'heterosexual' and 'homosexual,' like so many other conventional binaries, has always been constructed on the foundations of another related opposition: the couple 'inside' and 'outside.' The metaphysics of identity that has governed discussions of sexual behavior and libidinal object choice has, until now, depended on the structural symmetry of these seemingly fundamental distinctions and the inevitability of a symbolic order based on a logic of limits, margins, borders, and boundaries. Many of the current efforts in lesbian and gay theory, which this volume seeks to showcase, have begun the difficult but urgent textual work necessary to call into question the stability and ineradicability of the hetero/homo hierarchy, suggesting that new (and old) sexual possibilities are no longer thinkable in terms of a simple inside/outside dialectic. But how, exactly, do we bring the hetero/homo opposition to the point of collapse? How can we work it to the point of critical exhaustion, and what effects – material, political, social – can such a sustained effort to erode and to reorganize the conceptual grounds of identity be expected to have on our sexual practices and politics?

The figure inside/outside cannot be easily or ever finally dispensed with; it can only be worked on and worked over – itself turned inside out to expose its critical operations and interior machinery. To the extent that the denotation of any term is always dependent on what is exterior to it (heterosexuality, for example, typically defines itself in critical opposition to that which it is not: homosexuality), the inside/outside polarity is an indispensable model for helping us to understand the complicated workings of semiosis. Inside/outside functions as the very figure for signification and the mechanisms of meaning production. It has everything to do with the structures of alienation, splitting, and identification which together produce a self and an other, a subject and an object, an unconscious and a conscious, an interiority and an exteriority. Indeed, one of the fundamental insights of Lacanian psychoanalysis, influenced by a whole tradition of semiotic thought, is the notion that any identity is founded relationally, constituted in reference to an exterior or outside that defines the subject's own interior boundaries and corporeal surfaces.

But the figure inside/outside, which encapsulates the structure of language, repression, and subjectivity, also designates the structure of exclusion, oppression, and repudiation. This latter model may well be more insistent to those subjects routinely relegated to the right of the virgule – to the outside of systems of power, authority, and cultural legitimacy. Interrogating the position of 'outsiderness' is where much recent lesbian and gay theory begins, implicitly if not always directly raising the questions of the complicated processes by which sexual politics formulated. How do outsides and insides come about? What philosophical and critical operations or modes produce the specious distinction between a pure and natural heterosexual inside and an impure and unnatural homosexual outside? Where exactly, in this borderline sexual economy, does the one identity leave off and the other begin? And what gets left out of the inside/outside, heterosexual/homosexual opposition, an opposition which could at least plausibly be said to secure its seemingly inviolable dialectical structure only by assimilating and internalizing other sexualities (bisexuality, transvestism, transsexualism . . .) to its own rigid polar logic?

For heterosexuality to achieve the status of the 'compulsory,' it must present itself as a practice governed by some internal necessity. The language and law that regulates the establishment of heterosexuality as both an identity and an institution, both a practice and a system, is the language and the law of defense and protection: heterosexuality secures its self-identity and shores up its ontological boundaries by protecting itself from what it sees as the continual predatory encroachments of its contaminated other, homosexuality. Of course, any sexual identity, based on the complicated dynamics of object choice, works through a similar defensive procedure. Read through the language of psychoanalysis, sexual desire is produced, variously and in tandem, through acts and experiences of defense, ambivalence, repression, denial, threat, trauma, injury, identification, internalization, and renunciation. Indeed, sexual object choice is not even so 'simple' a matter of psychical identifications and defenses; it is also a result of the complex interaction of social conflicts, historical pressures, and cultural prohibitions.

The difference between the hetero and the homo, however, is that the homo becomes identified with the very mechanism necessary to define and to defend any sexual border. Homosexuality, in a word, becomes the excluded; it stands in for, paradoxically, that which stands without. But the binary structure of sexual orientation, fundamentally a structure of exclusion and exteriorization, nonetheless constructs that exclusion by prominently including the contaminated other in its oppositional logic. The homo in relation to the hetero, much like the feminine in relation to the masculine, operates as an indispensable interior exclusion – an outside which is inside interiority making the articulation of the latter possible, a transgression of the border which is necessary to constitute the border as such.

The homo, then, is always something less and something more than a supplement, and something more in that it signifies an addition to a lack, a lack which, importantly, may not be its own. Recent work on sexual subjectivities has begun to challenge the usual association, prevalent even in some poststructuralist thinking, of the outside (of sexual, racial, and economic others) with absence and lack. This work has begun to recognize that any outside is formulated as a consequence of a lack *internal* to the system it supplements. The greater the lack on the inside, the greater the need for an outside to contain and to defuse it, for with that outside, the lack on the inside would become all too visible.

To protect against the recognition of the lack within the self, the self erects and defends its borders against an other which is made to represent or to become that selfsame lack. But borders are notoriously unstable, and sexual identities rarely secure. Heterosexuality can never fully ignore the close psychical proximity of its terrifying (homo)sexual other, anymore than homosexuality can entirely escape the equally insistent social pressures of (hetero)sexual conformity. Each is haunted by the other, but here again it is the other who comes to stand in metonymically for the very occurrence of haunting and ghostly visitations. A striking feature of many of the essays collected in this volume is a fascination with the specter of abjection, a certain preoccupation with the figure of the homosexual as specter and phantom, as spirit and revenant, as abject and undead. Those inhabiting the inside, these essays collectively seem to suggest, can only comprehend the outside through the incorporation of a negative image. This process of negative interiorization involves turning homosexuality inside out, exposing not the homosexual's abjected insides but the homosexual as the abject, as the contaminated and expurgated insides of the heterosexual subject. Homosexual production emerges under these inhospitable conditions as a kind of ghost-writing, a writing which is at once a recognition and a refusal of the cultural representation of 'the homosexual' as phantom Other.

Paradoxically, the 'ghosting' of homosexuality coincides with its 'birth,' for the historical moment of the first appearance of the homosexual as a 'species' rather than a 'temporary aberration' also marks the moment of the homosexual's disappearance – into the closet. That the first coming out was also simultaneously a closeting; that the homosexual's debut onto the stage of historical identities was as much an egress as an entry; and that the priority of 'firstness' of homosexuality, which preceded heterosexuality in Western usage by a startling eleven years,[6] nonetheless could not preempt its relegation to secondary status: all these factors highlight, in their very contradictoriness, the ambiguous operations of ins and outs. 'Out' cannot help but to carry a double valence for gay and lesbian subjects. On the one hand, it conjures up the exteriority of the negative – the devalued or outlawed term in the hetero/homo binary. On the other hand, it suggests the process of coming out – a movement into a metaphysics of presence, speech, and cultural visibility. The preposition 'out' always supports this double sense of invisibility (to put out) and visibility (to bring out), often exceeding even this simple tension in the confused entanglement generated by a host of other active associations.

To be out, in common gay parlance, is precisely to be no longer out; to be out is to be finally outside of exteriority and all the exclusions and deprivations such outsiderhood imposes. Or, put another way, to be out is really to be in – inside the realm of the visible, the speakable, the culturally intelligible. But things are still not so clear, for to come out can also work not to situate one on the inside but to jettison one from it. The recent practice of 'outing,' of exposing well-known public figures as closet homosexuals, is (among other things) an attempt to demonstrate that there have been outsiders on the inside all along. To 'out' an insider, if it has any effect at all, can as easily precipitate that figure's fall from power and privilege as it can facilitate the rise of other gays and lesbians to positions of influence and authority. Because of the infinitely permeable and shifting boundaries between insides and outsides, the political risks or effects of outing are always incalculable.

Recently, in the academy, some would say that it is 'in' to be 'out.' An avant-garde affinity for the liminal space of the marginal energizes many of those disciplines and programs (Women's Studies, African-American Studies, Multicultural Studies) still routinely denied sufficient funding and support from their home institutions adequate to meet the excess in student demand. Supports of 'Gay Studies,' a recently emergent interdisciplinary yet autonomous field of inquiry, must grapple with many of the same issues its predecessors confronted, including the vexed question of institutionalization and the relation of gay and lesbian communities to the academy. The issue is the old standoff between confrontation and assimilation: does one compromise oneself by working on the inside, or does one short-change oneself by holding tenaciously to the outside? Why is institutionalization overwritten as 'bad' and anti-institutionalization coded as 'good'? Does inhabiting the inside always imply cooptation? (Can incorporation be so easily elided with recuperation?) And does inhabiting the outside always and everywhere guarantee radicality?

The problem, of course, with the inside/outside rhetoric, if it remains undeconstructed, is that such polemics disguise the fact that most of us are both inside and outside at the same time. Any misplaced nostalgia for or romanticization of the outside as a privileged site of radicality immediately gives us away, for in order to idealize the outside we must already be, to some degree, comfortably entrenched on the inside. We really only have the leisure to idealize the subversive potential of the power of the marginal when our place of enunciation is quite central. To endorse a position of perpetual or even strategic outsiderhood (a position of powerlessness, speechlessness, homelessness . . .) hardly seems like a viable political program, especially when, for so many gay and lesbian subjects, it is less a question of political tactics than everyday lived experience. Perhaps what we need most urgently in gay and lesbian theory right now is a theory *of* marginality, subversion, dissidence, and othering. What we need is a theory of sexual borders that will help us to come to terms with, and to organize around, the new cultural and sexual arrangements occasioned by the movements and transmutations of pleasure in the social field.

Recent and past work on the question of sexual difference has yet to meet this pressing need, largely because, as Stephen Heath accurately targets the problem, our notion of sexual difference all too often subsumes sexual differences, upholding 'a defining difference of man/woman at the expense of gay, lesbian, bisexual, and indeed *hetero* heterosexual reality.' Homosexuality is produced inside the dominant discourse of sexual difference as its necessary outside, but this is not to say that the homo exerts no pressure on the hetero nor that this outside stands in any simple relation of exteriority to the inside. Every outside is also an alongside; the distance between and proximity is sometimes no distance at all. It may be more accurate to say that the homo, occupying the frontier position of inside out, is neither completely outside the bounds of sexual difference nor wholly inside it either. The fear of the homo, which continually *rubs up against* the hetero (tribs-adic-style), concentrates and codifies the very real possibility and ever-present threat of a collapse of boundaries, an effacing of limits, and a radical confusion of iden-tities.

In its own precarious position at/as the border, homosexuality seems capable of both subtending the dominance of the hetero and structurally subverting it. Much has been made, in discussions of deconstruction's textual and political effi-cacy, of the tendency of hierarchical relations to reestablish themselves. Such retrenchments often happen at the very moment of the supposed transgression, since every transgression, to establish itself as such, must simultaneously resecure that which it sought to eclipse. Homosexuality, read as a transgression against heterosexuality, succeeds not in undermining the authoritative position of hetero-sexuality so much as reconfirming heterosexuality's centrality precisely as that which must be resisted. As inescapable as such a logic might be, it does not diminish the importance of deconstruction in addressing the admittedly stubborn and entrenched hetero/homo hierarchy. That hierarchical oppositions always *tend toward* reestab-lishing themselves does not mean that they can never be invaded, interfered with, and critically impaired. What it does mean is that we must be vigilant in working against such a tendency: what is called for is nothing less than an insistent and intrepid disorganization of the very structures which produce this inescapable logic. Perhaps what we, as gay and lesbian readers of culture, cannot escape at *this* moment in our histories is an 'analysis interminable,' a responsibility to exert sustained pressure from/on the margins to reshape and to reorient the field of sexual difference to include sexual differences.

But how do we know when the homo is contributing to the confirmation of the hetero and when it is disturbing it? How can we tell the difference – if we hold to the by no means certain assumption that there is a difference? Questions of epistemology ('how do we know?') enjoy a privileged status in theorizations of gay and lesbian identity. How does one know when one is on the inside and when one is not? How does one know when and if one is out of the closet? How, indeed, does one know if one is gay? The very insistence of the epistemological frame of reference in theories of homosexuality may suggest that we *cannot* know – surely or definitively. Sexual identity may be less a function of knowledge than perform-ance, or, in Foucauldian terms, less a matter of final discovery than perpetual reinvention. The essays in this collection, while not abandoning the demands of the epistemological, nonetheless mark an important shift away from the interrogative mode and towards the performative mode – toward the imaginative enactment of sexual redefinitions, reborderizations, and rearticulation.

'What we need,' Foucault writes in 'The Gay Science,' is 'a radical break, a change in orientation, objectives, and vocabulary.' While this writer remains suspi-cious of the faith Foucault places in epistemological 'breaks,' since such breaks inevitably seem to reassert what they sought to supersede, the call for new orien-tations, new objectives, and especially new vocabularies is still admittedly a seductive one. It would be difficult, not to say delusionary, to forget the words 'inside' and 'outside,' 'heterosexual' and 'homosexual,' without also losing in this act of willed amnesia the crucial sense of alterity necessary for constituting any sexed subject, any subject as sexed. The dream of either a common language or no language at all is just that – a dream, a fantasy that ultimately can do little to acknowledge and to legitimate the hitherto repressed differences between and within sexual identities. But one can, by using these contested words, use them up, exhaust them, transform them into the historical concepts they are and have always been. Change may well happen by working on the insides of our inherited sexual vocabularies and turning them inside out, giving them a new face.

On the cover of this book [from which this essay is extracted] is not a face (no attempt was made to select 'representative' gay and lesbian bodies, as if such a thing were possible) but a figure, a knot, a figure-eight knot or four knot to be precise. This three-dimensional geometrical domain, constituted by rings and matrices, loops and linkages, is nonetheless embodied, sexualized. The undecidability of this simple topology may be its greatest appeal, for it seems to signify at once an anal, a vaginal, a clitoral, a penile, and a testicular topography. The knot interlaces many orifices, many sites of pleasure, many libidinal economies. It visualizes for us in the very simplicity of its openings and closures, its overs and unders, its ins and outs, the contortions and convolutions of any sexual identity formation.

The figure-eight or four knot is intended as a twist or variation on Lacan's famous Borromean knot which, like several other of his favorite mathematical symbols (the Klein bottle, the Möbius strip), demonstrates how the unconscious itself has neither an inside nor an outside. Like the Borromean knot, the four knot, when pulled inside out, appears as its own mirror image; it is what mathematicians call an 'invertible' knot, and so might be glossed in the context of this book as a figure for (sexual) inversion. This invertible, three-dimensional four knot could even be seen as complementary to the more historically weighted and culturally recognizable symbol of identity in gay and lesbian communities, the pink triangle with its sharp angles, its straight undeviating lines, and its solid two-dimensional interior space. I offer it here, however, simply as a kind of shorthand notation for the nodular problems this book seeks to disentangle and to reweave: the entwining of identification and desire, of sexual difference and sexual differences, of heterosexuality and homosexuality, and, finally, of inside and out.

# Chapter 34

# Steven Seidman

## FROM IDENTITY TO QUEER POLITICS: SHIFTS IN NORMATIVE HETEROSEXUALITY

S INCE AT LEAST the 1950s, a social division between a dominant hetero-sexual majority and a subordinate homosexual minority has been central to American society. This hierarchy has been maintained, until recently, by primarily repressive practices. These practices create the idea of the heterosexual and the homosexual as antithetical human types and enforce the normative status of heterosexuality by polluting the homosexual. I will argue that, in the last decade or so, the norm of heterosexuality has been sustained less by social repression than by normalizing controls. Moreover, I suggest that if we understand gay identity politics as a response to a repressive social logic of normative heterosexuality, a historically unique type of sexual politics, so-called queer politics, can be viewed as a response to gay normalization. The normative grounds and political aims of queer politics, however, have been unclear. In the conclusion, I will propose an ethical-political elaboration of a queer, anti-normalizing politics.

Contemporary American gay culture can be dated from the 1950s. Two events occurred: first, the dominance of a view of homosexuality as a deviant minority identity; second, there occurred, perhaps for the first time historically, a national campaign to enforce normative heterosexuality by enlisting the state and other social institutions to control the homosexual. This societal mobilization deploying strategies of repression and pollution, gave birth to the era of the closet and iden-tity politics.

Central to this logic is the exclusion of the homosexual from public life. Constructing the homosexual as defiled justifies his/her exclusion from public life. Symbolically degrading the homosexual contributes to creating dominated gay selves – that is, individuals for whom shame and guilt are at the core of their sense of self; public invisibility becomes in part self-enforced. The exclusion of the homo-sexual from public life is reinforced by civic disenfranchisement: the denial of civil rights and political representation. Socially segregating the homosexual from the heterosexual is so basic to the repressive logic that everyday antigay violence is tolerated in order to protect the purity of the heterosexual. To the extent that the exclusion of homosexuals from public life fails, policing strategies focus on enforcing their social isolation and sequestration. Quasi-public gay spaces, well policed and removed from heterosexual public life, are permitted on the condition of their social segregation and containment. An example is gay bars that are often toler-ated but only on the territorial and social margins of cities, and only on the condition that this semi-public concentration of homosexuals is unseen by the respectable heterosexual citizen. A repressive logic enforcing heteronormativity operates then by strategies of cultural pollution and censorship, criminalization and civic disenfranchisement, sequestration and violence.

Repressive strategies do not aim to eliminate the homosexual, but to preserve the division between the pure heterosexual and polluted homosexual. Indeed, we might say that the polluted homosexual was invented in the 1950s and 1960s in order to maintain the purity of particular patterns of heterosexuality. It is not, in other words, the homosexual in general that is polluted, but a specific idea of the homosexual; for example, the homosexual as compulsively hedonistic and promiscu-ous. Accordingly, it is not just the homosexual that is defiled, but specific sexual-inti-mate practices such as pleasure-driven sex or multiple-partner sex. Heterosexuals who engage in such practices will experience something of the polluted status of homosexuals. Polluting homosexuality therefore purifies a particular normative het-erosexual order, for example, sex that is person- and love-centered and monogamous. Hence, regimes of heteronormativity not only regulate the homosexual but control heterosexual practices by creating a moral hierarchy of good and bad sexual citizens.

One unintended effect of a repressive social logic has been the development of gay social worlds. In these socially circumscribed private spaces, individuals can be recognized as homosexual. However, through at least the 1970s, these worlds survived on the margins of American society, largely hidden from the heterosexual public. To say it differently, a repressive social logic imposes on individuals the condition that we've come to call the closet – a pressure to project compulsively a public heterosexual identity by confining one's homosexuality to a private world of desire or sequestered gay enclaves. Living in the closet entails such intensive and extensive daily efforts at self-management that homosexuality often becomes the basis for a distinct social identity and way of life. This is the irony of the closet: intended to contain homosexuality the closet makes homosexuality into a primary identity and produces a desire to come out.

Thus, repressive strategies not only produce the closet but a politics aimed at gaining recognition. Gay identity politics has often been oriented to reverse a logic of homosexual repression. Thus, against the social imperative to make a secret of homosexuality, gay politics champions coming out; against the shame induced by pollution, gay pride is affirmed; against a fragmented, double life, gay politics pursues an ideal of an integrated and public gay life. Gay politics has not, however, challenged the construction of homosexuality as a minority identity, it has not contested the separation of sexual from gender, racial or class politics, and it has not politicized social norms that regulate gay selves apart from the norm of hetero-sexuality, for example, norms of sexual monogamy or public sex. In short, gay identity politics has challenged a repressive politics but largely in the terms set by this regime of normative heterosexuality.

Gay identity politics has had considerable success. The achievement of a wide range of civic rights; the decline of polluting representations in many sectors of public culture; the intermingling of straights and gays in public life; and the entry of gays into the political arena indicate a blurring of the boundary between the heterosexual and the homosexual and accordingly a weakening of a repressive heteronormative logic.

I have found evidence for the changing social status of the homosexual in interviews I have conducted. Targeting individuals who identify as gay, but who are not part of a public gay culture, and hence individuals I expected to be closeted, I found that most of them described lives beyond the closet.

Consider Clara, an 18-year-old black lesbian. Clara disclosed to her entire family when she was 14. Today, she says, 'I talk about everything with my mother and my sisters and one brother. They know about my lover [. . .] and just about everything about my lesbian life.' Her comments on disclosing to her father, a Jamaican described as less tolerant, illustrates the extent to which Clara has normalized her homosexuality: 'He had the biggest problem with it but it didn't matter to me because I just told him to be telling him. I wasn't telling him for approval.' The way Clara deals with peers likewise points to normalization. As a freshman living in a college dorm, Clara had to deal quickly with issues of disclosure. She reports being invited to a fraternity party. Clara declined. 'I'm not going, and they were like, "why?" I told them that I'm a lesbian.'

Clara's relatively painless integration of homosexuality into her life is exceptional. It was more common for respondents to narrate a change from a double life to a life beyond the closet.

For example, Bill is a white, 40-year-old, middle-level state worker who grew up in a working-class neighborhood in a small town. Bill was aware of his homosexual feelings as a child. These became more vivid when dating began in adolescence. Comments made by family, friends and his minister describing homosexuals in demeaning ways led Bill to follow the straight pattern of his peers. By early adulthood, he had married, joined the marines, and started drinking to manage what he described as a closeted life. Perhaps triggered by the end of his marriage and his decision to get sober, Bill, by now in his late-30s, decided to integrate his homosexuality into his life. He disclosed initially in the gay world and gradually to his entire family, and indeed to his hometown as Bill was interviewed by a local newspaper on being gay and Christian. Today, his homosexuality is conventionalized to such a degree that his life should not be described by the concept of the closet. For example, when his son was ten Bill tried to explain that he was gay. His son didn't respond. From time to time Bill would reintroduce this topic but his son showed little interest. Bill decided to be relaxed about it: 'I would be completely myself in front of him, and that included conversations with gay friends, or talking about gay people or places [. . .] I was in a relationship and I let him see us hugging and kissing. I was just trying to show him that [. . .] it was natural for us.'

Like Bill, Mike concealed his homosexuality from family and friends until he was 40. Since 1991, Mike has been deliberate in disclosing his homosexuality: 'I'm very free about being gay and don't want anybody to assume that I'm not.' In this regard, Mike has a picture of his partner on his desk at work. Mike does not, however, disclose to all his co-workers, but not for reasons of fear or shame, which would be indicative of the closet. With co-workers his decision to disclose 'depends on the way the conversation runs. If someone asks me if I'm married [. . .] I say that I'm with a man.' With some co-workers, Mike would not disclose because 'I probably would never have the opportunity to share anything personal with them.' Mike approaches his homosexuality as part of a class of 'intimate' or personal information, such as religion or financial matters. Disclosure decisions hinge on the degree of intimacy established or desired. In short, like Clara and Bill, Mike has normalized his gay identity (for a more elaborated statement of this argument, see Seidman *et al*. 1999).

Social resistance to normalizing gay identities remains strong. Many Americans still feel compelled to live closeted lives. Moreover, acceptance by family, friends and co-workers does not necessarily translate into institutional integration. Key social institutions, from families to schools and the military, continue to be organized by a norm of heterosexuality that is enforced by repressive strategies. My claim though is that for many individuals today managing homosexuality may involve episodic practices of concealment but these do not create a primary gay identity or a distinctive gay way of life. This argument suggests the end of the era of the closet, but not the end of normative heterosexuality as an institution.

If heteronormativity is sustained today less by repressive strategies, how is it maintained? To address this question, I studied American films between 1960 and 1997. I found that a shift is occurring from a dominant pollution logic, which pivots around a rigid social and symbolic division between the pure heterosexual and the defiled homosexual, to a normalizing logic. The latter recognizes gay identities but only on the condition that every other key aspect of the gay self exhibits what would be considered 'normal' gender, sexual, familial, work, and national practices. Ultimately, normalization is a strategy to neutralize the critical aspects of a gay movement by rendering sexual difference a superficial aspect of a self who in every other way reproduces an ideal of a national citizen.

Consider the film *Philadelphia*, in many ways a breakthrough movie as it brought the issue of homosexuality and AIDS to the American mainstream. You may recall that the story is about the firing of a lawyer (Andy, played by Tom Hanks) ostensibly because he has AIDS. Andy sues and wins. The film is also about the pathology not of homosexuality but of homophobia. It is the homophobia of the law firm that fires Andy and the bigotry of Joe, the lawyer who defends Andy, played by Denzel Washington, that is presented as a social problem. In other words, *Philadelphia* asserts the normal status of the homosexual. From the first scene, Andy is 'out' and reveals no moral anguish over his gay identity. If there is a coming-out story, it is Joe's struggle to normalize Andy's gay identity.

Through the figure of Joe, the film narrates a story of a shift in the logic of normative heterosexuality from pollution/repression to normalization. Joe initially pollutes homosexuals. Consider the scene where Andy approaches Joe for legal representation. As they are shaking hands, Andy tells Joe that he's seeking representation in an AIDS suit. Joe abruptly withdraws his hand, steps back, watches everything Andy touches on his desk, and declines to take the case for personal reasons, which he subsequently discloses as his hatred of homosexuals. In this scene, we can see normative heterosexuality operating as a repressive logic by establishing a hierarchical division between Joe – the normal, pure and powerful heterosexual – and Andy – the diseased, disgusting and disenfranchised homosexual.

As his relationship to Andy develops, Joe normalizes homosexuality as a minority identity. Anticipating his death, and the end of the trial, Andy has a party. At one point, Andy and Miguel are intimately embraced as they dance; Joe, who is similarly intimate with his wife, glances, then fixes on Andy and Miguel. Andy notices and smiles knowingly – as if he realizes in a way that Joe doesn't quite understand yet that he is beginning to normalize Andy by viewing Andy's love for Miguel as equivalent to his love for his wife. Joe's realization comes later that evening. After the guests leave, Joe and Andy are supposed to review Andy's anticipated testimony. Instead, in a poignant scene, Andy relates to Joe the story of a Maria Callas opera that is playing in the background. It's a sad tale of injustice, love, and tragic death. As Andy is fully absorbed in the operatic narrative, Joe is fixed intently on Andy. Tears begin to well up. No words are exchanged, nor do we learn Joe's thoughts. My reading is that for the first time Joe sees Andy as 'normal' or fully human. As Andy is dying in the hospital, he signals for Joe to sit next to him. This is a dramatic moment because such physical and emotional closeness marks the end of Andy's polluted status. Joe sits on the bed and touches Andy's face as he adjusts his breathing apparatus. This act signals for Joe – and presumably the viewer – the moral equivalence of the heterosexual and the homosexual.

If this film normalizes the homosexual, it still enforces a norm of heterosexuality. For example, homosexuality is confined to individuals whose lives in every way other than their sexual orientation fall within the realm of what America culture considers to be 'the normal'. Thus, Andy is conventionally masculine; he's in a quasi-marital intimate relationship; he is portrayed as hardworking and economically independent; and he is a champion of the rule of law – a core part of the American creed. Indeed, the figure of Andy not only reproduces the norm of heterosexuality by normalizing a binary gender order, but Andy epitomizes dominant American family, economic, and national values. As if to reassure the viewer that normalization does not threaten normative heterosexuality, Andy's parents' heterosexuality is portrayed in ideal terms. They have been happily married for 50 years, are lovingly involved with their children and grandchildren, and are unconditionally accepting of Andy. Likewise, Joe represents an idealized heterosexual figure: he's a masculine man, married, a father, homeowner, and a successful entrepreneur. The film's message is that only the homosexual who is a mirror image of the ideal heterosexual citizen is acceptable. To the extent that legitimation is conditional on the homosexual displaying dominant social conventions, normalization demands recognition only of a minority status, not the contestation of heteronormativity.

Normalization has been bravely fought for by the mainstream of the gay movement. A life beyond the closet, which is what normalization promises, affords a kind of personal integrity that has been unattainable for many individuals. However, legitimation through normalization leaves in place the polluted status of other marginal sexualities; it sustains the dominant norm that regulate our sexual intimate conduct apart from the norm of heterosexuality.

Two political responses to normalization stand out. First, new sexual identity movements have emerged. For example, marginal sexual groups within gay life have emerged advancing their own demands for rights based on claims of victimization. Indeed, their claims to sexual citizenship have been made against both the straight and the gay mainstream. For example, a bisexual and lesbian and gay S/M movement has had to struggle against the gay mainstream, which, in its quest for respectability, has echoed straight America's pollution of bisexuality and S/M. To the extent that bisexual and S/M politics aim at normalization they reproduce the identity political logic of the gay movement by claiming a distinct identity, by countering polluting with normalizing representation, and by inspiring to equal citizenship status.

A second response to normalization has been the rise of a queer politics. Whereas gay identity politics aims to change the status of homosexuality from a deviant to a normal identity, queer politics struggles against normalizing any identity. Queers are not against identity politics but aim to deflate its emancipatory narrative by exposing its exclusionary and disciplinary effects. For example, identity politics imposes a norm of sexual identification (for example, to identity as gay, straight or bisexual) and projects a normative construction of this identity (for example, of gays as white, young, lean-bodied men). Moreover, sexual identity politics is said to leave in place norms that sustain sexual hierarchies unrelated to gender preference, for example, a norm that privatizes sex or a norm of monogamy. Queers are not in principle against normative regulation but against normalizing social controls.

A queer perspective holds that normalizing social controls assigns a moral status of normal and abnormal to virtually every sexual desire and act. This creates a global division between good and bad sexualities and normal and deviant sexual citizens. Moreover, extensive institutional interventions into intimate life are justified for the purposes of preventing or minimizing the undesirable public consequences of sexual pathology. In short, by investing sexuality with heightened moral and social meaning, normalizing discourses justify and bring into being a wide network of controls that regulate sexual behavior. Queer politics is then critical of any political strategy that aims only to redraw moral boundaries to include a deviant practice within 'the normal' – without challenging the regulatory power of the category of the normal.

The queer critique of normalization underscores its aim to defend the social de-regulation of sex. Movements such as Queer Nation, Sex Panic! and Lavender Menace has struggled to remove large stretches of sexual intimate life from institutional control. But what moral and political ideal underpins this sexual politics?

By way of a conclusion, I want to comment on the normative grounds and political vision of a queer politics.

Queer politics assumes what I would call a 'communicative' sexual ethic. In contrast to a normalizing ethic, which holds that sex acts have inherent moral significance or that sexual desires can be classified as either normal or abnormal or good or bad by virtue of their intrinsic qualities, a communicative ethic maintains that sex acts are given moral meaning by their communicative context. In other words, the qualities of a sexual desire or act *per se* cannot be the basis for determining its moral status. Accordingly, the focus of normative evaluation shifts from the sex act to the social exchange. Instead of determining whether a specific sex act is normal, critical judgement would focus on the moral features of a social exchange; for example, does it involve mutual consent? are the agents acting responsibly and respectfully? is there erotic-intimate reciprocity? Thus, in assessing the legitimacy of S/M the relevant consideration would be the communicative practice of the agents, not the particular qualities of S/M such as the use of pain or role-playing.

A communicative sexual ethic suggests that most sexual practices should be viewed as matters of personal or aesthetic not moral choice. It follows that many sexual practices would lose their moral and hence broader social significance. There would be less justification for social intervention beyond regulating behavior that involves coercion or minors. Accordingly, the range of legitimate sexual choice would expand considerably beyond what is permissible in a normalizing sexual culture. Thus, if S/M were viewed as lacking intrinsic moral meaning, there would be no warrant for controlling this practice beyond regulating the social exchange. S/M between consenting adults would become a matter of aesthetic taste, not a focus of morality and not a site of social regulation.

A queer politics advocates, then, shifting large stretches of bodily, sexual, and intimate practice from the sphere of morality to that of aesthetics. This delegitimates extensive state and social institutional control over intimate life. At the root of queer politics is a libertarian standpoint.

In this regard, a queer politics draws heavily on liberal notions of bodily integrity and privacy. Sexual autonomy is said to presuppose individuals who can exercise a wide range of choice over bodily-based pleasures and intimacies. Accordingly, a queer concept of sexual freedom involves a robust defense of a private sphere that is juridically and socially protected from interference by the state and other citizens. However, in contrast to liberal traditions, which often anchor notions of bodily and self-integrity in natural law traditions, queers deconstruct appeals to a transcendent order of nature or reason. It is this natural law grounding, with its essentialist ideas about self and sexuality, that partially explains the historic alignment of liberalism with a normalizing sexual politics. For example, if sexuality is assumed by nature to be heterosexual or procreative, the range of legitimate forms of sexual identity and intimacy is greatly restricted. As sexual practices are reinterpreted as belonging to the realm of social convention, establishing moral boundaries becomes a site of contestation involving arguments that lean more on the justificatory language of context, consent, and consequence than that of nature and normality.

Yet, libertarianism is limited as a politics. A concept of sexual autonomy assumes individual access to social resources (expertise, financial assistance, and information). For example, a condition of sexual autonomy for women would surely include access to family planning services, including abortion. Given the economic inequality among women, sexual autonomy would have to include state aid to lower-income women as a condition of exercising their reproductive rights. Similarly, if a notion of sexual autonomy presupposes that individuals have sexual knowledge to make informed choices, state-enforced sex education in publicly funded schools should be part of a queer sexual politics. Hence, a queer politics would simultaneously advocate removing a wide range of sexual intimate practices

from institutional regulation, and offer democratic justifications for state intervention to create the material and cultural conditions of sexual autonomy.

## References

Seidman, Steven, Meeks, Chet and Francie Traschen (1999) 'Beyond the closet? The
     changing social meaning of homosexuality in the United States' *Sexualities* 2 (Feb.):
     9–34.

# RACE

- Anthony Appiah, African identities

- Michael Omi and Howard Winant, Racial formation

**Anthony Appiah** was born on 8 May 1954 in London, England. He currently teaches at Harvard University. His writings include *The Truth in Semantics* (1986) and *In My Father's House* (1992).

**Howard Winant** is a political sociologist at Temple University, Philadelphia. He received his undergraduate training at Brandeis University and did his graduate work at the University of California, Santa Cruz. **Michael Omi** teaches Ethnic Studies at the University of California, Berkeley. Omi and Winant are co-authors of *Racial Formation in the United States* (1994).

# Chapter 35

# Anthony Appiah

## AFRICAN IDENTITIES

THE CULTURAL LIFE of most of black Africa remained largely unaffected by European ideas until the last years of the nineteenth century, and
most cultures began our own century with ways of life formed very little by direct
contact with Europe. Direct trade with Europeans – and especially the slave trade
– had structured the economies of many of the states of the West African coast
and its hinterland from the middle of the seventeenth century onward, replacing
the extensive gold trade that had existed at least since the Carthaginian empire in
the second century BCE. By the early nineteenth century, as the slave trade went
into decline, palm nut and groundnut oils had become major exports to Europe,
and these were followed later by cocoa and coffee. But the direct colonization of
the region began in earnest only in the later nineteenth century, and European
administration of the whole of West Africa was only accomplished – after much
resistance – when the Sokoto caliphate was conquered in 1903.

On the Indian Ocean, the eastward trade, which sent gold and slaves to Arabia,
and exchanged spices, incense, ivory, coconut oil, timber, grain, and pig iron for
Indian silk and fine textiles, and pottery and porcelain from Persia and China, had
dominated the economies of the East African littoral until the coming of the
Portuguese disrupted the trade in the late fifteenth century. From then on European
trade became increasingly predominant, but in the middle of the nineteenth century
the major economic force in the region was the Arab Omanis, who had captured
Mombassa from the Portuguese more than a century earlier. Using slave labor from
the African mainland, the Omanis developed the profitable clove trade of Zanzibar,
making it, by the 1860s, the world's major producer. But in most of East Africa,
as in the West, extended direct contact with Europeans was a late nineteenth-
century phenomenon, and colonization occurred essentially only after 1885.

In the south of the continent, in the areas where Bantu-speaking people predominate, few cultures had had any contact with Europeans before 1900. By the end

of the century the region had adopted many new crops for the world economy; imports of firearms, manufactured in the newly industrialized West, had created a new political order, based often on force; and European missionaries and explorers – of whom David Livingstone was, for Westerners, the epitome – had traveled almost everywhere in the region. The administration of southern Africa from Europe was established in law only by the end, in 1902, of the Boer War.

Not surprisingly, then, European cultural influence in Africa before the twentieth century was extremely limited. Deliberate attempts at change (through missionary activity or the establishment of Western schools) and unintended influence (through contact with explorers and colonizers in the interior, and trading posts on the coasts) produced small enclaves of Europeanized Africans. But the major cultural impact of Europe is largely a product of the period since World War I.

To understand the variety of Africa's contemporary cultures, therefore, we need, first, to recall the variety of precolonial cultures. Differences in colonial experience have also played their part in shaping the continent's diversities, but even identical colonial policies identically implemented working on the very different cultural materials would surely have produced widely varying results.

No doubt we can find generalizations at a certain abstract level that hold true of most of black Africa before European conquest. It is a familiar idea in African historiography that Africa was the last continent in the Old World with an 'uncaptured' peasantry, largely able to use land without the supervision of feudal overlords and able, if they chose, to market their products through a complex system of trading networks. While European ruling classes were living off the surplus of peasants and the newly developing industrial working class, African rulers were essentially living off taxes on trade. But if we could have traveled through Africa's many cultures in those years – from the small groups of Bushman hunter-gatherers, with their Stone Age materials, to the Hausa kingdoms, rich in worked metal – we should have felt in every place profoundly different impulses, ideas, and forms of life. To speak of African identity in the nineteenth century – if an identity is a coalescence of mutually responsive (if sometimes conflicting) modes of conduct, habits of thought, and patterns of evaluation; in short, a coherent kind of human social psychology – would have been 'to give to aery nothing a local habitation and a name.'

Yet there is no doubt that now, a century later, an African identity is coming into being. I have argued throughout these essays that this identity is a new thing; that it is the product of a history, some whose moments I have sketched; and that the bases through which so far it has largely been theorized – race, a common historical experience, a shared metaphysics – presuppose falsehoods too serious for us to ignore.

Every human identity is constructed, historical; every one has its share of false presuppositions, of the errors and inaccuracies that courtesy calls 'myth,' religion 'heresy,' and science 'magic.' Invented histories, invented biologies, invented cultural affinities come with every identity; each is a kind of role that has to be scripted, structured by conventions of narrative to which the world never quite manages to conform.

Often those who say this – who deny the biological reality of races or the literal truth of our national fictions – are treated by nationalists and 'race men' as if they are proposing genocide or the destruction of nations, as if in saying that there is literally no Negro race, one was obliterating all those who claim to be Negroes, in doubting the story of Okomfo Anokye, one is repudiating the Asante nation. This is an unhelpful hyperbole, but it is certainly true that there must be contexts in which a statement of these truths is politically inopportune. I am enough of a scholar to feel drawn to truth telling, *ruat caelum*; enough of a political animal to recognize that there are places where the truth does more harm than good.

But, so far as I can see, we do not have to choose between these impulses: there is no reason to believe that racism is always – or even usually – advanced by denying the existence of races; and, though there is some reason to suspect that those who resist legal remedies for the history of racism might use the nonexistence of races to argue in the United States, for example, against affirmative action, that strategy is, as a matter of logic, easily opposed. For, as Tvetzan Todorov (1986) reminds us, the existence of racism does not require the existence of races. And, we can add, nations are real enough, however invented their traditions.

To raise the issue of whether these truths are truths to be uttered is to be forced, however, to face squarely the real political question: the question, itself, as old as political philosophy, of when we should endorse the ennobling lie. In the real world of practical politics, of everyday alliance and popular mobilizations, a rejection of races and nations in theory can be part of a program for coherent political practice, only if we can show more than that the black race – or the Shona tribe or any of the other modes of self-invention that Africa has inherited – fit the common pattern of relying on less than the literal truth. We would need to show not that race and national history are falsehoods but they are useless falsehoods at best or – at worst – dangerous ones: that another set of stories will build us identities through which we can make more productive alliances.

The problem, of course, is that group identity seems to work only – or, at least, to work best – when it is seen by its members as natural, as 'real.' Pan-Africanism, black solidarity, can be an important force with real political benefits, but it doesn't work without its attendant mystifications. (Nor, to turn to the other obvious exemplum, is feminism without its occasional risks and mystifications either.) Recognizing the constructedness of the history of identities has seemed to many incompatible with taking these new identities with the seriousness they have for those who invent – or, as they would no doubt rather say, discover – and possess them. In sum, the demands of agency seem always – in the real world of politics – to *entail a misrecognition of its genesis*; you cannot build alliances without mystifications and mythologies. And this chapter is an exploration of ways in which Pan-African solidarity can be appropriated by those of us whose positions as intellectuals – as searchers after truth – make it impossible for us to live through the falsehoods of race and tribe and nation, whose understanding of history makes us skeptical that nationalism and racial solidarity can do the good that they can do without the attendant evils of racism – and other particularisms; without the warring of nations.

Where are we to start? I have argued often in these pages against the forms of racism implicit in much talk of Pan-Africanism.

But these objections to a biologically rooted conception of race may still seem all too theoretical: if Africans can get together around the idea of the 'black person,' if they can create through this notion productive alliances with African-Americans and people of African descent in Europe and the Caribbean, surely these theoretical objections should pale in the light of the practical value of these alliances. But there is every reason to doubt that they can. Within Africa – in the OAU, in the Sudan, in Mauritania – a racialization has produced arbitrary boundaries and exacerbated tensions; in the diaspora alliances with other peoples of color, qua victims of racism – people of south Asian descent in Britain, Hispanics in the United States, 'Arabs' in France, Turks in Germany – have proved essential.

In short, I think it is clear enough that a biologically rooted conception of race is both dangerous in practice and misleading in theory: Africa unity, African identity, need securer foundations than race.

The passage from Achebe with which I began this chapter continues in these words: 'All these tags, unfortunately for the black man, are tags of disability.' But it seems to me that they are not so much labels of disability as disabling labels; which is, in essence, my complaint against Africa as a racial mythology – the Africa of Crummel and DuBois (from the New World) and of the *bolekaja* critics (from the Old); against Africa as a shared metaphysics – the Africa of Soyinka; against Africa as a shared metaphysics – the Africa of Diop and the 'Egyptianists.'

Each of these complaints can be summarized in a paragraph.

'Race' disables us because it proposes as a basis for common action the illusion that black (and white and yellow) people are fundamentally allied by nature and, thus, without effort; it leaves us unprepared, therefore, to handle the 'intraracial' conflicts that arise from the very different situations of black (and white and yellow) people in different parts of the economy and of the world.

The African metaphysics of Soyinka disables because it founds our unity in gods who have not served us well in our dealings with the world – Soyinka never defends the 'African world' against Wiredu's charge that since people die daily in Ghana because they prefer traditional herbal remedies to Western medicines, 'any inclination to glorify the analytical [i.e., the traditional] cast of mind is not just retrograde; it is tragic.' Soyinka has proved the Yoruba pantheon a powerful literary resource, but he cannot explain why Christianity and Islam have so widely displaced the old gods, or why an image of the West has so powerful a hold on the contemporary Yoruba imagination; nor can his mythmaking offer us the resources for creating economies and politics adequate to our various places in the world.

And the Egyptianists – like all who have chosen to root Africa's modern identity in an imaginary history – require us to see the past as the moment of wholeness and unity; tie us to the values and beliefs of the past; and thus divert us (this critique is as old as Césaire's appraisal of Tempels) from the problems of the present and the hopes of the future.

If an African identity is to empower us, so it seems to me, what is required is not so much that we throw out falsehood but that we acknowledge first of all that race and history and metaphysics do not enforce an identity: that we can choose, within broad limits set by ecological, political, and economic realities what it will mean to be African in the coming years.

I do not want to be misunderstood. We are Africans already. And we can give numerous examples from multiple domains of what our being African means. We have, for example, in the OAU and the African Development Bank, and in such regional organizations as SADDC and ECOWAS, as well as in the African caucuses of the agencies of the UN and the World Bank, African institutions. At the Olympics and the Commonwealth Games, athletes from African countries are seen as Africans by the world – and, perhaps, more importantly, by each other. Being African already has 'a certain context and a certain meaning.'

But, as Achebe suggests, that meaning is not always one we can be happy with, and that identity is one we must continue to reshape. And in thinking about how we are to reshape it, we would do well to remember that the African identity is, for its bearers, only one among many. Like all identities, institutionalized before anyone has permanently fixed a single meaning for them – like the German identity at the beginning of this century, or the American in the later eighteenth century, or the Indian identity at independence so few years ago – being African is, for its bearers, one among other salient modes of being, all of which have to be constantly fought for and rethought. And indeed, in Africa, it is another of these identities that provides one of the most useful models for such rethinking; it is a model that draws on other identities central to contemporary life in the subcontinent, namely, the constantly shifting redefinition of 'tribal' identities to meet the economic and political exigencies of the modern world.

Once more, let me quote Achebe:

> The duration of awareness, of consciousness of an identity, has really very little to do with how deep it is. You can suddenly become aware of an identity which you have been suffering from for a long time without knowing. For instance, take the Igbo people. In my area, historically, they did not see themselves as Igbo. They saw themselves as people from this village or that village. In fact in some places 'Igbo' was a word of abuse; they were the 'other' people, down in the bush. And yet, after the experience of the Biafran War, during a period of two years, it became a very powerful consciousness. But it was *real* all the time. They all spoke the same language, called 'Igbo,' even though they were not using that identity in any way. But the moment came when this identity became very, very powerful [. . .] and over a very short period.

A short period it was, and also a tragic one. The Nigerian civil war defined an Igbo identity: it did so in complex ways, which grew out of the development of a common Igbo identity in colonial Nigeria, an identity that created the Igbo traders in the cities of northern Nigeria as an identifiable object of assault in the period that led up to the invention of Biafra.

Recognizing Igbo identity as a new thing is not a way of privileging other Nigerian identities: each of the three central ethnic identities of modern political life – Hausa-Fulani, Yoruba, Igbo – is a product of the rough-and-tumble of the transition through colonial to postcolonial status. David Laitin has pointed out that 'the idea that there was a single Hausa-Fulani tribe [. . .] was largely a political claim of the NPC (Northern Peoples' Congress] in their battle against the South,' while 'many leaders intimately involved in rural Yoruba society today recall that, as late as the 1930s, 'Yoruba' was not a common form of political identification' (1986, 7–8). Nnamdi Azikiwe – one of the key figures in the construction of Nigerian nationalism – was extremely popular (as Laitin also point out) in Yoruba Lagos, where 'he edited his nationalist newspaper, the *West African Pilot*. It was only subsequent events that led him to be defined in Nigeria as an *Igbo* leader' (Laitin 1986, 7–8). Yet Nigerian politics – and the more everyday economy of ordinary personal relations – is oriented along such axes, and only very occasionally does the fact float into view that even these three problematic identities account for at most seven out of ten Nigerians.

And the story is repeated, even in places where it was not drawn in lines of blood. As Johannes Fabian has observed, the powerful Lingala- and Swahili-speaking identities of modern Zaire exist 'because spheres of political and economic interest were established before the Belgians took full control, and continued to inform relations between regions under colonial rule.' Modern Ghana witnesses the development of an Akan identity, as speakers of the three major regional dialects of Twi – Asante, Fante, Akuapem – organize themselves into a corporation against an (equally novel) Ewe unity.

When it is not the 'tribe' that is invested with new uses and meanings, it is religion. Yet the idea that Nigeria is composed of a Muslim North, a Christian South, and a mosaic of 'pagan' holdovers is as inaccurate as the picture of three historic tribal identities. Two out of every five southern Yoruba people are Muslim, and, as Laitin, [1986, 8] tells us:

> Many northern groups, especially in what are today Benue, Plateau, Gongola, and Kwara states, are largely Christian. When the leaders of Biafra tried to convince the world that they were oppressed by northern Muslims, ignorant foreigners (including the pope) believed them. But the Nigerian army [. . .] was led by a northern Christian.

It is as useless here as with race to point out in each case that the tribe or the religion, is, like all social identities, based on an idealizing fiction, for life in Nigeria or in Zaire has come to be lived through that idealization: the Igbo identity is real because Nigerians believe in it, the Shona identity because Zimbabweans have given it meaning. The rhetoric of a Muslim North and a Christian South structured political discussions in the period before Nigerian independence. But it was equally important in the debates about instituting a Muslim Court of Appeals in the Draft Constitution of 1976, and it could be found, for example, in many an article in the Nigerian press as electoral registration for a new civilian era began in July 1989.

There are, I think, three crucial lessons to be learned from these cases. First, that identities are complex and multiple and grow out of a history of changing responses to economic, political and cultural forces, almost always in opposition to other identities. Second, that they flourish despite what I earlier called our 'misrecognition' of their origins; despite, that is, their roots in myths and in lies. And third, that there is, in consequence, no large place for reason in the construction – as opposed to the study and the management – of identities. One temptation, then, for those who see the centrality of these fictions in our lives, is to leave reason behind: to celebrate and endorse those identities that seem at the moment to offer the best hope of advancing our other goals, and to keep silence about the lies and the myths. But, as I said earlier, intellectuals do not easily neglect the truth, and, all things considered, our societies profit, in my view, from the institutionalization of this imperative in the academy. So it is important for us to continue trying to tell our truths. But the facts I have been rehearsing should imbue us all with a strong sense of the marginality of such work to the central issue of the resistance to racism and ethnic violence – and to sexism, and to the other structures of difference that shape the world of power; they should force upon us the clear realization that the real battle is not being fought in the academy. Every time I read another report in the newspapers of an African disaster – a famine in Ethiopia, a war in Namibia, ethnic conflict in Burundi – I wonder how much good it does to correct the theories with which these evils are bound up; the solution is food, or mediation, or some other more material, more practical step. And yet, as I have tried to argue in this book, the shape of modern Africa (the shape of our world) is in large part the product, often the unintended and unanticipated product, of theories; even the most vulgar of Marxists will have to admit that economic interests operate *through* ideologies. We cannot change the world simply by evidence and reasoning, but we surely cannot change it without them either.

What we in the academy *can* contribute – even if only slowly and marginally – is a disruption of the discourse of 'racial' and 'tribal' differences. For, in my perfectly unoriginal opinion, the inscription of difference in Africa today plays into the hands of the very exploiters whose shackles we are trying to escape. 'Race' in Europe and 'tribe' in Africa are central to the way in which the objective interests of the worst-off are distorted. The analogous point for African-Americans was recognized long ago by DuBois. DuBois argued in *Black Reconstruction* that racist ideology had essentially blocked the formation of a significant labor movement in the United States, for such a movement would have required the collaboration of the 9 million ex-slave and white peasant workers of the South (Robinson 1983, 313). It is, in other words, because the categories of difference often cut across our economic interests that they operate to blind us to them. What binds the middle-class African-American to his dark-skinned fellow citizens downtown is not economic interest but racism and the cultural products of resistance to it that are shared across (most of) African-American culture.

It seems to me that we learn from this case what John Thompson has argued recently, in a powerful but appreciative critique of Pierre Bourdieu: namely, that it may be a mistake to think that social reproduction – the processes by which societies maintain themselves over time – presupposes 'some sort of consensus with regard to dominant values or norms.' Rather, the stability of today's industrialized society may require 'a pervasive *fragmentation* of the social order and a proliferation of divisions between its members.' For it is precisely this fragmentation that prevents oppositional attitudes from generating 'a coherent alternative view which would provide a basis for political action.'

Divisions are ramified along the lines of gender, race, qualifications and so on, forming barriers which obstruct the development of movements which could threaten the *status quo*. The reproduction of the social order may depend less upon a consensus with regard to dominant values or norms than upon a *lack of consensus* at the very point where oppositional attitudes could be translated into political action.

[Thompson 1984, 62–3]

Thompson allows us to see that within contemporary industrial societies an identification of oneself as an African, above all else, allows the fact one is, say, not an Asian, to be used against one; in this setting – as we see in South Africa – a racialized conception of one's identity is retrogressive. To argue this way is to presuppose that the political meanings of identities are historically and geographically relative. So it is quite consistent with this claim to hold, as I do, that in constructing alliances *across* states – and especially in the Third World – a Pan-African identity, which allows African-Americans, African-Caribbeans, and African-Latins to ally with continental Africans, drawing on the cultural resources of the black Atlantic world, may serve useful purposes. Resistance to a self-isolating black nationalism *within* Britain or France or the United States is thus theoretically consistent with Pan-Africanism as an international project.

Because the value of identities is thus relative, we must argue for and against them case by case. And given the current situation in Africa, I think it remains clear that another Pan-Africanism – the project of a continental fraternity and sorority, *not* the project of a racialized Negro nationalism – however false or muddled its theoretical roots, can be a progressive force. It is as fellow Africans that Ghanaian diplomats (my father among them) interceded between the warring nationalist parties in Rhodesia under UDI; as fellow Africans that OAU teams can mediate regional conflicts; as fellow Africans that the human rights assessors organized under the Banjul Declaration can intercede for citizens of African states against the excesses of our governments. If there is, as I have suggested, hope, too, for the Pan-Africanism of an African diaspora once it, too, is released from bondage to racial ideologies (alongside the many bases of alliance available to Africa's peoples in their political and cultural struggles), it is crucial that we recognize the independence, once 'Negro' nationalism is gone, of the Pan-Africanism of the diaspora and the Pan-Africanism of the continent. It is, I believe, in the exploration of these issues, these possibilities, that the future of an intellectually reinvigorated Pan-Africanism lies.

Finally, I would like to suggest that it is really unsurprising that a continental identity is coming into cultural and institutional reality through regional and subregional organizations. We share a continent and its ecological problems; we share a relation of dependency to the world economy; we share the problem of racism in the way the industrialized world thinks of us (and let me include here, explicitly, both 'Negro' Africa and the 'Maghrib'); we share the possibilities of the development of regional markets and local circuits of production; and our intellectuals participate, through the shared contingencies of our various histories, in a common discourse whose outlines I have tried to limn in this book.

'ɔdɛnky yɛm nwu nsuo-ase mma yɛmmɛfrɛ kwakuo sɛ ɔbɛyɛ no ayie,' goes an Akan proverb: 'The crocodile does not die under the water so that we can call the monkey to celebrate its funeral.' Each of us, the proverb can be used to say, belongs to a group with its own customs. To accept that Africa can be in these ways a usable identity is not to forget that all of us belong to multifarious communities with their local customs; it is not to dream of a single African state and to forget the completely different trajectories of the continent's so many languages and cultures. 'African solidarity' can surely be a vital and enabling rallying cry; but in this world of genders, ethnicities, and classes, of families, religions, and nations, it is as well to remember that there are times when Africa is not the banner we need.

# References

DuBois, W. E. B. 1935. *Black Reconstruction*. New York: Russel and Russel.

Fabian, Johannes. 1986. *Language and Colonial Power*. Cambridge: Cambridge University Press.

Gordon, David M., et al. 1982. *Segmented Work, Divided Workers*. Cambridge: Cambridge University Press.

Jameson, Fredric. 1981. *The Political Unconscious*. Ithaca, N.Y.: Cornell University Press.

Laitin, David. 1986. *Hegemony and Culture: Politics and Religious Change Among the Yoruba*. New York: Columbia University Press.

Olson, James S. 1969. 'Race, Class and Progress: Black Leadership and Industrial Unionism, 1936–1945.' In *Black Labor in America*, ed. M. Cantor. Westport, Conn.: Negro Universities Press.

Robinson, Cedric J. 1983. *Black Marxism: The Making of the Black Radical Tradition*. London: Zed Books.

Schuyler, George, 1931. *Black No More*. New York: Negro Universities Press.

Spivak, Gayatri Chakravorty. 1988. *In Other Worlds*. New York: Routledge.

Thompson, John B. 1984. *Studies in the Theory of Ideology*. Berkeley: University of California Press.

Todorov, Tzvetan. 1986. '"Race,' Writing and Culture.' In *'Race,' Writing, and Difference*, ed. Henry Louis Gates, Jr. Chicago: University of Chicago Press.

# Chapter 36

# Michael Omi and Howard Winant

## RACIAL FORMATION

[. . .]

### What is race?

**T**HERE IS A CONTINUOUS temptation to think of race as an *essence*, as something fixed, concrete, and objective. And there is also an opposite temptation: to imagine race as a mere *illusion*, a purely ideological construct which some ideal non-racist social order would eliminate. It is necessary to challenge both these positions, to disrupt and reframe the rigid and bipolar manner in which they are posed and debated, and to transcend the presumably irreconcilable relationship between them.

The effort must be made to understand race as an unstable and 'decentered' complex of social meanings constantly being transformed by political struggle. With this in mind, let us propose a definition: *race is a concept which signifies and symbolizes social conflicts and interests by referring to different types of human bodies*. Although the concept of race invokes biologically based human characteristics (so-called 'phenotypes'), selection of these particular human features for purposes of racial signification is always and necessarily a social and historical process. In contrast to the other major distinction of this type, that of gender, there is no biological basis for distinguishing among human groups along the lines of race. Indeed, the categories employed to differentiate among human groups along racial lines reveal themselves, upon serious examination, to be at best imprecise, and at worse completely arbitrary.

If the concept of race is so nebulous, can we not dispense with it? Can we not 'do without' race, at least in the 'enlightened' present? This question has been posed often, and with greater frequency in recent years. An affirmative answer would of course present obvious practical difficulties: it is rather difficult to jettison widely held beliefs, beliefs which moreover are central to everyone's identity and understanding of the social world. So the attempt to banish the concept as an archaism is at best counterintuitive. But a deeper difficulty, we believe, is inherent in the very formulation of this schema, in its way of posing race as a *problem*, a misconception left over from the past, and suitable now only for the dustbin of history.

A more effective starting point in the recognition that despite its uncertainties and contradictions, the concept of race continues to play a fundamental role in structuring and representing the social world. The task for theory is to explain this situation. It is to avoid both the utopian framework which sees race as an illusion we can somehow 'get beyond,' and also the essentialist formulation which sees race as something objective and fixed, a biological datum.[6] Thus we should think of race as an element of social structure rather than as an irregularity within it; we should see race as a dimension of human representation rather than an illusion. These perspectives inform the theoretical approach we call racial formation.

## Racial formation

We define *racial formation* as the sociohistorical process by which racial categories are created, inhabited, transformed, and destroyed. Our attempt to elaborate a theory of racial formation will proceed in two steps. First, we argue that racial formation is a process of historically situated *projects* in which human bodies and social structures are represented and organized. Next we link racial formation to the evolution of hegemony, the way in which society is organized and ruled. Such an approach, we believe, can facilitate understanding of a whole range of contemporary controversies and dilemmas involving race, including the nature of racism, the relationship of race to other forms of differences, inequalities, and oppression such as sexism and nationalism, and the dilemmas of racial identity today.

From a racial formation perspective, race is a matter of both social structure and cultural representation. Too often, the attempt is made to understand race simply or primarily in terms of only one of these two analytical dimensions. For example, efforts to explain racial inequality as a purely social structural phenomenon are unable to account for the origins, patterning, and transformation of racial difference.

Conversely, many examinations of racial difference – understood as a matter of cultural attributes *à la* ethnicity theory, or as a society-wide signification system, *à la* some poststructuralist accounts – cannot comprehend such structural phenomena as racial stratification in the labor market or patterns of residential segregation.

An alternative approach is to think of racial formation processes as occurring through a linkage between structure and representation. Racial *projects* do the ideological 'work' of making these links. *A racial project is simultaneously an interpretation, representation, or explanation of racial dynamics, and an effort to reorganise and redistribute resources along particular racial lines.* Racial projects connect what race *means* in a particular discursive practice and the ways in which both social structures and everyday experiences are racially *organized*, based upon that meaning. Let us consider this proposition, first in terms of large-scale or macro-level social processes, and then in terms of other dimensions of the racial formation process.

### Racial formation as a macro-level social process

To *interpret the meaning of race is to frame it social structurally*. Consider for example, this statement by Charles Murray on welfare reform:

> My proposal for dealing with the racial issue in social welfare is to repeal every bit of legislation and reverse every court decision that in any way required, recommends, or awards differential treatment according to race, and thereby put us back onto the track that we left in 1965. We may argue about the appropriate limits of government intervention in trying to enforce the ideal, but at least it should be possible to identify the ideal: Race is not a morally admissible reason for treating one person differently from another. Period.

Here there is a partial but significant analysis of the meaning of race: it is not a morally valid basis upon which to treat people 'differently from one another.' We may notice someone's race, but we cannot act upon that awareness. We must act in a 'color-blind' fashion. This analysis of the meaning of race is immediately linked to a specific conception of the role of race in the social structure: it can play no part in government action, save in 'the enforcement of the ideal.' No state policy can legitimately require, recommend, or award different status according to race. This example can be classified as a particular type of racial project in the present-day U.S. – a 'neoconservative' one.

Conversely, *to recognize the racial dimension in social structure is to interpret the meaning of race*. Consider the following statement by the late Supreme Court Justice Thurgood Marshall on minority 'set-aside' programs:

> A profound difference separates governmental actions that themselves are racist, and governmental actions that seek to remedy the effects of prior racism or to prevent neutral government activity from perpetuating the effects of such racism.

Here the focus is on the racial dimensions of *social structure* – in this case of state activity and policy. The argument is that state actions in the past and present have treated people in very different ways according to their race, and thus the government cannot retreat from its policy responsibilities in this area. It cannot suddenly declare itself 'color-blind' without in fact perpetuating the same type of differential, racist treatment. Thus, race continues to signify difference and structure inequality. Here, racialized social structure is immediately linked to an interpretation of the meaning of race. This example too can be classified as a particular type of racial project in the present-day U.S. – a 'liberal' one.

To be sure, such political labels as 'neoconservative' or 'liberal' cannot fully capture the complexity of racial projects, for these are always multiply determined, politically contested, and deeply shaped by their historical context. Thus, encapsulated within the neoconservative example cited here are certain egalitarian commitments which derive from a previous historical context in which they played a very different role, and which are rearticulated in neoconservative racial discourse precisely to oppose a more open-ended, more capacious conception of the meaning of equality, similarly, in the liberal example, Justice Marshall recognizes that the contemporary state, which was formerly the architect of segregation and the chief enforcer of racial difference, has a tendency to reproduce those patterns of inequality in a new guise. Thus he admonishes it (in dissent, significantly) to fulfill its responsibilities to uphold a robust conception of equality. These particular instances, then, demonstrate how racial projects are always concretely framed, and thus are always contested and unstable. The social structures they uphold or attack, and the representations of race they articulate, are never invented out of the air, but exist in a definite historical context, having descended from previous conflicts. This contestation appears to be permanent in respect to race.

These two examples of contemporary racial projects are drawn from mainstream political debate; they may be categorized as center-right and center-left expressions of contemporary racial politics. We can, however, expand the discussion of racial formation processes far beyond these familiar examples. In fact, we can identify racial projects in at least three other analytical dimensions: first, the political spectrum can be broadened to include radical projects, on both the left and right, as well as along other political axes. Second, analysis of racial projects can take place not only at the macro level of racial policy-making, state activity, and collective action, but also at the micro-level of everyday experience. Third, the concept of racial projects can be applied across historical time, to identify racial formation dynamics in the past. We shall now offer examples of each of these types of racial projects.

## The political spectrum of racial formation

We have now encountered examples of a neoconservative racial project, in which the significance of race is denied, leading to a 'color-blind' racial politics and 'hands-off' policy orientation; and of a 'liberal' racial project, in which the significance of race is affirmed, leading to an egalitarian and 'activist' state policy. But these by no means exhaust the political possibilities. Other racial projects can be readily identified on the contemporary U.S. scene. For example, 'far right' projects, which uphold biologistic and racist views of difference, explicitly argue for white supremacist policies. 'New right' projects overtly claim to hold 'color-blind' views, but covertly manipulate racial fears in order to achieve political gains. On the left, 'radical democratic' projects invoke notions of racial 'difference' in combination with egalitarian politics and policy.

Further variations can also be noted. For example, 'nationalist' projects, both conservative and radical, stress the incompatibility of racially defined group identity with the legacy of white supremacy, and therefore advocate a social structural solution of separation, either complete or partial. As we saw [. . .] nationalist currents represent a profound legacy of the centuries of racial absolutism that initially defined the meaning of race in the U.S. Nationalist concerns continue to influence racial debate in the form of Afrocentrism and other expressions of identity politics.

Taking the range of politically organized racial projects as a whole, we can 'map' the current pattern of racial formation at the level of the public sphere, the 'macro-level' in which public debate and mobilization takes place. But important as this is, the terrain on which racial formation occurs is broader yet.

### Racial formation as everyday experience

At the micro-social level, racial projects also  link signification and structure, not so much as efforts to shape policy or define large-scale meaning, but as the applications of 'common sense.' To see racial projects operating at the level of everyday life, we have only to examine the many ways in which, often unconsciously, we 'notice' race.

One of the first things we notice about people when we meet them (along with their sex) is their race. We utilize race to provide clues about *who* a person is. This fact is made painfully obvious when we encounter someone whom we cannot conveniently racially categorize – someone who is, for example, racially 'mixed' or of an ethnic/racial group we are not familiar with. Such an encounter becomes a source of discomfort and momentarily a crisis of racial meaning.

Our ability to interpret racial meanings depends on preconceived notions of a racialized social structure. Comments such as 'Funny, you don't look black,' betray an underlying image of what black should be. We expect people to act out their apparent racial identities; indeed we become disoriented when they do not. The black banker harassed by the police while walking in casual clothes through his own well-off neighborhood, the Latino or white kid rapping in perfect Afro patois, the unending *faux pas* committed by whites who assume that the non-whites they encounter are servants or tradespeople, the belief that non-white colleagues are less qualified persons hired to fulfill affirmative action guidelines, indeed the whole gamut of racial stereotypes – that 'white men can't jump,' that Asians can't dance, etc., etc. – all testify to the way a racialized social structure shapes racial experience and conditions meaning. Analysis of such stereotypes reveals the always present, already active link between our view of the social structure – its demography, its laws, its customs, its threats – and our conception of what race means.

Conversely, our ongoing interpretation of our experience in racial terms shapes our relations to the institutions and organizations through which we are imbedded in social structure. Thus we expect differences in skin color, or other racially coded characteristics, to explain social differences. Temperament, sexuality, intelligence, athletic ability, aesthetic preferences, and so on are presumed to be fixed and discernible from the palpable mark of race. Such diverse questions as our confidence and trust in others (for example, clerks or salespeople, media figures, neighbors), our sexual preferences and romantic images, our tastes in music, films, dance, or sports, and our very ways of talking, walking, eating, and dreaming become racially coded simply because we live in a society where racial awareness is so pervasive. Thus in ways too comprehensive even to monitor consciously, and

376 MICHAEL OMI AND HOWARD WINANT

despite periodic calls – neoconservative and otherwise – for us to ignore race and adopt 'color-blind' racial attitudes, skin color 'differences' continue to rationalize distinct treatment of racially identified individuals and groups.

To summarize the argument so far: the theory of racial formation suggests that society is suffused with racial projects, large and small, to which all are subjected. This racial 'subjection' is quintessentially ideological. Everybody learns some combination, some version, of the rules of racial classification, and of her own racial identity, often without obvious teaching or conscious inculcation. Thus are we inserted in a comprehensively racialized social structure. Race becomes 'common sense' – a way of comprehending, explaining, and acting in the world. A vast web of racial projects mediates between the discursive or representational means in which race is identified and signified on the one hand, and the institutional and organizational forms in which it is routinized and standardized on the other. These projects are the heart of the racial formation process.

Under such circumstances, it is not possible to represent race discursively without simultaneously locating it, explicitly or implicitly, in a social structural (and historical) context. Nor is it possible to organize, maintain, or transform social structures without simultaneously engaging, once more either explicitly or implicitly, in racial signification. Racial formation, therefore, is a kind of synthesis, an outcome, of the interaction of racial projects on a society-wide level. These projects are, of course, vastly different in scope and effect. They include large-scale public action, state activities, and interpretations of racial conditions in artistic, journalistic, or academic fora, as well as the seemingly infinite number of racial judgments and practices we carry out at the level of individual experience.

Since racial formation is always historically situated, our understanding of the significance of race, and of the way race structures society, has changed enormously over time. The processes of racial formation we encounter today, the racial projects large and small which structure U.S. society in so many ways, are merely the present-day outcomes of a complex historical evolution. The contemporary racial order remains transient. By knowing something of how it evolved, we can perhaps better discern where it is heading. We therefore turn next to a historical survey of the racial formation process, and the conflicts and debates it has engendered.

[. . .]


## Dictatorship, democracy, hegemony

For most of its existence both as European colony and as an independent nation, the U.S. was a *racial dictatorship*. From 1607 to 1865 – 258 years – most non-whites were firmly eliminated from the sphere of politics. After the Civil War there was the brief egalitarian experiment of Reconstruction which terminated ignominiously in 1877. In its wake followed almost a century of legally sanctioned segregation and denial of the vote, nearly absolute in the South and much of the Southwest, less effective in the North and far West, but formidable in any case. These barriers fell only in the mid-1960s, a mere quarter-century ago. Nor did the successes of the black movement and its allies mean that all obstacles to their political participation had now been abolished. Patterns of racial inequality have proven, unfortunately, to be quite stubborn and persistent.

It is important, therefore, to recognize that in many respects, racial dictatorship is the norm against which all U.S. politics must be measured. The centuries of racial dictatorship have had three very large consequences: first, they defined 'American' identity as white, as the negation of racialized 'otherness' – at first largely African and indigenous, later Latin American and Asian as well. This negation took shape in both law and custom, in public institutions and in forms of cultural representation. It became the archetype of hegemonic rule in the U.S. It was the successor to the conquest as the 'master' racial project.

Second, racial dictatorship organized (albeit sometimes in an incoherent and contradictory fashion) the 'color line' rendering it the fundamental division in U.S. society. The dictatorship elaborated, articulated, and drove racial divisions not only through institutions, but also through psyches, extending up to our own time the racial obsessions of the conquest and slavery periods.

Third, racial dictatorship consolidated the oppositional racial consciousness and organization originally framed by marronage and slave revolts, by indigeneous resistance, and by nationalisms of various sorts. Just as the conquest created the 'native' where once there had been Pequot, Iroquois, or Tutelo, so too it created the 'black' where once there had been Asante or Ovimbundu, Yoruba or Bakongo.

The transition from a racial democracy has been a slow, painful, and contentious one; it remains far from complete. A recognition of the abiding presence of racial dictatorship, we contend, is crucial for the development of a theory of racial formation in the U.S. It is also crucial to the task of relating racial formation to the broader context of political practice, organization, and change.

In this context, a key question arises: in what way is racial formation related to politics as a whole? How, for example, does race articulate with other axes of oppression and difference – most importantly class and gender – along which politics is organized today?

The answer, we believe, lies in the concept of *hegemony*. Antonio Gramsci – the Italian communist who placed this concept at the center of his life's work – understood it as the conditions necessary, in a given society, for the achievement and consolidation of rule. He argued that hegemony was always constituted by a combination of coercion and consent. Although rule can be obtained by force, it cannot be secured and maintained, expecially in modern society, without the element of consent. Gramsci conceived of consent as far more than merely the legitimation of authority. In his view, consent extended to the incorporation by the ruling group of many of the key interests of subordinated groups, often to the explicit disadvantage of the rulers themselves. Gramsci's treatment of hegemony went even farther: he argued that in order to consolidate their hegemony, ruling groups must elaborate and maintain a popular system of ideas and practices – through education, the media, religion, folk wisdom, etc. – which he called 'common sense.' It is through its production and its adherence to this 'common sense,' this ideology (in the broadest sense of the term), that a society gives its consent to the way in which it is ruled.

These provocative concepts can be extended and applied to an understanding of racial rule. In the Americas, the conquest represented the violent introduction of a new form of rule whose relationship with those it subjugated was almost entirely coercive. In the U.S., the origins of racial division, and of racial signification and identity formation, lie in a system of rule which was extremely dictatorial. The mass murders and expulsions of indigenous people, and the enslavement of Africans, surely evoked and inspired little consent in their founding moments.

Over time, however, the balance of coercion and consent began to change. It is possible to locate the origins of hegemony right within the heart of racial dictatorship, for the effort to possess the oppressor's tools – religion and philosophy in this case – was crucial to emancipation (the effort to possess oneself). As Ralph Ellison reminds us, 'The slaves often took the essence of the aristocratic ideal (as they took Christianity) with far more seriousness than their masters.' In their language, in their religion with its focus on the Exodus theme and on Jesus's tribulations, in their music with its figuring of suffering, resistance, perseverance, and transcendence, in their interrogation of a political philosophy which sought perpetually to rationalize their bondage in a supposedly 'free' society, the slaves incorporated elements of racial rule into their thought and practice, turning them against their original bearers.

Racial rule can be understood as a slow and uneven historical process which has moved from dictatorship to democracy, from domination to hegemony. In this transition, hegemonic forms of racial rule – those based on consent – eventually came to supplant those based on coercion. Of course, before this assertion can be accepted, it must be qualified in important ways. By no means has the U.S. established racial democracy at the end of the century, and by no means is coercion a thing of the past. But the sheer complexity of the racial questions U.S. society confronts today, the welter of competing racial projects and contradictory racial experiences which Americans undergo, suggests that hegemony is a useful and appropriate term with which to characterize contemporary racial rule.

Our key theoretical notion of racial projects helps to extend and broaden the question of rule. Projects are the building blocks not just of racial formation, but of hegemony in general. Hegemony operates by simultaneously structuring and signifying. As in the case of racial opposition, gender- or class-based conflict today links structural inequity and injustice on the one hand, and identifies and represents its subjects on the other. The success of modern-day feminism, for example, has depended on its ability to reinterpret gender as a matter of both injustice and identity/difference.

Today, political opposition necessarily takes shape on the terrain of hegemony. Far from ruling principally through exclusion and coercion (though again, these are hardly absent) hegemony operates by including its subjects, incorporating its opposition. *Pace* both Marxists and liberals, there is no longer any universal or privileged region of political action or discourse. Race, class, and gender all represent potential antagonisms whose significance is no longer given, if it ever was.

Thus race, class, and gender (as well as sexual orientation) constitute 'regions' of hegemony, areas in which certain political projects can take shape. They share certain obvious attributes in that they are all 'socially constructed,' and they all consist of a field of projects whose common feature is their linkage of social structure and signification.

Going beyond this, it is crucial to emphasize that race, class, and gender, are not fixed and discrete categories, and that such 'regions' are by no means autonomous. They overlap, intersect, and fuse with each other in countless ways. Such mutual determinations have been illustrated by Patricia Hill Collin's survey and theoretical synthesis of the themes and issues of black feminist thought. They are also evident in Evelyn Nakano Glenn's work on the historical and contemporary racialization of domestic and service work. In many respects, race is gendered and gender is racialized. In institutional and everyday life, any clear demarcation of specific forms of oppression and difference is constantly being disrupted.

There are no clear boundaries between these 'regions' of hegemony, so political conflicts will often invoke some or all of these themes simultaneously. Hegemony is tentative, incomplete, and 'messy.' For example, the 1991 Hill Thomas hearings, with their intertwined themes of race and gender inequality, and their frequent genuflections before the altar of hard work and upward mobility, managed to synthesize various race, gender, and class projects in a particularly explosive combination.

What distinguishes political opposition today – racial or otherwise – is its insistence on identifying itself and speaking for itself, its determined demand for the transformation of the social structure, its refusal of the 'common sense' understandings which the hegemonic order imposes. Nowhere is this refusal of 'common sense' more needed, or more imperilled, than in our understanding of racism.

## What is racism

[. . .]

We employ racial formation theory to reformulate the concept of racism. Our approach recognizes that racism, like race, has changed over time. It is obvious that the attitudes, practices, and institutions of the epochs of slavery, say, or of Jim Crow, no longer exist today. Employing a similar logic, it is reasonable to question whether concepts of racism which developed in the early days of the post-civil rights era, when the limitations of both moderate reform and militant racial radicalism of various types had not yet been encountered, remain adequate to explain circumstances and conflicts a quarter-century later.

Racial formation theory allows us to differentiate between race and racism. The two concepts should not be used interchangeably. We have argued that race has no fixed meaning, but is constructed and transformed sociohistorically through competing political projects, through the necessary and ineluctable link between the structural and cultural dimensions of race in the U.S. This emphasis on projects allows us to refocus our understanding of racism as well, for racism can now be seen as characterizing some, but not all, racial projects.

A racial project can be defined as *racist* if and only if it *creates or reproduces structures of domination based on essentialist categories of race*. Such a definition recognizes the importance of locating racism within a fluid and contested history of racially based social structures and discourses. Thus there can be no timeless and absolute standard for what constitutes racism, for social structures change and discourses are subject to rearticulation. Our definition therefore focuses instead on the 'work' essentialism does for domination, and the 'need' domination displays to essentialize the subordinated.

Further, it is important to distinguish racial awareness from racial essentialism. To attribute merits, allocate values or resources to, and/or represent individuals or groups on the basis of racial identity should not be considered racist in and of itself. Such projects may in fact be quite benign.

Consider the following examples: first, the statement, 'Many Asian Americans are highly entrepreneurial'; second, the organization of an association of, say, black accountants.

The first racial project, in our view, signifies or represents a racial category ('Asian Americans') and locates that representation within the social structure of the contemporary U.S. (in regard to business, class issues, socialization, etc.). The second racial project is organizational or social structural, and therefore must engage in racial signification. Black accountants, the organizers might maintain, have certain common experiences, can offer each other certain support, etc. Neither of these racial projects is essentialist, and neither can fairly be labelled racist. Of course, racial representations may be biased or misinterpret their subjects, just as racially based organizational efforts may be unfair or unjustifiably exclusive. If such were the case, if for instance in our first example the statement in question were 'Asian Americans are naturally entrepreneurial,' this would by our criterion be racist. Similarly, if the effort to organize black accountants had as its rationale the raiding of clients from white accountants, it would by our criterion be racist as well.

Similarly, to allocate values or resources – let us say, academic scholarships – on the basis of racial categories is not racist. Scholarships are awarded on a preferential basis to Rotarians, children of insurance company employees, and residents of the Pittsburgh metropolitan area. Why then should they not also be offered, in particular cases, to Chicanos or Native Americans?

In order to identify a social project as racist, one must in our view demonstrate a link between essentialist representations of race and social structures of domination. Such a link might be revealed in efforts to protect dominant interests, framed in racial terms, from democratizing racial initiatives. But it might also consist of efforts simply to reverse the roles of racially dominant and racially subordinate. There is nothing inherently white about racism.

Obviously a key problem with essentialism is its denial, or flattening, of differences within a particular racially defined group. Members of subordinate racial groups, when faced with racist practices such as exclusion or discrimination, are frequently forced to band together in order to defend their interests (if not, in some instances, their very lives). Such 'strategic essentialism' should not, however, be simply equated with the essentialism practiced by dominant groups, nor should it prevent the interrogation of internal group differences. [. . .]

Parallel to the debates on the concept of race, recent academic and political controversies about the nature of racism have centered on whether it is primarily an ideological or structural phenomenon. Proponents of the former position argue that racism is first and foremost a matter of beliefs and attitudes, doctrines and discourse, which only then give rise to unequal and unjust practices and structures. Advocates of the latter view see racism as primarily a matter of economic stratification, residential segregation, and other institutionalized forms of inequality which then give rise to ideologies of privilege.

From the standpoint of racial formation, these debates are fundamentally misguided. They frame the problem of racism in a rigid 'either-or' manner. We believe it is crucial to disrupt the fixity of these positions by simultaneously arguing that ideological beliefs have structural consequences, and that social structures give rise to beliefs. Racial ideology and social structure, therefore, mutually shape the nature of racism in a complex, dialectical, and overdetermined manner.

Even those racist projects which appear chiefly ideological turn out upon closer examination to have significant institutional and social structural dimensions. For example, what we have called 'far right' projects appear at first glance to be centrally ideological. They are rooted in biologistic doctrine, after all. The same seems to hold for certain conservative black nationalist projects which have deep commitments to biologism. But the unending stream of racist assaults initiated by the far right, the apparently increasing presence of skinheads in high schools, the proliferation of neo-Nazi computer bulletin boards, and the appearance of racist talk shows on cable access channels, all suggest that the organizational manifestations of the far right racial projects exist and will endure. Perhaps less threatening but still quite worrisome is the diffusion of doctrines of black superiority through some (though by no means all) university-based African American Studies departments and student organizations, surely a serious institutional or structural development.

By contrast, even those racisms which at first glance appear to be chiefly structural upon closer examination reveal a deeply ideological component. For example, since the racial right abandoned its explicit advocacy of segregation, it has not seemed to uphold – in the main – an ideologically racist project, but more primarily a structurally racist one. Yet this very transformation required tremendous efforts of ideological production. It demanded the rearticulation of civil rights doctrines of equality in suitably conservative form, and indeed the defense of continuing large-scale racial inequality as an outcome preferable to (what its advocates have seen as) the threat to democracy that affirmative action, busing, and large-scale 'race-specific' social spending would entail. Even more tellingly, this project took shape through a deeply manipulative coding of subtextual appeals to white racism, notably in a series of political campaigns for high office which have occurred over recent decades. The retreat of social policy from any practical commitment to racial justice , and the relentless reproduction and divulgation of this theme at the level of everyday life – where whites are 'fed up' with all the 'special treatment' received by non-whites, etc. – constitutes the hegemonic racial project at this time. It therefore exhibits an unabashed structural racism all the more brazen because on the ideological or signification level, it adheres to a principle of 'treating everyone alike.'

In summary, the racism of today is no longer a virtual monolith, as was the racism of yore. Today, racial hegemony is 'messy.' The complexity of the present situation is the product of a vast historical legacy of structural inequality and invidious racial representation, which has been confronted during the post-World War II period with an opposition more serious and effective than any it had faced before. [. . .] the result is a deeply ambiguous and contradictory spectrum of racial projects, unremittingly conflictual racial politics, and confused and ambivalent racial identities of all sorts. [. . .]

# POSTCOLONIALITY

- Edward Said, Orientalism

- Homi Bhabha, The other question: stereotype, discrimination and the discourse of colonialism

**Edward Said**, who was born in Jerusalem on 1 November 1935, immigrated to the United States in 1950. He has taught at various universities in the United States and Canada, among them Harvard, Columbia and Johns Hopkins. His writings include *Orientalism* (1978) and *Culture and Imperialism* (1993).

**Homi Bhabha** received a doctorate from Oxford University. He is a Professor of English at the University of Chicago and is the author of *The Location of Culture* (1994) and editor of *Nation and Narration* (1990).

# Chapter 37

# Edward Said

## ORIENTALISM

I HAVE BEGUN WITH the assumption that the Orient is not an inert fact of nature. It is not merely *there*, just as the Occident itself is not just *there* either. We must take seriously Vico's great observation that men make their own history, that what they can know is what they have made, and extend it to geography: as both geographical and cultural entities – to say nothing of historical entities – such locales, regions, geographical sectors as 'Orient' and 'Occident' are man-made. Therefore as much as the West itself, the Orient is an idea that has a history and a tradition of thought, imagery, and vocabulary that have given it reality and presence in and for the West. The two geographical entities thus support and to an extent reflect each other.

Having said that, one must go on to state a number of reasonable qualifications. In the first place, it would be wrong to conclude that the Orient was *essentially* an idea, or a creation with no corresponding reality. When Disraeli said in his novel *Tancred* that the East was a career, he meant that to be interested in the East was something bright young Westerners would find to be an all-consuming passion; he should not be interpreted as saying that the East was *only* a career for Westerners. There were – and are – cultures and nations whose location is in the East, and their lives, histories, and customs have a brute reality obviously greater than anything that could be said about them in the West. About that face this study of Orientalism has very little to contribute, except to acknowledge it tacitly. But the phenomenon of Orientalism as I study it here deals principally, not with a correspondence between Orientalism and Orient, but with the internal consistency of Orientalism and its ideas about the Orient (the East as career) despite or beyond any correspondence, or lack thereof, with a 'real' Orient. My point is that Disraeli's statement about the East refers mainly to that created consistency, that regular constellation of ideas as the pre-eminent thing about the Orient, and not to its mere being, as Wallace Stevens's phrase has it.

A second qualification is that ideas, cultures, and histories cannot seriously be understood or studied without their force, or more precisely their configurations of power, also being studied. To believe that the Orient was created – or, as I call it, 'Orientalized' – and to believe that such things happen simply as a necessity of the imagination, is to be disingenuous. The relationship between Occident and Orient is a relationship of power, of domination, of varying degrees of a complex hegemony, and is quite accurately indicated in the title of K. M. Panikkar's classic *Asia and Western Dominance*. The Orient was Orientalized not only because it was discovered to be 'Oriental' in all those ways considered commonplace by an average nineteenth-century European, but also because it *could be* – that is, submitted to being – *made* Oriental. There is very little consent to be found, for example, in the fact that Flaubert's encounter with an Egyptian courtesan produced a widely influential model of the Oriental woman; she never spoke of herself, she never represented her emotions, presence, or history. *He* spoke for and represented her. He was foreign, comparatively wealthy, male, and these were historical facts of domination that allowed him not only to possess Kuchuk Hanem physically but to speak for her and tell his readers in what way she was 'typically Oriental.' My argument is that Flaubert's situation of strength in relation to Kuchuk Hanem was not an isolated instance. It fairly stands for the pattern of relative strength between East and West, and the discourse about the Orient that it enabled.

This brings us to a third qualification. One ought never to assume that the structure of Orientalism is nothing more than a structure of lies or of myths which, were the truth about them to be told, would simply blow away. I myself believe that Orientalism is more particularly valuable as a sign of European-Atlantic power over the Orient than it is as a veridic discourse about the Orient (which is what, in its academic or scholarly form, it claims to be). Nevertheless, what we must respect and try to grasp is the sheer knitted-together strength of Orientalist discourse, its very close ties to the enabling socio-economic and political institutions, and it redoubtable durability. After all, any system of ideas that can remain unchanged as teachable wisdom (in academies, books, congresses, universities, foreign-service institutes) from the period of Ernest Renan in the late 1840s until the present in the United States must be something more formidable than a mere collection of lies. Orientalism, therefore, is not an airy European fantasy about the Orient, but a created body of theory and practice in which, for many generations, there has been a considerable material investment. Continued investment made Orientalism, as a system of knowledge about the Orient, an accepted grid for filtering through the Orient into Western consciousness, just as that same investment multiplied – indeed, made truly productive – the statements proliferating out from Orientalism into the general culture.

Gramsci has made the useful analytic distinction between civil and political society in which the former is made up of voluntary (or at least rational and noncoercive) affiliations like schools, families, and unions, the latter of state institutions (the army, the police, the central bureaucracy) whose role in the polity is direct domination. Culture, of course, is to be found operating within civil society, where the influence of ideas, of institutions, and of other persons works not through domination but by what Gramsci calls consent. In any society not totalitarian, then, certain cultural forms predominate over others, just as certain ideas are more influential than others; the form of this cultural leadership is what Gramsci has identified as *hegemony*, an indispensable concept for any understanding of cultural life in the industrial West. It is hegemony, or rather the result of cultural hegemony at work, that gives Orientalism the durability and the strength I have been speaking about so far. Orientalism is never far from what Denys Hay as called the idea of Europe, a collective notion identifying 'us' Europeans as against all 'those' non-Europeans, and indeed it can be argued that the major component in European culture is precisely what made that culture hegemonic both in and outside Europe: the idea of European identity as a superior one in comparison with all the non-European peoples and cultures. There is in addition the hegemony of European ideas about the Orient, themselves reiterating European superiority over Oriental backwardness, usually overriding the possibility that a more independent, or more skeptical, thinker might have had different views on the matter.

In a quite constant way, Orientalism depends for its strategy on this flexible *positional* superiority, which puts the Westerner in a whole series of possible relationships with the Orient without ever losing him the relative upper hand. And why should it have been otherwise, especially during the period of extraordinary European ascendancy from the last Renaissance to the present? The scientist, the scholar, the missionary, the trader, or the soldier was in, or thought about, the Orient because he *could be there* or could think about it, with very little resistance on the Orient's part. Under the general heading of knowledge of the Orient, and within the umbrella of Western hegemony over the Orient during the period from the end of the eighteenth century, there emerged a complex Orient suitable for study in the academy, for display in the museum, for reconstruction in the colonial office, for theoretical illustration in anthropological, biological, linguistic, racial, and historical theses about mankind and the universe, for instances of economic and sociological theories of development, revolution, cultural personality, national or religious character. Additionally, the imaginative examination of things Oriental was based more or less exclusively upon a sovereign Western consciousness out of whose unchallenged centrality an Oriental world emerged, first according to general ideas about who or what was an Oriental, then according to a detailed logic governed not simply by empirical reality but by a battery of desires, repressions, investments, and projections. [. . .]

My idea is that European and then American interest in the Orient was political according to some of the obvious historical accounts of it that I have given here, but that it was the culture that created that interest, that acted dynamically along with brute political, economic, and military rationales to make the orient the varied and complicated place that it obviously was in the field I call Orientalism.

Therefore, Orientalism is not a mere political subject matter or field that is reflected passively by culture, scholarship, or institutions; nor is it a large and diffuse collection of texts about the Orient; not is it representative and expressive of some nefarious 'Western' imperialist plot to hold down the 'Oriental' world. It is rather a *distribution* of geopolitical awareness into aesthetic, scholarly, economic, sociological, historical, and philological texts; it is an *elaboration* not only of a basic geographical distinction (the world is made up of two unequal halves, Orient and Occident) but also of a whole series of 'interests' which, by such means as scholarly discovery, philological reconstruction, psychological analysis, landscape and sociological description, it not only creates but also maintains; it *is*, rather than expresses, a certain *will* or *intention* to understand, in some cases to control, manipulate, even to incorporate what is manifestly different (or alternative and novel) world; it is, above all, a discourse that is by no means in direct, corresponding relationship with political power in the raw, but rather is produced and exists in an uneven exchange with various kinds of power, shaped to a degree by the exchange with power political (as with a colonial or imperial establishment), power intellectual (as with reigning sciences like comparative linguistics or anatomy, or any of the modern policy sciences), power cultural (as with orthodoxies and canons of taste, texts, values), power moral (as with ideas about what 'we' do and what 'they' cannot do or understand as 'we' do). Indeed, my real argument is that Orientalism is – and does not simply represent – a considerable dimension of modern political-intellectual culture, and as such has less to do with the Orient than it does with 'our' world. [. . .]

Here it seems to me there is a simple two-part answer to be given, at least so far as the study of imperialism and culture (or Orientalism) is concerned. In the first place, nearly every nineteenth-century writer (and the same is true enough of writers in earlier periods) was extraordinarily well aware of the fact of empire: this is a subject not very well studied, but it will not take a modern Victorian specialist long to admit that liberal cultural heroes like John Stuart Mill, Arnold, Carlyle, Newman, Macaulay, Ruskin, George Eliot, and even Dickens had definite views on race and imperialism, which are quite easily to be found at work in their writing. So even a specialist must deal with the knowledge that Mill, for example, made it clear in *On Liberty* and *Representative Government* that his views there could not be applied to India (he was an India Office functionary for a good deal of his life, after all) because the Indians were civilizationally, if not racially, inferior. The same kind of paradox is to be found in Marx, as I try to show in this book. In the second place, to believe that politics in the form of imperialism bears upon the production of literature, scholarship, social theory, and history writing is by no means equivalent to saying that culture is therefore a demeaned or denigrated thing. Quite the contrary: my whole point is to say that we can better understand the persistence and the durability of saturating hegemonic systems like culture when we realize that their internal constraints upon writers and thinkers were *productive*, not unilaterally inhibiting. [. . .]

# Chapter 38

# Homi Bhabha

## THE OTHER QUESTION
## Stereotype, discrimination and the discourse of colonialism

**A**N **IMPORTANT FEATURE** of colonial discourse is its dependence on the concept of 'fixity' in the ideological construction of otherness. Fixity, as the sign of cultural/historical/racial difference in the discourse of colonialism, is a paradoxical mode of representation: it connotes rigidity and an unchanging order as well as disorder, degeneracy and daemonic repetition. Likewise the stereotype, which is its major discursive strategy, is a form of knowledge and identification that vacillates between what is always 'in place', already known, and something that must be anxiously repeated . . . as if the essential duplicity of the Asiatic or the bestial sexual licence of the African that needs no proof, can never really, in discourse, be proved. It is this process of *ambivalence*, central to the stereotype, that this chapter explores as it constructs a theory of colonial discourse. For it is the force of ambivalence that gives the colonial stereotype its currency: ensures its repeatability in changing historical and discursive conjunctures; informs it strategies of individuation and marginalization; produces that effect of probabilistic truth and predictability which, for the stereotype, must always be in *excess* of what can be empirically proved or logically construed. Yet the function of ambivalence as one of the most significant discursive and psychical strategies of discriminatory power, whether racist or sexist, peripheral or metropolitan – remains to be charted.

The absence of such a perspective has its own history of political expediency. To recognize the stereotype as an ambivalent mode of knowledge and power demands a theoretical and political response that challenges deterministic or functionalist modes of conceiving of the relationship between discourse and politics. The analytic of ambivalence questions dogmatic and moralistic positions on the meaning of oppression and discrimination. My reading of colonial discourse suggests that the point of intervention should shift from the ready recognition of images as positive or negative, to an understanding of the *processes of subjectification* made possible (and plausible) through stereotypical discourse. To judge the stereotyped image on the basis of a prior political normativity is to dismiss it, not to displace it, which is only possible by engaging with its *effectivity*; with the repertoire of positions of power and resistance, domination and dependence that constructs colonial identification subject (both colonizer and colonized). I do not intend to deconstruct the colonial discourse to reveal its ideological misconceptions or repressions, to exult in its self-reflexivity, or to indulge its liberatory 'excess'. In order to understand the productivity of colonial power it is crucial to construct its regime of truth, not to subject its representations to a normalizing judgement. Only then does it become possible to understand the *productive* ambivalence of the object of desire and derision, an articulation of difference contained within the fantasy of origin and identity. What such a reading reveals are the boundaries of colonial discourse and it enables a transgression of these limits from the space of that otherness.

The construction of the colonial subject in discourse, and the exercise of colonial power through discourse, demands an articulation of forms of difference – racial and sexual. Such an articulation becomes crucial if it is held that the body is always simultaneously (if conflictually) inscribed in both the economy of pleasure and desire and the economy of discourse, domination and power. I do not wish to conflate, unproblematically, two forms of the marking – and splitting – of the subject nor to globalize two forms of representation. I want to suggest, however, that there is a theoretical space and a political place for such an *articulation* – in the sense in which that word itself denies an 'original' identity or a 'singularity' to objects of difference – sexual or racial. If such a view is taken, as Feuchtwang argues in a different context, it follows that the epithets racial or sexual come to be seen as modes of differentiation, realized as multiple, cross-cutting determinations, polymorphous and perverse, always demanding a specific and strategic calculation of their effects. Such is, I believe, the moment of colonial discourse. It is a form of discourse crucial to the binding of a range of differences and discriminations that inform the discursive and political practices of racial and cultural hierarchization.

Before turning to the construction of colonial discourse, I want to discuss briefly the process by which forms of racial/cultural/historical otherness have been marginalized in theoretical texts committed to the articulation of 'difference', or 'contradiction', in order, it is claimed, to reveal the limits of Western representationalist discourse. In facilitating the passage 'from work to text' and stressing the arbitrary, differential and systemic construction of social and cultural signs, these critical strategies unsettle the idealist quest for meanings that are, most often, intentionalist and nationalist. So much is not in question. What does need to be questioned, however, is the *mode of representation of otherness*.

Where better to raise the question of the subject of racial and cultural difference than in Stephen Heath's masterly analysis of the chiaroscuro world of Welles's classic, *A Touch of Evil*? I refer to an area of its analysis which has generated the least comment, that is, Heath's attention to the structuration of the Mexican/US border that circulates through the text affirming and exchanging some notion of 'limited being'. Heath's work departs from the traditional analysis of racial and cultural differences, which identify stereotype and image and elaborate them in a moralistic or nationalistic discourse that affirms the *origin* and *unity* of national identity. Heath's attentiveness to the contradictory and diverse sites within the textual system, which *construct* national/cultural differences in their deployment of the semes of 'foreignness', 'mixedness', 'impurity', as transgressive and corrupting, is extremely relevant. His attention to the turnings of this much neglected subject as sign (not symbol or stereotype) disseminated in the codes (as 'partition', 'exchange', 'naming', 'character', etc.), gives us a useful sense of the circulation and proliferation of racial and cultural otherness. Despite the awareness of the multiple or cross-cutting determinations in the construction of modes of sexual and racial differentiation there is a sense in which Heath's analysis marginalizes otherness. Although I shall argue that the problem of the Mexican/US border is read too singularly, too exclusively under the sign of sexuality, it is not that I am not aware of the many proper and relevant reasons for that 'feminist' focus. The 'entertainment' operated by the realist Hollywood film of the 1950s was always also a containment of the subject in a narrative economy of voyeurism and fetishism. Moreover, the displacement that organizes any textual system, within which the display of difference circulated, demands that the play of 'nationalists' should partic- ipate in the sexual positioning, troubling the Law and desire. There is, nevertheless, a singularity and reductiveness in concluding that:

> Vargas is the position of desire, its admission and its prohibition. Not surprisingly he has two names: the name of desire is Mexican, Miguel . . . that of the Law American – Mike. . . . The file uses the border, the play between American and Mexican . . . at the same time it seeks to hold that play finally in the opposition of purity and mixture which in turn is a version of Law and desire.

However liberatory it is from one position to see the logic of the text traced ceaselessly between the Ideal Father and the Phallic Mother, in another sense, seeing only one possible articulation of the differential complex 'race–sex', it half colludes with the proffered images of marginality. For if the naming of Vargas is crucially mixed and split in the economy of desire, then there are other mixed economies which make naming and positioning equally problematic 'across the border'. To identify the 'play' on the border as purity and mixture and to see it as an alle- gory of Law and desire reduces the articulation of racial and sexual difference to what is dangerously close to becoming a circle rather than a spiral of difference. On that basis, it is not possible to construct the polymorphous and perverse collu- sion between racism and sexism as a *mixed economy* – for instance, the discourses of American cultural colonialism and Mexican dependency, the fear/desire of miscegenation, the American border as cultural signifier of a pioneering, male 'American' spirit always under threat from races and cultures beyond the border or frontier. If the death of the Father is the interruption on which the narrative is initiated, it is through that death that miscegenation is both possible and deferred; if, again, it is the purpose of the narrative to restore Susan as 'good object', it also becomes its project to deliver Vargas from his racial 'mixedness'. [. . .]

The difference of other cultures is other than the excess of signification or the trajectory of desire. These are theoretical strategies that are necessary to combat 'ethnocentricism' but they cannot, of themselves, unreconstructed, represent that otherness. There can be no inevitable sliding from the semiotic activity to the unproblematic reading of other cultural and discursive systems. There is in such readings a will to power and knowledge that, in failing to specify the limits of their own field of enunciation and effectivity, proceeds to individualize otherness as the discovery of their own assumptions.

The difference of colonial discourse as an apparatus of power will emerge more fully as this chapter develops. At this stage, however, I shall provide what I take to be the minimum conditions and specifications of such a discourse. It is an apparatus that turns on the recognition and disavowal of racial/cultural/historical differences. Its predominant strategic function is the creation of a space for a 'subject peoples' through the production of knowledges in terms of which surveillance is exercised and a complex form of pleasure/unpleasure is incited. It seeks authorization for its strategies by the production of knowledges of colonizer and colonized which are stereotypical but antithetically evaluated. The objective of colonial discourse is to construe the colonized as a population of degenerate types on the basis of racial origin, in order to justify conquest and to establish systems of administration and instruction. Despite the play of power within colonial discourse and the shifting positionalities of its subjects (for example, effects of class, gender, ideology, different social formations, varied systems of colonization and so on), I am referring to a form of governmentality that in marking out a 'subject nation', appropriates, directs and dominates its various spheres of activity. Therefore, despite the 'play' in the colonial system which is crucial to its exercise of power, colonial discourse produces the colonized as a social reality which is at once an 'other' and yet entirely knowable and visible. It resembles a form of narrative whereby the productivity and circulation of subjects and signs are bound in a reformed and recognizable totality. It employs a system of representation, a regime of truth, that is structurally similar to realism. And it is in order to intervene within that system of representation that Edward Said proposes a semiotic of 'Orientalist' power, examining the varied European discourses which constitute 'the Orient' as a unified racial, geographical, political and cultural zone of the world. Said's analysis is revealing of, and relevant to, colonial discourse:

> Philosophically, then, the kind of language, thought, and vision that I have been calling orientalism very generally is a form or *radical realism*; anyone employing orientalism, which is the habit for dealing with questions, objects, qualities and regions deemed Oriental, will designate, name, point to, fix, what he is talking or thinking about with a word or phrase, which then is considered either to have acquired, or more simply to be, reality. [. . .] The tense they employ is the timeless eternal; they convey an impression of repetition and strength. [. . .] For all these functions it is frequently enough to use the simple copula *is*.

For Said, the copula seems to be the point at which western rationalism preserves the boundaries of sense for itself. Of this, too, Said is aware when he hints continually at a polarity or division at the very centre of Orientalism. It is, on the one hand, a topic of learning, discovery, practice; on the other, it is the site of dreams, images, fantasies, myths, obsessions and requirements. It is a static system of 'synchronic essentialism', a knowledge of 'signifiers of stability' such as the lexicographic and the encyclopaedic. However, this site is continually under threat from diachronic forms of history and narrative, signs of instability. And, finally, this line of thinking is given a shape analogical to the dreamwork, when Said refers explicitly to a distinction between 'an unconscious positivity' which he terms *latent* Orientalism, and the stated knowledges and views about the Orient which he calls *manifest* Orientalism.

The originality of this pioneering theory could be extended to engage with the alterity and ambivalence of Orientalist discourse. Said contains this threat by introducing a binarism within the argument which, in initially setting up an opposition between these two discursive scenes, finally allows them to be correlated as a congruent system of representation that is unified through a political–ideological *intention* which, in his words, enables Europe to advance securely and *unmetaphorically* upon the Orient. Said identifies the *content* of Orientalism as the unconscious repository of fantasy, imaginative writings and essential ideas; and the *form* of manifest Orientalism as the historically and discursively determined, diachronic aspect. This division/correlation structure of manifest and latent Orientalism leads to the effectivity of the concept of discourse being undermined by what could be called the polarities of intentionality.

This produces a problem with Said's use of Foucault's concepts of power and discourse. The productivity of Foucault's concept of power/knowledge lies in its refusal of an epistemology which opposes essence/appearance, ideology/science. '*Pouvoir/Savoir*' places subjects in a relation of power and recognition that is not part of a symmetrical or dialectical relation – self/other, master/slave – which can then be subverted by being inverted. Subjects are always disproportionately placed in opposition or domination through the symbolic decentring of multiple power relations which play the role of support as well as target or adversary. It becomes difficult, then, to conceive of the *historical* enunciations of colonial discourse without them being either functionally overdetermined or strategically elaborated or displaced by the *unconscious* scene of latent Orientalism. Equally, it is difficult to conceive of the process of subjectification as a placing *within* Orientalist or colonial discourse for the dominated subject without the dominant being strategically placed within it too. The terms in which Said's Orientalism is unified – the intentionality and unidirectionality of colonial power – also unify the subject of colonial enunciation.

This results in Said's inadequate attention to representation as a concept that articulates the historical and fantasy (as the scene of desire) in the production of the 'political' effects of discourse. He rightly rejects a notion of Orientalism as the misrepresentation of an Oriental essence. However, having introduced the concept of 'discourse' he does not face up to the problems it creates for an instrumentalist notion of power/knowledge that he seems to require. This problem is summed up by his ready acceptance of the view that, 'Representations are formations, or as Roland Barthes has said of all the operations of language, they are deformations'.

This brings me to my second point. The closure and coherence attributed to the unconscious pole of colonial discourse and the unproblematized notion of the subject, restrict the effectivity of both power and knowledge. It is not possible to see how power functions productively as incitement and interdiction. Now would it be possible, without the attribution of ambivalence to relations of power/knowledge, to calculate the traumatic impact of the return of the oppressed – those terrifying stereotypes of savagery, cannibalism, lust and anarchy which are the signal points of identification and alienation, scenes of fear and desire, in colonial texts. It is precisely this function of the stereotype as phobia and fetish that, according to Fanon, threatens the closure of the racial/epidermal schema for the colonial subject and opens the royal road to colonial fantasy.

There is an underdeveloped passage in *Orientalism* which, in cutting across the body of the text, articulates the question of power and desire that I now want to take up. It is this:

> Altogether an internally structured archive is built up from the literature that belongs to these experiences. Out of this comes a restricted number of typical encapsulations: the journey, the history, the fable, the stereotype, the polemical confrontation. These are the lenses through which the Orient is experienced, and they shape the language, perception, and form of the encounter between East and West. What gives the immense number of encounters some unity, however, is the vacillation I was speaking about earlier. Something patently foreign and distant acquires, for one reason or another, a status more rather than less familiar. One tends to stop judging things either as completely novel or as completely well-known; a new median category emerges, a category that allows one to see new things, things seen for the first time, as versions of a previously known thing. In essence such a category is not so much a way of receiving new information as it is a method of controlling what seems to be a threat to some established view of things. . . . The threat is muted, familiar values impose themselves, and in the end the mind reduces the pressure upon it by accommodating things to itself as either 'original' or 'repetitious'. [. . .] The orient at large, therefore, vacillates between the West's contempt for what is familiar and its shivers of delight in – or fear of – novelty.

What is this other scene of colonial discourse played out around the 'median category'? What is this theory of encapsulation or fixation which moves between the recognition of cultural and racial difference and its disavowal, by affixing the unfamiliar to something established, in a form that is repetitious and vacillates between delight and fear? Does the Freudian fable of fetishism (and disavowal) circulate within the discourse of colonial power requiring the articulation of modes of differentiation – sexual and racial – as well as different modes of theoretical discourse – psychoanalytic and historical?

The strategic articulation of 'coordinates of knowledge' – racial and sexual – and their inscription in the play of colonial power as modes of differentiation, defence, fixation, hierarchization, is a way of specifying colonial discourse which would be illuminated by reference to Foucault's poststructuralist concept of the *dispositif* or apparatus. Foucault insists that the relation of knowledge and power within the apparatus are always a strategic response to *an urgent need* at a given

historical moment. The force of colonial and postcolonial discourse as a theoretical and cultural intervention in our contemporary moment represents the urgent
need to contest singularities of difference and to articulate diverse 'subjects' of
differentiation. Foucault writes:

> the apparatus is essentially of a strategic nature, which means assuming
> that it is a matter of a certain manipulation of relations of forces, either
> developing them in a particular direction, blocking them, stabilising
> them, utilizing them, etc. The apparatus is thus always inscribed in a
> play of power, but it is also always linked to certain coordinates of
> knowledge which issue from it but, to an equal degree, condition it.
> This is what the apparatus consists in: strategies of relations of forces
> supporting and supported by, types of knowledge.

In this spirit I argue for the reading of the stereotype in terms of fetishism.
The myth of historical origination – racial purity, cultural priority – produced in
relation to the colonial stereotype functions to 'normalize' the multiple beliefs and
split subjects that constitute colonial discourse as a consequence of its process of
disavowal. The scene of fetishism functions similarly as, at once, a reactivation
of the material of original fantasy – the anxiety of castration and sexual difference
– as well as a normalization of that difference and disturbance in terms of the
fetish object as the substitute for the mother's penis. Within the apparatus of colonial
power, the discourses of sexuality and race relate in a process of *functional over-
determination*, 'because each effect [. . .] enters into resonance or contradiction with
the others and thereby calls for a readjustment or a reworking of the heterogeneous
elements that surface at various points.'
  There is both a structural and functional justification for reading the racial
stereotype of colonial discourse in terms of fetishism. My rereading of Said establishes the *structural* link. Fetishism, as the disavowal of difference, is that repetitious
scene around the problem of castration. The recognition of sexual difference – as
the precondition for the Symbolic – is disavowed by the fixation on an object that
masks that difference and restores an original presence. The *functional* link between
the fixation of the fetish and the stereotype (or the stereotype as fetish) is even
more relevant. For fetishism is always a 'play' or vacillation between the archaic
affirmation of wholeness/similarity – in Freud's terms: 'All men have penises'; in
ours: All men have the same skin/race/culture' – and the anxiety associated with
lack and difference – again, for Freud 'Some do not have penises'; for us 'Some
do not have the same skin/race/culture.' Within discourse, the fetish represents
the simultaneous play between metaphor as substitution (masking absence and
difference) and metonymy (which contiguously registers the perceived lack). The
fetish or stereotype gives access to an 'identity' which is predicated as much on
mastery and pleasure as it is on anxiety and defence, for it is a form of multiple
and contradictory belief in its recognition of difference and disavowal of it. This
conflict of pleasure/unpleasure, mastery/defence, knowledge/disavowal, absence/
presence, has a fundamental significance for colonial discourse. For the scene of
fetishism is also the scene of the reactivation and repetition of primal fantasy –

the subject's desire for a pure origin that is always threatened by its division, for the subject must be gendered to be engendered, to be spoken.

The stereotype, then, as the primary point of subjectification in colonial discourse, for both colonizer and colonized, is the scene of a similar fantasy and defence – the desire for an originality which is again threatened by the differences of race, colour and culture. My contention is splendidly caught in Fanon's title *Black Skin, White Masks* where the disavowal of difference turns the colonial subject into a misfit – a grotesque mimicry of 'doubling' that threatens to split the soul and whole, undifferentiated skin of the ego. The stereotype is not a simplification because it is a false representation of a given reality. It is a simplification because it is an arrested, fixated form of representation that, in denying the play of difference (which the negation through the Other permits), constitutes a problem for the *representation* of the subject in significations of psychic and social relations.

When Fanon talks of the positioning of the subject in the stereotyped discourse of colonialism, he gives further credence to my point. The legends, stories, histories and anecdotes of a colonial culture offer the subject a primordial Either/Or. *Either* he is fixed in a consciousness of the body as a solely negating activity *or* as a new kind of man, a new genus. What is denied the colonial subject, both as colonizer and colonized, is that form of negation which gives access to the recognition of difference. It is that possibility of difference and circulation which would liberate the signifier of *skin/culture* from the fixations of racial typology, the analytics of blood, ideologies of racial and cultural dominance or degeneration. 'Wherever he goes', Fanon despairs, 'the Negro remains a Negro' – his race becomes the ineradicable sign of *negative difference* in colonial discourses. For the stereotype impedes the circulation and articulation of the signifier of 'race' as anything other than its *fixity* as racism. We always already know that blacks are licentious, Asiatics duplicitous. . . .

There are two 'primal scenes' in Fanon's *Black Skins, White Masks*; two myths of the origin of the marking of the subject within the racist practices and discourses of a colonial culture. On one occasion a white girl fixes Fanon in a look and word as she turns to identify with her mother. It is a scene which echoes endlessly through his essay 'The fact of blackness': 'Look a Negro [. . .] Mama, see the Negro! I'm frightened.' 'What else could it be for me', Fanon concludes, 'but an amputation, and excision, a haemorrhage that spattered my whole body with black blood.' Equally, he stresses the primal moment when the child encounters racial and cultural stereotypes in children's fictions, where white heroes and black demons are proffered as points of ideological and psychical identification. Such dramas are enacted *every day* in colonial societies, says Fanon, employing a theatrical metaphor – the scene – which emphasizes the visible – the seen. I want to play on both these senses which refer at once to the site of fantasy and desire and to the sight of subjectification and power.

The drama underlying these dramatic 'everyday' colonial scenes is not difficult to discern. In each of them the subject turns around the pivot of the 'stereotype' to return to a point of total identification. The girl's gaze returns to her mother in the recognition and disavowal of the Negroid type; the black child turns away from himself, his race, in his total identification with the positivity of whiteness which is at once colour and no colour. In the act of disavowal and fixation the colonial subject is returned to the narcissism of the Imaginary and its identifica-tion of an ideal ego that is white and whole. For what these primal scenes illustrate is that looking/hearing/reading as sites of subjectification in colonial discourse are evidence of the importance of the visual and auditory imaginary for the *histories* of societies.

It is in this context that I want to allude briefly to the problematic of seeing/being seen. I suggest that in order to conceive of the colonial subject as the effect of power that is productive – disciplinary and 'pleasurable' – one has to see the *surveillance* of colonial power as functioning in relation to the regime of the *scopic drive*. That is, the drive that represents the pleasure in 'seeing', which has the look as its object of desire, is related both to the myth of origins, the primal scene, and to the problematic of fetishism and locates the surveyed object within the 'imaginary' relation. Like voyeurism, surveillance must depend for its effectivity on 'the *active consent* which is its real or mythical correlate (but always real as myth) and establishes in the scopic space the illusion of the object relation' (my emphasis). The ambivalence of this form of 'consent' in objectification – real as mythical – is the *ambivalence* on which the stereotype turns and illustrates that crucial bind of pleasure and power that Foucault asserts but, in my view, fails to explain.

My anatomy of colonial discourse remains incomplete until I locate the stereo-type, as an arrested, fetishistic mode of representation within its field of identification, which I have identified in my description of Fanon's primal scenes, as the Lacanian schema of the Imaginary. The Imaginary is the transformation that takes place in the subject at the formative mirror phase, when it assumes a *discrete* image which allows it to postulate a series of equivalences, samenesses, identities, between the objects of the surrounding world. However, this positioning is itself problematic, for the subject finds or recognizes itself through an image which is simultaneously alienating and hence potentially confrontational. This is the basis of the close relation between the two forms of identification complicit with the Imaginary – narcissism and aggressivity. It is precisely these two forms of identi-fication that constitute the dominant strategy of colonial power exercised in relation to the stereotype which, as a form of multiple and contradictory belief, gives know-ledge of difference and simultaneously disavows or masks it. Like the mirror phase 'the fullness' of the stereotype – its image *as* identity – is always threatened by 'lack'.

The construction of colonial discourse is then a complex articulation of the tropes of fetishism – metaphor and metonymy – and the forms of narcissistic and aggressive identification available to the Imaginary. Stereotypical racial discourse is a four-term strategy. There is a tie-up between the metaphoric or masking func-tion of the fetish and the narcissistic object-choice and an opposing alliance between the metonymic figuring of lack and the aggressive phase of the Imaginary. A reper-toire of conflictual positions constitutes the subject in colonial discourse. The taking up of any one position, within a specific discursive form, in a particular historical conjuncture, is thus always problematic – the site of both fixity and fantasy. It provides a colonial 'identity' that is played out – like all fantasies of originality and

origination – in the face and space of the disruption and threat from the heterogeneity of other positions. As a form of splitting and multiple belief, the stereotype
requires, for its successful signification, a continual and repetitive chain of other
stereotypes. The process by which the metaphoric 'masking' is inscribed on a lack
which must then be concealed gives the stereotype both its fixity and its phantasmatic quality – the *same old* stories of the Negro's animality, the Coolie's
inscrutability or the stupidity of the Irish *must* be told (compulsively) again and
afresh, and are differently gratifying and terrifying each time.

In any specific colonial discourse the metaphoric/narcissistic and the
metonymic/aggressive positions will function simultaneously, strategically poised
in relation to each other; similar to the moment of alienation which stands as a
threat to Imaginary plenitude, and 'multiple' belief' which threatens fetishistic
disavowal. The subjects of the discourse are constructed within an apparatus of
power which *contains*, in both senses of the word, an 'other' knowledge – a knowledge that is arrested and fetishistic and circulates through colonial discourse as
that limited form of otherness that I have called the stereotype. Fanon poignantly
describes the effects of this process for a colonized culture:

> a continued agony rather than a total disappearance of the pre-existing
> culture. The culture once living and open to the future, becomes closed,
> fixed in the colonial status, caught in the yolk of oppression. Both
> present and mummified, it testifies against its members. [. . .] The
> cultural mummification leads to a mummification of individual thinking.
> [. . .] As though it were possible for a man to evolve otherwise than
> within the framework of a culture that recognises him and that he
> decides to assume.

My four-term strategy of the stereotype tries tentatively to provide a structure and a process for the 'subject' of a colonial discourse. I now want to take
up the problem of discrimination as the political effect of such a discourse and
relate it to the question of 'race' and 'skin'. To that end it is important to remember
that the multiple belief that accompanies fetishism not only has disavowal
value; it also has 'knowledge value' and it is this that I shall now pursue. In
calculating this knowledge value it is crucial to consider what Fanon means when
he says that:

> There is a quest for the Negro, the Negro is a demand, one cannot get
> along without him, he is needed, but only if he is made palatable in a
> certain way. Unfortunately the Negro knocks down the system and
> breaks the treaties.

To understand this demand and how the native or Negro is made 'palatable'
we must acknowledge some significant differences between the general theory of
fetishism and its specific uses for an understanding of racist discourse. First, the
fetish of colonial discourse – what Fanon calls the epidermal scheme – is not, like
the sexual fetish, a secret. Skin, as the key signifier of cultural and racial difference in the stereotype, is the most visible of fetishes, recognized as 'common

knowledge' in a range of cultural, political and historical discourses, and plays a public part in the racial drama that is enacted every day in colonial societies. Second, it may be said that sexual fetish is closely linked to the 'good object'; it is the prop that makes the whole object desirable and lovable, facilitates sexual relations and can even promote a form of happiness. The stereotype can also be seen as that particular 'fixated' form of the colonial subject which *facilitates* colonial relations, and sets up a discursive form of racial and cultural opposition in terms of which colonial power is exercised. If it is claimed that the colonized are most often objects of hate, then we can reply with Freud that

> affection and hostility in the treatment of the fetish – which run parallel with the disavowal and acknowledgement of castration – are mixed in unequal proportions in different cases, so that the one or the other is more clearly recognisable.

What this statement recognizes is the wide *range* of the stereotype, from the loyal servant to Satan, from the loved to the hated; a shifting of subject positions in the circulation of colonial power which I tried to account for through the motility of the metaphoric/narcissistic and metonymic/aggressive system of colonial discourse. What remains to be examined, however, is the construction of the signifier of 'skin/race' in those regimes of visibility and discursivity – fetishistic, scopic, Imaginary – within which I have located the stereotypes. It is only on that basis that we can construct its 'knowledge-value' which will, I hope, enable us to see the place of fantasy in the exercise of colonial power.

My argument relies upon a particular reading of the problematic of representation which, Fanon suggests, is specific to the colonial situation. He writes:

> the originality of the colonial context is that the economic substructure is also a superstructure [. . .] you are rich because you are white, you are white because you are rich. This is why Marxist analysis should always be slightly stretched every time we have to do with the colonial problem.

Fanon could either be seen to be adhering to a simple reflectionist or determinist notion of cultural/social signification or, more interestingly, he could be read as taking an 'anti-repressionist' position (attacking the notion that ideology as miscognition, or misrepresentation, is the repression of the real). For our purposes I tend towards the latter reading which then provides a 'visibility' to the exercise of power; gives force to the argument that skin, as a signifier of discrimination, must be produced or processed as visible. As Paul Abbot says, in a very different context,

> whereas repression banishes its object into the unconscious, forgets and attempts to forget the forgetting, discrimination must constantly invite its representations into consciousness, reinforcing the crucial recognition of difference which they embody and revitalising them for the perception on which its effectivity depends .[. . .] It must sustain itself on the presence of the very difference which is also its object.

What 'authorizes' discrimination, Abbot continues, is the occlusion of the preconstruction or working-up of difference: 'this repression of production entails that the recognition of difference is procured in an innocence, as a "nature"; recognition is contrived as primary cognition, spontaneous effect of the "evidence of the visible".'

This is precisely the kind of recognition, as spontaneous and visible, that is attributed to the stereotype. The difference of the object of discrimination is at once visible and natural – colour as the cultural/political *sign* of inferiority or degeneracy, skin as its natural *'identity'*. However, Abbot's account stops at the point of 'identification' and strangely colludes with the *success* of discriminatory practices by suggesting that their representations require the repression of the working-up of difference; to argue otherwise, according to him, would be to put the subject in 'an impossible awareness, since it would run into consciousness the heterogeneity of the subject as a place of articulation'.

Despite his awareness of the crucial recognition of difference for discrimination and its problematization of repression, Abbot is trapped in his unitary place of articulation. He comes close to suggesting that it is possible, however momentarily and illusorily, for the *perpetrator* of the discriminatory discourse to be in a position that is *unmarked by the discourse* to the extent to which the *object* of discrimination is deemed natural and visible. What Abbot neglects is the facilitating role of contradiction and heterogeneity in the construction of authoritarian practices and their strategic, discursive fixations.

My concept of stereotype-as-suture is a recognition of the *ambivalence* of that authority and those orders of identification. The role of fetishistic identification, in the construction of discriminatory knowledges that depend on the 'presence of difference', is to provide a process of splitting and multiple/contradictory belief at the point of enunciation and subjectification. It is this crucial splitting of the ego which is represented in Fanon's description of the construction of the colonized subject as effect of stereotypical discourse: the subject primordially fixed and yet triply split between the incongruent knowledges of body, race, ancestors. Assailed by the stereotype, 'the corporeal schema crumbled, its place taken by a racial epidermal schema. [. . .] It was no longer a question of being aware of my body in the third person but in a triple person. [. . .] I was not given one, but two, three places.'

This process is best understood in terms of the articulation of multiple belief that Freud proposed in his essay on fetishism. It is a non-repressive form of knowledge that allows for the possibility of simultaneously embracing two contradictory beliefs, one official and one secret, one archaic and one progressive, one that allows the myth of origins, the other that articulates difference and division. Its knowledge 'value' lies in its orientation as a defence towards external reality, and provides, in Metz's words,

> the lasting matrix, the effective prototype of all those splittings of belief which man will henceforth be capable of in the most varied domains, of all the infinitely complex unconscious and occasionally conscious interactions which he will allow himself between believing and not-believing.

It is through this notion of splitting and multiple belief that, I believe, it becomes easier to see the bind of knowledge and fantasy, power and pleasure, that informs the particular regime of visibility deployed in colonial discourse. The visibility of the racial/colonial Other is at once a *point* of identity ('Look, a Negro') and at the same time a *problem* for the attempted closure within discourse. For the recognition of difference as 'imaginary' points of identity and origin – such as black and white – is disturbed by the representation of splitting in the discourse. What I called the play between the metaphoric/narcissistic and metonymic/aggressive moments in colonial discourse – that four-part strategy of the stereotype – crucially recognizes the prefiguring of desire as a potentially conflictual, disturbing force in all those regimes of 'originality' that I have brought together. In the objectification of the scopic drive there is always the threatened return of the look; in the identification of the Imaginary relation there is always the alienating other (or mirror) which crucially returns its image to the subject; and in that form of substitution and fixation that is fetishism there is always the trace of loss, absence. To put it succinctly, the recognition and disavowal of 'difference' is always disturbed by the question of its re-presentation or construction.

The stereotype is in that sense an 'impossible' object. For that very reason, the exertions of the 'official knowledges' of colonialism – pseudo-scientific, typological, legal–administrative, eugenicist – are imbricated at the point of their production of meaning and power with the fantasy that dramatizes the impossible desire for a pure, undifferentiated origin. Not itself the object of desire but its setting, not an ascription of prior identities but their production in the syntax of the scenario of racist discourse, colonial fantasy plays a crucial part in those everyday scenes of subjectification in a colonial society which Fanon refers to repeatedly. Like fantasies of the origins of sexuality, the productions of 'colonial desire' mark the discourse as 'a favoured spot for the most primitive defensive reactions such as turning against oneself, into an opposite, projection, negation'.

The problem of origin as the problematic of racist, stereotypical knowledge is a complex one and what I have said about its construction will come clear in this illustration from Fanon. Stereotyping is not the setting up of a false image which becomes the scapegoat of discriminatory practices. It is a much more ambivalent text of projection and introjection, metaphoric and metonymic strategies, displacement, over-determination, guilt, aggressivity; the masking and splitting of 'official' and phantasmatic knowledges to construct the positionalities and oppositionalities of racist discourse:

> My body was given back to me sprawled out, distorted, recoloured, clad in mourning in that white winter day. The Negro is an animal, the Negro is bad, the Negro is mean, the Negro is ugly; look, a nigger, it's cold, the nigger is shivering, the nigger is shivering because he is cold, the little boy is trembling because he is afraid of the nigger, the nigger is shivering with cold, that cold that goes through your bones, the handsome little boy is trembling because he thinks that the nigger is quivering with rage, the little white boy throws himself into his mother's arms: Mama, the nigger's going to eat me up.

It is the scenario of colonial fantasy which, in staging the ambivalence of desire, articulates the demand for the Negro which the Negro disrupts. For the stereotype is at once a substitute and a shadow. By acceding to the wildest fantasies (in the popular sense) of the coloniser, the stereotyped Other reveals something of the 'fantasy' (as desire, defence) of that position of mastery. For if 'skin' in racist discourse is the visibility of darkness, and a prime signifier of the body and its social and cultural correlates, then we are bound to remember what Karl Abrahams says in his seminal work on the scopic drive. The pleasure-value of darkness is a withdrawal in order to know nothing of the external world. Its symbolic meaning, however, is thoroughly ambivalent. Darkness signifies at once both birth and death; it is in all cases a desire to return to the fullness of the mother, a desire for an unbroken and undifferentiated line of vision and origin.

But surely there is another scene of colonial discourse in which the native or Negro meets the demand of colonial discourse; where the subverting 'split' is recuperable within a strategy of social and political control. It is recognizably true that the chain of stereotypical signification is curiously mixed and split, polymorphous and perverse, an articulation of multiple belief. The black is both savage (cannibal) and yet the most obedient and dignified of servants (the bearer of food); he is the embodiment of rampant sexuality and yet innocent as a child; he is mystical, primitive, simple-minded and yet the most worldly and accomplished liar, and manipulator of social forces. In each case what is being dramatized is a separation – *between* races, cultures, histories, *within* histories – a separation between before and *after* that repeats obsessively the mythical moment or disjunction.

Despite the structural similarities with the play of need and desire in primal fantasies, the colonial fantasy does not try to cover up that moment of separation. It is more ambivalent. On the one hand, it proposes a teleology – under certain conditions of colonial domination and control the native is progressively reformable. On the other, however, it effectively displays the 'separation', makes it more visible. It is the visibility of this separation which, in denying the colonized the capacities of self-government, independence, Western modes of civility, lends authority to the official version and mission of colonial power.

Racist stereotypical discourse, in its colonial moment, inscribes a form of governmentality that is informed by a productive splitting in its constitution of knowledge and exercise of power. Some of its practices recognize the difference of race, culture and history as elaborated by stereotypical knowledges, racial theories, administrative colonial experience, and on that basis institutionalize a range of political and cultural ideologies that are prejudicial, discriminatory, vestigial, archaic, 'mythical', and, crucially, are recognized as being so. By 'knowing' the native population in these terms, discriminatory and authoritarian forms of political control are considered appropriate. The colonized population is then deemed to be both the cause and effect of the system, imprisoned in the circle of interpretation. What is visible is the *necessity* of such rule which is justified by those moralistic and normative ideologies of amelioration recognized as the Civilizing Mission or the White Man's Burden. However, there coexist within the same apparatus of colonial power, modern systems and sciences of government, progressive 'Western' forms of social and economic organization which provide the manifest justification for the project of colonialism – an argument which, in part, impressed

Karl Marx. It is on the site of this coexistence that strategies of hierarchization and marginalization are employed in the management of colonial societies. And if my deduction from Fanon about the peculiar visibility of colonial power is justified, then I would extend that to say that it is a form of governmentality in which the 'ideological' space functions in more openly collaborative ways with political and economic exigencies. The barracks stands by the church which stands by the schoolroom; the cantonment stands hard by the 'civil lines'. Such visibility of the institutions and apparatuses of power is possible because the exercise of colonial power makes their *relationship* obscure, produces them as fetishes, spectacles of a 'natural'/racial preeminence. Only the seat of government is always elsewhere – alien and separate by that distance upon which surveillance depends for its strategies of objectification, normalization and discipline.

The last word belongs to Fanon:

> this behaviour [of the colonizer] betrays a determination to objectify, to confine, to imprison, to harden. Phrases such as 'I\know them', 'that's the way they are', show this maximum objectification successfully achieved. There is on the one hand a culture in which qualities of dynamism, of growth, of depth can be recognised. As against this, [in colonial cultures] we find characteristics, curiosities, things, never a structure.

# Index

ethnomethodology 2
Evans-Pritchard, E.E. 62–3
exchange theory 2
expressivism 2, 317–20

Fabian, Johannes 59, 62, 367
Face 143
Falk, Richard 274
Fanon, Fritz 395, 398, 402
feminism 22, 84, 85–6, 156, 209, 210, 282,
    364; Anglo–American 322–31; and
    common denominator 324–5; and
    consciousness 325–9; epistemology 325–6;
    and gender relations 323–4, 325, 329;
    humanist 205, 206; impact on culture
    99–100; language of 328–9; meaning of
    328; modal person in 322; multiple
    registers of 330; and philosophy 157–8,
    160–1; and politics of unity 329; and
    postmodernist retreat from utopia 161–2;
    racial/ethnic aspects 206; separatist
    205–6; as situated criticism 158–61;
    socialist 327; and women of colour 323,
    324, 328–31
Finkielkraut, Alan 140
Flaubert, Gustave 385
Flax, Jane 323, 325
Fletcher, Angus 57
Fordism 180–3
Foucault, Michel 7, 25, 76, 77, 83, 98, 294,
    297–302, 351, 392, 393–4
foundationalism 1–2, 3
Frankfurt School 4, 190
Franklin, Aretha 344
freedom 307–9, 311
Freeman, Derek 59–60
Freud, Sigmund 343, 394, 399
Frye, Northrop 8, 59, 105–6

gay politics 292; and
    affirmative/transformative remedies
    291–2; background 294; and closet life
    355–6; and normalization 356–9; as
    reverse discourse 295–7; and sexual
    autonomy 359–60; and shift from morality
    to aesthetics 359; social resistance to 356;
    and strategies of repression/pollution
    353–5; success of 355
gay rights 204–5
gender 18, 21–2, 282, 378; as bivalent
    collectivity 288–9, 290; and identity

323–4, 325, 328, 329, 341–2; and notion
    of proper 339; reality-effects of 340–1; as
    site of psychic miming 343
genealogy 70–2
Gershon, Richard K. 277–8
Glenn, Evelyn Nakano 379
globalization 1; cultural/economic
    relationship 264–5; defined 245; and
    deterritorialization 261–2; dimensions of
    245–52; disjuncture/difference in cultural
    economy 253–65; ethnoscapes 257, 258,
    263–4; financescapes 259; from
    above/from below 273–5; ideoscapes
    259–60; and industrial development
    251–2; and international relations 246–7;
    mediascapes 259; military order 250–1;
    and modernity 245–6; and nation-states
    248–50, 262–3; and sovereignty 246–7;
    technoscapes 258; threats 272–3; and
    world-system theory 247–8
Gramsci, Antonio 79, 82, 96–8, 191,
    377, 385

Habermas, Jürgen 3–4, 25, 154, 170, 174,
    180, 187, 191, 192
Halperin, David 18
Haraway, Donna 20, 269
Harding, Sandra 324
Hayles, Katherine 279
Heath, Stephen 350, 389–90
Hegel, G.W.F. 39, 40, 43, 157, 167, 228
hegemony, articulation/discourse 76–83;
    cultural 385; genealogy of 76–86; racial
    377–9; and structuralism 96–7; subject
    83–6
Heidegger, Martin 105, 150, 156–7
Herder, J.G. 318
heterosexual/homosexual binary, and change
    in language 351–2; and coming out
    349–50; difference 348, 350; ghosting
    effect 349; hierarchy of 353; and identity
    348, 349, 351; inside/outside rhetoric
    347–8, 349, 350, 352; philosophical
    opposition 347; pure/polluted aspect
    354
heterosexuality 23–4, 291, 294;
    homosexuality as derivative of 336,
    339–41; as normal 356–8
history 102–3
Hobbes, Thomas 157, 274–5
homophobia 296–7, 334, 339